Pokes & Jabbs:
The Before, During and After of the Vim Films Corporation

by
Rob Stone

Split Reel LLC
Culpeper, Virginia
2022

Pokes & Jabbs:
The Before, During and After of the Vim Films Corporation

© Rob Stone

All rights reserved.

Published in the United States by:

Split Reel LLC
P.O. Box 946
Culpeper, VA 22701
split-reel.com
info@split-reel.com

Cover design by Marlene Weisman

ISBN 978-0-9652384-1-0 (Paperback)
ISBN 978-0-9652384-8-9(Hardcover)

TABLE OF CONTENTS

FOREWORD

A book on Pokes & Jabbs??!!

Quick quiz – which one was Pokes, and which was Jabbs?

Well, the good news is that the book in front of you will not only give all the information on Pokes & Jabbs (i.e. Bobby Burns and Walter Stull) and the Vim Company, but you'll also get the lowdown on the Lubin Manufacturing Company, Wizard Comedies, Harry Myers & Rosemary Theby, the Jaxon Film Corporation, Mae Hotely, Kate Price, Billy Ruge, and a young actor named "Babe" Hardy (better-known as Oliver).

And that's just scratching the surface.

Much of Rob's research was begun for his excellent 1996 book *Laurel or Hardy: The Solo Films of Stan Laurel and Oliver "Babe" Hardy* (one of the essential silent comedy studies). At that time you couldn't just sit in your pajamas and go online to use Lantern Search for the Media History Digital Library – you had to go page by page through the motion picture trade magazines – and on top of that you had to go where the collections of trade magazines were kept.

And that he did – traveling on his own dime to places like New York City, Washington, D.C. and Philadelphia. Since then Rob has continued to scour the trades, plus newspapers, synopses of missing films, genealogical information, pressbooks, interviews, and copies of surviving films. Also working as a professional film archivist, he's even helped to locate and preserve a fair share of the missing films.

So in *Pokes and Jabbs: The Before, During and After of the Vim Films Corporation* not only do you get a cornucopia of information on individual films – detailed casts and crews, synopsis, and reviews – the book also gives a nuanced view of the larger world of silent comedy.

We silent comedy film lovers owe a huge debt of gratitude for this labor of love. Rob's dogged determination and accurate eye has brought light and life to this dark and neglected corner of movie history.

I can't wait for the next book.

Steve Massa
New York, New York

For all those that appreciate the mostly lost.

ACKNOWLEDGEMENTS

The acknowledgement section of a book can often be a mine field. Remembering all that have contributed in the research, writing and illustrating of a book often results in some being forgotten or being given too little credit (or too much) for their contribution. Apologies in advance to those who are unintentionally slighted. The community of film lovers, collectors, researchers and archives provide so much and they make projects such as this book a pure joy to attempt.

Thankfully there are numerous institutions that facilitate the study of motion pictures and those institutions that were sourced for this book are named below. But it is the individuals that in many various ways perpetuate film history that must be thanked first (*alphabetically, of course*): Robert Arkus, Peter Bagrov, Bob Birchard, Lisa Bradbury, Serge Bromberg, Rachel Del Gaudio, David Denton, Robb Farr, Joe Eckhardt, Carol Galbraith, Sam Gill, Paul Gierecki, David Glass, Michael Hayde, Dave Lord Heath, Nelson Hughes, Jim Kerkhoff, Robert Kiss, Herman McEachin, Steve Massa, Nicola Mazzanti, Ben Model, Elif Rongren-Kaynakci, Thomas Reeder, Steve Rydzewski, Richard M. Roberts, Rick Scheckman, Randy Sktrevedt, Lynanne Schweighofer, Larry Smith, Mark Wanamaker, Marlene Weisman, Todd Wiener, George Willeman, Dave Wyatt, Wayne Wood, Jordan Young, and others certainly but not maliciously forgotten. A special shout out to my son Ben who made some last minute observations that helped make this a better publication than it would have been.

Institutions and companies that provided onsite and/or online resources and assistance (*in no particular order*): George Eastman Museum, Library of Congress, Museum of Modern Art, UCLA Film & Television Archive, Academy of Motion Picture Arts & Sciences' Margaret Herrick Library, Lobster Films, EYE (Amsterdam), Royal Film Archive of Belgium, State Archives of Florida, Harry Ransom Center at University of Texas, University of North Florida, New York Public Library, Lantern (Media History Digital Library), British Film Institute, Free Library of Philadelphia, Slapsticon, Cinefest, Mostly Lost, Nitrateville, YouTube, NewspaperArchive, Newspapers.com, The British Newspaper Archive, Ancestry.com, Family Search.org, Copyright Descriptions at the Library of Congress, and the many trade magazines that shed so much light on the silent era of movies including *Moving Picture World, Motion Picture News, Motography, Motion Picture Stories, Reel Life, Kalem Kalendar, The Bioscope, Kinematograph Weekly, New York Dramatic Mirror*. Not to forget the local Jacksonville newspapers: *Florida Metropolis* and *Florida Times-Union*.

With this publication Split Reel LLC is embarking on a quest to present more and more publications focusing on little known and esoteric aspects of film history. To do so we have been able to assemble a great team. Michael Hayde, a great author in his own right, serves as the editor for this and future books. Marlene Weisman, graphic artist extraordinaire, not only designs the front covers but also crafted the Split Reel logo. Rob Arkus does magic making the photos, some from very poor source material, look the best they possibly can. Rob Farr, who had little to do with this book, is key to Split Reel in that his book *Presenting Mr. & Mrs. Drew* will be the first published by Split Reel written by someone not named Rob Stone. Steve Massa lends an ear and an eye to help identify players and fact checking. Ben Model consults on matter such as Kickstarter and other ways to bring the odd, forgotten or overlooked back to life, he doing so successfully with his Undercrank endeavor. Not to forget my wife Jodi who not only lets her husband dig deep into silent film esoterica, but proofreads, critiques, and provides moral support beyond belief. Quite a nice group I might say (and I just did).

A special thank you must be given to the many Kickstarter backers who made the publication of this book possible. Your money is very much appreciated, but more importantly your personal investment and interest in sustaining such efforts to document our filmic past is to be applauded. My sincerest thanks to:

Luke Primak	Pam Burrows	Vanessa Garlock
Kevin Rollason	Eric Cohen	Sam Gill
Russ Arnold	Frank Thompson	T. Willis
Nelson Hughes	Jim Reid	Edward Watz
Richard Lewis Ward	Kenneth Cone	Nico Cartenstadt
Neeraja V	Everett Haagsma	Jeff Rapsis
Sergey Kochergan	Dave Glass	Terry Baxter
Richard Scheckman	George B. Schramm III	Daniel Bourque
Michael Aus	Larry Smith &	Ryan Chattaway
Karen Owen	Jenny Paxson	Jason Kinsey
Brent Walker	David Eickemeyer	Krith and Cheri Martin
Bruce Calvert	Todd Hitchcock	Todd Terpening
Steve Massa	C. James Cook	Bil Barrett
David Denton	Steve Zalusky	David Perlmutter
Kirk Gardner	Debbie MacEwen	Jennifer Adams
R. Michael Pyle	Ron Spayde	Curtis B. Edmundson
Robert Lipton	Ronald Larimore	Jason Boles
Michael Gebert	Elizabeth J Maxim	Robert Siwczyk
Lisa Stein Haven	John Michael Jones	Dennis Smit
Thomas Reeder	Asher and Hazel	Beth Ann Gallagher
Brian Cruz	Dodge	Frank Thielmann
David L. Gill	Bianca Baynum	Frank Flood
Lisa Bradberry	Linda Keenan	Myrhat Eliot
Steven Rowe	Jill Feldman	David Samuelson
Joe Moore	Susan Selig	Stephen M.
Rowby	Shane Bliss	Wolterstorff
Barbara C. Wingo	Steven Nordhougen	Julie Phillips
Anonymous	George Watt	Stan Taffel
Ray Frieders	Pete Bainbridge	Rob Farr
T. Dennis Reece	Ben Model	Raif & Rebecca Barnes
Darlene Jacob	Michael Meltzer	Florian Schiffmann
Jim Kerkhoff	Nicholas Hatcher	Jan L. Will
Robert Arkus and	Jennifer Keenan	
Jeni Rymer	Kevin Shannon	

ILLUSTRATIONS

Many of the illustrations in this book were sourced from the previously mentioned trade publications and from various internet sites. Fortunately, many collectors also provided rare photographs including Bob Birchard, Joe Eckhardt, Herman McEachin (*with photos from Ray Godfrey's personal scrapbook*), Randy Skretvedt (*numerous Vim photos from Babe Hardy's personal scrapbook*), Marc Wanamaker and Wayne Wood. Photos were also obtained from the following institutions: Cinemtek (Brussels), State Archives of Florida (*photos from Ethel Burton's personal scrapbook*), Free Library of Philadelphia, George Eastman Museum, Museum of Modern Art, New York Public Library, University of Washington – J. Willis Sayre Collection, and even a few from me.

Bob Birchard:
11, 15, 347, 381.

Joe Eckhardt:
378-379, 390, 392-394.

Cinemtek (Brussels):
332.

Free Library of Philadelphia:
20-24, 31-32, 45, 49, 53,55,57-58, 60-62, 64, 67-69, 71-72, 74-76, 79-81, 83-91.

George Eastman Museum:
291, 299.

Herman McEachin:
252-253, 264, 275.

Museum of Modern Art:
421-422.

New York Public Library:
15.

Randy Skretvedt:
153, 168, 173, 232, 236, 243-249, 254, 256-258, 260-261, 280, 311, 317-318, 322-323, 325.

State Archives of Florida:
5, 135, 164, 180, 185, 191, 201, 207, 213,219, 223.

Marc Wanamaker:
239, 326.

University of Washington:
12, 342, 386.

Wayne Wood:
349.

Many of the still used are from the personal scrapbook of Ethel Burton.

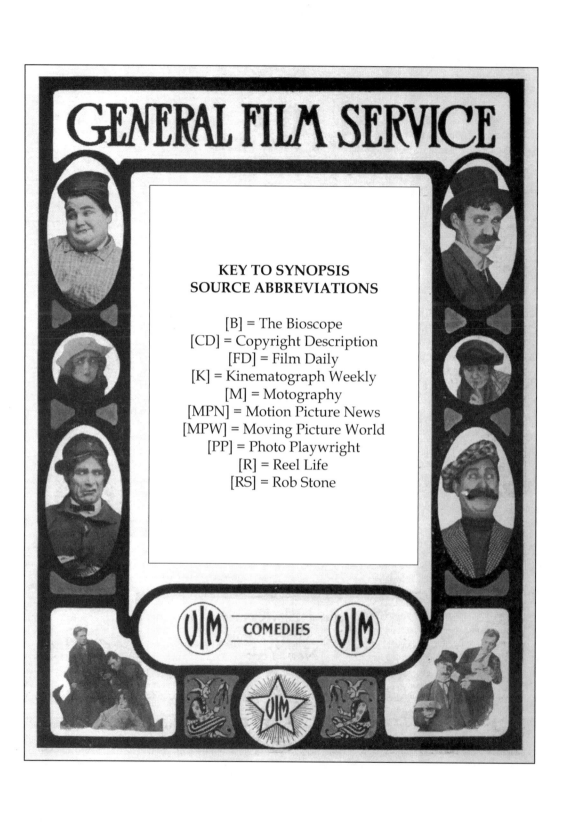

GENERAL FILM SERVICE

**KEY TO SYNOPSIS
SOURCE ABBREVIATIONS**

[B] = The Bioscope
[CD] = Copyright Description
[FD] = Film Daily
[K] = Kinematograph Weekly
[M] = Motography
[MPN] = Motion Picture News
[MPW] = Moving Picture World
[PP] = Photo Playwright
[R] = Reel Life
[RS] = Rob Stone

COMEDIES

INTRODUCTION

In the early days of filmmaking there were hundreds and hundreds of small production companies that were formed and operated to exploit the public's newly found desire to see movies. Most worked in the shadows of the big "trust" studios like Edison or Vitagraph, some aligned with the likes of Universal and openly competed with the "licensed" releases of the Motion Picture Trust. Many just worked on a shoestring and sold their product to any taker they could find that had money. Later the larger companies, be they independent or licensed, needed more product and contracted with smaller film companies to produce product for them. Success and even fortunes could be had if an enterprising person or two could find a couple of nickels to rub together, purchase some film, get a camera and find some people who could mug in front of it. At least that is what many thought; in reality it was a tough business and the more mature the movie industry became the more pressure there was for these small companies to produce a quality product. One of those companies that worked to fill not only the larger companies' void in their release schedules but also the large hole in the availability of quality short comedies was the Vim Films Corporation.

By 1915, when the Wizard Film Corporation (the direct predecessor to Vim) was formed it was a great advantage to have a front office with experience as Louis Burstein (a former executive at Reliance) had; and important to have talent with, if not film experience, then extensive work on the stage (comedians Bobby Burns and Walter Stull had both). Throw in technicians that had been turning a crank, writing a scenario or building a set for a decade or longer in the still-in-its-infancy film business and Wizard Comedies were bound to succeed. Business dealings, not quality of product, caused Wizard to morph into Vim and even later into Jaxon, but the little film studio that not only could but did is a prime example of one of the better of those hundreds of film companies that sprang up during the first quarter of the 20th Century.

So why write about Vim? One could argue (as I just did) that they were one of the better small film companies, but it would be foolish to suggest they were the *only* good one or even the best. Perhaps it is the condensed existence of the company, having lasted only three years through three different iterations, that makes it an interesting study. Too, Vim tells many stories about early filmmaking, such as New York City being the center of the industry until the desire to move out of the Big Apple and its surrounds led to Jacksonville, Florida becoming a large film production center for most of the 'teens; or the transient nature of a film actor's life; or an understanding of the kinds of things that made people laugh in the early 20th century. Calling this book a "case study" would be too lofty a term to use, but it does provide a quick, concentrated glimpse at a gone-by era when movies were movies, and fun to make to boot.

Oliver Hardy, or more correctly Babe Hardy (as he was known during his days at Vim and throughout his personal life), often commented that his happiest days making movies were those spent in Jacksonville, Florida working at the small film studio located at 750 Riverside Avenue. Others also told stories of their days as

Vimmies and the pure fun they had working and playing in JAX. But the story of Vim doesn't begin with Babe Hardy, but with Walter Stull.

A Philadelphia native that found success traveling on the vaudeville circuit only to come home and go into movies, Stull became an immediate asset to the Lubin studios. There he soon gained a friend and co-worker named Bobby Burns. The two, along with another comedian George Reehm, become key players in Lubin's Gay Time comedies. Eventually the three moved on to Komic and, sans Reehm, Burns & Stull then began making their own comedies as Pokes & Jabbs with the advent of the Wizard Comedies. From Wizard to Vim to Jaxon, the two wrote, directed and acted in numerous comedies. Through financial scandals, business intrigue, and a changing filmmaking landscape they continued making what were then pretty good comedies and are today much overlooked films. When Walter Stull left the film business in 1917 so did Pokes & Jabbs and so did the last iteration of what was Vim, but then it could be said that neither Pokes, Jabbs or Vim would have ever happened in the first place without him.

So it is appropriate to start with Walter Stull, the man in plaid…

THE ORIGINS OF POKES & JABBS

Walter Howard Stull was born on September 28, 1875 in Philadelphia, Pennsylvania to Aaron and Harriet Stull, a street cleaning inspector and his wife. Both were born in Philadelphia but their parents came to America from Germany and Switzerland. Young Stull trained to be a telegraph operator, but something else caught his attention that would influence his life for the next twenty-five years.

By the early 1890s Philadelphia was a city of over a million people and had become a very important stop on the thriving vaudeville circuit. All the big acts would come through town and with vaudeville doing so well, many Philadelphia theaters also formed their own stock companies to perform for the locals between bookings of the traveling performers. Stull would slip away from his studies of dots and dashes to attend as many theatrical performances as he could. He became a student of the dramatic, learning the various parts, and in 1894 was offered a position in the Forepaugh Stock Company, which he gladly took. Also in the company at that time were future Kalem actor and film director George Melford, as well as Earl Metcalfe, an actor who would later begin his film career working in the dramatic unit at Lubin.

The Forepaugh Stock Company was formed in April 1893 by John A. Forepaugh, who had taken over management of the Forepaugh Theatre (located at 251 North 8th Street) from his Uncle Adam, a long-time circus and theater entrepreneur. John suddenly passed away in June 1895, and for the next seven years the theater was managed by his widow Luella, one of the first female theater manager-operators. The Forepaugh Theatre was highly regarded in Philadelphia and Stull was fortunate to start his career with such a first class organization. Stull quickly improved his position within the company, moving from supporting roles to leads through his talent and ability to memorize. He'd competently learn all the male parts within the production being staged and was thus able to jump into any role at a moment's notice. This and Stull's overall good acting ability made him popular to theatergoers and other theater owners. Stull left the Forepaugh Company after four years, moving over to work with the actors in residence at the Standard Theatre located at 1124 South Street. A new theater in an upper middle class area of Philadelphia, the Standard would later gain attention when it was purchased in 1914 by John T. Gibson, a Black businessman. Gibson turned around the by-then failing theater and parlayed his purchase into a string of highly successful theaters that catered to Black audiences.

Stull only stayed at the Standard for two years. In 1900, he moved on to the Durban & Sheeler Stock Company working at the Girard Avenue Theatre located at 621 West Girard Avenue. Stull showed his worth to the company early on when, according to the *Philadelphia Inquirer* on October 20, 1900, just before the curtain was to go up on their new play *"A Colonial Girl"* another actor fell ill and "Walter Stull essayed the role at a moment's notice, and before the performance was half ended he had a thorough understanding of the character, and is to be commended for his smooth rendition of the lines. The management is also to be complimented on having as capable an actor as Mr. Stull shows himself to be." Another actor in the company was Edwin Middleton who would go on to direct Casino Star Comedies for Gaumont, the most famous being W.C. Fields' film debut, *Pool Sharks* (1915). On October 28, 1903, a fire gutted the Girard, but by then Stull was no longer employed there, having been lured away by a national touring stock company.

Mamie Fleming opened at the Kensington Theatre in Philadelphia on September 14, 1903 in one of the productions she was preparing to take on tour, *"The Lion and the Mouse."* Walter Stull played Fleming's main male support, and also included in the new company, listed as stage manager, was Harry Myers. After two weeks the Fleming company would move on to Red Bank, New Jersey and then to other stops, including Baltimore, Maryland and a place Walter Stull would later become very familiar with, Providence, Rhode Island.

For at least two summers, 1904 and 1905, concurrent with his work with other companies, Stull worked as the director and lead actor in a summer stock troupe in Du Bois, Pennsylvania. James Kirkwood, who a few years later found work as leading man in D.W. Griffith's early Biograph films, was in the company, as were Natalie Perry, Ellen Bover, Grace Whitcher, Mrs. Emma Ballard, A. W. Morfarty, Eugene A. Phelps, Walter Gilbert and Walter O'Hern. Florence Murphy was in charge of the music. Harry Myers, promoted from stage manager to actor, came along with Stull and the two would work together often over the next few years.

Stull continued with Fleming for two years but left in the fall of 1905 to work with Emma Bunting. However, when his replacement proved to be unsatisfactory, he returned to work with Fleming for one more year. Stull was becoming better known and print advertisements for Mamie Fleming appearances often prominently displayed the line "supported by Walter H. Stull," a definite indication of Stull's popularity and pulling power. At the end of the Summer season in 1906, Stull didn't return to the Fleming Company but took the logical next step and formed the Walter H. Stull Company (although there is evidence the two did work together some in 1908). Coming along with Stull was stage manager-turned-actor Harry Myers. The Stull Company quickly gained a reputation as a highly

Emma Bunting

professional group and had no trouble finding attractive bookings over the next couple of years. The Highland Democrat published in Peekskill, New York had, in September 1907, the highest praises, "The Stull Company is headed by the sterling young romantic actor Walter Stull, which in itself is an absolute and positive guarantee that every performance presented will be of the most artistic and detailed class, as he will be remembered as heretofore always being identified with only the better class of attractions, and is this season supported by a cast of extraordinary strength". One of the company's big hits was the comedic sketch *"How Baxter Butt In"* with other sketches such as *"The Great Diamond Robbery"*, *"Beyond the Lines"*, *The Finger of Scorn"* and *"All for Gold"* included in their repertoire.

Despite the company's great success at the end of the 1908 season, Stull disbanded his touring stock company and returned to live in Philadelphia. Not, as later publicity would suggest, to take a big offer from the movies but because his mother was gravely ill. For the next few years Stull stayed close to home. There is little to no mention of him in the trade papers except for an engagement in July 1909 in nearby Atlantic City. He appeared on stage with the stock company of Blaker's Theatre in a production of *"Bess"* which was written by his future Lubin co-star Eleanor Caines and directed by Edwin Middleton.

On April 5, 1911, Stull's mother passed away and, no longer needed in the role of caretaker, he went back to work full time (he had briefly worked at the Lubin studios late in 1910). In all likelihood, Stull had remained in contact with his protégé Harry Myers who was now appearing in moving pictures at the Lubin studios, and used their friendship as a means of gaining employment at the studio, until his mother's health became his main focus. With Lubin being located in Philadelphia, entering the movies would allow Stull to keep acting but not have to leave home. This was important because Stull's father was also in ill health, plus Stull had become enamored with a local girl named Virginia Foreman, whom he ended up marrying in December 1912.

The Lubin Manufacturing Company's film studios were located at 20th and Indiana Streets in Philadelphia. The company was a natural progression for Sigmund Lubin, who as an optometrist became interested in manufacturing lenses, and then cameras and projectors for the new moving picture industry. As early as 1897, Lubin was shooting moving pictures for commercial release, and with that being a successful venture a studio was the next step. As an inventor and film producer, Lubin was a contemporary and competitor of Thomas Edison. At first, Lubin would copy other studios' films either by reshooting them, as he did with his 1904 version of *The Great Train Robbery*, or by simply duping his competitors' releases. Many legal battles ensued but by the mid-aughts the Lubin Manufacturing Company became an honorable member of the Motion Picture Trust and released their films through the Trust's distribution arm known as the General Film Company.

Lubin's Philadelphia Headquarters

Like most other film studios of the time, Lubin shot actuality footage of major and not-so-major events around the country, giving audiences a chance to see people and places they would never otherwise have a chance to see. But like the others, Lubin also made fictional films, both comedies and dramas. By 1910, Lubin had set up a comedy company under the direction of Arthur D. Hotaling, who had already been with the company for over a decade, and which featured Hotaling's wife Mae Hotely (her stage name being an intentional play on their legal last name). Hotely, the star of the company, stood out as being not only a gifted comedienne but also a rather tall one (measuring exactly 6 feet in height). Making what became known as "Gay Time" comedies, this unit would be the main source of comedy films at Lubin for the next five years.

Walter Stull's first few films with Lubin were with a unit directed by Wilbert Melville, and featuring Myers, that was making both comedies and dramas. However, it soon became evident that Stull was more effective in comedic roles, and he went to work with the "Gay Time" unit that made comedies exclusively. The unit at that time featured Billy Louis (later known as Will Louis, the director of the Plump & Runt comedies), Spottiswood Aitken, Elsie Green, Gladys Cameron, Bernhardt Niemeyer (with an occasional appearance by Harry Myers who would come over from the Lubin dramatic company) and George Reehm.

George Reehm

The first film at Lubin known to feature Reehm (at that time reporting actors' names was taboo) was *Martyr or Crank?* released in 1909. For the rest of that year, through 1910 and into 1911, Reehm was mainly working in support of Harry Myers. Around the same time that Walter Stull transferred over to the all-comedy unit, so did Reehm. It was with Reehm that Stull first formed an on-screen comedic partnership. While working with the ensemble cast, with Hotely firmly established as its star, Stull and Reehm stood out enough to be informally known as the "Lubin Twins." In addition to acting in the films, Reehm often served as Arthur Hotaling's assistant director, honing a talent that would serve him well later in his career.

The Gay Time troupe went down to Jacksonville, Florida in late 1911 and made their comedies at a studio they built at 750 Riverside Avenue, taking over the old yacht club. The company had gained some new faces with the addition of Jack O'Neil, May Owens, Will Hopkins, Helen Marten, Walter Kendig (who would gain some short lived fame in 1915 as the Louie of the "Heinie & Louie" comedies), Jerold T. Hevener, and Robert Burns who went by the nickname of Bobby.

Born September 1, 1878 in Philadelphia, Pennsylvania to James and Julia Burns, one of eight sons, little is known about the early life of Robert Paul Burns. With such a large Scotch-Irish contingent on the East Coast of America at the time, most of the press surrounding "Robert Burns" concerned the popular 18th century Scottish poet. There were societies, lodges, songs, plays and even cigars named after the literary Burns, making it hard to discern him from the acrobatic comedian of the same name (or from hundreds of others named Robert Burns, being the Scottish equivalent of John Smith).

Evidence suggests that the comedian began full time vaudeville work sometime in 1899. A very agile performer, Burns quickly found work on the stage with his first known credit being part of the cast of *"The Devil's Auction."* It was his work in this play that led him to the role that first gained him some notoriety. Producer Fred R. Hamlin and Director Julian Mitchell were staging Victor Herbert's *"Babes in Toyland"* and Burns secured the role of the Spider (in a cast that also featured future Biograph comedian Gus Pixley) . The play opened in Chicago on June 17, 1903, then ran briefly in Washington, DC before moving to Broadway that Fall for an extended run. Burns' turn as the Spider was a highlight of the show and reviewers as well as audiences marveled at his acrobatic abilities.

It was with this company that Burns visited San Francisco in April 1906, and ended up being an eyewitness and unwilling participant in the great earthquake and fire that nearly destroyed the city by the Bay. Mark Whiting, a fellow *"Babes"* cast member, recounted the catastrophe in a letter home that was published by his hometown newspaper, *The Arkansas Democrat*. Whiting noted that he and Burns had gone to sleep when "Not to exaggerate, the building I was in swayed like a drunken man: the fire escapes fell off, the bricks fell all through the room and hall, to say nothing of the plaster." Whiting also wrote that, once outside, they saw a number of fires and knew they needed to evacuate the area, eventually sleeping in a cemetery, and discouraging vandals and would-be robbers with a revolver he was carrying. Four days later Burns, Whiting and a number of their fellow cast members were able to arrange transportation heading towards New York City. The theater that had been staging "Babes in Toyland" was at the center of the worst devastation, and all was lost; with the company's scenery and props destroyed, the troupe was disbanded.

With *"Babes"* gone, Burns went over to the producers' other show *"The Wizard of Oz,"* taking the role of the Cowardly Lion with the main road company. *"Oz"* had opened on Broadway in early 1903 (after a run in Chicago) and featured the team of (David R.) Montgomery and (Fred) Stone who until the 1939 MGM musical were the performers most associated with the L. Frank Baum story. The road company starred George Stone as the Scarecrow and a revolving door of actors essaying the Tin Man role including Fred Nice, Billy Baker, Frank Hayes and others.

Since the play had been written for the duo of Montgomery & Stone, the Cowardly Lion became a secondary character, but that did not stop Burns from captivating the audience and he was often singled out when the play was reviewed. The constant in the company beside Stone was Joseph Schrode, who played Imogene the Cow (who replaced the excluded Toto the Dog, a large animal being needed in order for a human to play the part). There were many Dorothys also, with Minerva Coverdale being the most memorable. For a time Rosa Gore, who had a long career as a film comedienne, played the role of Cynthia Cynch.

Between engagements as the Cowardly Lion, Burns showed real courage and was married on February 28, 1908 to the former Violet Comaford. Violet would later appear in some of the Vim comedies and likely some of the Jaxon films. For her the move by Jaxon from Jacksonville to her hometown of Providence, Rhode Island would be a bittersweet and tragic homecoming. Born in Providence in 1887, she would pass away there on October 3, 1917, her illness perhaps influencing Bobby's involvement with Jaxon.

Burns left the *"Oz"* company in mid-1909, and went to work for famed producer Florenz Ziegfeld, Jr. in his latest production *"The Ziegfeld Follies of 1909."* The show featured an act with performers dressed in animal costumes, Burns' forté. Of course the real appeal of the show, which ran from June 14 to August 7, was the sight of a Ziegfeld girl not wearing much of a costume at all. After the closing of the show, Burns disappears for the rest of 1909, most all of 1910 and most of 1911. He reportedly reprised his role as the Cowardly Lion in a short series of Oz films made in Chicago by Selig in 1910. Since his Oz character was in a full animal costume his appearance cannot be confirmed, however, he is known to have appeared in at least one Selig comedy released July 25, 1910, *A Sleep Walking Cure*. His reappearance in mid-1911 at the very same moving picture studio that employed Walter Stull set the stage for what would eventually become Pokes and Jabbs.

Walter Stull and George Reehm, eventually along with Bobby Burns, became the main supporting players for Mae Hotely. In various configurations the trio began

Mae Hotely

obtaining more and more screen time and a certain level of their own notoriety. For the next few years, Burns, Stull, Reehm and the rest of the "Gay Times" company would get into the routine of shooting in Jacksonville during the winter, and in Philadelphia and/or Atlantic City the rest of the year, with occasional excursions to other locations.

Concerning the winter move South, the *New York Dramatic Mirror* noted in January 1912 that the unit "carries a Pullman standard sleeping coach, and a day coach; also a seventy-foot baggage car containing a big outfit of scenery and the probable necessary props and furniture. The first stop will be made at Jacksonville, the itinerary to follow being Daytona, Miami, St. Augustine, Knights Key, and thence to Cuba, returning by way of New Orleans and up the Mississippi River."

With the possible exception of St. Augustine, the Lubin players never left Jacksonville in the winter of 1912 until returning up North once Summer reached Florida. The Hotaling unit would retrace their steps the following winter and again shoot in Jacksonville. For the Summer of 1913, the unit traveled back north and set up camp, not at the home base of Philadelphia, but in nearby Atlantic City. The troupe at that point consisted of Mae Hotely, Bobby Burns, George Reehm, Walter Stull, Frances Ne Moyer and her sister Marguerite, and Julia Calhoun taking most of the larger roles with Ella Reehm, Florence Leslie, Violet Burns, Raymond McKee, Walt. Leslie and Jack Willard in support. Garry Hotaling, the brother of the director and head of the "Gay Time" unit was the cameraman and Reehm was assistant director.

The relatively close proximity of the Lubin activities to the movers and shakers in New York City may have assisted in the departure of Burns, Reehm and Stull. By mid-Summer 1913, the trio had shot their last films for Lubin walking the famous seaside boardwalk one last time and then headed about 150 miles north and went to work for Reliance and their Komic brand.

A side note to the trio's defection from Lubin. The loss of such key players was hard for the remaining members of the Gay Time troupe to absorb. This less-than-favorable situation kept on for a time until, during the unit's 1913-14 winter trip to Jacksonville, they added some local talent to the company roster. One of those was a former movie theater operator and would-be comedian named Oliver Hardy, who when visiting the Lubin studio merely to watch the production, found himself appearing, front and center, in a film called *Outwitting Dad*. The rest being history, and our good fortune.

The Lubin Comedy Company

Under the direction of Arthur D. Hotaling

Standing, from left to Right: Mrs. George Reehm, Jack O'Neil, May Owens, Will Hopkins, Mae Hotely, Jerold T. Hevener, Halen Marten, Bobby Burns, Betty Cameron. Sitting: Walter Kendig, Will Louis, Arthur D. Hotaling, Leola Hotaling, Walter Stull, George Reehm.

LUBIN FILMS

Only films known to feature Walter Stull and/or Bobby Burns are listed. Since cast lists were rarely published, and since most of the films are lost, it is impossible to know what other Lubin films they may have appeared in. The cast lists supplied here include only those performers verified as having appeared in the films. Mae Hotely and other regular Gay Time cast members most certainly appeared in many of these films uncredited. Directorial credits are only given if known for certain. Most of the Gay Time comedies were directed by Arthur D. Hotaling, with some being directed by Jerold T. Hevener, and perhaps a few by George Reehm or Will Louis.

Spoony Sam

Released December 1, 1910. Lubin Manufacturing Co.-General Film Company release. One reel (950 ft.).

Filmed in Philadelphia, Pennsylvania.

With George Reehm (*Spoony Sam*), Walter Stull.

Sam could not help spooning any more than he could help eating. He had three square meals a day and spent the remainder of the time spooning pretty Sue. Sue was quite willing to be spooned though there was another chap who wanted to marry her and Sam had a fine time. But Pa Sprague, Sue's father, had forgotten long ago the time when he himself was young and he had no sympathy with spooners. He told Sue she could not see Sam except in the house where Pa and Ma could keep an eye on them and Sue, like a dutiful daughter, sent word to Sam. But that didn't help matters much. Sam spooned just the same. That was too much for Pa Sprague and he went after the minister. Immediate marriage took Sam all of a heap and he made a sprint for the door that was a record breaker and he didn't stop running until the sight of a young married couple admiring their first baby. That gave Sam the idea that he would like to get married and he went back after Sue but meantime the other fellow had come along and Sue had decided that she would rather marry a man who did not spoon so much but who meant it more. The minister was still there and the knot was tied before Sam poked his face through the doorway and announced that after all he thought he would rather be married if it wasn't too much trouble to the minister. Pa Sprague told him what he thought of him and Sue added an appendix. Then Pa Sprague took a malicious delight in putting Sam out of the house so Sam went and spooned somewhere else. [Nickelodeon & Film Index]

The character of Spoony Sam had been the subject of a vaudeville play circa 1907, and there was also a popular song called *"Everlovin' Spoony Sam."* While hard to determine if this was Walter Stull's film debut it is his first known film work. The film was remade in 1912 again with Reehm and Stull.

"Sam undoubtedly is funny. Anyhow everybody laughed at him where this picture was seen. But Sue's character seems in some ways a travesty upon womanhood. No woman worth considering would be as inconsistent as this one is represented to be, marrying a man apparently because he appeared at the time when the minister was there. Spoony Sam is not improbable. Indeed, there are a good many like him. But Sue can scarcely be swallowed. Women are not like that and there is nothing funny in representing them so. This picture would be improved by changing that wedding scene to make it appear that Sam was put off for a time, but eventually accepted, after he had received his lesson." -- *Moving Picture World*

Their Mother-In-Law

Released April 13, 1911. Lubin Manufacturing Co.-General Film Company release. One reel (1000 ft.).

With Mae Hotely (*Mrs. Jones*), Walter Stull (*Peter Smith*).

Young Mrs. Smith, becoming weary of housework, sent for her mother to pay her a visit. The same day Mr. Smith, wishing to help his wife, sent for his mother. Both arrived in one time, and when they met — well, if looks could kill, they both would have died on the spot. The Smiths had only one spare room, and, as it was impossible for both mothers to occupy this, they had to give up their own room to one of them and sleep in the attic themselves. There was all kinds of trouble, while the mothers were disputing which should be head of the household. If Mrs. Smith started to fry a steak, Mrs. Jones flew to the range and tried to do it. If Mrs. Jones in sweeping the parlor, placed a chair in one position, Mrs. Smith came in later and put it somewhere else. The young Smiths soon found this state of affairs intolerable. So one day they quietly planned a little trip, leaving the note: "Dear Mothers — We have gone away for a rest. Lovingly, Peter and Mary." When Mrs. Jones and Mrs. Smith read the note they fell into each others' arms for comfort. [MPW]

"One mother-in-law is usually thought to be sufficient to create enough trouble in one household. The situation can be imagined when the second one appears. As may well be expected the young married couple are unable to stand the strain and decamp, leaving the mothers to find out who is who, by themselves. When they get the letter, addressed 'To Our Dear Mothers,' they fall into each other's arms." -- *Moving Picture World*

A Hero -- Almost

Released May 22, 1911. Lubin Manufacturing Co.-General Film Company release. Split reel (370 ft.) on the same reel with *The Gambler's Chance* (605 ft.).

With Walter Stull (*Walter*), Jack Regan (*Jack*), Miss Harvey.

Walter and Jack were both in love with Mildred. She told them that she would marry no one but a hero. So of course it was up to them to become heroes. Their first stunt was to rescue Mildred's little dog from being run over by an automobile. But she told them that the man she would marry must save a human life. Next day Jack was out walking. While passing a building he heard a wild cry for help. Jack dashed into the building and saw a young girl being strangled by a man. Bravely and fearlessly he leaped upon the villain. A moment later he was leaped upon by a crowd of angry people, for he had interrupted the taking of a moving picture. After he had been thrown out he was considerably disheartened with the hero business. Then he thought of a scheme whereby he could do a noble deed without any harm to himself. He hired a tramp to waylay Mildred as if meaning to steal her money and jewels. At the right moment Jack was to appear on the scene and rescue her. The plan worked out all right except that Jack was delayed in doing the rescue stunt. Walter, by a lucky chance, happened to be there and heard Mildred's cry for help. He certainly did handle that, tramp

without gloves. He nearly killed the poor fellow. Jack arrived soon after and the tramp gave him a beating up that was not any make believe. In addition Jack had the sorrow to see Mildred walking off in arm with the real hero, Walter." [MPW]

"*A Hero – Almost* is a very funny Lubin comedy, full of laughs from start to finish." -- *Binghamton (N.Y.) Press*

"This comedy will keep them laughing. It tells the story of a romantic girl with two lovers. She will only marry a hero. The subject is not very fresh, but is lively and holds the attention from beginning to end." -- *Moving Picture World*

A Gay Time in Atlantic City

Released July 20, 1911. Lubin Manufacturing Co.-General Film Company release. One reel (945 ft.)

Directed by Arthur D. Hotaling. Filmed in Atlantic City, New Jersey.

With Jack Hopkins (*Fred Perkins*), George Reehm (*George Smith*), Mae Hotely (*Mrs. Perkins, Fred's wife*), Glady Cameron (*Betty*), Elsie Glynn (*Peggy*), Bobby Burns, Will Louis.

The call of summer was in the blood of Fred Perkins and George Smith. They longed to disport themselves upon the sands and in the waves by the seaside. But, alas! They were married. Fearful handicap! Still being brave and also clever, they proceeded to overcome this disadvantage. Fred suddenly had a nervous breakdown, shaking all over most fearfully in the presence of his wife. Just at the right time, George brought around a doctor, who was something of a sport himself. Doc looked serious. He must go away for a couple of weeks to the mountains, said Doc. Friend George nobly presented himself to be his caretaker, waving aside all considerations of neglect to his business or other inconvenience. Noble man! In due time, the invalid and his friend, roughly dressed and carrying kettles, pans and other camping paraphernalia, said good-bye to their wives. Then they hit the high places for a thick wood, not far distant where they had hidden two suitcases full of clothes. After dressing in their gay garments, Fred had entirely recovered from his nervous breakdown; they took the fastest train for gay Atlantic City. There they met a couple of young ladies, with whom they rode along the boardwalk in rolling chairs, and later went in bathing. Meanwhile, Mrs. Perkins and Mrs. Smith, being lonely, decided to spend a couple of days in Atlantic City. Thither they went in Mrs. Smith's motor car. Their room in the hotel overlooked the beach, and there after talking for a while and wondering how their husbands were getting along in the lonely mountains, far from civilization's comfort, they sighed and looked out over the beach, where a great crowd of bathers were enjoying themselves. They looked through field-glasses. Suddenly, Mrs. Perkins ejaculated, "Oh!" She handed the glasses to Mrs. Smith. Mrs. Smith looked and she also ejaculated, "Oh!" for they had recognized their husbands with the two girls in the surf, and they certainly did not look as though they were ill. If did not take Mrs. Perkins and Mrs. Smith very long to get to the beach. Their husbands saw them coming and tried to escape by running into the water. But that did not stop the angry wives for an instant. Into the water they waded. Each grabbed her recreant spouse by the hair and led him upon the shore, where they administered a just punishment. [MPW]

It is more than likely that the same cast made up the 1912 comedy *A Hot Time in Atlantic City* (a remake of a 1909 Lubin comedy with the same title) which was apparently shot at the same time as *Gay Time in Atlantic City"* but cast and crew credits cannot be confirmed. This film was one of a series of *Gay Time In…* films that also included New York City, Quebec, Canada and Washington, D.C. (and eventually Jacksonville, Florida).

"The Lubin comedy *A Gay Time in Atlantic City* is the feature reel at the Hudson Theatre to-night. 'Hubbies Tried to Fool Wifeys with the Nervous Breakdown Stuff.' Did it go? Well, you want to see the picture. Wifeys accidentally met them on the beach with two dashing ladies. Shed a tear for hubbies. They fret theirs. The beach boardwalk and famous sights of the resort are shown." -- *The Hudson Evening Register (Hudson, NY)*

Love's Labor Lost

Released December 7, 1911. Lubin Manufacturing Co.-General Film Company release. One reel (990 ft.).

With Walter Stull (*Walter*), Harry Myers (*successful suitor*), Jack Hopkins (*John*), Elsie Glynn (*Elsie*).

John Hopkins and Walter Stull were deep, deep in love with Peggy Glenn. It happened that they both called on the same evening. They could not conceal their hatred of each other. The first word led to the retort courteous and then swiftly to the quip modest – the reply churlish – the reproof valiant and finally to the lie direct. Pretty Peggy left the room and then the two young men left the house. They went to their respective clubs, where they told their respective friends of their respective hatreds. John's friends advised a duel. The challenge was sent and Walter readily accepted. Both arrived with their friends at the dueling ground by the old mill. It so happened that that same day Harry Myers, an old admirer of Peggy, returned unexpectedly from the West. He lost no time in calling on the girl he could not forget. He had the pleasure of seeing that he was not forgotten. Just at this moment a stable boy rushed in to tell Peggy about the duel. Harry seized the psychological moment, proposed and was accepted. Then Peggy sent the stable boy with a note to the duelists announcing her engagement. [MPW]

"[*Love's Labor Lost*] is a modern comedy that is not very amusing. The audience looked at it in silence except at two instances, when a messenger in a hurry slipped skillfully while going down some steps, and again when the same man took a plainly premeditated header down a bank. It was conducted with not much skill, but there are some very pretty pictorial effects in it. Two men chance to meet at the same girl's. They quarrel; the girl leaves the room; the maid brings their hats. Each at his own club excites much sympathy. A challenge is accepted; about ten men in tile hats arrive at the dueling place, but none among them knows how to conduct a duel, so they toss up to see who shall choose the weapons. This gives time for the messenger from the girl to arrive with the news that she is going to marry a third man. The way the girl got news of the duel was not at all realistic; it hardly could have happened as shown." -- *Moving Picture World*

A Dark Deception

Released January 17, 1912. Lubin Manufacturing Co.-General Film Company release. Split reel on the same reel with *The Peanut Industry*.

With George Reehm, Peggy Glenwood, Walter Stull (*Walter*), Bobby Burns.

George Reehm and Peggy Glenwood are sweethearts, but Peggy could not resist the temptation of inviting Count De Tears to call on her one evening, she having met the count at a reception a few nights previous. She does not love the count, but merely invited him to furnish a little amusement. George calls one afternoon and accidentally picks up a note, which happens to be the one the count had written to Peggy, accepting her invitation, saying he will call that evening. George thinks the count is trying to rob him of his love. He says nothing to Peggy about this note, but that same afternoon he tells his troubles to his room-mate, who figures out a scheme whereby he can watch the count. George and his friend persuade the colored butler to follow "them" (George and his friend). The journey ends, after a taxicab ride of several blocks, at the stage door of a theater. Another friend, who is an actor, is now pressed into service, who, with the aid of black cork, makes George up to look like the butler, leaving the butler in the dressing room. After borrowing his livery, George returns to the Glenwood household, just in time to admit the count. George makes it very uncomfortable for the count that evening, and when the count left he went out a different way than which he entered, as George assisted him out of the rear window. George now explains to Peggy that he is not the butler, and admits to Peggy that he was a little jealous. Peggy now sees the humorous side of the situation, and assures George that she does not love the count. They forgive each other and with the engagement kiss, predict a very happy future. [MPW]

The first known appearance of Bobby Burns and Walter Stull in the same film. With most of the Lubin films lost, sparse company records, and trade papers that still did not overly concern themselves with the actors' names in films it is near impossible to know for sure if the two had made a film together before this one.

"A rough farce to please the gallery. A girl, her lover, a count and a negro butler are the principals. The lover knows that the count is to call. He is jealous, captures the butler and, with the help of theatrical friends, makes up to look like him. He then abuses the count. It is funny." -- *Moving Picture World*

A Compromise

Released January 20, 1912. Lubin Manufacturing Co.-General Film Company release. Split reel (417 ft.) on the same reel with *A Boardinghouse Romance* (433 ft.) and *Making Hay* (175 ft.).

With Bobby Burns (*husband*), Elsie Glynn (*wife*), Mae Hotely.

Mr. Wallace, a traveling salesman, just returned home to find that Mrs. Wallace has all new servants and very pretty at that. Mr. Wallace just can't resist the temptation of kissing them. It does not take his wife long to see what is going on and she immediately discharges them. The nect day he finds all new male help. Mrs. Wallace thinks up a scheme whereby she will cure her husband of flirting. She starts in flirting with the help. Mr. Wallace gets sore and fires all the men. Mr. and Mrs. compromise and now we find all colored servants in the Wallace household. [MPW]

"A very short farce that never falls down from start to finish. The idea is fresh and in the atmosphere of a farce, amusing and it is handled as was proper. It is bright and laughable." -- *Moving Picture World*

A Midwinter Night's Dream

Released February 19, 1912. Lubin Manufacturing Co.-General Film Company release. Split reel (878 ft.), on the same reel with *Army Aviation Practice* (140 ft.).

Filming started in Philadelphia, Pennsylvania and finished in Jacksonville, Florida.

With Walter Stull (*tramp of the orange grove*), Bobby Burns (*tramp in the freight car*), Helen Martin [Marten].

A tramp is asleep on the end of a freight car on a railroad siding. He awakes — snow covers the ground. He makes a snowball and throws it. It strikes another tramp asleep in an orange grove. The tramp awakes. The other tramp leaves the snow, walks over to the orange grove. It is too hot so he walks back to the snow with the other tramp. Two girls appear in the orange grove. The tramps take the girls over in the snow. The girls are cold and run back. The tramps write a note asking the girls to meet them at a certain place, and placing it in a snowball, throw it to the girls. The girls receive the note and agree to meet the tramps. While the hoboes are walking down the street they see an actor taking clothes from his trunk in front of a theater. He gives each of them a costume and they dress up and meet the girls. They discover a big wad of stage money in the pocket of the coat and proceed to spend it with a lavish hand. They have a great time until the money is discovered to be stage money, when they are chased by a large crowd until one of the tramps falls down. A policeman is fanning his foot with a club, when he wakes up on the freight car and is ordered away by the policeman. [MPW]

Starting a film in Philadelphia (in order to show the cold, snowy conditions) and then finishing the film down in Florida had been done before by Lubin with 1910's *A Honeymoon Through Snow to Sunshine.*

"The Lubin people have a company at Palm Beach. In this picture a tramp in a snowy freight yard falls asleep and dreams that he and a pal are having the time of their lives in tropical parks and groves. The ideas are very fresh and amusing. The effect of the combination of summer and winter in one picture is delightfully ludicrous and it kept the house in roars of laughter. In one scene a snowball is chucked from the freight yard and lands in the next scene at the feet of two girls at Palm Beach, who flirt with the tramps in the snowdrift. The photographs are very good." -- *Moving Picture World*

Willie the Hunter

Released February 24, 1912. Lubin Manufacturing Co.-General Film Company release. Split reel (700 ft.), on the same reel with *Pottery Making in America* (300 ft.).

With Walter Stull (*Willie Tait*), Robert Burns (*the "bear"*), George Reehm (*club member*), Walter Kendig (*club member*).

Willie Tait appears one day at the club room, dressed in a new hunting suit. The boys enjoy a good laugh over his costume. While in the club, some of the boys extract the shot from his shells and then hurry off to a costumer's and rent a bear suit. One of the boys dresses up like a bear and, followed by the other members of the club, hurries to the woods to overtake Willie. Willie is frightened to death at the sight of the bear, drops his hunting bag and gun. He is chased some distance by the supposed bear, and when he finds the bear close upon his heels, he climbs a tree, only to be pulled down by the bear. He is finally allowed to escape, and the boys hurry back to the club house to hear Willie's story, Willie tells the boys of his terrible battle. The boys give him the ha ! ha ! and produce the bear. [MPW]

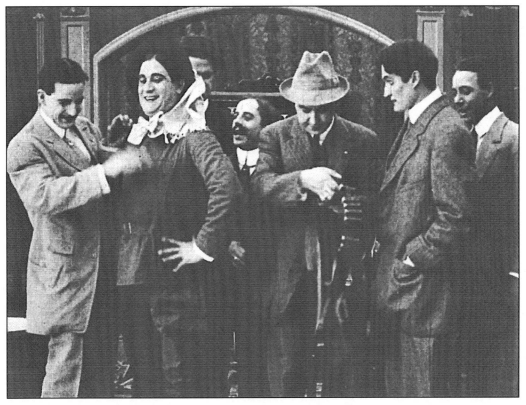

A Lubin ad describes Willie as a "somewhat ladylike member of the Oakland Club" and Walter Stull's character does dress a bit like a dandy and acts a little effeminate. This, of course, leads the macho men of the club to want to prank Willie all the more. Bobby Burns take on the role of playing the bear, imitating animals being nothing new to Burns nor something he wouldn't do frequently in the future. Stull gets to ham it up a bit when back at the club he tells his great story of triumph, only to faint when Burns (in the bear costume) comes up from behind and puts his arm around him. As of the writing of this book this is the oldest extant film to feature both Walter Stull and Bobby Burns.

"The man who played the Willie-boy hunter in this picture could hardly have enjoyed his job. He plainly wasn't that kind. It is a very unpleasant character; the farce has nothing fresh whatever and it is somewhat vulgar. The photographs are good." -- *Moving Picture World*

"*Willie the Hunter* is an admirable film to see when depressed, as one is bound to laugh as the ludicrous situations follow one another on the screen." -- *Nothern Whig (Antrim, Northern Ireland)*

His Little Sister

Released April 11, 1912. Lubin Manufacturing Co.-General Film Company release. Split reel (652 ft.), on the same reel with *That Chicken Dinner* (374 ft.).

With Walter Stull (*brother*), Leona Devoe (*sister*), Raymond McKee.

Hans, an amiable Dutchman who keeps the Red Dog Delmonico, tells the boys that his little sister is coming from Germany and shows them the photograph of a beautiful young girl. She is the first woman to come to Red Dog Gulch, and the residents of the Arizona town prepare to welcome her in their triad rags. When she does come they find she does not come up to the photograph and after an indignation meeting demand an explanation of Hans. He shows the photograph and explains that he forgot to tell that the picture was made in 1883. Minna pursues all the men and they fight shy of the Delmonico, bringing Hans to the verge of bankruptcy. A horse thief is captured and they are about to lynch him when Pete suggests that they make him marry Minna. After he has seen her the thief begs them to lynch him, but they are hard-hearted and refuse. He is married to Minna and with tearful farewells they ship them out of camp. [MPW]

Publicity for *That Chicken Dinner*, the other half of the reel, describes the lead character as "Rummy George" likely inferring that George Rehm played the part. That in turn may indicate the presence of Stull or Burns in the cast, but without the ability to actually view the film that will remain an unknown as is the case with casts for so many early comedy short subjects.

"A Western farce on the same reel; it made a good many more laughs than the other. The boys had seen little sister's photograph taken years before and expected her to look like it. She disappointed them; her face, especially her nose, spoilt business at the restaurant for cowboys, her brother kept. The boys got a horse thief and made him marry her. He asked them to go on with the hanging." -- *Moving Picture World*

A Gay Time in Jacksonville, Florida

Released April 18, 1912. Lubin Manufacturing Co.-General Film Company release. One reel (1,042 ft.).

Directed by Arthur D. Hotaling. Filmed in Jacksonville, Florida.

With Mae Hotely, Walter Stull, George Reehm (*smooth faced German*).

Fritz and Hans decide that they will take a trip to Jacksonville, Fla. They arrive in the city and board a car, and after riding through many of the principal streets, reach the ostrich farm. They see the ostriches driven hooked up to a buggy and also ridden bareback. They then go to the alligator farm and are shown the alligators in all the various stages from their infancy to old age. They see the alligators hooked up to a wagon and driven; also see the alligators shoot the chutes. Then after taking a few rides on the roller-coaster, they make up their minds to again tour the city proper. They hire an automobile and ride through the beautiful residential section of the city. On their way they pass a couple of pretty girls, and now the auto has no attraction for them. They hop out and try to scrape up an acquaintance with the girls, but receive a severe beating at the hands of two of the young ladies' gentlemen friends. They cannot resist the temptation of picking a few oranges from an orange tree and for this receive another beating. While passing the Morocco Temple, where the Shriners hold forth, they hear voices inside and decide to go in and see what is going on. Their presence not being desirable, and not being able to give the proper signs, Fritz and Hans are roughly thrown out. Poor Fritz and Hans meet their Waterloo while standing beside a fire alarm box. They do not know what it is and start an inspection. Upon opening the door they see a little handle and while one is lighting his pipe the other pulls the little handle down. They have unconsciously sent in a general fire alarm. We now see the doors of all the fire houses in the city thrown open and the engine and apparatus depart for the fire. The chief speeds out in his auto. The fire department arriving at the scene from where the alarm was turned in are unable to locate the fire. The chief seeing the two Germans standing by the open alarm box, asks them, 'Where the fire is?" They, always ready for a joke, tell the chief that the fire is in Fritz's pipe. The chief fails to see the humor of it and orders the firemen to put the fire out. Frits and Hans receive a good wetting after they are taken in hand by the police and placed in a patrol wagon. The next morning Fritz and Hans wishing to return home and in order they get in no more trouble, a squad of police escort them to the station and see them safely aboard the train. [MPW]

By the time *Gay Time in Jacksonville* was released the Lubin Stock Company under Arthur D. Hotaling had left Florida and returned to their Philadelphia home base. *Moving Picture World* noted that they had made a number of pictures while on the "Peninsula" and more specifically that "with the exception of two slight automobile collisions, no mishap occurred. One of them cut up the Lubin machine rather badly, but Hans and Fritz, who were seeing the sights of Jacksonville, were not hurt. The company will take work easy at the home plant for a few months and then make another trip, probably to Alaska." Other trade paper articles inferred that the Company was headed for Europe. Neither trip ever happened.

The Lubin studio backlot in Jacksonville.

The May 18, 1912 issue of *Moving Picture World* detailed the shooting of *Gay Time in Jacksonville* and of the Lubin Company's activities in Florida during the winter and early spring of 1912 in an article entitled "The Dare-Devil Comedians": "The Lubin stock company just returned from Jacksonville, Fla., among other anecdotes, have a good joke on two of the troupe who like to hear themselves spoken of as 'dare-devils.' Walter Stull often says, 'dare all that man dare, he who dares more is no man.' He claims to be willing on any emergency to face a wolf or wild cat, rescue a babe from the angry deep or take any risk where prowess is required. Geo. Reehm's hardihood is even more thrilling, he will (in the photoplays) leap from the window of a ten-story skyscraper, roll down the side of a mountain or loop the loop in a bi-plane. So many of these thrillers occur in the moving pictures that Reehm is always accompanied with a dummy to take his place should he by chance be killed. One day at Jacksonville several of the company visited a reptile farm and Mae Hotely dropped her handbag in the snake pit. The pit was alive with the squirming reptiles among which was two Gila monsters, Stull and Reehm were called upon to recover the bag, they quickly got busy throwing aside their hats and coats, each looked at the other with a kind of Alphonse and Gaston expression, the situation was tense for a few seconds, then they remembered that whiskey was the antidote for snake bites and rushed to the 'German Village' thinking that it was also a preventative. Five minutes passed and they had not returned. Miss Hotely looked and waited in vain, presently she noticed that a bystander had a hooked walking cane. She hastily borrowed it and when the dare-devils returned, the bag had already been rescued by the fair owner, and it was noticed that the snakes had not even bitten the cane."

"As usual in these Lubin "Gay Time" pictures, a couple of comic characters, Germans, are used to give human interest to the views and make a few laughs. The views take in the chief streets and parks of the city. Some are very beautiful; some are extremely hard on the eyes. The spectators seemed to like it." -- *Moving Picture World*

"George E. Reehm was the smooth-faced German In *A Gay Time in Jacksonville.* He used only straight make-up, getting his expressions through the control of his facial muscles. In point of service he is one of the oldest photoplayers in the business and it is this long practice which enables him to dispense with lining paints in his make-up box." –*Moving Picture World column*

The Tramp Elephant

Released June 28, 1912. Lubin Manufacturing Co.-General Film Company release. Split reel (732 ft.), on the same reel with *Bridget's Explanation* (321 ft.).

With Walter Stull (*second tramp*), Robert Burns (*first tramp*), Joe Reilly (*tramp*).

Three weary travelers, having arrived somewhere in their special box, see in front of them some bills of a circus. Looking around the yard after making their somewhat incomplete toilet, they see the cars of the show quite close to them. It was natural for them to inspect. They find one open to enter. Seemingly it was the wardrobe car for on the floor lay an elephant skin and head waiting for two human forms to introduce themselves inside to make a funny imitation of the real animal. The thought is suggested to the weary travelers that it might be a means to an end to procure breakfast, so they quickly avail themselves of the gift fate had sent them. Two of the liveliest quickly insert themselves, while the other donning a keeper's uniform, straightway start to test their fortunes. Unfortunately the inmates of the elephant were not satisfied with their condition as the keeper and they found ample cause to grumble. For instance when the meals came round for the employees of the circus the keeper got a full meal, while the poor elephant got a bundle of hay. Finally the elephant holds the police force at bay by squirting a hose of water through his trunk and escapes. [MPW]

"Three weary travelers see some bills of a circus, and looking around, also discover the cars of the show. It was the wardrobe car, and on the floor lay an elephant skin and head. Two of them donned the hide, and with the other in a keeper's uniform, started to test their fortunes. Unfortunately, the inmates of the elephant were not as satisfied, for when the meals came round for the employees, the keeper got a full meal, while the poor elephant got a bundle of hay. The elephant goes on strike, and wild flurries to get out of his way causes tents to fall and numberless novel chases." -- *New York Clipper*

Over the Hills to the Poor House

Released July 12, 1912. Lubin Manufacturing Co.-General Film Company release. Split reel (368 ft.), on the same reel with *The Hypnotist* (688 ft.).

Directed by Arthur D. Hotaling.

With Robert Burns (*The husband*), Mae Hotely (*Martha Downs, the wife*).

Jim Downs is an habitual drunkard and leaves his home, wife and children. The poor woman in despair writes to her husband, telling him that unless he sends money quickly she and the children will have to seek refuge in the poor house, Saturday. Jim, when he receives the letter, is as usual, three parts full, but he scrawls a letter which reads: "Dear Martha. — Try and not move until Monday, and I will arrange my affairs so that we can all go to the poor house together. Lovingly, Jim." [MPW]

Although Biograph shot a film in 1908 based on the now classic poem it is highly unlikely that this film, other than title, had much to do with Will Carleton's literary work. The poem written in 1872 was in 1912 still the basis for a play performed by a number of touring stock companies. Carleton would pass away before the end of 1912 (December 18).

"You will find the laughing road early in this one." -- *The Missoulian (Missoula, Montana)*

The Stranded Actors

Released July 13, 1912. Lubin Manufacturing Co.-General Film Company release. One reel (1,065 ft.).

Directed by Arthur D. Hotaling.

With Mae Hotely, Walter Stull.

Two actors, who are down on their luck and out of an engagement, are walking the ties to the next town, carrying their trunk. They sit down to rest when one of them, who has a nail in his shoe which has been annoying him, sees a newspaper, which he picks up and tears off a piece. The other actor starts to read the paper and an article on the front page attracts *his attention. It is to the effect that should John Silas Higgins return to his native village he would find a fortune of $75,000 and his old sweetheart awaiting him. He has an idea immediately, that here is a chance to get a good square meal and possibly some ready money. He at once tells his partner of his scheme and the partner agrees. They go to the edge of a wood and opening their trunk, proceed to make themselves up to appear like what they suppose the advertised personage would look like. Having gotten themselves up in true western style, they*

start, and on the way they perceive a bottle of gold paint on a table in front of a second-hand store. This they appropriate, and, picking some stones up from the street, they paint them so that they will look similar to nuggets. Armed with all the proofs (and the get up), that they are fresh from the West, they go to the girl's house, where they are wined and dined. Everything is going nicely until the old girl receives a letter from the real Silas Higgins. She then discovers that they are imposters. She excuses herself in order to notify the police. In the meantime the actors get a peep at the letter that she has left in the adjoining room, and they think it best to be on their way. A lively chase then follows. In order to throw off the pursuers, they try to get away in autos, motor boats, etc. They finally succeed in losing the crowd and make their way to where their trunk is hidden, and quickly change into their street clothes. They have a lively time, and although had a run for it they are amply repaid by the good square meal that they have had. [MPW]

"*The Stranded Actors* caused the biggest laugh throughout ever drawn for one picture. It was real comedy. There have been many funny things in pictures but the way the motor boats were handled has never been produced before." -- *The Auburn Citizen (Auburn, NY)*

The Uninvited Guests

Released July 19, 1912. Lubin Manufacturing Co.-General Film Company release. Split reel (513 ft.), on the same reel with *Buster's Dream* (554 ft.).

With Walter Stull, Robert Burns, Raymond McKee.

Two convicts, who make their escape from jail, take advantage of a masquerade ball which is in progress. They steal a couple of masques, and enter the ball room as masqueraders. For the first time in some months they are enjoying themselves to the strains of sweet music on a ballroom floor. They induce two gentlemen, who are masquerading as policemen, to exchange clothes with them. They make their "getaway" at an early hour in the morning in their police uniforms. They breakfast on bread and milk, which they get from the early merchants. In the meantime the guards are on the track of the convicts, and mistake the two gentlemen wearing the convict clothes home. Here a lively chase follows. While the prison guards are chasing the supposed convicts, another crowd is chasing the real convicts, whom they think are police, and wondering why policemen got frightened at burglars and ran away. The whole affair comes to a lively finish when the two crowds meet. The guards are rewarded for their chase by catching the right men. [MPW]

"Fast comedy toward the end, this is a travesty that is amusing in plot and action." -- *The Rome Daily Sentinel (Rome, NY)*

"A story of mixed identities which untangled themselves satisfactorily to the accompaniment of a good laugh." -- *Bedfordshire Times and Independent (U.K.)*

A Visit to Lively Town

Released July 24, 1912. Lubin Manufacturing Co.-General Film Company release. Split reel (436 ft.), on the same reel with *The Talker* (599 ft.).

Filmed in Atlantic City, New Jersey along Atlantic Avenue, the Boardwalk and on the beach.

With Robert Burns (*Si Barbour*), Walter Stull (*Seth Jones*).

While Si Barbour and Seth Jones are at work on the farm Si, who has been chopping wood, suddenly becomes thirsty and goes to the pump to have a drink. On his way back he passes the mail box and thinks that he will look in to see if there is any mail for himself or the family. He finds a large booklet which he looks over and is quite surprised at the things he finds pictured in the book. He at once goes over to where Seth is at work, and tells him of the wonders that are hidden in the book, and shows him the pictures. These pictures, which are views of Lively Town, so enthuse the two that they decide on a visit to the place. They leave the farm in charge of the hired man, and get on their best clothes and start. We next see them arriving at the station where things are in such a bustle, and confusion, that they are quite bewildered. They stroll around the town taking in the sights and amusements, until they are standing looking at a rough and tumble scrap. A policeman appears on the scene at which time the participants run away and the officer seizes the two rubes and gives them a severe shaking. This wakes them up for a minute and they move with the alacrity of the people of Lively Town. But the exertion is so great and different from what they have been accustomed to that they are quite dizzy. They decide that they have had enough for one day and return home. [MPW]

The film is almost more travelogue than comedy. It gives the audience a great view of the famous seaside attraction with an extended view of the Atlantic City Boardwalk including the fun house and shops such as Flett's, Huyler's Confectioners, Reliance Tailoring Co., Cassman's Milliners, and Fralinger's Salt Water Taffy (this company is still open for business in Atlantic City). Also the Hotel Malatesta and the Criterian Theatre are seen. Neither Burns nor Stull have much to do in the film, and it is the trick photography that is the real star.

"This makes a unique trick picture that strikes one's sense of the incongruous, and therefore humor. The city farmer and his son visit Atlantic City, which they find an exceedingly lively place. They walk with slow and stately tread through the various amusement resorts, while other persons and things move with lightning rapidity before their eyes. It is a good caricature of the way a city might appear to a country gentleman who came hither for the first time." -- *New York Dramatic Mirror*

"It is one of those lovable human interest dramas, *A Visit to Lively Town*. A comedy in which two country farmers visit a big city and find themselves in a maze of fast-moving people that proves too bewildering to them. The street scenes are well taken and the comic antics of the rubes will amuse all who see it." -- *The Home Daily Sentinel (Rome, NY)*

His Vacation

Released July 26, 1912. Lubin Manufacturing Co.-General Film Company release. One reel (1053 ft.).

Filmed in Atlantic City, New Jersey.

With Robert Burns (*Bobby*), George Reehm (*His employer*), Walter Stull (*His chum, Walter*), Mae Hotely (*The chaperon*), Frances Ne Moyer and Eleanor Brenner (*The two girls*).

Bobby Burns, one morning while working in the office, receives a photograph from a friend of his, who is in Atlantic City. The photograph is a picture of his friend and two young ladies in bathing suits. On the back of the photograph a note is written telling Bobby of the swell time they are having at the shore. Bobby loses no time in cooking up a scheme to get away for a few days. He has a friend send him a fake telegram to the effect that his mother met with an accident, spraining her ankle while at Atlantic City. Bobby's employer, a sympathetic old gentleman, gives Bobby some money and hurries him off to his mother's side. While Bobby is enjoying himself with the party in Atlantic City, his employer finds the photograph and, after reading the note, decides to go to Atlantic City to find Bobby and fire him. The next morning finds Bobby's boss in Atlantic City. Bobby and his friends are about to leave to go sailing when the girls' chaperon, afraid of sea-sickness, remains on shore. While the party is out sailing a flirtation has taken place between Bobby's boss and the chaperon. He is so taken up with the chaperon that he forgets all about looking for Bob. The party has returned from their yachting trip and are on their way to the hotel in an automobile, when Bob is discovered by his boss, who runs after the automobile. Bob sees the boss and thinks the gig is up. They hunt up the chaperon and make her act as mother with the sprained ankle. Handkerchiefs are tied around the ankle of the chaperon. When Bob introduces the boss to his supposed mother, they are all surprised to see that the boss and the chaperon are friends and have met before. The boss is so pleased to meet the chaperon again that he forgets all about firing Bob. The picture closes with the boss and the chaperon leaving the party for a stroll. [MPW]

The reviews for *His Vacation* highlight the reception that the Gay Time comedies generally received. Some critics looked upon the films favorably ("funny and has been acted with much intelligence"), others held the comedies in much disdain ("more painful than amusing"). Lubin's films overall were more popular with audiences than they were with film critics.

"In a quiet way the story is funny and has been acted with much intelligence. Bob misses out a little in his part at the time of his interview with the boss after the alleged accident to his mother, for his efforts at comedy are much too obvious, but for the most part the characters are well done." -- *New York Dramatic Mirror*

"An Atlantic City farce picture. When seen by a large audience, the few laughs that it made were due to one or two good situations rather than to the acting. This, excepting the two older people, was poor. In the case of the young man who took the vacation, it was exaggerated so much that it was more painful than amusing. Yet the picture has some excellent things and will get past." -- *Moving Picture World*

A Farmer's Son

Released July 29, 1912. Lubin Manufacturing Co.-General Film Company release. Split reel (293 ft.), on the same reel with *Pueblo Indians, Albuquerque, New Mexico* (765 ft.).

With Robert Burns, Raymond McKee (*Silas, the farmer's son*).

Silas, son of old Farmer Simpkins, is very tired of farming, and, while his father and the hired man are out in the fields working, he is soundly sleeping by the stable door. The old man brings the hay rake and horse into the stable about dinner time, and inquires of the hired man where Silas is. The man shows him his son fast asleep, He calls Si, who wakes and goes to his father. The father sends him to the pump to draw a bucket of water. While at the pump he decides to go to the city and on his return to where the old man is he states the fact to him. The father tries to dissuade him, but the boy is persistent, so the father decides to allow him to go. We next see him leaving the old home and all the farm hands bidding him good-bye. It is haying season and the farmer, who is busy at his daily toil, wonders what has become of his boy. We are very soon enlightened, for while the father makes hay the son shines. [MPW]

"On the same reel [with *Pueblo Indians, Albuquerque, New Mexico*] is this short picture, which is of the slightest. It hardly tells a story, just sketches a situation for us. It is in comedy vein and will probably make a laugh or two." -- *Moving Picture World*

The Hindoo's Charm

Released August 16, 1912. Lubin Manufacturing Co.-General Film Company release. One reel (1058 ft.).

Filmed in Philadelphia, Pennsylvania.

With Mae Hotely (*Mrs. Washbuckel*), George Reehm (*Mr. Washbuckel*), Robert Burns (*the Hindoo*), Walter Stull (*doctor*), Frances Ne Moyer (*the maid*), Raymond McKee (*the Hindoo's assistant*).

Mr. Washbuckel, a good-natured middle-aged gentleman, keeps his wife on the verge of distraction because he persists in flirting with every woman he meets. Mrs. Washbuckel learns of a mystic Hindoo who claims to possess a remedy for evil habits. She calls on the Hindoo, who presents Fetich (a miniature clay figure of a man), which is supposed to represent the wayward husband. If a pin is stuck into the Fetich the husband will feel the prick in the corresponding part of his body. Mrs. Washbuckel has abundant opportunity to test its efficacy. It works like a charm. Mr. Washbuckel, feeling the mysterious pin pricks and unable to account for the cause, first consults a dentist, then a doctor, and finally takes to his bed, where he is tended by a pretty nurse. Mrs Washbuckel discovers him flirting with the nurse, and in a rage she returns to the drawing-room, where she abandons herself to a savage attack on the Fetich. Mr. Washbuckel, unable to stand the assault, makes his way to the drawing-room, where he discovers the cause of all his agony; Mrs. Washbuckel explains matters and Mr. Washbuckel promises to behave in the future. [MPW]

George Reehm produces most of the comedy as he flinches and jumps from the phantom pains he endures when his wife pokes the miniature of him. Bobby Burns is barely recognizable with dark face makeup and a goatee beard (Raymond McKee also in dark face is more than equally hard to recognize). Walter Stull sports some very large handlebar sideburns, but Mae Hotely plays it with normal make-up showing that she was not at all unattractive, which puts to question why Reehm had the wandering eye.

"A picture that made one or two laugh; but distressed, or seemed to distress, the majority of the spectators. Anyone who can laugh at such a picture must have had a pitiable education, in fact, must be inhuman; its fun comes solely from its suggestion of vulgar possibilities." -- *Moving Picture World*

A Red Hot Courtship

Released September 11, 1912. Lubin Manufacturing Co.-General Film Company release. Split reel (432 ft.), on the same reel with *His First Auto* (625 ft.) with *His Pair of Pants* in the U.K.

Directed by Jerold T. Hevener.

With Eleanor Caines, Walter Stull (*Folsom Barrymore*).

Nellie Nugent, an attractive young actress, is stranded in a small, one-night stand. She remains at the boarding house while her husband goes to New York. Nellie makes a hit among the rubes. Hoyt Heffoner and Folsom Barrymore, two village dandies, both forsake their sweethearts, who also board at Mrs. Heffoner's. Then they start an ardent courtship for Nellie. After many love situations, Folsom is driven to desperation. He thinks of some way to eliminate his rival. He passes a drug store, enters and asks the clerk for two pills—one deadly poison, the other harmless. The drug clerk sizes up Folsom as a "bug," but to humor him, gives him two pills. Both are red-pepper. At the boarding house he bursts Into Hoyt's room. "Choose one of these," he commands, holding out the box to Hoyt, who is too frightened to refuse. He swallows one pill, Folsom swallows the other. Hoyt almost immediately begins to scream with pain. Folsom laughs. Then he too is convulsed with pain. Both run madly through the door. Outside in the yard they encounter the hired man with two buckets of water. They grab these, drink part of them. Not having yet quenched the horrible fire inside, they run madly to the front yard. Here they beg the man who is sprinkling the lawn to soak them with water. They feel no better. They then rush wildly upstairs into the bathroom. One of the boarders, peering into an upper shelf, is standing on the edge of the tub. In their mad rush to plunge into the water, Hoyt and Folsom upset the balance of the third man, and he too splashes into the tub. The water runs over and trickles down into the dining room below, deluging the table where the boarders are eating, with the exception of Nellie, who, in her bedroom, has just received a wire from hubby saying he will arrive that morning for her. She starts to pack up. The water causes a panic among the boarders. Headed by the landlady they rush upstairs and put Hoyt and Folsom to flight. While they are upstairs, Nellie's husband arrives, meets Nellie, and they hurry from the house to catch the train. In the front yard they meet Hoyt and Folsom. Then the bucolic swains discover to their intense chagrin that Nellie is married. They collapse and their two sweethearts, whom they had forsaken, agree to take them back. [MPW]

This comedy was not made by the "Gay Time" company, but rather by the main unit of Lubin that alternated between dramas and comedies, and even Westerns. By 1912 though direction of the comedies from this unit was handed over to Jerold T. Hevener (who also often appeared in the films). The star frequently was Eleanor

Caines, yet another native Philadelphian, who beginning in 1909 split time between stage work and making movies for Lubin. She also occasionally wrote the scenarios for the films she made. In early 1913 she (along with Hevener) left Lubin to work for the Scarlett Motion Picture Company making Westerns. Unfortunately, in June 1913, while filming only their second production, Caines fell off her horse and the injuries led to her death on June 3, 1913. Hevener would return to Lubin. It is interesting to note that Walter Stull's character was named Folsom Barrymore. John Barrymore was a frequent star for this Lubin unit, although whether he appeared in this film is unknown.

"Nellie Nugent, a stranded actress but married, flirts with the country boys until she gets two of them crazy jealous. One of them resolves that he or his rival must die. He goes to a drug store and asks for two pills, one poison and the other harmless. The clerk gives him two pills made of red-pepper. The rivals each take a pill, and the result is excruciating pain and laughter." -- *Lubin ad*

No Trespassing

Released September 20, 1912. Lubin Manufacturing Co.-General Film Company release. Split reel (600 ft.), on the same reel with *Turpentine Industry* (400 ft.).

With Walter Stull, Robert Burns, Frances Ne Moyer.

Geo. Engle, surveying on a country road, sees Mabel Long pass by. He is infatuated, but unfortunately, Mabel has heard him address his assistant in very forcible language. Mabel meets her uncle at the entrance of their place and shows a letter from brother Jack that he is coming home next week on a leave of absence. Engle's duty takes him surveying on the Long's place. In spite of a "No trespass" sign. Long and the hired man capture him up in a tree. Long goes for an officer. Later they get an axe, but Mabel pretends fainting and in the excitement Engle escapes. Later brother Jack arrives and recognizes Engel as an old chum, but Mabel declines an introduction. Proceeding thoughtfully in the neighborhood of the tree she bumps into a cow tethered there. Frightened, she climbs the tree. Engle sees her and hurries to the rescue. He imposes the condition that she marry him if he rescues her. Long and the hired man see him and come on the run. Mabel yields, and when shown that the cow is tied is indignant. Long and the hired man assault Engle and dire things are about to happen when Jack arrives, introduces and explains. Uncle says "Yes" and all is over. [MPW]

"On the same reel [with *Turpentine Industry*] is this farce on a farm. It is plainly 'put together' and is not a convincing story, but it has a pretty heroine, some lovely scenes, a daisy meadow, and rural views, and it has one or two amusing situations. It is not very substantial. " --*Moving Picture World*

His Pair of Pants

Released September 21, 1912. Lubin Manufacturing Co.-General Film Company release. Split reel (630 ft.), on the same reel with *His Trade* (422 ft.). with *A Red Hot Courtship* in the U.K.

With Walter Stull.

Enthused by the warm weather, Mr. Horatio Smith yields to his wife's entreaties to dig up the back yard truck garden. He gets halfway through his work before he sees that he is soiling his pants, and he goes to the garret, dons a pair of overalls and leaves his pants up there and, incidentally, his month's salary in the same. While he is digging the garden an old clothes peddler calls at the front door. Mrs. Smith sees a chance to get some money for buying garden seed and sells the pants Smith left up in the garret. Poor Smith discovers the awful truth and he and his wife hurry frantically after the peddler. They swoop down upon him and scatter his clothes right and left before he can explain to them that he has just sold the pants to a tramp. Mr. and Mrs. Smith leave the indignant peddler and continue the search after the tramp. Meanwhile the hobo has put on the pants in a convenient shed nearby, has discovered the roll of greenbacks and is spending Smith's wad right and left on ice cream and peanuts for kids. About this time the Rev. Jones, a minister, hurriedly leaves his house with a pair of pants that he has to have pressed (they are an exact duplicate of Smith's) ; he is overtaken by Smith and wife. Smith, in his excitement, declares the minister has his pants and tries to pull them away from him. They are ripped in two, and the minister and Smith begin hitting each other right and left with the two halves. A cop separates the combatants and is just about to arrest them when Smith sees the tramp down the street. The tramp has come out of the saloon, gloriously drunk, and is throwing Smith's money right and left to a big crowd of men, women and children. Smith, the minister, the cop and Smith's wife rush up to the tramp, but he sees them coming and the crowd chase him down the street. The tramp, during the chase, crawls through a barbed wire fence. It is not until he stumbles and falls into a shallow pool of puddle water that the cop and Smith can lay hands on him. Smith then discovers, to his great grief, that the pants are not only ruined but that little of the money is left. [MPN]

"A rather slow-moving farce that has an old situation and nothing that is truly fresh. Eccentric camera work made a number of good laughs near the end of it." -- *Moving Picture World*

"It's a corker and the title does not do justice to the story. A ragman, tramp, policeman and preacher all figure very prominently and the stirring action of the story does not lag for a moment." -- *Fort Wayne (Indiana) Journal-Gazette*

Spoony Sam

Released October 4, 1912. Lubin Manufacturing Co.-General Film Company release. Split reel (450 ft.), on the same reel with *Collection Day* (600 ft.). Sometimes listed as *Spooney Sam*.

With George Reehm (*Spoony Sam*), Walter Stull, Tommy Aiken (*Cy*), Frances Ne Moyer (*Sis Perkins*).

Spoony Sam and Sis Perkins think they are in love with each other. Sam is too spoony in his courtship to suit old man Perkins. Sam has a hated rival in the person of Cy Hawkins.

Sam takes a desperate chance and buys a ring, engages the parson and boldly presents himself to old man Perkins, as a prospective son-in-law. The old man is furious at first, but finally weakens. Just as the parson is about to perform the ceremony, Sam runs away. Just then Cy Hawkins happens along and wants to know what the excitement is. He is informed that Sam and Sis were about to be married when Sam got cold feet and ran away. Cy tells the old man that there is no danger of him getting cold feet if placed in the same position. The parson starts to marry them when they discover that they have no ring. Just then Sam returns. Old man Perkins takes the ring away from Sam, and informs him that the best he will get is that Cy will marry Sis with his (Sam's) ring. In order that the ceremony may continue peacefully, old man Perkins Is compelled to hold Spoony Sum's head in a bucket of water. [MPW]

A remake of sorts of the same titled one reel 1910 Lubin comedy that also featured Walter Stull and George Reehm. Lubin also used the character name "Spoony Sam" earlier in 1912 when Jerold T. Hevener played the part in the film *A Prize Package*. Loosely based on the comic song *"Everloving Spoony Sam"* (Andy Rice/Fred Fischer) recorded by Edison artist Bob Roberts in 1907. Walter Stull and George Reehm must have made a particularly good impression with this film. Upon their departure from Lubin to work at Reliance with the Komic brand most of the publicity referred to Stull and Reehm as "of Spoony Sam fame."

"Spoony Sam is exceedingly humourous." -- *Dundee Courier (Angus, Scotland)*

Meeting Mamie's Mother

Released October 18, 1912. Lubin Manufacturing Co.-General Film Company release. Split reel (600 ft.), on the same reel with *Rube's Mistake* (400 ft.).

With Mae Hotely (*mother*), Frances Ne Moyer (*Mamie*), Robert Burns (*Josh Bentham, the husband*).

Josh Bentham is married to a pretty little doll, but she is shrewish. Josh is henpecked aud altogether his life is far from a happy one. No matter how attentive and kind he is, Mamie responds with every lack of appreciation. When Maude informs Josh that her mother is coming on to visit for a while. he makes up his mind that life will be unbearable. Mamma arrives and much to the surprise of Bentham she is all right, alright. She quickly regulates her angel child and transforms the shrew into a consistent and well behaved little woman. Mamie is broken of her habit of nagging and meets her husband with due affection and appreciation. Having accomplished the beautiful change in the atmosphere of the home, Mamma prepares to leave the now happy couple. Josh nails her trunk to the floor in hopes that he can keep her there forever. [MPW]

"Josh Bentnam is married to a pretty little shrew, who makes his life a misery. Mamie's Mother, however, comes to visit and quickly regulates her angel child, and Joan nails her trunk to the floor hoping to keep his Mother in law forever." -- *Lubin ad*

Down With the Men

Released October 25, 1912. Lubin Manufacturing Co.-General Film Company release. Split reel (590 ft.), on the same reel with *The Noodle Industry* (450 ft.).

With Mae Hotely, Walter Stull (*Paul*), Marguerite Ne Moyer (*Mabel*).

Mabel Mordant is a militant suffragette and when the men won't let the agitators hold their meetings in peace, the girl's real mad. Determining to fight the issue, she secures a detective's badge from a correspondence school of detectives. She has a uniform suit made and when Paul Arthur, one of her tormentors, gets gay she pinches him. The police guy her and the justice tries to flirt and gets sore when Mabel refuses to respond. As a last resort she tries a Justice of Peace to listen to the ridiculous complaint. To end the farce, Paul proposes marriage and persuades her that it is a much better game than trying to be a man. Mabel is won over and gives up the fad much to the disgust of her associates. [MPW]

"A comedy designed to show that when some women are put to the test they will go back to first principles—i.e. to the men." -- *Moving Picture World*

Fixing A Flirt

Released November 1, 1912. Lubin Manufacturing Co.-General Film Company release. One reel (1000 ft.). Listed in some publications as *Fixing The Flirt*.

With George Reehm (*Bill Bruce*), Frances Ne Moyer (*Bess Bradley*), Walter Stull (*waiter*), Robert Burns (*cashier*), Spottiswoode Aiken, Mae Hotely.

Bill Bruce is an imitation of "a man about town." He starts a flirtation with Bess Bradley, a stenographer, who has little use for a "make believe." He, however, invites her to dinner. Bess tells the head clerk, who outlines a scheme. The invitation is accepted, and Bess and Bill are seated at a table in a rather pretentious cafe. Presently two other girls "blow in" and Bess greets them cordially. Of course, It is up to Bruce to ask them to sit down, which they do and commence to study the bill of fare. In a few minutes two more "drift in" and the other girls are delighted; the newcomers are invited by Bess to join the party. Before the orders are given three more turn up, and Bill finds that he has eight girls to feed. The dinner is most enjoyable until Bruce calls for the bill, which is much higher than his money roll will stand. He excuses himself for a few minutes and interviews the cashier, who will hear of no compromise except the money. Bill has to strip himself of his watch and other ornaments and is carefully watched by the eight girls. Finally, he makes his escape and upon reaching his home is tackled by his landlady, who talks money and nothing else. She is so hard-hearted that poor Bruce has to sleep on the doorsteps. [MPW]

George Reehm spends half of the movie chasing a girl, and the second half wishing he didn't. Of course, his intention was just to spend time with the one girl and not a crowd of them. Perhaps he could have picked a better restaurant than one manned by Burns and Stull, neither of which have much to do in the film.

"A young man predisposed to flirtation with nearly every girl he sees is 'fixed' good and plenty. One of seven girls receives a letter inviting her to dinner. She accepts. As the two are seated in a restaurant two of the girls join them and are invited to sit down. When the last of the party have been fed the flirt is broke. The restaurant man takes his watch, stick and several other articles for security. As the party leaves the restaurant, all bid the young man good-bye. To make the discomfiture complete the man's landlady shuts him out of his home. It is fair comedy." -- *Moving Picture World*

Love and Treachery

Released November 21, 1912. Lubin Manufacturing Co.-General Film Company release. One reel (1021 ft.).

Written by William C. Carr.

With Walter Stull (*Jacques*), Robert Burns (*The Captain*), George Reehm (*Jean*), Frances Ne Moyer (*Marie*), Thomas Aiken (*halfwit*).

In a fishing village dwells Marie, a fisher maiden, who is loved by Jean and Jacques. Jacques meeting Marie one day proposes marriage to her, but is refused. Happening to pass Jean's cabin, Jacques sees Marie in Jean's arms. Jacques meets the coast guard, who tells him that smugglers are about. This puts an idea in Jacques' mind, and he with his pal, Francois, starts to put it into execution. They go to Jean's cabin and take Jean's hat and coat. Then he and Francois go where they have a boat moored and Jacques puts on the stolen clothes. A coast guard sees the launching of the boat, and recognizing Jean's coat and hat, becomes suspicious of Jean. Jacques and Francois proceed to their cave, as they are smugglers. Arriving at the cave they get a bundle of lace which has been smuggled and returning to Jean's cabin they cut off several yards and place it in the pocket of Jean's coat. They leave the cabin and are returning to the cave when they meet the captain of the coast guards. They inform him that Jean is a smuggler. The captain accuses Jean of smuggling. He is placed under arrest. Francois and Jacques gloating over their success, return to the cave and are making a division of their spoils when a quarrel ensues and Jacques insults Francois. Francois leaves the cave. He runs to Jean's cabin and tells Marie how the affair was accomplished, and they start after the captain and the guard. Overtaking them, Francois tells the captain. The whole party then proceed to the cave where Jacques is. After surrounding the cave with guards, the captain, Marie and Jean go inside. Jacques is accused and denies, but when Francois appears and confronts him with the balance of the lace he is arrested. [MPW and PP]

"A theatrical story of smugglers in which there are no new characters, just the stock villain, hero, heroine and half witted man. with the soldiers, etc. We find the usual rocky beach scenes, etc. The author is William C. Carr, who has followed the approved formula for fabricating a melodrama. The hero is played by Geo. E. Reehm, the villain by Walter Stull. The heroine by Frances de Moyer; the halfwit by Thomas Aiken and the captain by Robert Burns." -- *Moving Picture World*

Nora the Cook

Released December 20, 1912. Lubin Manufacturing Co.-General Film Company release. Split reel (691 ft.), on the same reel with *Hogan vs. Schmidt* (362 ft.).

With Mae Hotely (*Nora*), Jack Ridgeway (*Mike McCloskey*), Robert Burns.

Nora, a young Irish girl, is a tarter, and puts several households into discord. Every day Nora is looking for a new job. While working in one place she meets Mike McCloskey, the Iceman. The courting is short and they are soon married. Nora, who has never been bossed by anyone, is soon tamed by love, and we see Mike sitting and smoking at his ease, while Nora who takes in washing to support him, is busy at the wash-tub. [MPW]

"Mae Hotely, as Nora, a cook with an independent opinion of her own, but who, after marriage, is a willing slave to her husband the iceman, makes many a good laugh in a farce almost a whole reel in length and with much that is fresh in it. The cast is a large one and we do not recognize them all; but see a good deal to commend in the acting throughout." -- *Moving Picture World*

Stage-Struck Sally

Released January 10, 1913. Lubin Manufacturing Co.-General Film Company release. Split reel (363 ft.), on the same reel with *An Accidental Dentist* (674 ft.).

Directed by Arthur D. Hotaling, written by Epes W. Sargent.

With Mae Hotely (*Sally*), Ben Walker (*her sweetheart*), Julia Calhoun, Jack Ridgeway, Robert Burns, Raymond McKee, Walter Stull and George Reehm.

Sally is a new girl at the Cort's, who do not know that she has an ambition to go on the stage. When she studies her part in the kitchen, Mrs. Cort comes to the conclusion that Sally is crazy and is made nervous. Meantime Sally finds the butcher knife too dull to cut the bread, and goes to ask her mistress that it be sharpened. Mrs. Cort is certain that she is to be killed and faints. Sally, all excitement, runs for the doctor, forgetting to put down the knife. The doctor thinks she is crazy and telephones the police. The reserves come and cart her off to the station-house, where Terrance her policeman sweetheart, offers explanation, and Sally is turned loose. Sally has a bad case of "stage struck," but Terrance will try to cure her. [MPW]

"Mae Hotely, in this farce, plays a cook who is studying out of a book the mysteries of acting. Her mistress overhearing a rehearsal, takes her for mad and is frightened almost to death. Mae has a dull knife. She takes it to the mistress to have it sharpened ard that is both end and beginning, for Mae goes for the doctor without putting down the knife." –*Moving Picture World*

Fooling Their Wives

Released January 17, 1913. Lubin Manufacturing Co.-General Film Company release. Split reel (510 ft.), on the same reel with *Quarantined* (494 ft.).

Written by Epes W. Sargent.

With Robert Burns, Walter Stull, Raymond McKee, Mae Hotely, Frances Ne Moyer, Marguerite Ne Moyer.

Brown, Jones, Smith and Black are camping. The wives of the first three find things rather dull. They decide to take their turns when the men come back. They do. The husbands think they will have a fine time with their wives away, but they get lonesome and try to scare the women back to town by posing as tramps and attacking the camp. It's a good scheme, but it works the wrong way, for the women chase them from the camp and run them up to their necks into the lake, where they reveal their identities. They are permitted to come out again and all start for home. [MPW]

When the wives are gone on their camping trip Burns meets Stull on the street and the two have a joint sigh as they pine for their sweethearts. Usually in these situations the husbands are trying to gather the wives back up since they can't cook, or care for the children, or generally are just incapable of any domestic efforts at all. In this film the husbands just do sincerely miss their wives. Of course, they can't just say so, they have to attempt to scare the ladies back home. The ladies for their part seem to be doing just fine camping out sans any men. In the end they do not punish the husbands for their ill-fated ruse, which again is a bit off the norm for these comedies.

Epes W. Sargent in his *Moving Picture World* column *The Photoplaywright* writes about his own near plagiarism when writing *Fooling Their Wives:*

"Not So Certain. We used to think that it was safe to follow the usual practice of working over a newspaper paragraph, so long as the paragraph only gave impetus to a train of thought, but we're not so certain now. Last October we wrote *Fooling Their Wives* and sold it to the Lubin company. It was developed from a newspaper paragraph in the *Morning World* of October 4th, which told of eight women going camping. They left their husbands behind. With this for a starter, we developed a plot in which the wives' husbands were rejoiced at the promised liberty of action, but grew tired and sought to enforce a return of their spouses by a fake attack on the camp. We were doing two services a week then, in an effort to get away on a vacation, and did not

Epes W. Sargent

have time to read the *Stories of the Films* a week or so later, which carried the Thanhouser story, *Petticoat Camp,* and our first knowledge of a pretty close duplication of incident came when the *Telegraph* called attention to the similarity. Investigation seems to prove that some newspaper correspondent fancied the theme of *Petticoat Camp,* which he learned from some Thanhouser actor, and sent in to his paper an item founded on the main idea. In twisting this around we almost duplicated the original story by Lloyd Lonergan, except that in his story the men and women were camping as a party, and the women went on strike against overwork, establishing a special camp, which the men raided. If you take inspiration from a newspaper item, be certain it does not hail from a town where there is a picture company. Newspaper correspondents, dependent on their 'space,' are none too careful as to what they send out. We're not so certain now that any paragraph is safe."

[no review available]

Pizen Pete

Released January 24, 1913. Lubin Manufacturing Co.-General Film Company release. Split reel (720 ft.), on the same reel with *Making a Baseball Bug* (316 ft.).

With Walter Stull.

Bad Bill has Catamount Creek terrorized. He is so bad it burns his boots, but he hazes Pete Green, a raw tenderfoot, and Pete gets the idea he can play the game, too. He gets a make-up that beats Bill's for fierceness, and he puts Bill out of the running. But he, too, meets his Nemesis in the shape of a stranger who discovers that his guns are not loaded. Blanks are inserted and when Pete accidentally discharges one he thinks someone is shooting at him and he starts to run. A boy is sent after him with the gun, but even the youngster can frighten Pete. He surrenders and goes back to town, where he shares with Bill the tyranny of the Chinese cook of the Catamount Cafe. [MPW]

"On the same reel [with *Making a Baseball Bug*] is this burlesque of a bad man brought to grief by a timid soul rigged up as another bad man by a strolling actor. Both come to grief. The reel is all right." -- *Moving Picture World*

She Must Elope

Released January 30, 1913. Lubin Manufacturing Co.-General Film Company release. Split reel (600 ft.), on the same reel with *What's In A Name?* (400 ft.).

Directed by Arthur D. Hotaling, Written by Epes W. Sargent.

With Mae Hotely (*Mary*), Robert Burns (*Harry*), Spottiswoode Aitken.

Mary, a novel reading old maid, is courted by Harry, who needs the money. Father is willing enough to have her off his hands, but Mary insists that they elope, so father helps Harry get a ladder. That night they start out, but the auto breaks down and Mary, fearful

that they are pursued, will not wait for Harry to fix it, but starts off on foot. She grows tired and they take a dray, changing to a boat when they pass the water; but the boat overturns and Harry catches a donkey for her. She doesn't like riding without a saddle. so she tries the road again and arrives at the minister's in a wheelbarrow. There they hire a rig to take them back to the auto and the journey is completed in the car. Mary kneels for forgiveness and father, not only forgives, but hands Harry a bunch of money, which Mary takes away from him, letting him have half a dollar. [MPW]

"Mae Hotely gives a capital performance in this half reel subject that is played in a farcical manner throughout. The story would not permit of more serious treatment. In its present form it should draw a few good laughs. Harry is penniless with 'prospects' of receiving a fortune from an aunt whose early death is expected. He can wait no longer and jumps at the chance to marry a romantic old maid, whose wealthy father is anxious to see her wedded. To satisfy her romantic cravings she insists that they elope, and to carry out the idea the father must greet their return with a storm of abuse, which he does. Then he hands Harry a roll of bills which the wife quickly appropriates and in their place gives the husband a little small change, as an indication of what he may expect. Just at this point, to add to the misery of the bridegroom, a telegram is delivered stating that his aunt is dead and the will allows him $50,000. Miss Hotely is well supported by Robert Burns and Spottiswoode Aitken." -- *New York Dramatic Mirror*

"There is a good deal of fun in this brisk farce, but it is hard to tell whether the author or the producer deserves the credit. The treatment of her poor boarder by the landlady shows knowledge of the world, and the best that the picture has is this fun of wisdom. These details and the clever fresh way in which the old situation has been handled make it go. Its most noticeable shortcoming is that Spottiswoode Aitken is not old enough to play a doddering old man — it is noticeable that he has all his teeth. Mae Hotely, as the romantic old maid, is very funny, and she is well supported by Robert Burns, Author, E. W. Sargent, and producer, A. Hotaling." -- *Moving Picture World*

The Missing Jewels

Released February 4, 1913. Lubin Manufacturing Co.-General Film Company release. Split reel (600 ft.), on the same reel with *A Motor Boat Party* (400 ft.).

Directed by Arthur D. Hotaling, Written by Elsie Kiesler.

With Robert Burns (*James Henry*), Mae Hotely (*Mrs. Henry*), Frances Mann (*Miss Violet*), Walter Stull (*Parker*), Thomas Aiken.

Just as James Y. Henry is about to leave home for his office, his wife requests him to place her pearl necklace in the bank safe deposit. She places the bag in his overcoat pocket. Then he remembers that he has forgotten his watch. In her husband's absence, Mrs. Henry receives a 'phone message to attend a bridge party, and desiring to wear the necklace, takes the bag out of

Henry's pocket and forgets to tell him of it. In the employ of Henry is Miss Violet, a stenographer, Parker, the bookkeeper, and Sam, the shipping clerk. Sam is very fond of Miss Violet and invites her to a dance, which she refuses. Sam is much chagrined and makes an angry exit. Later Henry remembers the bag with the necklace. He finds that it has disappeared and makes inquiry. Still later Sam, through the window, sees Miss Violet place a small bag in her stocking and informs Mr. Henry. The girl is summoned and requested to produce the bag. Parker fights hard for the stenographer, but Sam, feeling sure of his game, telephones for the police. They force Violet to show the bag, which she digs out and displays the contents to be her powder puffs. In the meantime, Mrs. Henry has phoned to her husband to inform him that she has won the prize at bridge. He in return tells her of the missing necklace. This explains the mystery and Henry proposes to raise the girl's salary, but she advises that he shall raise Parker's salary instead, as they are about to be married. [MPW]

"Through a coincidence, the little stenographer is able to rightly choose between two suitors. The comedy-drama on the same reel with *A Motor Boat Party*, is particularly engaging considering the amount of space that has been given to the working out of the plot. The situation, where the girl is accused, might have been made a trifle more gripping through a stronger display of indignation by the successful suitor but even as it is there is much to interest and hold us. Robert Burns does creditable work as James Henry, the husband who imagines he has lost his wife's jewels. Mrs. Young is played by Mae Hotely. The stenographer is enacted with considerable emotion by Frances Mann. Walter Stull and Thomas Aiken play the clerks her two admirers."
-- *New York Dramatic Mirror*

"A melodrama produced by Arthur Hotaling for the laugh's sake and played by the company that has been putting over the Lubin farce comedies. Mae Hotely plays a young society matron who has told her husband (Robert Burns) that she has placed her jewels in his overcoat pocket and then has changed her mind, but has neglected to tell him that she has taken them out. He goes to his office and she to a bridge party. At the office there is a girl and two rival clerks. But by the time we get through with the office love story we have forgotten the real situation and have begun to feel that this part was made long, mostly to fill out the reel. The situation is taken up again in time and on account of the acting, not of the story, makes a few laughs. We cannot say that the authoress, Elsie Kiesler, has done anything very remarkable. The office force is played by Frances Mann with Walter Stull and Thomas Aiken." -- *Moving Picture World*

Training A Tightwad

Released February 17, 1913. Lubin Manufacturing Co.-General Film Company release. Split reel (505 ft.), on the same reel with *Wild Man For A Day* (520 ft.).

With Mae Hotely (*Mrs. Wad*), Robert Burns (*Mr. Wad*), Frances Ne Moyer (*Nell, their daughter*), Marguerite Ne Moyer (*Bess, their daughter*), Raymond McKee, William H. Hopkins (*the policeman*).

Mrs. Wad wants some money, but Wad reminds her that he gave her a dollar the week before, and goes to his office to fire the boy, because he finds a penholder in the waste paper basket. The Wad girls get the idea of having a rummage sale to get the money from their father, and win their mother's consent. The papers get hold of the story, and Wad rushes home to stop the sale. The bystanders prevent any action, and when he appeals to a policeman, the officer buys an old hat and tells Wad to chase himself. Wad goes to the station house, but gets thrown out. He then comes home to buy out his wife's business, which is offered for $5,000. The lesson lasts. [MPW]

"On the same reel with *A Wild Man for a Day*, this light comedy is quite out of the ordinary and is productive of considerable amusement. Robert Burns assumes the role of Tightwad. Mae Hotely Mrs. Wad, and Frances Ne Moyer and Marguerite Ne Moyer the daughters. The father refuses to allow his wife enough money to properly

Arthur D. Hotaling

furnish the girls with clothing. In a fit of anger, the three women decide on a plan to bring him to terms. They establish a public auction of all their castoff clothes, and then advertise the affair through the newspapers, featuring the fact that they are compelled to do it because of the tightness of the father in money matters. The father catches sight of the notice, and rushes to the auction to guard the dignity of his position. The women refuse to give up the business for less than $5,000. which the old man is finally forced to pay." –*New York Dramatic Mirror*

"Good comedy along original lines, Mae Hotely has the role of the woman who sets out to teach her stingy husband a real lesson. She succeeds." -- *Moving Picture World*

Sixes and Nines

Released March 14, 1913. Lubin Manufacturing Co.-General Film Company release. Split reel (403 ft.), on the same reel with *Jane's Waterloo* (648 ft.).

Directed by Arthur D. Hotaling, Written by Epes W. Sargent.

With Earl Metcalfe (*Jim*), Marguerite Ne Moyer (*Bess*), Robert Burns (*constable*), William Hopkins (*constable*), Walter Stull.

Jim Nugent and his sweetheart, Bess Forrest, go auto riding. They break the speed limit law, but manage to get away. The auto number is 666 and Jim reverses it so that it reads

999. Later they are arrested and it is discovered that 999 belongs to a car used by a couple of bank robbers who have just made a good haul. Jim and Bess are pretty badly scared until the robbers are caught and brought in. Of course Jim declares that the number was hung upside down in the garage, and promises to make his machine behave in the future. [MPW]

"A farce that depends on the number plates of two automobiles. One is 999 and the other is 666; both drivers get into trouble and both turn their plates upside down. The idea is certainly fresh, and it makes a laughable picture, but there is very little to it, and it might have been carried much further. William Hopkins and Robert Burns play two rural constables. The other players are not so noticeable. The photography is clear. It was written by E. W. Sargent and produced by Arthur Hotaling." -- *Moving Picture World*

The Fixer

Released March 25, 1913. Lubin Manufacturing Co.-General Film Company release. Split reel (456 ft.), on the same reel with *Such An Appetite* (600 ft.).

With Walter Stull (*the fixer*), Robert Burns (*Jim Gray, the husband*).

Jim Gray is a hen-pecked old man who can't make his eyes behave. The only thing that saves him from being a gay libertine is that the girls only laugh at him. He gets caught by his wife chasing Tess Ne Moyer, at a time, when, according to his card on the office door, he is out on important business. Gay ducks, but when he turns up at the house that evening, he is loaded down with presents for his wife. When she gets them all she enters the house but Gay is given the sign to go away. He goes to his friend, Fixer, who promises to fix it. His scheme is to make love to Mrs. Gay, and let Gay burst in, but as Gay approaches the house, the noise warns him to keep on walking. Fixer is thrown out of the house and June Ne Moyer, his fiancé, comes to his relief when she learns that he tried to kiss Mrs. Gay, she hands back the ring and Fixer fades away. In Fixer's bachelor apartment there is deep gloom. Fixer is sad because he isn't married and Gay is sadder because he is. [MPW]

"This is a story of a hen-pecked husband who thinks be is also a gay boy. He is detected by his wife in one of his flirtations, and she makes things warm for him. To get revenge he induces a friend to try a flirtation with his wife. The friend tries and fails miserably, and besides gets in trouble with his sweetheart. There is mild fun." -- *Moving Picture World*

The Fake Soldiers

Released April 1, 1913. Lubin Manufacturing Co.-General Film Company release. Split reel (600 ft.), on the same reel with *Shipping A Clock* (400 ft.).

Written and directed by Arthur D. Hotaling.

With Walter Stull (*Marks*), Robert Burns (*Johnson*), Mae Hotely (*Mrs. Marks*), Julia Calhoun (*Mrs. Johnson*), Frances Ne Moyer, Marguerite Ne Moyer.

Marks and Johnson, two businessmen, receive notice of a special meeting of the board of directors of the bank. This notice they lose no time in showing to their wives. It is a good excuse to attend the regular weekly card game at the club. While the club is in session, it is suddenly interrupted by the police. During the raid, Marks and Johnson make their escape. They are closely pursued by two cops. They finally make their get away on a freight train. In the morning when the train stops they find they are in a town that is under martial law. They think it is a good idea to deceive their wives and have a good time and a few days sport. They borrow a couple of soldiers suits, have their pictures taken which they send back to their wives, saying that they have been drafted in the army. The wives, hearing of the hardships of the soldiers, decide to visit their husbands with baskets of food. They arrive in town and go from camp to camp. The soldiers do not know their husbands. A friend of Marks and Johnson meets the wives and puts them on the right track. He learns of the deception and fixes things up. Marks and Johnson meet their wives and get away with the joke, and return to their wives love and confidence. [MPW]

"*Shipping a Clock* and *The Fake Soldiers,* on the same reel, are cracking good comedies. The former, however, is much the better of the two." -- *Motion Picture News*

"This is a real farce and we can report that it pleased, for there was a good deal of laughter. It is made by adding to an old farcical plot a new situation and the result gives fresh entertainment and amusement. The author is Arthur Hotaling and his leading characters are played by Walter Stull and Robert Burns, the fake soldiers, and by Mae Hotely and Julia Calhoun, their wives. It is a better farce than usually found found on the screen." -- *Moving Picture World*

Collecting the Bill

Released April 5, 1913. Lubin Manufacturing Co.-General Film Company release. Split reel (517 ft.), on the same reel with *His Widow* (400 ft.).

Directed by Arthur D. Hotaling, written by Epes W. Sargent.

With Jack Ridgeway (*Marks*), Marguerite Ne Moyer (*stenographer*), Walter Stull (*Walter, a clerk)*, George Reehm (*clerk*), Robert Burns (*John*).

John Scott always refuses to pay his bills. He owes a bill to Archibald Marks. Marks, having a number of clerks in his office, decides that he will send them one after the other, until Scott being dunned so much will pay. The first clerk that receives the bill with instructions that he call upon Scott is rather alarmed at the prospect of what will happen to him. However, he has to make a trial. He finds Scott in his office and receives a rather cold reception until he is so persistent that he is thrown out of the window after being beaten soundly. Upon his return, to the office another clerk is entrusted with the bill. He meets Scott on the street, presents the bill and receives in return a pair of black eyes instead of the money. Marks then offers half of the amount of the bill to the one who will collect it. At this offer another clerk decides to try. He meets with the same dose that was administered to his predecessors. Marks then comes to the conclusion that he will try in person. He does so and Scott becomes enraged at him and throws him out of the office. Upon his return to the office Marks meets the three other victims of Scott's wrath and they are consoling themselves as best they can, when the stenographer, a pretty little miss, asks Mark's permission to try her hand. He willingly gives his consent. She takes the bill and calls upon Scott and with her woman's wit and cleverness collects the bill and receives half of the amount for the trouble. [MPW]

Epes W. Sargent writing in *Moving Picture World* about his scripts:

You Never Can Tell. No author can judge his own work, no matter how cleverly he may appraise the work of another, and so, when that pet script of yours gets turned down in a dozen studios don't declare that there is no intelligence among the studio editors. Be willing to admit that fifty per cent, of the fault lies with the script. The script of *Collecting the Bill* didn't look very promising to us, but on the screen it is getting lots of laughs while its companion picture, *His Widow,* is given second place, though we liked this much the better of the two when we wrote it. When you get $20 for that corking good story that you wanted to make into two reels and are paid $35 for another not half so good, wait until you see the picture on the screen before you throw rocks at the Editor. You stand too close to your own work to get a proper perspective. Be willing to trust to the man who stands far off and can get the true values. Because you got $25 for a story that should have brought you $50 do not price everything you send out. We never have priced either a fiction story or photoplay and we never will; In the long run the profit is on our side.

"Before this half-reel farce is finished one is in the midst of uproarious laughter. Among the comedies or farces that this company has produced, it is one of the best. To whoever collects the bill the employer offers half. Each one of his clerks, in turn, makes an attempt, but each fails not only in collecting the bill, but returns with mussed clothes and a bruised countenance. The employer himself tries, and he gives the old 'tightwad' a tough battle, but in the end he is vanquished. It finally rests upon the girl, his stenographer, to succeed. She succeeds in a woman's way. Instead of using harsh methods, she rubs the old man in the right direction and he pays. The Lubin Company is to be congratulated on such a lively farce." -- *New York Dramatic Mirror*

"This little farce kept the audience in a roar of laughter. It has a good amusing situation and good comic acting. It is the kind of picture to make the audience forget its troubles. Jack Ridgeway has in his office Marguerite DeMoyer and two clerks: Walter Stull and George Reehm. He has a bill against Robert Burns, who goes into a rage whenever asked to pay. Each of the men tries to collect. We are shown what happens and see the hapless ones come back to the office needing bandages. The girl volunteers and tries gentler methods with success. That is all, but it is done in a very clever way and both author, E. W. Sargent, and producer, Arthur Hotaling, deserve praise." -- *Moving Picture World*

His Widow

Released April 5, 1913. Lubin Manufacturing Co.-General Film Company release. Split reel (540 ft.), on the same reel with *Collectung the Bill* (517 ft.).

Directed by Arthur D. Hotaling, written by Epes W. Sargent. Filmed in Jacksonville, Florida.

With Walter Stull (*Walter Faust*), Robert Burns (*Edwin Barbour, his godfather*), Mae Hotely (*Mrs McGoon, his landlady*), Frances Ne Moyer (*Frances, his sweetheart*), George Reehm (*policeman*), Jack Ridgeway (*policeman*).

Walter Faust gets a letter from his god-father. Edwin Barbour, whom he has not seen in ten years, stating that the old man is coming to make a long visit. Walter does not enjoy the prospect and gets his landlady, Mrs. McGoon to pretend that she is his widow, he having died lately. By this ruse it is expected that the old man will quickly turn back. Barbour, however, likes the looks of the "widow" and resolves to stick. He also phones the sad news of

Walter's passing to Frances, his sweetheart. Later in the day Walter comes back to the house to get some clean linen and old Barbour, thinking him to be a burglar, has him arrested. The policeman knows Walter well, but getting the wink takes his prisoner away. Later the god-father sparks the landlady and going to buy an engagement ring, runs into Walter and his sweetheart on the street. He again demands that the burglar be re-arrested, but when the cop tells the story all the party go home and the widow announces her willingness to become Mrs. Barbour. [MPW]

The New York Dramatic Mirror thought *His Widow* was "based upon a fresh idea, well developed, and ably presented by the Lubin players." And that "It is all very funny." But while they liked the film didn't seem to know who they were watching, they identified Francis N. Moyer as the actor playing the uncle. However, it was Bobby Burns that played the godfather (not Uncle) and the very feminine Frances Ne Moyer was the sweetheart.

"On the same reel [with *Collecting the Bill*] is this farce by the same author and producer; but of not quite the same quality, being less spontaneous. It made a good deal of laughter. The acting is very commendable. Walter Stull hears that his godfather (Robert Burns) is coming to visit him. To escape he gets his landlady (Mae Hotely) to say she is his widow. Frances Ne Moyer plays Walter's sweetheart, and George Reehm and Jack Ridgeway play policemen." -- *Moving Picture World*

Angel Cake and Axle Grease

Released April 10, 1913. Lubin Manufacturing Co.-General Film Company release. Split reel (445 ft.), on the same reel with *The Magic Shoe* (400 ft.).

With Walter Stull (*Pete*), Robert Burns (*the father*), George Reehm (*Bob*), Frances Ne Moyer.

Col. Hopkins, Betty, his daughter, Bob and Pete, play a game of quoits. The colonel and Bob have a quarrel and Pete, who is Bob's rival for Betty's love, urges the colonel on till Bob is discharged and Pete himself is made foreman. Bob gets work in the store, and writes to Betty of the fact, and sends the letter by Buck. When Buck gets to the ranch, Betty has just finished baking some angel cakes. She packs a large cake in a box and writes a note to Bob, telling him that if he does not eat it all, she will not love him anymore. She gives Buck a piece

of cake to carry the box to Bob. While Buck is sitting by a tree eating his cake, Pete gets the box and butters the cake with a generous layer of axle grease. When Buck is nearing the store, he is stopped by five or six Indians and they take the cake away from him and have a feast. Buck, seeing it disappear so fast, grasps a piece and eats it himself. Rob and the storekeeper are soon busy doping a lot of sick Indians with pain killer. Betty, on her road to the store for supplies, comes upon the crowd, and Bob points to the terrible work of her cake. Betty cannot believe that her nice-looking cake was capable or laving out a half-dozen Redskins. She begins an investigation and scents axle grease. Suspicion points to Pete, and a plot is hatched to make him confess. Betty sends a note to the Colonel. "I am in trouble, come quick and bring Pete." When they arrive the sheriff pretends to arrest Betty for poisoning the Indians. Pete confesses and the colonel fires him and Bob is restored to favor. [MPW]

"The story found here is no more than a mechanical arrangement of events leading up to the situation that gives the picture its strange title. The daughter of a ranch owner has two cowboy lovers, and the father objects to the one she prefers. When her beloved Bob is banished he finds employment at the country store. Betty sends him an angel cake, which Pete, the second suitor, intercepts and turns into an axle grease layer cake. The big comedy moment is supposed to come when a number of Indians eat the doctored cake and suffer violent indigestion. Then for a climax Pete confesses, having been fooled into believing that Betty is to be arrested for circulating poisoned cake. The father shakes hands with Bob and all is well. Frances Ne Moyer, George Reehm, and Walter Stull have the principal roles." -- *New York Dramatic Mirror*

"A well worked-up comedy with the standard ranch setting. It might have been even more amusing, if the title had not let the 'cat out of the bag' before the right moment. The two on this reel make a very fair offering. George Reehm and Frances Ne Moyer play the leads with Walter Stull as the villain, Robert Burns, the objecting father and a large cast including Indians, cowboys, etc. The photography is very fair." -- *Moving Picture World*

Minnie the Widow

Released April 14, 1913. Lubin Manufacturing Co.-General Film Company release. Split reel (400 ft.), on the same reel with *One on Romance* (600 ft.).

Directed by Arthur D. Hotaling. Written by Epes W. Sargent.

With Mae Hotely (*Minne Windom*), Frances Ne Moyer (*Clara Windom*), L.A. Howard (*Major Dowling*), Julia Calhoun, Bobby Burns, George Reehm, Raymond McKee, Will Louis.

Minnie Windom, a fascinating widow, and her daughter, Clara, being moderately well to do, are spending the winter on the southeast coast. They are having a good time, for the widow is charming. The daughter feels that her mother is beating her. She must tell somebody, so she writes of her vexation to a girl chum and cries herself to sleep. The mother comes in, sees her daughter and tells her that she shall have her chance when she (the mother) has perfected her own affair. Major Dowling is pressing the widow pretty hard, and to give Clara her chance they remove from St. Augustine to another resort. Mrs. Windom does her best to distract attention; she dresses plainly and makes her eyes behave, but the major still pursues her, and in the end persuades her to say "Yes." After the marriage the widow resumes her attractive personality, and the major chases the young swells after Clara, so all is love and kisses. [MPW]

"A farce in a summerland setting and with a hotel-life flavor. It is an amusing picture, but not one that makes much loud laughter. There were some laughs and many smiles, Mae Hotely plays the lead as the widow, so charming that she quite eclipses the chances of her daughter (Frances Ne Moyer) and who, when she finds how things are, dresses in a different style and the men crowd around Elsie. It was produced by Arthur Hotaling from the script of E.W. Sargent. The scene-making and the photography are commendable." -- *Moving Picture World*

Beating Mother to It

Released April 18, 1913. Lubin Manufacturing Co.-General Film Company release. Split reel (793 ft.), on the same reel with *Baby's New Pin* (268 ft.).

Written by Epes W. Sargent.

With Walter Stull (*John Parker*), Frances Ne Moyer, Frances Mann (*Miss Violet*), Robert Burns (*the husband*), Julia Calhoun (*Mrs. Ray*), Earl Metcalfe (*Tom*).

Mrs. Ray's daughter, Bess, loves Tom Travers. But mother objects. Mrs. Ray has a love affair with John Jackson, who seeks her hand. The two love affairs clash frequently. Jackson hires an automobile to elope with mother, Tom and Bess get his note. Tom hires a car and plays chauffeur, while Bess delivers the note to her mother, after turning the clock back one hour. Bess, in the car with Tom, disguised as chauffeur, call for Jackson. Bess being veiled, Jackson thinks her to be the widow. They drive to a minister, where Tom and Bess are married, with Jackson as an unwilling witness. Mother forgives them later. [MPW]

"On the same reel [with *Baby's New Pin*] is this good comedy. It did seem as if the fun might have been extended by having the self-substituted chauffeur, accompanied by his bride, drive the major and the widow to the minister's and stand up with them. E. W. Sargent wrote the script." -- *Moving Picture World*

Sunshine Sue

Released April 22, 1913. Lubin Manufacturing Co.-General Film Company release. Split reel (640 ft.), on the same reel with *A Slight Mistake* (400 ft.).

Directed by Arthur D. Hotaling, written by Epes W. Sargent.

With Frances Ne Moyer (*Sunshine Sue*), Walter Stull (*the boss*), Julia Calhoun (*stenographer*), Raymond McKee (*office boy*), Robert Burns (*Bobby*), George Reehm.

Everybody has a grouch on Friday at the Bronson office. Bobby hates to get up, and his mother pours a pitcher of water over him. When he gets to the office he salutes the bookkeeper, who does not answer. Presently the clerk arrives. He again says good morning, but the others are dumb. The bookkeeper points to the clock and the clerk growls. Bobby has a run-in with the scrubwoman and throws things about. Bronson is late leaving home, and a man with a ladder bumps into him. Bronson knocks the man down, and a policeman comes to arrest him. Bronson gives the cop a five and rushes to the office. The typist arrives late, and she gives a letter to the boss which reads: "Please get another typist. I was married last night." Bronson is crazed; he phones to the employment agency and they send a Miss Prim, who proves to be absolutely incompetent. The boss fires her. Finally another typist arrives; she is a pretty little doll. She immediately proves her ability. Everybody waits upon her. The boss is restored to good humor, and as the day ends all bid her a cheery good night, Bobby, left alone, goes to Sue's vacant chair and pats it, smiling. [MPW]

An article written as part of Epes Wintrop Sargent's regular column for the *Moving Picture World* entitled *The Photoplaywright* discusses *Sunshine Sue* and a few other Lubin comedy productions:

We Will Try and Explain. A brutally frank person down in Texas wants to know what we think of a couple of our stories. He states that he has had stories returned by companies with the statement that the plot was too slight or that it lacked comedy. He says they were written "as tersely as was wise." He adds: "The author has about four pages on which to write the action of a thirty-five scene scenario and to hit even the high points he has a lot of figuring to do and cannot possibly include all of the details of comedy." Then comes the cruel blow. He says: I might mention one or two of your own stories to show you that I am partly right, at least. I do not mean to discredit your ability when I call your attention to your *Sunshine Sue* and *Collecting the Bill*, but to ask you if you really believe that there is much of a plot in either of them. These two stories could have been almost turned into almost a tragedy and without the slightest trace of comedy if the director had have wanted to produce it that way, or if the company had not have been capable of handling comedies. Do you think that I am right? The correspondent mentions two stories that have been pleasantly commented upon by the critics and which seem to have made a laughing hit. Neither story had much plot. *Sunshine Sue* was the story of a grouchy office that began to smile when Sue came into the place. *Collecting the Bill* was the story of a girl typist who collected an account from a grouch through feminine wiles when masculine force had failed to accomplish the purpose. We are willing to admit that the stories lacked strong plots, indeed *Sunshine Sue* can boast of little or no plot, but we'll be hanged if we will admit that either story would have made a good tragedy without alteration. It is not possible to put a finger on any specific line in the long letter that distinctly asks how it was we came to sell such stuff when his own superior product doesn't sell, but the whole tenor of the letter is one of inquiry and we are going to answer the unasked question. In the first place we did not even write four pages of script for either of these stories. We have not the carbons at hand and cannot give exact lengths, but it is seldom indeed that we turn the third page on a half-reel story and we did not even do any figuring to get the high points into such narrow compass. We sat down and wrote them off and mailed them and in the course of time they were made and released. We gave the director all he needed to have in the way of comedy business and let it go at that. That we did our share of the work seems to be shown by the fact that sticking to these scripts, the director, who is Arthur D. Hotaling, by the way, made successful stories. But the reason these scripts sold is not that they were so infinitely superior to all other comedy scripts. They sold because the full story was presented in such a form that Mr. Hotaling could take the script and make it. He did not have to lay his company off for a couple of days while he wrestled with some good idea poorly displayed. All that there was to the script was right there on the paper ready to be made from that script. *His Widow* seems to have been pleasantly received by the papers and the public. It was put in work the day we left Jacksonville, last winter, after a brief visit to the studio. The night before, Mr. Hotaling came into the room after we had turned in and wanted to know if the widow required real widow's weeds. We waked up sufficiently to explain that in our opinion a maiden lady, widowed on the spur of the moment, would not have crepe in the house. Then we went to sleep again. The next morning the picture was started, the outside scenes being made while the stage settings were being prepared. Had it been necessary to get the crepe, some other story would have been taken up in the wait. That's why we can sell scripts. We offer a reasonably sufficient idea displayed in such a form that the director can make it from our script. We do not try to get a two-reel idea into a half-reel script, but we do try to make it possible for the director to put in plenty of comedy and we write two to four line scenes so tersely that the director can get the idea and work it out as his surroundings and his people best permit. Many writers on photoplay subjects profess a fine indifference to the form in which a story is written. They argue that the idea is the thing and that the technical form is unimportant, but we have found that the good idea properly displayed is ten times as likely to sell as the splendid idea that may require a day to straighten out. That's why *Collecting the Bill* sold and our correspondent's stories didn't. We are sending out the same sort of script that an editor or director would write. We are writing stuff that sells and not the sort of stuff we think ought to sell. It is practical, complete, comprehensive and not too costly. That's why we preach technique of form and technique of plot development. It sells scripts.

"*Sunshine Sue* was a comedy which caused a few laughs. Little time was spent on the film and the comedy is overdrawn." -- *Variety*

"On the same reel [with *A Slight Mistake*] is this comedy, showing the difference on the temper of an office force exerted by a woman of pleasing appearance compared with one of lesser charms. Frances Ne Moyer has the title role. Walter H. Stull is the boss. Between these two and the office force much hearty laughter is created." -- *Moving Picture World*

Fixing Auntie Up

Released May 3, 1913. Lubin Manufacturing Co.-General Film Company release. Split reel (659 ft.), on the same reel with *Clarence at the Theatre* (350 ft.). Directed by Arthur D. Hotaling, written by Epes W. Sargent.

With Mae Hotely (*Miss Bayne*), Robert Burns (*Old man Carson*), George Reehm (*Jack Carson*), Marguerite Ne Moyer, Frances Ne Moyer, Raymond McKee, Len Brooks.

Miss Bayne is much perturbed because her nieces. Bertha, Bess and Nan, are beating her badly at the game of hearts, and she strenuously objects to their getting married until she secures a husband. Jack Carson has a widowed father and he coaxes dad to keep an eye on the spinster. He tells him that she is rich and beautiful, but when old man Carson sees her he is much disappointed. The girls see what is the trouble and they determine to doll auntie up. By many little arts they improve her every day until she looks perfectly human, and it is not long before the old man capitulates. When he proposes, of course, auntie says, "This is so sudden," but she is too wise to lose her chance. Jack Carson is rewarded with the hand and heart of Bertha. George Radnor wins Bess and Ray Hewitt gets Nan, and the path is paved for four happy marriages. [MPW]

"On the same reel [with *Clarence at the Theatre*] is this farce in the well known style of A. D. Hotaling's company. We found it fairly entertaining ourselves and it seemed to please the audience. Aunty, played by Mae Hotely, won't let her three nieces get married to their three lovers till she is herself disposed of in wedlock. George Reehm writes to his dad, Robert Burns, to come and marry her. Tired of widowerhood, he comes; but is repelled by her looks, so the girls "fix her up" and she comes out of it a most charming young woman. Dad is now glad he came." –*Moving Picture World*

She Must Be Ugly

Released May 8, 1913. Lubin Manufacturing Co.-General Film Company release. Split reel (470 ft.), on the same reel with *Hattie's New Hat* (553 ft.).

Directed by Arthur D. Hotaling, written by Epes W. Sargent. Filmed outside the Burbridge Hotel and Riverside Park in Jacksonville, Florida.

With Mae Hotely (*the ugly stenographer*), Robert Burns (*W. Kerry, the employer*), Raymond McKee (*his assistant*), Marguerite Ne Moyer (*first job applicant*), Frances Ne Moyer (*second job applicant*), Ben Walker (*park policeman*), Walter Stull (*Kerry's friend*).

Robert Bums is tired of having his stenographers quit their jobs to get married. He hits upon an idea — to advertise for a stenographer that is so ugly there is no chance for her to get married. Pretty girls apply for the position, but are decidedly turned down on account of their good looks. Mae Hotely decides to make herself ugly and applies for the position. The boss engages her. One Sunday afternoon, while he is out walking in the park, he meets her in her own proper person, and falls violently in love, not knowing that she is his own stenographer. He tries to scrape up an acquaintance with her, but she appeals to a policeman for protection. He is utterly miserable until one day in the office, when Mae's smoked glasses fall off. He sees through the rest of her make-up; she is the girl of his dreams. Everything ends happily, as she promises to be his stenographer for life. [MPW]

Frances Ne Moyer as the second attractive applicant struts into the office with an attitude and chomping on chewing gum. When Burns turns her down she pats him on the chest, snaps her fingers at him and struts right back out of the office. She does this all for very good comic effect. Mae Hotely then is seen making herself ugly. While a very tall women Hotely was actually fairly attractive but like many other comediennes (Louise Fazenda comes to mind) more often than not wore make-up that hid her beauty. Walter Stull appears for a total of about five seconds as a friend Burns meets on the street.

"A picture that made plenty of laughter and seemed to be well liked. The idea it uses—the pretty typist getting married and making her discouraged boss advertise for an ugly one—has been used a number of times, but there is freshness enough in the picture to justify it. One would say that its author, E. W. Sargent, had seen the others and then shown how they might have been made so as to approach possibility. It is funnier than any of the others that we remember. Of course, it isn't high art." -- *Moving Picture World*

"Epes Winthrop Sargent is the author of this half reel farce produced by the Lubin Company. Though not glittering with originality or adroit business, the slight affair is surprisingly laugh provoking. Mae Hotely as the ugly duckling, and the fair maiden does well. As the head of a business, the old bachelor is disgusted at the fact that all his stenographers marry and leave him. He advertises for one that is ugly. More as a joke than anything else, a charming young woman makes herself up and secures the job. How she wins her boss's love without him knowing it is the substance of the remaining part." -- *New York Dramatic Mirror*

Hattie's New Hat

Released May 8, 1913. Lubin Manufacturing Co.-General Film Company release. Split reel (553 ft.), on the same reel with *She Must Be Ugly* (470 ft.).

Directed by Arthur D. Hotaling, written by Epes W. Sargent.

With Mae Hotely (*Hattie Hotaling*), Robert Burns (*Arthur, her husband*).

Mrs. Jones and Mrs. Smith, neighbors of the Hotalings, have new hats, and Mrs. Hotaling tells her husband that she really must have a new lid to be equal with the others. Arthur demurs, but Hattie not only gets the price, but takes her husband with her to bring the package home. When Arthur sees the box he nearly swoons. It is big enough to hold a rocking chair. To navigate the streets and get by without injuring people, requires all of his optic measurement, and with all of his care he runs a-foul of many offensive and inoffensive pedestrians, which cause arguments that are annoying. Reaching home Mrs. Hotaling shows the neighbors the largest box and dearest little hat ever seen, Arthur is worn out with the jolt and well nigh demented, attempts suicide by getting into the box and attaching a gas heater hose. Hattie rescues him and administers a spanking to make him behave. [MPW]

"With the foregoing [*She Must Be Ugly*] this farce by the same author, producer and company, also made laughter. Like the other, it pleased many, but there was no time when it made the whole house laugh. Its quality comes from its unexpected things. We see, for instance, a man cutting a hole in big, empty hat box and wonder what he is going to do with it. We are not permitted to know for some time and then when we find it on his head and connected with the gas, it is in this case, very amusing."
-- *Moving Picture World*

"For a farce-comedy *Hattie's New Hat* partakes too much of burlesque in the spirit, acting, and general business. For certain kinds of audiences, the piece will, no doubt, prove advisable, but it will not amuse those demanding a high standard. There is not the humor in it that marks *She Must Be Ugly*. Hattie wants a new hat. Her husband is loath to buy one, but wifey's determined will prevails after considerable horseplay." -- *New York Dramatic Mirror*

Lucky Cohen

Released May 12, 1913. Lubin Manufacturing Co.-General Film Company release. Split reel (286 ft.), on the same reel with *A Ten Acre Gold Brick* (746 ft.).

Directed by Arthur D. Hotaling.

With Mae Hotely, Walter Stull, George Reehm.

Sol Cohen, a Jew peddler, has the whole village of Pikeville buying the cheap jewelry that he has for sale. He tells them that it is solid gold, and they fall for the "stall" and many of the men and women make purchases. Sol leaves them well satisfied, and he is also satisfied, for he has made a fine profit. Not long after one of the jays, while washing his hands, makes the discovery that the ring that he has bought is nothing more than brass, and wild with excitement, he informs the constable and townspeople, who have also been stung. They immediately get clubs and other weapons and start in pursuit of the Jew. In the meantime, he has wandered along and a tramp, who is hiding behind a tree, holds him up with his empty hand covered with a handkerchief, takes his pack and clothes away from him and leaves him bewailing his fate. The crowd catch sight of the tramp, now dressed up in the Jew's clothes, and give chase. They catch him after he has dropped the pack and tray, right at the foot of the

tree behind which the Jew is hiding. They beat the tramp up thinking that he is the Jew, while lucky Sol recovers his goods and goes on his way rejoicing. [MPW]

"A half reel farce, acted in an amusing manner by Walter Stull and George E. Reehm. Cohen sells his wares about the village, and the villagers believe they have real gold and silver jewelry. As Cohen is passing out of the village he is held up and robbed of everything by Happy Jones, and Jones returns to the village just in time to catch the wrath of the villagers after they have discovered the cheat. Cohen saves his money and goods and doesn't get the licking. He is lucky and one laughs necessarily." -- *New York Dramatic Mirror*

"A laughable little farce by Mae Hotely. It is not wholly new, but has enough freshness to make it entertaining. The audience seemed to like it." -- *Moving Picture World*

A Ten Acre Gold Brick

Released May 12, 1913. Lubin Manufacturing Co.-General Film Company release. Split reel (746 ft.), on the same reel with *Lucky Cohen* (286 ft.).

Directed by Arthur D. Hotaling, written by Epes W. Sargent, Filmed in Jacksonville, Florida.

With Mae Hotely (*farmer*), Robert Burns (*farmer*), Walter Stull (*agent*), J. Irving White (*agent*).

Jed Bascom and his wife, who live in the Middle Atlantic States, where the winters are noted for their severity, are about tired of the cold and snow. One evening, after Jed has put in a hard day's work on the farm, and has arrived home with an armful of wood, he receives a prospectus and reading matter concerning Tropical Farms. He answers the letter and tells the real estate men that he will come on as a prospective purchaser. Skin & Dolle, the real estate men, who are land sharks, upon receiving Jed's reply decide to fix up a fake fruit farm on one of the worthless pieces of land that they have. Accordingly they buy a quantity of grape fruit, oranges, bananas and pine apples. These they give their men instructions to tie upon the trees with twine, so that when the unsuspecting buyer arrives they can show him the wonderful bargain they are going to sell him. Jed arrives and falls into the trap. He buys the farm, but he pays the bill with a check. The next day he takes a survey of his purchase, and finds out the deception. Instead of raising a row, he and his wife borrow a hundred dollars from the land sharks. Then he wires the bank to stop payment on the check. He then sends Skin & Dolle a letter, telling them what he has found out. When they receive the letter they faint. [MPW]

"A farce that made laughter and seemed to be liked. It deals with a rural pair who are swindled by being persuaded to buy a few acres of sand in Florida, but who are too crafty to stay swindled. It is amusingly acted." -- *Moving Picture World*

"Though acted and produced in the usual commendable style of the Lubin Company, this half reel farce discloses itself as rather below standard in theme and originality. It was not long ago that another Licensed company used the same idea of fastening fruit onto a tree with strings in order to sell property. Robert Burns and Mae Hotely are good as the farmers, and Walter H. Stull and J. Irving White act up to their roles as the swindlers." -- *New York Dramatic Mirror*

His First Experience

Released May 23, 1913. Lubin Manufacturing Co.-General Film Company release. Split reel (564 ft.), on the same reel with *Detective Dot* (453 ft.).

Directed by Arthur D. Hotaling, written by W.H. Kitchell. Filmed in Jacksonville, Florida.

With Mae Hotely (*Roxanne*), Robert Burns (*Wiggins*), Frances Ne Moyer (*Maggie*), Leon Brooks (*the bachelor*), Buster Johnson (*her little boy*).

John Joline, who is old enough to be married and happy, comes home from his office with a headache, to find a new family moving in next door, and his valet, Muggins, already in love with the new maid. Muggins is lectured severely. Joline learns that the new neighbors are Rosanne Cameron, a widow, and Buster, her little boy. Joline detests boys as much as he detests women. As soon as he finds that Buster has slipped through a hole in the fence to make friends with his collie dog, he captures him and takes him home. He is overwhelmed by the charms of Roxanne. and instead of repeating his lecture, he stammers an apology and falls in love with her. Some time later Roxanne goes on a visit, leaving Buster in charge of her maid. Joline takes her to the train and has reason to be encouraged over the progress of his suit. The same afternoon Muggins and Maggie elope, leaving Buster asleep in Mr. Joline's study, with a note beside him. John returns and finds the note and then Buster. Joline has grown fond of the boy, but the responsibilities of temporary charge of a five-year old seem infinite. Muggins gone and nobody home next door, he gets a good supper for Buster, and failing nerve to undress the youngster, rocks him to sleep in his arms. Roxanne is expected back the next day and Joline and the boy watch for her. She arrives and Joline sends Buster to meet her. Buster before going, hands Joline a painfully written letter, which Joline reads as follows: "I like you because you have a nice dog. I like you too. So does my mama. If you was my papa I guess you would let me play with the dog whenever I wanted to. I wish you was my papa. Your friend. Buster Cameron." This is enough for even an old bachelor to enthuse over, and Joline has grown tired of bachelor life. There was but one way to end it and the way led him into the house next door, and into Roxanne's arms. So Mr. Joline's first experience in love, ended in a honeymoon, and it was Buster who lit the moon. [MPW]

"On the same reel [with *Detective Dot*] is this comedy love story, which also pleased the audience. The bachelor (Leon Brooks) falls in love with the widow in the next house, played by Mae Hotely. Her little boy (Buster Johnson) plays the part of a human cupid. The script is by W. H. Kitchell and was produced by Arthur Hotaling." -- *Moving Picture World*

Kate the Cop

Released June 5, 1913. Lubin Manufacturing Co.-General Film Company release. Split reel (731 ft.), on the same reel with *Bob Builds a Chicken House* (305 ft.).

Directed by Arthur D. Hotaling, written by Epes W. Sargent.

With Walter Stull (*timid cop*), Mae Hotely (*Kate, his sweetheart*), Robert Burns (*burglar*), Jack Ridgeway, Mrs. Clayton.

Casey is not much of a policeman, but he and the old Chief of Police are all the force Beckvllle boasts. Casey is like a big-town cop and is popular with the servant girls. Kate is his favorite. Kate's mistress catches a burglar in her bedroom and phones for the chief. Then she finds Casey in the kitchen and Kate makes Casey go after the burglar. Casey is scared by a noise and rushes back to the kitchen. Kate goes after the intruder herself and makes the arrest, and the disgusted chief appoints Kate the cop and makes Casey turn cook. A week later the cop is invited in for lunch, but this time Casey does the inviting and Kate is the uniformed guest. [MPW]

"Running somewhat over a half-reel this is a burlesque satire on country policemen, with Walter Stull, Mae Hotely, Jack Ridgeway, Robert Burns, and Mrs. Clayton in the principal roles. Casey (Mr. Stull) makes up half the village police force. He is better, adapted to paying court to his sweetheart (Mae Hotely) than capturing burglars, it would appear. When a call for assistance comes the sweetheart, Kate, is forced to take his place. She captures the burglar, but thereafter insists on wearing the policeman's clothes. Casey has to take her place in the kitchen. Tightening up the action and shortening the sketch in proportion would give more 'punch' to the picture. It is fairly amusing, on the whole, and occasionally highly laughable." -- *New York Dramatic Mirror*

The Professor's Predicament

Released June 12, 1913. Lubin Manufacturing Co.-General Film Company release. Split reel (600 ft.), on the same reel with *Nearly in Mourning* (400 ft.).

Directed by Arthur D. Hotaling, written by Epes W. Sargent.

With Mae Hotely, Bobby Burns, George Reehm.

Professor Silas Bingle, a staunch temperance advocate, starts out on a crusade against the "demon drink." He stops in front of a saloon and the first to emerge therefrom is a son of Erin, Pat Lafferty, with a kettle of beer. Bingle follows him and takes the can of foaming beverage away from him and dumps it over the fence, where it falls accidentally in the hat of Dusty Dawkins. Dusty is about to drink when the temperance lecturer reaches over the fence with his cane and upsets the beer all over him. He again stations himself in front of the saloon, where a young fellow coming out bumps against him and knocks him down. He loses his eye glasses in the altercation which follows, and, being very nearsighted, meets with several unpleasant happenings. But in the end virtue triumphs and receives its reward. [MPW]"

"A farce with broad humor that made a great deal of laughter among an East Side audience. The professor is a temperance advocate and, following "the cause," he comes in contact not only with drunkenness, but with that which makes it. In a scrimmage with a barkeeper he loses his glasses and now he can't see and, smelling of liquor, he must walk as though he were drunk. The poor professor has a hard time." -- *The Moving Picture World*

"A rather tiresome effort in the comedy line, with hackneyed situations. The makeup of the Irishman is very stereotyped and burlesquy. Direction and playing good, considering commonplace story. Photography good." -- *The New York Clipper*

The Zulu King

Released June 24, 1913. Lubin Manufacturing Co.-General Film Company release. Split reel (874 ft.), on the same reel with *At the Telephone* (153 ft.).

With Mae Hotely (*wife*), Walter Stull (*Brown*), Robert Burns (*The White King*).

John Smith is abused and henpecked. He is left at home to wash the dishes, while his wife has a good time. Brown and Jones sympathize with him and carry some of their sympathy in a bottle. Smith revolts and ships as a cook on a steamer bound for Africa. It is one slavery for another, and when a party is landed to get fresh water, he beats it up the beach and runs into a party of Zulus, who drive off the others and make him their prisoner. They take him before their king and when Smith deceives them by telling them he is bullet proof, and giving them a pistol loaded with blank cartridges with which to fire at him. they are so surprised that the shots have no effect upon Smith. They think he is supernatural and proclaim him king. The original king gives the crown and scepter to Smith. Later Mrs. Smith has turned missionary. She is shipwrecked on the very coast where Smith is king. Smith is delighted at the news of a new queen, until he finds out who it is. He then tries to commit suicide by abusing the sacred idol. But Mrs. Smith saves him. She drives off his numerous brunette wives and dethrones him. She becomes the ruler and makes Smith take the place of the fan boy and he becomes the humblest of her subjects. [MPW]

In the Spring of 1913 Arthur D. Hotaling set up a second unit of the Lubin company working in Jacksonville to exclusively make films with an all Black cast (or at least Black actors in the lead parts), eventually in 1914 building a second studio exclusively for these comedies (located on the corner of Park & Dora in Jacksonville) about six blocks from the main Lubin facility at 750 Riverside Avenue. For a time the stars of that company were Mattie Edwards and John Edwards, and Will Louis the primary director. However, most of the early "colored" comedies made prior to 1914 were directed by Hotaling with Jerold T. Hevener occasionally running things. The motivation as to whether these comedies were made for Black audiences or made merely to perpetuate stereotypes and provide some cheap laughs for unenlightened White audiences may never be known. Yet some of these films survive and show that the Lubin "colored" players were just as skilled as their White counterparts and that the storylines did not seem to more adversely target the Black community than other films made that attacked and/or made fun of other ethnic or racial minorities. It is known that Hotaling recruited Walter Stull and George Reehm to conduct an acting school for the Black players since most were local Jacksonville talent rather than the few seasoned actors they imported from New York.

"It is almost a shame to take the terrible theme of Cannibal Savage history and reduce it to comedy, but there is a humor in the condition, which may induce a laugh so long as the white man comes out on top. The picture is not intended to horrify the audience, but more to induce a scream of laughter, at the beautiful stupidity of the aborigines and how easily they were conquered by modern tact and wit. The picture is wonderfully true to the atmosphere of the pictorial savage and an excellent example of the Lubin director's thoroughness." –*Moving Picture World article*

"A much henpecked husband becomes transformed by a few drinks into a man of courage, whereupon he embarks as a cookee on a long voyage. He finds this nearly as bad as his old condition, however, and when the ship touches at the coast of Africa, he deserts. He is taken prisoner by a band of Zulus, but awes them by withstanding the shots from a pistol loaded with blank cartridges, and is acclaimed their king. His bliss is perfect until his wife arrives as a missionary and recognizes him. By pure force of tongue and arms she deposes him and becomes queen, and we may surmise that he serves her with the natives ever after, for so the picture closes. This sort of thing is endless. It may continue forever, inventing complications to suit any length of film. However, being farcical, it is not to be criticized too harshly. It is full of animation and has several good situations. The king is spiritedly done by Robert Burns and Mae Hotely as the wife is quite as sincere." -- *New York Dramatic Mirror*

The Beaut From Butte

Released June 27, 1913. Lubin Manufacturing Co.-General Film Company release. Split reel (699 ft.), on the same reel with *Bob Buys An Auto* (338 ft.).

With Walter Stull (*Bill, The Beaut*), Frances Ne Moyer, Mae Hotely, George Reehm, Marguerite Ne Moyer.

Bill Bragg comes East to visit relatives and friends. He is in full cowboy regalia, and cuts a wide swath while he is the guest of Mrs. Eayne, whose pretty daughter, Nell, throws over Jack Scott for the dashing westerner, who is not afraid to shoot up a sheriff's posse. Bill tells all the girls exciting stories of his wonderful adventures and thrilling rescues. They think he is quite a hero and adore him. When Bill goes home, he leaves his photograph with all the girls, and they remain true to the attractive stranger. Then comes a letter from one of the town boys who went West. He has looked Bill up and encloses a snap-shot of Bill in his true colors, which shows him to be far from the romantic cowboy which he represented himself to be. The boys take the snap-shot over to the sewing circle to show the girls, and cupid gets on the job once more. [MPW]

"This farce, on the same reel with *Bob Buys an Auto*, has the virtue of giving room for laughter, even though the theme is conventional with usage. Visiting his cousins in the East the young man wins all the girls with his tales of wonderful adventures in the West. Later, after his return home, one of the boys, after investigation, learns that the fellow is a driver of a sprinkling wagon." -- *New York Dramatic Mirror*

"This, on same reel with above [*Bob Buys an Auto*], is longer and stronger than the other. Bad Bill comes on a visit from the East and tells big stories of his prowess. But later, it is learned that he drives a sprinkling wagon in his home town. Some good laughs in this." -- *Moving Picture World*

The Wrong Hand Bag

Released July 4, 1913. Lubin Manufacturing Co.-General Film Company release. Split reel (532 ft.), on the same reel with *The Waiter's Strategy* (400 ft.).

With Mae Hotely (*Mrs. Hanson*), Robert Burns (*Mr. Jones*), George Reehm (*Mr. Hansom*).

Mrs. Hanson reminds hubby that it is her birthday as he is about to leave for his office. On the way, he stops in a jewelry store, and purchases for her a silver mesh bag, which he sends home by a messenger. When Mrs. Hanson receives the bag she cannot resist the temptation to show it to her next-door neighbor, Mrs. Jones, who at once becomes jealous. When Jones returns home she makes him promise that he will buy her one. This promise she persuades Jones into with the aid of a broom. Jones buys his wife a bag exactly like the one which Mrs. Hanson has. Mrs. Hanson mislays her bag, and seeing Mrs. Jones with one, she immediately decides that the one Mrs. Jones has is hers. She attacks Mrs. Jones and quite a fight ensues. The husbands arrive on the scene, become involved. In the meantime the maid of the Hanson family discovers the hand bag in the exact spot where Mrs. Hanson had laid it. During a lull in hostilities the maid informs Mrs. Hanson of her find. Mrs. Hanson, anxious to straighten the matter out, rushes to the Jones home and arrives just as the husbands are about to be arrested. She makes explanation, and everything is satisfactorily adjusted. The two husbands look as if they had gone through a threshing machine. But in these days of women's rights what does a poor husband do. [MPN]

The second team must have photographed *The Wrong Hand Bag*. There are a limited number of scene set-ups, much of the action is filmed in long shot, and the climatic fight between the two husbands barely keeps the two combatants in frame. Doesn't seem to be reflective of the usual good direction that Arthur D. Hotaling provided for the Gay Time comedies.

"The lovers of comedy will not be forgotten, several of the best procurable have been included in the list. "The Wrong Hand Bag" will perhaps prove the best. It is a Lubin film and one that will provoke a thousand laughs. The Lubin people make a specialty of humorous pictures and this one is a record breaker." -- *The Niagara Falls Gazatte*

"Amongst other items is a humorous film, *The Wrong Handbag,* in which a domestic contretemps concerning a wife's birthday gift causes amusing warfare between two neighboring households, with a ludicrous ending." -- *Leeds Mercury (U.K.)*

Building A Trust

Released July 10, 1913. Lubin Manufacturing Co.-General Film Company release. Split reel (600 ft.), on the same reel with *When Love Loses Out* (400 ft.).

Directed by Arthur D. Hotaling, written by Epes W. Sargent. Filmed December 1912.

With Mae Hotely (*Mary Murphy*), Robert Burns (*Wan Lung*).

Wan Lung and Mary Murphy are business rivals — both running laundries. Lung does fairly well, but Mary gets the best of the game, as the policeman naturally would work for his countrywoman. Then Mandy Jackson opens another "white as snow" laundry and Lung and Mary hold a conference of war, united against the colored lady. Mrs. Murphy reads the papers and gets much knowledge of the advantages of the big laundry trusts and, with the co-operation of Lung, she organizes a trust. They scoop in all of the washerwomen of the neighborhood and boom prices. The scheme is a big success; the new acquisitions are proud of the institution and work hard, while "the trust" sits at ease and bosses things. [MPW]

Epes W. Sargent seemed a bit obsessed with this film writing not one but two articles in *Moving Picture World* detailing some of the circumstances of the film's production. First article:
We wrote a little farce last winter that just barely got on the screen. It was not great, but it was a pleasant little thing and well produced. It was titled *Building a Trust* and was produced by the Lubin company. It is rather lively in action, but not heavy in idea. An Irish washerwoman and a Chinese laundryman constantly scrap. The woman has the best of it because the patrolman on the beat is himself an Irishman. Presently a darkey lady down the street opens a laundry. Past differences are forgotten and the Irishwoman and the Chinaman join hands against their

competitor. That's farcical enough, and yet it has the same basis as a score of plays dealing with the oppressions of the trusts and other plays dealing with racial prejudice. Dozens of race prejudice plays are written but not produced because of their bias. Several trust plays have been done and many more have been turned back to the writers. The idea of making it into a farce was more original and so it sold in that form. It gave the audiences, the children and the ignorant something to laugh at, and yet, below the surface, there was thought and satire. This is a rather crude illustration, perhaps, but it gives a hint. Originality should not be directed toward getting so far away from the common things of life as to require a highly trained intellect to appreciate the idea. It must appeal to the children and to those with the intelligence of children, and yet it should be capable of appealing to the better informed as well. If editors cannot get that, they have to take the same old themes, but they are looking for originality of the right sort and are taking it when they can find it and asking for more.

Second article:

Coincidences. John William Kellette, who is all right even if he does live in New Rochelle, drops us a line on the yellowest kind of yellow paper. We hope some time that Kellette will write William Lord Wright, who opines that our own green paper makes more noise than a circus calliope. The Kellette paper is still louder, but he writes sensible things. A recent duplication moves him to this: "Until today I was serene in the belief that I had something original, only to find out that you beat me to it. Strange, at that, for yours was *Building a Trust*, and *The Trust that Was Busted* was mine, and while they differed in several instances, the underlying germ was the same. I simply indite this to show that had I seen the Lubin and I was prone to believe things, and having sent Lubin mine (which I didn't) I might think they 'pinched it.' Whenever I see anything similar to something I wrote produced by a company rejecting the script, I simply feel that somebody beat me to it. I think that is the better way, don't you? Too many embryo photoplaywrights get the idea that what they write is as fresh as a new laid egg, when, as a matter of fact, hundreds of aspiring future greats may have, at that time, Uncle Sam's mail packs burdened with just such scripts. And as to titles: I have found titles that I believed original with me later produced, only to find that the stuff was made up weeks before my script reached the studio. *The Little Girl Next Door*, for instance, produced by Thanhouser, was identical in name, but not in theme, to one I submitted, but their story was filmed and finished more than a week before I put mine into the mails. When the aspiring photoplaywright gets feeling that he is being robbed, he ought to hie himself into the woods and give himself a good licking. The things he believes original with him, he is simply sending out weeks and months after somebody else had beaten him to it." *Building a Trust* was written in October, made in December, but not released until July. Meantime Mr. Kellette had written a story that dealt with a Chinaman and an Irish woman and that had our title in reverse. He didn't accuse us of theft of suggestion because he knew we never had seen the script and we do not believe that he would have made the suggestion, anyhow. But he wrote a trust story with an Irishwoman and a Chinaman and we wrote one with an Irishwoman, a Chinaman and a negress. This is threshing out old wheat, but there are too many persons who still cling to the belief that if they see a story that is something like the other, they know the company steals. If they never sent it there, they are certain that some editor who did it stole the idea and sold it elsewhere. Just get it into your head that it is possible for two persons to thick up substantially the same idea, and you'll never get over that belief in the whole dishonesty in the studios.

"An Irish washerwoman and a Chinese laundryman are doing business side by side. The former throws mud on the other's wash and cuts the lines, and the latter retaliates in kind, matters reaching a crucial stage when a negress starts up a business nearby. The two quondam enemies now combine to drive out the common competitor. So effectually is this plan carried out. that the Celestial and daughter of Erin become partners, hiring the negress and a number of others to do the work while they take it easy. This little comedy is well conceived, well acted, and well done generally. It is clean fun of the best sort, and should prove a favorite on any bill. As the washerwoman and the Chinaman Mae Hotely and Robert Burns are excellent." –*New York Dramatic Mirror*

"On the same reel with the forgoing [*When Loves Loses Out*], this farce comedy by E. W. Sargent and produced by Arthur Hotaling seemed to make a hit with the audience. The Chinese laundryman's getting the Irish cop to keep his rival on the other side of the fence, Mrs. Murphy by name (Mae Hotely), from splashing the clothes on his line with mud, gives a taste of the quality of the fun in this picture. The situation is changed several times as the plot develops, but there is enough truth and freshness every time to get real laughter." –*Moving Picture World*

The Hidden Bank Roll

Released July 18, 1913. Lubin Manufacturing Co.-General Film Company release. Split reel (319 ft.), on the same reel with *When Mary Married* (600 ft.).

With Walter Stull (*Weary Willie*), Robert Burns (*Bob Prichard*), George Reehm (*Sleepy Sam*), Mae Hotely (*the maid*).

Bob Prichard, who has spent a very lively night at the club, approaches his home very tipsy. Upon arriving at the door he thinks it best to remove his shoes, which he does. Then, after drinking the water from the flower vase, and trying for some time to open the door with a cigar while he has the key in his mouth, he succeeds in getting the door open. He is about to enter the house when he thinks that he had better hide his bank roll, which he puts safely in one of the shoes. He decides to go to bed, and unconsciously picks up a flower pot instead of the shoes. He retires, leaving the shoes with the money on the front porch. About five minutes after Bob has gone upstairs, Weary Willie, a hobo, happens along, sees the shoes and no one in sight, puts them under his coat and goes away, he finds a quiet spot and sits down to put on the new shoes. They are a little tight but he gets them on and starts off again. But the money stuffed in the toe of one of the shoes makes it so uncomfortable that he cannot stand the pain, so he takes them off and walks back to the place, and after putting on the old shoes, starts out to dispose of the new ones. He meets Sleepy Sam, who is busily engaged devouring a lunch. Weary makes a trade of the shoes for a sandwich and goes on his way. Sam picks up the shoes and starts on his way. Happening to pass Bob's house, where by this time the maid is sweeping the sidewalk, and the baker, having just delivered the morning rolls, Sam asks her for one. She gives him a roll and recognizes her master's shoes. Sam at the same time sees a cop on the corner, drops them and takes to his heels. About this time Bob has awakened, and, in searching for the shoes, he comes out of the house and sees them in the maid's hand. He feels for the money and finds it safe. He is so overjoyed he rewards everybody and starts to kiss the maid when his wife catches him and she, with the maid, gives him a good beating. [MPW

The first half of the film has Bobby Burns in top hat and tails arriving at home after a long night drunk as can be. While Chaplin in a similar situation in *One A.M.* cannot find his house key, Burns is just too drunk to use it. While Burns' forte was acrobatics and mimicking animals he also does quite fine at playing a drunk, dare say at least equal to the other above-mentioned comedian.

"A drunk getting home late at night, or early, in the morning, hides the remainder of his bankroll in his shoes, which he promptly forgets, on the front porch. A tramp happening that way picks them up, and trades them off with another of his kind for something to eat. This hobo stops to beg from the drunk's servant girl when a cop appears on the scene. He drops the shoes and runs. The drunk comes out, now sober, recognizes his shoes, takes his money from the toes, and joyfully rewards both the policeman and the tramp he has now captured with a fiver apiece. Trivial and long drawn out in the extreme, but with a laugh here and there that makes it more readily forgiven." -- *New York Dramatic Mirror*

"*The Hidden Bankroll* is an excellent Lubin comedy, with a plot that never bores." -- *Oregon (Portland) Daily Journal*

Rastus Among the Zulus

Released July 28, 1913. Lubin Manufacturing Co.-General Film Company release. Split reel (452 ft.), on the same reel with *The Widow's Wiles* (678 ft.).

Directed and written by Arthur D. Hotaling. Filmed in Jacksonville, Florida.

With Joseph Outen (*Rastus*) [?], Walter Stull, George Reehm.

Rastus Johnson, a happy-go-lucky coon, after eating a large meal, lies down on the dock to take a nap. While he is slumbering three roughs happen along and see him, and knowing a sea captain who is in need of men to fill out his crew, they seize Rastus and shanghai him. He is placed aboard the ship and the voyage started. The vessel is wrecked off the African coast, and poor Rastus is the only survivor. While wandering along the beach he is seen by the Zulus, who

immediately give chase. Rastus runs through the jungle, but is compelled to give up. They capture him and take him before their king, who orders him to be cooked. One of the women of the tribe, who happens to be present when Rastus is brought in, knowing the king's daughter is ambitious to be married to some man outside of her own tribe, runs off to tell her of the captive. Rastus is led to the royal kitchen, where the cook pot is prepared. They are just about to thrust him in when the daughter pleads with her father for Rastus' life. This he grants on one condition, that Rastus must marry the daughter. This he tells to Rastus, and Rastus after a good look at the daughter, decides to take to the cook pot. This enrages the king so that he orders Rastus to be seized and given a sound beating. They seize him and throw him on the ground and commence. They beat him so hard that he wakes up to find a policeman tapping him with his club. The blue coat orders Rastus to move on his way which he does, little the worse for his terrible dream. [MPW]

Rastus Among the Zulus is a remake of the 1910 film *Rastus in Zululand*, also a Lubin and also directed by Arthur D. Hotaling. The big difference is that in the 1910 all the natives are played by white actors in blackface, but the 1913 film features Black actors in those roles. Lubin's all-colored unit was a pet project of Hotaling's and his recruiting of Walter Stull among others to be acting coaches for the players in the company seemed to be a great success. Many of the novice Black actors proved to be quite capable, and the scene where Rastus must choose between the king's daughter or the boiling pot is hilarious.

"On the same reel with the foregoing [*The Widow's Wiles*] is this slight but lively and very acceptable picture an extravagant fares. The scenes are like those in other recent Zulu offerings by the same company and producer, and it has much the same kind of action. It was produced by Arthur Hotaling from his own script." -- *Moving Picture World*

The Widow's Wiles

Released July 28, 1913. Lubin Manufacturing Co.-General Film Company release. Split reel (678 ft.), on the same reel with *Rastus Among the Zulus* (452 ft.).

Directed by Arthur D. Hotaling, written by Epes W. Sargent.

With Mae Hotely (*Mrs. Bruce, the widow*), Robert Burns (*John Scott*), Walter Stull (*Henry Carlton*), George Reehm (*Jack Scott*), Ben Walker (*successful suitor*), Frances Ne Moyer (*Mamie Carlton*).

John Scott and Henry Carlton are old cronies, and it is their delight that young Jack Scott and Mamie Carlton are to be married some day. The Widow Bruce comes to town and both Scott and Carlton become infatuated. In their rivalry they forbid Jack and Mamie to marry. The widow discovers the trouble and has Jack make love to her. Carlton and Scott see and each withdraws his objection to the marriage of Mamie and Jack, thinking by this means to get rid of their younger rival. But Mamie has seen Jack's love making, too, and the widow has to square Jack there. This she does and when Scott and Carlton find out. they race for the widow's house, only to find that she has just become engaged to a younger man. [MPW]

"Robert Bums and Walter Stull, in this picture, play two old cronies. The former has a son (George Reehm), the latter has a daughter (Frances Ne Moyer) and the young people are engaged. The widow (Mae Hotely) comes in a stylish plush dress and two old men lose their heads over her; fall out, and try to break up the love story of the young people. It is not wholly new, but some new things are rung in, and it makes a very fair offering, because the players seem to be in good spirit for fun making and the situation gave them a good chance. The audience seemed to like it very much." -- *Moving Picture World*

Roses For Rosie

Released August 5, 1913. Lubin Manufacturing Co.-General Film Company release. Split reel (422 ft.), on the same reel with *Getting Married* (600 ft.).

With Walter Stull (*Jack Hall*), George Reehm (*Dick Hendricks*), Frances Ne Moyer (*Rosie Forrest*), Robert Burns (*florist*).

Dick Hendricks and Jack Hall are militant rivals for the favors of Rosie Forrest. One day Dick sends the young lady a box of roses, and Jack, being present, gets awfully peeved. There is a lover's quarrel and Jack leaves in a huff. As he passes the store his tailor gives him a box containing a pair of trousers which had been left to be pressed. Still on his way home Jack passes a florist, and entering, buys a box of roses for Rosie, as a peace offering. He attaches a note to the flowers requesting that she wear them in place of Dick's. In his excitement he puts the card on the box containing the pants and carries home the box of roses. Arriving at his lodging he discovers his mistake and rushes frantically back to the florist, but the boy has just started on the errand to deliver. Jack chases the boy, but a policeman stops him, wanting to know why he is running. Then he proceeds, and on arriving at Rosie's house, lacks the courage to pull the bell. Rosie comes around the corner with a handsome bunch of roses. Jack is dumbfounded, and goes to see what has become of his pants. Meantime the box has been delivered to an old maid, who goes to the store to get explanation. By the time Jack gets there the store is wrecked, so is the florist, so is the boy, so are the trousers, and Jack has a narrow escape. [MPW]

"Jack has a rival for the hand of Rosie. He stops to get a pair of trousers at the presser's and then buys a box of roses and orders them sent to Rosie. He leaves the trousers at the florist's and walks off with a box of flowers addressed to an old maid's sewing circle. At home he discovers his mistake, but thinks the trousers have been sent to Rosie. He makes frantic efforts to have the delivery stopped and has a pleasant shock to find Rosie with the flowers. What the old maid did to the florist was plenty. A snappy little comedy." -- *Moving Picture World*

Her Wooden Leg

Released August 25, 1913. Lubin Manufacturing Co.-General Film Company release. Split reel (380 ft.), on the same reel with *On the Dumbwaiter* (663 ft.).

Directed by Arthur D. Hotaling, written by Epes W. Sargent.

With Mae Hotely (*Alice, a dashing widow*), Mr. Rechard (*one legged man*), Walter Stull (*Mr. Smith*), Robert Burns (*Mr. Jackson*), George Reehm (*constable*), Frances Ne Moyer, Marguerite Ne Moyer.

Alice, a dashing widow, takes up a collection for a wooden leg. She doesn't look as though she needed one, but most of the men fall for her plea and contribute. Seeing her continue the collection for some time and getting together and comparing notes, they decide that she is a swindler. They seek the constable to have her arrested, but as Alice has passed the constable many times and given him very sweet smiles in her good-humored way the constable argues the question with them. At length he is persuaded that it is his duty to carry out the law. The constable and the angry crowd come upon the widow just as she is coming from the express office. She has a large box in her arms and they are all anxious to know what it contains. Upon the officer's demand for an explanation of affairs, she leads the crowd to the poorer quarter of the town to a dilapidated dwelling and there sitting on the steps is a poor man with only one leg. This is the man that she was taking up the collection for. [MPW]

"The little comedy depicts the frailty of mere man in such a way as to create and hold a five-minute smile. Mae Hotely gives a capital performance." -- *New York Dramatic Mirror*

"In this picture a very slight plot gives the Lubin people of Producer Arthur Hotaling's Company a good chance to be entertaining in their delineation of farcical characters. Mae Hotely's asking on the street for 'help in getting a wooden leg' amuses, because it has so plainly nothing to stand on. There is a good deal of fun in the offering that is not at all boisterous. There is, by the way, a corking chance for a good story of sentiment in the picture's idea." -- *Moving Picture World*

An Exclusive Pattern

Released September 12, 1913. Lubin Manufacturing Co.-General Film Company release. Split reel (621 ft.), on the same reel with *Panama Hat Industry* (423 ft.).

With Robert Burns (*Tom White*), Mae Hotely (*Nan White*), George Reehm (*haberdasher*), Raymond McKee (*man on street*), Walter Stull (*Dusty Dawkins, a tramp*), Frances Ne Moyer (*woman with vest*).

A haberdasher sells to a young man a vest that he declares to be an absolutely exclusive pattern. The design is unique and startling, and Tom wears it home to luncheon with much pride. He immediately spills soup on it, but Nan, his wife, promises to clean it. After the wife has cleaned it she hangs it in the backyard to dry. It is stolen by a tramp. She telephones Tom of the theft, and notifies the police, giving a description of the vest. Nan goes on a shopping expedition, and the first man she sees on the street is wearing the stolen vest, or at least she thinks it is the stolen vest. She endeavors to recover it and the man, deeming her a lunatic, flees in horror. Meanwhile Tom has seen the vest adorning the figure of a suffragette, a prize fighter, and the original tramp, and his attempts to recover it have been highly disastrous. The police now busy themselves and the tangle comes to a head at the station house, where the simultaneous appearance of half a dozen persons wearing the vest, tends to disprove the haberdasher's assertion, that the one sold to Tom was without a duplicate. Freed from the clutches of the law, Tom and the other battered and furious vest owners, proceed to wreak vengeance on the haberdasher. They treat him to a bath under the fire hydrant. [MPW]

Part of the humor in the reel is that the vest is rather ugly; white cloth with exaggerated black stitching, it would be hard to miss seeing it being worn. The fact that so many seemed to like the style enough to spend hard-earned cash on the vest, and that the clothier thought he could get away with selling multiple copies of his "one of a kind" garment add to the insanity. The reviewer for the *Moving Picture World* took exception to an early example of "product placement." The practice is almost as old as the movies themselves. Need a store front? Be sure to get the establishment's name in the shot. Want a free meal for the crew? Be sure the restaurant is featured in the action.

"A comedy which will mildly amuse. A vest is sold by a haberdasher, who informs the buyer that it is an exclusive pattern. When the vest is stolen from a clothesline by a tramp and a search is begun it is developed that there are duplicates of the garment in the neighborhood. It was hardly necessary for the director to feature in his exterior view and his interior as well a particular brand of collars." -- *Moving Picture World*

Her Present

Released September 20, 1913. Lubin Manufacturing Co.-General Film Company release. Split reel (508 ft.), on the same reel with *His Reward* (495 ft.).

With Mae Hotely (*Laura*), Robert Burns (*Ben*), Wilmer Cahill (*Tom*), Walter Stull (*Jack*), Raymond McKee (*Sam*).

Laura Bell, a winsome young miss, while spending her vacation at a fashionable summer resort, is besieged with suitors. She announces that she will marry the one who gives her the

most acceptable present within a week. Jack gives her candy, by the ton, Tom sends her flowers every hour in the day, but Sam goes in to the fight more extravagantly and buys jewelry. Ben, the last, but not the least (in Laura's mind), can think of nothing that will put him in the race. Time wanes and the last day has arrived; they all, with the exception of Ben, go bathing. While the boys and Laura are enjoying themselves in the ocean. Ben is walking the beach. At a lucky moment, for Ben, while the boys are talking to some other girls, Laura meets with an accident. Ben, who has been watching her, sees the predicament she is in, rushes away and soon returns with a paper of safety pins, which proves by far to be the most acceptable offering. [MPW]

"The girl agrees to marry the one of her four admirers who brings her the best present. The last one succeeds by bringing her a safety pin when she is taking a dip in the ocean. Very fair light comedy." -- *Moving Picture World*

His Reward

Released September 20, 1913. Lubin Manufacturing Co.-General Film Company release. Split reel (495 ft.), on the same reel with *Her Present* (508 ft.).

Filmed in Atlantic City, New Jersey.

With Julia Calhoun (*Auntie*), Frances Ne Moyer (*Nina, Jim's sweetheart*), Walter Stull (*Jim*), Robert Burns, Raymond McKee.

Auntie, who is exceedingly homely, is always fond of butting in on the young girls' fellows and trying to steal them away. One day at the seashore, while they are all enjoying themselves, auntie appears in a bathing suit. She is compelled to go in bathing alone, because no one wants to go in with her. While she is in the water she pretends to drown, and Jim, who is sitting with the crowd on the beach, thinking she is really in the precarious situation, starts in the water to rescue her. He carries her out of the water, and, while the crowd is cheering, auntie declares that she will marry her preserver, but Jim swears that she won't. He climbs on top of the boardwalk, and throws shells at her to drive her away and at last succeeds. She decides to lay for another victim, and when she sees Paul walking along the beach she drowns for his benefit. Paul is about to make a heroic rescue, when Jim arrives on

the scene and dissuades him. About this time Jack happens along and seeing auntie in the water, is about to rush in and save her, when he is stopped by Jim, Paul and the crowd, and told that this is her scheme for getting a man and that she will want to marry him. He, like the rest, is willing to let her drown. While they are all watching her antics in the water, she decides that no one is coming to rescue her, so she calmly stands up in the water which is only waist deep and walks ashore. The crowd enjoys a good laugh at auntie's expense. [MPW]

"This, on same reel with above, is a sprightly little comedy. Auntie has a habit of pretending to drown. The hero saves her once, but as she wants to marry him as a reward, he refuses to go after her a second time. A pleasing idea in this." -- *Moving Picture World*

This Isn't John

Released September 22, 1913. Lubin Manufacturing Co.-General Film Company release. Split reel (638 ft.), on the same reel with *Poker Paid* (400 ft.).

Directed by Arthur D. Hotaling, written by Epes W. Sargent.

With Robert Burns (*John Hickey, a henpecked husband*), Julia Calhoun (*Mary, his wife*), Frances Ne Moyer (*Maud, his daughter*), Marguerite Ne Moyer (*Nell, his daughter*), Raymond McKee (*Harry, Maud's sweetheart*).

The boys are going camping and they send John Hickey a letter asking him to accompany them. He wants to go, but his wife objects. He has to fake a plan, which he does. He arranges a fake drowning. He gets a fisherman friend to wet his clothes in the river, and return them to his wife and daughters with the story that they were found on the bank. While the fisherman is sousing the garments in the water, and John is standing by watching the proceeding, his youngest daughter and her sweetheart, Harry, happen to pass on the pier above and see them. They hurry home to inform the folks and arrive just after the fisherman has delivered the clothes and told the falsehood. They explain the whole affair as they saw it, and upon inspection they find the tell-tale letter still in the pocket. They accept Harry's idea that if John wishes to be a dead one, it will be a good plan to let him be dead. John returns from the trip dead broke, poker cleaned him out. His wife and daughter refuse to recognize him, even his office employees, who have been put wise, ignore him. He tries to send a telegram, but the operator refuses to accept it collect. He goes home to make one last appeal and is taken back on the condition that he eat the letter that led him into the trouble. He does so, but Maud pleads, and he gets a concession in the shape of permission to eat it between two slices of bread. [MPW]

"This farce gives laughable nonsense which is in part really laughter making and in part is not. The ending is especially good — shows a man having to eat his note to his wife, who knows that he has lied. He puts it in a sandwich. There was some laughter, which at no time became general." -- *Moving Picture World*

The Actress and Her Jewels

Released September 30, 1913. Lubin Manufacturing Co.-General Film Company release. Split reel (520 ft.), on the same reel with *The Constable's Daughter* (480 ft.).

With Mae Hotely (*Dottie Dare*), Robert Burns (*Bill, the burglar*), George Reehm (*Plantem, the press agent*), Walter Stull (*Dick, the fake burglar*).

Dottie Dare, an actress who has not had the press attention that she thinks she should have, hires a personal press agent. He, very desirous of getting employer all the notice that is possible, arranges to have her diamonds stolen. While he is planning with a fake crook to steal the diamonds, a real thief overhears the plan and beats it to the hotel first. Dottie, never having the acquaintance of a burglar and not being informed that this particular crook was to look like, meets him when he enters the hotel room and blows him to champagne, gives him an autographed photograph, and on the whole they spend a very pleasant little time. He decides that it is about time to go with all the Jewels and he departs. Shortly after the real crook has gone, the press agent and his burglar arrive, and much to their surprise Dottie informs them that the burglar has been there and has taken her Jewels. The two of them are nearly knocked off their feet and think that the best thing that they can do is to make their escape. They do so down the fire escape and when they arrive at the bottom the fellow that the press agent has hired with the promise of a handsome reward, seeing the reward had disappeared, gives the agent a thrashing for his trouble. [MPW]

"Mae Hotely is interesting as the actress who in search of publicity connives at the theft of her jewels, only to learn later that the bogus thief has been anticipated by the real article. It is good drama; it carries a few laughs, too." -- *Moving Picture World*

The Constable's Daughter

Released September 30, 1913. Lubin Manufacturing Co.-General Film Company release. Split reel (480 ft.), on the same reel with *The Actress and Her Jewels* (520 ft.).

With Arthur Hotaling (*Ray Jordon*), Walter Stull (*Jack Clifford*), Robert Burns (*Constable Hackard*), Frances Ne Moyer (*Maud Hackard*), George Reehm (*Justice of the Peace*).

Ray Jordon, having just purchased a new automobile, invites his friend Jack Clifford, to go with him while he tries the new machine out. While they are speeding over a country road, they attract the attention of Constable Hackard, who instructs his daughter to get his six shooter and his club, so he can catch the speeders. He loses no time in jumping in front of the machine with drawn revolver. Naturally Ray and Jack, with a six shooter staring them in the face, come to a stop. An argument is started as to the speed the car was traveling, when the constable's daughter Maud puts in an appearance. It is a case of love at first sight on Jack's part: he immediately withdraws from the argument and starts in talking to Maud. Ray and the constable can come to no agreement, and Ray is ordered to drive to the Justice of the Peace; the constable takes a seat along side of Ray while Jack takes a seat in the rear of the machine and waves a goodbye to Maud. On their arrival at the Justice of the Peace, Ray is still putting up an argument but Jack cheerfully pays the fine, thinking the price is well worth meeting the pretty daughter. Jack becomes a persistent suitor and is constantly being chased away from Constable Hackard's house. He frames up a scheme with his friend Ray to go out on the road and speed, so the constable will arrest him. When he gets the constable in the car, he is to drive him at break neck speed, in a round-about way to the Justice of the Peace. While Ray is driving the constable around Jack has made a short cut to the Justice and by the time Ray and the constable arrive, Jack and Maud have been married. After the constable sees the humor of the affair he blesses them both but makes Ray pay a fine. [MPW]

"The policeman owes the wealthy lover several grudges, but the latter gets even in a delightful way" -- *The Bioscope*

The Drummer's Narrow Escape

Released October 10, 1913. Lubin Manufacturing Co.-General Film Company release. Split reel (490 ft.), on the same reel with *Going Home To Mother* (524 ft.).

With Walter Stull (*Walter Wilson*), Robert Burns (*Abner Peabody*), Mae Hotely (*Priscilla Peabody*), Frances Ne Moyer (*Bess Peabody*).

Walter Wilson, a traveling man, arrives in the village of Mt. Pleasant. While he is talking to the proprietor of the hotel, he sees the charming daughter of Abner Peabody passing on her way to the store. He is attracted and asks the proprietor to introduce him. This is done and Bess, the daughter, merrily trips on her way. Walter walks over to the store and assists Bess with her basket of groceries to the crossroads. Here she tells him he must leave her, which he does after arranging another meeting. Bess returns to the house and tells her older sister, Priscilla, of the fine young man she has met. Priscilla, anxious to meet most any young man as she is getting to the shelving age decides to pass the hotel and see if she cannot attract Walt's attention. Walt is seated in front of the hotel when Priscilla arrives on the scene. She does not make a hit and goes off disgruntled. The following day Walt passes the Peabody residence, bumps into Priscilla and she throws a fake faint. The father sees her in Walt's arms and thinks he is a suitor. That afternoon when he receives a note from Walt asking permission to call and be a suitor for his daughter's hand he, thinking it means Priscilla, willingly consents. Walt calls and the old man meets him, and being anxious to get Priscilla off his hands he leaves Walt while he goes to tell her. Walt waits in anticipation and when a female hand is placed in his he is thrilled, but on turning around and seeing who it is he beats it, with Priscilla and her father in pursuit. Bess sees the chase from the porch and follows. They catch Walt at the edge of the woods. Explanations are made and when the old man looks Priscilla over he with a suggestive wink declares that he cannot blame Walt, and a good laugh is enjoyed by all at Priscilla's expense. [MPW]

"A big topliner in the way of a photoplay will head today's list in *The Drummer's Narrow Escape*, and it is a peach, that will especially appeal to every 'knight of the grip.'" -- *The Wilmington Morning Star* (Wilmington, North Carolina)

Going Home to Mother

Released October 10, 1913. Lubin Manufacturing Co.-General Film Company release. Split reel (524 ft.), on the same reel with *The Drummer's Narrow Escape* (490 ft.).

With Walter Stull (*Will Black, the husband*), Frances Ne Moyer (*Nell, his wife*), Marguerite Ne Moyer (*the maid*).

Will Black gets up late and his hurried dressing leaves him in a bad temper. The morning mail brings only a bunch of Nell's bills, and he goes up in the air. Nell declares that she will go home to her dear mother and Will dares her to. He gives her the money for railroad fare and leaves. Down at the office he cannot work, and sadly he returns to the deserted home. He has not the heart to enter, but sits on the steps in deep dejection. Meantime, Nell has fallen for the lure of the shop windows and by the time she reaches the station she has spent every cent, so she goes home and she and Will forgive each other. [MPW]

Epes W. Sargent, in his column *The Photoplaywright* featured in *Moving Picture World* was often critical of the way some studios or distributors did business. He was particularly critical of the way *Going Home to Mother* was marketed:

More care should be taken with the announcements of the reels. There is no pull in the paragraphs. A two-part Essanay, *Tony, the Fiddler*, is announced: Here is another example of fine stage direction and acting, as well as a story of strength and worth to be credited to the Essanay producers. Natural expressive and unconscious acting, by all the principals and support was pleasingly conspicuous. Lubin's *Going Home to Mother* is one of those comedies that always raise a smile. And it's a perfectly possible event, therefore its realism adds greatly to the humor. A glance at the synopsis should have given something more like this: She started to go home to mother — but she passed a dry good's store window. She did not get very far past it and instead of going home to mother, she went back to Hubby because her money was all gone — but she had a lot to show for it. Instead of studying the synopses, the announcements have been faked, and like all fake stuff, it is unconvincing and uninteresting.

"Good comedy, don't miss it." –*The Evening Herald (Ottawa, Kansas)*

Father's Choice

Released October 20, 1913. Lubin Manufacturing Co. - General Film Company release. Split reel (508 ft.), on the same reel with *All on Account of Daisy* (517 ft.).

Directed by Arthur D. Hotaling, written by Harry Hoyt.
With Frances Ne Moyer (*Ruth Harris*), Marguerite Ne Moyer (*Mabel Dean*), Ray McKee (*Bob Watt*), Walter Stull (*Pa Watt*), George Reehm (*Jack*).

Bob Watt's father wants him to marry Mabel Dean, but Bob can't see her, because he is strong for Ruth Harris. Pa Watt tries to break up the combination by offering Ruth a diamond ring in exchange for the gold seal ring Bob has given as a love token. Bob hiding behind a tree sees the negotiation and motions Ruth to take the diamond, which she does. A week later Pa Watt is threatened with a lawsuit by Ruth, for breach of promise. The ring being the prime exhibit, then he switches and wants Bob to marry Ruth. The boy, however, also switches and pretends a liking for Mabel. It takes a $25,000 check for Ruth to settle the tangle. Father thinks he has done a pretty good day's work, as the money is still in the family. Ruth and Bob are satisfied and Mabel has to be content with her second best boy. [MPW]

"A farce with a laughable idea. It is broad and somewhat rough in parts. That scene in which the father blows smoke in the face of his son's sweetheart, whom he dislikes, is inelegant. Harry Hoyt wrote the script which Arthur Hotaling produced it[sic]." -- *Moving Picture World*

All on Account of Daisy

Released October 20, 1913. Lubin Manufacturing Co. - General Film Company release. Split reel (517 ft.), on the same reel with *Father's Choice* (508 ft.).

Directed by Arthur D. Hotaling, written by Violet Adams.

With Walter Stull (*Bill Thomas*), Frances Ne Moyer (*Mrs. Bill Thomas*), Julia Calhoun (*Mrs. Thomas's mother*), Marguerite Ne Moyer (*Mrs. Tom Jones*), George Reehm (*Tom Jones*), Raymond McKee.

Bill Thomas, a young happily married man, meets Tom Jones on the street one day and buys a ticket for a chance on a dog. The drawing takes place. Bill wins the dog and Tom informs him by letter. Bill's wife, who is a little jealous, is present when the letter arrives and as Bill hurriedly goes out without explaining to her, she becomes suspicious. As Bill has left the letter in his house coat, which she finds after his departure laying on the floor, she notices the hanger is broken and starts to fix it, when she discovers the letter in the pocket. She reads the letter and at once makes up her mind that Bill is false to her. She follows him and sees him talking to Mrs. Tom Jones, while Tom is inside of the house getting the dog for Bill to take home. Enraged she, rushes home and smashes things up. Bill in the meantime has gotten the dog and is trying to feed it everything that he can buy on the way home. The house is a wreck and Mrs. Bill rushes off to her mother's, leaving a note on the table. Bill arrives at the house and thinking to surprise his wife enters quietly, but is astonished at the condition of things. He finds the note on the table and leaving the dog rushes off to find his wife.

Arriving at the mother's Bill is set upon by the wife and mother, and he has to retreat to save himself further punishment. They follow him and when they all arrive at Bill's house the affair is satisfactorily explained and the little dog, Daisy, is the favorite of all. [MPW]

"Parts of this offering on the same reel with the other farce tickled the audience; for, though old, it is very well handled. But it is too long." -- *Moving Picture World*

Paying the Bill

Released October 27, 1913. Lubin Manufacturing Co. - General Film Company release. Split reel (551 ft.), on the same reel with *She Should Worry* (422 ft.).

With Walter Stull (*Joe Wood/Jimmy*), Robert Burns (*Jno. Mark/Mack*), George Reehm (*the waiter*).

Jimmy owes Mack a considerable sum and is very much upset when he receives a letter telling him that the debt must be met at once. He starts off to the city to have have it out with Mack, who is unknown to him personally. Just as Jimmy is leaving the station, he nearly gets run over by a passing car, and only escapes through the assistance of a stranger, who is no other than Mack. The two men become great pals and after sundry drinks go off to a baseball match. They increase the interest of the game by betting, which results in Jimmy clearing out his creditor. A very funny scene takes place when the men become aware of each other's identity, and Jimmy, who is now very flush, settles with Mack out of his winnings. [KW]

This reel is mentioned in a secondary ad of the *Moving Picture World* and not the regular ad that Lubin placed in the front of the magazine each week. In that ad another title is listed as the October 27 release, and no synopsis was published of either title in *Moving Picture World* or any American trade publication.

"If you like a good laugh, see this comedy." -- *The Fort Wayne Journal-Gazette* (Fort Wayne, Indiana)

She Should Worry

Released October 27, 1913. Lubin Manufacturing Co - General Film Company release. Split reel (422 ft.), on the same reel with *Paying the Bill* (551 ft.).

With Robert Burns (*Martin Slink*), Marguerite Ne Moyer (*Nell Shipman*), George Reehm (*Joe Shipman*), Raymond McKee (*Jack Shipman*).

Ethel resented the attentions of a dude that haunted the beach. He thought she gave him the glad eye, but he was wrong, for it was a smacked face. But he was not to be thus choked off. The " boys " lay a plan. Ethel sits with her legs buried in the sand, with a pair of stuffed out stockings laid against her knees. The dude approaches and starts to pinch the calves. Suddenly she jumps away, leaving him horror stricken with a " leg "in his hand. After which the boys fling the intruder into the sea. [KW]

The character names were provided by domestic (American), sources but the synopsis comes from a British trade paper. It was not uncommon for characters' names to be changed when shown in another country.

"A fair comedy of the seashore, with some good bathing costumes introduced. A flirt goes after every girl with nice-looking lower extremities, and he is cured of this by 'the bunch.' False legs and "the water cure" play a big part in the education of the 'pest.'" –*Motion Picture News*

George Reehm, Walter Stull and some of the Lubin ladies picnicking.

Will Louis, George Reehm, Walter Stull, Bobby Burns and a cast of one thousand in Philadelphia.

The Lubin Company in Washington, DC.

Left to right: Will Louis, Spottiswood Aiken, Elsie Green, George Reehm, Mae Hotely, Walter Stull, Gladys Cameron, Bernhardt Niemeyer, Arthur D. Hotaling.

Jacksonville, November 1912.

Top row: Francis Ne Moyer, Harry Marks, Marguerite Ne Moyer, Gus Anderson, Catherine Anderson. Bottom row: Ray McKee, Walter Stull, Ben Hopkins.

Atlantic City, 1912.

Bobby Burns and Walter Stull enjoying the day with a couple young ladies.

KOMIC and ROYAL

Sometime in the Autumn of 1913 the "Lubin Twins" (with Bobby Burns in tow) packed up their bags, bid farewell to Lubin and headed for the big city. Or at least nearby the big city, going to the Reliance Film Corporation studios in Yonkers, New York. There's no real evidence on why the three made the move, but conjecture would indicate that they sought a situation where they would be the lead comedians and have some control over their films. At Lubin, while the Gay Time comedies made good use of an ensemble of comedians, Mae Hotely was decidedly the star. George Reehm at times found his way behind the camera working as an assistant to director Arthur Hotaling, but for the most part the three seemed to have little say in the films they were making at Lubin. Thus the move.

As with many of the larger film companies at the time, the Reliance Film Corporation focused its attentions on their feature film productions, which were under the supervision of D.W. Griffith. However, needing to provide a full range of films to their distributor, the Mutual Film Corporation, Reliance had smaller subsidiaries making their short subjects. These brands were presented to the public as stand-alone entities, and as was the case with both the Komic and Royal brands at Reliance, the actual relationship between the parent company and the smaller groups making the shorts was never made clear. It was to the former brand, Komic, that Stull, Reehm and Burns reported for work. It should be noted that by the time of Burns & Stull's arrival at Reliance that the company had merged with Majestic, so the films are occasionally referred to as Majestic products.

The trio of comedians got what they wanted at Komic; not only did they star in the films but they also wrote and directed them. The system for directing was simple: whoever was out of the shot took hold of the megaphone. It's unclear who was in charge when all of them were in the same scene, but then with three confirmed hams before the lens it probably didn't matter anyhow.

Another unit at Komic featured Fay Tincher and a young Max Davidson. Both series seemed to be very successful and contemporary reviews showed then to be popular and well made (attested when viewing the few extant Komic titles). However, at the end of April 1914 the Komic brand was discontinued by Reliance, with Stull, Reehm and Burns moving over to the company's Royal brand. Exhibitor objections forced Reliance to quickly reverse their decision and bring back the Komic comedies, but the trio remained at Royal until the middle of Summer 1914 when they left Reliance.

With the Komic and Royal comedies, the trio assembled a stock company of players that would work as support to their efforts, and occasionally take some of the lead roles. Louise Ducey, Maxine Daintry and Maxine Brown were the key female players while Walter Kendig, James Harris and Jack Peters provided the main male support. Daintry had made a few films for Thanhouser and would later make a few for Éclair America but the bulk of her work was in these Stull, Burns and Reehm comedies. Much the same could be said of the other supporting players; they had done little film work before these films and most all made just a few films afterwards. The most notable exception to this is Walter Kendig.

Having appeared uncredited in some of the Lubin comedies that the boys had made, Kendig moved over to work with them under the Reliance banner. Among the scant evidence that exists about these films is that Kendig became a very key player, often taking the third male lead instead of George Reehm. So talented was Kendig that the Mittenthal Brothers, who also shot in Yonkers, pulled him away and gave him the co-lead in a series of comedies begun in late 1914 featuring James Aubrey, entitled "Heinie and Louie." But Aubrey wasn't inclined to share the screen the way Burns and Stull did, and Kendig's Louie often ended up playing second fiddle to a comedian whose ego knew no end.

Despite this, the series would last almost three years, but tragically Walter Kendig did not. On October 13, 1915, Kendig died when the motorcycle upon which he was a passenger struck a trolley car. Only the briefest reports of the accident were published in the trades and a faux Louie was quickly cast to replace him; the Mittenthal Brothers never really making it clear to the public that there was a replacement Louie (played by Elmer E. Redmond). The series became an out-and-out star vehicle for Aubrey, with the Louie character often making only a token appearance in each film.

Louis Burstein, one of the executives at Reliance, took a liking to Komic's new comedians, and struck up a friendship with Bobby Burns and Walter Stull in particular. Burstein first started in the movie business in 1909 when as an attorney he successfully represented the New York Motion Picture Company in a suit brought by the Motion Picture Patents Company. By 1914 he had worked for a number of production entities, including Equitable/Reliance and even made an aborted attempt earlier in 1914 at setting up his own company (Hartigan Comedies). Sensing that the boys were still looking for a way to more freely make their own comedies, and again looking for a way to set himself up as an independent producer, Burstein convinced Burns & Stull to jettison Reliance and form a working partnership with him, with the intent to develop their own brand and their own company.

Why at this point the trio again became a duo, but with Burns instead of Reehm, is a mystery. Perhaps Reehm had taken more to the behind-the-camera work; after Reliance he would go on to direct at Biograph. This would also explain the added prominence that Kendig had achieved. Stull and Reehm had seemed to be the best of friends and it certainly is no coincidence that Reehm would later find work at Vim (although with the Myers-Theby unit). For whatever reason, Burns & Stull bid adieu to both Reehm and Yonkers, bound for parts unknown and opportunities equally mysterious.

Burns & Stull, along with Louis Burstein, left Reliance in the Summer of 1914, and the last Royal comedy that they are known to have appeared in was released July 4. A couple of the films they made at Reliance would strangely appear via Kalem the next year. The second, *He Was a Traveling Man*, is truly odd in that none of the cast is credited by their real names, Walter Stull being called "George H. Wheeler" and Bobby Burns carrying the name "Gerald Meyton". Perhaps there was some contractual issue, but it brings home the point that with mostly only written, and very little photographic, evidence it is impossible to fully know who actually made what films and where. As with the Lubin films, it is highly likely that Burns and/or Stull appeared in other Komic or Royal comedies but we simply cannot verify the appearances.

A side note to Burns & Stull's tenure at Reliance was the presence of another actor named Robert Burns, leading obviously to some confusion with their respective filmographies. The other Burns was primarily a dramatic actor and had worked on the stage with his brother Fred in an act appropriately called The Burns Brothers.

The Lead Nickel

Released September 4, 1913. Komic-Mutual Film Corporation release. Split reel (509 ft.), on the same reel with *Hiding the Wad From Wifey* (421 ft.).

Written and directed by Walter Stull, George Reehm and Robert Burns. Filmed in Yonkers, N.Y. at the Reliance studios.

With Walter Stull, George Reehm, Robert Burns.

The lead nickel has many adventures, passing from one to another. Finally, although the coin is a bad one it brings Cohen luck. [KW]

An odd way to start a new series for a new company. Other than the briefest announcement that most of the trade papers printed the "Reliance triplets" came in with a whimper. Not only was *The Lead Nickel* the first Stull, Reehm and Burns offering it was also the very first Komic brand release. With this film the trio did take over directing their own films, something Burns & Stull would carry on for the rest of their partnership, and also wrote their own scenarios.

"'The Lubin Twins' have become 'The Reliance Triplets,' and are now preparing a series of comedies for early Reliance releases. Reehm and Stull, of *Spooney Sam* fame with the addition of Bobby Burns, make an interesting trio and will first be seen in a comedy entitled *The Lead Nickel*." -- *Motion Picture News*

"But while the Keystone comedies have always been popular, the new brand of 'Komic' film being shown today bids fair to become just as popular. If all releases are as good as *The Lead Nickel* and *Hiding the Wad from Wifey*." -- *Palladium-Item (Richmond, Indiana)*

Hiding the Wad from Wifey

Released September 4, 1913. Komic-Mutual Film Corporation release. Split reel (421 ft.), on the same reel with *The Lead Nickel* (509 ft.), released with *Old Heads and Young Hearts* (444 ft.) in the U.K.

Written and directed by Walter Stull, George Reehm and Robert Burns. Filmed in Yonkers, N.Y. at the Reliance studios.

With Walter Stull, George Reehm, Robert Burns.

The husband comes home intoxicated, and after hanging his hat upon the gas bracket and hiding his money under the bed, goes to sleep. The wife throws the hat out of the window, and it is picked up by a tramp. When the husband dresses in the morning his hat is missing, and his wife tells him that she threw it away; he commences a search for his hat, with disastrous consequences to himself. [KW]

A slight variation on *The Hidden Payroll* filmed earlier in the year by Lubin featuring Stull, Reehm and Burns.

[no review available]

Father And The Flies

Released October 30, 1913. Royal-Mutual Film Corporation release. Split reel (530 feet), on the same reel with *The New Curate* (411 feet).

Written and directed by Walter Stull, George Reehm and Robert Burns.

With Walter Stull, Robert Burns.

A highly amusing number in which dear father is very much troubled by flies. It does not matter where he goes the flies are always attracted to his bald head. Father decides to purchase some fly paper (10 dollars' worth). He places these papers all over the house, causing great inconvenience to its inmates. Finally father employs men to do the dreadful execution. They do so, and father remembers it for many a day. [KW]

The obscurity of these films is somewhat puzzling. Even the distributor's house organ *Reel Life* only mentions these early Komic comedies in the release charts with no photographs, synopses, or advertisements to be found.

"Showing how the boys swat the flies and don't seem to be particular where, when father's bald head is a convenient place." -- *The Daily Gazette (Lawrence, Kansas)*

"This is a real funny reel, and really, it will make you laugh even if you don't want to." -- *The Central New Jersey Home News (New Brunswick, New Jersey)*

Poor John

Released November 6, 1913. Komic-Mutual Film Corporation release. Split reel (416 feet), on the same reel with *Caused by a Clock* (545 feet).

Written and directed by Walter Stull, George Reehm and Robert Burns.

With Robert Burns.

[no synopsis available]

"Good photography helps along this half-reel depicting the troubles of a henpecked husband. Some of the scenes are amusing." -- *Moving Picture World*

"The troubles of a henpecked husband are shown in some cleverly photographed episodes of happy (?) domestic life." -- *The Bioscope*

An Affair of Honor

Released November 13, 1913. Komic-Mutual Film Corporation release. Split reel (617 feet), on the same reel with *Biddy on Her Mettle* (500 feet).

Written and directed by Walter Stull, George Reehm and Robert Burns.

With Walter Stull, George Reehm.

[no synopsis available]

"A sort of roughhouse comedy, in which a thief plays a prominent part. He is discovered during a hand to hand conflict in the bedroom. Love and jealousy are at the bottom of the trouble. A fair comedy number." -- *Moving Picture World*

Making Himself a Hero

Released November 20, 1913. Komic-Mutual Film Corporation release. Split reel (464 feet), on the same reel with *Murphy's New High Hat* (518 feet).

Written and directed by Walter Stull, George Reehm and Robert Burns.

With Robert Burns (*Adam Jones*), Isabel Daintry (*Mrs. Jones*), George Welch (*Mr. Smith*).

Mr. and Mrs. Jones, on their way home from market, found a crowd in front of the village store. "Our esteemed townsman, Smith," explained the head selectman, "has become a hero. Last night, he captured a burglar, unarmed and single-handed." Mrs. Jones was tremendously impressed—and Jones shrank before her withering look. He was notoriously henpecked—not at all the stuff heroes are made of. Staggering along under the huge market basket, piled high with his wife's purchases, he listened humbly to her rating all the way home. Why, for goodness' sake, hadn't he a spark of courage, now? And why shouldn't she have a husband to be proud of, as well as Minnie Smith! Lord knows she deserved the bravest man in Jigabee Junction – and why Providence had shoved off on her Adam Jones – a mere excuse for a man – who shook in his shoes if you so much as looked at him – That night the burglars invaded the Jones's house. Adam was at last persuaded to go downstairs. The thieves heard him, and fled – dropping the plunder. Jones had a brilliant thought. He rolled himself in a dirt pile – returned to his wife in triumph with the silver – and told her he had wrenched it away in a hand to hand fight with six desperate men. The next morning found Jones six times a hero – and Mrs. Jones the most submissive wife in town. [RL]

"Good photography makes this half-reel offering quite pleasing. The husband scares away the burglars and tells his wife a great story of his bravery. Just an ordinary comedy." -- *Moving Picture World*

Murphy's New High Hat

Released November 20, 1913. Komic-Mutual Film Corporation release. Split reel (518 feet), on the same reel with *Making Himself A Hero* (464 feet).

Written and directed by Walter Stull, George Reehm and Robert Burns.

With Robert Burns, Walter Stull [both unconfirmed].

Murphy, who has just purchased a new high hat is invited to the wedding of Kelly. He goes and during the excitement he leaves his hat on a chair. A large, fat woman sits on the chair. The hat is sent out by the groom and fixed. Murphy and Nolan plan to play a joke on Casey and put his hat on the chair. They are trying to persuade the fat woman to sit on it when Casey enters, sees the joke, and substitutes Murphy's hat for his own. The fat woman is then placed on the chair. Murphy asks Casey out for a walk and Casey consents. Murphy takes a hat from the piano and finding it too small discovers that it is Casey's hat. He pulls the fat woman from the chair and finds his own flattened worse than before. Filled with rage, he rushes out, takes all the other hats and stamps upon them. The guests are about to attack him when Casey, who is the only one with a whole hat plays an Irish jig on the piano. At the sound of Erin's music, all hat is forgotten, and a dance begins. [MPW]

"On same reel with above. A rather amusing slapstick offering, in which the chief fun centers about breaking up hats by Murphy and Casey." -- *Moving Picture World*

Method In His Illness

Released November 27, 1913. Komic-Mutual Film Corporation release. Split reel (5890 feet), on the same reel with *The Man With a Razor* (390 feet).

Written and directed by Walter Stull, George Reehm and Robert Burns.

With Robert Burns, Walter Stull [both unconfirmed]

Grey, a very much henpecked husband, has an engagement with his friend Batch, and two girls. Everything seems to conspire against him to keep him from going to meet them. He feigns illness and is immediately almost smothered in blankets. His wife sends for a doctor, who knowing what his illness is, prescribes that he be kept in bed. Mrs. Grey goes to the door with the doctor, and Grey, seeing his chance, jumps from the window. As he nears the cafe he sees Batch and the girls coming out. His wife, who has discovered his flight appears on the scene. He gets an inspiration and falls to the ground, feigning insanity. His wife has started to berate his companions, but is overcome with pity for her spouse and all is forgiven. [MPW]

"A breezily presented half reel, in which a very gay married man plays sick. His wife takes him at his word and puts him to bed. Later he escapes and joins his friends, but his wife follows. Fairly amusing." -- *Moving Picture World*

The Man With the Razor

Released November 27, 1913. Komic-Mutual Film Corporation release. Split reel (390 feet), on the same reel with *Method In His Illness* (5890 feet).

Written and directed by Walter Stull, George Reehm and Robert Burns.

With Robert Burns, Walter Stull [both unconfirmed]

    A customer enters a barber shop and asks for a shave. The barber starts the process, lathers his face and begins to strop the razor. An organ grinder stops in front of the shop and starts to play a "Turkey Trot." The music is so inspiring that the barbers cannot resist it and begin dancing. This so infuriates the customer that he chases them out of the barber shop with a razor in his hand. In their mud flight the barbers upset the organ grinder, scare a number of policemen, break up a woman's suffrage meeting, drench a dude in a watering trough, deluge two milkmen in forty quarts of milk, and give a negro woman a bath in the tub with her washing, The chase is brought to an end when the customer catches up with a barber who has fallen exhausted on the ground, and insists that he finish shaving him right where he is. [MPW]

"On same reel with above. The half-shaved customer objects when the barbers begin dancing about the shop to hand organ music. The chase was very well done and the close of the film is laughable. An entertaining split reel." -- *Moving Picture World*

How He Won

Released December 4, 1913. Komic-Mutual Film Corporation release. Split reel (451 feet), on the same reel with *The Actor Book Agent* (560feet).

Written and directed by Walter Stull, George Reehm and Robert Burns.

With Robert Burns, Walter Stull [both unconfirmed]

    Hy and Cy, two country bumpkins, are rivals for the hand of Sue Higgins, whose father does not approve of their attentions. They both try to outdo each other to win Sue's affection. While they are wasting valuable time, Tom Tracey, a fine looking city chap, arrives in the village, and, meeting Sue one day on her way from the store with a heavily laden basket, offers his services. The chance acquaintance ripens into love, but his two rivals must be gotten rid of. Tom arranges for them to fight a duel for the hand of Sue. At first they object, but when Tom insists, and drags them off to the store to purchase the pistols, there is no other way out of it. Tom loads the pistols with blank cartridges unknown to Hy and Cy. They fight the duel with no deadly results, but badly frightened, they take refuge behind a tree. Old man Higgins sees them, and mistaking them for hoboes, treats them to a load of shot and rock salt. While bemoaning their discomfort they have insult added to injury, by seeing Tom, the city fellow, become the accepted suitor of the girl they have been fighting for. [MPW]

"A half reel of the knockabout variety. The lover accidently throws a bucket of water on the girl's father and trouble naturally ensues. This is rather laughable." -- *Moving Picture World*

The Actor Book Agent

Released December 4, 1913. Komic-Mutual Film Corporation release. Split reel (5600 feet), on the same reel with *How He Won* (451 feet).

Written and directed by Walter Stull, George Reehm and Robert Burns.

With Robert Burns, Walter Stull [both unconfirmed]

William Jones, an actor, being out of work and his room rent due, becomes desperate. While walking along the street he sees a sign "Book Agent Wanted." He applies, and is engaged. His first customer is a broker named John Dobson. This is supposed to be a sure sale. Jones calls upon Dobson and is promptly ejected. He disguises himself, and appears before Dobson in various characters, and at last persuades Dobson to buy a copy of the book, entitled "Hours at Home." Upon Dobson's returning home, he finds that his wife and daughter have also purchased the same book. Enraged, he nearly has a fit and to give him air they open the window, when, to their surprise, they see the agent-actor walking up the street. They call to a lady friend who happens to pass, and ask her to overtake the man and tell him that Dobson wants him. She overtakes the actor agent, and he shrewdly tells her that he cannot return to see Dobson, as he has a train to catch, but that he is fully aware of what Mr. Dobson wants. It is the book. She says she will take it to him and gives the actor the money, and they separate. Upon her returning to the Dobson home with the book and explaining, Dobson falls into a fit and becomes so violent that he eats the books, covers and all. [MPW]

"This, on same reel, is better. It shows an actor out of employment who decides to be a book agent. He rings in many changes of disguise upon his victims and the result is very funny. A good split reel." -- *Moving Picture World*

The Wild Indian

Released December 11, 1913. Komic-Mutual Film Corporation release. Split reel (532 feet), on the same reel with *How It Worked* (440 feet).

Written and directed by Walter Stull, George Reehm and Robert Burns.

With Robert Burns, George Reehm.

Whilst two out of work actors, Messrs. Long & Short, are "footing it" along the railway track, they receive some food wrapped in a local paper in which they read that a wild Indian is at large. Long disguises himself and, on entering the local store, is taken to be the escaped man, consequently he soon has the place to himself, to be joined later by Short, who has got the people to believe him a great Indian slayer. After a good feed they depart, and have scarcely resumed their ordinary clothing when the real Indian arrives. However, he does nothing worse than to lead them to a circus at which he performs. Long and Short are engaged by the manager, who also pays the store-keeper for his losses — a profitable advert. [KW]

[no reviews available]

The Wild Indian

How It Worked

Released December 11, 1913. Komic-Mutual Film Corporation release. Split reel (4400 feet), on the same reel with *The Wild Indian* (532 feet).

Written and directed by Walter Stull, George Reehm and Robert Burns.

With Robert Burns.

He was the husband of a suffragette, and his friends told him that they were surprised at his weakness and gave him a few hints as to what to do with such a wife. He plucked up courage one night and commenced ordering his wife about, but it did not work as well as expected, and he came in for a very bad time indeed. [KW]

[no reviews available]

At the Cabaret

Released December 18, 1913. Komic-Mutual Film Corporation release. Split reel (452 feet), on the same reel with *The First Prize* (571 feet)

Written and directed by Walter Stull, George Reehm and Robert Burns.

With Robert Burns.

   Brown sends a note to Jones asking him to come at once, as he has had a bad attack of Terabac. Jones sets out to visit Brown, and they proceed to the cabaret. Mrs. Jones goes to console with Mrs. Brown, and finds out that it is a hoax. Taking the note with them, they explain matters to a police constable, who on reading the note discovers the catch, and informs the wives that the men hay gone to the cabaret. On arrival they find their husbands highly amused with several young ladies, and naturally an exciting time follows. [KW]

[no reviews available]

The First Prize

Released December 18, 1913. Komic-Mutual Film Corporation release. Split reel (571 feet), on the same reel with *At the Cabaret* (452 feet)

Written and directed by Walter Stull, George Reehm and Robert Burns.

With Robert Burns, Walter Stull.

Mrs. Newlywed is asked out to a euchre party, and is fortunate enough to get the first prize, a beautiful puppy, whose name is "Baby." Knowing her husband's dislike for dogs, she gets a friend to care for it. After keeping the dog a little while the friend sends a note to say "come and get your baby." Hubby sees the note and is mad. He gets a policeman and goes in search of his wife, who arrives home in time to deposit " baby " in her husband's wearing apparel. When Hubby returns he is raving to see the baby and is shown the dog. Seeing that he is cornered and has no grounds for his rage, the overcomes his dislike for dogs and makes up for lost time with his wife and "Baby." [KW]

[no reviews available]

Wifey's Christmas Present

Released December 25, 1913. Komic-Mutual Film Corporation release. Split reel (662 feet), on the same reel with *The Live Wire* (460 feet)

Written and directed by Walter Stull, George Reehm and Robert Burns.

With Walter Stull.

Hubby buys a tiger-skin hearth rug for his wife, and when he gets home with it, not without adventure, he spreads it out on the floor and sits down to admire it, but goes to sleep. In his dream the tiger comes to life and, chases him out of the house and all over the countryside. Eventually it catches him, and whilst struggling Hubby awakens to find it is but his wife who has her arms around his neck. [KW]

[no reviews available]

Walt's Photograph

Released January 15, 1914. Komic-Mutual Film Corporation release. Split reel (548 feet), on the same reel with *The Vapor Bath* (441 feet). Also known as *Walt's Photo*.

Written and directed by Walter Stull, George Reehm and Robert Burns.

With Walter Stull.

The plot is laid in a boarding house: we are introduced to the boarders at their meal and their table manners are most diverting. One young man of the establishment makes love to two of the young ladies, to the servant girl and to the landlady, who lets him off paying his account. He presents each of his conquests with a signed photo, and when the servant is dusting the rooms she finds these copies, and then things get fast and furious. [KW]

"Walt has all the photographs he needs and all inscribed to the girl he loves most devotedly. He distributes them too widely. There's a laughable moment when we see him coming home to the boarding house all unconscious that there is trouble waiting for him in the hall. He gets his." -- *Moving Picture World*

The Wild Man From Borneo

Released January 22, 1914. Komic-Mutual Film Corporation release. Split reel (438 ft.), on the same reel with *What the Burglar Got*.

Written and directed by Walter Stull, George Reehm and Robert Burns.

With Walter Stull.

Reading in the daily paper that a wild man has escaped from a show, an actor dresses for the part and goes out into the streets to liven things up. This he succeeds in doing — in fact, we leave him very much regretting having started the joke [KW]

"Wild Man From Borneo in which an actor posing as a wild man escapes from a show involves himself in a series of disasters which make for irresistible merriment." -- *The Bioscope*

He Who Laughs Last

Released March 18, 1914. Komic-Mutual Film Corporation release. Split reel (687 feet), on the same reel with *Snowball Pete* (410 feet).

Written and directed by Walter Stull, George Reehm and Robert Burns.

With Walter Stull (*Tom*), Joe Schroeder (*Jim*), Jack Burns (*Reggie*), Elsie Balfour, Miss Brown, Mr. Peters (*landlord*), Mr. Harris (*policeman*), George Reehm (*burglar*), Miss Ducey (*landlady*).

Landlord Peters has two pretty girls as guests in his boarding house. Tom and Jim are rather smitten on the young women, but Reggie is the favored one in their eyes. When Reggie walks off with the young women Tom and Jim vow to be avenged. They rig up a dummy and put it in Reggie's clothes closet. When Reggie opens the door the dummy falls out upon him *and he takes to his heels. Tom and Jim then put the dummy in Reggie's bed while the landlord and his frightened guests rouse the cop at the corner. The policeman, with revolver wavering in his hand, is pushed up toward Reggie's bedroom. The dummy is taken into custody and Reggie is in danger of being arrested, when a real burglar, who has wandered into the house during the excitement, jumps from the closet door and bowls everyone over. Reggie captures the burglar and at once becomes even a greater favorite both with the landlord and the girls because of a $500 reward which has been posted for the capture of the burglar.* [RL]

"A somewhat broad comedy with a superfluity of rapid action which causes hearty laughter. The acting is well done and the direction and photography up to the standard." -- *Moving Picture World*

Snowball Pete

Released March 18, 1914. Komic-Mutual Film Corporation release. Split reel (410 feet), on the same reel with *He Who Laughs Last* (687 feet)

Written and directed by Walter Stull, George Reehm and Robert Burns.

With Robert Burns (*Snowball Pete*), Walter Stull (*the old George Reehmouch*), Joe Schroeder (*the young sport*), Mr. Peters (*policeman*), Miss Ducey (*the lady*).

Pete had spent the best years of his life — and some of the worst — panhandling in every city of the Union. When winter came and the park benches were covered with snow, Pete picked out a rose bush and found himself wrapped up in burlap by mistake one night by an enterprising florist. In his burlap wraps Pete started out the next morning making his customary round of possible "touches." One woman, from whom he had successfully begged before, advises him to eat snow if he is hungry. Pete instantly adopts the suggestion on the nearest street corner, with great success. Passersby tip him liberally. One old grouch, however regrets having given Pete anything when he returns and finds Pete counting his morning's profits. He tells a patrolman and others who have been duped and Pete is given a lively time before he is led off to jail. [RL]

"This comedy is on the same reel with *He Who Laughs Last*. While ridiculous in many ways it is a laugh producer, and will hold its own with the other comedy. Well done in every respect." -- *Moving Picture World*

Sadder But Wiser

Released April 4, 1914. Royal-Mutual Film Corporation release. One reel.

Written and directed by Robert Burns, George Reehm and Walter Stull.

With Robert Burns (*Jack Smith*), Walter H. Stull (*Will Jones, his partner*), George E. Reehms (*Tom Jenkins*), Louise Ducey (*Hazel Grey*).

Smith and Jones, two actors "at liberty'" have not eaten in several days. After making the round of the agencies in vain, Jones looks through the want columns of a daily paper. In doing so he runs across a news item which tells of an heiress in Lowerre, N.Y., who is grieving her life away for her sweetheart, who went West to hunt for gold. The two actors jump aboard a passenger train and ensconce themselves in the parlor car. They continue to argue with the conductor until they are put off. During their sparing for time, however, the train has reached Lowerre and the pair make their way to the address given in the newspaper article. They find that the "heiress" is an elderly spinster, who sews for a living. Jack's makeup convinces the spinster that he is her long-lost sweetheart and when he presents her with a gilded lump of coal and tells her that he is now a millionaire, she doubts his love no longer. The actors are busily encompassing the first meal they have had in several days, when there is a knock at the front door and in walks the spinster's real sweetheart. At almost the same time the spinster's maid discovers that the "gold nugget" is a gilded lump of coal. Smith and Jones attempt to escape when they realize that their perfidy has been discovered. Spinster Hazel, however, seizes Smith and attempts to restrain him. A sofa pillow proves more effective and Smith is about out for the count when Hazel gives him the coup de grace by sitting with a dull thud upon his midriff. Jones gives the police and Hazel's maid a battle with the bric-a-brac before he is finally taken into custody. Hazel, her true sweetheart and the maid follow the actors to the door, belaboring them soundly until the patrol wagon arrives. [RL]

Reliance announced that they were discontinuing the Komic brand after the release of *Izzy and The Bandit* on April 29. Two weeks later they announced that "due to the high demand for comedy subjects" the Komic brand would return on May 10 with a split reeler *The Scene of His Crime* and *A Race for a Bride* as the release. Komic had been the regular Wednesday release on the Mutual schedule by Reliance. The Royal brand was the regular Saturday release from Reliance and the Stull, Reehm and Burns unit were moved to that brand even before the brief exit and return of Komic.

"This plot could have been vamped into a fine little comedy had it been properly produced. Exaggeration abounds that is far from being laugh-producing or sensible; in that they are passé." –*Moving Picture World*

"A humorous comedy which, although impossible in reality, will 'get across.' Two actors impersonate a lost sweetheart, but unfortunately he turns up at the inopportune moment." –*Motion Picture News*

Hubby's Surprise

Released April 11, 1914. Royal-Mutual Film Corporation release. Split reel (497 feet), on the same reel with *It Came By Freight* (480 feet).

Written and directed by Walter Stull, George Reehm and Robert Burns.

With Robert Burns, George Reehm.

Wifey informs Hubby she has a surprise for him. He thinks it is a baby, but learns to his disgust that it's only a dog. [MPN]

"This is a laughable production that is not new, by any means, as several other photoplays have been based on the same theme." -- *Moving Picture World*

Good short-length comic, the distracted hubby coming in for "a hot time." -- *The Bioscope*

Collecting the Rent

Released April 18, 1914. Royal-Mutual Film Corporation release. One reel (982 feet).

Written and directed by Robert Burns, George Reehm and Walter Stull.

With Walter H. Stull (*Tom Drake*), Robert Burns (*Bill Rough*), Jack Peters (*Collector*), James Harris (*Janitor*), Walter Kendig (*Milo*), Maxine Brown (*Stenographer*), Isabel Daintry (*Nancy Jackson*), Louise Ducey (*Miss Prim*).

Nancy Jackson, a spinster of mature years, has a pronounced aversion to paying her rent. Tom Drake, real estate agent for the flat in which she lives, tries one collector after another in an effort to get her to pay up but without success. A collector, experienced in handling such hard cases, returns to the office badly battered up and without the money he has been sent out to get. Drake next sends out his stenographer, but she also fails in her mission. Determined to get the money at all hazards, Drake next goes out to visit Nancy himself. He meets with an experience similar to those of his employees. Driven to desperation and determined now to get the money, Drake employs a prize-fighter. The latter returns in short order with a black eye and badly bruised countenance. Finally, there walks into Drake's office a nice, sweet little chap with a cerise necktie, a handkerchief up his sleeve and a wristwatch. Daintily he trips across the floor and applies for a position as collector, "if you please, sir." Drake, with his head in his hands, engages him on the spot without looking up. The young man is sent around and smilingly returns in a few moments with the money. Just how Milo collected the money from the sullen old spinster makes a good comedy in itself. [RL]

"A very laughable rough comedy which introduces several diversified characters attempting to collect rent money from a garrulous and parsimonious old maid. After the boss, the stenographer and prizefighter fail it is amusing to see dear little Milo get the money and a job for life." -- *Moving Picture World*

The Tale of a Coat

Released April 25, 1914. Royal-Mutual Film Corporation release. Split reel, on the same reel with *Two Hungry Tramps* (418 feet). Listed as *The Tale of a Cat* in some trade papers.

Written and directed by Robert Burns, Walter Stull and George Reehm.

With Isabel Daintry, Walter Stull, Robert Burns.

[no synopsis available]

"A poor comedy in which two automobilists are mistaken for bears because of their fur coats." -- *Motion Picture News*

Two Hungry Tramps

Released April 25, 1914. Royal-Mutual Film Corporation release. Split reel (418 feet) on the same reel with *The Tail of a Coat*. Listed as *The Hungry Tramps* in some trade papers.

Written and directed by Robert Burns, Walter Stull and George Reehm.

With Walter Stull, Robert Burns [unconfirmed].

[no synopsis available]

"The tramps are clever acrobats, but at times are a little disgusting. Their antics are humorous and the way they try to get a meal is as novel as it is funny." -- *Motion Picture News*

"The Royal 'Two Hungry Tramps' proved so absurdly silly that it was taken off the program after the first run." -- Santa Barbara News and the Independent (Santa Barbara, California)

A Boy For A Day

Released May 16, 1914. Royal-Mutual Film Corporation release. Split reel (640 feet), on the same reel with *I Should Worry* (340 feet). Erroneously listed as *At Bay For A Day* in some trade papers.

Written and directed by Robert Burns, Walter Stull and George Reehm.

With Isabel Daintry *(Carrie "Snips" Devine)* , Walter H. Stull *(Silas Smith, the boss)*, James Harris *(policeman)*, George E. Reehm *(rag man)*, Robert Burns *(man on crutches)*, Walter Kendig *(office boy)*, Maxine Brown *(stenographer)*, Helen La Verne *(Mrs. Devine, Snips' mother)*, Jack Peters *(costumer)*.

"Now, Carrie, I expect you to do some real studying while I am gone. Your report card shows that you need to," remarked Mrs. Devine in a righteously firm voice, as she closed the sitting room door on a very pouty little girl. Carrie's pouts increased while she manhandled her "jography." "Gee, I wish I was a boy, an' then I'd get a job, an' never have to study any more," she exclaimed, thumping the book down to the floor. Then an idea arrived, not pertaining to geography, and she slipped out of the house to a costume shop near by. When she went home she carried under her arm a complete masculine regalia from knickerbockers to a mop of brown hair. The next morning when Carrie crawled out of bed she purposed to emerge into a new world. Tossing her scorned little gingham dress to one side she insinuated herself into the uniform of masculinity, and as she pulled the cap down over her hair, carefully inspecting herself in the mirror, she concluded that she made a pretty good looking boy. "Gee," she exclaimed, out loud, feeling justified in promiscuous slang, "no more school for me. I'm always goin' to play hooky like this," and she swaggered along till she came to a sign that read " Boy Wanted." She accosted Silas Smith in his office and soon found herself on a chair beside another office boy, waiting for orders. There wasn't much to do that morning, and at lunch time Sandy took her along intending to initiate her into the recreations the region offered. Wandering past the river he suggested that it would be kind of fun to go swimmin', Carrie looked at the dark, thick water, and with difficulty restrained her teeth from chattering when she said, " Naw, I don't want to." That amusement failing, Sandy led her to a low building on the wharf where a crowd of boys were imitating the acrobatic stunts they had observed at the circus. Carrie joined in, but found it more difficult than she had supposed to stand on her head and wave her feet in the air. When the boys laughed at her she hit one and got a bloody nose in return. Privately she was thankful when lunch hour was over and it was time to go back to the office. That afternoon her courage returned and she felt quite like a real boy, until the mischievous Sandy, planning a treat for the stenographer, set

a little tin mouse spinning on the floor. The stenographer didn't get on, her chair a minute before Carrie did; Carrie screaming with fear and losing her wig. She made a break for the door, followed by everybody in her race home, accumulating a long line of escorts, until finally on her front steps she landed in her mother's arms prepared for the spanking that mother was prepared to administer. [Chicago Daily Tribune]

"A split reel that will go well as both of its offerings are laughable and have broadly humorous incidents. The first part is a rough and tumble farce with a girl enjoying a day's escapade in boy's clothes. An amusing clown policeman helps it out." -- *Moving Picture World*

"In the same program of the New Majestic Company are two good comedy releases, though "A Boy for a Day" might be more accurately described as a comic. It is a film of a type commoner three or four years ago than now, but a revival of which will, we believe, prove very acceptable to the public. It is a 'Royal' release and tells how a young lady who has. always wanted to be a boy had an opportunity of posing as one for a day. The experiences she encounters quite cure her and, incidentally, provide a series of scenes of genuine unforced humour." -- *Kinematograph Weekly*

I Should Worry

Released May 16, 1914. Royal-Mutual Film Corporation release. Split reel (340 feet), on the same reel with *A Boy For A Day* (640 feet).

Isabel Daintry

Written and directed by Robert Burns, Walter Stull and George Reehm.

With Walter H. Stull (*Abe Rosinsky*), Robert Burns (*tramp*), Walter Kendig (*Joe*), George E. Reehm (*sheriff*), Isabel Daintry, Maxine Brown.

Abe Rosinsky, a prosperous Jewish peddler, is selling goods in the country, when he is held up on a stretch of lonely road by two tramps in need of funds. They drag him on the rocks and relieve him of all he has. On his way home, lamenting, a bright scheme strikes him. Returning to the tramps, he requests that they shoot some holes in his clothing so that his wife, Becky, may be convinced that he has really been robbed. They comply, firing five shots through various parts of his wearing apparel, and then he asks for a hole in his hat. They tell him that, as they have no more bullets, they cannot gratify this last request. Realizing the defenseless position they are now in, Rosinsky knocks them down and recovers his property. In the next town he meets the sheriff searching for the tramps. The Jew leads him to their hiding place and wins a large reward. Then counting his gains, he remarks: "Well, I should worry about a few holes in my new suit!" [RL]

"The second part uses and develops a fine farce idea that once made a good Biograph picture—the sheeney Cheap John who is robbed by two tramps and persuades them to shoot holes in his coat until they have no more bullets. It is still good fun and this picture's producer has added to it something else, but of thinner quality." -- *Moving Picture World*

"A humorous offering depicting the experiences of two tramps and a Jewish peddler." -- *Motion Picture News*

Handle With Care

Released June 13, 1914. Royal-Mutual Film Corporation release. One reel (992 feet).

Written and directed by Walter Stull, George Reehm and Robert Burns.

With Robert Burns, Walter H. Stull, Stanley Ferguson, Jack Peters, Walter Kendig, James Harris, Isabel Daintry, Louise Ducey, Maxine Brown.

Ben Binks is such a favorite at the boarding-house in the country where he spends his vacation that on his departure he is presented with a can of strained honey. On his way to the depot, he stops in the village saloon to have a parting drink and to say good-bye to the boys. There he forgets the can of honey on the counter, where the barkeeper discovered it and puts it in the cellar for safe-keeping. A tramp, called Shift Pete, is employed at the saloon as a roustabout. He wanders into the cellar, and after sampling several wines and whiskies, drinks the honey. Meanwhile, Binks, thinking to keep all hands off his delectable gift until he can come for it, writes the bartender that the can contains nitroglycerine. From the revelation that Pete has consumed the contents of Bink's can, a doctor is summoned in great haste, who pronounces Pete highly explosive, and orders that he be handled with care. The police are notified and a special guard detailed to attend Pete. The tramp walks around like some scared victim of the scourge of God in the ancient days, until a tough character who happens that way pitches into him without waiting for an explanation. It is sufficiently demonstrated that Pete is in no danger of exploding, and everybody in town turns in and finishes him up. [MPW]

"There is plenty of good stuff in this rough and tumble farce to make it go well. The principal idea — the peculiar immunity of a man who is supposed to have drunken nitroglycerine and is being protected by the police from being jarred by anybody — has been used and even more felicitously by another company in a farce; but it is still very funny and will make laughter again. Some of its funny clown work is comical and some is 'worked to death' by repetition. A very fair offering." -- *Moving Picture World*

"An abundance of the slapstick variety of comedy appears in this reel, which is extremely amusing. A tramp drinks a can of honey which is thought to be nitroglycerine. A number of comical events follow." -- *Motion Picture News*

The Busy Man

Released June 20, 1914. Royal-Mutual Film Corporation release. Split reel (337 feet), on the same reel with *Such A Business* (652 feet). Also known as *A Busy Man*.

Written and directed by Robert Burns, George Reehm and Walter Stull.

With Walter H. Stull (*Squire Higgs*), Robert Burns (*Tom*), James Harris (*Jim*), Walter Kendig (*Joey, the boy*), George E. Reehm (*Reggie, a love sick youth*), Maxine Brown (*Mae, his bride-to-be*), Jack Peters (*Bill Jones*), Louise Ducey (*His wife*), Isabel Daintry (*His daughter*).

Squire Higgs was the busiest man in Dogs' Corners. He was fire department, minister, doctor, constable, postmaster — everything, in fact, in way of a public official. One hot day, returning from sundry duties he was summoned to stop a street fight. He put on his police hat, but had scarcely arrived upon the scene when the fire bells began to clang. Tearing back to the office, he hastily exchanged police hat for fire helmet and rushed to the burning property. But no sooner was he getting the flames under control than he was pulled off the job to prevent the fighters murdering each other. A lightning change of hats saw the squire separating the bloodthirsty combatants, when the fire broke out afresh. The helmet hack in vogue, he was handling the conflagration heroically when he was attacked by a love-sick young man who insisted that he perform his marriage ceremony on the spot. Back to the office flew the first citizen of Dogs' Corners, hustled into his clerical hat and was about to pronounce the matrimonial blessing, when the town arrived in a body to drag him back to the fire. The lovesick young man and his bride went too, clinging onto the squire's coat tails. Higgs put the bridegroom in the bucket brigade, swashed out the fire, called in the erstwhile fighters to stand as witnesses, married the young couple, and collected his fee. [RL]

Tagline in *Reel Life*: "The story of Squire Higgs who had to do everything at the same time."

"Another one of [the] Burns, Reehm and Stull Royal comedies. Squire Higgs, of Dog's Corners, is the fire department, minister, doctor, constable, postmaster—in fact, the pooh-bah of the whole durn village. 'Hats in his specialty,' begosh, and the whole community recognize the fact. Gee, but it's funny—and he always collects his fee." -- *Moving Picture World*

"Higgs is the police force, fire department, justice of the peace, et al., and has his hands full. An uproarious comedy." -- *Motion Picture News*

Such A Business

Released June 20, 1914. Royal-Mutual Film Corporation release. Split reel (652 feet), on the same reel with *The Busy Man* (337 feet).

Written and directed by Robert Burns, George Reehm and Walter Stull.

With Robert Burns (*Ike*), Isabel Daintry (*Percy*), Walter Kendig (*Sammy*), Stanley Ferguson (*Mrs. Ike*), Walter H. Stull (*Pugilist*), Louise Ducey (*Old woman*), James Harris (*Dutchman*), Jack Peters (*Lawyer*), Maxine Brown (*Lena*).

Ike Levy, hatter, finds business dull. He is raving up and down in front of his store, when two Irishmen get into an argument across the street and one of them throws a brick. Ike is hit in the back, which doesn't improve his temper, until he is seized by a bright idea. He calls his son, Sammy, and arming him with the brick sends him up the street to break some gentleman's hat. The scheme works. A tall silk hat is sacrificed, and the owner hurries to Ike's shop to buy a new one. Sammy doubles his ammunition, with a brick in either hand, proceeds far and wide to demolish headgear and to drive the trade into the parental establishment. There is such a thing as choosing one's victims sagaciously. When Sammy, who is not an infallible marksman, bricks a celebrated pugilist in the chest, his little game abruptly comes to a close. The prizefighter rounds him up in Ike's shop and by the time he gets through with the place, the hatter has decided that honesty is the best policy. [RL & MPW]

"By Burns, Reehm and Stull who essay the leading parts, assisted by Isabel Daintry and others of equal ability. Ike Levy, a hatter, finds business dull and he seeks to improve it through his son Sammy, who follows the bright idea of his bright parent and the results of his endeavors furnish the comedy. This offering creates laughter." -- *Moving Picture World*

"Advice to hatters when business is poor: Send your son out with bricks and instructions to break everyone's hat. It worked for a while, but the evil plan was discovered later, after it had produced a good laugh." -- *Motion Picture News*

A Hasty Exit

Released June 27, 1914. Royal-Mutual Film Corporation release. One reel (987 feet).

Written and directed by Walter Stull, George Reehm and Robert Burns.

With Robert Burns, Walter H. Stull, George Reehm, Maxine Brown, Isabel Daintry, Louise Ducey.

Jones is the darling of the girls, and two suitors determine to get even with him. A widow writes to Jones and asks him to meet her at a certain spot as she has fallen in love with him. Susceptible Jones keeps the appointment. He gets a rude shock, however, when the lady's "husband" turns up and gives him a good hiding. Jones locks himself in a room, and the "husband" hammers at the door. The joke is turned into a tragedy (as he thinks) when he hears a shot from the room and thinks Jones has committed suicide. Jones, however, did this so as to throw him off his guard, and escapes out of the window, glad enough to go. [KW]

"The boys play a joke on Jack and make him think the widow is married, in the end he wins her hand. A lot of slapstick work appears, which makes the comedy an unusually amusing one." –*Motion Picture News*

Did She Run?

Released July 4, 1914. Royal-Mutual Film Corporation release. One reel (992 feet)

Written and directed by Walter Stull, George Reehm and Robert Burns.

With Robert Burns.

[no synopsis available]

"Very little fun comes directly from the situations in this rough and tumble farce. It has a comedy force of cops and a lot of comedy neighbors, especially one woman who is made to put on trousers by her "skirt" friends. There is very little reason for this step, but from it there follows plenty of the usual farcical happenings, for she is chased by the cops and takes refuge in a house from which she pours water down upon them. It will make laughter in most places; but it is not the kind of picture that would make a reviewer laugh." -- *Moving Picture World*

"A fine comedy in which the town gossip almost precipitates a quarrel between husband and wife. The police force enter and a chase results." -- *Motion Picture News*

How Ida Got A Husband

Released March 5, 1915. Kalem-General Film Company release. One reel (1,046 feet).

Written and directed by Walter Stull, George Reehm and Robert Burns. Filmed circa Summer 1914 in Yonkers, New York.

With Louise Ducey (*Mrs. Needham*), Walter H. Stull (*Mr. Needham, her husband*), Robert Burns (*Bill Saddle, Justice of the Peace and Rancher*), Walter Kendig (*Slippery Pete, a second story man*), Isabel Daintry (*Ida Claire, the Needhams' servant*), Walter Hiers (*cowboy*).

Although the Needham's servant, Ida, is anxious to be married, her face is against her. An ad inserted by Bill Saddle in a matrimonial paper, gives Ida a ray of hope. She answers the ad enclosing Mrs. Needham's photo in her letter. Bill promptly loses his heart when he sees this picture. He leaves for the city. Meeting the original of the photo on the street, Bill follows Mrs. Needham home. In the meantime, Slippery Pete, a second-story man, breaks into the house. Hearing someone coming, the man hides behind the portieres. Saddle enters the house and is confronted by Ida. Although Ida protests that it was she who wrote the answer to his ad, the rancher demands to see the original of the picture in his possession. Hearing Mrs. Needham coming Ida thrusts Saddle into a closet and locks the door. But the man raises such a rumpus that Mrs. Needham opens the door to ascertain the cause. The sight of the stranger who had followed her home affords the woman the fright of her life. Mr. Needham enters the house. In his desire to hide, Saddle approaches Slippery Pete's place of concealment. An inspiration seizes the rancher. As a Justice of the Peace, he is empowered to perform the marriage ceremony. Seizing Slippery Pete and Ida, he joins their hands and makes them one just as Mr. Needham enters the room. While Ida's employers are busy offering their congratulations. Saddle makes his escape. Once out of the house, he tears up Mrs. Needham's photograph and the matrimonial sheet. Raising his right hand, he vows, "Never Again". [MPW & KK]

A discarded Komic or Royal comedy picked up by Kalem for release. The *Kalem Kalendar* published a full synopsis and photograph from the film, something that the folks over at Reliance rarely did. Kalem putting forth some effort that Reliance didn't raises the question as to who ultimately was to blame for the discontinuation of the Stull, Reehm and Burns series at Reliance? Most reviews show that the series was well received.

Walter Hiers appears ever so briefly when Ida dreams of her ideal man at the beginning of the film. He is dressed as a cowboy and is simply sitting counting his cash. By the time of the film's actual release, Walter Kendig had started his brief stint as "Louie" to James Aubrey's "Heinie" in a series made at the Mittenthal Studios, also in Yonkers, New York. Isabel Daintry does well in the film as the love struck maid. Although not the last film she made (Daintry briefly worked at Éclair American after leaving Reliance), this was her last appearance released.

"There is good fun in the unfolding of the plan by which the young woman of the title enters the married state. She endeavors to capture a husband by mailing the gentleman who advertises for a wife, the picture of her mistress, a much prettier woman. An old device! Perhaps! but still vigorous, and capable of exciting honest laughter in the hands of experts of the Kalem calibre. The table scene, as played by Ida, Slippery Jim and the Westerner, is farce of the merriest and swiftest kind." -- *Moving Picture World*

He Was a Traveling Man

Released April 9, 1915. Kalem-General Film Company release. One reel (1,016 feet).

Written and directed by Walter Stull, George Reehm and Robert Burns.

With Walter Stull [as George H. Wheeler] (*Jim Flip, hosiery salesman*), Mildred Pierce (*Marietta, a Spinster*), Bobby Burns [as Arthur Werner] (*Driggs, a hotel clerk*), Gerald Meyton (*Charlie Jones – Bellboy*), Walter Kendig [as Walter B. Etton] (*Billy Peeker – Bellboy*).

The inquisitiveness of the employees and guests of the little country hotel causes Jim Flip, hosiery salesman, to make up his mind to teach them a lesson. When Marietta, an old maid, displays her hosiery in going upstairs, she innocently gives Jim an idea. Charlie Jones, one of the bell boys, peers into Jim's room via the keyhole. He sees a pair of legs sticking out of the hosiery salesman's sample trunk. A slight jar causes the legs to move. The hose on the legs is similar to that worn by Marietta. Charlie promptly speeds down to the hotel clerk and declares that Jim had slain the old maid and was hiding her body in his sample trunk. The clerk takes a peek to satisfy himself and then summons the entire village police force. His alarm approach Jim's room. They finally muster up sufficient courage to smash the door. They come just in time to see the salesman reach into his trunk and pull out a pair of leg dummies such as are used for the purpose of displaying stockings in show windows. With one accord, the intruders turn upon the clerk and the bellboy and kick them from the room.
[MPW & KK]

Why Stull, Reehm and Burns (and even Walter Kendig) are given pseudonyms for this film is both a curiosity and a mystery. With the way many comedians bounced from company to company, and with the various companies releasing films shot months or even years before it seems any kind of contractual issue wouldn't be the cause. No other film featuring "George H. Wheeler" et al has ever surfaced. Adding to the confusion is that with the exception of these two Kalem releases there is a year gap in the boys' filmography.

"This one-reel farce is a 'happy thought' on the part of the author. Life on the road may not resemble the adventures of this 'Knight of the Grip,' but his troubles are the source of much amusement, so no further excuse is needed. George H. Wheeler is the traveling salesman. Gerald Meyton and Walter B. Etton are a pair of lively bellboys." –*Moving Picture World*

"This is a slapstick comedy in which the only approach to humor is an unending succession of punching, slapping and general rough- house. It will appeal to audiences who like the most extreme of this sort of thing, with nothing else in the picture." –*Motion Picture News*

STERLING COMEDIES

For about a year, from around June 1914 until May 1915, Bobby Burns and Walter Stull seemed to just disappear. Little is known about their activities during this time, with only scant mention of them in the trades. A few of their Komic/Royal titles from 1914 were released by Kalem, and Kriterion announced that the pair would appear in a new series for C.K. Comedies, but despite a couple of advertisements in the trade journals there is no solid evidence that a series was ever made.

What's certain is that the trio that left Lubin and starred at Komic were no longer a trio. George Reehm, who had been Walter Stull's main collaborator since Stull entered pictures, left the others and by February 1915 was working as a director at Biograph. Burns and Stull gained a new partner, albeit of a different kind. Louis Burstein, the lawyer who had been instrumental in the early days of the New York Motion Picture Company and was by 1914 an executive at Reliance, saw the business potential in the teaming of Bobby Burns and Walter Stull. He convinced the two that the next step they needed to make if they wished to control their own product was to form their own production company. Together, all three set out to do just that.

Whether the seemingly aborted venture with Kriterion was just a stop-gap intended to raise funds for the new venture, or whether the new production company was to supply product for the C.K. brand (instead of Burns and Stull merely being employed by C.K.) is also a mystery. Advertising inferred that the C.K. Comedies were to be made in Santa Barbara, California but there is no evidence that Burns, Stull or Burstein ever left the East Coast during this time.

Kriterion was one of those companies that arrived with a big bang, then disappeared with a whimper. The plan was that Kriterion would be a large distribution entity with multiple companies (both subsidiaries and independent producers) supplying content, enabling Kriterion to offer a full slate of films to exhibitors, essentially trying to beat the General Film Company at their own game. After a year in existence, with only a handful of verifiable titles released and amidst legal proceedings, Kriterion ceased to exist.

During the Spring of 1915, the new trio of Burns, Stull and Burstein did finally go into production on some new comedies that they hoped would be the basis for funding to firmly establish their new production company. Burstein found the money, and Burns and Stull would write, direct and star in the films. When explaining this new endeavor, Louis Burstein commented: "We want to get a name for these pictures which will show that there are a lot of pokes and jabs in it." An unknown participant in the conversation replied: "That's the very name you want – Pokes and Jabbs."

A common practice among start up production companies was to produce a pilot film representative of the product for which they were attempting to secure a long-term deal. Burstein, Burns and Stull actually made three films: *Pokes and Jabbs*, *The Tangles of Pokes and Jabs*, and *Two For A Quarter*. With "Pokes" and "Jabbs," Burns & Stull settled on the comedy personas that would serve them well for the next three years across three different (and yet the same) production companies, but establishing a comedy series didn't yield immediate success.

One of the films, *Pokes and Jabbs*, was sold to the Sterling Film Company. Sterling was one of the many companies providing content for Universal. Initially established in mid-1914 to produce films starring the former Keystone star Ford Sterling, the company struggled to stay afloat when its namesake returned to Keystone in early 1915. With Sterling in trouble it is likely that a production deal was never on the table; rather it was the practice at the time for production companies and distributors to buy outside product to quickly (and cheaply) fill gaps in their release schedule. As it turns out *Pokes and Jabbs* was the penultimate release by the Sterling Film Company, which by the end of May 1915 no longer existed. The lawyer, the acrobat and the man in plaid would have to look elsewhere to get firmly established, but at least with Sterling Pokes and Jabbs had come to life.

Pokes and Jabbs

Released May 13, 1915. Sterling Company-Universal Film Mfg. Company release. Copyrighted May 5, 1915 (LP5222) by Universal Film Mfg. Co. One reel (970 feet).

Produced by Louis Burstein. Directed by Bobby Burns & Walter Stull.

With Bobby Burns (*Pokes*), Walter Stull (*Jabs*).

The Pokes and Jabbs families, neighbors, live across the hall from each other in the same apartment house. The fearless Mr. Pokes is very much bossed by his wife, a suffragette, while Mr. Jabbs is the ruler in his own home. Mrs. Jabbs has just been presented with a new coat by her husband, and meeting Mr. Pokes in the hall, asks his opinion of it. While Pokes is admiring the coat, his wife, hearing his voice in the hall, peers through the keyhole and mistakes his admiration of the coat for affection for Mrs. Jabbs. Jabbs, at the same time, also hearing voices in the hall, looks through the keyhole and decides to punish Pokes for his familiarity with his wife. Jealousy is aroused in both families and Jabbs and his wife quarrel, the result of which is that she leaves to go to her mother. Mrs. Pokes leaves home to attend a suffragette meeting and Jabbs, learning of a mask ball, persuades Pokes to go as his escort. Jabbs dresses as a woman. Arriving at the hall, they learn that the ball has been postponed. Disgustedly, they start toward home. A policeman gives them quite a chase, but they elude him by dodging into a saloon. The kindly bartender gets in wrong by offering his services and when they beat a hasty exit through the side door, they are confronted by another policeman. Pokes gets rid of him in a peculiar fashion. after several mishaps they arrive home. Jabbs has forgotten his keys. Pokes, becoming brave immediately, offers to put him up for the night They proceed to retire without removing their clothes. The suffragette meeting being over, Mrs. Pokes returns. A horrible discovery meets her gaze upon entering her bedroom.

Jabbs, in female attire, occupies her bed. Wild with rage, she rushes to the Jabbs apartment to inform Mr. Jabbs of his wife's actions. Jabbs, hearing the clatter on the door, beats it out the window to the fire escape. About this time, Mrs. Jabbs returns repentant. Entering her own apartment, she sees a woman lying on the couch and fails to recognize it as her husband. With a piercing shriek, she rushes to the hallway and faints. Jabbs again aroused, makes his exit through the window, and for the fire escape to the Pokes' apartment, begging Mr. Pokes to hide and protect him. Mrs. Pokes arrives on the scene and Jabbs makes for the hallway, but in so doing leaves his skirt clutched in the hand of Mrs. Pokes. Explanations follow, and what at first appeared to be a horrible catastrophe, turns out an innocent prank. [MPW]

Reviews of this first Pokes & Jabbs effort were mixed. *Moving Picture World* referred to the film as a "low comedy number" and thought the knockout incidents were "rough but not quite laughable." *Motion Picture News* was more accepting noting the film's direction and mentioning that Sterling was "honored" to have the film on its release schedule.

The question of how many B's are in Walter Stull's character's name is raised with this initial film. It is advertised using the singular "B" in Jabs but then the studio-supplied synopsis reprinted by the trade magazines uses the double "B" Jabbs. Once at Wizard the character's name settles in with the single "B" version. Then at Vim, Jabbs regains the second "B" until it is finally lost for good with the Jaxon brand... usually.

"A strenuous slapstick, in which two henpecked husbands go out for a "time," one of them dressing as a woman. The situations resulting on their home-coming and during their tour of the saloons are humorously conceived and very well carried out by the cast. The majority of the male comedians who appear seem confirmed acrobats, and their actions have obviously been well guided by a director who knows his business. This was made by an outside company, but the Sterling brand has seldom been honored with a more acceptable slapstick." -- *Motion Picture News*

"A very involved comedy in which the humour is not entirely free from suggestiveness." -- *The Bioscope*

WIZARD COMEDIES

The Wizard Motion Pictures Corporation was incorporated in the Commonwealth of Virginia in December 1914. Intended to be the entity to supply comedies for the Equitable Film Corp. (also incorporated in 1914 in Virginia and having some of the same board members), Wizard sat dormant without making a single film for over six months. Equitable was set up to be one of the many companies that would feed into the World Film Corporation, providing both features and short films. However, Equitable also was a film company in name only for much of 1915.

World, which had started in 1913, not only was a distributor of other brands (an arrangement not unlike Universal at the time) but also a producer of their own product. Like the other contributing producers who focused on feature films, World either contracted with small companies to produce short films for them or formed such companies themselves as somewhat independent subsidiaries. Such was the World Comedy Star Film Corporation (known as the World Comedy Star Corps) which began providing titles for the World release schedule in early 1915. The World Comedy Star Film Corps made a number of comedies with nondescript actors, such as Jeff De Angelis and Richard Carle, but then finally secured Weber & Fields for a series of comedies. The Weber & Fields films, shot in Chicago, were made independently and released by World. The rest of the World Comedy Star Corps product was shot at the Doc Willat Studio in Fort Lee, New Jersey.

Wanting more product, World also made an arrangement in February 1915 for the Flamingo Film Company to provide a series of Flamingo Comedies to strengthen World's slate of releases. Flamingo had previously been released by Sawyer, Inc. and even had A.H. Sawyer on its board until the move to World. Fred Mace, the former and future Keystone player, had been Director General at Flamingo but was released soon after the move, being replaced by former Lubin director Charles Murphy.

With the World Comedy Star Film Corps and Flamingo, a full complement of comedies were available to World but suddenly they had no comedy product whatsoever. The Flamingo deal never really worked out. There were a few releases in the Spring and early Summer of 1915 but Flamingo would eventually sue World for breach of contract only to go out of business altogether in 1916. One of the trade journals announced that the World Comedy Star Film Corps would cease production around May 1915; no official explanation was given, although inability to meet payroll was suspected. Parent company World Film Corporation desperately needed to fill their release schedule, and quickly. Enter Burstein, Burns and Stull.

The film *Pokes & Jabbs* had accomplished its goal. Shot as a pilot to attract a future production deal, the film had done just that. The World Film Corporation secured a deal with Louis Burstein for the production of a series of Pokes & Jabbs comedies. Instead of forming a new corporation, Burstein was put on the board of the dormant Wizard Motion Pictures Corporation. With the establishment of the Pokes & Jabbs series, the corporation (with the slightly altered name, Wizard Films Corporation) reincorporated in New York, and placed Burstein in charge of that entity's productions.

Further complicating the business relationships, Wizard actually bought the first two Pokes & Jabbs that were already completed from Milton E. Hoffman (a member of their board) who had bought them from Louis Burstein (who had just been added to the board). Reports noted Burstein joining the Equitable Film Corporation with the intent for Wizard to be a subsidiary, yet since Equitable was just gearing up to start their own productions, there was no real affiliation between them. A final interesting note in the oft-twisted legal dealings among film companies was the outright sale of the World Comedy Film Corporation to Wizard in August 1915. Since Wizard comedies were filling the World Comedy Film Corps' slot on the release schedule, the releases were sometimes erroneously listed as such. Confusing legal documents aside, the happy result was that Pokes & Jabbs would live beyond their single namesake title film.

OFFERS TO LIVE EXHIBITORS WHO WANT COMEDY FILMS THAT CAUSE LAUGHTER. THE FUNNIEST FILM PRODUCTS OF THESE TRIED & TESTED

Laugh Creators De Luxe

BURNS & STULL POKES & JABS
WIZARD FILMS

BURNS & STULL PIONEERS AMONG FILM LAUGHTER CAUSERS - AVAILABLE FOR BOOKING AT ALL OUR BRANCHES

Production of the Pokes & Jabs series began in late May 1915, keeping in mind that *The Tangles of Pokes & Jabs* and *Two For A Quarter* were already completed (shot around the same time as the Sterling *Pokes & Jabbs*). As with the pilot, and all of the Pokes & Jabbs comedies, Bobby Burns and Walter Stull would not only star but also direct. Burstein would fulfill the role of producer handling the finances and publicity. A supporting cast was hired to work with Burns & Stull including a beautiful quartet of ingenues consisting of Helen Von Huben, Pearl Shepard, Ethel Burton, and Betty Holton. All were fairly new to film and, with the exception of Shepard and Burton, did little after appearing in the Wizard comedies. Pearl Shepard would remain in New York after Burns &

Stull et al moved to Florida and would make Three C Comedies and a number of others (sometimes as the lead) before eventually working in features.

The keeper was Ethel Burton who would be Pokes & Jabs' leading lady through all the Wizard and Vim comedies. Other players added to the company include Edna Reynolds, Billy Ruge and eventually Babe Hardy.

The first Pokes & Jabs Wizard comedy was released in July 1915 and Burstein immediately made plans to expand Wizard with the addition of a second production unit to be headed up by Jerold T. Hevener. A semi-regular in the Gay Times comedy unit at Lubin, Hevener acted in many of the Mae Hotely comedies and would direct the company when Hotely and husband/director Arthur Hotaling took time off or was directing the all-Black cast comedy unit. But like Babe Hardy, with whom he regularly appeared and directed, Hevener was let go by Lubin in early 1915 when Billie Reeves was signed by the company and their comedy unit retooled.

The new Wizard unit was supposed to make films with name stars (like the Casino Star comedies or the later Hal Roach All-Star comedies) surrounded by a veteran group of film comics. Among those announced to star in these comedies were Sliding Billy Watson, Ed Lee Worthe, Weber & Fields, Johnny & Emma Ray and Clara Kimball Young. It appears that only the first two actually went before the Wizard cameras.

Included in the supporting cast were Betty Holton (Pokes & Jabs not needing that many ingenues), contortionist comedian Billy Ruge, Billy Bletcher and Hevener's former Lubin cohorts Mabel Paige, Charlie Ritchie (also known as C.W. Ritchie), Billy Bowers and Babe Hardy. Paige can be seen as the servant girl in one of Babe Hardy's earliest extant films *The Servant Girl's Legacy*, and Bowers appears in Hardy's film debut *Outwitting Dad*. Ruge and Hardy would go on to form the core of the Vim stock company and then graduate to their own series. Excluding Bletcher, Hardy and Ruge, none of the other Jerold Hevener unit cast would move on to Vim (Betty Holton has a few Vim credits but those films were originally shot for Wizard).

Initially the two production units worked out of different rental studios, Burns & Stull at the Speedway Inn on Dyckman Street in Yonkers and Hevener at the Equitable studio in Flushing on Long Island. In August both units moved into the newly-built Wizard studio on 310 52nd Street near 8th Avenue in New York City. However, just a week later the new studio experienced heavy rain damage causing a delay in production.

Wizard Comedies disappeared from the World schedule after the release of *In Clover* on August 16, 1915. However, there were a number of other completed comedies that could have filled the release schedule while Wizard reset after the storm, so the stoppage wasn't for lack of product. The unreleased Wizard-Pokes & Jabs would eventually be released as Vim comedies, yet there is no evidence that any of the Hevener-directed comedies were ever released.

Storm damage may not have had any direct influence on the end of Wizard. More likely, it again came down to legal matters. Burstein's original contract was for six films, and it seems after delivering seven he chose to end his relationship with Wizard, officially resigning from the board on October 14, 1915. Lewis J. Selznick, who had become Vice President of both World and Equitable, joined the board of the Wizard Motion Pictures Corporation but no further productions were made by the company and it was dissolved in 1917.

While Wizard Comedies had a short life, existing for only six weeks on the release charts, Pokes and Jabbs had just begun. For years the only known Wizard Comedy to exist was a short fragment of *Juggling the Truth*; more recently, nearly-complete prints of *In Clover* and *A Quiet Game* have been discovered. To date, none of the second unit Wizard Comedies survive. Such is the case for many a film company's product from the silent era, especially from the many fleeting companies like Wizard that came and went in a heartbeat back in the 'teens.

POKES & JABS COMEDIES

The Tangles of Pokes and Jabs

Released July 5, 1915. Wizard Comedies-World Film Corporation release. One reel. No copyright registered.

Produced by Louis them from Burstein. Directed by Bobby Burns and Walter Stull. Filmed prior to June 1915 in New York City.

with Bobby Burns (*Pokes*), Walter Stull (*Jabs*), Helen Von Huben, Pearl Shepard, Ethel Burton, and Betty Holton.

Pokes and Jabbs are neighbors; each has a wife. And there is a fifth character, Miss Tattler, who is the authoress of all the mischief of the comedy. She thinks she sees Pokes kissing Mrs. Jabbs and then she goes and spreads the scandal. Jabbs madly jealous, tries to shoot Pokes, who escapes! Next day Pokes, who has lost some money in the Jabbs home tries to recover it but is again detected by the malicious Miss Tattler. After many exciting adventures and escapes. Pokes recovers his money, but has it taken from him by his wife, who will no longer trust him out of her sight. [MPW]

One of two comedies, along with *Two For A Quarter*, completed before Louis Burstein signed a contract with Wizard on June 7, 1915.

"Another riotous slapstick featuring the same two comical gentlemen who appeared in *Two For a Quarter*. While not possessed with much original plot, the actions of the comedians are productive of much laughter. This film was shown for a week at the New York Hippodrome, where it well upheld the comedy end of the bill." -- *Motion Picture News*

Two For a Quarter

Released July 12, 1915. Wizard Comedies-World Film Corporation release. One reel. No copyright registered.

Produced by Louis Burstein. Directed by Bobby Burns and Walter Stull. Filmed prior to June 1915 in New York City.

with Bobby Burns (*Pokes*), Walter Stull (*Jabs*), Helen Von Huben, Pearl Shepard, Ethel Burton, and Betty Holton.

Two penniless hoboes contrive to procure a square meal. At last they discover a very large suit, so both of the gentlemen enshroud themselves therein and repair to an eating house. Their ruse is discovered, but not until they have well appeased their appetites. [MPN]

Published biographies give this as Ethel Burton's film debut. Both this film and *The Tangles of Pokes and Jabs* were delivered to World for approval at the same time. It is entirely possible that this was the first of the two to be made.

"This reel features two capable comedians, one long and the other short. Their antics throughout the picture, chiefly while encased in the suit are uproarious. For a slapstick comedy this well fills the bill, and as the offensive is almost totally lacking it should prove fit entertainment for all classes of houses." -- *Motion Picture News*

One Busy Day

Released July 19, 1915. Wizard Comedies-World Film Corporation release. One reel. No copyright registered.

Produced by Louis Burstein. Directed by Bobby Burns and Walter Stull. Filmed in Yonkers, New York.
with Bobby Burns (*Pokes*), Walter Stull (*Jabs*), Helen Von Huben, Pearl Shepard, Ethel Burton, and Betty Holton.

[no synopsis available].

[no reviews available]

A Quiet Game

Released July 26, 1915. Wizard Comedies-World Film Corporation release. One reel. No copyright registered.

Produced by Louis Burstein. Directed by Bobby Burns and Walter Stull. Filmed in New York City.

with Bobby Burns (*Pokes*), Walter Stull (*Jabs*), Walter Hiers (*poker player*), Billy Bletcher (*poker player*), Louis Burstein (*poker player*), Ethel Burton (*maid*), Joe Cohen (*burglar*), Helen Von Huben.

Top left: Billy Bletcher, Bobby and Walter Hiers. Top Right: Walter and Ethel. Bottom Left: The back of Billy's head, Louis Burstein, Bobby and some guy. Bottom Right: Walter, Ethel and Bobby.

Pokes gets a note telling him his presence is required at the club that evening. He fakes an illness so that the wife will leave him at home alone and give him the opportunity to sneak out to the club. She overhears his phone call to his buddies and his plan is spoiled. She instructs him not to leave the house and goes upstairs. Meanwhile Jabs the cop flirts with the maid allowing Pokes to borrow his uniform and sneak out. At the club some of the members think it is a raid since Pokes is dressed as a cop. But Pokes' poker playing buddies remain and he sits in on the game at which they all cheat. A burglar breaks into the Pokes' home and Jabs catches him in the act. The burglar doesn't believe Jabs is a cop since he doesn't have his uniform, so Jabs goes out in search of it. Pokes returns home, scares off the burglar, puts the uniform back in its place. He is taking his belongings out of the bag left by the burglar and is mistaken for the thief. He tells an outlandish story about how he came to possess the bag. [RS]

Most of the action follows Bobby Burns with Walter Stull only appearing intermittently…. and much of that time was spent having Ethel Burton sit on his lap. It is understandable why Ethel endured as Pokes & Jabbs' main female support. Beauty aside, she glides through this film with a bounce in her step and playful smile on her face. Walter Hiers and Billy Bletcher as Pokes' poker playing buddies are a nice surprise and even the boss, Louis Burstein, is seen playing poker early in the film. Bletcher, originally thought to have not joined the Vim forces until after the move to Jacksonville, is seen in a few of the Wizard comedies. Bletcher started his film career the year before working at the Vitagraph Studios in Brooklyn. While there he supported the likes of Mr. & Mrs. Sidney Drew, Lillian Walker and Billy Quirk.

"Pokes and Jabs are the most consistently comic film creators being presented today." -- *Twin Falls Times (Twin Falls, Idaho)*

Mashers and Splashers

Released August 2, 1915. Wizard Comedies-World Film Corporation release. One reel. No copyright registered.

Produced by Louis Burstein. Directed by Bobby Burns and Walter Stull. Filmed in Yonkers, New York and at the Palisades Park pool near Fort Lee, New Jersey.

with Bobby Burns (*Pokes*), Walter Stull (*Jabs*), Helen Von Huben, Pearl Shepard, Ethel Burton, Laurie Mackin, Nora Sprague, Betty Holton, Corinne Malvern, Edna Reynolds, Mabel Greene (*diver*), Lenore Courtney (*diver*), Marie Jensen (*diver*), Helen Constance (*diver*).

Mr. Jabbs tells his wife that he must go away to a watering place for his health. Mr. Pokes informs his wife that he must look after a sick friend. Jabbs and Pokes journey to a surf bathing summer resort where they meet a friend with a bevy of pretty girls. They take the girls away, and the irate escort travels back to town. He meets Mrs. Jabbs and Mrs. Pokes, and, wishing to get even, tells of their husband's whereabouts. Jabbs and Pokes are caught by their spouses and hustled home in a hurry, while the bevy of girls disband. [M]

Pokes and Jabbs tell the wives that they are going to ""Loopsedasilap" in order for Jabbs to recuperate. Perhaps merely spelling "Palisades Pool" backwards wasn't the best idea the boys ever had. The wives quickly decipher the name and head out to stop their husbands' fun. Reportedly over fifty ladies tried out for the film by exhibiting their diving and swimming abilities. Six women were chosen to augment the troupe's regular cast of beauties. *Moving Picture World* (erroneously referring to the film as *Mashers and Smashers*) noted that "girls in attractive bathing suits and high diving are among the attractions of the picture." One story was published that Pearl Shepard not only didn't know how to dive, she didn't know how to swim. But knowing it was required for the film went down to the Brighton Baths and learned how to swim and dive including inventing her own "Flop back" dive.

The central locale for the film was most commonly known as the Palisades Amusement Park or just Palisades Park, originally having the much more clumsy yet geographically sound name "The Park on the Palisades." In 1910 the park was purchased by Nicholas and Joseph Schenck, who worked in the film business in the nearby town of Fort Lee, and for the next twenty five years held the official name Schenck Bros. Palisades Park. This was the same Joseph Schenck that married Norma Talmadge and was a major film studio executive. He divorced Talmage and sold Palisades Park around the same time in 1934. The subject of Freddy Cannon's rock and roll hit song Palisades Park closed in 1971, not because it wasn't still successful but because the land had become too valuable and the traffic a nuisance to the surrounding upscale neighborhood.

"One of the Pokes and Jabs series in which the two indomitable husbands take a little trip to Palisades Park as recreation, and also vacation from their wives. The incidental part, which will hold these in search of fancy diving, is the finished performance by several young ladies most adept in the art. Of course, their wives locate them, and take them protestingly home." -- *New York Dramatic Mirror*

Juggling the Truth

Released August 9, 1915. Wizard Comedies-World Film Corporation release. One reel. No copyright registered.

Produced by Louis Burstein. Directed by Bobby Burns and Walter Stull. Filmed in Yonkers, New York.

with Bobby Burns (*Pokes*), Walter Stull (*Jabs, the butler*), Helen Von Huben, Pearl Shepard, Ethel Burton, Laurie Mackin.

[no synopsis available].

Only a brief fragment of this film survives, less than 45 seconds total running time. It shows Bobby Burns prancing around and acting insane, apparently as part of his efforts to deceive the wife of his philandering as mentioned in the review of the film. Other than Burns breaking a mirror with a chair there is little to describe, but the

fragment does show that the Wizard version of Pokes & Jabbs looked pretty much the same as the Vim and Jaxon incarnations. The title cards note the film as *"Pokes and Jabbs in Juggling the Truth."* At Wizard there is a lack of consistency concerning Jabs vs. Jabbs.

"Pokes thinks to fool his wife when she accuses him of being seen in the company of two bewitching young girls, and tells her that this man was his double. Matters become seriously complicated when a real double does put in an appearance. This is a very funny reel and should create just as much laughter as the previous experiences of Pokes." *-- Motion Picture News.*

In Clover

Released August 16, 1915. Wizard Comedies-World Film Corporation release. One reel. No copyright registered. Also known as: *Pokes and Jabs In Clover.*

Produced by Louis Burstein. Directed by Bobby Burns and Walter Stull. Filmed in Yonkers, New York.

with Bobby Burns (*Pokes*), Ethel Burton (*farmer's daughter*), Helen Von Huben, Pearl Shepard (*the other daughter*), Laurie Mackin, Joe Cohen (*plaid dressed suitor*), Billy Bletcher (*farm hand*), Billy Ruge (*Silas Higgs, the constable*).

The newspaper reports that Farmer Brown saw a ghost in the field. What he did see for sure was his daughter pitching woo with her beau the farm hand. The farmer throws a pumpkin at the beau but hits the constable instead who returns the volley. Meanwhile, Pokes the vagabond exits the train boxcar in search of breakfast. The beau sees Pokes and thinks he is poacher and shoots at him, hitting the farmer's other daughter instead. As Pokes runs away he comes across a scarecrow in the field and seeing that it is better dressed than he switches clothes with the dummy. He sees the farmer coming and pretends to be the scarecrow and when he moves it gives the farmer credence to his belief of a ghost in the field. The other daughter's suitor shows up dressed in plaid. Pokes then unintentionally scares the farmer, the beaus and the daughters who run and get the constable. They then go in search of the ghost scarecrow. [RS]

Walter Stull does not appear in the film and why he is missing from the film is not explained, but was well noted by reviewers. It is interesting to note that Joe Cohen appears dressed in Jabbs' trademark plaid suit, so in essence was playing a faux Jabbs. This, the last Wizard Comedy released, was deemed to be "well up to the standard of previous offerings" and "acted with spirit" according to *Moving Picture World*. Another handful of productions were completed but held back from distribution, finally being released when Pokes and Jabbs moved over to the Vim Films Corporation.

"Although the title says 'Pokes and Jabs,' Jabs is conspicuous only by his absence in this slapstick number. Pokes is the main gentleman. He appears in his usual ridiculous makeup and affects the same idiotic mannerisms. All the action takes place on a farm, and while the plot is reminiscent of many others, there are several original touches that, combined with the queer antics of Pokes, lend it an air of unconventionality. Pokes' private box car lands him in an unfamiliar town, very much in need of food and amusement. He raises havoc by clothing himself in the garments of a scarecrow. It is a very good slapstick comedy, exhibiting nothing of a vulgar sort and pleases with much that is humorous." -- *Motion Picture News (review by Peter Milne)*

SECOND UNIT

The Crazy Clock Maker

Intended for release circa September 1915. Wizard Comedies-World Film Corporation release. One reel. No copyright registered.

Produced by Louis Burstein. Directed by Jerold T. Hevener. Filmed circa August 1915 at the Equitable studio in Flushing, Long Island.

With Sliding Billy Watson (*Herman Ludwig*), Babe Hardy, Betty Holton, Mabel Paige, Batrice Miller, Nan Egleson, Myrtle Gilbert, Ray Ford, Myra Brooke, Billy Bowers, Charlie Ritchie, Clay Grant, Hod Weston, Walter Schimpf.

Slidin' Billy Watson

Mr. Watson leads his assistants on a lively chase after he is mistaken for a lunatic, and evades capture by assuming the coat and cap of a policeman, and when he takes a real policeman to the sanitarium a veritable riot ensues in the house where he is to fix the clock. When he discovers the lady in pajamas, and dishes crash, doors slam, and pistols track before he makes his getaway. [New York Clipper review of stage play]

Wizard's second unit appears to have adopted the same strategy as Mutual's Casino Star Comedies being made at the same time: assembling a troupe of film comedians to support a well known stage performer that would come in for a film or two between stage engagements, or to film during the day while appearing on New York stages in the evening (W.C. Fields made two Casino Star films before Flo Ziegfeld made him quit citing his "daylighting" as harming the quality of his performances at night).

The first of these for Wizard featured Slidin' Billy Watson who was enjoying much success on the vaudeville circuit in a program co-billed (but not teamed) with Ed. Lee Worthe. It was reported that Watson would appear in an adaptation of *Happyland* (another of his stage plays that dated as far back as 1911) for Wizard. Whether that was in addition to this film, or if this was shot instead is unknown. But *Crazy Clock Maker* was in essence just a filming of Watson's stage act usually known simply as *The Clockmaker*, appealing to both performer and film company. Though it required some staging, plot and action had long been in existence, making this pretty much an easy, cheap production.

By the time this film was mentioned in a brief article in the August 21, 1915 issue of *Motion Picture News* (which was repeated in the September 4, 1915 issue of *Moving Picture World*) Louis Burstein was already looking to shut down Wizard and create Vim. There is no mention in the trades of a release date, and most likely it was never released in America. However, newspapers reported that it did screen in Australia in 1921. It is the first known association between Burstein and the soon-to-be key Vim player Babe Hardy.

[no reviews available]

The New Butler

Little Jerry

Intended for release circa September 1915. Wizard Comedies-World Film Corporation release. One reel. No copyright registered.

Produced by Louis Burstein. Directed by Jerold T. Hevener. Filmed in New York City.

with Jerry "Little Jerry" Austin (*the butler*), Babe Hardy [?], Betty Holton.

[no synopsis available].

The existence of *The New Butler* is only known from one single article in the *Moving Picture World* that noted "Little Jerry, perhaps one of the most versatile of the "little people" there is, is working with Jerold Hevener, the Wizard Motion Pictures Corporation director, in a picture entitled *The New Butler*, which will be released through the World Film Corporation. Little Jerry will play the role of the butler. Little Jerry, although he is only a little over two feet tall, is possessed of a marvelous voice, and he has sung both at the Hippodrome (New York) and in large auditoriums with a brass band. While he is most fond of the operas and classical songs, he is a great lover of ragtime, too. He says that he does not care what it is he is singing, just so he can make his audience respond. Jerry was born in Russia, and he reads and speaks Russian, French and German. Singing and dancing are merely his avocations." Little Jerry did work often in films reportedly at Keystone and Fox among other studios but his real claim to fame was in vaudeville. Often billed as "The Smallest Man with the Biggest Voice," his greatest asset was one that didn't transfer to silent film.

There was a 1914 Joker comedy by this title and in June 1915 Lubin released a one-reeler starring starring Billie Reeves entitled *The New Butler* all which may add to the confusion regarding Babe Hardy's participation. Many filmographies list Hardy as appearing in *The New Butler* but it was assumed to be an erroneous reference to the Lubin film, his recent former employer, that definitely does not feature Hardy. However, those filmographies may have been right on the title of the film and just missed the mark on which company's production features Hardy.

Betty Holton's entry in the Studio Directory Section of the *Motion Picture News* lists a Wizard comedy entitled *Guilty Consciences*. Whether that is another film, an alternate title or an erroneous entry in Holton's filmography is not known.

[no reviews available]

Janitor Higgins

Intended for release circa September 1915. Wizard Comedies-World Film Corporation release. One reel. No copyright registered.

Produced by Louis Burstein. Directed by Jerold T. Hevener. Filmed circa August 1915 at the Equitable studio in Flushing, Long Island.

with Ed. Lee Wrothe (*Janitor Higgins*), Betty Holton, Alma Murray, Billy Bletcher and Billy Ruge.

The janitor becomes a husband for a few moments to gain $25,000 for the wife of an absent naval officer. [Variety, review of stage play]

Ed. Lee Wrothe toured extensively between 1914 and 1918 with variations of the Janitor Higgins character. Early in his stage career, around the turn of the century, Wrothe had worked as part of a trio including George Bickel and Harry Watson that would go on to make comedies for Kleine, most famously with Watson as Musty Suffer.

[no reviews available]

Untitled Hevener Wizard Comedy

Intended for release circa September 1915. Wizard Comedies-World Film Corporation release. One reel. No copyright registered.

Produced by Louis Burstein. Directed by Jerold T. Hevener. Filmed in New York City.

with Joe Schrode, Pearl Shepard.

[no synopsis available]

Other than one very brief single-sentence mention of the film in a *Moving Picture World* article there is no information on this film including its title.

[no reviews available]

VIM FILMS CORPORATION

Having severed his business arrangement with the World Film Corporation, Louis Burstein needed a new deal in order to continue to produce the Pokes & Jabbs comedies. Enter the Melies Manufacturing Company which was the American branch of George Melies' Paris-based Star Films. Gaston Melies, George's older brother, was in charge of the subsidiary which adopted the same brand name, Star Films, as the parent company. Gaston had come to America in 1902 and made some films, but the Star Film Company became fully established in 1908 when Melies joined the General Film Company, a move that included a number of obligations to the "Trust," not least the requirement to supply a mimimum amount of footage for release each week. The older Melies moved his operation around from Chicago, to San Antonio (where the company seemed to have done its best work), to Santa Paula, California and finally the southern Pacific Ocean with stops in New Zealand, Tahiti and Singapore.

Eventually the poor condition of the footage sent back to the States, resulting in a lack of releasable product for General Film, led to the bankruptcy and dissolution of the American version of the Star Film Company. However, the obligation to General Film had become an asset; money was still to be made filling the Melies slot on the General Film Service release schedule, and as such the Melies Manufacturing Company, although not producing anything themselves, remained active for a number of years by subcontracting their required footage to other producers.

Added to the mix was Pathé Freres' exit from General Film in early 1915, and along with some companies' increasing focus on feature films, there was a potential shortage of short film product looming over the General Film Service. Enter David Horsley.

One of the first truly independent film producers and the first to openly contest the monopoly held by the Motion Pictures Patents Company, Horsley was finally convinced to deal with the enemy. At the time he was producing comedies at his Centaur Studios in Bayonne, New Jersey. While continuing the Centaur product on the independent market, Horsley contracted to supply the General Film Company, through Melies, three one-reel comedies each week (Thursdays and Fridays were his usual release days) under a new brand name. Announced initially as Ace Comedies, the brand was changed to MinA (Made in America) before any products were released. Harry La Pearl, and then George Ovey were the featured comedians for MinA.

However, as Horsley became more and more involved in the planning and building of a Los Angeles area studio, the less interested in the General Film Company he became. Not long after completion of the California studio, Horsley shifted all production to the west coast. At the same time he severed his association with the General Film Company. The last MinA product was released on Thursday, August 5, 1915. Horsley changed the name of his Ovey series to Cub Comedies, and made a distribution arrangement with the Mutual Film Corporation.

General Film would continue to release some films under the brand name MinA for some time, but there was no production company to supply any new product and there was a need for a new subcontractor. As had been the case with the creation of the Wizard brand, Burstein, Burns and Stull were again the benefactor of good timing. Burstein quickly established the Vim Films Corporation (incorporating on October 22, 1915 with his niece Mildred Burstein as one of the directors and stockholders), and with a small backlog of films made at the Wizard studios but unreleased, moved into the recently vacated Centaur Studios on Avenue E and East 43rd Street in Bayonne, New Jersey and began production on comedies for General Film Company release, the first scheduled for Friday, November 12, 1915.

Vim arrives in Jacksonville.

Back Row: Fred T. O'Neil, Frank Hanson, Robin Williamson. Middle Row; Babe Hardy, Ione Lyle, Helen Gilmore, Ethel Burton, Edna Reynolds, Mildred Burstein, Anna Mingus, Harry Naughton. Front Row: Bobby Burns, Louis Burstein, Walter Stull.

The initial cadre of performers at Vim were carry-overs from Wizard. In addition to Walter Stull and Bobby Burns the first Vims featured the likes of Babe Hardy, Billy Ruge, Billy Bletcher, Joe Cohen, and thankfully Ethel Burton.

Early in November 1915, the Vim company packed their bags and left Bayonne for the warmer, sunnier Jacksonville, Florida. For Bobby Burns, Walter Stull, and Babe Hardy the move South was a welcome return to their old stomping grounds. Vim leased the old Lubin studio at 750 Riverside Avenue where the "Gay Times" comedies with Mae Hotely had been shot until February 13, 1915 (and after a brief pause, where the Billie Reeves comedies, with virtually a whole new company of actors, were made until the studio closed in mid-May 1915), and the three had at various times been a part of that Lubin stock company.

Arriving in Jacksonville with Burns, Stull and Hardy on November 3, 1915 were Billy Ruge, Frank "Spook" Hanson, Robin Williamson (who worked both as an actor and as an assistant director), Harry Naughton (writer, assistant director, sometime actor and eventually studio manager), Ethel Burton, Helen Gilmore, Edna Reynolds, Anna Mingus, Mildred Burstein (company secretary and bit player Virginia Coffee, Violet Adams Ione Lyle, Fred T. O'Neil, Louis Burstein and Herman Obrock (cameraman). Since the studio was familiar territory to many in the troupe they were able to jump into production on the next Pokes & Jabbs comedy quickly.

The new year found the Vimmies settling into their new studio on Riverside Drive and hitting their stride. With the popularity of the Pokes & Jabbs comedies building, Burstein was able to start up a second unit to produce additional comedies to expand Vim's release schedule. Veteran film director Will Louis was hired to direct, while Babe Hardy and Billy Ruge, both chief support for Pokes & Jabbs, were tabbed to head up the new series to be known as Plump & Runt comedies. Louis, who had most recently been directing at Edison, was no stranger to either JAX or his lead comedians. Billy Ruge worked briefly with Louis at Edison, and Babe Hardy worked with Louis more at Lubin and Edison than he did any other director.

While still providing occasional support in the Pokes & Jabbs films, the new team of Hardy & Ruge (as they were often billed) began filming comedies that would take the Thursday slot in the General Film Service program. In addition to Hardy & Ruge, the series would feature Bert Tracy providing not only great comic support but also most of the scenarios for the films (although specifc titles are hard to verify). Local beauty Florence McLoughlin was added to the unit to provide some female flavor, with the rest of the cast coming from the stock company that worked in both series, but more often than not Billy Bletcher, Edna Reynolds and Helen Gilmore would help out Plump & Runt.

Yet even with the new homegrown series just starting production, Burstein was planning for even more expansion. On February 13, Louis Burstein left Jacksonville for New York City to handle some business matters, including adding new on-screen talent, and left his niece Mildred in charge of the studio. Albeit temporary, this was one of the earliest occurrences of a woman as a studio head. While in New York, Burstein apparently obtained a partner in the person of Mark Dintenfass. Although credited with co-founding Vim, there are no references to Dintenfass being connected to Vim until this period in mid-February 1916. Referred to in the trade papers as the Treasurer of the Vim Films Corporation, Dintenfass may have been brought on to attract new investors (he was a well established film producer, having been involved in the formation of Universal, in particular the Champion and Victor brands), or perhaps he was brought on by a specific investor (perhaps marking the beginning of the Eastern Film Corporation's involvement, of which more anon).

The war in Europe was in full swing by 1916 and amongst the many businesses that suffered was their film industry. Production and attendance were down, and many of those making movies began looking elsewhere for employment. One of these was the comedian Marcel Perez, known in Europe as Robinet or Tweedledum, and Louis Burstein signed him.

Manuel Fernandez Perez or Fernandea Perez as he was known (it would be some time before the billing of Marcel Perez would become the standard) in early 1916 was contracted by Burstein to make a comedy series for Vim as the character Bungles. The

Marcel Perez aka Bungles aka Tweedledum

Bungles comedies would be released on alternating Thursdays, sharing their release schedule with the Plump & Runt series taking over the final MinA slot. Why Burstein decided to change Perez's on-screen name to Bungles from the pre-sold Tweedledum is unknown; strangely, even the publicity surrounding his signing referred to the Tweedledum comedies. Regardless, working in America away from the chaos of the Great War certainly must have been an attractive notion to Perez.

Added to the Vim company to provide comic support for Perez was comedienne Elsie McLeod. A veteran of the film industry herself, McLeod, a pretty blonde with big eyebrows, had been working in pictures since 1911, most often at Edison in support of Wadsworth & Housman. McLeod had even appeared in the first film Perez made in the States in late 1915, a one-off for Universal called "A Day At Midland Beach." McLeod reached Jacksonville ahead of Perez and had actually taken a turn in a Plump & Runt production before settling down to her work as Bungles' leading lady. No stranger to Jacksonville, she was part of the Edison troupe that filmed there during the winter of 1913/14, and was even known to have attended a "Poodle Roast" dance held at the Lubin studio to celebrate the arrival of the Edison and Kalem companies to Jacksonville, so she certainly was known to the heavily-populated-by-ex-Lubin-players troupe working at Vim. The trade papers had announced that Perez would direct himself assisted by translator Ernest Boehm, but photographic evidence appears to show that Will Louis assisted by Babe Hardy were behind the camera on at least some of these comedies.

But as quickly as Perez came to Vim he left. Arriving sometime in January 1916, Perez was gone by March, moving about six miles to the North and across the St. Johns River to the Eagle Film Company where he would successfully make a number of well-received comedies. His time at Vim was brief but Marcel Perez had begun a successful and significant career in America as a comedian and comedy film director. None of his Bungles comedies survive today, so it's unknown how good they were or weren't. That only four were made doesn't speak to their reception by the public, since Perez left Vim just as the films were being released.

Around this time the Gaumont Studio (located just across the St. Johns River) cast and crew had formed a baseball team, and wearing striped uniforms (actually leftover costumes from a prison film) won their first game decisively against a local team. They then challenged the Vim to a game, so a team was formed. Playing on March 12, the final score of 20 to 13 did not favor the Vim team, despite the pitching efforts of James Renfro and Al Ray. By an account given by Bert Tracy in the local *Florida Metropolis* newspaper the following was evident: Harry Naughton was out of shape, Joe Schrode and Walter Stull nailed the concept of chatter and Babe Hardy's imagination regarding the number of runs he scored mirrored the comedian's physical size. Tracy did say that had he, Louis Burstein and James Carleton played the outcome would have been different, although the Englishman Tracy confessed he knew nothing about baseball, illustrated by his request for a cup of tea at "half time." Joe Cohen brought along his camera and took photos of the game causing a lament as to their current where-abouts. Gaumont, then very sure of themselves and bragging in the local newspapers, challenged the Eagle Film Company to a game the next weekend. The Eagle team, with the newly acquired Marcel Perez playing third base, beat the Gaumont team so badly (27 to 3) that the Gaumont players quit before playing the final two innings.

After their loss on the baseball diamond, the Vim actors generally stuck to what they knew and that was entertaining people. Just two days after their baseball game against Gaumont, the Vimmies put on a full minstrel show for the Jacksonville Chamber of Commerce (which they would repeat for a local charity ball), and when not filming or rehearsing for a live show, many could be found singing or performing in some of the local clubs. The lineup for the March 14 minstrel show had the entire company singing an opening chorus. Billy Ruge and James McGowan performed a comedy sketch entitled "A Man and a Half." Musical selections from Bert Tracy and then Babe Hardy followed just before James Carlton gave a recitation. Mabel Best sang, and then Billy Bletcher sang and gave recitations, after which Elsie McLeod gave one. Harry Burns played the banjo and danced, Joe Cohen sang a song, Robin Williamson accompanied by his Anna Mingus on piano sang a character song and then Babe Hardy and Elsie McLeod sang a duet, Bert Tracy and Harry Burns performed a musical selection before the entire company sang a closing chorus. A standout of the show was Hardy, the *Florida Metropolis* commenting, "As we have said before, Babe Hardy has a great voice."

Burstein and company took the loss of Marcel Perez in stride, made the Plump & Runts a full time series and added Elsie McLeod into the Hardy-Ruge unit, often getting equal billing and even got the top spot in *What's Good for the Goose?* But April brought many changes to Vim. Elsie McLeod left the company to initially make films for the United States Motion Picture Co. where she was to write, direct and star in a series of films (although there is no record of her filming any of these Black Diamond comedies; documentation of that series is scant). She ended up getting work back in New York City in features supporting the likes of Viola Dana, but disappears from film altogether by 1921. Ray Godfrey (whose first name would be altered to "Rae" later in her career) arrived on April 12, replacing the just departed McLeod, and would make her first appearance in the Plump & Runt release *Sea Dogs* which was filmed the week of her arrival at Pablo Beach (a popular spot for the Vim folks during their leisure time). But the biggest change was, on or about April 15, the addition of Harry Myers and Rosemary Theby.

Myers & Theby had met while working at Lubin in 1913. Theby had started her career at Vitagraph in 1911 working in both comedies and dramas. She appears in a few John Bunny comedies, and often appeared in Maurice Costello, Clara Kimball Young or Norma Talmadge films. After working at Reliance for most of 1913, Theby ended up at the Lubin studios at the end of the year. Hired specifically to appear opposite Harry Myers, their first work together was in *A Question of Right* (released January 15, 1914).

Harry C. Myers had entered pictures in 1910 after having spent a mumber of years on the vaudeville stage in the Walter H. Stull Company among others. When Stull folded the company Myers went to work for Lubin initially in supporting roles for Florence Lawrence. But like Theby, Myers bounced from comedy to drama and from support to lead. By 1912, he was frequently cast with May Buckley and then by 1913 often with Ethel Clayton. Although he often appeared in comedies, Myers only worked a handful of times in the "Gay Time" comedy unit that was so much the genesis of the Vim stock company. He appeared only once at Lubin, in 1911's *Love's Labor Lost*, with his former boss and future fellow Vimmie Walter Stull.

The Myers-Theby films were popular, so much so that the pair, along with their chief support Binsley Shaw, left Lubin to star in a series of films (both dramas and comedies) for the Victor Comedy Company in late 1914. Myers, who had directed some of their Lubin films not only directed all of the Victors but was also responsible for the set design, something he continued at Vim with surreal result.

It was at Universal (parent company of the Victor brand) that Myers & Theby first worked with Mark Dintenfass, who was responsible for signing them to Vim (and this signing might best explain Dintenfass' joining Vim himself). A number of the Victor Myers-Theby titles ended up being released well after their move to Vim and some were in concurrent release with the Vim films. Even though they didn't work directly with many of the Vim players, they all knew each other and so it was no surprise that Walter Stull, Bobby Burns, Babe Hardy, Billy Ruge and Elsie McLeod joined Louis Burstein at the train station to welcome the pair to Florida. It should be noted that while Myers & Theby often played a married couple on screen they were not at this time married. They acted off-screen as if they were, but Myers had a wife and children back home in Philadelphia. It wouldn't be until 1928 that the two were married in California.

Vim was operating pretty much as an independently owned subsidiary of the Melies Manufacturing Company but around this time Melies sold their rights to the Eastern Film Corporation of Providence, Rhode Island. Started in 1915 by millionaire Frederick S. Peck, he apparently had more cents than sense. Dozens of films were shot over the next two years starring the likes of Dan Mason and George

Bunny, given the brand name of Pelican Comedies, yet none were released. When Frank Tichenor took over the managing of the studio the idea of not only producing but presenting films was put into action, and the purchase of the Melies slots on the General Film Service schedule was the first move. This resulted in Eastern being a bit more directly involved in the operation of Vim, first by controlling the cash flow to Vim and eventually by taking over operation control of the productions.

With three units now in full production, the Vim studio was really hitting its stride, and the rest of the Spring and early Summer was uneventful. There had been talk of moving up North during the Summer months but plans to send the entire operation north in June were dropped.

At the start of 1916 nearly a dozen film studios were in operation in Duval County many with numerous production units working. Thanhouser moved North for the Summer as did many other studios, beating the heat of the deep South. Eventually Vim reversed its decision and ended up sending just the Myers-Theby unit up to Providence, Rhode Island. This was the first operational indicator that the Eastern Film Corporation was now involved with Vim. While the Jacksonville studio continued to be under the direction of Louis Burstein with the occasional visit by Mark Dintenfass, filming in Providence was directly supervised by Frank Tichenor of Eastern.

Added to the players working with the Theby-Myers unit were William Chamberlain, Jennie Nelson and an old friend of Burns & Stull, George Reehm. It is unclear what films Reehm made for Vim (with *The Chalk Line* being the only known credit) or whether he went with the unit back down to Jacksonville, thus being reunited with his former comedy partners. It is known that the three (Reehm, Chamberlain and Nelson) would in 1919 make up the core of the Peerless Film Players, a group that would travel the South putting on a vaudeville show and also filming a story using local talent to augment their company, then selling the film to the locals.

Even though Robin Williamson, Anna Mingus and Ray Godfrey had left Vim for Hollywood, early September 1916 found Jacksonville film production as busy as it had even been, and would ever be. Eagle Film Company was gearing up production on its Tweedledum series and built a new indoor studio in the Arlington area of Jacksonville. Richard Garrick, who had been studio manager for Gaumont, took over the Gaumont lot (located in the old Dixieland amusement park) when that company left for good, and opened a studio rental facility aptly called the Garrick Studios.

The Regent Photo Film Trust, headed by Walter Shumway and Walter Richard Stahl, a new outfit out of Cleveland, Ohio was Garrick's first tenant (although not starting production umtil December). Shumway was married to actress Corra Beach and she starred in one of the few Regent products to actually be released, *What Becomes of the Children?* Prior to Regent, Stahl had been a writer on the Casey Comedies made in Cleveland that starred Johnny and Emma Ray (who would shoot in Jacksonville much of 1916 for another company) and filled the director's chair at Regent. Other companies would follow the Regent company to the Garrick lot, making it for a brief time a very busy place.

The Vim lot was running at full speed, and yet there were changes. Feeling that the Plump & Runt comedies had run their course, Burstein and Dintenfass brought in Kate Price and Raymond McKee to start a new series of films with Babe Hardy. Price, being a rather large person, was to be a female equivalent of Hardy while

McKee would be a younger, more attractive and more talented replacement for Billy Ruge. For the remainder of his time at Vim, Ruge would bounce from working in the "Babe Hardy unit" or back in his old role as support for Pokes & Jabbs.

Kate Price was a well known and much liked comedy star. Beginning at Vitagraph in 1910 she often played in support of John Bunny and Hughie Mack when not taking the lead role herself (*Office Kate* and *Cabman Kate.*) in the comedies produced at the studio. Price was highly prolific and can be seen in most of the Vitagraph dramas produced in the early teens usually playing supporting character roles. Her last role before coming to Vim was also her only appearance ever in a Keystone comedy: *The Waiter's Ball*, which starred Roscoe Arbuckle.

Raymond McKee started in film in 1912 working in the Lubin "Gay Time" comedies alongside Walter Stull and Bobby Burns amongst others. By 1914 McKee often worked with Babe Hardy (he appears in Hardy's debut film *Outwitting Dad*), and like Hardy lost his job at Lubin in 1915 when the comedy unit was restructured around the hiring of Billie Reeves. Both McKee and Hardy traveled north to New York City and both found work with the Edison studio working most often with future Vim director Will Louis. McKee ended working in only two films while at Vim (*A Maid to Order* and *Twin Flats*) and was announced for a third (*A Warm Reception*) before leaving Florida and returning to work at Edison in New York City. It seems that McKee's mother was hoping for a Florida vacation and McKee accommodated her by obtaining work in the Sunshine State. When Mom was ready to go home, McKee quit.

The last days of October and the beginning of November brought the lull before the storm that would hit Vim. The first reference to Amber Star, a subsidiary that Eastern Film established to run Vim, made the trade papers on October 28, noting that there would be no changes in the operation of Vim. Initially incorporated in Rhode Island, the Amber Star Films Corporation had its first meeting on August 11, 1916 with Herbert S. Tillinghast elected President. One week later, he was out and Mark Dintenfass became the President while Louis Burstein served as a director of the corporation.

Ethel Burton was one of the nominees for the top honor in the "Queen of Fall" festival held in town, and after a lengthy newspaper campaign and vote beat out four other local lovelies and was crowned Queen, her award being a $250 diamond ring, 10 pounds of chocolate, a bouquet of roses, perfume, fancy stationery and a set of photographs. On November 2, it was announced that a Screen Club was being formed for the purposes of giving the movie folks a place to socialize and also to provide additional entertainment to the community. This would be a companion to the already-in-operation Cinema Club which catered to behind-the-camera personnel. Storm Boyd, Louis Burstein and Harry Myers were officers in the new organization and big plans (few of which were ultimately realized) were made.

But then things turned for the worse. The "Raymond McKee and Mom" fiasco was the first in a flurry of negative activity that ultimately would result in the end of Vim. In early November, Harry Myers, who had gone North in August to film in Providence, found working directly under Frank Tichenor intolerable and packed up the Myers-Theby unit, left Providence, and returned to Jacksonville. His displeasure with the arrangements up north did not go unnoticed in the moving picture trade papers.

Bert Tracy's take on the Vim people.

What happened next may never be fully understood or explained. Supposedly Babe Hardy found discrepancies in how the payroll funds were being handled by Louis Burstein, leading to an audit of Vim's finances. An article in the November 7

Florida Times-Union entitled "Old Vim Film Concern Bawled Up In Finances" explained that "While Mr. Tichenor did not go into details as to the company's affairs, he declared that the shortages were thought to have been caused by padding of the payrolls and redating of old accounts held against the Vim Company by local concerns." The article also noted that the large shortage of funds was being traced by "expert auditors." It was mentioned that Amber Star had leased space at the Garrick Studios and much of the Vim cast and crew had moved to that facility the previous day. Mark Dintenfass, Walter Stull, Bobby Burns, Frank Hanson and Billy Ruge were amongst those to leave Vim (Will Louis would follow the next week). Remaining at Vim would be Harry Myers, Rosemary Theby, Kate Price, Babe Hardy, Ethel Burton, Harry Naughton, Florence McLoughlin, Bert Tracy, Joe Cohen and Jerold T. Hevener (who had just joined the company).

Hardy's remaining with the Burstein-controlled Vim would seem to indicate that if he did find discrepancies, he didn't find Burstein at fault. Ethel Burton's remaining at Vim ended her long tenure as chief support for the antics of Pokes & Jabbs, and was perhaps the most surprising of the choices when sides were being taken. Burton had briefly considered the move over to Amber Star but reconsidered and stayed with what was left of Vim, her strong friendship with Babe Hardy likely to have influenced her decision.

The day before the newspaper broke the story, new Articles of Incorporation were filed with the State of Florida for Amber Star; the day after the story, incorporation documents were issued for the company. The rift among those that had been working at 750 Riverside Avenue would be a permanent one. Apparently Louis Burstein still controlled the studio itself and the release schedule for Vim, while Amber Star continued to have the financial backing of the parent Eastern Film Corporation. Burstein did go to New York City around this time, either to conduct legitimate business (Vim announced they had signed Leah Baird although that never was realized) or just to get out of town.

While the executives went about taking legal action, the players went back to work. Vim brought in Herman Keepers to be the new cameraman for the Myers-Theby comedies, and Herman Obrock was added to do the same for the Babe Hardy unit. A new stage was completed on the Vim lot (probably intended for the aborted Leah Baird company), and additional players were hired including Tom Murray and his wife Louise Carver who had been working over at Eagle. Kate Price and Babe Hardy, usually with Ethel Burton, stayed busy shooting comedies under Babe Hardy's direction. Harry Myers took advantage of the new set on the lot and built even bigger surreal sets for the comedies he was directing and appearing in with Rosemary Theby, now ably assisted by Jerold Hevener.

Over at Amber Star, the cameras rolled on November 9 with a new Pokes & Jabbs comedy the objective; the first few of these Amber Star-produced Pokes & Jabbs were released under the Vim banner. The following week, the newest addition to Amber Star, Will Louis, started shooting a comedy with Billy Ruge and Spook Hanson in the cast. Working at Amber Star proved to be quite different than at Vim. While the studio lot at 750 Riverside Avenue was Vim's alone, the Garrick Studios that housed Amber Star also rented space to Regent, Anchor, Klever Comedies and other production companies.

On November 15, Frank Tichenor swore out an arrest warrant for Louis Burstein which was announced in the local papers. Indicators were that Louis Burstein was the bad guy in the unfolding drama until Mark Dintenfass, at the time President and board member of Amber Star, asked to look at the accounts books himself. Tichenor quickly denied him access, accused him of being party to the alleged misdeeds by Burstein and moved to remove Dintenfass from the board (he was removed from the presidency on December 6, 1916 and the board altogether on the 14th of the same month), giving some strong indicators as to who may have really been at fault in the rift.

Dintenfass filed suit against Amber Star and eventually won, although his access was limited to only some of the business records "except certain payroll books contained in a safe to which the respondents (Tichenor et al) did not have the key." This was likely the same evidence, or lack thereof, that started the whole mess. The case Dintenfass v. Amber Star Films Corp. was eventually argued before the Supreme Court with the rights of a director of a corporation to view the accounting of said corporation at issue (it is still used today as a case study for similar litigation). But while that was being settled, Dintenfass was out of a job since making his initial alliance with Tichenor over Burstein ended any cordial business he might ever have with Louis Burstein, and any hope of returning to Vim. The lack of cordiality between Dintenfass and Burstein would continue when latter sued the former in July 1918. A ship carrying Vim films to Europe was attached by a German submarine. The films were thought to have been lost, but Dintenfass knew otherwise, exhibited the films in Europe and pocketed the proceeds which should have been jointly shared with Burstein. No honor among thieves, or film executives apparently.

In the midst of all the turmoil caused by studio executives the film players in Jacksonville kept their comradery at the forefront. On November 17 Vimmies, ex-Vimmies as well as actors from the other companies in town formed a Screen Club. Seems the arrest warrant for Louis Burstein could have easily been served to him at the Hotel Mason where that night he was elected First Vice President of the new Jacksonville Screen Club. Not to be outdone the technicians from the various film companies under the leadership of cameramen Harry Keepers and Herman Obrock formed a Cinema Club for their ilk on November 28, and appropriate to their station the Cinema Club meeting was held down at the local motion picture exchange rather than at one of them fancy downtown hotels.

By the end of November things seemed to calm down. Amber Star added Lucille Taft and Roland Hill to their roster, both to work with the Will Louis company. A big vaudeville show featuring the players from various studios was held at the Armory on November 27 to a full house and rave reviews. Babe Hardy and Ethel Burton did an act, and Bert Tracy, Tom Murray and Florence McLoughlin also were on stage representing Vim, while Billy Ruge, Spook Hanson and others appeared on behalf of Amber Star.

Some of the disfunction started to become evident in the trades when published release schedules featured "title to be announced later" notices rather than the forthcoming film's title. In one case, the *Moving Picture World* even lists an erroneous title, "Have You Heard About Little?" as a December 1st release. It was announced in early December that Raymond McKee would again be joining Vim, an event that never happened. Apparently the senior Mrs. McKee didn't need another vacation after all. However, there was one more move made: Kate Price defected to Amber

Star. Tichenor quickly teamed her with Billy Ruge and initially, due to their size difference, called the new Price and Ruge series by a familiar name: Plump & Runt. One of the first of the Price and Ruge collaborations was released as a Vim (*Bad Kate*), the rest had to wait for Vim to die altogether and Amber Star to rebrand itself as Jaxon before any other were released.

Babe Hardy continued to make comedies on Vim lot sans Kate Price for a few weeks until it was announced around Christmas that the Vim companies would be shutting down for about two weeks to allow the hard working cast and crew a respite. In reality Louis Burstein, who was in New York City at the time, was having difficulty finding new financing for what was left of Vim while at the same time dealing with legal issues with the Eastern Film Corporation. A Christmas greeting published in the *Florida Metropolis* provides a list of the what would be the last cadre of Vim players: Rosemary Theby, Harry Myers, Tom Murray, Louise Carver, Harry Keepers, Florence McLoughlin, Joe Cohen, Jerold T. Hevener, Babe Hardy, Louis Burstein, Harry Naughton, Jack Rose, and Bert Tracy. Many of the company took the opportunity to go North for the holidays and it was left to Babe Hardy to answer any questions brought up locally about the future of Vim. Assured by Burstein that a reopening of the studio was imminent, Hardy passed along that hope and waited. In the meantime, to keep the brand alive Burstein made sure that the Vim slots in the General Film Company schedule were filled into the early months of 1917 using Vim films already in the can, inexplicably some Amber Star productions, and leftover unreleased films bought from various film exchanges. After a few hopeful but eventually false announcements about reopening, the Vim Films Corporation ceased to exist.

VIM COMEDY COMPANY. Bottom row, left to right: BERT TRACY, ROY GAHRIS, HARRY NAUGHTON. Second row: WILL LOUIS, FERNANDEZ PEREZ (BUNGLES), EDWARD McWADE, LOUIS BURSTEIN, BABE HARDY, BILLY RUGE, BOBBY BURNS, WALTER STULL.

Moving Picture World omitted the names of those in the back rows. Third row: Helen Gilmore, Anna Mingus, Elsie McLeod, Ethel Burton, unid., Mildred Burstein, Florence McLoughlin and Edna Reynolds. Frank Hanson, Joe Cohen and Billy Bletcher can be seen among the others.

POKES & JABBS COMEDIES

The Midnight Prowlers

Released November 12, 1915. Vim Comedies - General Film Company release. One reel. No copyright registered. Release number 19439.

Produced by Louis Burstein. Directed by Bobby Burns and Walter Stull. Filmed circa August 1915 as a Wizard Comedy in New York City.

with Bobby Burns (*Loos Pokes*), Walter Stull (*Jabbs*), Ethel Burton (*female detective*), Edna Reynolds (*Mrs. Jabbs*), Spook Hanson, Billy Ruge, Babe Hardy [?].

Mr. and Mrs. Jabbs live in a suburban retreat where the police force is conspicuous by its absence. Burglaries are rife in the neighborhood. The Jabbs family get the scare of their lives one night when the cat pulls a vase from the table in trying to get out of the house for a midnight prowl. A detective must get hired is the secret resolve of both Mr. and Mrs. Jabbs and forth with they proceed to hire one. But one does not inform the other which results in Mrs. Jabbs hiring a male sleuth in the person of Loos Pokes and Mr. Jabbs hiring a female Sherlock Holmes. The two sleuths are unaware of each other's identity and there the trouble begins. Gum Shoe Peter, the cracksman, gets into the house. Mr. and Mrs. Jabbs hear the noise but think it is "only the detectives." Meanwhile the two detectives have met and are spooning in the

moonlight (they should worry about burglars). While Pete is pilling his booty in his sack, and by unlucky chance, he stumbles and the pack falls, burying him. The detectives hear the noise. So do Mr. and Mrs. Jabbs. All four appear on the scene. The female sleuth grabs Mrs. Jabbs and the male sleuth grabs Mr. Jabbs and start for the station house. But explanations follow and just as the real crook is discovered and all ends as it should. [MPW]

The Midnight Prowlers was mentioned in a September 11, 1915 *Moving Picture World* article as the next Pokes and Jabs to be released by Wizard. It seems there were quite a few Pokes and Jabs filmed at Wizard yet withheld from release until Vim came along (*A Pair of Birds* and *Speed Kings* also being Wizard vintage). Complete cast lists for the Vims (or most any silent shorts) are not usually found, and the extant portion of this film is incomplete, so the inclusion of Babe Hardy in the cast cannot be verified.

"This single reel offering is up to their [Burns and Stull] usual amusing style, and though the story is slight there is enough of it to carry the picture along to a good amusing climax. The picture has been well staged and directed, and should form a welcome addition to the programme on which it is released." -- *New York Dramatic Mirror*

A Pair of Birds

Released November 19, 1915. Vim Comedies - General Film Company release. One reel. No copyright registered. Release number 19501.

Produced by Louis Burstein. Directed by Bobby Burns and Walter Stull. Filmed August 1915 as a Wizard Comedy in New York City, and at Palisades Park near Fort Lee, New Jersey.

with Bobby Burns (*Pokes*), Billy Ruge (*Runt*), Edna Reynolds (*woman on street*), Harry Naughton (*prison guard*), Pearl Shepard (*girl at amusement park*), Ethel Burton (*girl at amusement park*), Joe Cohen (*man hit by ice cream*), Helen Von Huben, and Betty Holton.

Pokes and Runt are in jail. Tired of the lockstep and hard labor, they try many times to escape, but meet with little success. Their latest trial — the rubbish route — lands them back where they started from when Runt gets a bright idea. With the aid of a burlap bag, they scale the walls and make their get-a-way. Fatty is taking a stroll by the river and, the day being hot, he decides to take a swim. He does so and hides his clothes under a tree. Pokes and Runt pass this spot and, seeing Fatty's suit, decide that "one suit will do in a pinch for two." Fatty finishes his swim and returns for his clothes. By this time guards have discovered the escape and are in hot pursuit of anything wearing stripes. They see an object among the underbrush and fire at it, chase it for some distance, but upon catching it find that it is not their quarry, but Fatty in a suit of striped B. V. D.'s searching for his clothes. Meanwhile Pokes and Runt have met a couple of fair charmers and, with the money they find in Fatty's suit, they are having a fine time. They go to the summer amusement park and try all the amusements. The guards, still in pursuit, also spy a couple of vivacious chickens and also seek the amusement park. When they see the guards, Pokes and Runt run for all their lives. After many mishaps and a watery plunge they surrender to the guards and are once more happy to receive the protection of the striped suits and stone walls and glad to return to the task of making little ones out of big ones. [MPW]

The absence of any mention of the character "Jabbs" in the studio supplied synopsis makes clear that, as with the Wizard comedy *In Clover*, Walter Stull is missing in action. The reviewer for the *Motion Picture News* was apparently not familiar enough with series to know the difference between Stull and Ruge. It is interesting to note this is the first time that Ruge's character is referred to as "Runt", and it is Ruge playing "Runt" and not Frank "Spook" Hanson as some of the early Vim publicity states. The reference to "Fatty" which was Babe Hardy's character's name briefly (before they settled on "Plump") made it appear that this film might also include Hardy. However, a print of the film exists and upon viewing reveals that another large comedian (his name unknown) played the part of "Fatty."

The Third Degree, "House of Fun and Gaity", a main attraction at Palisades Park during its early days is seen to good effect in the film as are a number of the various vendors that populated the famous amusement park. Also seen at the end of the film is the Hudson River the obstacle that necessitated a ferry ride from New York City, a service still available today.

"There's a new brand of comedies out—'Vim' is the title—and they star those two inimitable comedians, Pokes and Jabs, who were formerly on the World Film Comedy Star program. The first one is at the Grand today, entitled, *A Pair of Birds*, and it's simply a scream from beginning to end. Don't miss it." -- *Wilmington Morning Star*

"Pokes and Jabbs, garbed in prison stripes, break from the lockstep line, and after several humorous experiences, make their escape from prison, They encounter an especially heavy man who has left his clothes on the bank while he bathes in the river, and they find his suit large enough to envelop them both. As one man they visit the fair, and when pursued by police, manage not only to dive off the pier, but to bring the pursuers into the water after them. Burns, Stull and Ethel Burton are in the cast." -- *Motion Picture News*

Pressing Business

Released November 26, 1915. Vim Comedies - General Film Company release. One reel. No copyright registered. Release number 19559.

Produced by Louis Burstein. Directed by Bobby Burns and Walter Stull. Filmed in Bayonne, New Jersey.

With Bobby Burns (*Pokes*), Walter Stull (*Jabbs*), Billy Ruge (*bellboy*), Billy Bletcher (*desk clerk*), Spook Hanson (*man with gout*), Ethel Burton (*party attendee*), Edna Reynolds (*hotel guest*), Clay Grant.

Plaid Jabbs is quite a fellow among the ladies. Arriving at the hotel at Pumpkinville he finds an invitation awaiting him from his friend, Billy Bean, to attend an afternoon tea given by Bean's sister. Jabbs is long on nerve but short on wardrobe, having only one suit of clothes to his name. It sadly needs pressing. He sends the suit to the tailor to get it pressed. Awful to relate, the tailor's shop burns down while his suit is there. Jabbs has just learned his awful predicament when Loos Pokes, a modern Raffles, enters the rear window of the hotel and makes his way to the very room occupied by the unfortunate Jabbs. Jabbs hides at the approach of the stranger but when he notices the intruder has on just the clothes that he needs and being about the same size as himself, Jabbs pounces upon him, holds him up, relieves him of the dress suit and dashes off for the afternoon tea, leaving Pokes in his room rather negligee. Pokes must get out; but how? He stealthily skulks along the hallway and after entering various rooms much to his discomfort and that of the guests, he makes his get-a-way down the fire escape with the whole crowd at his heels. The police also join the chase. Jabbs returning from the tea meets Pokes at a watering trough. A struggle for possession of the suit takes place. Pokes gets back his suit. The police arrive and Jabbs is compelled to take refuge in the water trough much to the amusement of all assembled. [MPW]

Walter Stull is the center of the action in the first third of the film. When Bobby Burns finally appears he takes the lead for the rest of the film being the one everyone is after during a big chase thought the hotel halls, up and down stairways then eventually outside. Ethel Burton appears in the film just ever so briefly in the party scene with a group of other young ladies and then later as one of the two ladies walking with Stull after leaving the party. The reviewer in the *Idaho Statesman* mentions that the other film on the bill (Maurice Costello's *Saints and Sinners*) was "a serious film but *Pressing Business* makes up for any lack of comedy in the other photoplay, it is so full of laughs." One of the quirky little oddities that seem to be frequent occurrences when they would publicize a film back in those days: The studio-supplied synopsis mentions Billy Bean as Jabbs' friend whereas in the film the invitation sent to Jabbs is signed Percy Long.

"A generous supply of knockabout comedy will be found in this one reel farce. The producer kept everyone moving to quick time, and each individual of the cast seem to enjoy their work. That seemed to be a trademark of the Vim Comedies, their high energy and constant movement, their 'vim'." -- *Moving Picture World*

Love, Pepper And Sweets

Released December 3, 1915. Vim Comedies - General Film Company release. One reel. No copyright registered. Release number 19621.

Produced by Louis Burstein. Directed by Bobby Burns and Walter Stull. Filmed in Bayonne, New Jersey.

with Bobby Burns (*Pokes*), Walter Stull (*Jabbs*), Billy Ruge (*Runt*), Ethel Burton (*Ethel*), Babe Hardy, Spook Hanson, Edna Reynolds.

Jabbs is the star boarder and favorite of Betty, the landlady, while Pokes and Runt – two other boarders – always suffer the worst end of things. After a very scant breakfast Pokes and Jabbs take a walk through the park when Ethel – some queen! – attracts their attention. An acquaintance is soon formed, but, as usual, Jabbs spoils their happiness by passing along and taking Ethel away. She invites Jabbs into her house and he accepts the invitation. The indignant Pokes and Runt, who have been following, decide to bombard the house. Their bombardment is unsuccessful, however, and the two conspirators are treated to a bath of milk and milk bottles for their pains. Jabbs decides to play a joke on them and has Ethel invite them to call upon her that afternoon at the same hour ; but neither knows that the other has been

invited. Overjoyed, they prepare for the call — one with candy and the other with a bouquet of flowers. Jabbs prepares to receive them. The result of his preparations are that the candy and flowers are smeared with pepper, which is the cause of Ethel's fainting. Jabbs, disguised as her father, follows them with a pistol and their affections are cooled by a refreshing ducking in the lake. Oh, you can't get ahead of a star boarder! [MPW]

Perhaps Burns & Stull were missing their old friend George Reehm. They revert to working as a trio since Billy Ruge is given near equal status in this and a number of the other early Vim Pokes and Jabbs entries. *Moving Picture World* noted the trio: "This Vim release of December 3 promises to be particularly funny, as this is the first Vim release in which the three comedians—Pokes, Jabbs and Runt—all work together. Pokes is the star boarder, while Jabbs and Runt are the neglected ones. Even in the matter of love Pokes has the best of them, while Jabbs and Runt are the "also rans." The efforts of Jabbs and Runt to beat out Pokes furnish the plot, but they find their task is a Herculean one." The abilities of Ruge, along with Louis Burstein's previously known admiration for Babe Hardy's work, would lead Burstein to soon start another comedy company. So, after a brief detour Pokes and Jabbs would remain a comedy duo, and not the trio that the addition of Ruge would have made.

"Jabbs, Pokes and Runt enter a race for love of the same girl, in this one reel comedy, and punch, slap and kick each other, after the highest style of the art known to the demonstrators of their strenuous and broadly comic school of fun." -- *Motion Picture World*

Strangled Harmony

Released December 10, 1915. Vim Comedies - General Film Company release. One reel. No copyright registered. Release number 19675.

Produced by Louis Burstein. Directed by Bobby Burns and Walter Stull. Filmed in Bayonne, New Jersey.

with Bobby Burns (*Pokes*), Walter Stull (*Jabbs*), Billy Ruge (*Runt*), Ethel Burton (*Ethel*), Babe Hardy, Spook Hanson, Edna Reynolds.

Ethel a penniless orphan upon the death of her father, goes to her Uncle Greedy Grab's home to live. With her is a note from the attorneys telling the Uncle "she has music born in her," but the only music to Grab's ear is the jingle of coin in his pocket. So Ethel becomes the household drudge. Jabbs, the handsome stranger, happens to pass that way, and, seeing Ethel, falls in love with her. Having plenty of money he is acceptable to Uncle Grab, but not to Ethel, whose soul is full of music. Pokes, the fiddler, is the apple of her eye. Pokes sees that he can never hope to win out without coin, so when Mr. Rich offers to buy his fiddle for $1,000 Pokes doesn't let the grass grow under his feet but consummates the bargain then and there. Returning to Ethel with a bunch of greenbacks, she tells him she ceases to love him without his fiddle. Pokes starts out to recover it. Meanwhile Jabbs wins Ethel's hand and Pokes returns with the fiddle only to find Ethel married to Jabbs. Pokes dreams of the happiness he *has missed; but he doesn't know that Jabbs is Ethel's henpecked husband, the father of ten children, all with music born in them and their mother trying to bring it out – while Jabbs labors over the wash tub. Pokes doesn't realize that it is sometimes better we do not get what we strive for the most, for Ethel improves her mind by reading novels and the children make father's life miserable improving their musical education.* [MPW]

It should be noted that although these films are listed as being produced in Bayonne, New Jersey, the film companies who had their studios on the Jersey side would often take their crews into New York City, across to Brooklyn and even up to Yonkers for filming.

"The efforts of Pokes and Jabbs to win the love of pretty Ethel Burton will cause many a laugh and the troubles of Mr. Jabbs, who finally wins, are just as funny to an audience as they are serious to Mr. Jabbs." -- *San Bernardino News (San Bernardino, California)*

"The strenuous action that has erstwhile marked as Pokes and Jabbs is somewhat modified in this one reel farce. Perhaps the notes of music from Pokes' violin may have had something to do with it, that gentleman having taken to horsehair and cat gut. However, the spirit of fun in the picture has by no means been strangled and the grotesque capers of the comedians are as amusing as ever." -- *Moving Picture World*

Speed Kings

Released December 17, 1915. Vim Comedies - General Film Company release. One reel. No copyright registered. Release number 19733.

Produced by Louis Burstein. Directed by Bobby Burns and Walter Stull. Filmed early August 1915 as a Wizard Comedy in New York City and on the streets of Yonkers.

with Bobby Burns (*Pokes*), Walter Stull (*Jabbs*), Billy Ruge, Ethel Burton, Spook Hanson, Edna Reynolds.

Pokes and Jabbs are golf enthusiasts. While playing one day, Pokes makes a phenomenally long drive and loses the ball. Willie Slim and his sweetheart are out in Willie's flivver; and while Pokes is in the middle of the road hunting the ball, Willie's car runs him down. Jabbs appears on the scene and demands reparation for Pokes but Willie, having no excess funds and fearing prosecution, squares himself by giving Pokes and Jabbs the auto. The time they have learning to run the auto is something terrible but at length they do succeed and the auto fever is upon them. Jabbs trades in a flivver for a real car and he and his friend Pokes go for a ride. Trouble overtakes them whey they are held up by two auto bandits, robbed of all their money and their car. They apply to a farmer for permission to work for a meal. He thinks

they are two bandits who have been prowling about the neighborhood so humors them along until the sheriff comes upon the scene and arrests them. Meanwhile the bandits have driven the car to a saloon to get a supply of drinks for a long trip. Mrs. Pokes and Mrs. Jabbs pass the saloon and recognize the car. They think their husbands are drinking again so they get in the car to wait. The bandits try to oust them which results in the arrest of the real bandits. Pokes and Jabbs are freed and the picture fades out with a happy reunion. [MPW]

The last of the filmed-as-a-Wizard-but-released-as-a-Vim comedies. Burns & Stull reportedly got on the bad side of the real Yonkers police when filming this comedy and were given a ticket for excessive speed.

"*Speed Kings* is the story of a couple of men –Pokes and Jabbs—who receive an automobile in payment for a debt and proceed to get the speed fever. The picture is marked by the explosion of an automobile which is said to be a most realistic bit of photography." -- *Motion Picture News*

Mixed And Fixed

Released December 24, 1915. Vim Comedies - General Film Company release. One reel. No copyright registered. Release number 19770.

Produced by Louis Burstein. Directed by Bobby Burns and Walter Stull. Filmed November 1915 at the former Lubin Studios in Jacksonville, Florida.

with Bobby Burns (*Pokes*), Walter Stull (*Jabbs*), Billy Ruge, Ethel Burton, Babe Hardy, Spook Hanson, Edna Reynolds.

Pokes and Jabbs are still living in the same apartments and are on friendly terms as usual. On her birthday, Jabbs presents the Mrs. with a pearl necklace. Pearls are an ill omen and bring tears and this case was no exception. Mrs. Jabbs, about to go upon an errand for her husband, meets Mr. Pokes in the hallway, and while examining the new necklace is seen through the keyhole by Mr. Jabbs. Trouble is at once started. Mrs. Pokes, also peeping through the keyhole, sees what she thinks is her husband with Mrs. Jabbs held in tender embrace. More trouble. Mrs. Pokes and Mr. Jabbs seize the things handiest and start for the hallway, but Mr. Pokes and Mrs. Jabbs have gone and they pounce upon a poor, unsuspecting lodger from the upper floor. Pokes telephones to Jabbs to meet him. Jabbs seizes the opportunity of his wife's absence and does so. Over a friendly drink in the saloon, they are presented with a ticket for a mask ball. Meanwhile, Mrs. Pokes, who is a member of the society giving the ball, has invited Mrs. Jabbs to attend as her escort. Mrs. Pokes, in Jabbs' clothes, starts out with Mrs. Jabbs. Pokes and Jabbs return home and Jabbs, disguising himself as a woman, joins Pokes and they leave for the ball. Numerous events take place when the two couples come face to face in the saloon. Mr. Pokes is anxious to get Jabbs away so that he will not see his wife with another man and Mrs. Jabbs is anxious to get Mrs. Pokes away so that she will not see her husband with another woman. After a trying ordeal they do so, and return home. Mistaking each other for intruders, a lively chase ensues, which is ended in the hallway by Jabbs losing his skirt and Mrs. Pokes almost losing her trousers. Things are explained and all is forgotten. [MPW]

This was the first film shot by Vim in Jacksonville. Burstein leased the old Lubin studio at 750 Riverside Avenue where the "Gay Times" comedies with Mae Hotely had been shot until February 13, 1915 (and after a brief pause, where the Billie Reeves comedies, with virtually a whole new company of actors, were made until the studio closed in mid-May 1915). For many Vimmies, including Walter Stull, Bobby Burns, Babe Hardy and later Will Louis, it was a homecoming for the former Lubin players.

"A masked ball in which none of the characters in this one reel farce arrive, although they make great preparations to that end, is the 'cause of the trouble' in this knockabout comic. Messrs. Pokes and Jabs and the rest of the cast, see to it that the photoplay does not belie its title or the name of the brand." -- *Moving Picture World*

Ups And Downs

Released December 31, 1915. Vim Comedies - General Film Company release. One reel. No copyright registered. Release number 19805.

Produced by Louis Burstein. Directed by Bobby Burns and Walter Stull. Filmed in Riverside Park and the Vim Studios in Jacksonville, Florida.

With Bobby Burns (*Pokes*), Walter Stull (*Jabbs*), Babe Hardy (*Shifty Mike*), Ethel Burton (*Ethel*), Spook Hanson (*Runt*), Edna Reynolds (*washer woman*), Billy Ruge (*butler*), Harry Naughton (*job applicant*).

Plaid Jabbs has lots of money and a beautiful daughter. While out in the park one day feeding the ducks, the beautiful daughter, Ethel, is accosted by Shifty Mike, who has endeavors to carress her and impress a kiss upon her lips. Jabbs, nearby, hears her scream and hurried to the rescue. Administering a sound thrashing to Shifty Mike, he kicks them away. Buft Shifty Mike is not so easily gotten rid of. He immediately summons his two assistants and with orders to them to repair to their rendezvous, he proceeds to follow Jabbs home. Pokes is Ethel's favorite and arrives upon the scene shortly after Jabbs leaves. Ethel, forgetting her troubles, reposes comfortably in the arms of her sweetheart. Marriage is the question, but Pokes is broke and Ethel informs him work he must get. So he starts out to hunt it. The confederates about this time have finished their task of getting ready a warm reception for Jabbs. Shifty arrives, but a brave man is needed to put their scheme into execution. A poster card is written and placed upon the front of their residence. Numerous applicants arrive and last of all, Pokes who, upon seeing the sign "Little work and big pay," immediately applies. As we might expect, Pokes is the successful applicant, and with Shifty's two assistants as watchers, he starts out to perform his task. Numerous obstacles present themselves, which are finally overcome. Arriving at the side of Jabbs' residence, Pokes throws the missile through the window. It travels some distance and is handled by various people when it arrives back at Pokes' feet, it explodes. In his journey up and down he passes through a room full of card players and the sides of a house, only to fall back into the very room where Jabbs is sitting, unhurt. Shifty, during this time, has captured Ethel upon the street, while she was walking with a friend. Pokes and Jabbs rough it up a bit, and Jabbs tosses Pokes through the open window. Unconsciously, but just in time, Pokes knocks Shifty head first into a rail barrel and rescues his sweetheart Ethel, proving "it is indeed an ill wind that blows nobody good." [MPW]

In his attempt to deliver the bomb, Pokes throws it in the window of the house only to have various people pass it along until, back in Pokes' hand, it explodes. He is catapulted to the roof, crashing down through each floor and into Jabbs' room where he is beaten, hence the title *Ups and Downs*.

This is one of Babe Hardy's first appearances as a villain with bushy mustache and heavy brows similar to those of Eric Campbell, the memorable villain in Charlie Chaplin's Mutual comedies. Although purported to be a common role during Babe's Lubin days, he more often played a cop, foreman or cowboy in those films. Looking at his solo career in total, Babe rarely played a melodramatic villain. But he certainly is one in this film, complete with two anarchist henchmen who appear and disappear at Babe's command.

Chickens was originally announced for this release date but was postponed and *Ups and Downs* released in its place. A still from the film with Ethel Burton's handwriting on the reverse notes that the film was made in New York City. However, upon viewing the film it obviously was shot in and around Riverside Park in Jacksonville, Florida (palm trees being the most obvious clue).

"*Ups and Downs* is another one of those Vim comedies, featuring Burns and Stull as Pokes and Jabs. A very thrilling and funny situation in the picture is where Pokes gets blown up with a 'bomb' intended for Jabs, and in his trip up and down he is blown through a room full of card players and the side of a house only to fall back in the very room where Jabs is sitting unhurt. This is a comedy that will bring laughs." *–San Bernadino Daily Sun (San Bernardino, California)*

This Way Out

Released January 7, 1916. Vim Comedies - General Film Company release. One reel. No copyright registered. Release number 19842.

Produced by Louis Burstein. Directed by Bobby Burns and Walter Stull.

with Bobby Burns (*Pokes*), Walter Stull (*Jabbs*), Babe Hardy (*Plump*), Billy Ruge (*Runt*), Ethel Burton, Spook Hanson, Helen Gilmore.

Hotel men have their troubles and the Eagle Hotel is no exception. All the help have quit and the place is in pandemonium. Something must be done and quick. The clerk rushes out. Plump & Runt are plying their trade, street cleaning. The clerk rushes out, sees them, brings them into the hotel and presses them into service as porter and bellboy. Baths are being rung for and ice water, too. The new crew starts to work and after administering a bath to the cranky old grouch who had been ringing for an hour for ice water and eating part of the cake that the waitress had baked for her sweetheart, the clerk, order is once more restored. Jabbs and his wife arrive at the hotel accompanied by mother-in-law. They are no sooner in their room when a telegram calling Jabbs out of town arrives. Mother-in-law and wifey accompany him to the station. On their return, an insipid flirt accosts them. He is repulsed, but follows them home, even into the hotel. The wife and mother-in-law ring for the porter and bellboy and demand protection, which is gladly given. In return, the porter and bellboy are treated sumptuously to cake and wine. Jabbs misses the train and returns home. He being the first arrival, after the porter and bellboy have agreed mutual protection, he is promptly ejected as the suspect. Jabbs must get into his room. He tries the ladder route, but is bustled out again. He secures a hamper,

has himself expressed to the hotel, is delivered and signed for. The flirt, who has been in the room all this time, thinks it is about time to make his getaway and tries to get out just as wifey and mamma are returning. The porter and bellboy are again summoned and are going to throw the hamper down the stairs, when Jabbs emerges from it. Recognition takes place. The flirt is found, and but for the appeal of the women would have received a sound thrashing. So he quickly slinks away from the porters' words ringing in his ears, "This Way Out." [MPW]

This is the first time Babe Hardy's character is given the name "Plump" instead of the formerly (and unfortunately) used "Fatty" and is working alongside Billy Ruge as "Runt", making this film the first appearance both in name and in teaming of "Plump & Runt."

"The ins and outs of hotel life is made possible by a skilled director of comic situations and the efforts of a cast that hesitate at no known variety of 'funny fall,' combine to shape this one-reel farce into a worthy Vim. The trio of 'knockabout' comedians employed in this brand of pictures have full scope of their best endeavors." -- *Moving Picture World*

Chickens

Released January 14, 1916. Vim Comedies - General Film Company release. One reel. No copyright registered. Release number 19880. Originally scheduled for release December 31, 1915 but was withheld.

Produced by Louis Burstein. Directed by Bobby Burns and Walter Stull. Filmed in Jacksonville, Florida.

with Bobby Burns (*Pokes*), Walter Stull (*Jabbs*), Babe Hardy, Spook Hanson, Ethel Burton (*Ethel*), Helen Gilmore, Billy Ruge, Harry Naughton.

Hiram Gothrocks, having recently acquired wealth, desires to enter into society and agrees to marry his daughter, Ethel, to Count Chasem, who is coming to visit Gothrocks at his summer home. Jabbs, who until now has been Ethel's sweetheart, is ordered by Gothrocks to cease paying attentions to her and in despair seeks the advice of his friend, Pokes, the village barber. Pokes, learning from Jabbs of the count's intended visit, advises his friend to impersonate the count, which Jabbs agrees to do. On his way to the residence of Gothrocks the count and his valet are held up by two tramps who are enjoying a meal at the roadside of chickens they have stolen from the hencoop of a nearby girls' seminary. They force the count and his valet, after first exchanging clothes with them, to enter the seminary by way of the window, where they are arrested as the tramps who recently stole the chickens. In the meantime. Pokes and Jabbs have been disporting themselves in the Gothrocks home at the expense of Gothrocks' furniture. The tramps having found in the clothes of the count the letter of introduction to Gothrocks think that they shall pass themselves off as the titled nobleman and his valet, but instead find themselves marched off to jail by the irate Gothrocks. In the station house, when Gothrocks learns that the count is the husband of the matron of the seminary, his dream of society vanishes and he gladly gives Ethel into the arms of Jabbs. [MPW]

The chickens in the story are stolen from a girls school and Vim, needing a large number of female extras, advertised in the society pages of the local newspaper. On the day of the shooting, a long line of limousines and touring cars was found along Riverside Drive, just outside the studio. Seems it was the dream of nearly all of the Jacksonville debutantes to appear in the movies. Critics generally liked the Pokes and Jabbs comedies and *Chickens* was no exception. However, not everybody was happy with them. Censors in Ohio condemned the film on grounds of being "harmful." They must have feared copycat chicken poaching.

"'Needles and pins, needles and pins! When a man starts to flirt, his trouble begins.' This slight change in the old saw is the keynote to the plot of *Chickens*. Pokes and Jabs keep up their reputation as comedic despoilers of domestic happiness, and the picture has the requisite quantity of Vim comedy." *--Moving Picture World*

Frenzied Finance

Released January 21, 1916. Vim Comedies - General Film Company release. One reel. No copyright registered. Release number 19918.

Produced by Louis Burstein. Directed by Bobby Burns and Walter Stull. Filmed in Jacksonville, Florida.

with Bobby Burns (*Pokes*), Walter Stull (*Jabbs*), Babe Hardy, Spook Hanson, Ethel Burton (*Ethel*), Mildred Burstein (*Millie*).

As brokers Pokes and Jabbs certainly live up to the name, for outside of the office furniture, their one asset is their nerve. Added to business troubles Jabbs as the real business man of the firm is driven to distraction by Pokes who, instead of attending to the office affairs, devotes all his time in flirting with Ethel, the stenographer. In despair Jabbs discharges Ethel, much to the chagrin of Pokes, who, however, dare not interfere. In vain Jabbs seeks to engage a new stenographer, but the applicants sent to him by the employment bureau only add to the worries of poor Jabbs, while Pokes sits by and enjoys the proceedings. Finally, Jabbs is forced not only to re-engage Ethel but also to employ Millie, Ethel's friend, as his own stenographer. One of their clients enters with a large deposit which he entrusts with Pokes and Jabbs. The deposit is the largest that either members of the firm has ever handled and extraordinary precautions are employed to insure its safety. However, the modern crook resorts to unusual methods in his manner of plying his trade, so that when the client, having changed his mind about leaving the deposit in the office, returns to claim it, the partners suddenly realize that not only have the crooks stolen the money, but the safe as well. While Jabbs and the

client seek the assistance of the police, Pokes devotes himself to the pursuit of the crooks and the safe. Catching up with them, he overpowers them, but during the struggle, the safe, released from control, rolls downs to the docks and falls into the harbor. However, undaunted, Pokes dives into the water after the safe and when Jabbs arrives with the police, Pokes has succeeded in salvaging the precious money. [MPW]

The role of Millie the stenographer was played by Louis Burstein's niece Mildred, who worked in the Vim offices in that capacity (when not running the studio in her uncle's absence). Playing the friend of Ethel Burton would not have been much of a stretch for Mildred, since they were very close friends, as were most of the performers that made up the Vim Company. Harry Naughton who served as studio manager and bit player with Vim (and later King Bee) fell in love with Millie at first sight. It was that infatuation that caused Naughton to seek and retain employment with Millie's Uncle Louis Burstein's various filmmaking effort. The couple's romance was readily evident during the days of Vim in Jacksonville, and the two would marry (and live happily ever after) not long after King Bee moved to Hollywood.

Harry and Millie

"Pokes and Jabs, brokers, have trouble with stenographers. Pokes spends all his time flirting with Ethel, the stenographer. Jabs "fires" her, but has trouble in getting another that pleases him. He is forced to hire her again, and also her friend Millie, an arrangement which works out well. The robbers steal the office safe. Pokes, after many mishaps, recovers it." -- *Motography*

"*Frenzied Finance* is a good Vim comedy featuring Pokes and Jabs. As financiers they are not much of a success, but as laugh producers they are fine. They are supported by pretty Ethel Burton." –*San Bernardino Daily Sun (San Bernardino, California)*

Busted Hearts

Released January 28, 1916. Vim Comedies - General Film Company release. One reel. No copyright registered. Release number 19956.

Produced by Louis Burstein. Directed by Walter Stull and Bobby Burns. Filmed in Jacksonville, Florida.

with Bobby Burns (*Pokes*), Walter Stull (*Jabbs*), Babe Hardy (*Peggy Plump*), Spook Hanson (*Runt*), Ethel Burton.

Peggy Plump, the good-natured daughter of old farmer Plump, never had but one beau. Many times she tried for more, but father always prevented. Pokes, after many days travel in his box car, arrives at Pumpkinville, the home of the Plumps. Peggy is milking. Pokes passes and after a rather rough flirtation they become friends. Peggy takes Pokes home with her. Marks, the village lawyer, is at the Plump house paying Farmer Plump a large sum of money. Peggy and Pokes arrive and Pokes sees the money through the window. Immediately he wants to get it and persuades Peggy to invite him in the house. Once inside, Pokes hypnotizes Peggy and she takes the money. Pokes and Peggy elope. When they arrive in the city Pokes sees a fairer charmer and deserts Peggy. Flat broke, Peggy gets a job in Jabbs' restaurant as a waitress. The cook and waiter become infatuated with her, much to the discomfort of the dishwasher. A rough house ensues and is at its height in the kitchen when Pokes and his fair charmer enter the restaurant to have dinner. Peggy is thrown into the dining room and when her eyes meet those of Pokes she recognizes the man who deserted her. She seizes the opportunity and gives Pokes a sound thrashing, much to the amusement of Jabbs and the rest of the diners. Runt, Peggy's first love, arrives just in time in the restaurant in search of Peggy to receive her in his arms after the fray and soothes her busted heart." [MPW]

Likely shot before the establishment of the Plump & Runt unit, Hardy or Ruge only on the rarest of occasions would appear in a Pokes & Jabbs comedy after this film. Another clue to when the film was made is the naming of Spook Hanson's character as "Runt", something that wouldn't have been done once Plump & Runt were established. Babe Hardy, again playing the distaff version of himself, received praise in the trades for his performance.

"Babe Hardy enacts the plump and beauteous maiden that fractures the hearts of Pokes and Jabbs in this one real farce. Bobby Burns and Walter Stull find a worthy confrere in Babe and the trio hops friskily from one bit of funny business to the other. Vim is the watchword for everyone concerned in the farce." -- *Moving Picture World*

"Busted Hearts if not the most amusing of the Vim comedies, is at least notable from the fact that it employs the services of the quartette of comedians, Plump, Runt, Pokes, and Jabbs, and in a roughly knock-about style is likely to please a public which has clearly shown its appreciation of this class of work. Without exceeding previous records, it is up to the average of this series of comedies." -- *The Bioscope*

The Getaway

Released February 4, 1916. Vim Comedies - General Film Company release. One reel. No copyright registered. Release number 19994. Listed in some sources as: *Their Getaway*, or *The Cold Feet Getaway*.

Produced by Louis Burstein. Directed by Bobby Burns and Walter Stull. Filmed in Jacksonville, Florida.

with Bobby Burns (*Pokes*), Walter Stull (*Jabbs*), Ethel Burton, Edna Reynolds (*Mrs. Jabbs*), Helen Gilmore (*Mrs. Pokes*).

When Mrs. Pokes, the ruler of the Pokes domicile, intercepts an invitation for her better half to sit in a friendly little card game, she marches the unfortunate bread winner of the family off to bed. Thinking that since Pokes is now safely enthroned in bed and his clothes safe in her possession, Mrs. Pokes ceases to worry. Pokes, however, escapes via the window route and, joining his pal Jabbs, they make their way to the card game. Here Pokes' hard luck again visits him, for just as he is about to scoop in the banner pot of the session, the house is raided and Pokes and Jabbs have a very eventful time marking their escape. In trying to reach the street in safety they become bewildered, and instead of locating the door to the street, succeed only in disturbing the other occupants of the house. Their retreat being cut off both from the street and the fire escape, they finally take refuge in the chimney of the house of the very police official who had raided the card game. After an eventful period of hiding in the chimney, during which time the two friends are subjected to the delightful sensation of being roasted from below and stunned from above, they are finally dislodged, and to crown their misfortunes find themselves in the presence of their respective wives. [MPW]

"The Getaway is one of those successful Vim Comedies. Pokes and Jabbs make an exciting 'getaway' from a card game. Madam Pokes heads the pursuers. They are stranded between earth and sky: finally land at the feet of the furious female." -- *Leavenworth Times (Leavenworth, Kansas)*

"Mrs. Pokes tries to keep her husband from a card party. He escapes. During the game, the place is raided. Pokes and Jabbs, evading the police, hide in the chimney. When finally dislodged they fall into the hands of their angry wives." -- *Motography*

The High Sign

Released February 11, 1916. Vim Comedies - General Film Company release. One reel. No copyright registered. Release number 20032.

Produced by Louis Burstein. Directed by Bobby Burns and Walter Stull. Filmed in Jacksonville, Florida.

with Bobby Burns (*Pokes*), Walter Stull (*Jabbs*).

Although one of the leading bankers of the city, Jabbs, is also a member of the Mysterious Seven, an organization that passes out regular cash dividends to its members. Pokes has incurred the enmity of Jabbs by attempting to perform the wonderful mystic egg trick in Jabbs' new silk hat. Poor Pokes not knowing that his new sweetheart is the daughter of Jabbs, purloins from Mrs. Jabbs the new necklace that her husband has recently given to her. Pokes thinks only of re-establishing himself firmly in his sweetheart's affections and to further his suit, gives to Ethel the very necklace that he has stolen from her mother. When Jabbs and his wife meet Pokes, they quickly recognize him as the man who has caused them so much annoyance and Jabbs summons his trusty fellow members of the secret organization. They chase unfortunate Pokes up through the house to the roof-tops from where Pokes succeeds in escaping, but only to stumble into the meeting rooms of the society. Here Pokes succeeds in turning the tables on Jabbs and his fellow conspirators and completely routs the entire society. [MPW]

"A remarkable secret society gives the one-reel comedy its title, and Robert Burns and Walter Stull rush through the action with their usual speed, dropping seeds of laughter at frequent intervals. The portal through which the lodge room is entered is in a class by itself and must be seen to be appreciated." -- *Moving Picture World*

Pluck and Luck

Released February 18, 1916. Vim Comedies - General Film Company release. One reel. No copyright registered. Release number 20069.

Produced by Louis Burstein. Directed by Bobby Burns and Walter Stull. Filmed in and around Riverside Park and at the Vim Studios in Jacksonville, Florida.

with Bobby Burns (*Loose Pokes impersonating the piano tuner, Prof. Sauernote*), Walter Stull (*Jabbs*), Helen Gilmore (*Jabbs' wife*), Ethel Burton (*their daughter*), Joe Cohen (*one of the anarchists*), Harry Naughton (*policeman*).

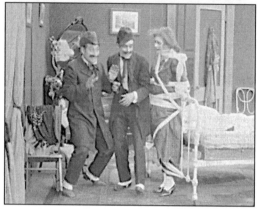

When Pokes, a plumber, is dispossessed from his humble place of business owing to his inability to pay his rent, he accepts the invitation from a neighbor, the piano tuner, to share his store. Jabbs' wife is socially ambitious, and to advance herself into the ranks of the elite of her native city has decided to give a musicale at her home. In order to have the piano in excellent condition for the great event she sends Ethel, her daughter, to notify the tuner to come and inspect the piano. During this time, Jabbs by his overhearing manner has incurred the hostility of two anarchists, tenants in one of his houses. To avenge themselves on their landlord they manage to hide a time clock bomb in the piano at Jabbs' home. When Ethel arrives at the piano tuner's she finds only Pokes present and he is so smitten with her charms that he cannot resist the desire to impersonate the tuner as he realizes that he will have an opportunity to make Ethel's acquaintance. On Ethel's arrival home she surprises the anarchists at their nefarious work and is seized by them and carried upstairs where they have her bound and helpless. Pokes' attempt to tune the piano is a dismal failure for he succeeds in demolishing all parts of it until he finds the bomb hidden in the inside. He calls the attention of Jabbs to the bomb, driving both Jabbs and his wife in a frenzy of fear as the clock lacks only a few seconds of the time set for the explosion. After they reach the street in safety, their attention is called to Ethel on the upper floor and Pokes proves his nerve by dashing into the house and saving the girl at the peril of his life. [MPW]

The two anarchists that appeared in the earlier *Ups And Downs* show up again in *Pluck and Luck* albeit without Shifty Mike their leader (played by Babe Hardy in the first film). This time around Joe Cohen plays one of the agitators. When Pokes the plumber, who is sharing a shop with the piano tuner, takes a job on the musician's behalf he writes a note stating, "I pity the piano" and he does then proceed to utterly destroy the instrument.

"Robert Burns and Walter Stull, assisted by a much-enduring piano and a kit of plumber's tools, manage to keep the fun moving right along through this one-reel farce. Acrobatic comedies, in which the funny fall is the piece de resistance, many persons find vastly amusing, and the Vim pictures are equal to the best of them." -- *Moving Picture World*

Love and Lather

Released February 25, 1916. Vim Comedies - General Film Company release. One reel. No copyright registered. Release number 20106.

Produced by Louis Burstein. Directed by Bobby Burns and Walter Stull. Photography by James Carlton. Filmed Mid- January 1916 in Jacksonville, Florida.

with Bobby Burns (*Pokes, the street cleaner*), Walter Stull (*Jabbs*), Ethel Burton (*the barber's daughter*), Spook Hanson (*barber*), Robin Williamson.

Spook, the barber, is in despair because he is unable to accompany his friend on a fishing trip owing to the fact that he has nobody to take care of the shop during his absence. In looking about for a substitute, he chances to see Pokes, the street cleaner and mistaking Pokes' white wing suit for barber's clothes, he tries to press him into service for the day. Pokes is willing to accept the offer once he catches sight of Spook's daughter, Ethel, the manicurist of the shop, under whose charms he immediately succumbs. The unfortunate customers who happen to fall into the none too gentle hands of Pokes suffer all kinds of tortures, even Ethel herself receives rather rough usage from him. Pokes is notified by the police to be on the look-out for a desperate convict who has recently escaped from jail, and whose chief mark of identification is the absence of one-half of his mustache. The police realize that the convict will head for a barber shop as soon as possible in order to remove the tell-tale half of his mustache, so hence after the warning to Pokes, they set in to watch the shop. The police warning gives Pokes the idea of securing revenge on Jabbs, Ethel's sweetheart, whose face is adorned by a beautiful hirsute growth of which both he and Ethel are inordinately fond. Finding Jabbs asleep in the barber chair, Pokes seizes the opportunity to shave off one half of his rival's mustache. That incident succeeds in getting Jabbs very much in wrong with the police who happen to see him walking from the shop and give chase. In the station house Jabbs finds Spook and his pal who have also been arrested in the meantime, is brought in. On being cleared of the charges, Jabbs accompanies Spook home where they wreak the full vengeance upon Pokes for the trouble that he has brought upon them. [MPW]

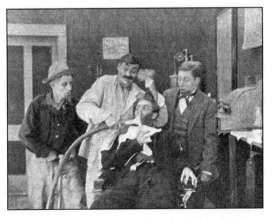

"The Vim comedy release for Feb. 25 is one of the funniest in the Pokes and Jabbs series, which features Robert Burns and Walter Stull. Pokes is a member of the brigade of 'White Wings' of the street: easily taken for a barber, he takes the place of Spook, the village barber, and is soon enmeshed in the attractions of the manicurist of the shop. Complications build up as the ingenious 'White Wings' tests new appliances for shaving the unsuspecting customers. The comedy includes an escaped convict, Jabbs, who suffers at the hands of Pokes and a general mixup of the police. Pokes, however, suffers for his escapades and the escaped convict wins the girl and the graces of the barber. The General Film program will carry this release." -- *Moving Picture World*

"Love and Lather and Nerve and Gasoline two 1,000 ft. "Vim" comedies,. featuring Pokes and Jabbs and Plump and Runt, respectively, were shown at the same time. Neither calls for any detailed description. Bewilderingly rapid in their action, they are irresponsible, playful and amusing, and possess a certain amount of novelty of incident and treatment. The knockabout fun is neat, and there is no vulgarity." -- *Kinematograph Weekly*

The Artist's Model

Released March 3, 1916. Vim Comedies - General Film Company release. One reel. No copyright registered. Release number 20143.

Produced by Louis Burstein. Directed by Bobby Burns and Walter Stull. Filmed circa January 1916 at the Vim Studios and outside the Heard National Bank at 110 Forsyth Street in Jacksonville, Florida.

with Bobby Burns (*Pokes, the porter*), Walter Stull (*Jabbs, the baggage man*), Ethel Burton (*artist*), Helen Gilmore (*landlady*), Spook Hanson (*flirty landlord*), Robin Williamson (*bum*), Harry Naughton (*police captain*), Mildred Burstein (*stenographer*), Joe Cohen (*bum*).

Pokes, the porter poses for Ethel, a struggling young artist. Ethel unfortunately is very short of ready money and in consequence is asked by her landlord to vacate her room at once. As a last desperate resort, Ethel tries to sell a painting of Pokes posing as an archer, but the rebuff handed to her by the critical and unsympathetic art dealer, is the final blow to her spirit, so she resolves to make a get-a-way from the apartments. She conspires with Pokes to smuggle her trunk from the studio and when the latter comes to remove the trunk he unwittingly locks it, the landlord, who, while inspecting its contents and hearing his wife's voice on the corridor outside, had taken refuge in the trunk. Pokes starts to carry the trunk to the railroad station where Jabbs, the baggage man is anxiously awaiting the arrival of a trunk containing a shipment of gold consigned to a local bank. Some crooks, who have learned of the expected shipment of gold mistake Ethel's trunk for that of the treasure chest, overpower Jabbs, and load the trunk with the unfortunate landlord inside, upon a truck which they have commandeered. Upon Ethel's arrival, Jabbs plight is discovered, the alarm given and the pursuit of the fleeing crooks is started. The police follow the desperate thieves and overtaking them through the help of Pokes and Jabbs finally succeed in releasing the landlord from his perilous position. [MPW]

Ethel Burton as the artist is the main focus of the first two-thirds of the film aided by a frantic Bobby Burns. She tries to paint Pokes, and then sell the painting to pay her rent all the time trying to avoid the advances of the amorous landlord (himself hiding from his wife for good reason). Ethel finally has enough of the landlord and smashes the painting over his head. Another, albeit too few, extant example of Ethel Burton's comic abilities. Jabbs finally makes an appearance as the baggage man down at the train station where Ethel's trunk is sent. The last third of the film features a rather Keystonesque car chase with cops included. Pokes can't seem to quite catch up with the car that is pursuing the thieves so we get a series of stunts and pratfalls (many appropriately undercranked) as he attempts to get into the speedy car.

The subject of female nudity in film was a hot topic in early 1916. Audrey Munson, who had gained fame as an artist's model, appeared nude in the feature film *Inspiration* released in November 1915 by Mutual. This caused much debate and also many imitations with the use of an artist's model to bring nudity into a film, because it would be "art" not just salaciousness. With tongue firmly in cheek the Vim folks broach the subject but with Bobby Burns as the model, though thankfully not nude.

"Robert Burns and Walter Stull, in the Vim Pokes and Jabbs series are distinguishing themselves for their originality. Their comedies always spring some new situations. Among the best is *The Artist's Model*. This comedy includes no beautiful female model, rather, Pokes himself is the model, driven to it by straitened circumstances. While the girl, Ethel, is the struggling artist. Ethel's picture is a failure, debts accumulate, and Pokes endeavors to aid her in her escape from her quarters, where rent is long overdue. All went well until Jabbs the baggage man butts in. The trunk of Ethel is mistaken for the trunk of gold, being shipped at that time to a local bank. The trunk is stolen by crooks, Jabbs overpowered. The trunk is found to contain a half alive landlord, but the gold saved, while Pokes, Jabbs and Ethel have exciting experiences in their chase for the supposed treasures of Ethel." -- *Moving Picture World*

Their Wedding Day

Released March 10, 1916. Vim Comedies - General Film Company release. One reel. No copyright registered. Release number 20174.

Produced by Louis Burstein. Directed by Bobby Burns and Walter Stull. Filmed circa February 7-11, 1916 in Jacksonville, Florida.

With Bobby Burns (*Pokes*), Walter Stull (*Jabbs*), Ethel Burton, Helen Gilmore, Frank Hanson, Jane "Tiny" Wills.

To find proper husbands for two marriageable daughters is a hard proposition to confront any father. But when one of them happens to be extremely fat, then indeed, it is a very serious task. Yet such was the dilemma that Judge Findem had to face, for his elder daughter, Tiny, the fat duckling, always found herself to be amongst those also present. Ethel, the youngest daughter, was Tiny's exact antithesis and had the local swains all out of breath in pursuing her. To settle Tiny's future, the Judge finally inserts a personal advertisement. This ad attracts the attention of Jabbs, the town sport, who is in financial distress, and also of Pokes,

the village loafer, who must find a wife before he can secure employment. Both Pokes and Jabbs call upon Tiny at different times, only to desert her once they happen to see the pretty sister Ethel. Unknown to each other, Pokes and Jabbs scheme to kidnap Ethel and engage two different pairs of thugs to carry out their instructions. However, as the thugs have never seen Ethel, the plans miscarry, Jaggs' thugs carting off the mother. While Pokes' pair abduct Tiny. The thugs carry their respective victims to the Judge's office, where Pokes and Jabbs are anxiously awaiting the girl. Great is their consternation when instead of the girl of their dreams, they find Tiny and her irate mother confronting them when the thugs remove the coverings. The Judge determined, however, to force somebody to marry Tiny, now that he has a chance, tries to force either Pokes or Jabbs to become her husband. Pokes and Jabbs, however, manage to escape and the desperate father succeeds only in marrying Tiny to one of the thugs who kidnapped her. Pokes and Jabbs make haste back to the Judge's residence to capture Ethel, but after their hard run, arrive on the scene in time to find Ethel content in the arms of her sweetheart, Roy. [MPW]

With this film, Jane Wills, previously with Eagle, makes her only confirmed appearance in a Vim comedy.

"The Pokes and Jabbs series of comedies, made by the Vim Films Corporation, are constantly offering new situations and ideas. Among the comedies of this series there is none better than *Their Wedding Day*, in which Pokes and Jabbs, as usual, raise a cyclone of action in laugh-provoking situations. Jabbs is the town sport and financially equal to the heavy demands on his generosity, while Pokes, the village loafer, is down and out. Both men are attracted by an advertisement in a paper from a wealthy man offering a dowry to anyone who would marry his daughter. The effort to come up to the demands of the wealthy father and the hopeless struggle for the hand of the girl by these rivals makes the fun of the film, while in the end both lose out as the girl, Ethel, claims the man of her own choice. Robert Burns and Walter Stull, as Pokes and Jabbs, are well supported by Ethel Burton, Helen Gilmore, Frank Hanson, and Tiny Wills." -- *Moving Picture World*

"Pokes and Jabbs both try to elope with the same lady, there are numerous comedy mix-ups, and a third party becomes the happy bridegroom. One of the best 'knockabouts' in which Burns and Stull have appeared." -- *Moving Picture World*

A Pair of Skins

Released March 17, 1916. Vim Comedies - General Film Company release. One reel. No copyright registered.

Produced by Louis Burstein. Directed by Bobby Burns and Walter Stull. Filmed in Jacksonville, Florida.

with Bobby Burns (*Pokes*), Walter Stull (*Jabbs*), Ethel Burton.

Up to the time that Prof. Chasebugs received a letter announcing the arrival of Jabbs, the four-flush hunter, Pokes had been the accepted suitor of Ethel's hand. However, once her father, the Professor, hears Jabbs describe the manner in which he killed the ferocious man-eating tiger in the jungles of India, he resolves that Ethel shall belong to no other man. As the Professor is interested in the study of bugs of various kinds, it is only natural that he should fall a victim to Jabbs' stories of his skill as a hunter, so he naturally succumbs to Jabbs' proposition to go hunting. Pokes in the meantime has been practicing up in his efficiency as a marksman much to the discomfort of his two friends who volunteer to hold the target for Pokes, forgets all about the target and shoots his friends instead. When Jabbs, Ethel, the Professor and his wife arrive at the hunting grounds, Jabbs proceeds to give a demonstration of his skill as a marksman and all is well until a bear creeps out from the underbrush and chases the Professor and his family from the place. Jabbs calmly proceeds with his demonstration unmindful of the hurried departure of the Chasebug family until a friendly bug notifies him of the presence of the bear. Once he becomes cognizant of the bear's presence, Jabbs proceeds to break all speed records back to the Chasebug bungalow passing the Chasebug family en route. Arriving at the bungalow, the once mighty hunter rushes up to the roof, where he locks the skylight and peers down upon the family frantically trying to force their way up from the attic in a vain attempt to escape from the pursuing bear. Great, however, is his chagrin when on looking down again he finds Ethel lying contently n the arms of the bear and to his horror the supposed bear is none other than his despised rival, Pokes. [MPW]

Bobby Burns is again dressed as an animal. Not only a great acrobat, Burns also had the ability to mimic the movements of the various animals he impersonated, he was able to convince audiences that they were seeing a real animal only to humanize or exaggerate the beast's behavior to great comic effect.

"Vim comedies are great fun. Pokes and Jabbs, too, are great comedians, so these two, and a good cast of players are entertaining nicely in *A Pair of Skins* wherein Pokes, who is a 'four flush' hunter, disturbs the romance of Jabbs, the ambitious lover." -- *Leavenworth Times* (Leavenworth, Kansas)

"[*A Pair of Skins*] is really good fun, and we give pride of place to the animal impersonators who play the lion and the tiger that the bold hunter professes to have destroyed. "Pokes" and "Jabbs" are the featured comedians. Pokes is a funny lover whose are clever and laughable. Jabbs is the mighty hunter (and liar) who would win the pretty daughter of the quaint old butterfly catcher. Pokes wins by disguising as a bear and frightening Jabbs out of the game. Children especially will enjoy this." -- *The Bioscope*

Behind the Footlights

Released March 24, 1916. Vim Comedies - General Film Company release. One reel. No copyright registered. Release number 20254.

Produced by Louis Burstein. Directed by Bobby Burns and Walter Stull. Filmed circa February 10, 1916 in Jacksonville, Florida.

with Bobby Burns (*Pokes*), Walter Stull (*Prof. Plaid Jabbs*), Billy Bletcher (*theatergoer*), Ethel Burton (*Pokes' girl*), Edna Reynolds (*theatergoer*), Joe Cohen (*man in audience*), Helen Gilmore (*theatergoer*), Harry Naughton (*theatergoer*), Robin Williamson (*theater manager*), Florence McLoughlin (*theatergoer*), Mildred Burstein (*theatergoer*), Tiny Wills [?].

Pokes, the property man at the Vim theater, incurs the hostility of Prof. Jabbs the wonderful Escape King on the opening day of the performance. Jabbs is very fond of posing in the lobby of every theater where he is featured as the star act. Here he meets Ethel, Pokes' sweetheart, and invites her into the theater to watch his act. Pokes sees his fickle sweetheart in the front row flirting with Jabbs and in his rage he resolves to get even with his lordly rival. Discovering that the secret of Jabbs' escape from the padlocked barrel consists in a false bottom, Pokes maliciously nails up the bottom securely. Jabbs does not discover the trick until after he has been securely locked into the barrel by Pokes in full sight of the audience who become alarmed. Pokes with fiendish glee packs dynamite into the barrel on top of the almost suffocated Jabbs and after lighting the fuse rolls the barrel out of the theater. Then seizing Ethel, who of all the audience has remained in the theater, the arch villain rushes her to the

office of a Justice of the Peace. Just as the marriage ceremony is about to commence, Jabbs who has been hurled high in the air by the force of the explosion, falls into the same office, and throwing Pokes out through the window, proceeds to marry the now-willing Ethel himself. [MPW]

The first Pokes & Jabbs film to be centered around the vaudeville stage, something they would go back to often with films such as *Anvils & Actors* and *The Property Man* (among others). According to the sign appearing at the Vim Theater were Prof. Plaid Jabbs (Escape King), the Limber Bros. (Acrobats), Long & Short (Song Dance Artists), Willie Balance (Wire Walker), the Dropp Family (Jugglers) and Lily Lemon (A Sweet Singer). After the barrel is filled with explosives and rolled out of the theater a long chase ensues. First by Ethel and others in an effort to save Jabbs, but then running away from the barrel when it starts chasing them with the explosion imminent. Using stop motion photography the barrel turns corners, goes up stairs and the action goes back and forth on who actually is after who or what.

"Burlesques on life behind the footlights are no novelty, but are often amusing. The one now in question is one of the best so far produced. Its humor is continuous, being spurred on by Pokes and Jabs. The finish is a scream." -- *Moving Picture World*

Anvils and Actors

Released March 31, 1916. Vim Comedies - General Film Company release. One reel. No copyright registered. Release number 20291. Working title: *Something Doing.*

Produced by Louis Burstein. Directed by Bobby Burns and Walter Stull. Filmed in Jacksonville, Florida.

with Bobby Burns (*Pokes*), Walter Stull (*Jabbs*), Ethel Burton (*Ethel*), Elsie McLeod, Edna Reynolds.

Ethel, the daughter of the village blacksmith, is greatly admired by both Pokes and Jabbs. Pokes is the apprentice at the blacksmith shop and has the inside track of his rival, Jabbs, who has ambitions to become an actor. Ethel ridicules Jabbs' histrionic efforts and gives her heart to the honest son of toil, Pokes. After Pokes has presented an engagement ring to Ethel, poor Jabbs is heartbroken and hides away to the distant city to follow the career he loves. Ethel's joy is short-lived, for the black-heated villain Pokes, securing the return of the ring by a crafty excuse, places it on the finger of a city girl who chances to visit the village. Crushed in spirit at her sweetheart's parody, Ethel leaves her rural home to seek fame and fortune in the city. Years afterwards, Pokes deciding to enjoy a well-earned vacation, visits the city and finds his way inside a theater to witness the performance of a repertory company. When the theater curtain rises, to the horror of Pokes, there on the stage he sees his erstwhile sweetheart Ethel and his former rival Jabbs enacting a melodramatic play that portrays the exact conduct of Pokes toward Ethel in former days. Forgetful of the fact that the play is based upon his own acts, and thinking that Jabbs is really treating Ethel shamefully, Pokes climbs on the stage and, opening fire with his revolver, chases the performers into the wings. Seeking refuse in a corner, Jabbs and Ethel spy a fire hose hanging nearby and opening the nozzle full force they turn the water upon the oncoming Pokes. The current is so strong that Pokes is swept completely out if the theater and out into the alley, while Jabbs and Ethel look on convulsed with laughter. [MPW]

With the departure of Marcel Perez, Elsie McLeod became a bit of a free agent and while she would soon settle in as Plump & Runt's chief support she makes this one-off appearance with Pokes & Jabbs.

"A Pokes and Jabs comedy that will be found moderately amusing. The comedians in love with the blacksmith's daughter are bitter rivals. Jabbs becomes an actor and Pokes in search of the girl who has suddenly disappeared from her home comes upon Jabbs and his troops in a theater in a neighboring town. Pokes makes a great deal of disturbance, and in fact, breaks up the show by jumping on the stage at the climax of a tragic scene. A good number." -- *Moving Picture World*

In the Ring

Released April 7, 1916. Vim Comedies - General Film Company release. One reel. No copyright registered.

Produced by Louis Burstein. Directed by Bobby Burns and Walter Stull. Filmed circa February 29, 1916 in Jacksonville, Florida.

with Bobby Burns (*Pokes*), Walter Stull (*Jabbs*), Ethel Burton, Robin Williamson (*fighter*), Harry Naughton (*fighter*).

Jabbs having bet all his capital on the Gashouse Kid to win the fight with Locomotive Steve, decides to safeguard his chances by hiring Pokes to referee the bout. On the evening of the fight Jabbs acting as the Fixer, enables Pokes to escape from the vigilant eye of Mrs. Pokes, by telling that lady that he is bringing Pokes to attend a Strawberry Festival. Pokes takes his place in the ring and tries his hardest to aid Jabbs' fighter to win, but only succeeds in having the latter knocked out. Chagrined at his failure to help his friend, Pokes puts on the gloves himself and starts to fight. After some rapid fighting, Locomotive Steve delivers a terrible blow on Pokes' jaw, and Pokes is knocked unconscious. The club is raided, and Pokes and Jabbs with the other principals are arrested. When brought before the Magistrate, Jabbs still continuing in his role as Fixer, whispers in the Magistrate's ear, whereupon the Magistrate immediately discharges the other prisoners, but sentences Pokes and Jabbs to five years at hard labor. The wives believing that their husbands are away in the country recuperating from a severe attack of strawberry rash, join the Women's Reform League and visit the County Jail. Here Pokes and Jabbs, now prisoners, are ordered by the Warden to wait on the table where the wives are being feasted by the Jail Officials. Infuriated by the Warden's attentions to their wives, Pokes and Jabbs start in to assault the unfortunate Warden and are ordered by him to receive old water treatment. When the hose is turned on, Jabbs succeeds in eluding the guards, and getting possession of the hose, turns it upon the officials and after chasing them up the prison corridor, starts in to drown poor Pokes. When the water hits Pokes he begins to revive and opening his eyes finds himself still in the ring with Jabbs anxiously throwing water into his face and the other principals all grouped around him praying for his recovery. [MPW]

"A lively mix-up in the squared circle with Pokes and Jabs taking active part furnishes most of the laughs in this one-reel farce. It is a funny knockout skit in every sense of the word." -- *Moving Picture World*

The Sleuths

Released April 14, 1916. Vim Comedies - General Film Company release. One reel. No copyright registered. Release number 20365.

Produced by Louis Burstein. Directed by Bobby Burns and Walter Stull. Filmed in Jacksonville, Florida.

with Bobby Burns (Pokes), Walter Stull (Jabbs), Ethel Burton.

When Mrs. Newlywed received the sacred jewel from her uncle in the Far East with a note telling her that the jewel had once adorned the famous idol in one of the temples, she naturally was anxious to have her friends admire it. Wearing it to a dance, the jewel received much comment from the papers. The newspaper articles are seen by some Arabs who have been commissioned by the Sheik to follow the jewel to the end of the world and recover it. The Arabs force an entrance into the house, but are discovered by the Newlywed family as they are blowing the safe. Missing the jewel, the Newlyweds call in Pokes and Jabbs, "the world-famous detectives," who undertake to recover the precious stone. The Arabs, who really did not succeed in gaining possession of the jewel, learn that Pokes and Jabbs are on their trail. Luring them into the house of one of the band, the Arabs finally succeed in imprisoning the sleuths in the torture chamber. Once the sleuths are safely imprisoned the Arabs start the mechanism controlling the chamber and which forces the walls to compress. While the Arabs are gloating over the untimely end of the sleuths, the latter are anxiously waiting the moment when the walls shall crush them. At the last minute, however, the detectives seeking comfort from the horror of their position indulge in some snuff that causes them to sneeze. The mighty blast blows down the torture chambers, wrecks the entire house and liberates the sleuths who triumphantly emerge from the wreck. [MPW]

"Pokes and Jabbs on the trail of a famous jewel from the forehead of an idol, leads to number of amusing situations in this one-reel comedy. The finish is particularly clever." -- *Moving Picture World*

Hired And Fired

Released April 21, 1916. Vim Comedies - General Film Company release. One reel. No copyright registered. Release number 20402.

Produced by Louis Burstein. Directed by Bobby Burns and Walter Stull. Filmed in Jacksonville, Florida.

with Bobby Burns (*Pokes*), Walter Stull (*Jabbs*), Ethel Burton, Florence McLoughlin, Babe Hardy, Al Ray.

Pokes and Jabbs both being broke, see an ad in the paper stating that Mr. Ginks, a wealthy and dyspeptic old grouch is in need of a secretary and a butler. They secure the positions and being installed in the house, both fall victims to the smiles of Ethel, the pretty maid. Ginks gives a large reception and among the guests is the Countess de Splash, famed for her jewels and her sweetheart, Cyril Cerise. Pokes and Jabbs get one flash of the diamond anklet worn by the Countess and both resolve to secure possession of it. in the hope that thereby they can win the affections of the charming Ethel. However, among the guests is also Rattles, the society crook, and Ethel's real lover, who also has designs upon the anklet. Pokes manages to secure the anklet from the Countess during the dance and hastens to conceal his ill-gotten spoils. When the Countess discovers the loss of her jewel, the Ginks summon the police, who insist upon all the guests submitting to a rigid search. Pokes hears the call for the police and breaks into trembling and perspiration for fear of arrest. Suddenly thinking that now would be the time to get even with his detested rival, and at the same time cover up his theft, he slips the anklet into Jabbs' coat pocket. With fiendish glee Pokes awaits the moment when the police will find the anklet in Jabbs' pocket, but the latter discovering the stolen jewel in time, in turn slips it into the pocket of Rattles. The crook knowing that should the police discover him among the guests, they would immediately arrest him, manages to make his escape after first telling Ethel to meet him in the garden prepared to elope. While waiting for Ethel he discovers the anklet in his pocket. The police learning that Rattles had been a guest at the party, throw up their hands in despair and inform the Countess that her precious anklet is now beyond recovery. Seeking some victim upon whom he can vent his wrath. Gink turns his attention upon the unfortunate Pokes and Jabbs and chases them out of the house, and they are once again broke and homeless. [MPW]

Researching silent films, particularly silent short comedies, and constructing accurate filmographies can be a dauting and confusing task. In addition to this Pokes & Jabbs comedy, there was also a Ben Turpin Vogue comedy called *Hired and Fired* and a Carter De Haven comedy titled *Hired and Fired*, as well as a two-reel Universal dramatic serial entitled *Timothy Dobbs — That's Me* which featured *Hired and Fired* as the title of episode five, all released in 1916. Some filmographies credit Kate Price with an appearance in this film. Although Price would eventually work for Vim, at the time this film was made she was working in New York and those listings are in error. During her time at Vim and at Jaxon Kate Price actually never appeared in any Pokes & Jabbs comedy.

Appearing in *Hired and Fired* was a brief addition to the Vim forces, a young man named Al Ray. The publicity surrounding Ray touted him as the youngest director in the business and noted that he also wrote and starred in own productions. There is little evidence, virtually none, that Ray fulfilled any of those roles at Vim and was primarily a bit player. It is possible that he may have served as an assistant director but he was never mentioned by name in regards to any specific Vim production in the trade papers, with the exception of a single comment made that he appeared in this film. The same article mentioned that in all Ray appeared in 15 Vim comedies. He would exit Vim in the early Fall along with Robin Williamson and others who headed West. Ray would first stop at Vogue and then spend some time at Keystone.

"A Vim comedy with lots of pep." –*Altoona Times (Altoona, Pennsylvania)*

The Rivals

Released April 28, 1916. Vim Comedies - General Film Company release. One reel. No copyright registered.

Produced by Louis Burstein. Directed by Bobby Burns and Walter Stull. Filmed in Jacksonville, Florida.

with Bobby Burns (*Pokes*), Walter Stull (*Jabbs*), Frank Hanson (*Lumber King*), Ethel Burton (*His Daughter*), Helen Gilmore (*His Wife*).

Pokes incurs the bitter enmity of Jabbs, his foreman, at the lumber yard where he is employed by winning the affections of Ethel, the employer's daughter. To get revenge, Jabbs orders the unfortunate Pokes to carry one of the heaviest logs he can find from one end of the lumber yard to the other. The terrible weight causes Pokes to bend almost double, and when Ethel and her father arrive and find him in this condition they are forced to use a heavy roller to straighten him out. Later, when Jabbs is discovered in a drinking bout by the Lumber King, he is discharged from his position and Pokes is appointed fore- man in his stead. Believing that turn about is fair play, Pokes now commands Jabbs to carry the same log that he had struggled with a few hours before. Smarting under the humiliation caused by his discharge, Jabbs plots with two of his confederates to kidnap Ethel. After knocking Pokes unconscious, Jabbs and his men throw Ethel into her father's auto and drive off. Recovering from the blow, Pokes seizes a bicycle and starts in pursuit of the fleeing auto. He overtakes the car and scrambling aboard, hurls the conspirators and Jabbs over the side and down an embankment. Not being familiar with the mechanism of the auto Pokes harnesses himself to the front and drags the car back to the lumber yard. Desperate at being balked in his nefarious scheme Jabbs orders his confederates to plant a bomb in the pocket of Pokes' coat. Discovering the smoke issuing from his clothes and not knowing the cause, Pokes dashes after Jabbs and his men, who seek safety in the powder house. Pokes dives into the house after them, and immediately after the bomb exploding, the entire house with Jabbs and his men are blown skyward. Pokes drops safely to the ground after shaking himself from the branches of a tree, where he has lodged and, viewing the ruins of the powder house, hies himself back to Ethel and his well earned reward. [MPW]

"Robert Burns and Walter Stull pursue the heroine of this one-reel comedy with such vigor that it is a wonder enough of the lady is left at the finish to serve for her identification. The expression 'knockabout' comedy will not cover this case; 'slam-about' or 'catapult comedy' comes nearer the mark. Those who like their fun fired at them in broadsides, will furnish an excellent target for *The Rivals*." -- *Moving Picture World*

Home-Made Pies

Released May 5, 1916. Vim Comedies - General Film Company release. One reel. No copyright registered. Release number 20483.

Produced by Louis Burstein. Directed by Bobby Burns and Walter Stull. Filmed in Jacksonville, Florida.

with Bobby Burns (*Pokes*), Walter Stull (*Jabbs*), Ethel Burton (*Ethel*), Edna Reynolds.

No one could blame Jabbs for being disgusted when he was forced to attempt to eat some of the biscuits made by his daughter, Ethel, a recent graduate of the Culinary Correspondence Course. Not discouraged by her first failure, Ethel bravely attempts a second trial under the supervision of her mother. This time she tries her hand at home-made pies, using all the ingredients she can find in the kitchen. When she places the pies outside the window to cool, the aroma attracts the attention of Pokes, who is badly in need of a meal. Pokes attempts to get away with the pies, but succeeds only in separating himself from some of his teeth. Finally, when he is contentedly munching one of the pies made by the mother and which he has found amongst the sad efforts of Ethel, he is attacked by a policeman and a farmer whom he previously insulted. Vigorously defending himself by using the pies as ammunition, which proves most effective, Pokes manages to seize Ethel and carry her off. Followed by the crowd, Pokes carries Ethel off to the quarry which Jabbs owns. Here he pauses to rest and sits on an old log where an irate employee, whom Jabbs had discharged, had planted a keg of powder in an attempt to blow up Jabbs. Unheedful of the burning fuse stealing quickly up to the keg, Pokes tells Ethel of his love for her, when the explosion occurs. The blast hurls both Pokes and Ethel high in the air and Ethel falls in on top of her mother and astonished crowd. When they look off in horror expecting to see the mangled remains of Pokes, to their chagrin they see him perched on top of a high tree calmly devouring the last of the home-made pies. [MPW]

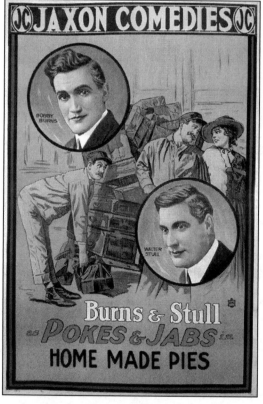

As illustrated by the poster seen here many of the Vim Comedies were reissued by Jaxon, an indication that the parent company (Eastern Film Corporation) retained the films themselves when Vim imploded in late 1917. Note that Jaxon, even with reissues, used the single "b" spelling for Walter Stull's character. It is likely that these reissues retained Vim titling and as such the double "b" version of Plaid Jabbs' name would appear on the movie screen.

"The Vim comedies with their slogan of 'slapsticks and stories' have struck the popular keynote. Slapstick is popular to a certain extent but too much of any good thing is distasteful. The moving picture public has been educated to the extent that they do not care to have a series of incidents carrying no plot whatever presented to them. They want the humor but at the same time they demand the reason back of it. In the latest Vim releases *The Brave Ones* and *Home Made Pies*, this combination of pie-throwing and plot is well combined and the result is both laughable and pleasing. The champion pie-thrower also has to be able to extricate himself from some good plot situations and the result is comedies of a high character." -- *Motography*

The Pretenders

Released May 11, 1916. Vim Comedies - General Film Company release. One reel. No copyright registered. Release number 20521. Erroneously listed in Pennsylvania Board of Censor records as *The Pretender.*

Produced by Louis Burstein. Directed by Bobby Burns and Walter Stull. Filmed in Jacksonville, Florida.

with Bobby Burns (Pokes), Walter Stull (Jabbs), Ethel Burton, Robin Williamson, Helen Gilmore, Frank Hanson, Edna Reynolds.

A foreign count, representing his government, advertises for a new instrument of war. Prof. Micum has just invented a flying torpedo and determines to win the award. He is robbed of his invention by two crooks, Pokes and Jabbs, who visit the count and try to get the money. But they cannot make the contrivance work. The professor comes on their trail and denounces them. They are chased off and he sets the flying torpedo after them. They climb a telegraph pole to escape, but the torpedo cuts the pole in two and they come down with a bump. Convinced that the torpedo is just what he wants, the count pays the award to the professor. [M & MPW]

"Pokes and Jabs play the gentlemen referred to in the title of this one-reel farce. They steal an aerial torpedo from an aged inventor and try to sell it to the representative of a foreign government. The torpedo proves their Nemesis and blows them up. A quick moving farce that contains amusing situations." -- *Moving Picture World*

A Fair Exchange

Released May 19, 1916. Vim Comedies - General Film Company release. One reel. No copyright registered. Release number 20562.

Produced by Louis Burstein. Directed by Bobby Burns and Walter Stull. Filmed in Jacksonville, Florida.

with Bobby Burns (*Pokes*), Walter Stull (*Jabbs*), Ethel Burton, Robin Williamson, Frank Hanson, George Marks.

Squire Higgs is ordered on a vacation by his doctor. He asks Squire Perkins to substitute for him. Perkins is off on a fishing trip, and Jabbs, the gardener, whom he has left in charge, opens the telegram. Jabbs decides to act and, putting on a suit of the squire's, sets out for the village. On the way he passes a lake and goes in swimming. An escaped convict, named Pokes, steals his clothes and runs away. Jabbs is forced to don the convict's clothes. Pokes discovers the telegram in the squire's clothes and decides to act as substitute squire. A young policeman elopes with a girl and comes to be married. Pokes takes a fancy to the girl and abducts her. Jabbs finds the policeman's spare uniform and puts it on. Marching toward the squire's house he comes on Pokes with the girl, overpowers him and forces him to put on the prison clothes again. Pokes escapes and climbs unobserved into an automobile, which drives in at the prison gates, making him a prisoner once more. [M & MPW]

"The exchange consists of swapping a suit of prison stripes for a frock coat and all that goes with it. Pokes and Jabs are the swapees and the two suits of clothes are made to contribute largely to the fun of the reel. A lively and comical Vim." -- *Moving Picture World*

Villains and Violins

Released May 26, 1916. Vim Comedies - General Film Company release. One reel. No copyright registered. Release number 20605.

Produced by Louis Burstein. Directed by Bobby Burns and Walter Stull. Filmed in Jacksonville, Florida.

with Bobby Burns (*Pokes*), Walter Stull (*Jabbs*), Ethel Burton (*Ethel, Cohen's daughter*), Joe Cohen (*Cohen*), Robin Williamson (*Robin*).

Pokes and Jabbs, two stranded minstrels, see in a local newspaper an ad stating that high prices will be paid for all musical instruments. They concoct a scheme whereby they can secure enough funds to carry them back home. After Pokes has pawned his violin for a ridiculously small amount, Jabbs enter the store supposedly in search of a violin. Of all the violins in the store none suits his fancy but the one pawned by Jabbs, for which he offers a large price. The pawnbroker, frantic at his inability to sell the pledged article, begs Jabbs to return after he has had an opportunity to see the owner of the instrument. When Pokes returns to redeem the violin, the pawnbroker offers him a large sum to sell him the instrument and Pokes apparently unwilling to part with his beloved violin, finally consents to the sale. The pawnbroker in vain awaits the return of Jabbs, and later seeks the advice of his friend Cohen. Cohen's daughter, Ethel, is greatly admired by Robin, an insurance agent who has been seeking to sell a policy to the old pawnbroker. After being continually chased way from the house by Cohen, Robin takes the matter in his own hands by eloping with Ethel and by surreptitiously making out a fire insurance policy on the store in his own favor. When the first pawnbroker arrives at Cohen's store he is surprised to find Pokes inside again pawning the violin. The instant Pokes leaves, the pawnbroker running inside tells Cohen of the scheme, and they decide to spring a trap on Jabbs when he enters. Cohen demands that Jabbs show the money with which he desires to purchase the violin, and the moment he displays the roll of "long green" both pawnbrokers try to capture him. Pokes comes to the assistance of his partner and in the melee the stove is overturned and the store destroyed by the flames. After Pokes and Jabbs are led away to jail, Cohen is wringing his hands and bemoaning his hard lot, when Ethel and Robin appear and tell of their marriage. When the old man sees the policy his tears are turned to smiles, and he quickly forgives the elopers and decides that after all, fire insurance is not a bad idea. [MPW]

"A Vim comedy, the kind that will make you laugh." -- *Mount Carmel Item (Mount Carmel, Pennsylvania)*

The Land Lubbers

Released June 2, 1916. Vim Comedies - General Film Company release. One reel. No copyright registered. Release number 20651.

Produced by Louis Burstein. Directed by Bobby Burns and Walter Stull. Filmed in Jacksonville, Florida.

with Bobby Burns (*Pokes*), Walter Stull (*Captain Plaid Jabbs*), Ethel Burton (*the Captain's daughter*), Joe Cohen (*leader of the club*), Harry Naughton (*club member*), Robin Williamson (*waiter*), Edna Reynolds (*maid*), Frank Hanson, Billy Bletcher.

Plaid Jabbs, a retired sea captain, being accustomed to the motion of his ship to lull him to sleep, finds it impossible to rest ashore. He therefore devises a specially constructed room which he has built into his house and which operated by levers gives the same effect as the motion of a ship at sea. While he is peacefully enjoying his sleep in the rocking room with the lever at the point which operates the effect of a calm sea, Pokes, the new butler in the family household, while making love to Ethel, the Captain's daughter, accidentally releases the lever which controls the effect of the hurricane motion. The violent pitching and tossing of the room causes Captain Jabbs to be hurled out of his bunk and in a rage he discharges Pokes. Later, Pokes is induced to join a correspondence school for burglars and is subjected to the various tests for courage and endurance which are called for by the curriculum of the school. Having successfully passed these tests, two of the band lead Pokes out for some practical instruction in the art of entering and robbing houses. Pokes is routed from the first house which he attempts to burglarize, and the conspirators then lead him to the home of Captain Jabbs for a second attempt. When Pokes learns that the house which he is to rob is the home of his sweetheart, he tries to induce the conspirators to select some other house and failing this, he flatly refuses to follow their orders. However, terrified by their threats of dire punishment if he should refuse to follow their instructions, Pokes musters sufficient courage to climb in through the window of the house leading into the rocking room. The other two conspirators not trusting Pokes, decide to follow him and enter the room after him. In the room in which the levers are located, Captain Jabbs is entertaining some friends and for their benefit decides to demonstrate the wonderful possibilities of the rocking room. Pokes and the burglars are dismayed at the violent motion of the room when the Captain operates the levers from without, but the climax is reaches when the professor's boy to whom the Captain is demonstrating the levers accidentally breaks the lever which causes the machinery controlling the room to run amuck and Pokes and his fellow villains are left to their fate whirling round and round in the now rapidly revolving room. [MPW]

The name of the burglary school is Rogue's Club and it seems to be more of a hangout for anarchists than a place of learning. Joe Cohen and another comedian are dressed much like the anarchist duo seen in other Pokes and Jabbs films around this time. The surviving fragment of the film shows Walter Stull's character to apparently be suffering from a case of the gout.

"The familiar but none the less effective device, the revolving stateroom, is the big comic hit of this one-reel farce. Pokes and Jabbs are the leading funmakers, and the finish is rapid of movement and prodigal of laughs." -- *Moving Picture World*

"A rocking room, which gives the players and the spectators the same effect as that produced by a ship on a storm-tossed ocean, makes this slapstick of novel interest. The comedy is of the usual Burns and Stull type." -- *Motion Picture News*

"A hilarious production of a "dry land " captain and some giddy burglars, in which Burns and Stull are featured with much success. With comedies such as these available no more should be heard of dull and dreary performances. Exhibitors who appreciate how much their patrons enjoy a good hearty laugh, which leaves no regrets behind, will see that Direct Comedies are often featured on their programmes." -- *The Biscope*

"The mechanical device of the rocking cabin is well carried out—otherwise, the comedy is very ordinary stuff." -- *Kinematograph Weekly*

A Dollar Down

Released June 9, 1916. Vim Comedies - General Film Company release. One reel. No copyright registered. Release number 20689.

Produced by Louis Burstein. Directed by Bobby Burns and Walter Stull. Filmed in part outside of F.O. Miller Music Co. at 39 W. Forsyth Street and at the Vim Studios in Jacksonville, Florida.

with Bobby Burns (*Pokes*), Walter Stull (*Jabbs*), Ethel Burton (*Ethel Darling*), Helen Gilmore (*Ethel's mother*), Robin Williamson (*street cleaner*), Harry Naughton (*piano salesman*), Spook Hanson (*old man*).

Pokes decides to present his sweetheart, Ethel, with a piano, in order to win her love. On her birthday, Jabbs, another suitor for Ethel's hand, appears at the home of his beloved with a large bouquet of flowers. Pokes, in the meantime, has invested his entire capital of $1 for a piano, to be paid for on the installment plan of $1 per week. When the piano is installed, to the disgust of Jabbs, who seeks to avenge himself upon his hated rival. The smoke issuing from the chimney of Ethel's home gives Jabbs an idea of how he can secure his revenge, and immediately he begins upon his nefarious scheme. By sitting upon the chimney he succeeds in forcing the smoke back into the parlor of the house. Here Pokes and Ethel are spooning, *while Ethel's mother is executing some harmonious selections on the piano. When the smoke fills up the room Pokes' first thought is to save Ethel, while the mother rushes for help. However, the awful thought of paying $1 a week for the rest of his life for a piano that is about to be lost decides Pokes' conduct, so he forgets Ethel, thinking only of his beloved piano. Dropping Ethel on the couch, Pokes drags the piano outside, when Jabbs from the roof above begins to spill water down on top of the piano. Pokes covers up the piano to protect it, but more trouble comes to him when the mother returns accompanied by two white wings armed with a street cleaning hose. Acting under the instructions of the revengeful Jabbs, the white wings turn the hose upon Pokes and his piano and sweep them down the street, over the dock and into the river.* [MPW]

As with the Plump & Runt team, Pokes & Jabbs are sometimes on the same side and at other times rivals. In *A Dollar Down* they are rivals for the affections of Ethel Burton, certainly a worthy endeavor. Pokes thinks he has one up on Jabbs with the gift of the piano. However, neither he or Ethel are very happy once her mother starts to play and sing. Eventually, due to the water hose used by the street cleaners, the prized piano with Pokes atop of it sails down the street and apparently (the end is missing from the extant print) into the St. John River. As a press release by the studio notes, "There isn't much left of the instrument after Pokes and Jabbs get through with it." Something that could be said about most props, sets and costumes involved in the making of one of these frantic Vim comedies.

"The dollar applies to the first installment paid on a piano by Pokes. His adventures with the instrument are surprising, to say the least. He plays upon it, then sits astride of it and rides it down the street. Jabbs is also in the picture and holds up his end of the merry-making. A novel reel." -- *Moving Picture World*

The Raid

Released June 16, 1916. Vim Comedies - General Film Company release. One reel. No copyright registered. Release number 20730. Title mentioned as *Undress Poker* in *Motography* article.

Produced by Louis Burstein. Directed by Bobby Burns and Walter Stull. Filmed in Jacksonville, Florida.

with Bobby Burns (*Pokes*), Walter Stull (*Jabbs*), Mabel Best (*Mrs. Pokes*), Ethel Burton (*Mrs. Stull*), Robin Williamson (*policeman*).

If a man bets his clothes in a poker game he should take the precaution to have some way by which he could reach his home safely in case he loses. However, Pokes failed to take this precaution, so after having lost everything in the game he suddenly realizes his predicament and refuses to give up his trousers. When his fellow players insist on the payment of his bet, Pokes seeks refuge in flight, clad only in his undershirt and pants. Pokes steals a policeman's coat and hat and wends his way back to the clubroom. When he bursts in on the players they are terrified at the uniform and, failing to recognize Pokes in his disguise, they dive pell mell through the window, leaving all the money on the table. Failing to find his clothes, which have been removed. Pokes appropriates the money in payment for his lost attire and starts for home. On his way he passes a saloon, where Jabbs is engaged in an altercation. In the fight Jabbs' new silk hat is knocked off his head and flies outside the saloon, landing on Pokes' head, who wears it away in glee. He conceals the money inside the band of the hat and crawls through the window of his house, where he finds his wife awaiting him with open but far from loving arms. Hanging the hat on a burning gas bracket, Pokes falls asleep, but his wife smells the blazing hat and hurls it out the window. The hat fails on Jabbs, who lives next door, just as he is about to enter his home. Recognizing the hat as his own, Jabbs is delighted, but fails to find the money. The next morning Pokes, on missing the hat and being informed by his wife that she had hurled it from the window, is in despair over the loss of the money. On searching for the hat he sees it lying on the table in Jabbs' home, but is unable to reach it. He enlists the aid of a policeman, but Jabbs, entering the room at this moment, wrecks all the well-made plans of Pokes and his ally and routs them ignominiously. [MPW]

"This is some comedy number. Come have a laugh and forget the heat." -- *The Danville Morning News (Danville, Pennsylvania)*

"Pokes and Jabbs engaged in a deadly struggle for a hat in which the former has hidden his ill-gotten poker winnings, but which is really the property of the latter, who greatly prizes the ancient specimen of head-gear. Their struggle is enhanced by a well sketched policeman." -- *The Bioscope*

For Better or Worse

Released June 23, 1916. Vim Comedies - General Film Company release. One reel. No copyright registered. Release number 20773.

Produced by Louis Burstein. Directed by Bobby Burns and Walter Stull. Filmed in Jacksonville, Florida circa April 1916.

with Walter Stull (*Jabbs, the Police chief*), Bobby Burns (*Pokes*), Robin Williamson (*His pal*), Helen Gilmore (*Mrs. Gothrox*), Ethel Burton (*her maid*), Edna Reynolds (*woman on street*), Harry Naughton (*store owner*), Billy Bletcher (*striking worker*).

Jabbs, the Chief, and Pokes, one of the members of the local police force, are both suitors for the hand of Ethel, the maid at the home of Mrs. Gothrox. While Jabbs is calling on Ethel they hear somebody at the door and, fearing the return of Mrs. Gothrox, Ethel locks Jabbs into the closet. To her dismay, it is Pokes at the door, and refusing to listen to Ethel's entreaties that he remain outside, the doughty policeman enters the kitchen, where he partakes of the repast set on the table for the Chief. Mrs. Gothrox having died, Ethel receives from her late mistress a legacy which causes Pokes and Jabbs to press their suits with still greater ardor. Taking advantage of his position as Chief, Jabbs discharges Pokes from the police force and wins Ethel. Later, when Jabbs and Ethel are having their new home renovated, a strike of paper hangers is called, and the men employed by the newly married couple join the strikers, leaving the house in an unfinished condition. Pokes, now broke and out of work, is pressed with a pal into service as a strike breaker and sent to finish the wall

papering job at Ethel's house. Here Pokes and his pal succeed in papering the room according to their ideas of paper hanging, but in a fashion which would hardly be approved of by interior decorators. When Jabbs, who is now a poor henpecked husband, and Ethel return from a shopping trip they are horrified to see the condition of their once beautiful home. Filled with rage, when he recognizes Pokes, Jabbs chases his former rival and his pal around the room, out of the window and into the water trough beneath. [MPW]

As the object of the amorous efforts of both Walter Stull and Bobby Burns, Ethel Burton gets the bulk of the screen time in the first half of the film as Pokes and then Jabbs visit her in the kitchen only to have to hide from her employer. Mrs. Gothrox, played by Helen Gilmore, dies suddenly leaving her wealth to her maid Ethel. The added incentive of Ethel having money causes the two comedians to again seek her hand. Jabbs wins out only to become a henpecked husband forced to meet his wife's every whim, and Ethel plays her conversion to bossy and even cruel wife well. Pokes for his part now an ex-policeman, does his best to imitate Charlie Chaplin's efforts (á la his 1915 Essanay short, *Work*) at wallpaper application with equal result.

One of the key elements to identifying or confirming identification of a film are clues such as a calendar hanging on the wall. In *For Better Or Worse* those best practices of identification would be thrown a curve. The calendar in the kitchen is turned to April 1915, in this case more evidence of the production budget than the timing of the filming.

"A knockabout comedy of the kind usually made by Bob Burns and Walter Stull in the characters of Pokes and Jabs. The story has little continuity, but the action is swift and rough enough to give the elementary appeal to be expected in productions of this description." -- *Moving Picture World*

For Value Received

Released June 30, 1916. Vim Comedies - General Film Company release. One reel. No copyright registered. Release number 20819.

Produced by Louis Burstein. Directed by Bobby Burns and Walter Stull. Filmed in Jacksonville, Florida.

with Bobby Burns *(Pokes)*, Walter Stull *(Jabbs)*, Ethel Burton *(Ethel Burton)*, Robin Williamson *(her brother)*.

Circumstantial evidence is not always conclusive and it is sometimes wiser to wait until sufficient proof is collected before one jumps to a conclusion. If Ethel had done this when she discovered her sweetheart, Jabbs, with his arm about a young lady in a public cafe, she would have learned that her fiancé was only trying to caress her. Instead of listening to an explanation, Ethel tells Jabbs that the engagement is at an end and that she will marry the first man whom she happens to meet. After several rebuffs she finally discovers Pokes, a tramp, who has been chased by a dog through the window of Ethel's house and into her kitchen, where he is making himself at home. Ethel places her proposition before Pokes, telling him that she will give him a good salary to marry her and to be her husband in name only. Pokes, thinking of the good food and easy money, consents, but balks when it comes to shaving and taking a bath. However, through the cajoling of Ethel's maiden aunt and the assistance of the butler, Pokes is finally cleaned up and looks fairly presentable. The possession of so much money turns Pokes' pocket, and his first thought is for a long drink to quench his thirst, so he sends the butler for a supply of liquid refreshments. The aunt catches him in the attempt and throws the beer away. Nothing daunted, Pokes makes a second and even a third attempt, but each time the aunt interferes so that poor Pokes is almost dying for want of his beloved beer. Finally, in a last desperate endeavor, Pokes thinks of a scheme whereby the butler, with the aid of a hose and funnel, can supply the cherished drink. The scheme almost succeeds until the last minute, when the entrance of the aunt and one of her old admirers spoils the well-made plans of Pokes' and ends in the deluging of aunt and her sweetheart. On the night of the wedding, Jabbs reads of the coming marriage ceremony and makes a last effort to have Ethel listen to his explanation. Ethel, now too willing to be convinced, listens to Jabbs' pleadings and renews the engagement. The problem of what to do with Pokes confronts the happy lovers until Jabbs suggests that rather than disappoint the assembled guests they substitute Auntie and Pokes for the bridal ceremony. Pokes, who has been imbibing rather free in the interim, does not learn of the substitution until the last moment, when he raises the wedding veil and there discovers the aunt. In despair, he falls through the window, rushes back to his old haunts in the freight yards and leaves Jabbs and Ethel to the tender mercies of the minister. [MPW]

"The acrobatic proficiency of Walter Stull and Bob Burns is amply revealed in this Pokes and Jabbs number, which introduces several ingenious bits of low comedy business. As usual, the plot is of secondary importance." -- *Moving Picture World*

Furnished Rooms

Released July 7, 1916. Vim Comedies - General Film Company release. One reel. No copyright registered. Release number 20854.

Produced by Louis Burstein. Directed by Bobby Burns and Walter Stull. Filmed in Jacksonville, Florida.

with Bobby Burns (*Pokes*), Walter Stull (*Jabbs*), Frank Hanson (*Professor Wisem*), Edna Reynolds (*His Wife*), Ethel Burton (*His Daughter*), Robin Williamson (*Her Sweetheart*).

When a person rents a furnished room he should be careful to find first out [sic] something about his fellow roomers. However, Jabbs, a stranded actor, failed to take this precaution. Therefore when he receives from a theatrical agent a part in a drama, he rushes back to his room where he expected to study in quiet. To his consternation, however, Pokes, a one-man orchestra who occupies the opposite room, selects the same time to practice some new music. Driven desperate by the awful bedlam in Pokes' room and finding that all his appeals to the noisy musician to keep quiet are useless, Jabbs packs his belongings and vacates his room. He rents a room in the home of Prof. Wisem who is working on a wonderful rain-making bomb. The Professor's daughter Ethel is in love with Robin and the Professor has promised the young couple that he will give his consent to their marriage when his bomb is proven a success. In the Prof.'s home, Jabbs believes he has found the quietude he needs to study his part, but to his dismay he finds that Pokes, who has been ordered out of his former room, has rented the same room of which Jabbs has already taken possession. In the fight that follows for possession of the room, both Jabbs and Pokes are badly mussed up and in the end agree to be friends and share the room together. That night Robin and Ethel, after having witnessed several futile attempts of the Prof, to produce rain, decide to take matters in their own hands. They rig up a fire hose and arrange that when the bomb explodes, the water shall be turned on and in this way hope that the Prof, shall be deceived into giving his consent to their marriage. The plan proves a great success as far as the young couple are concerned, but not so with Pokes and Jabbs. These two worthies, who happen to be in bed asleep, have the misfortune to have their bed placed directly beneath a broken skylight upon which the hose is turned. The water pours into the room drenching the pair of them and before they can escape from their predicament the rising waters flood the entire room. [MPW]

"A would-be rain-maker is an important character in this one-reel farce. The picture has a well defined plot and a good supply of amusing incidents. Pokes and Jabs head the cast and contribute their usual amount of ginger." -- *Moving Picture World*

The Great Safe Tangle

Released July 14, 1916. Vim Comedies - General Film Company release. One reel. No copyright registered. Release number 20889.

Produced by Louis Burstein. Directed by Bobby Burns and Walter Stull. Filmed circa May 21, 1916 in Jacksonville, Florida.

with Bobby Burns (Pokes), Walter Stull (Jabbs), Harry Naughton (Ima Shark), Ethel Burton (his stenographer), Frank Hanson (Ima Lark) and Robin Williamson (clerk).

When a man is anxiously awaiting the arrival of a safe at his office, it is a calamity that the safe should have been entrusted to the tender mercies of Pokes and Jabbs for safe delivery. The only thing that Pokes and Jabbs know or cared about was that they were ordered to deliver one safe and return with another one. Lark, the lawyer, who had ordered the new safe had accepted from his friend Shark some valuable papers, which Robin, a clerk in Shark's office, but in reality the spy of a foreign government, was anxious to obtain. After an arduous journey Pokes and Jabbs arrive at the office building where despite the protests of Lark that it was he and not Shark that had ordered the new safe, the terrible truckmen deliver the safe in Shark's office. Then they forcibly take from Lark's office his own safe in which Robin disguised as a girl had concealed himself. On their way back to the store with Lark's safe, Pokes and Jabbs get stuck fast on the railroad tracks in front of an oncoming express. With a crash and thud the train hurls them high in the air but with the good luck that always accompanies the pair they fall through the roof of the office building and back into Lark's office, safe, Robin and all. [MPW]

"Pokes and Jabbs lead the fun-makers in this one-reel comedy. The material is original and gives the stars a chance to create a lot of laughs." -- *Motion Picture World*

This farce is chiefly remarkable for the adventures of Pokes and Jabbs, who deliver a safe by donkey cart (which is rough on the donkey) containing instead of valuables a real live male anarchist in female attire. There is a fearful collision with an express train, donkey cart, safe, and our heroes are all blown sky-high, which enables them to deliver the goods through the roof. A very useable, well-acted absurdity." -- *The Bioscope*

Help! Help!

Released July 21, 1916. Vim Comedies - General Film Company release. One reel. No copyright registered. Release number 20923.

Produced by Louis Burstein. Directed by Bobby Burns and Walter Stull. Filmed late February- early March 1916 in Jacksonville, Florida.

with Bobby Burns (*Pokes*), Walter Stull (*Jabbs*), Ethel Burton (*girl*), Robin Williamson (*her sweetheart*), Harry Naughton (*member, Strong Arm Club*).

Because Robin happened to be a much smaller man and not fond of rough play, Pokes was able to frighten him away from Ethel's side. This incident makes Pokes a hero in the eyes of Ethel, who admires manly men. Pokes is getting away with a great amount of talk concerning his ability as a fighter until Jabbs strolls along. Then it is all over with Pokes, who is forced to witness Jabbs coolly walk home with Ethel while he sits disconsolate in the park. Thirsting for revenge, he secures the services of a professional strong arm agency to mete out to Jabbs a well-deserved beating, but not knowing Jabbs' name merely tells the agent to bruise the man with the mustache sitting on Ethel's porch. Little does Pokes realize that Robin has also hired the agency to send Norton one of the bruisers to beat up Pokes, also leaving the same instructions as to the man with the mustache. Jabbs is really another member of the Strong Arm Club and he is sent out on the second order, little knowing that he is really supposed to be out looking for himself. When Norton and Jabbs reach Ethel's house they find only Pokes, and as he has a mustache they go after him with a vengeance. But as even the worm will sometimes turn, so Pokes turns and routs both of the thugs only to find that after all his strenuous fighting Ethel thinks him too rough and gives her affections to gentlehearted Robin. [MPW]

"Another one of those funny Vim comedies with Pokes and Jabs in the feature roles, will be seen today. It is called *Help, Help* and is everything but a story with plot." -- *Hartford Courant* (Hartford, Connecticut)

What'll You Have?

Released July 28, 1916. Vim Comedies - General Film Company release. One reel. No copyright registered. Release number 20959.

Produced by Louis Burstein. Directed by Bobby Burns and Walter Stull. Filmed in Jacksonville, Florida.

with Bobby Burns (*Pokes*), Walter Stull (*Jabbs*), Robin Williamson (*Robin, the bartender*), Ethel Burton.

Jabbs' steady customers try to persuade him that Robin, the bartender he has just discharged, is a member of the Black Hand organization and decide to perpetrate a little joke on him. By the time Pokes appears in the barroom and proceeds not only to eat all the free lunch, but even to get away with a cigar and leaves nothing in the line of cash behind, Jabbs is willing to believe that perhaps the Black Hand is really after him. After Pokes' meeting Robin on the street and purloining a watermelon from him he seeks refuge in Jabbs' saloon, poor Jabbs is so scared that he runs for assistance. While Jabbs is seeking help, Pokes makes himself at home in the saloon, sampling everything in sight. When Jabbs finally returns to the café with police aid, Pokes is having the time of his life. When the police order Pokes to come outside he threatens them with the watermelon and the police believing that it is a bomb, open fire on him with their revolvers. The bullets hit the beer kegs behind which Pokes is hiding, with the results that the entire place is wrecked and both Pokes and Jabbs are deluged with the streams pouring out of the kegs. [MPW]

A printed advertisement for *What'll You Have?* states "The awful results of free lunch – a glorious adventure of the inimitable Pokes. Credit one assist to friend Jabbs." Not so sure Jabbs is ever really much help to Pokes, and more often not even a friend.

"Jabs goes into the saloon business in this one-reel comedy and Pokes at once becomes his best customer. The trick business in the picture is handled cleverly and will prove very amusing." *–Moving Picture World*

Wait a Minute

Released August 4, 1916. Vim Comedies - General Film Company release. One reel. No copyright registered. Release number 20986.

Produced by Louis Burstein. Directed by Bobby Burns and Walter Stull. Filmed in Jacksonville, Florida.

with Bobby Burns (*Pokes*), Walter (*Jabbs*), Helen Gilmore (*Jane Higgs*), Robin Williamson (*Robin*), Ethel Burton (*his sweetheart*), Edna Reynolds (*her sister*), Harry Naughton (*Thirsty Norton*), Bert Tracy (*saloon customer*), Spook Hanson (*Ethel's father*).

Jane Higgs is admired by Pokes, who tries in every possible way to win her affections but to no avail. Jane is not only the village constable, but the head of the Fire Department and the local Justice of the Peace. Being suddenly called to assist the sheriff of the adjoining county, Jane appoints Pokes as her substitute to take charge of the office in her absence. Jane has scarcely departed when Pokes receives word that Bad Jabbs is shooting up Thirsty Norton's Café. Putting on his police hat, Pokes starts out to capture Jabbs, but one look at the bad man and Pokes seeks refuge back in the office and emerges only at the call of fire from a near barn. While busy at the fire, Robin rushes in and demands that Pokes act as justice of the peace and marry him immediately. Pokes quits the fire and proceeds with the wedding service, but the call for help coming again from the dance hall stops the marriage while Pokes again rushes forth. Then the various calls coming for Pokes that are part of the duties of the many offices he holds keeps him rushing madly in all directions. He finally discovers that Robin has eloped not with his real sweetheart, but with her older sister who has disguised herself in Ethel's clothes. However, now that he has a couple of young people in front of him, Pokes is determined to fulfil the duties of the justice of the peace and is going to marry them regardless of Robin's vehement protests. By a clever scheme Pokes succeeds in capturing Jabbs and putting out the fire in the barn and proudly returns to the office with his prisoner. When Pokes arrives at the office, he finds that in his absence Jane has returned with Robin's real sweetheart, Ethel, and has already performed the wedding service. Moreover, instead of being praised for his daring capture of Jabbs, he sees his admired Jane clasp the bad man to her bosom and proclaim him as her long lost husband. Picking up the presents he has given Jane, Pokes, heartbroken, wends his weary way over the hills to another village. [MPW]

[no review available]

Rushing Business

Released August 11, 1916. Vim Comedies - General Film Company release. One reel. No copyright registered. Release number 21019.

Produced by Louis Burstein. Directed by Bobby Burns and Walter Stull. Filmed in Jacksonville, Florida.

with Bobby Burns (*Pokes*), Walter Stull (*Jabbs*), Ethel Burton (*cashier*), Frank Hanson (*Tough*).

Pokes and Jabbs, having come into possession of a fortune, decide to invest it in a business enterprise. After examining and deciding against several places of business that are for sale, the attention of the two is drawn to a hat store, outside of which a crowd of men are struggling to enter. They decide that this certainly is a prosperous business and after a fierce fight finally succeed in entering the store. Quickly making terms with the proprietor, they buy the store and make ready to attend to the wants of the customers, only to discover to their chagrin that the struggling customers are seeking not to buy hats but to pay their poll taxes before the legal limit expires. Nothing daunted, Pokes and Jabbs plan to make business for themselves by breaking the hat of every man they find. While Pokes attends to the breaking end, Jabbs busies himself with selling new hats to all the men that Pokes has caused to patronize the store. Their Waterloo comes, however, when Pokes in his zeal to help business accidentally hits the tough guy of the district with one of his well aimed brick throws. The tough catching sight of Pokes, gives chase and Pokes seeks refuge in the hat store followed by the irate tough. In the melee that follows the entire store is wrecked, Pokes and Jabbs receive the beating of their lives and the tough proudly emerges from the store the possessor of a new hat and the affections of the charming cashier. [MPW]

"Pokes and Jabbs become the owners of a hat store at the opening of this one-reel comedy. They are tricked into thinking that the establishment does a large business, but quickly discover their error. Pokes hits upon a scheme to bring in customers: he gathers an armful of bricks and bombards the hat of every man that passes the corner. The store is soon filled with buyers and Pokes and Jabbs are rapidly becoming rich when Pokes smashes the head covering of a heavy-weight tough, is caught in the act, chased into the store and the place wrecked. The grotesque acting of Robert Burns and Walter Stull make the reel amusing. Ethel Burton and Frank Hanson are worthy of mention." -- *Moving Picture World*

Comrades

Released August 18, 1916. Vim Comedies - General Film Company release. One reel. No copyright registered. Release number 21045.

Produced by Louis Burstein. Directed by Bobby Burns and Walter Stull. Filmed in Jacksonville, Florida.

with Bobby Burns (*Pokes*), Walter Stull (*Jabbs*), Helen Gilmore (*Mrs. Goodgrub, Landlady*), Ethel Burton (*Miss Goodgrub, her daughter*), Edna Reynolds (*boarder*), Harry Naughton (*policeman*).

Comrades in many a midnight burglary and cellmates in the prison where they are spending their summer vacations, Pokes and Jabbs have formed a friendship that seemed unbreakable. When their sentences are served Pokes tells Jabbs that henceforth he will follow the path of honest living. Scornfully, Jabbs parts from his old comrade, and hies himself back to the old surroundings. Pokes, however, seeks shelter in a boarding house to which he has been attracted by the charms of the landlady's daughter. Pokes by his manner, quickly wins the smiles of fair Ethel, much to the disgust and envy of the other lodgers, especially two young men who have also sought to charm the capricious damsel. In order to secure revenge upon the man who has not only stolen away from them their share of the meals and the affections of Ethel, the two roomers plant a dummy in Pokes' room and succeed in convincing the latter that a robber has entered the room. Frightened nearly to death after alarming all the other boarders of the boarding house and scaring them also, Pokes is induced by the two schemers to call the police. While seeking police assistance, Jabbs, who has reverted to his old profession of housebreaking, has entered the room of Pokes and sought shelter in the closet. Pokes returns with a worthy representative of the law, who, after exposing the dummy, berates Pokes for having sought to ridicule him. Pokes, left in the room with the dummy, discovers Jabbs hiding in the closet and learns that in the absence of the household Jabbs has purloined Ethel's beautiful pearl necklace. Ethel, discovering the loss of the necklace, gives the alarm and the policemen and others immediately suspect Pokes of the theft. Pokes has been struggling desperately in his room with the villain Jabbs for the possession of the necklace and succeeds in wrestling it from the latter, after, which he hurls his old partner in *crime out through the window. When the policeman rushes in the door, Pokes is in the act of admiring the necklace, preparatory to returning ot to Ethel. However, circumstantial evidence causes it to look black for Pokes, and quickly realizing the fact, the would-be hero dives out through the window and away before the law can again fasten its grasp upon him.* [MPW]

Pokes and Jabbs are released from jail together but then spend the bulk of the film apart only to come together, and in trouble, in the end. Bobby Burns gets most of the screen time and while everyone in the boarding house is fed up with his antics, be it spreading pepper around the dinner table or playing the piano horribly, Ethel Burton just seems to love his every move. Apparently love is blind, and that fact is used for comic effect.

"A comic 'crook' drama with Pokes and Jabbs as a pair of thieves, this one-reeler has incessant action and is good for a number of laughs. The principal scenes take place in a boarding house, and the two heroes are mixed up in a love affair, their love for their profession being the means of their undoing. Robert Burns and Walter Stull are as acrobatic and as humourous as ever. Helen Gilmore and Ethel Burton are members of the cast." -- *Moving Picture World*

The Tryout

Released August 25, 1916. Vim Comedies - General Film Company release. One reel. No copyright registered. Release number 21079.

Produced by Louis Burstein. Directed by Walter Stull and Bobby Burns. Filmed at the Vim Studios in Jacksonville, Florida.

with Bobby Burns *(Pokes)*, Walter Stull *(Jabbs)*, Ethel Burton *(Ingenue)*, Robin Williamson *(Tramp)*, Harry Naughton *(Cameraman)*, Spook Hanson, Babe Hardy.

Pokes is told by his landlady not to return unless he brings the money necessary to pay up his back board bill. Therefore, when Pokes sees a sign hanging in front of one of the picture studios "Extra Wanted," he jumps at the opportunity and is told to report the following morning for a tryout. Jabbs, the director of the company to which Pokes is assigned is in no pleasant mood when Pokes reports on the following morning. Instead of taking heed to his cues and entering the stage in the proper moment Pokes is either busy rehearsing his business behind the sets or thinking of the reward that is coming to him when he rescues the pretty ingenue from the villainous tramp that is to attack her. After several rehearsals Jabbs is almost frantic and determines to give Pokes only one more chance. This time when the cameraman is grinding and everything is running smoothly, Pokes really does appear, but instead of following the routine ordered by Jabbs, runs amuck and starts shooting at everybody in the cast. At the time that Jabbs' scene is taken place, several other directors are working on the stage and each company is busy with its respective scenes. When Pokes emerges from the set chasing everybody before him at the point of his revolver, consternation reigns on the big studio stage, and all of the members of the various companies seek refuge behind wings and chairs. Pokes continues on his wild journey until finally Jabbs in self-defense unites all the studio employees to turn upon the luckless Pokes and succeed in subduing him after a hard struggle. [MPW]

Since films that give the viewer a glimpse behind the camera are always fun to watch, it is too bad this one no longer exists. Walter Stull's mad rampage through the movie studio would have been an interesting look behind the scenes of Vim Studios. Most all of the Vim contingent appear briefly during the final scenes involving the disruption of all the companies' filming.

"The scene of the tryout is a motion picture studio. Pokes gets a job as a actor and the dream he has the night before he goes to get work becomes the plot of the comedy. The reel is an amusing burlesque on the making of a motion picture, the slap dash acting of Robert Burns and Walter Stull being right in line with the scenario. Ethel Burton, Robin Williamson and Harry Naughton complete the cast."
-- *Moving Picture World*

The Reward

Released September 1, 1916. Vim Comedies - General Film Company release. One reel. No copyright registered. Release number 21104.

Produced by Louis Burstein. Directed by Bobby Burns and Walter Stull. Filmed in Jacksonville, Florida.

with Bobby Burns (*Pokes, a secret service man*), Walter Stull (*Jabbs, the pseudo doctor*), Robin Williamson (*Butler, also a secret service man*), Mabel Best (*The Girl*), Frank Hanson (*Her Father*), Helen Gilmore (*Her Mother*).

Masked behind the garb of respectability accomplished by the pseudo title of doctor, Jabbs conducts a gambling den in one of the most exclusive districts of the city. Although warned by a confederate that the hand of the law is about to grasp him, Jabbs refuses to leave. Pokes, a secret service man, who is delegated to watch Jabbs, saves Mabel from death at the peril of his own life. Jabbs, however, claims the credit for the rescue and later entices Mabel to come to his office. Once he has Mabel inside the office, Jabbs drops his mask and attacks the girl. Pokes on guard outside hears the noise of the struggle and the screams of the girl and dashes into the waiting room. He finds his way to the private office barred, but nothing daunted, Pokes batters down the doors, and enters the private office. In the private office Jabbs, hearing the hammering on the doors, throws Mabel into a back room and now awaits Pokes' rush. The two men clinch and a struggle ensues during which both Pokes and Jabbs fight for the possession of a knife. Locked in a death-like clinch the fighting men roll out of the window and off the roof to the yard below. Eluding Jabbs again, Pokes risks his life once more and reaches the room where Mabel is confined. Just as Jabbs enters the room Pokes seizes Mabel in his arms and dives out of the window into a passing machine. Inside the room, Jabbs is raging as Robin, another secret service man posing as a butler in Jabbs' office, clamps the handcuffs on the ruthless villain, while in the car Pokes now discloses his identity to Mabel, and wins his just reward. [MPW]

"Popular melodrama is amusingly burlesqued in this one-reel farce. As a secret service man, Pokes gets in the trail of Jabbs the villain, and saves the heroine from some kind of terrible fate. The acrobatic stunts performed by the two, while locked in a deadly embrace on the roof of a house, give the reel a strong finish." -- *Moving Picture World*

A Bag of Trouble

Released September 8, 1916. Vim Comedies - General Film Company release. One reel. No copyright registered. Release number 21136.

Produced by Louis Burstein. Directed by Bobby Burns and Walter Stull. Filmed in Jacksonville, Florida.

with Bobby Burns (*Pokes*), Walter Stull (*Jabbs*), Helen Gilmore (*Mrs. Pokes*), Mabel Best (*Mrs. Jabbs*), Edna Reynolds (*maid*).

Even if he were certain that the act would cost him his life. Pokes would take a chance and flirt if a pretty girl happened to pass him. Therefore, it is nothing unusual when Pokes finds a beautiful handbag lying on the street that he should give it to the maid living next door and with whom he carried on a flirtation. Pokes little realized that this bag is one which his wife just purchased but lost on her return home. Later, however, when he meets Melba in the park, he regrets his hasty action in giving the bag to the maid and returns to gain possession of it. After securing the bag. Pokes meets Jabbs, the pride of the local police force, and terrified Pokes drops the bag and makes a hasty exit. Jabbs decides that the bag is just the thing he

needs as a present for his wife in honor of her birthday. When the maid a few hours afterward espies Mrs. Jabbs displaying the bag, she recognizes it as the one which Pokes gave her, and sends him after Mrs. Jabbs to demand an explanation. Mrs. Pokes, in the meantime, having missed her bag, begins a frantic search for it and forces Jabbs to assist her. Coming upon Pokes and Jabbs struggling for possession of the bag, Mrs. Pokes proves her ownership to it and marches away in triumph, leading the unfortunate Pokes with her. Arriving home, she discovers that by mistake she has taken two bags, and sends Pokes back to the jeweler's with one of them. Pokes really intends to return it safely, but meeting Melba once more, he succumbs to her wiles and gives her the bag. But this time Mrs. Pokes catches him, and the result is anything but favorable to Pokes. [MPW]

With a few alterations in the plot and the roles played this is basically a remake of the 1913 Lubin short *The Wrong Handbag*. In that earlier film is Bobby Burns and George Reehm that learn the purse is truly a bag of trouble.

"Pokes and Jabbs, in the persons of Robert Burns and Walter Stull, get into a lot of trouble in this one-reel comedy over the question of ownership of a handbag. Poke's flirting with and subsequent gift to Jabbs' wife of Mrs. Pokes' new handbag starts things going, and the following many involved situations are humorous." -- *Moving Picture World*

" … another Pokes and Jabbs story with Jabbs as a policeman, and has an ending reminiscent of Maskelyne and Devant. Pokes' wife loses a smart handbag in a collision with P.C. Jabbs, and hubby, finding it, presents it to a lady. The bag causes many amusing incidents, being at various times in possession of half a dozen ladies in the district. Mrs. Pokes in a jealous rage takes hubby to task and he melts away to nothing before the wrath of his better half, While she nonchalantly picks up his bundle of clothes and goes home. It is quite an amusing comedy and the disappearance of Pokes is quite effectively conceived." -- *Kinematograph Weekly*

Payment in Full

Released September 15, 1916. Vim Comedies - General Film Company release. One reel. No copyright registered. Release number 21160.

Produced by Louis Burstein. Directed by Bobby Burns and Walter Stull. Filmed circa August 1916 in Jacksonville, Florida.

with Bobby Burns (*Pokes*), Walter Stull (*Jabbs*), Ethel Burton (*Pokes' sweetheart*), Frank Hanson (*her father*), Robin Williamson (*Pokes' friend, an actor*).

Forced by the threat of old Moneybags to foreclose the mortgage unless he receives the hand of Ethel in marriage Jabbs reluctantly pleads with his daughter to accept the old miser's proposal. Ethel, in love with Pokes, is torn between love and duty, but finally consents to act according to her father's wishes. Pokes, heartbroken, confides in his friend, Robin, an actor, who promises to help him out of his difficulties. Robin succeeds in making Pokes up to resemble

Jabbs and after sending Jabbs downtown by a decoy message, Pokes invites Moneybags to the Jabbs' home to receive Ethel's answer. Once he has the mortgage in his possession Pokes demands that Moneybags, who has not penetrated the disguise of Pokes, to give a demonstration of his muscular prowess and forces him through a series of gymnastic exercises that nearly kill the old man. The test is too much for Moneybags and, after surrendering all claims to Ethel, he wrathfully quits the house. When Jabbs returns home disgusted with the fool's errand on which he has been sent, he is dumbfounded to find himself face to face with his double. Believing that he is confronted by a madman, Jabbs secures a revolver and shoots and is then terrified by the conviction that he is a murderer. However, when Pokes comes to life after pulling off his disguise and produces the mortgage papers, Jabbs is only too happy to give Ethel into Pokes' outstretched arms. [MPW]

"More comedy here than "slapstick" and the darling child is a particularly sweet child." --*The Bioscope*

"Pokes and Jabbs do several new stunts in a gymnasium in this one-reel knockabout comedy. Pokes puts one over on Jabbs when he disguises himself as Jabbs and gets rid of Old Moneybags, who also wants to marry Jabbs' daughter. Pokes gets the mortgage, though, and also gets the girl." -- *Moving Picture World*

"The plot is not stimulating, nor original. There are some neat feats of tumbling and some dexterity of action. The girl is attractive and there is no vulgarity." -- *Kinematograph Weekly*

The Man Hunters

Released September 22, 1916. Vim Comedies - General Film Company release. One reel. No copyright registered. Release number 21192.

Produced by Louis Burstein. Directed by Bobby Burns and Walter Stull. Filmed in Jacksonville, Florida.

with Bobby Burns (*Pokes*), Walter Stull (*Jabbs*), Ethel Burton (*postmistress*), Frank Hanson (*storekeeper*), Harry Naughton (*outlaw*), Robin Williamson (*outlaw*).

The local police force and all the inhabitants of the town are in mortal fear of two outlaws who have been terrorizing the neighboring townships. Pokes, the village boob, who is a graduate of a correspondence school for detectives, volunteers to safeguard the town and arrest the outlaws, but his efforts are ridiculed by the populace. Pokes, however, follows the trail of every stranger who enters the town. When Jabbs, the famous city detective summoned by the local police to assist them in guarding the post-office, appears in town, Pokes follows him and observes Jabbs disguising himself as a woman. That is enough evidence for Pokes, and when Jabbs, dressed as a woman enters the post-office to introduce himself, Pokes summons the police and despite Jabbs' protests has him marched off to the police station. While Jabbs is establishing his identity, Naughton and Robin, the two outlaws, ride up to the post-office and overpowering the postmaster and his assistant, seize the safe and the contents of the cash drawer and gallop off to their cabin.

Later when Jabbs and the police return to the post-office, they discover the robbery. Realizing that Pokes' act has been responsible for the affair, they rush to seek the would-be detective. Catching sight of him they give chase, but Pokes manages to elude them. Just as he believes himself secure, Pokes blunders in upon the outlaws who are surprised at the sudden appearance and allow themselves to be captured by Pokes with the aid of their own guns. As Pokes marches his captives to the front of the post-office, as Jabbs is praising him for his wonderful feat, as the village belles rush to kiss him, fate steps in and instead of a hero, Pokes finds himself once again the village boob. [MPW]

"Pokes and Jabbs dole out considerable comedy in this reel, which contains more story than several of their recent releases. Pokes, as a correspondence school detective, captures the outlaws in spite of himself, but, nevertheless, is proven a boob. Jabbs gets over considerable comedy as the city detective." –*Moving Picture World*

Tangled Ties

Released September 29, 1916. Vim Comedies - General Film Company release. One reel. No copyright registered. Release number 21219. Erroneously called *Tangled Hearts* in some publications.

Produced by Louis Burstein. Directed by Bobby Burns and Walter Stull. Filmed in Jacksonville, Florida.

with Bobby Burns (*Pokes*), Walter Stull (*Jabbs*), Mabel Best (*Mrs. Pokes*), Ethel Burton (*Mrs. Jabbs*), Harry Naughton (*Mr. Newlywed*), Melba Andrews (*Mrs. Newlywed*), Frank Hanson (*hotel proprietor*), Edna Reynolds (*old maid*).

Pokes, a supposed nervous wreck, is sent by his wife to a hotel in the country that he may enjoy a well-earned rest. However, instead of resting, Pokes begins to flirt desperately with the wives of Jabbs and Newlywed. Both husbands are incensed at Pokes' conduct and finally their patience is exhausted, so they agree that Jabbs must be taught not to flirt so promiscuously. Jabbs' wife, overhearing her husband's plan to punch Pokes, tries to warn the latter to escape, but when her husband discovers her in Pokes' room he is infuriated and refuses to listen to her explanations. In the fight that follows Pokes defeats both Jabbs and Newlywed, but when his wife suddenly appears at the hotel, he seeks refuge in flight. He escapes from the hotel via the telegraph wire, but slips and falls into the well, out of which he is dragged in a half-drowned condition, but upon his recovering consciousness, rather than face his irate spouse, he again falls to the bottom and rises no more. [M]

"An average knockabout comedy reel with numerous lively spots. Pokes and Jabs sow considerable "pep" in this number. Pokes goes to country hotel for a rest, and begins to flirt with the wives of Jabbs and others. This starts the complications that lead to Pokes' escaping from his pursuers via a telegraph wire. He sinks into a well, rises again, but once more sinks at sight of his angry wife." -- *Moving Picture World*

Strictly Business

Released October 6, 1916. Vim Comedies - General Film Company release. One reel. No copyright registered. Release number 21247.

Produced by Louis Burstein. Directed by Bobby Burns and Walter Stull. Filmed in Jacksonville, Florida.

with Bobby Burns (*Pokes*), Walter Stull (*Prof. Jabbs*), Mabel Best (*Mrs. Jabbs*), Ethel Burton (*Miss Jabbs*), Harry Naughton (*superintendent*), Spook Hanson (*worker*).

Pokes, the porter in an office building, has several times by his acts of omission incurred the wrath of the superintendent, but each time he has been forgiven and granted another chance. Finally, after a clash with Jabbs, a new tenant in the building, Pokes is discharged. Securing a position as book agent, Pokes is filled with one ambition to sell a book to Jabbs. Stalking his intended victim like a jungle tiger, Pokes becomes Jabbs' shadow and haunts him in both his working hours and in his dreams. No matter how often Jabbs and the Superintendent throw him out from the office. Pokes turns up in the most unexpected manner, until Jabbs, in a frenzy, decides that the only way to rid himself of the pest is to buy one of the books. Having made the purchase, Jabbs returns home, secure in the belief that at last he is safe from Pokes salesman's urgings. But to his horror finds not only the members of his family but even the butler the proud possessors of the despised books. [MPW]

The door on Jabbs' office notes that he is an economy expert. The book that Pokes is trying to sell is entitled *How To Save Money*, the answer being what any economy expert would tell you: don't buy useless books. This Pokes and Jabbs outing was much more situational than slapstick but still gave Bobby Burns a number of opportunities to get in a tumble or two. As Pokes, he does everything from walking across telephone wires to getting rolled up in a carpet as ways to gain entrance into Pokes' office.

"A quite lively knockabout number. Pokes and Jabbs are the funmakers in this reel. Pokes gets a job as a book agent and insists on selling Jabbs a book. Pokes is relentless in his pursuit of Jabbs, and no matter how many times he is thrown about he sticks to his ambition. Finally Jabbs capitulates, only to find that the book agent has sold every one in his household a book. Besides Pokes and Jabbs, there appear on the screen Mabel Best, Ethel Burton and Harry Naughton." -- *Moving Picture World*

Watch Your Watch

Released October 13, 1916. Vim Comedies - General Film Company release. One reel. No copyright registered. Release number 21277.

Produced by Louis Burstein. Directed by Bobby Burns and Walter Stull. Filmed in Riverside Park, along Riverside Avenue and in downtown Jacksonville, Florida.

with Bobby Burns (*Pokes*), Walter Stull (*Jabbs*), Melba Andrews (*Mrs. Jabbs*), Ethel Burton (*Miss Jabbs*), Harry Naughton (*crook*), Frank Hanson (*Professor E.Z. Mark*), James Renfro (*butler*), Mabel Best (*maid*).

Jabbs, falling asleep at his club one evening, is made the victim of a practical joke by his fellow club mates, who relieve him of his watch. On his way home, he collides with Prof. E. Z. Mark, who, having been presented with a beautiful watch by his fellow professors, is naturally somewhat still under the influence of the happy event. Missing his watch, a minute later, Jabbs naturally suspects that the professor was none other than a clever pick pocket who had used the collision to cover up his light fingered operating. Running back Jabbs catches up with the professor and after administering a severe beating to him forces the professor to hand over his own cherished watch. Not until the following morning when he reads of the robbery of which the professor is the victim does Jabbs realize his error. In terror that he may at any moment be arrested. Jabbs seeks several ways by which he can rid himself of the watch, which is plainly marked with the professor's name. All his schemes failing, he throws it out of the window to be found by Pokes who gives it to his sweetheart, Ethel, Jabbs' daughter who proudly displays it to her father, Jabbs employs a professional crook to rob his house. The crook forces Pokes to assist him in the robbery. They fight over possession of the watch and both are marched off to jail. Jabbs' home is demolished by the crook and Pokes. In despair he rushes out and seeing the professor calls to him to come and get the watch, but the professor, fearing another beating, hurries away. He is followed by Jabbs. The professor seeks refuge in the police station just as the crook and Pokes are being arraigned. The crook catches sight of Jabbs and accuses him of hiring him to rob his home and the professor also accuses him of being the man who assaulted him and robbed him of his beautiful watch. The evidence being conclusive all three, Pokes, Jabbs and the crook are led away to the cells, where the crook and Pokes proceed to mete out to Jabbs dire punishment for having been the direct cause of their predicament. [MPW]

Walter Stull as the man unable to discard a watch gets the lion's share of screen time in this comedy. And while more times than not it is Pokes that gets the beating for odd behavior this time around it is Jabbs that receives the greater punishment. While an often used premise, that of an object always coming back even against the disposer's best efforts, the different methods and situations that arise in *Watch Your Watch* are amusing.

"A good number of the Pokes and Jabbs comedies. Fast knockabout work keeps the spectator chuckling. Pokes has a hard time getting rid of the watch he took from the professor, believing it to be his. The outcome is that Pokes, Jabbs and the crook hired by Pokes to steal the watch Pokes stole are all three led to jail." -- *Moving Picture World*

Here and There

Released October 20, 1916. Vim Comedies - General Film Company release. One reel. No copyright registered. Release number 21304.

Produced by Louis Burstein. Directed by Bobby Burns and Walter Stull. Filmed in Jacksonville, Florida.

with Bobby Burns (*Pokes*), Walter Stull (*Jabbs*), Ethel Burton (*Flossie Footlights*).

Pokes, coming home late one night, is ordered out of the house by his wife. Seeking refuge in a side-door Pullman, Pokes falls asleep, little knowing that his train de luxe is bound for Cyclone Gulch, miles way in the desert. Here Jabbs, the local sheriff, realizing the need of a loving female to mend his socks and sew a few buttons on his shirts, advertises for a wife. The "ad" catches the eye of Flossie Footlights. Flossie, knowing that the early bird catches the worm, burns up the road in getting out to Cyclone Gulch to land the lonesome sheriff. Pokes has been hired by Jabbs as a cowpuncher and when Flossie breezes into the Gulch, Pokes immediately

poses as the sheriff and makes a rapid play for the erstwhile Broadway chicken. Jabbs, learning of the deception, wrathfully confronts the artful Pokes, but in the fight that follows Pokes, by a trick, send the sheriff on a "flying" trip to dreamland. After securing the sheriff's badge from the vanquished opponent, Pokes receives from Flossie all the adulation due a conquering hero. Later, however, Jabbs, posing as a real old time bad man, meets with Pokes just as the latter is feasting on the plaudits of the townspeople gathered in the local dance hall. Caught at a disadvantage and his wits refusing to come to his assistance, Pokes seeks safety in putting as much distance as possible between himself and Jabbs. At the station Pokes comes face to face with his irate spouse, who, having learned of Pokes' whereabouts, has come in search of him. When Mrs. Pokes learns from Jabbs of her husband's flirtation with Flossie she sets out to finish in her own manner the task Jabbs had begun. [MPW]

"Pokes and Jabbs do considerable fast knockabout work in this reel. The film is a fair comedy. Pokes lands in a Western town where the sheriff, Jabbs, has advertised for a wife. The ad is answered by a showgirl and Pokes makes a play for her favor. He gets rid of Jabbs for a while, but the latter comes back in the guise of a bad man, and to add to Pokes's worries his wife appears on the scene." -- *Moving Picture World*

The Frame-Up

Released October 27, 1916. Vim Comedies - General Film Company release. One reel. No copyright registered. Release number 21334.

Produced by Louis Burstein. Directed by Bobby Burns and Walter Stull. Filmed in Jacksonville, Florida.

with Bobby Burns (*Pokes*), Walter Stull (*Jabbs*), Frank Hanson (*Mr. Spookem*), Edna Reynolds (*Mrs. Spookem*), Ethel Burton (*Miss Spookem*), Billy Ruge (*former cellmate*).

When Pokes, the butler in the Spookem home, see Jabbs, a young man about town, making love to Ethel, the daughter of the household, his jealousy knows no bounds. He plans revenge by putting the family silver in Jabbs' pocket where Spookem is bound to see it. Spookem enraged, orders Jabbs to leave the house. Pokes' happiness at the success of his little scheme is short lived, for soon he comes face to face with Ruge, formerly a cellmate in the penitentiary. Ruge has been discharged by Spookem, and has come to the house to blow up Spookem and his family. Through fear that Ruge will betray him to his master, Pokes is forced to carry the bomb into the house, but later hurls it back at Ruge, who is blown into the river. Jabbs sends a box of candy to Ethel, but as it is similar in shape to Ruge's bomb, Pokes is almost frantic with fear. In terror he notifies the entire household, who look in deadly fright at the queer-acting "bomb." The "bomb" seems possessed of spirits moving here and there about the house, until Jabbs returns and explains the mystery to the discomfort of Pokes. [MPW]

"Another great feature, the latest Vim comedy scream, "The Frame-Up" is as full of laughs as you usually get in these great comedy creations." -- *Wilmington Morning Star (Wilmington, North Carolina)*

In the Ranks

Released November 3, 1916. Vim Comedies - General Film Company release. One reel. No copyright registered. Release number 21362.

Produced by Louis Burstein. Directed by Bobby Burns and Walter Stull. Filmed in Jacksonville, Florida.

with Bobby Burns (Pokes), Walter Stull (Jabbs), Frank Hanson (A Deserter), Ethel Burton (Pokes' Sweetheart).

Realizing the peculiar attraction that soldiers' uniforms seem to possess for all girls, Jabbs, after being rejected by Ethel, in favor of Pokes, decides to enlist in the army. In this case, however, the exception seemed to be the rule, for instead of admiring glances from Ethel, Jabbs receives only laughter and sarcasm. Later, Ethel has cause to regret her decision, for Pokes coming to Ethel's lawn fete attired in a soldiers uniform, which he has secured from a deserter, becomes enamored of the danseuse whom Ethel has engaged to entertain her guests. Enraged at Pokes' perfidy, Ethel, to secure revenge, informs the soldiers who are seeking the real deserter that Pokes is the man for whom they are searching. Pokes is led back to the camp grounds despite his protests that he is only wearing the uniform as a masquerade. At the camp he is brought before Jabbs (who is now a general) and other officers for trial, and Jabbs immediately sentences Pokes to be shot. Pokes is led off by a firing squad for execution but chance intervenes and Pokes, making the most of his advantage, pulls the bullets from the cartridges and makes a dash for liberty. [MPW]

"Pokes and Jabbs are seen in this comedy reel. The reel is not as lively as some of the recent Pokes and Jabbs numbers, but embraces a number of laughs. Pokes and Jabbs both take a chance at soldiering this time, and a little knockabout work gets over. To cap the climax Pokes is shot from a cannon and is seen catapulting through the air." *-- Moving Picture World*

Hot Dogs

Released November 10, 1916. Vim Comedies - General Film Company release. One reel. No copyright registered. Release number 21392. [Some release charts list *Gay Deceivers* as being released on this date]

Produced by Louis Burstein. Directed by Bobby Burns and Walter Stull. Filmed in the Riverside district and at Riverside Park in Jacksonville, Florida.

with Bobby Burns (*Pokes*), Walter Stull (*Jabbs*), Ethel Burton, Billy Ruge (*dog owner*), Edna Reynolds (*Mrs. Pokes*), Harry Naughton (*man in park*).

Nobody could ever accuse Pokes of being afraid of hard work; he likes it so well that he could sleep right alongside of it. The morning Mrs. Pokes receives word that her husband has received an appointment as City Dog Catcher, she loses no time in routing her tired spouse from his doway bed and rushes him over to the dog pound, where Jabbs is waiting for him. Jabbs instructs Pokes in the gentle art of swinging the net on all stray dogs and orders him to go out and make good. In his anxiety to win the medal as champion dog catcher. Pokes tries to capture every dog he spies, no matter where they are or to whom they belong. After getting into all kinds of trouble because of his misplaced zeal, Pokes decides to partake of a little liquid refreshment. Inside the cafe, his attention is attracted by the free lunch. After devouring about a ton of "hot dogs," Pokes is transformed into a dog, and only after the strenuous action on the part of Jabbs and Mrs. Pokes is the would-be dog catcher subdued and safely muzzled. [MPW]

Trying to make good with Jabbs the veteran dog catcher, Pokes attempts to capture anything that even slightly looks canine. At one point he grabs a little girl's stuffed puppy that eventually gets thrown in the house, hitting Ethel and knocking her out. She awakes, sees Billy Ruge on the porch and in a fit of rage throws the stuffed animal at him. He in turn being a somewhat innocent bystander throws the animal at Pokes, who after being knocked to the ground picks up the stuffed toy and throws it back again hitting Ethel. When the dog hits Ethel, who is leaning out the window, she gets a very comical look on her face and faints across the window sill. The brief sequence makes up Ethel's entire appearance in the film but shows she could be very funny.

Billy Ruge drifts in and out of the film dressed as an Italian immigrant with a big bushy mustache, whose dog keeps getting taken away by Jabbs. At this point, with the demise of Plump & Runt, there wasn't really a place for Ruge except working in support of Burns and Stull. Providing support sums up what Walter Stull was doing in this film, with most all of the screen time chewed up by Bobby Burns.

"Pokes and Jabbs get across considerable knockabout comedy in this reel. Pokes is taught the gentle art of dog catching by Jabbs. Pokes gets into trouble over some of his catches. The action is quite fast." -- *Moving Picture World*

Good and Proper

Released November 17, 1916. Vim Comedies - General Film Company release. One reel. No copyright registered. Release number 21420.

Produced by Louis Burstein. Directed by Bobby Burns and Walter Stull. Filmed in Jacksonville, Florida.

with Bobby Burns (*Pokes*), Walter Stull (*Jabbs*), Ethel Burton (*Mlle. Zee-Bra*), Harry Naughton (*her husband*), Edna Reynolds.

Pokes and Jabbs, two rare sports, become enamored of Mile. Zee-Bra, the dashing comedienne appearing at one of the local theaters, and invite her out to supper after the show. When Mile. Zee-Bra appears at the stage entrance, the two sports are there with flowers and candy, but Jabbs, with fiendish skill, double crosses his pal, and after getting in solid with the actress himself leaves Pokes to pay for the taxi while he enters the cafe with the girl. Pokes, however, disguises himself as the waiter, enters the private room where Jabbs and the Mile. are dining, and proceeds to wreak vengeance upon his false friend. While Pokes and Jabbs are trying to arrange a plan whereby one of them can be eliminated, leaving the field open to the other, the husband of the actress appears at the cafe and demands an explanation. Mile. tearfully begs her husband to spare the two cringing sports, but the husband is obdurate and refuses to show them mercy. However, at length he consents to spare one of them, but they themselves must decide who will be the unfortunate one. Pouring a vial (which all think contains poison) into the coffee, the husband orders Pokes and Jabbs to choose between the cups. Pokes loses, and, in a frenzy of fear, after drinking the fatal dose, implores Jabbs to save him from death. This Jabbs tries to do to the best of his ability, and the punching which Jabbs hands to Pokes according to his ideas of resuscitation makes Pokes regret that any such person as Mile. Zee-Bra ever crossed his path. [MPW & Studio synopsis]

"A moderately fast knockabout comedy with Pokes and Jabbs rivals for the favor of an actress. Jabbs manages to get the actress to dine with him. Pokes disguises as the waiter, and things start going rapidly when the actress's husband appears. The reel closes with a whirlwind fight." -- *Moving Picture World*

Money Maid Men

Released November 24, 1916. Vim Comedies - General Film Company release. One reel. No copyright registered. Release number 21450.

Produced by Louis Burstein. Directed by Bobby Burns and Walter Stull. Filmed at the Vim studios in Jacksonville, Florida.

with Bobby Burns (*Pokes*), Walter Stull (*Jabbs*), Ethel Burton.

Both Pokes and Jabbs, clerks in Grabem's counting rooms, are in love with Ethel, the stenographer. Grabem himself, becomes enamored of the pretty stenographer, much to the disgust of his two clerks, who realize the difference between their lowly wages and the great wealth of their employer. Jabbs determines that if it is money and ability to buy expensive gifts that prevents him from winning Ethel's love, then he will, in some manner, secure the necessary riches. Late one night, while Ethel is out to dinner with Grabem, Pokes is working over his books in the counting room. Suddenly he is startled by a sound from the private office. Rushing inside he is confronted with a masked burglar, who, at the point of a gun, orders Pokes to help him open the vault. Against his will Pokes is forced to assist the crook, but once the vault is opened, Pokes pushes the burglar inside the vault and locks the door. Pokes calls for help, and Grabem, Ethel and the watchman rush into the office. At first they think that Pokes is the crook, and are about to arrest him, when he begs them to listen to his explanations. Telling Grabem to open the vault, Pokes drags the almost suffocated crook into the office, where, upon unmasking him, the group is shocked to see that the masked burglar is Jabbs. Overjoyed at Pokes' honesty and bravery, Grabem thrusts a huge sum of money upon his bewildered clerk, and Ethel, not to be outdone in generosity, coyly tells Pokes that now she is willing to be his forever, but, after a few seconds of thought Pokes chooses which --ah! that is the question. [MPW]

"A rather slow-moving comedy reel, with Pokes and Jabbs in the role of bookkeepers, and rivals the favor of the stenographer. A few laughs come through antics with a sliding chair. Pokes decides to get money in robbing the safe, and is discovered by Jabbs. The boss, as a reward to Jabbs, make him choose between money and the girl. He takes the money." -- *Moving Picture World*

Ambitious Ethel

Released December 1, 1916. Vim Comedies - General Film Company release. One reel. No copyright registered. Release number 21478.

Produced by Louis Burstein. Directed by Bobby Burns and Walter Stull. Filmed in Jacksonville, Florida.

with Bobby Burns (*Pokes*), Walter Stull (*Jabbs*), Ethel Burton (*Ethel*).

[no synopsis available].

From the scant information available, Ethel Burton took a more prominent role in this Pokes and Jabbs offering. A beautiful woman and skilled comedienne, Burton often seemed under utilized in the Vim comedies. It is a shame that a chance to see her front and center, at least via this film, is not possible.

"Pokes and Jabbs always get off some good comedy, and this reel is up to their standard." -- *Fairmont West Virginian (Fairmont, West Virginia)*

"A fair number of the Pokes and Jabs comedies. Ethel Burton is seen with Robert Burns and Walter Stull. The film embraces a quite funny burlesque to *Romeo and Juliet*. When Ethel sees it she becomes fired with ambitions to become a movie actress, and it is in the course of her instruction that most of the laughs come." – *Moving Picture World*

A Rare Boarder

Released December 8, 1916. Vim Comedies - General Film Company release. One reel. No copyright registered. Release number 21508.

Produced by Louis Burstein Directed by Bobby Burns and Walter Stull. Filmed in Jacksonville, Florida.

with Bobby Burns (*Pokes*), Walter Stull (*Jabbs*), Ethel Burton, Edna Reynolds..

Pokes, a traveling salesman for cheap diamond rings, visits the city where his pal Jabbs, the well-known actor, is playing a week's engagement at the local theater. Jabbs' specialty is female impersonation, while Pokes' speed is to woo and inflame the hearts of all damsels that cross his path. In the boarding house where he is staying, he finds several of the fair sex, and thinking that he will help push the sale of his bum jewelry, he begins to lay siege to the affections of all of them, but at different intervals. To each and all of them he presents a sparkler and a photo of himself with the inscription "To my future wife" on the back of them. Each girl considers herself the fiancée of the charming Pokes, and secretly laughs at her less fortunate fellow roomers. However, when May discovers in Nellie's room the photo of Pokes adorning her dresser and on the back of the photo the same inscription as Pokes had written on the one he had presented to her, there is an awful scrimmage. The fight attracts the attention of the other roomers, and after truce has been declared, all discover that Pokes has been trifling with them. The girls all join against the unlucky Pokes and the only thing that saves his life is his promise to marry the girl his mother chooses. In desperation he implores Jabbs to impersonate his mother, and this the actor consents to do. So clad in full regalia he accompanies Pokes to the boarding house where the two deceivers are getting away with the bluffing until Jabbs is unmasked by the lawyer who is acting in the interests of the girls. This double deception at the hands of Pokes makes the fury of the women break all bounds; but in the end the two conspirators manage to escape from destruction with the solemn assurance to each other of "NEVER AGAIN." [MPW]

By this time Burns & Stull had been working over at Amber Star for some time. While it is possible this comedy was filmed there , the presence of Ethel Burton (who chose to stay at Vim and move over to work in the Babe Hardy unit.) seems to indicate that this was a true Vim product made at the Riverside Avenue studio.

"Pokes and Jabbs are the comedians in this comedy-reel, which is a fair knockabout reel. Pokes, as a jewelry salesman, makes love to all his female prospects in a boarding house, which leads to many complications. Jabbs comes to the rescue, disguised as Pokes' mother, but the women get wise and the two are barely able to escape." – *Moving Picture World*

What's the Use?

Released December 15, 1916. Vim Comedies - General Film Company release. One reel. No copyright registered. Release number 21533.

Produced by Louis Burstein [or Frank Tichenor]. Directed by Bobby Burns and Walter Stull. Filmed in Jacksonville, Florida [whether at the Vim studios or at the Amber Star studios is unknown].

with Bobby Burns (*Pokes*), Walter Stull (*Jabbs*), Ethel Burton [?], Edna Reynolds.

Mrs. Pokes is president of the Gossip Club. Pokes, her husband, very much hen-pecked, is chief cook, dishwasher and general maid of all work about the house. Mrs. Gift of Gab is scheduled to speak on "How to Keep Husbands at Home" at the club that afternoon. When Mrs. Pokes receives this notice she puts Pokes to work at the dishpan and leaves at once for the club. Pokes drowsily continues his task. His manhood, however, asserts itself and he resolves to declare his independence. Forthwith he takes off the apron. After writing his wife

a farewell note and taking an affectionate leave of the dog, his only friend, he leaves the house. Finding shelter in a moving freight car, he rolls on his way to liberty. Mrs. Pokes returns only to find Pokes gone. Thrown on her own resources, she hangs out a sign "Rooms and Board." The side-door Pullman in which Pokes is traveling stops, and Pokes emerges in a strange town. Walking down the street he sees a sign "Furnished Rooms" and decides to rent one. Mrs. Jabbs keeps the rooming house and her politician husband has her under his thumb. Pokes sympathizes with her, so when Jabbs returns home and demands the room rent money that Pokes has just paid, threatening his wife with blows, Pokes bravely interferes and drives Jabbs away. To cool his temper, Jabbs takes a trip on a train and gets off in the very town that Pokes has left. By a strange fate, he takes board at the home of Mrs. Pokes. Time passes. If the newspapers had been carefully scanned, two divorce and two marriage notices might have been read. Two honeymoons are next in order and at a quiet little hotel well named "Harmony," the Pokes and Jabbs and Jabbs and Pokes meet. Such complications! They beggar description. Mrs. Pokes arming herself with a tray of dishes decides to take the law in her own hands and settle affairs. Jabbs is knocked out and so is Mrs. Jabbs. Pokes arrives just in time to get a crack on the head with a plate which rudely awakens him from his slumber, and he realizes he is still in the kitchen. Still maid-of-all-work, still hen-pecked. Pokes longs for the day when dreams come true. [MPW]

"Pokes and Jabbs are seen in this comedy reel. While there is humor in the reel, there are touches that could have well been left out. Two divorces and two marriages take place, Pokes and Jabbs thereby changing wives; but as it is only a dream everything ends as happily and as mirthfully as could be expected." -- *Moving Picture World*

Reckless Romeos

Released December 22, 1916. Vim Comedies - General Film Company release. One reel. No copyright registered. Release number 21562 (per MPN), 21606 (per ETR), 21563 (per Motography).

Produced by Mark Dintenfass or Frank Tichenor. Directed by Bobby Burns and Walter Stull. Filmed at the Garrick Studios in Jacksonville, Florida. Produced as an Amber Star production.

with Bobby Burns (*Pokes*), Walter Stull (*Jabbs*), Edna Reynolds.

Pokes, Jabbs and Reggie Gotrox are all members of the same club and at the same time rivals for the hand of La Belle Edna, a popular actress. Things being dull at the club, Pokes decides to call on Edna. With a headache for an excuse he slips away, procures a large bunch of chrysanthemums, presents himself at Edna's house and is admitted. Reggie, bored by a fellow club member, also decides to call on Edna. When Reggie arrives at Edna's home. Pokes is compelled to hide under the arm chair cover. Reggie is getting along very well when the door bell rings and none other than Jabbs is announced. Reggie takes refuge in the fireplace. Jabbs is smoking a cigar when ushered in the room, and throwing it in the fire place, the legs of his trousers become ignited and he has to crawl out, the chair cover is torn from Pokes and the three meet face to face. Trouble is in the air, and they nearly come to blows when Edna enters the room and stops them. At her request they all adjourn to the club to await her decision. They finally receive a note at the club from Edna saying; "That the one who will escort her to a swell cafe and prove his love, she will marry." They are all willing, so much so that the dice cup is brought into play to decide. Pokes wins and starts out. He meets Edna just as she is coming out of her home and they go to the Palms Cafe. Dinner is ordered when Edna raises her veil and Pokes discovers he is escorting a mulatto. Horror-stricken, he rushes from the place. Edna discloses her identity to the proprietor and the guests and they all enjoy the joke. She then telephones to Reggie at the club and he hastens to rescue her. She is seated when he arrives at the cafe and the dinner is served. When he offers to give her a piece of steak she removes her cape, and when he beholds the colored lady that he is dining with he takes a fit and beats it. Passing the club he meets Jabbs, and tells him that it is he (Jabbs) that Edna wants. Jabbs arrives at the cafe. When Edna throws back her cape and also removes her veil Jabbs, who is ready for the play, laughs and tells her to eat and enjoy herself. Edna, to all appearances, is fairly caught, when in struts a big burly black man and demands that Edna accompany him. Jabbs interferes and is knocked out. Edna takes to her heels with the black man in pursuit. The chase leads her to her own home, where she is overtaken by her pursuer. In the kitchen, while the black man flourishes a razor. Edna begs for mercy. The black man grabs a wet towel and wiping off the paint from one side of his face discloses the countenance of Pokes. At this juncture Jabbs arrives. Seeing Edna in Pokes arms is too much; he rushes on Pokes but is promptly pushed back on the hot stove. Reckless Pokes by his reckless ways is the most reckless Romeo and carries off the prize. [MPW]

"Pokes and Jabbs are seen in this comedy reel—an average number. Pokes, Jabbs and Reggie are rivals for the hand of Edna, and they go to reckless lengths to win her. Considerable knockabout work is done by Pokes and Jabbs, and lively action is seen in the reel. There is quite a fast finish." –*Moving Picture World*

The Property Man

Released December 29, 1916. Vim Comedies - General Film Company release. One reel. No copyright registered. Pre-release title: *Before the Show*, reviewed under that title in some sources. Release number 21585 (per *Motion Picture News* as *Before the Show*) then 21629 and release date January 12, 1917 as *The Property Man*, 21639 (per *Exhibitors Trade Review*).

Produced by Frank Tichenor. Directed by Bobby Burns and Walter Stull. Filmed late November-early December 1916 at the Garrick Studios in Jacksonville, Florida. Produced as an Amber Star production.

with Bobby Burns (*Slippery Pokes, property man*), Walter Stull (*Jabbs, stage manager*), Edna Reynolds (*Stylish Kate, scrub woman*), Jobyna Ralston (*one of the Fickel Sisters*), Billy Quirk (*Mrs. Hamm*), Spook Hanson (*the shorter Limber Brother*).

The smalltown vaudeville manager, before the afternoon performance, discovers his property man has quit without notice, so is compelled to hire one of the hangers-on, Slippery Pokes. Pokes is installed and made man of all work. Bills are to be posted, props collected, scenery put in place, trunks delivered to dressing rooms. This all falls to Pokes' lot. Stylish Kate, the scrub-woman, is secretly in love with Jabbs, the manager. Jabbs objects to her attentions and several times has to call her down and remind her of her position. The Limber Brothers arrive and after tipping Pokes, are shown to the dressing room. The Ham Family also arrives. The greatest trouble is created when the Fickle Sisters put in an appearance and smile upon Jabbs. Jabbs places them in the star room. Pokes discovers Jabbs making love to the sisters and informs Stylish Kate, who, with a pistol, makes things so lively that had the police not interfered the afternoon performance would have been delayed. [MPW as BEFORE THE SHOW]

Pokes and Jabbs are once again backstage at a vaudeville theater. However unlike previous adventures the theater is not named the Vim but rather the Amber Star, an on-screen indication of the changing circumstances surrounding the making of the Pokes & Jabbs comedies. This time the advertisement board lists the following performers: the Fickle Sisters, the Hamm Family, Dewdrop Juggler and the Limber Bros. Acrobats. It is noted within the film that the Limber brothers first names are Nimble and Agile, somewhat questionable in reality since they carry a five gallon jug of liniment with them upon arrival at the theater. Bobby Burns has trouble getting all the steamer trunks backstage since the stairs turn into a ramp at will, and not his will. However, when Edna Reynolds uses the stairs they work perfectly. Edna, who has plenty to do in this film, gets pushed and shoved by Walter Stull frequently leading to her obtaining a gun with the requisite chase to follow. The Amber Star (soon to be Jaxon) version of Pokes & Jabbs did not include Ethel Burton who chose to stay with the Vim company, and her absence is felt. The loss of Ethel is tempered somewhat by the presence of Jobyna Ralston as one of the Fickle sisters in her earliest known film appearance. She would go on to support Bobby Burns in his Cuckoo comedies and more famously as one of Harold Lloyd's leading ladies.

"A side-splitting Vim comedy, with a good laugh in every foot of film, featuring Burns and Stull." -- *Republican and Herald (Pottsville, Pennsylvania)*

War Correspondents

Released January 19, 1917. Vim Comedies - General Film Company release. One reel. No copyright registered. Release number 21647.

Produced by Frank Tichenor. Directed by Bobby Burns and Walter Stull. Filmed at the Garrick Studios in Jacksonville, Florida. Produced as an Amber Star production.

with Bobby Burns (*Pokes*), Walter Stull (*Jabbs*).

Pokes and Jabbs have been sent to the border to report events for a sensational daily newspaper, but things are quiet and news is scarce. A telegram telling them to send in some thrilling news items or quit arouses them to action. A Mexican is seen skulking through the woods clutching a jewel box. Their attention is attracted and they see visions of columns of thrilling news, so decide to follow the mysterious stranger. The trail leads to the foot of a tree, where the stranger digs a hole, plants the box and then departs. Pokes and Jabbs start to dig the box out and have almost reached their goal, when the stranger returns. They take refuge in a tree. The stranger, noticing that someone has discovered his hiding place, digs up the box and is about to depart when Pokes and Jabbs demand to know his business and the contents of the box. The stranger relates a wonderful and thrilling tale of persecution, privation and hardship. Pokes and Jabbs take down the main facts for publication, but when the stranger tells of his wife and two pretty daughters being held in captivity, they volunteer to rescue his loved ones. The stranger accepts their assistance and agrees to lead them to the dungeon on which his wife and children are confined. The way leads through weird places and strange mishaps are encountered, but all obstacles having been surmounted, the three arrive at their destination, where Pokes and Jabbs are thanked for the return of Mysterious Pedro, whose mania is hiding empty jewel boxes of sand. [MPW]

"There are several laughs in this comedy reel in which Pokes and Jabbs are the stars. They are seen as war correspondents and they run across some mysterious happenings. They trace these to their source and are treated to a surprise. Action throughout is fairly fast, considerable knockabout work being done with good comedy result." -- *Moving Picture World*

The Masher Mashed

Released late March 1917. Vim Comedies - General Film Company release. One reel. No copyright registered. Release number not listed.

Produced by Louis Burstein [or Frank Tichenor]. Directed by Bobby Burns and Walter Stull. Filmed in Jacksonville, Florida [whether at the Vim studios or at the Amber Star studios is unknown].

with Bobby Burns (*Pokes*), Walter Stull (*Jabbs*) [?].

[no synopsis available].

Easily the least documented Pokes & Jabbs comedy ever, be it Wizard, Vim or Jaxon. Whether this film was shot by Vim or by Amber Star is unknown, although it would seem to be somewhat incongruent for Amber Star to still be providing product to Vim (and the General Film Company) with their soon-to-be-announced plans to release future films via states rights. If it was a Vim production it would the last in-house made film released by the company.

"Completing the program will be a comedy picture with a laugh a second guaranteed entitled *The Masher Mashed*." *-- The Morning Call (Allentown, Pennsylvania)*

Jabbs (Stull) and Pokes (Burns) with their boss during the Wizard and Vim days, Louis Burstein.

PLUMP & RUNT COMEDIES

A Special Delivery

Released January 27, 1916. Vim Comedies - General Film Company release. One reel. No copyright registered. Release number 19950.

Produced by Louis Burstein. Directed by Will Louis. Filmed in Jacksonville, Florida.

with Babe Hardy (*Plump*), Billy Ruge (*Runt*), Edna Reynolds, Helen Gilmore.

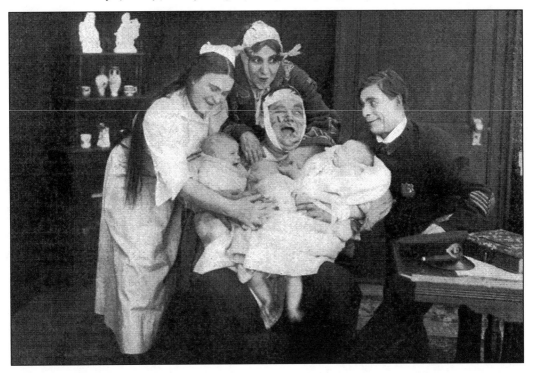

When Plump is informed that the stork is expected to visit his home shortly, he rushes to summon medical assistance. His peculiar actions and wild haste arouse the suspicion of the police officials, who have been on the lookout for some burglars who have recently been operating in the vicinity of the sanatorium. Runt, the pride of the police force, follows Plump, but in the tussle is severely worsted. The nurses in the sanatorium are in a very nervous state owing to their dread of burglars and the least noises drives them into a panic. Plump reaches the sanatorium followed by Runt and other policemen, whom he has summoned to assist him. Plump's entrance at the sanatorium in a wild and disheveled condition throws the nurses into a frenzy of fear, and they attempt to phone for help only to learn that a real burglar has entered the house during the excitement and has cut the telephone connection. The screams of the nurses have been heard by Runt and his fellow-policemen and, rushing to the house, they overpower the unfortunate Plump and drag him off to the station, where the head nurse lodges a complaint of burglary against Plump. He begs the officials to release him and explains his predicament, and is finally able to convince them of the truth of his statements. On his release he rushes madly to his home, accompanied by the doctor and the head nurse

and, as if Fate, desirous of making amends for his misfortunes of the earlier part of the night, Plump is rewarded by the appearance of the doctor bearing in his arms not one, but three bouncing boys. [MPW]

Although the characters of Plump & Runt had appeared before, this film was the first of their own series of comedies. Often billed as Hardy & Ruge, the two only irregularly actually worked as a team in the various entries in the series. More often than appearing as buddies, the two were rivals, even enemies, working against one another. When they are cast as adversaries, they have little screen time together. All of the Plump & Runts were released on Thursdays, so fans of the series knew what to expect when seeing the "Thursday Vim."

"Babe Hardy as Plump and Billy Ruge as Runt are the leading fun makers in this one reel farce produced by the new Vim Company. There is a striking resemblance to the other Vim comedies-- a twin brother in fact--and is a succession of quick moving antics by the entire cast." -- *Moving Picture World*

A Sticky Affair

Released February 3, 1916. Vim Comedies - General Film Company release. One reel. No copyright registered. Release number 19988.

Produced by Louis Burstein. Directed by Will Louis. Filmed in Jacksonville, Florida.

with Babe Hardy (*Plump*), Billy Ruge (*Runt*), Elsie McLeod, Billy Bletcher, Edna Reynolds.

The home of Prof. Perkins, the inventor of a wonderfully adhesive glue, is under the supervision of Lena Brown, who has a penchant for brass buttons. Plump and Runt, the pride of the local police force, are rivals for Lena's hand, but Lena refuses to accept either one until they have proven themselves heroes. Each one strives to outdo the other in deeds of bravery in order to win the affections of Lena, but without success. The city is visited by two famous crooks, who after looking over various suitable locations, finally decide to rob the house of the professor. While they are engaged in burglarizing the house, both Plump and Runt are enjoying the hospitality of Lena. The lovemaking is interrupted by the appearance of the professor, and Lena hides both Plump and Runt in the closet. They try to make their escape from there disguised in women's attire, but are discovered by the irate professor, who has also summoned the police to come to his assistance. Plump and Runt followed by the professor and their fellow policemen are chased through the house to the roof-tops from which they try in vain to escape. In the meantime an explosion has occurred in the laboratory of the professor, causing the glue to run over the floor, firmly entrapping the two burglars at work on the safe. They find themselves stuck fast to the glue and unable to extricate themselves from their plight. On the roof-tops Plump and Runt after having been chased by the other policemen and the professor, hide behind the skylight through which the professor in his rush to seize the two offenders, falls through, which mishap causes Plump and Runt to follow him headlong in his descent. They fall through the entire three floors of the house and finally land on the floor of the laboratory where they also find themselves stuck fast in the glue beside the two burglars. When they recover from the shock of the fall, Plump's first thoughts are to rescue Lena who has also been stuck fast in the glue. He succeeds in saving her thereby causing Lena to acknowledge him as her hero to the chagrin of Runt. [MPW]

Elsie McLeod makes her first appearance in a Vim comedy here. McLeod first appeared in movies in 1911 at the Edison Company working often with Arthur Housman and William Wadsworth but left that company in late 1914. For the next year or so she would bounce around the various New York-based production companies from Rex to Victor, Kalem to Powers to Universal. One of her roles at Universal was in a comedy called *A Day at Midland Beach* which featured Marcel Perez in his first American film. Early in 1916 she was brought into Vim to be the leading lady to Perez in the Bungles series, but appeared in the Plump & Runt comedies when not occupied with the other series.

Vim really played up the sticky aspects of this film in their trade advertisements: "Everybody Sticks; The hero and heroine Stick; The terrible villains Stick; The staid professor Sticks. A Glorious Gambol in a Geyser of Glue. Mr. Exhibitor: Glue this ad in your VIM Book and make your patrons Stick!!"

"Babe Hardy and Billy Ruge impersonate a pair of comedy cops in this one reel farce and make love to the hired help of an inventor of a wonderful glue. The picture lives up to its title when a large quantity of the liquid is spilled on the floor. The supply of 'rough house' comedy does not run short during the reel.." -- *Moving Picture World*

One Too Many

Released February 17, 1916. Vim Comedies - General Film Company release. One reel. No copyright registered. Release number 20063.

Produced by Louis Burstein. Directed by Will Louis. Filmed in Jacksonville, Florida.

with Babe Hardy (*Plump*), Billy Ruge (*Runt, the janitor*), Billy Bletcher (*unhappy boarder*), Edna Reynolds (*woman across the hall*), Madelyn Hardy (*woman on street*), Florence McLoughlin (*newlywed*).

Plump, a carefree bachelor, after a stormy night, awakes to find a letter from his rich uncle, stating that he is going to pay him a visit in order to meet his wife and baby. Plump who has been getting an income for this mythical wife and baby, is frantic. He employs Runt, the Janitor, and also seeks the services of Doris, an actress, to get him the much needed frau and kidlet. Runt scurries around and corrals a bunch of babies. A male friend of the actress searches the apartment house for a child, a series of complications arise in which one baby answers the purpose of all the parties who are trying to help Plump. Plump, in order to play safe, persuades Madame Nitouch, a French woman, to pose as his wife for the afternoon. Runt also commands his wife to help out Plump. Mrs. Newlywed. who needs $50.00 to pay for a new dress also agrees to be his wife. The time is near at hand for the uncle to arrive. The baby has disappeared from Plump's room and Runt is forced to be the baby. The uncle, who is near-sighted, arrives. The deception is proving a success when the uncle asks to see the wife. To Plump's horror the three women make their appearance at the same time. The uncle gets wise and Plump is on the verge of losing his income when Doris, the actress, who is an old flame of the uncle, arrives. The uncle acknowledges defeat, gives Plump a fat check and hikes back home, while Plump and Runt divide the spoils. [MPW]

Much more a bedroom farce than the normal knockabout comedies that featured Plump & Runt. The stealing, borrowing, renting, and retrieval of babies happens at such a rapid pace it is hard to follow. Billy Bletcher, as the only resident of the apartment building that isn't involved in the deception of the uncle is very much irritated by the goings on. Early in the picture Babe Hardy comes across him in the hallway and knocks him about, and then does pretty much the same to Billy Ruge. Seeing Babe next to the two men in fairly identical scenes visually supports Arline Bletcher's belief that her husband Billy would have been a better teammate for Babe than Billy Ruge. Although *One Too Many* does give the two comedians a few occasions to work together, yet there is no great rapport between Hardy and Ruge. Rather, we see just two comedians being funny, separately, in the same frame.

Madelyn Hardy, Babe's wife, appears briefly as a woman who allows Runt to borrow her baby briefly. Harold Lloyd and Snub Pollard would use the same premise for their 1917 Rolin comedy *Bashful*, as did numerous other silent comedies.

First known appearance of Florence McLoughlin in a Vim comedy. A local Jacksonville girl Florence worked first at Vim in the Plump & Runts then later with the Babe Hardy company. She was with King Bee when they moved to New York City but left the company when they headed for California, and went back South. She made a few films with the Florida Film Corporation, then met and fell in love with a returning veteran. Their marriage ended her film career.

"Babe Hardy and Billie Ruge lead the list of sprinting comedians in this one reel farce. Somewhat familiar young man who is forced to borrow a wife and a baby before the arrival of his uncle is the character assumed by Mr. Hardy. His histrionic equipment enables him to amply fill the role. The picture is a good example of the Vim brand of quick-fire farce." -- *Moving Picture World*

The Serenade

Released March 2, 1916. Vim Comedies - General Film Company release. One reel. No copyright registered. Release number 20137.

Produced by Louis Burstein. Directed by Will Louis. Filmed along Riverside Drive (including at the corner of Osceola Street) in Jacksonville, Florida.

with Babe Hardy (*Plump*), Billy Ruge (*Runt*), Billy Bletcher (*Schmitte*), Florence McLoughlin (*Florence, Schmitte's daughter*), Edna Reynolds (*downstairs neighbor*), Ed Lawrence (*grouchy upstairs neighbor*).

Schmitte, the leader of a street band is the proud father of Florence whose love is eagerly sought after by Plump and Runt, both members of the band. The fickle Florence not caring for either one, as her affections are centered around Harry Hick, determines to create trouble between Plump and Runt by deliberately making love to Runt. Inflamed by jealousy when he sees his little rival cuddled up in Florence's arms, Plump chases Runt out of the apartment by the aid of his bass horn. During their day's work on the streets the band is invited by a kind-hearted saloon keeper to refresh themselves at his bar. He tells them that they can have all the liquid refreshment that their musical instruments will hold. This delights Plump who is the possessor of the bass horn, but infuriates Runt who plays the clarinet, hence he is unable to get enough beer to even wet his lips. Chagrined by this experience Runt enlists the aid of his fellow bandsmen with the exception of Plump and serenades Florence at her home. Plump also attempts to serenade the sweet miss but finding his solitary efforts unavailing against the united forces of Runt and the other members of the band, basely attempts to bribe the men to desert Runt and come to his assistance. Just as the serenade is about to commence, both Plump and Runt are dismayed to see the fickle Florence at the window enjoying the performance while reclining in the arms of her lover Hick. At this moment, a neighbor who is unable to appreciate the musical entertainment furnished by Plump and Runt, throws water upon them which landing in Plump's big horn just at the moment when Plump is blowing his hardest. The result is that Florence and her lover are drenched by the blast which showers upon them, to the delight of Plump and Runt who agree to forget their rivalry and be friends once more. [MPW]

Plump plays a horn, while Runt blows on a clarinet. The similarity of instruments and occupation are about the only ties between this film and Laurel & Hardy's *You're Darn Tootin'*. But *The Serenade* does foreshadow the film work of Babe Hardy and Stan Laurel together in one way. The difference in size between Babe and Billy Ruge is emphasized in the film. When the band is required to walk from location to the next, Babe exchanges his large instrument with Billy's smaller, lighter clarinet. Then when the band is set to play again, he switches instruments back. The bigger Plump takes charge, to the detriment of the smaller Billy, although neither benefit from the arrangement.

A running gag throughout the film is Babe's ability to blow away (or suck in) people, cars and other objects using his bass horn. When he has had enough of Runt, Plump blows his horn. When he wants the other band members he sucks them in. This device works on bothersome children, and causes cars to blast away swerving down the street. The size of the horn comes into play when the saloon keeper offers to fill the musician's instruments with beer. This obviously pleases Plump, while Runt is disappointed with his small clarinet.

The opening titles of this film are written on sheet music, and in the final title Babe and Billy Ruge pop their heads through a couple of the notes and a title reads "Try This On Your Piano" (since the main title is missing from the print at the Museum of Modern Art it was incorrectly catalogued under this title). Although spelled Schmitte in the studio publicity, the name of Billy Bletcher's band as noted within the film is "Schmidt's Weiner Band."

"A little German Band of which Plump and Runt are members supplies a serenade. It furnishes more fun than melody and the execution that Plump does on his bass horn knocks out his hearers in more ways than one. An amusing knockabout farce." -- *Moving Picture World*

Nerve And Gasoline

Released March 16, 1916. Vim Comedies - General Film Company release. One reel. No copyright registered. Release number 20211.

Produced by Louis Burstein. Directed by Will Louis. Filmed in Jacksonville, Florida.

with Babe Hardy (*Plump*), Billy Ruge (*Runt*), Florence McLoughlin (*Florence*).

When Runt is sent by his wife to seek employment, he takes great care to avoid all places where he may find work. Even the "Help Wanted" columns of the paper are distasteful to him as the only part of the paper in which he is interested is the Sporting Page. Plump on the other hand is so industrious that he could sleep at any position he ever held. Plump succeeds in rescuing Florence, the stenographer, at the garage from rough treatment at the hands of some striking employees, for which act he is rewarded by the position of mechanic. While Runt is enjoying himself in the park, Mrs. Runt's brother, whom Runt has never met, arrives at the Runt home and takes his sister out for a ride in a taxi. During their ride the car becomes stalled in the park near where Runt is reading, and the chauffeur is induced by the delegate of strikers to quit the job, so he deserts the car. When the garage receives the hurry call for help from Mrs. Runt's brother, Plump is sent out with his little "Flivver" to aid them. As Plump knows less about an auto than he does about the North Pole, his efforts to drive through the streets are laughable in the extreme. Runt seeing the antics of Plump and the little "Flivver" follows the big fellow to the spot where Mrs. Runt and her brother are anxiously awaiting help. When Runt sees his wife in the arms of an unknown man his anger knows no bounds and in his rage he starts to make a general "cleanup" of the entire crowd. In the melee that follows, Plump's auto explodes blowing Plump back to the garage while Mrs. Runt succeeds in calming her irate little husband sufficiently long enough to introduce her brother to him and explain the entire situation to the satisfaction of Runt. [MPW]

The flivver used in this short was actually owned by Babe Hardy who drove the rather unique car around Jacksonville. Not to be outdone, Billy Ruge, and later Harry Myers and Kate Price would also buy rather flamboyant automobiles and conduct a parade of auto one-upsmanship around town, one of several things about the "movie people" that did not amuse many of the regular folks living in Jacksonville.

"Plump and Runt and a brokedown 'flivver' suffering from auto-intoxication supply most of the hilarity in this one-reel farce. Those who love to laugh at the antics of clever knockabout comedians will give this picture a hearty greeting." -- *Moving Picture World*

"Plump gets a job at a motor garage, and, as mechanic, gets mixed up in a row between the jealous Runt, whose wife has gone for a joy ride with her brother. A wild chase of motors, cycles, and patrol wagons ends in a great explosion. Though containing no new features, this is full of amusing situations, brightly played and effectively produced." -- *The Bioscope*

Their Vacation

Released March 30, 1916. Vim Comedies - General Film Company release. One reel. No copyright registered. Release number 20285.

Produced by Louis Burstein. Directed by Will Louis. Filmed in Jacksonville, Florida.

with Babe Hardy (*Plump*), Billy Ruge (*Runt*), Bert Tracy, Florence McLoughlin.

With bursting pocket books, Plump and Runt put up at the swellest hotel to spend the first stage of their vacation. For safety's sake Runt entrusts Plump with his wallet, and all goes well until Plump becomes enchanted with a pair of bright eyes belonging to a charmer who inveigles the big fellow into an invitation for an expensive dinner, during the course of which the pocket book mysteriously disappears. Runt, in the interim, has been making the most of his opportunities with the landlord's daughter, and he presents her with a large box of candy. On asking Plump for the "necessary," Plump discovers the loss. The irate landlord puts them both to work cleaning shoes to pay for their board. Meantime, the fair crook and her partner, fearing a hue and cry after the lost cash, hide the wallet in a pair of shoes. Plump, gathering up the guests' footwear, takes away an identical pair and gives them to his little pal in distress, to clean. Hardly believing his eyes, Runt recovers their lost property and with howls of joy they awaken the landlord, pay their bills and are just in time to capture the evildoers as they attempt to escape. [MPW]

Throughout his career Babe Hardy was often teamed with a smaller comedian in an attempt to find humor highlighting his thick stature aside a slighter man. From Billy Ruge at Vim, to Bobby Ray at Arrow, and finally his historic pairing with Stan Laurel, the practice usually found good success. It was Bert Tracy, while both he and Hardy worked at Lubin, who was the first small comedian placed aside the large Babe. The two were best buddies at Lubin, and it is in *Their Vacation* that Tracy makes his first appearance in a Vim Comedy. Tracy would work as a comedian, assistant director and write scenarios while at Vim. Later in life Bert worked as a prop man on Laurel & Hardy's 1947-48 European tour.

"Plump and Runt carry the weight of the fun in this one-reel farce. Plump appearing as a susceptible young gentleman with considerable ready money, and Runt as his valet. There is a number of lively mix-ups during the action of the reel and strenuosity is the watchword of the entire cast." -- *Moving Picture World*

Mamma's Boys

Released April 6, 1916. Vim Comedies - General Film Company release. One reel. No copyright registered.

Produced by Louis Burstein. Directed by Will Louis. Filmed in Jacksonville, Florida.

with Babe Hardy (*Plump*), Billy Ruge (*Runt*), Bert Tracy.

Way back in the woods, Plump and Runt, the apples of their mother's eye, work on the farm. Unfortunately, their pranks get them into trouble with the neighbors and as mother takes in summer boarders, the boys are always in hot water. One of the guests, an old grouchy dyspeptic, is the object of their attention. The arrival of a golfing enthusiast diverts their ideas into new channels and they forthwith steal his clubs and proceed to play the "ancient and noble game." The fact that the balls are missing does not in any way prevent our heroes from becoming champions for they use all the available eggs they can find. Their first shot flies far and true, finding a billet in old grouch's face. The second hits their distracted mother as she is doing the family wash, while the third puts to flight a jovial party of picnickers. Tried beyond all patience and hoping that the change will improve them, mother arranges for them to visit her brother, a captain of police, and they depart for new lands to conquer. In the city, they make a slight mistake in the directions given to them and enter a strange house, where they find a nice dinner awaiting. Putting an end to this, they feel tired and enter a bedroom and go to sleep. They are rudely awakened by the owner's entrance, who promptly empties his gun and chases Plump out in the streets. Runt, from under the bed, crawls into the place vacated by his pal and again goes to dreamland, only to be aroused out by the horrified screams of the wife. Up and down the street they are chased, finally captured and hauled to court where they discover the presiding officer to be their much sought relative, and the old boy, listening to their story, promises that he, at least will give a good time to mamma's boys. [MPW]

The second half of this film is a reworking of the Lubin short *Back To The Farm*, which shows that Bert Tracy, who appears in both films, undoubtedly contributed to the writing of both films. The premise of Plump & Runt going to the wrong house is used again by Laurel & Hardy in *Scram!* The portrayal of golfing in the film foreshadows the pastime that would eventually consume Babe Hardy's off-screen life later in his career.

"Plump and Runt are the two little heroes of this one reel farce. They are anything but angel children and are at all sorts of tricks. One of the most amusing is playing golf with hen fruit for balls. The reel will bring the laughs." -- *Moving Picture World*

"Plump" and "Runt" are two bucolic practical jokers, farm hands who specialize in making everybody uncomfortable chiefly by breaking eggs all over them. They are inclined be coarse without being particularly humorous, although there are plenty of laughs absurd predicaments they find themselves in when they visit uncle in New York." -- *The Bioscope*

The Battle Royal

Released April 13, 1916. Vim Comedies - General Film Company release. One reel. No copyright registered. Release number 20359.

Produced by Louis Burstein. Directed by Will Louis. Filmed mid- February 1916 in Jacksonville, Florida.

with Babe Hardy (*Plump*), Billy Ruge (*Runt*), Elsie McLeod (*Runt's sister*), Billy Bletcher (*Grandpa Runt*), Will Louis (*revenue officer*), Joe Cohen (*revenue officer*), Billy Slade (*mother*), Florence McLoughlin (*Runt's sister*), Edna Reynolds (*Mother Plump*), Joe Schrode (*brother Plump*).

Far away in the Kentucky hills live the families of Plump and Runt. The former were all big and fat — the latter small and wiry. Never a cross word passed between them. The oldest Plump son was the future husband of the Runt girl and the stocky sons and heir of the Runts was the betrothed of the two hundred and sixty pound daughter of the Plumps. Life flowed in one happy stream — the two fathers ran the old still undisturbed by either conscience or Revenue — the hills resounded with the joyous cries of the boys and girls, until the fatal day arrived, and then, Ye Gods, how the blood and feathers flew. Plump and Runt happened to hook the same fish. Argument, hot words and blows followed and the Feud was born. Each fired on the others at sight, and had their marksmanship in any way equaled their intentions, the two families would have been wiped out. Grandma Runt was the fiercest and most blood thirsty of all. Bred in the Feudist country, a fight was the breath of life to her, but as she has the unfortunate knack of getting in eveyone's way, her family had their hands full in taking care of her. Inspired by thought of deepest revenge her son and his family dig a large hole and cover it with leaves and wait for their mortal enemies to fall into the pit. Grandma, determined not to miss anything, falls in and is rescued only with the greatest difficulty. The Plump stronghold is attacked by the Runts, when some unfortunate Revenue officers find their way to the hills and become targets for the combined fire of both families. The joyful discovery that they are fighting the law, blinds the Feudists to their personal quarrel and joining forces, they pepper the fleeing officers – then a general handshake takes place and once more harmony reigns. [MPW]

This is pretty much the Plump & Runt unit just frolicking around the backwoods of northern Florida. There is some rough and tumble action and Babe Hardy pretty easily throws the smaller Billy Ruge about. Anyone who knows anything about hillbillies knows that they don't take too kindly towards any government types that try to close down their moonshining. One of the revenue officers is the film's director, Will Louis, playing a bit part.

"This is a very amusing comedy in which a feud arises between two mountain families over a most trivial matter. One son of each house loves the daughter of the other, and even the sweethearts are forced to take to the gun much against their inclinations. The visitation of a common enemy, the revenue officer, who has nosed out the fact that moonshining is in the business of the respectable families, makes the two families companions in misery and cements the friendship." -- *Moving Picture World*

All For A Girl

Released April 20, 1916. Vim Comedies - General Film Company release. One reel. No copyright registered. Release number 20396.

Produced by Louis Burstein. Directed by Will Louis. Filmed in Jacksonville, Florida.

with Babe Hardy (*Plump*), Billy Ruge (*Runt*), Elsie McLeod (*Elsie*).

Plump and Runt are in love with Elsie, who informs them that the first one to make good in a position will win her hand. Runt secures a position as office boy in a bank and Plump because he rescues the president's daughter from certain death is made superintendent of the bank. Plump, using his newly acquired power, fires Runt, who secures a job in a pressing club. Plump gets an invitation from Elsie to attend a dance in her home and on his way to the party calls into the pressing club where Runt is employed to have his clothes pressed. Runt finds the invitation and attends the party himself, leaving Plump sitting in a barrel. Finally Plump arrives at the scene and his entrance in the barrel breaks up the party. Explanations ensue and the fat boy wins his love, much to the disgust of his Runty rival. [M]

The similarity of plot with the earlier Lubin film *Shoddy the Tailor*, the idea of the wronged person coming into control of his rival's clothes because he is a tailor, that also featured Babe Hardy tends to show that Babe helped develop some of the situations being presented in the Plump & Runt comedies. Again Plump & Runt are rivals rather than partners, and as such a comedy team in name only.

"Plump and Runt are rival suitors for the same young lady and Plump wins her, although he is obliged to press his suit while wearing the latest style in flour barrels. A good knockabout comedy." -- *Moving Picture World*

What's Sauce For The Goose

Released April 27, 1916. Vim Comedies - General Film Company release. One reel. No copyright registered.

Produced by Louis Burstein. Directed by Will Louis. Filmed in Jacksonville, Florida.

with Elsie McLeod (*Mrs. Boob*), Babe Hardy (*Mr. Boob Plump*), Billy Ruge (*Runt*), Bert Tracy.

Mrs. Boob was pretty; Boob himself was a good-looking chap and each loved the other to distraction. Naturally, this state of affairs gives an opening for the entrance of the Green Demon. Boob was busy, so busy that he could not get home till late. Meeting with a very cold reception, the meal is disturbed by the telephone's chirpy call. His better half answers and is astonished to bear a woman's inquiring for Boob. He explains that it is the janitress telling him that he has left the safe open and leaves for his office. Wifey, now aroused, decides to follow him, and putting on a suit of hubby's clothes, sallies forth. Her departure is noticed by the returning husband who is mystified at the sight of a strange man leaving his house. Hastily entering, he calls for wifey. No reply forthcoming, his worst fears are realized and he dresses in wifey's clothes and the hunt commences. Wifey, becomes scared and enters a café. Here she is molested by a couple of toughs, whose cupidity is aroused by the sight of her money. Boob, thirsty by now, stops into the café, and his manhood is aroused at the sight of supposedly innocent-looking boy becoming the victim of the crooks, he follows after them. Choosing a quiet spot, the two pounce on Wifey, but Boob with a good right and left scares them off. The heat of battle passed, Boob does not know what to do. However, he lifts the almost fainting stranger and makes tracks for home. Arriving at last, recognition takes place, and as darkness falls, all else is forgotten in the joy of reconciliation. [MPW]

Elsie McLeod is the star of this comedy, and although released in the regular Plump & Runt slot this is Elsie's film. The trade papers noted McLeod as the star, and it is possible that Billy Ruge doesn't even appear in the film.

"Elsie McLeod stars in this one reel farce and her acting justifies the designation. The reel depends upon its comic complications for its funmaking and is plentifully supplied with laughs." -- *Moving Picture World*

The Brave Ones

Released May 4, 1916. Vim Comedies - General Film Company release. One reel. No copyright registered. Release number 20477.

Produced by Louis Burstein. Directed by Will Louis. Filmed in Jacksonville, Florida.

with Babe Hardy (*Plump*), Billy Ruge (*Runt*), Billy Bletcher (*Sheriff*), Elsie McLeod (*Sheriff's daughter*), Edna Reynolds.

Plump and Runt are once again in hard luck. Footsore and weary they arrive at a village and after devouring a plate of newly-made pies, proceed to make love to the Sheriff's daughter, who is rescued from their attentions by the worthy official himself. Not having the necessary money to pay for their meal, the old man tells them that if they will sleep for one night in an untenanted house on his property, he will not have them jailed. Our two heroes agree to his proposal and take up their new quarters. As midnight approaches, they are disturbed by unearthly noises, creakings and shadow-like apparitions. Finally, giving up hope of sleeping, they lay awake. Their door slowly opens and in the wall appears a ghost like shape. This puts the finishing touch to their nerves and they bury their heads under the bed clothes. Meanwhile, a gang of counterfeiters who have long used the house as their headquarters discover the presence of the new tenants and decide to scare them off. Dressing in white sheets, they invade the bedroom, but Plump and Runt, now thoroughly aroused, attack and make them prisoners. The Sheriff's daughter, thinking to have a joke, also dons a sheet and is mistaken by the coiners for one of themselves. Confusion now reigns. The two boys try to escape. The Sheriff fires at them. Elsie screams as the villains vamoose and inform the police that the Sheriff is a coiner. A posse is dispatched, the Sheriff arrested and only released on the explanation from Plump and Runt who are now hailed as the saviours of the village, for were they not truly the means of making the ghost walk? [MPW]

"Plump and Runt are called upon to occupy a haunted house, can be entertained by a number of ghosts in this one reel farce. The spooks turn out to be a party of counterfeiters (ghosts generally are by the way). Lively doings in the house when the Sheriff takes a hand in the matter. Babe Hardy, Billy Ruge, Billy Bletcher and Elsie McLeod are the star cut ups of the cast. An average Vim." -- *Moving Picture World*

The Water Cure

The cast of The Water Cure pose for the camera at Pablo Beach.

Released May 11, 1916. Vim Comedies - General Film Company release. One reel. No copyright registered. Release number 20515. Erroneously listed in Pennsylvania Board of Censor records as *The Water Clue*.

Produced by Louis Burstein. Directed by Will Louis. Filmed in Jacksonville, Florida.

with Babe Hardy (*Plump*), Billy Ruge (*Runt*), Elsie McLeod, Florence McLoughlin, Edna Reynolds, Bert Tracy, Joe Cohen, Billy Bletcher, Joe Schrode.

As a result of business worries, Plump and Runt determine to take a holiday and get the doctor to prescribe a week at the seashore. Away from their wives, they have a good time with two girls whose beaux have temporarily departed. Their wives follow them and, to escape, they are forced to enter the women's bathhouse, where they put on ladies' bathing suits and caps. After harrowing adventures they are finally run down, and rather than face their outraged partners they swim out to sea, leaving their wives pleading for them to return. [M & MPW]

Not the last time Babe Hardy and a buddy try to take a vacation without the wives, see *Be Big* and *Sons of the Desert* (where Mr. Laurel was the co-conspirator). Unlike many of the early Plump & Runts it seems Hardy & Ruge are acting more like a comedy team in this entry in series.

"Plump and Runt attempt to deceive their wives in this one-reel farce in order to take a vacation at the seashore. The two worthies start a flirtation on the sand that leads to numerous comic mishaps. The regulation Vim speed is maintained through the picture." -- *Moving Picture World*

Thirty Days

Released May 18, 1916. Vim Comedies - General Film Company release. One reel. No copyright registered. Release number 20556.

Produced by Louis Burstein. Directed by Will Louis. Filmed in Jacksonville, Florida.

with Babe Hardy (*Plump*), Billy Ruge (*Runt*), Elsie McLeod, Florence McLoughlin, Bert Tracy, Billy Bletcher [?].

Billy Bletcher on the set of Thirty Days with Babe Hardy, but is he in the film?

Plump and Runt get into a poker game at the club and are arrested. The judge gives them thirty days, and before going to jail they phone their anxious wives that an important business trip will keep them away from home for a month. In the jail they meet a hobo who attaches himself to them and, released, they find that the knight of the road cannot be shaken off; so they are forced to introduce him to their wives as a friend, a famous detective in disguise. He makes life a burden for them until the wives, taking matters into their own hands, drive off the hobo with carving knives. [M & MPW]

As in the previous film, Hardy & Ruge are again working as a team, and at the same time are still trying to deceive the wives. When will they learn? Apparently never for Babe Hardy. He will move across the country, change movie studios and gain a new comedy partner and still not understand honesty is the best policy when dealing with one's wife.

"The material for this one-reel farce has been selected with excellent judgment. It has had a long honorable career upon the French, English and American stages, and its powers of creating laughter are still unimpaired. Plump & Runt are very funny as the two married men who are forced to serve a jail sentence and deceive their wives concerning their whereabouts." -- *Moving Picture World*

Baby Doll

Released May 25, 1916. Vim Comedies - General Film Company release. One reel. No copyright registered. Release number 20599.

Produced by Louis Burstein. Directed by Will Louis. Filmed late February 1916 in Jacksonville, Florida.

with Babe Hardy (*Plump*), Billy Ruge (*Runt*), Elsie McLeod.

Business having slackened with Plump and Runt, our small friend decides to write to his uncle for a little cash. Uncle tells him to make a man of himself by marrying. To this. Runt immediately replies saying that he has taken a spouse, and arranges with Plump to impersonate the lady. Uncle leaves the farm to visit his new relative and on his way is inveigled into a flirtation with Plump who is returning from the costumer arrayed in female attire. So delighted is Plump with his powers of deception, that he encourages the old man to the point where the gay old sport will not quit. Time is passing and Plump has to rid himself of his too ardent admirer by dropping him into the river. Poor Runt, meanwhile, is in a fever of anxiety at his proud wife's non-appearance. Finally, Plump arrives and relates his experience as a female impersonator. On the point of giving up hope of the uncle's visit, Plump is about to disrobe, when Uncle arrives and meeting his erstwhile charmer, bursts out into rage. Unhappily for him, his wife, who has also determined to visit her nephew, appears on the scene. Caught between two fires, poor Uncle has to keep quiet and incidentally part with the $5,000. [MPW]

A reworking of the Lubin short *An Expensive Visit*, the earlier Plump & Runt effort, *One Too Many* and a forerunner of Laurel & Hardy's *That's My Wife* (with Stan Laurel in the dress). This time Babe Hardy takes his turn to dress in drag.

"Hardy and Ruge, the Vim comedians, appear in this as Plump and Runt. It is an ultra slapstick, with several situations which might have been omitted. The humor is not equal to other Vim comedies and the story could have been improved." -- *Motion Picture News*

"Rump [sic] and Plump are the chief offenders in this comic. Plump is a "vampire," and does a considerable business in blackmail. This female impersonation is not in the best of taste." -- *The Bioscope*

Dressed as a woman Plump is a comic sight, and the reason is to provide a wife for his friend Runt in order to impress an uncle from the country. The uncle meets Plump earlier in the day, and his amorous attentions are recalled when he sees his sham niece." --*The Bioscope*

The Schemers

Released June 1, 1916. Vim Comedies - General Film Company release. One reel. No copyright registered. Release number 20645.

Produced by Louis Burstein. Directed by Will Louis. Filmed in Jacksonville, Florida.

with Babe Hardy (*Plump*), Billy Ruge (*Runt*), Elsie McLeod (*Elsie*), Florence McLoughlin (*the stenographer*).

Plump was a young man. His thoughts were of love, also of his spring, for it that was to bring him a fortune. Runt, his rival, thought otherwise. Elsie the object of their affections, was undecided, and so the story opens. First she bestowed her favors on Plump, then on Runt. The spring on Plumps farm is known to possess valuable mineral qualities and a larger offer is made to Plump to sell. He leaves for the city to escort the financier over his property and during his absence, Runt persuades the fickle Elsie to marry him. Accompanied by his pretty stenographer, the promoter arrives at the farm, where poor Plump learns of his rival's wedding. However, the blow is softened by the little stenographer's sympathy. Not satisfied with winning Elsie, Runt plans to ruin the spring and runs oil into it. Arrived at the spring, Plump is on the point of accepting the cash, when the stenographer discovers that it is an oil well and whispers to Plump to double his price. This he does and once more virtue triumphs over villainy. [MPW]

Hardy and Ruge are back in their more common places as adversaries in this film but this time with a twist. Usually Runt is the troublemaker that loses in the end, but this time around it is Plump that gets the short end. This is Elsie McLeod's final released film for Vim. It was announced that she would move over to the United States Motion Picture Company where she was to write, direct and star in her own series. There is no evidence that these films were made. McLeod ended up working in New York City appearing in the occasional dramatic feature before disappearing from the screen by 1921.

"Plump and Runt are rivals for the hand of a fickle young woman and Plump is the loser. Not satisfied with winning the lady, Runt turns villain and tries to ruin the waiting but always virtuous Plump. The way in which the fat person is rewarded by fate is highly edifying. It is also a pleasure to state that the reel has the additional virtue of being equipped with frequent and well developed laughs." -- *Moving Picture World*

Sea Dogs

Released June 8, 1916. Vim Comedies-General Film Company release. One reel. No copyright registered. Release number 20683.

Produced by Louis Burstein. Directed by Will Louis. Filmed circa April 7, 1916 at Mayport along the St. Johns River in Jacksonville, Florida.

with Babe Hardy (*Plump*), Billy Ruge (*Runt*), Ray Godfrey, Bert Tracy.

Basking in the rays of the sun, Plump and Runt are rudely awakened by some overworked sailors and offered work. "Who ever worked, while the larder was full?" answers Plump, showing their larder, a two-week old weeny. Disgusted, the sailors plan to shanghai the two loafers and our two heroes, some days later, awake to find themselves at sea. They are put to work now, but, diving overboard, after a three days' swim land on a desert isle, where they meet a family of castaways. Here an ideal life is led. Between intervals of eating the tropical fruits and sleeping, the pair make love to the daughters of the family and everything goes happy as the marriage bell. One day a small boat is sighted and the whole crowd embark, only to find that the oars are missing. What is to be done? An idea strikes one of their number. A rope is tied around Plump's neck, and, much against his wish, he is pushed into the water and the long voyage starts. After several days the loiterers on a distant shore observe a boat approaching with no visible means of propulsion. Nearer and nearer it comes and to their amazement, a head appears from the depths, followed by the big body of Plump terribly tired, but happy after his long walk on the ocean's bed. [MPW]

The addition of Ray Godfrey to the female side of the Vim stock company was announced on May 6, 1916. Seemingly a direct replacement for Elsie McLeod the two women were quite different. McLeod a blonde and Godfrey a brunette had very dissimilar looks. Godfrey was very athletic, she was a great swimmer, and her physical abilities add greatly to the Plump & Runt unit.

"Several of the incidents in this one-reel farce are not only good for hardy laughs, but require a deal of hard work and expense to transfer them to the screen. Plump and Runt are the chief fun-makers and the scenes where Plump is forced to tow the boat while walking on the bottom of the sea is one of the best features of the reel." -- *Moving Picture World*

"*Sea Dogs*, Vim Comedy No.5, is a 1,000 feet of Plump and Runt antics, and, as the title implies, is a sea comic. The underwater effect is cleverly arranged and the photography remarkably fine. The party reach a new country and we leave Plump in the role of a modern Columbus. Quite an amusing little picture." -- *Kinematograph and Lantern Weekly*

"Plump and Runt are shanghaied. They desert and get to an island where they meet nice girls. The four escape in a washed ashore boat, Plump providing the motive power by walking under the waves, towing the frail craft. The chimpanzee who escapes with them is an amusing creature. This is really - funny." -- *The Bioscope*

"CLEVER UNDER-SEA PHOTOGRAPHY. Remarkable scenes photographed under water enhance the brisk comedy of *The Sea Dogs*, the Vim release of June 8. The rescue of a family of castaways is effected by the simple expedient of towing a boat which drifts to their island. The towing is done by Babe Hardy, the famous 'Plump,' who walks along the sea bottom, pulling the painter of the boat, in which six persons are seated. Several other cleverly devised scenes lift this picture out of the ordinary run, including the antics of a hawser which obligingly ties itself into knots at the right moment." -- *Moving Picture World* article

Hungry Hearts

Released June 15, 1916. Vim Comedies - General Film Company release. One reel. No copyright registered. Release number 20724.

Produced by Louis Burstein. Directed by Will Louis. Filmed in Jacksonville, Florida.

with Babe Hardy (*Plump*), Billy Ruge (*Runt*), Ray Godfrey (*model*), Edna Reynolds (*the widow Sharp*), Bert Tracy (*art connoisseur*), Joe Cohen.

Photo from the collection of Herman McEachin

Plump and Runt artists, find that the combined results of their efforts in colors do not pay even for the hire of their pretty model. However, an angel appears in the person of an old connoisseur, who offers them a large sum of money for a finished picture of the model. The old chap's too evident admiration of the girl's shape arouses Plump's jealousy and in a rage he slashes the canvas to bits, thus ruining their opportunity of getting the greenbacks. Attracted by their door sign, a wealthy widow commissions Plump to paint her portrait. Plump tries, but her attempts at lovemaking disgust him and he leaves the work for Runt to finish. Runt, with an eye to the widow's wealth, makes hay while the sun shines and wins her hand, leaving the poor but pretty model for Plump. The tables are turned when it is discovered that the little girl is an heiress and her fat hero is happy, possessing both wealth and beauty, while poor Runt finds that he has tied himself to a muchly over-rated piece of second hand femininity.. [M]

Plump & Runt start out friends and end up rivals. As usual Plump forsakes both friendship and fortune for love. Throughout the film, Babe Hardy plays the part of the lovesick yet starving artist with much flair. His emotional overplaying, grand gestures and all, hits right on the mark. Exaggerated poses, arm-over-brow gestures of grief, and a cry that would make Stan Laurel proud are all well played by Babe. At one point he cries so hard his whole body quakes. While Babe does well in this short, there is little for Billy Ruge to do, which is exactly what he does.

The painting of Ray Godfrey that is to be sold is a joint effort by the two artists. Plump paints the young lady's body waist up on one canvas, while Runt paints from the waist down. This sets up a funny bit after Plump declines to sell the painting. Once he has put a knife through the canvas (in order to void the sale), Plump picks up the top half of the painting and tenderly kisses the likeness of the model he loves. He then picks up the other canvas and begins to kiss it also but realizes what part of the anatomy is depicted and thinks better of his actions.

Photo from the collection of Herman McEachin

"Plump and Runt are rival artists in this one reel farce. They both become involved in a love affair which gets them in trouble and furnishes a corresponding amount of amusement for all disinterested persons. Not the funniest of the Vims but a laughable reel with fair average." -- *Moving Picture World*

Never Again

Released June 22, 1916. Vim Comedies - General Film Company release. One reel. No copyright registered. Release number 20767.

Produced by Louis Burstein. Directed by Will Louis. Photographed by Garry Hotaling. Filmed early April 1916 in St. Augustine, Florida.

with Babe Hardy (*Plump*), Billy Ruge (*Runt*), Bert Tracy (*Pop Dale*), Helen Gilmore (*his wife*), Florence McLoughlin (*their daughter*), Ray Godfrey (*their daughter*), Joe Cohen, Mabel Best, Edna Reynolds.

Pop Dale determines to go on a trip to Spain and at a day's notice orders the family to pack up. This upsets the little daughters. A hasty farewell and the girls are rushed down to the boat, leaving our heroes in a sad frame of mind. However, they also act with precision, and as the boat is drawing away, two forms dash madly over the rail and again the lovers are together, much to Pop's disgust. Arrived in Spain, the charm and romance of the country appeal to the male members of the family, so much so that serious trouble ensues. Falling victims to the enticing guiles of a Spanish dancer, the two boys, forgetting their fiancées, become her admirers. Pop, attempting to break up this awkward state of affairs, is himself made a fool of and we have the three of them, each ready to cut the other's throat. The girls complain to their mother. She, in turn, appeals to her husband, but discovers that the old scamp is as bad as the boys. A plan is made to catch the three culprits and they are followed by the three women on their next expedition. The boys and the old man take bouquets and different roads to the dancer's home. Here, on the point of presenting the orchids, she introduces them to her husband and six children. Disgusted, the lovers return, only to find that their women-kind have seen the whole performance and, making the best of a bad job, they decide that the old friends are the best and with rather forced smiles offer the bouquets, which are this time accepted. [MPW]

St. Augustine is located about 40 miles south by southeast of Jacksonville and was not new to filmmaking. Gaumont, Kalem and Thanhouser (among others) made films down in St. Augustine during the time those studios were based in Jacksonville. Occasionally some of the larger feature film companies would visit the city. Theda Bara made a number of films in the city. During their short stay in the city the Vim company stayed at the Hotel Keystone. Thankfully, there's no evidence Vim actresses were ever accidentally locked out of their rooms and accosted by flirtatious, drunken, derby-wearing tramps.

"Babe Hardy and Billy Ruge lead the fun-makers of this one reel farce. As Plump and Runt take a trip to Spain and make the acquaintance of a real Spanish dancer, get in wrong with their sweethearts and are glad to return to America. Up to the usual Vim standard." -- *Moving Picture World*

Better Halves

Released June 29, 1916. Vim Comedies - General Film Company release. One reel. No copyright registered. Release number 20813.

Produced by Louis Burstein. Directed by Will Louis. Filmed in Jacksonville, Florida.

with Babe Hardy (*Plump*), Billy Ruge (*Runt*), Florence McLoughlin (*Mrs. Plump*), Ray Godfrey (*Mrs. Runt*).

Plump and Runt are benedicts, but their "benedictives" are of different brands. Little Runt is the boss of his house. Fatty is nothing more than a jelly fish in the hands of his wife. Shopping one day, Plump helps a damsel in distress by tying her bootlace and is caught by Mrs. Plump. Sherman's famous remark might by aptly applied to the ensuing dispute. Runt, rescues Plump and after the pair have imbibed a little refreshment, the latter is inflamed by his little pal's sarcasm and resolves to cast off the shackles of slavery and assert himself. Full of his newly-found courage, they repair to their home, only to find that in their absence Mrs. Plump has likewise educated Mrs. Runt and successfully proven to her that woman should be the boss of the house. But Plump and Runt are averse to their demands, and in the end they win out. [MPW]

Another battle of the sexes, and another film that uses the premise of the large, strong Babe Hardy being dominated by the diminutive wife.

"The situations in this one reel farce have long served to make people merry. However, they were ripe good material in the days of their youth and have lost but little of their vitality. Two married couples figure in the plot and are cleverly acted by Babe Hardy, Billy Ruge, Florence McLoughlin and Ray Godfrey." -- *Moving Picture World*

"Apart from the knockabout side of the comedy, there are several humorous passages." -- *Kinematograph Weekly*

A Day At School

Released July 6, 1916. Vim Comedies - General Film Company release. One reel. No copyright registered. Release number 20848.

Produced by Louis Burstein. Directed by Will Louis. Filmed in Jacksonville, Florida.

with Babe Hardy (*Plump*), Billy Ruge (*Runt*), Joe Cohen (*father*), Ray Godfrey (*daughter*), Bert Tracy (*janitor*), Anna Mingus (*principal*).

Ray is sent to boarding school. With the connivance of her maid, her lover is apprised of her destination and he goes to rescue his lady love. He succeeds in entering her room, but is seen by the inquisitive janitor, who informs the principal. A grand sortie is made by the whole school, but on bursting into Ray's room, nothing is seen but a man's hat and glove. This is conclusive evidence and the father is sent for. Meanwhile, scared but undismayed, Plump dresses as a girl, is admitted as a pupil and plans an elopement. Once more the ever busy janitor intervenes and again the alarm is raised. Fortunately for the two an enterprising burglar chooses this moment for an entrance and he, alarmed by the commotion, hides in a closet. Their escape cut off, Plump and Ray dash into their room, and our hero takes refuge in the burglar's closet, from which he forces the crook. Rushing through the assembled pupils the prowler dives through the window and meeting the father downs him, after stealing his clothes. This leaves open the way of escape and the lovers, jumping into the father's auto, wave a kiss as the crook climbs on behind, leaving dad now mistaken for the burglar to be almost annihilated by the excited girls. [MPW]

Perhaps one of the reasons Babe Hardy always said he had the fondest memories of his Vim days.

Babe Hardy once again dons a dress for a good portion of a film. As evidenced by existing stills, he seems to very much enjoy such parts. Some reviewers listed Bill Ruge as the janitor; the synopsis supplied by Vim to the trades lists Bert Tracy in the role. With the film among the missing, neither comedian's part can be confirmed.

"Babe Hardy's sweetheart is sent to boarding school in this one reel comedy and Babe as Plump gets into a girlish, but expensive frock and follows her after the manner of Mary's lamb. Runt is the janitor and the mix-up that bound to occur is quite full of pretty girls in pajamas and nighties as the situations give warrant." -- *Moving Picture World*

"The plot is prehistoric; but Plump is such a pleasing fat creature in his female impersonation of a school girl, and the school girls that he mixes with are such jolly, pyjama-clad creatures, that the age of the theme is forgiven. There are plenty of laughs in this comic, which is quite devoid of offence" -- *The Bioscope*

Spaghetti

Released July 13, 1916. Vim Comedies - General Film Company release. One reel. No copyright registered. Release number 20883.

Produced by Louis Burstein. Directed by Will Louis. Filmed around May 11, 1916 in Jacksonville, Florida.

with Babe Hardy (*Plump*), Billy Ruge (*Runt*), Ray Godfrey (*cashier*), Bert Tracy (*waiter*), Harry Burns (*chef*), Joe Cohen (*Italian customer*). Moving Picture World lists Bert Tracy as the Italian customer and makes no mention of Joe Cohen.

Between attending to business calls and endeavoring to keep his assistants from making love to his pretty cashier, Runt has his hands full. To mend matters, his chef spoils the meal of a regular customer and he, being a typical son of Sunny Italy, shows his disapproval by trying to divert the circulation of the culinary artist's blood. In despair, Runt employs Plump as head chef. The latter's gifts are more in the line of lovemaking than in preparing the menu, and Runt discovers to his horror that he has only added another nuisance to his establishment. Things go from bad to worse. The Italian gentleman calls for another meal and Plump's cooking sends him into a couple of fits, in the course of which he makes good his threat and cleans up the whole place. Spaghetti flies through the air. Plump runs away with the cashier and poor Runt, trying to quell the disturbance, is finally buried under volley after volley of the stringy mixture. [M & MPW]

Some of the publicity surrounding the Plump & Runt comedies liked to play up Babe Hardy's size, even exaggerating it somewhat. The following blurb printed in the *Richmond Times Dispatch* lists Babe at a weight he was not likely to reach until much later in life: "Two hundred pounds of spaghetti, all cooked up a l'Italienne, was served up in one of the early scenes of a forthcoming Vim comedy, and Babe Hardy, who only weighs 325 pounds in his stocking feet, started to eat it. But somebody interrupted him, and a battle royal ensued, which resulted in a first-page story for the Jacksonville, Fla. Reporters. Meanwhile the camera man was grinding away, and it's all in the film—probably the first time anybody ever really saw what eight yards of spaghetti looks like." Another referred to Hardy as a "Spaghetti Cook's Dream."

"It is, perhaps, too much to say that spaghetti plays the leading part in this one reel comedy, but it is star "prop." Plump and Runt assisted by the entire cast consume, juggle and bombard each other with it and finally bury one of their numbers under gallons of Dagoe's Delight. Persons who relish this brand of humor will have a feast." -- *Moving Picture World*

Aunt Bill

Released July 20, 1916. Vim Comedies - General Film Company release. One reel. No copyright registered. Release number 20917.

Produced by Louis Burstein. Directed by Will Louis. Filmed in Jacksonville, Florida.

with Babe Hardy (*Plump*), Billy Ruge (*Runt*), Ray Godfrey (*Mrs. Plump*), Florence McLoughlin (*Mrs. Runt*), Bert Tracy (*Aunt*), Billy Bletcher (*bogus aunt*), Joe Cohen (*club friend*), James Renfro (*club friend*), Joe Schrode (*club friend*).

The families, Plump and Runt, although in fairly good circumstances, live a little beyond their means, so that the arrival of a letter from their wives' unknown and wealthy aunt is the cause of general rejoicing. Brimming over with anticipation of the good things to come, Plump confides in his club friends and they plan this joke: that one of them shall dress up and pose as the aunt. The plot is overheard by Plump's best pal and he informs Plump of the *pending deception. Unfortunately, the real aunt appears earlier than expected, and our heroes, thinking that she is the impersonator lead her the life of a dog -- much to the old lady's amazement. At last, driven wild by her relatives' unexplainable conduct, Aunty gathers her clothes and steals out in time to meet the bogus one, who promptly retreats. Explanations ensue, but to no avail, for the now-thoroughly disgusted lady tears up the $10,000 check and departs, leaving her would-be heirs frozen with disappointment.* [MPW]

Two tried and true comedic premises meet in this short: mistaken identity and attempting to bilk rich relatives. Billy Bletcher plays one of the buddies that impersonates the aunt, but Bert Tracy plays the aunt. Unlike most of the Vim comedies filmed in Jacksonville this one shows very little of the Florida city. With the exception of a few brief scenes in front of the boarding house where Plump & Runt live, all of the action takes place inside the boarding house and an actual hotel lobby. All three of Babe Hardy's diminutive male co-stars from his time at Vim appear in this film: the genuine Runt (Ruge), the should-have-been Runt (Bletcher) and the could-have-been Runt (Tracy). The pairing of Hardy with a more slight in stature partner was an oft-used practice long before he teamed up with Chaplin's understudy.

"Plump and Runt are the stars of this one reel comedy. It has a well-defined plot that has seen considerable service in the cause of dramatic art, mistaken identity being the foundation for the fun. Florence McLoughlin, Ray Godfrey, Bert Tracy, Billie Bletcher give Babe Hardy and Billy Ruge a helping hand with the acting." -- *Moving Picture World*

"This is the most old fashioned and futile feature described as comedy we have seen or heard of for some years. The story is the same one which has provided the basis for many a stage farce and screen comedy, and the producers have not even taken the trouble to try to clothe it in a slight disguise of originality. Its one redeeming feature is its cleanliness. The production is ordinary in every way, and the acting is equal to the story." -- *Kinematograph Weekly [reviewed in 1920]*

"The fun is rather boisterous than humorous, and certainly lacks subtlety." -- *The Bioscope*

The Heroes

Released July 27, 1916. Vim Comedies - General Film Company release. One reel. No copyright registered. Release number 20953.

Produced by Louis Burstein. Directed by Will Louis. Filmed in Jacksonville, Florida.

with Babe Hardy (*Plump*), Billy Ruge (*Runt*), Ray Godfrey (*Sweetheart of Plump & Runt*), Bert Tracy (*schoolmaster*), Joe Cohen (*circus agent*), Harry Burns.

Day succeeded day in one happy sequence for Plump and Runt. Occasionally they caught the drift of their teacher's meaning: often they did not, but what matter? Had they not beanshooters, tacks and other little things with which to annoy him? Was not Ray the object of their youthful passion, also a member of their class and did they not rob every orchard for her delectation? One day the circus arrived in town and then began the trouble. Fascinated by the tales of the flashy agent, Ray vanishes and Plump and Runt are left alone. Like true knights they take up the trail and at last locate the circus in a distant town. To their horror they recognize Ray as the high diver as she stands poised for her terrific drop through space. As she hits the water her lovers also dive in and pandemonium reigns. Down comes the tent, over goes the tank, and the villainous circus men count more stars than ever were in the firmament as the reunited trio set out for their peaceful country home. [M & MPW]

The tagline on an ad for *The Heroes*: "Exploits of the yellow-haired kid who ran away with the wicked circus man and became a diving Venus. Plump and Runt to the rescue." But in reality Ray Godfrey was an expert swimmer, a talented high diver and needed no real rescue. This short gives her the chance to show off her skill in the water and her beauty. Why Plump & Runt ever thought they would have a chance with such a beauty is a mystery, although the fact that they are often successful is an even greater mystery.

"The story tells how Plump and Runt, two schoolboys, discover to their horror that their sweetheart has joined a circus, impelled thereto by the fascinating tale of the flashy agent. They rescue her from the villainous circus man, but not before they have wrecked the circus."
-- *Motion Picture News*

Human Hounds

Released August 3, 1916. Vim Comedies - General Film Company release. One reel. No copyright registered. Release number 20983.

Produced by Louis Burstein. Directed by Will Louis. Filmed in Jacksonville, Florida.

with Babe Hardy (*Plump*), Billy Ruge (*Runt*), Bert Tracy (*General Debility*), Ray Godfrey (*his wife*), Joe Cohen (*Count de Lummox*), Mudge Cohen (*Mudge de Lummox*).

With the secrets of a nation entrusted to his care, General Debility cautiously places them in his bureau as his charming friend, the Countess Mudge, enters his room. Her fascinating manner entirely puts the old chap off his guard and she discovers the hiding place of the papers. The old general's wife, tired of his everlasting flirtations, decided to divorce him and with the divorce papers calls on the famous detectives Plump and Runt to serve them. At the same time the general discovers that his valued plots are missing and also employs them to find them. Not gifted with any great amount of intelligence our two worthies manage to muddle things up in splendid style. They find the plots, mistake them for the divorce papers, are themselves robbed, and finally blunder into the right course, owing to the indecision of the female mind, as the general's wife, changed her mind in regards to the divorce, and returns to them the missing plots which she fondly imagined were her divorce papers. [MPW]

The premise of two well-meaning but not so bright guys thinking their logical career path is as detectives must be a sure fire comedy set-up because it is so often used. And as many times as it is used, it doesn't work out. One really must question the mental capabilities of the ones that seem to always hire these kind of guys. *Do Detectives Think?*, well Plump & Runt (or Laurel & Hardy) certainly try, however, thinking is something their would-be employers seem to not even attempt.

"Plump and Runt are a pair of detectives in this one-reel farce. Their efforts to help a client secure a divorce from her husband leads to considerable broad fun. The number has the vigor of action that is generally to be found in a Vim comedy."
-- *Moving Picture World*

Dreamy Knights

Released August 10, 1916. Vim Comedies - General Film Company release. One reel. No copyright registered. Release number 21013.

Produced by Louis Burstein. Directed by Will Louis. Filmed in Jacksonville, Florida.

with Babe Hardy (*Plump*), Billy Ruge (*Runt*), Ray Godfrey (*maiden in distress*), Bert Tracy.

The fish were to blame, they would not bite, so Plump and Runt dozed off and dreamed. The bottle containing a message is picked up from the waves and they start out to rescue the beauteous damsel, writer of the script. Mounted on a mule and goat and armed to the teeth, they encounter many and various adventures. Deceived by the voice of a porker they become lost in the forest and wander upon a pirate stronghold, where they are scared almost to death by the appearance of the pirate chief. Once more on the trail and more by good luck than management, they blunder upon the haunted house where the maid is imprisoned. Here they arrive in time to save the girl from being forced into an unwelcome marriage. Love hits them both and they are in a quandary how to solve the situation, when the fish begin to bite. Two or three vicious tugs at the lines and they wake up to find that though their qualifications as Knights Errant leave much to be desired, still as fishermen, they are in a class by themselves.
[M]

The dream sequence is another comedic tool often used which allows for the action to be bizarre and even unbelievable. It is good that Will Louis employed such a technique in this short lest the stark, true to life, believable antics of Plump & Runt seen in their other films be tainted... Okay, so the dream sequence doesn't really serve much purpose. This short is a take-off on that guy from La Mancha, Don Quixote, the absence of windmills notwithstanding. *Motion Picture* magazine reviewed the film: "The usual slapstick, burlesque farce; but there are things in this that make it better than the average-- particularly the appearance of a young lady, whose name is not given, but who gives promises of even better things." The lady in question was Ray Godfrey.

"An amusing burlesque of Cervantes' immortal Don Quixote is the theme of this one reel farce, Babe Hardy, Billy Ruge and Ray Godfrey heading the cast. Plump and Runt are discovered fishing from a boat, they go to sleep and dream they are heroes of a great adventure. Although still in the present century they imagine they are a pair of bold knights, who mission is to rescue beauty in distress and defeat villainy at every turn. A captured maiden is freed by them and a pirate stronghold overthrown. Their gallant steeds are an undersized donkey and an underfed goat. Plump and Runt make a ludicrous pair of swashbucklers until awakened from their pleasant dreams by the unsettling of the boat." -- *Moving Picture World*

Life Savers

Released August 17, 1916. Vim Comedies - General Film Company release. One reel. No copyright registered. Release number 21043.

Produced by Louis Burstein. Directed by Will Louis. Filmed in Jacksonville, Florida.

with Babe Hardy (*Plump*), Billy Ruge (*Runt*), Ray Godfrey (*Miss Aqua*), Helen Gilmore (*old maid*), Dad Bates (*Neptune, Miss Aqua's husband*).

Though Plump and Runt had yet to save the first life, it was through no fault of theirs, the one with his antediluvian flivver and the other with his leaky old boat spent the days hoping that someone would give them the opportunity they so anxiously longed for. The visit of the beautiful young diver, Miss Aqua, accompanied by her manager, caused the break between our heroes. Each fell for her charms and sought means to humiliate the other. Love and jealousy occupied all their thoughts. First one, then the other would be favored by the diver's smiles, until, driven almost crazy, Runt decides to get rid of his fat rival by digging a hole under the water, and enticing there his hated one-time pal. A kittish old maid is the first victim, and poor Plump, attempting to rescue her, himself falls in and the two are buried in the ocean bed. The victor now escorts his loved one into the water, thinking to gloat over his rival's destruction, but, remorse seizing him, he aids in the rescue of the almost choked Plump. The diver now gives an exhibition of her powers and, pretending to be overcome, the two gallants dash to her rescue by boat and flivver. The flivver arrives first, but explodes, throwing its occupants high in the air and upsetting Runt, who is now over the spot in his boat. However, their united efforts bring the charter safely to land, where, to their horror, they are met and thanked by the lady's husband. Once more, their best intentions foiled, Plump and his pal cool their fevered and disappointed brows beneath the salty waves. [MPW]

Ray Godfrey, who is once again clad in swim gear and portraying a diver, must have been something in a bathing suit. As in *The Heroes*, Plump & Runt are dazzled by her beauty. This time around their rivalry for the bathing beauty is for naught, there being a Mr. Aqua. Trick photography is effectively used for the underwater scenes, and during the attempted rescue scene Plump races to the scene only to have his car explode and capsize Runt's boat.

Photo from the collection of Herman McEachin

A dead whale washed up at Pablo Beach. The Vimmies jumped into action and filmed Life Savers.

"Several of the scenes in this one-reel comedy take place on the bottom of the ocean, and the illusion is skillfully maintained. Plump and Runt are the leaders in the cast and the director has devised considerable amusing business. The finish is novel." -- *Moving Picture World*

"The Vim comedy, *The Life Savers* is a delightful satire on seashore amusements. Babe Hardy and Billy Ruge, as Plump and Runt, fall in love with a beautiful diver, only to find, after they have jeopardized their friendship for her favor, that she is already married." -- *Hartford Courant*

Their Honeymoon

Released August 24, 1916. Vim Comedies - General Film Company release. One reel. No copyright registered. Release number 21073.

Produced by Louis Burstein. Directed by Will Louis. Filmed in Jacksonville, Florida.

with Babe Hardy (*Plump*), Billy Ruge (*Runt*), Edna Reynolds (*mother-in-law*), Ray Godfrey (*Mrs. Plump*), Frank Hanson (*Tramp*).

Starting on their honeymoon, young Mrs. Plump decides to carry their cash in the form of gold pieces sewed on her coat as buttons. Attacked by tramps, the coat is stolen and the shock makes Ma-in-law ill. Wifey telephones to Mr. Plump to hasten home. He is arrested for speeding and put in jail. Here he recognizes one of the thugs, pinched for another crime. The judge is told of the thug's attack and Plump phones to tell wifey of his capture. The lost coat is discovered among the tramp's belongings and Plump, tearing off one of the buttons, cheerfully pays his fine and once more breathes the fresh air. [M & MPW]

The ongoing existence of the comedy team of Hardy & Ruge appeared to be in jeopardy by this time. Yet again the action centers around Babe Hardy, with Billy Ruge mainly playing a supporting role. Perhaps the Vim bosses were never quite sold on the Plump & Runt series. Frank "Spook" Hanson, who was working regularly over in the Pokes and Jabbs company, does a rare turn with Plump & Runt likely due to Bobby Burns and Walter Stull having taken a mid-summer vacation to New York City.

"Plump becomes a bridegroom in this one-reel farce, and makes the mistake of turning over the money for the bridal tour to his wife. The fate of the money, which is stolen, furnishes the fun of the reel. The acting of Babe Hardy, Billy Ruge, Frank Hanson, Ray Godfrey and Edna Reynolds bring out the good points of the picture."
-- *Moving Picture World*

An Aerial Joyride

Released August 31, 1916. Vim Comedies - General Film Company release. One reel. No copyright registered. Release number 21101.

Produced by Louis Burstein. Directed by Will Louis. Filmed in Jacksonville, Florida, outside Jacksonville Electric Garage at 618-626 Riverside Avenue, around the Riverside district including Riverside Park, downtown and at the Claude Nolan Cadillac building at 937 N. Main Street in Jacksonville.

with Babe Hardy (*Plump*), Billy Ruge (*Runt*), Ray Godfrey (*his sweetheart*), Will Louis (*man kicking Plump*), Florence McLoughlin (*one of Ray's friends and a shop girl*), Joe Cohen (*cop*), Bert Tracy (*man at auto dealer*).

Runt is a sport and he leads his girl to believe that he is about to buy a swell auto. He examines several, but the prices do not suit him and he finally gets what he thinks is a bargain — a broken down flivver for a small sum. Plump, an out of work chauffeur, is engaged as driver and they sally forth for the girl's house. Being a two-seated car, Runt is obliged to sit on the axle and during the ride is lost. He calls the police and they pursue the flying couple, who leap through the clouds in their attempts to escape. A shot from below blows up the flying flivver and in the ensuing excitement the police car is driven clean through the wall of a garage just in time to catch Plump and the girl who unfortunately drop through the ceiling. [M & MPW]

Runt gets a rare turn in the lead role, and Billy Ruge is dressed rather nicely in a summer business suit and straw hat. Babe Hardy, on the other hand, is dressed like a country bumpkin, although he does wear a derby. *An Aerial Joyride* allows us a great look at Jacksonville and at some great vintage cars (many of them the personal vehicles of the cast). Runt goes from dealer to dealer in search of an affordable car and test drives a number of them. His sweetheart sees him pass by and is impressed, but when he shows up with a lousy flivver she is disappointed (yet gamely puts on a brave face). After he is thrown from the car, Ruge gets the police. Apparently in hibernation since the demise of the Lubin studios, the Riverside police force make an inept (and, yes, very Keystone Kop-ish) return to films. The scenes of the car flying pleased reviewers and was apparently very well done, but sadly is missing from the only print known to exist.

The Claude Nolan Cadillac dealership is still an ongoing concern in Jacksonville. The dealership is now located elsewhere in Jacksonville but the original building on Main Steet remains. Built in 1911, the building was designated a historical landmark in 2016 and as of that date was being refurbished.

"Runt determines to present his wife an automobile but finds he only has money to purchase a flivver. To make matters worse he engages Plump to chauffeur, and that heavyweight loses control of the machine to such an extent that it refuses to stay upon the solid ground. The effect of the auto sailing through the air is cleverly handled. There are both excitement and amusement before the machine quits the earth." -- *Moving Picture World*

Sidetracked

Released September 7, 1916. Vim Comedies - General Film Company release. One reel. No copyright registered. Release number 21130.

Produced by Louis Burstein. Directed by Will Louis. Filmed in Jacksonville, Florida.

with Babe Hardy (*Plump*), Billy Ruge (*Runt*), Robin Williamson (*Negro porter*), Melba Andrews (*Mrs. Runt*).

The newlyweds, Mr. and Mrs. Runt, start out on their honeymoon, and through the extreme affability of Plump, a drummer, trouble commences. Longing for a smoke, the bridegroom strolls to the smoker. Here he falls asleep, and the switching during the night of his end of the train leaves him miles away from his little wife. Meantime Plump does all he can to allay her anxiety, eventually escorting her to a hotel and promising to find her missing spouse. Runt manages to start on his return journey. He gets into trouble again with the minions of the law. Arriving at the hotel, he rushes to his wife's room in time to meet Plump leaving. Jealousy, rage and murder fly through the air, and the innocent drummer makes a hurried exit to the accompaniment of a fusillade of pistol shots. Through the street, up and down fire-escapes they go while the hotel is in an uproar. Fortunately, or otherwise, the pursued one finds his way unseen, as he thinks, into one of the rooms and proceeds to hide himself. Runt, exhausted with his murderous chase, returns to his room and, seeing his loved one in tears, relents and takes wifey in his arms. Plump, cramped in his hiding place and thinking the coast clear, emerges and disturbs the little scene. Once more the dogs are let loose and Runt gets up on his hind legs. Oil is poured on the troubled waters by a double explanation and instead of being carried out in bits Plump is admitted into the bosom of the Runt family. [MPW]

"Plump & Runt are featured in this one-reel farce. While on his wedding tour, Runt falls asleep on the smoking car that is separated from his bride. Plump attempts to adjust matters and is nearly murdered for his pains. There is a lively chase at the finish, but the reel is not one of the best of its brand." -- *Moving Picture World*

Stranded

Released September 14, 1916. Vim Comedies - General Film Company release. One reel. No copyright registered. Release number 21157.

Produced by Louis Burstein. Directed by Will Louis. Filmed in Jacksonville, Florida.

with Babe Hardy (*Plump*), Billy Ruge (*Runt*), Frank Hanson (*Millionaire Slocum*), Ray Godfrey (*Slocum's daughter*), Florence McLoughlin (*Slocum's daughter*), Robin Williamson (*Ray's unwanted suitor*), Bert Tracy, Helen Gilmore.

Tired of business worries and an endless round of social activities, Plump & Runt board their speed boat, the Scum, and sail for the wilds. At sea their attention attracted by a strange object, they make a close examination and then — Crash! Bang! Oblivion. Consciousness returned, their boat in splinters and all but dead, the conclusion slowly forces itself on them that they landed on a target at the very moment the artillery let loose. After a long swim they crawl ashore and fall asleep. Time passes and millionaire Slocum and friends choose the same spot for their camp. His daughter's wealth and beauty have attracted the attention of an adventurer and he arrives to press his suit, in spite of the girl's evident dislike. Out hunting, the beauty disturbs Plump's slumbers by a shot thus bringing about an introduction. A sportsman to the backbone, the old man goes fishing and loses his artificial teeth. Our heroes restore them. The villain, mad with jealousy, seizes the girl and sails away with her. A wonderful shot from Plump's rifle and down comes the sail. Foiled again, the bad man places a bomb on the craft, ties up the girl, and leaves her to her fate. Plump & Runt rescue her, throw away the bomb, which blows up the escaping scoundrel. [MPW]

Much was made of the fact that Babe Hardy actually shot the rope with the rifle, although likely an exercise in printing the legend rather than the fact. In a *Moving Picture World* article entitled "Vim Comedian Proves Prowess With Rifle" it was noticed that "Babe Hardy, who is Plump in the Plump and Runt series of Vim comedies, weighs as much as four ordinary men, but is a wonderful rifle shot in spite of his bulk." Also interesting to note that the publicity surrounding the Plump & Runt comedies always exaggerated Babe Hardy's weight, who probably was at his most trim in his career during the Vim years.

"Plump and Runt meet with adventure when they decide to quit the high life. They board a motor boat, planning a quite day's fishing, but the boat gets in the way of soldiers at target practice and is wrecked. Ham and Bud swim to shore and find themselves in the midst of a group of picnickers. They have a good time and prove themselves heroes when they rescue the Poor Young Girl from the clutches of the Dastardly Villain." -- *Moving Picture World*

Love and Duty

Released September 21, 1916. Vim Comedies - General Film Company release. One reel. No copyright registered. Release number 21186.

Produced by Louis Burstein. Directed by Will Louis. Story by Bert Tracy. Filmed early August 1916 in Jacksonville, Florida.

with Babe Hardy (*Private Plump*), Billy Ruge (*Lieutenant Runt*), Bert Tracy (*Colonel Tracy*), Florence McLoughlin (*his daughter*), Ray Godfrey (*pet of the regiment*), Edna Reynolds (*woman with baby*), James Renfro (*jailer*).

The bugle's call rouses Private Plump and he hurries to Lieutenant Runt's tent to aid his pompous little superior's dressing. Secure in his authority, the officer tortures poor Plump with unnecessary drilling and departs for the day's work. The colonel's daughter loves Plump. The lieutenant loves her. Plump's heart is given to the little pet of the regiment, so that things are rather mixed. A trumped up charge places Plump in the court-martial's hands and unthinkingly the colonel sentences him to death. Risking her life, the pet aids him to escape. About this time the maneuvers are taking place and the bursting of a cannon scatters the troops and sends the colonel's horse away on a mad gallop ending in a flying jump into the river. Plump sees this and rushes off to a crane, jumps into the scoop and with a mighty heave drags out the drowning colonel. Before the whole regiment the hero is now restored, decorated and promoted, and with the pet in his arms, his happy future is assured. [M & MPW]

When the troops are in pursuit of the escaping Plump, they shoot a cannon at him. An amusing scene follows, with Babe running about the countryside avoiding the cannonball which follows him round and about. He finally catches the cannonball and throws it back at his pursuers, destroying their cannon in the process. Babe Hardy adds a bit of flair and confidence to Plump that was not apparent in previous turns. He smokes a cigarette, flipping the butt about and tipping his hat just so. Plump ends up getting the girl in the end but this time around so does Runt so while Babe embraces Ray as the film fades to black Billy gets to hug Florence, not a bad consolation prize.

"Plump and Runt as soldiers in this film are funny. Crisscrossed love affairs between Private Plump, Lieutenant Runt, the Colonel's daughter, and the pet of the regiment lead to complications. Plump is sentenced to die but the pet aids him to escape. An explosion throws the colonel into the water and Plump rescues him. He is who's given the hand of the pet and everybody including Runt is happy. Cast is made up of Babe Hardy, Billy Ruge, Florence McLoughlin and Ray Godfrey." -- *Moving Picture World*

The Reformers

Released September 28, 1916. Vim Comedies - General Film Company release. One reel. No copyright registered. Release number 21213.

Produced by Louis Burstein. Directed by Will Louis. Filmed in Jacksonville, Florida.

with Babe Hardy (*Plump*), Billy Ruge (*Runt*), Florence McLoughlin (*vampire*), Edna Reynolds (*Mrs. Ogden*), Ray Godfrey (*her daughter*), Bert Tracy (*her son*), Helen Gilmore, Anna Mingus (*maid*).

The fact that an unfortunate member of the canine race possesses a rather lurid appellation should not necessarily mean hat the free passage of his breath ought to be prevented by means of a piece of hemp. Plump and Runt were jail birds – thieves from the day they first stole a mouthful of air. A religious revival hits some buried chord in their beings and they reform so much as they get jobs as butler and chef. The same household shelters a wayward son, who is being bled by a woman of the world. To meet his demand for money his sister steals her friends' money and jewels, the blame falling upon our (this time innocent) heroes. How they emerge from the cloud of suspicion and finally bring the real culprits to justice is graphically told in the picture for the closing scenes show them, covered with virtuous indignation, vegetables, and a few clothes, enthroned among the household gods. [M]

Plump & Runt are never allowed to be downright bad (well, Plump at least is always a good guy). Why they were in jail in the first place is unknown. It is also uncertain if, while working as domestic help, Plump & Runt served the salad undressed.

"A fair comedy reel. Plump and Runt get over quite a few laughs. Convicts, they reform and obtain positions as menials. The daughter of the house steals to silence the enchantress of her wayward brother and Plump and Runt are accused of the crime. Through a series of rather cleverly burlesqued events, the guilty person is brought to book." -- *Moving Picture World*

Royal Blood

Released October 5, 1916. Vim Comedies - General Film Company release. One reel. No copyright registered. Release number 21242. Working title: *Counts and No-Counts.*

Produced by Louis Burstein. Directed by Will Louis. Filmed mid-August 1916 in Jacksonville, Florida partially at the Hotel Mason.

with Babe Hardy (*Plump*), Billy Ruge (*Runt*), Edna Reynolds (*Mrs. Vandergift*), Ray Godfrey (*her daughter*), Bert Tracy (*the Count*), Florence McLoughlin (*country*), Harry Naughton.

Though Ray's mother has a decided preference for blue blood, her daughter plainly showed that the old-fashioned color was good enough for her. Plump's life stream was red, while that of the Count was supposed to be tinged with cobalt. To mystify mother, Plump and his pal, Runt, make up as "Bluebloods" and gain the old lady's approbation. All goes well until the real aristocrat appears on the scene and then blood of all shades flies about. Mother finally comes to the conclusion that the old tinge is the best and allows the willful maid to have her own way. [MPW]

The *Florida Metropolis*, the local Jacksonville newspaper, ran a story that a Frenchman staying at the Mason Hotel mistook Babe Hardy, Billy Ruge and Bert Tracy as real German spies. The Frenchman assaulted Babe before Johnny Murnan the desk clerk at the Mason could convince him that it was all for the movies. While an unlikely tale in reality it does point out the current sentiment at the time in America regarding the war being fought across the Atlantic.

"A fair comedy number with Plump and Runt doing their best with a rather poor story. The girl's mother wants her to marry nobility, she chooses red rather than blue blood. Plump and Runt get over a few laughs in their attempts to appear aristocratic and the fur begins to fly when the real count appears." -- *Moving Picture World*

The Candy Trail

Released October 12, 1916. Vim Comedies - General Film Company release. One reel. No copyright registered. Release number 21271.

Produced by Louis Burstein. Directed by Will Louis. Filmed outside Atlantic Stores Co. at 120 Forsyth Street and at the Vim Studios in Jacksonville, Florida.

with Babe Hardy (*Plump*), Billy Ruge (*Runt*), Florence McLoughlin (*village belle*), Bert Tracy, Will Louis (*stranded motorist*), Spook Hanson, Edna Reynolds (*saloon customer*), James Renfro (*gang member*).

Florence, the village belle and heiress, accepts the invitation of Runt, the local sport, for a ride in his new flivver, much to the heartache of Plump, her true but rustic sweetheart. Runt, by his tales of wonderful adventure to be gained in the city he himself soon plans to visit, causes Florence to yearn to be one of the myriad lights that help to make the great White Way burn so brightly. When Runt reaches the city he falls into the clutches of a lawless gang and soon becomes one of its most ardent members. Scheming to gain possession of her riches, Runt writes to Florence telling her to come to town where he will show her the sights. Poor Plump is heartbroken at the departure of his sweetheart. Premonition tells Plump that his loved one is in danger. He hastens to the city where he finds a clue to Florence's whereabouts and follows her trail to the den where she is about to fall a victim at the hands of the gang's leader. Using all of his strength Plump routs the gang and rescues Florence. [MPW]

Before following his girl to the big city, Plump imagines Florence being attacked by Runt, and we see in this sequence Runt as a real bad guy. But when he gets to the city only a portion of his fears are realized. Runt turns out to be not so bad, but Florence is in a desperate struggle to preserve her virtue when attacked by one of Runt's fellow crooks. Plump cleans up the whole gang of crooks, throwing many of them about the room as if they were stage dummies (it is obvious they are not, and is an exhibition of some real strength by Babe).

Early in the film there are a few other amusing sequences. Desperately trying to get a car to follow Florence McLoughlin and Billy Ruge, Babe Hardy attempts to hit a parked motorist over the head with a stick. Just at the moment of impact the motorist turns around and Babe quickly goes into a lecture about the fine grain in Florida wood. Billy drives by and splashes Babe, who is standing near a puddle, but gets a flat tire in the process. Babe goes over to assist, removes the plunger from the air pump, and blows up the tire with his mouth. It over inflates, explodes, and sends Billy into the mud puddle.

"A funny reel with Plump and Runt doing good knockabout work. There are more laughs in this reel than have been in many of the recent Plump and Runt releases. When the girl goes to the city with Runt the sport, Plump, her faithful village sweetheart, is sick at heart. However, he follows her to the city and finds her via the candy trail." -- *Moving Picture World*

"There is something more in the nature of a connected story in this than in some single reel comedies, and Plump, with his big baby smile, imparts more humour than is to be found in mere slapstick. Plump's sturdy frame is the prop which supports the fabric of the comedy, and his contest with his rival Runt, who joins the band of crooks, affords a fair amount of amusement." --*Kinematograph Weekly*

The Precious Parcel

Released October 19, 1916. Vim Comedies - General Film Company release. One reel. No copyright registered. Release number 21299.

Produced by Louis Burstein. Directed by Will Louis. Filmed late September 1916 in Jacksonville, Florida.

with Babe Hardy (*Plump*), Billy Ruge (*Runt*), Florence McLoughlin (*Runt's accomplice*), Edna Reynolds (*telegraph operator*).

News flies swiftly in small communities, and although it is supposed to be an official secret that Edna, the telegraph operator at Lonesome Gulch, has been notified of a valuable assignment of gold soon to arrive, it was a matter of a few hours before the entire town knew of it. It reaches the ears of Runt and his accomplice, Florence, and they plan to gain possession of the gold. While Florence by her wiles keeps Plump, Edna's sweetheart, engaged in a flirtatious conversion, Runt and his man, Friday, seize Edna and tie her on the tressle over which the Overland Mail is due to pass in a few minutes. Then safe from interruption, Runt opens the strong box and the three conspirators drive off with the gold in their possession. Edna, by aid of a broken telegraph wire, manages to send out a call for help which Plump receives. Running to the trestle he releases her just as the train thunders past. Mounting their horses, Plump and Edna ride after the fleeing ensues in which Runt and his assistant receive a terrible beating and are hurled into the river by Plump. [MPW]

This is the last Plump & Runt film. After completing this film around September 25, 1916, Babe and Billy Ruge, along with Babe's wife, took a vacation at Atlantic Beach. Louis Burstein went north to Providence, Rhode Island where the Myers & Theby unit was working. When Burstein returned, Kate Price had been signed to star along with Babe in a new series of comedies and Ruge was left odd man out (foreshadowing things that would come yet again for Mr. Runt). The fact that Hardy and Ruge still socialized makes it appear the split was a studio decision and an effort to elevate Vim's second series.

While individual films in the series showed promise, the series itself failed because Hardy and Ruge simply did not work as a team. Sometimes they were friends, other times rivals, and at times downright enemies. Billy Ruge would move into supporting roles at Vim (both with Pokes & Jabbs and with Babe and Kate Price), and only after the split with Vim and formation of Amber Star would Ruge get his own series again and then was teamed with Kate Price in "Sparkle" comedies.

"A quite humorous reel with Plump and Runt as the chief laugh makers. The story burlesques in an entertaining manner the old plot of a shipment of gold to a lonely express office, and the conspiracy to steal it. Runt is the bad man and Plump is the hero." -- *Moving Picture World*

Photo from the collection of Herman McEachin

Much of the Plump & Runt Company. Top row: Ray Godfrey, Billy Ruge. Bottom Row: James Renfro, Anna Mingus, Robin Williamson, Frank Hanson, Mabel Best, Joe Schrode, Joe Cohen.

BUNGLES COMEDIES

Bungles' Rainy Day

Released February 10, 1916. Vim Comedies - General Film Company release. One reel. No copyright registered. Release number 20026.

Produced by Louis Burstein. Directed by Fernandea Perez, assisted by Ernest Boehm Boehm [photographic evidence indicates that Will Louis and/or Babe Hardy were involved in the production of the Bungles films]. Filmed in Jacksonville, Florida.

with Fernandea Perez [Marcel Perez] (*Bungles*), Elsie McLeod, Babe Hardy.

Not being anxious to have his new suit spoiled, Bungles was greatly worried over the important question of whether he should carry his umbrella or not. But because of his inability to arrive at any decision, he allows himself to be influenced by trivial circumstances, the result of which is that Bungle starts off the day disastrously to himself. Added to his misfortunes of the morning, he finds his sweetheart being beset by two tramps who are trying to rob her of her purse. After he puts the tramps to rout, he is amazed to discover that his sweetheart has deserted him, and he wanders through the city in a vain search of her. Finally, when he does find her. In his eagerness to be with her again, he succeeds in incurring the hostility of some piano movers, who swear to get revenge on poor Bungle. The tramps also plan to avenge themselves

on Bungle, and when they see the poor fellow being driven from his sweetheart's home by her irate mother, who has been insulted by Bungle, they join forces with the piano men. In the resultant melee that follows, Bungle is the recipient not alone of a beating, but of one of the most complete drenchings at the hands of the fire department. [MPW]

Marcel Perez a.k.a. Manuel Fernandez Perez a.k.a. Fernandea Perez (as the Vim publicity referred to him) was a moderately well known film comedian working in Europe, mainly with Pathé and Éclair under the character names of Robinet or Tweedledum. Why Vim changed Perez's character's name from the fairly well known "Tweedledum" to "Bungles" isn't known, but the move didn't have much tweedle and was a lot of dumb.

Perez at the time spoke no English, but reportedly directed his own films assisted by Ernest Boehm who interpreted for him. Existing stills, however, seem to indicate that Will Louis and Babe Hardy were involved in the production of the Bungles comedies, perhaps even directing the films. The two were easily available since the Bungle comedies were released every other Thursday which was Plump & Runt's regular day, and it appears the two production units may not have both been working at the same time or certainly had to share studio space.

"A new 'comic' has come to town! His name is Fernandea Perez and is a remarkable gentleman. His head long dives into an empty barrel are both startling and amusing. He has plenty of other tricks up his sleeves, at the end of his toes, and inside his coattails. He is getting to make to make a place for himself right along side the top row of knockabout comedians. His work in *Bungles' Rainy Day* proves this absolutely! He is from Italy and has a huge European reputation; he deserves it. He is a huge success in his first Vim release." -- *Moving Picture World*

Bungles Enforces The Law

Released February 24, 1916. Vim Comedies - General Film Company release. One reel. No copyright registered. Release number 20100.

Produced by Louis Burstein. Directed by Fernandea Perez, assisted by Ernest Boehm [photographic evidence indicates that Will Louis and/or Babe Hardy were involved in the production of the Bungles films]. Filmed in Jacksonville, Florida.

with Fernandea Perez [Marcel Perez] (*Bungles*), Elsie McLeod, Babe Hardy.

Owing to the disturbed financial affairs in their respective countries, three impoverished noblemen, Counts Boolum of Germany, Pierre of France and Shamus of Ireland, decide to marry the daughter of the wealthy Mayor of Mudton. The local police, distinguished for their absolute lack of even the smallest grain of intelligence, have failed in their efforts to drive the foreigners from the town and their worthy chief wires for the world-famed Bungles to bring his mighty brain to bear on the problem. The latter arrives in a cloud of mystery, electricity and uncertainty and forthwith lives up to his name by arresting the Mayor and placing him in the calaboose. The three rivals unfortunately choose the same hour for their proposal and challenged to mortal combat fly through the air. At last Bungles gets on the trail. He gathers his forces and arrives on the field of battle in time to become a billet for the first shot fired. Undaunted, however, he surrounds the combatants and marches both them and the girl off to jail, where all are jammed in to keep the now frothing Mayor company. Leaving his valiant force on guard, he, almost bursting with pride, hurries off to tell the chief of his success. Fortunately for the prisoners, the jail is very old and rickety and they walk off with it. Scared to death, the guards dash off to tell of the escape. Mad with rage, Bungles pursues, catches up with his quarry as it walks on to the ferryboat which is just pulling out. Resourceful as ever, Bungles orders his men to pull back the boat. They try but the ferry wins and they are on the point of being dragged into the water when Bungles grasps the rope and with a superhuman effort pulls the boat back to the slip. Pride once again proves his fate, for as he poses to receive the admiration of his followers, the boat again departs. This time, Bungles' effort is too late and the whole force is dragged into the water. Spitting out teeth, water and revenge, Bungles manages to hang on to the side of the boat and on its arrival at the opposite side, climbs over and strides to the calaboose. Horrors, he opens the door, only to find that the prisoners have escaped. Hardly believing his eyes, he enters the jail. A flash of golden hair dashes from behind and Bungles finds himself locked in and looking at him from the outside, is the mischievous face of his erstwhile captive. [MPW]

"The finishing episode of this one reel farce is enough to insure its success. The picture is only fair up to this point, but the stunt performed by Bungles that closes the reel is in a class by itself. He is dragged off the dock by a ferry boat and towed through the water at a lively pace." -- *Moving Picture World*

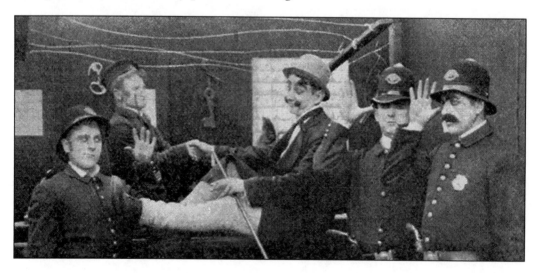

Bungles' Elopement

Released March 9, 1916. Vim Comedies - General Film Company release. One reel. No copyright registered. Release number 20174.

Produced by Louis Burstein. Directed by Fernandea Perez, assisted by Ernest Boehm [photographic evidence indicates that Will Louis and/or Babe Hardy were involved in the production of the Bungles films]. Filmed in Jacksonville, Florida.

with Fernandea Perez [Marcel Perez] (*Bungles*), Elsie McLeod, Babe Hardy.

Bungles earned his bread by painting houses and engaged in this pursuit, his "Heagle heye" led him to gaze into the fair face of a damsel in evident distress. Hoisting himself up to her window, he learned that she was to be forcibly married to a silly old beau by an ambitious father. That was enough for Bungles. Immediately he became a knight. She, eager to escape, throws a knotted sheet down and he climbs to the window and enters her room, where the young lovers have their first kiss. The father hears them and peeping through the keyhole sees cash and notes strewn on the floor, same having rolled from the pockets of our Romeo. The old beau, having returned home and discovered his loss receives a message from the father, asking him to return at once. Arriving at the house, the door is burst in, but Bungles escapes up the chimney, and after an exciting escapade wins the girl and punishes the pursuers. Then all is forgotten in the joy of his brilliant elopement. [MPW]

"The agile Mr. Bungles performs a number of startling acrobatic stunts in this one-reel farce, but he succeeds in running off with the lady fair. There is plenty of live action in this reel, and the laughs are frequent and hearty." -- *Moving Picture World*

Bungles Lands A Job

Released March 23, 1916. Vim Comedies - General Film Company release. One reel. No copyright registered. Release number 20248.

Produced by Louis Burstein. Directed by Fernandea Perez, assisted by Ernest Boehm [photographic evidence indicates that Will Louis and/or Babe Hardy were involved in the production of the Bungles films]. Filmed in Jacksonville, Florida.

with Fernandea Perez [Marcel Perez] (Bungles), Elsie McLeod, Babe Hardy.

The great and only Bungles, treated with scorn, contempt and later violence, wandered despairingly along the streets. Everything seemed at an end, so far as he was concerned. Seeing a trolley car approach, he laid his head across the rails and awaited death with a calm face. To his horror he found that the car had turned down another track and that he was still in the land of the living. Resting for a moment beneath a hotel window he found himself suddenly enveloped in the folds of something soft and filmy. Then he is flattened to the earth by a pair of shoes landing upon his head. A change takes place. A piece of glass does the duty for a razor and off comes his mustache. A few movements and his old rags are thrown aside and he becomes some female. Then follows a series of exciting experiences as Bungles, impersonating a woman, seeks employment and friends. He finds both with the theater folks, and finds in addition to work, trouble that ends his delicate plot. [MPW]

Bungles lands a job... at another studio. After this film Bungles disappears forever and Tweedledum reemerges, but not at Vim. This is the last of the Bungles films, and as such is the last work Marcel Perez would do for Vim. By the time this film was released, Perez was already working just north of the Vim Studios at the Eagle Film Co. A reason for the abrupt departure is not recorded in the trades or local newspapers, but Perez working at Eagle instead of at Vim is presented as a mere matter of fact. Some of Perez's work at Eagle, such as *A Bathtub Elopement*, still exist and give us a glimmer of what a Vim comedy with the great Marcel Perez might have looked like.

"Bungles lands a job and the job that Bungles lands almost lands Bungles in jail. Bungles finds that no one will employ him while in his proper person. He disguises himself as a tall and willowy member of the opposite sex. The trouble keeps right on his trial, although covered with skirts he makes a record as a bicycle rider and performs other amusing and reckless feats. The reel is right in line with the other Vim comedies." -- *Moving Picture World*

Marcel Perez (with some language assistance) reportedly directed the Bungles comedies. This photo seems to indicate that Will Louis and Babe Hardy were involved in the direction of the films to some extent. Also note that Bert Tracy appeared in at least one of the Bungles comedies.

MYERS & THEBY COMEDIES

Housekeeping

Released July 5, 1916. Vim Feature Comedies - General Film Company release. One reel. No copyright registered. Release number 20843.

Produced by Louis Burstein. Directed by Harry C. Myers. Photographed by Harry Keepers. Sets by Harry Myers. Filmed early April 1916 in Jacksonville, Florida.

with Harry Myers (*Hubby*), Rosemary Theby (*bride*).

The young married couple have a few pieces of home-made furniture in their flat. The bride's uncle sends her all his old heirlooms, which fill the flat to overflowing. Hubby buys a rocking chair and brings it home. He thinks he is in the wrong flat until the janitor reassures him. He has to use great care in navigating and gets stuck while trying to get into the kitchen. The bride and the janitor release him. He determines to sell the heirlooms and buy some real furniture. No sooner is the flat furnished with modern pieces when uncle comes to visit the couple. They dare not face him and escape to the roof. The scuttle is closed, and they are left in a rainstorm without shelter. [MPW]

The first of the Vim Feature Comedies which were intended to be a bit more refined than your run-of-the-mill Vim. Harry Myers and Rosemary Theby did bring a more sophisticated approach (á la Mr. & Mrs. Sidney Drew) to their films than the basic slapstick nature of the other two Vim units. Often compared to the Drews these domestic comedies benefited from Myers' direction but also his surreal set designs.

The Lois Weber-Phillip Smalley feature *Idle Wives* which was filmed in late July through August, 1916 features a scene outside a cinema where the principals pass by the outdoor lobby on their way into the theater. A poster for *Housekeeping* is clearly visible to the actors' right as they go inside the door.

"Harry C. Myers and Rosemary Theby are the stars of this domestic comedy which illustrates the troubles of a newly-married couple. The subject is treated in a broadly farcical manner and capitally played by Mr. Myers and Miss Theby." -- *Moving Picture World*

A Spring Cleaning

Released July 12, 1916. Vim Feature Comedies - General Film Company release. One reel. No copyright registered. Release number 20878. Some newspaper ads refer to the film as: *A Spring House Cleaning*. Working title: *House Cleaning Time*.

Produced by Louis Burstein. Directed by Harry C. Myers. Photographed by Harry Keepers. Sets by Harry Myers. Filmed late April 1916 in Jacksonville, Florida.

with Harry Myers (*Hubby*), Rosemary Theby (*Wifey*).

Hubby gets home from the road and prepares to enjoy a few days at home, when Wifey announces that she will begin her spring cleaning. Hubby immediately has business at the office, but the boss is heartless and sends him home. He meets Bill, a trusty friend, and arranges with him to send a telegram demanding Hubby's immediate presence in Jersey City on business. All day Hubby looks for the telegram to arrive. In the interim he gets in bad with Wifey over the spring cleaning. His meals are irregular and unsatisfying; he cannot sleep after 5 a. m. At last the telegram arrives and he tells Wifey he must be off. She advises him to read the message. He does so and reads: "Stay home and help your wife. Bill." Then he sinks through the floor. [M & MPW]

Charles Ellsworth Grapewin of New Jersey sued the General Film Company, Vim and Melies claiming he wrote *Spring Housecleaning*. He contended that he wrote on September 30, 1913 a vaudeville act entitled *Poughkeepsie* which was produced in Union Hill, New Jersey and duplicates what is presented in this film. It was not uncommon for the various film productions companies to solicit stories from the public. Whether Grapewin claims that he had done that and was just not paid, or if someone saw the stage production and lifted the idea suggesting outright theft is not known. It is also entirely possible that the similarity is pure coincidence, the plots of one reel comedies not being all that complicated to start with.

"Gentlemen: Your comedy *Spring House Cleaning* was shown with Harry Myers and Rosemary Theby at this theater the week of July 2nd, and caused general satisfaction. It was clean and the situation at the end of the film accorded a good laugh." -- *Letter from The Rialto (Times Square, NYC) to the Melies Manufacturing Company.*

The Connecting Bath

Released July 19, 1916. Vim Feature Comedies - General Film Company release. One reel. No copyright registered. Release number 20912.

Produced by Louis Burstein. Directed by Harry C. Myers. Photographed by Harry Keepers. Sets by Harry Myers. Filmed circa May 11, 1916 in part at the Hotel Seminole in Jacksonville, Florida.

with Harry Myers (*Hubby*), Rosemary Theby (*Wifey*), Billy Bletcher, Joe Schrode.

Hubby and Wifey part company and their divorce suit comes off. They arrive in the city and, unconsciously, put up at the same hotel. There is only one bath left, connecting between two rooms, and they are assigned to these rooms. The similarity of their names causes the house detective to watch the rooms. Wifey goes to take a bath and is scared away by Hubby's sneezing. Hubby enters the bath room and locks the communicating door. Wifey, indignant, beats on the door. Hubby sniffs the perfume she has left behind, and thinks of his wife. He writes a note of apology and retires. Wifey sniffs the cigarette butt he has left and thinks of her husband. She also writes a note. The house detective, his suspicions aroused by the constant slamming of doors, enters and arrests Hubby for playing Bo-peep under the door. Then he goes to arrest Wifey. Each gets into the other's room and sees his or her photograph on the dressing table. With a cry of joy they clinch as they meet in the bathroom, and when the detective interferes they drown him in the tub. [MPW]

"Harry C. Meyers and Rosemary Theby supply most of the acting in this one-reel comedy. They appear as an about-to-be-divorced couple who occupy rooms connected by a bath, and play hide-and-seek from one room to another until they discover that they haven't the slightest use for a divorce. Most of the stage business is clever, and the stars are easy and natural." -- *Moving Picture World*

Will a Woman Tell?

Released July 26, 1916. Vim Feature Comedies - General Film Company release. One reel. No copyright registered. Release number 20948.

Produced by Louis Burstein. Directed by Harry C. Myers. Photographed by Harry Keepers. Sets by Harry Myers. Filmed May-June 1916 in Jacksonville, Florida.

with Harry Myers (*Hubby*), Rosemary Theby (*Wifey*), Helen Gilmore.

Wifey gossips and stirs up the neighborhood. Hubby determines to teach her a lesson, and, having prepared her mind by pretending to be greatly worried, sends her to bed with the injunction not to look out of the window facing the woodshed. Her curiosity gets the better of her, and she sees Hubby bury something in a hole under a tree. That night he talks in his sleep and confesses a murder. Next morning as soon as he is gone, she confides in a neighbor, who informs the police. The "criminal" is arrested and taken to the scene of the crime, where the box is dug up. On the lid is the inscription: "You can't keep a secret but you can keep this." The laugh is on Wifey, and we hope she is cured of her propensity to tell everything she knows. [M & MPW]

The *Photoplayers Weekly* magazine published the following about this film: "Will a Woman tell? 'You bet she will,' says Harry Myers, co-star and director with Rosemary Theby in Vim feature comedies. Of course, every woman will rally to the defense of her sex against this base calumny, but Mr. Myers pleads extenuating circumstances. He has just finished a comedy with the above title, in which Miss Theby, as his wife, is tortured by the possession of a terrible secret after she has set the neighborhood in an uproar by her tattling of scared confidences. As a matter of precaution, Mr. Myers wishes it distinctly understood that this is only his professional opinion of the fair sex, and not what he really thinks."

"The husband of the lady on this one-reel comedy is fully convinced that his wife can't keep a secret, and puts up a job on her to prove that he is right. The plot is neatly worked out and played with equal deftness by Harry C. Myers and Rosemary Theby." -- *Moving Picture World*

Hubby's Relatives

Released August 2, 1916. Vim Feature Comedies - General Film Company release. One reel. No copyright registered. Released 20981.

Produced by Louis Burstein. Directed by Harry C. Myers. Photographed by Harry Keepers. Sets by Harry Myers. Filmed in Jacksonville, Florida.

with Harry Myers (*Hubby*), Rosemary Theby (*Wifey*).

Lothario has many girls and is pursued by creditors. He falls in love with a new girl and marries her, having told his creditors that she is wealthy. His old flames read of the marriage and descend upon him. Likewise the creditors come to collect. Hubby in despair introduces them as his cousins, sisters, uncles, aunts and other relatives. He gets them out of the house, but they become suspicious and return. After he has exhausted every effort to keep the facts from wifey he is exposed. [M & MPW]

Motion Picture magazine didn't pull any punches with their opinion of the Myers-Theby comedies and this one specifically commenting that "Rosemary Theby, who was so enthralling as an emotional actress, seems wasted on such clap-trap." Although they did appreciate Harry Myers' talents as a set designer stating "A lot of nonsense in unusually artistic settings." It should be noted that the Myers-Theby comedies were generally enjoyed by critics and audiences alike.

"Harry C. Meyers and Rosemary Theby continue their domestic difficulties in this one-reel comedy. Hubby's relatives turn out to be bill collectors, for the most part, and he is put to rid the house of their presence. The reel is capitally played and the situations are fairly funny." -- *Moving Picture World*

That Tired Business Man

Released August 9, 1916. Vim Feature Comedies - General Film Company release. One reel. No copyright registered. Release number 21009.

Produced by Louis Burstein. Directed by Harry C. Myers. Filmed in Jacksonville, Florida.

with Harry Myers (*Hubby*), Rosemary Theby (*Wifey*).

Hubby after the day's work is done usually stops for a little lunch and a few cocktails while Wifey waits at home for him with a hot supper. Hubby usually reaches home in an ugly mood finding nothing to his liking for supper and usually leaving the table without eating. Wifey finally insists on knowing what is wrong when Hubby tells her if she had to work for one day as hard as he has to she would be tired too. Wifey thinks for a moment and tells Hubby that she will take his place at the office for one day and he must take her place at home. Hubby thinking he has a snap consents. The next morning Wifey gives Hubby a taste of what

she receives each morning, eating in silence and then asking what time it is to find she must rush off to the office. Hubby asks if she hasn't forgotten something. She remembers and gives him a long list of things to be done for the day. That does not satisfy him as he wants to be kissed. She hastily kisses him and leaves. Hubby goes over the list then decides that his wife has been too easy with the maid. He goes into the kitchen and the discovers a speck on a dish.

The maid is very angry, looks at the plate and slams Hubby with dish cloth and quits her job. Hubby does not know what to do, he phones his wife who now is in the office working, that the maid has left. Wifey tells hubby the work must be done and that he should do it. Hubby does not like the idea, but decides he might try. He goes into the kitchen and begins to wash the dishes, but somehow cannot do it. After an hour or two of waiting without having washed the dishes he empties them into the ice chest and phones his wife again to send up a maid, but to his surprise the clerk answers the phone. When Wifey finds her husband is on the phone, she tells the clerk to tell him that she has gone to get a drink with a friend. [MPW]

"A Vim feature comedy with Harry C. Myers and Rosemary Theby as the stars, this one-reel photoplay cleverly satirizes the domestic side of married life. The male member of the household thinks that he is terribly overworked and that his wife's duties are anything but onerous. When he makes the mistake of telling her so, she promptly suggests that they exchange work for a day—she will run the office for him, while he has an easy time at home doing the household tasks. Hubby accepts joyfully, but soon learns his mistake. The cook leaves him in a huff and, after trying in vain to put his house in order, he is glad to phone for his wife and acknowledge his defeat. The picture is well staged and acted, the easy method of the two stars fitting smoothly the requirements of the comedy." -- *Moving Picture World*

Their Dream House

Released August 16, 1916. Vim Feature Comedies - General Film Company release. One reel. No copyright registered. Release number 21039.

Produced by Louis Burstein. Directed by Harry C. Myers. Photographed by Harry Keepers. Filmed May-June 1916 in Jacksonville, Florida.

with Harry Myers (*Hubby*), Rosemary Theby (*Wifey*).

A bad real estate man sells a phoney house to the young couple. They are delighted with it until things begin to happen. The water won't run until after they have turned on every tap; then it runs too much and floods the house before they are aware of what is happening. The gas works on the installment plan and then won't behave. Things go from bad to worse until the house starts to leak in a heavy storm. Hubby steals a big umbrella from the real estate man's buggy and comes home. The wind blows the door shut, and when he kicks it the panel bursts, being made of paper. With the umbrella the couple are sheltering themselves as best they may when the roof of the house blows away and they are engulfed in the rain. What happens afterward is left to the imagination. [M & MPW]

"A feature comedy in which Harry C. Meyers and Rosemary Theby are the stars, this one-reel satire on the joys of married life will awaken a responsive chord in hearts of many a spectator. The mishaps to the beautiful home, unloaded on them by the real estate agent, will remind other victims of the way they were stung. The production and acting are both of a high order." -- *Moving Picture World*

The Lemon in the Garden of Love

Released August 23, 1916. Vim Feature Comedies - General Film Company release. One reel. No copyright registered. Release number 21066.

Produced by Louis Burstein. Directed by Harry C. Myers. Written by Watkins Eppes Wright. Likely filmed in Jacksonville, Florida although Myers & Theby were in Providence, Rhode Island by the time of this film's release.

with Harry Myers (*Hubby*), Rosemary Theby (*Wifey*).

Hubby (Harry Myers) and wifey (Rosemary Theby) are happy but for Fido,"the lemon in their garden of love." Wifey showers more attention on Fido than upon her husband, which makes hubby angry. They quarrel and leave breakfast unfinished. When hubby gets to the office everything he touches or looks at turns into a little dog. Later hubby is notified that Fido has been killed, having fallen from a window sill where wifey placed him to get a sun bath. Hubby thinks he will be the "peach" in their garden of love and everything runs along "smoothly until a package arrives. Hubby is advised that it contains the ashes of wifey's Fido. Dinner is being served and the maid has just placed a plate of hot dogs on the table. Wifey attempts to place the jar containing Fido's ashes on the table and trouble commences again. He declares he will live with live dogs, eat hot dogs, but will not have his table decorated with cremated dogs. In reaching for the jar he accidentally knocks it over and breaks it. Wifey insists that he have it repaired. Realizing that he must get rid of this "lemon," hubby throws the jar away and concocts a story that he was held up and robbed of everything, even the jar. Although she is sorry for the dog, wifey is also very sorry for poor hubby. Later on, when she is out walking, she is attracted by the sale of an antique jar, and returning home for her check book tells hubby, who has been reading about the jar, that it reminded her so much of the dog's jar that she must try to get it. Realizing that it must be the jar, hubby also decides to attend the auction and try to prevent wifey from getting the

jar; he has a man bid against her. When the bid finally reached $1,500 hubby stops and wifey gets the jar. Upon returning home they discover that the jar is the one containing Fido's ashes. Wifey never intends to leave the jar out of her sight again and places it by her bed after kissing it good night. Upon seeing the jar turn into a dog hubby throws a pillow and knocks the jar to the floor. Wifey woke and tells him it is time for him to go. He goes as the picture fades out. [MPW]

Watkins Eppes Wright was one of the many, many would-be screenwriters that answered Vim's advertisement soliciting film scenario submissions. Wright was from Asheville, North Carolina and the local papers proudly announced that Wright and a co-writer (Steve McEniry) had just received notice that their comedy entitled *Glittering Gems and Broken Hearts* had been accepted by Vim. The article also noted that Wright had written a number of successful screenplays including *Two Girls of the Hills, Mumps, Comedy of Terrors* and *Miss Judis*. One of the screenplays, *Mumps*, was for a Myers & Theby comedy made for Victor in 1915; it is unknown if any of the other titles actually made it to the screen. As of 1936 Wright had written 65 short stories, four novels and a number of screenplays; he gets a story credit for a film as late as 1932 for a Mayfair feature entitled *Sister for Judas*. Wright ended up writing pulp fiction under the name Wright Williams and did so late into the 1950s.

"Another of the Harry C. Meyers and Rosemary Theby one-reel feature comedies, this photoplay turns on the love of a young wife for her poodle. She carries it to such an extreme that her husband becomes jealous and secretly rejoices when the dog dies. But his joy is short-lived. His wife has her pet cremated and the ashes of the dear departed become as great a nuisance as was the dog himself. The reel is enhanced in value by the skillful acting of Mr. Meyers and Miss Theby." -- *Moving Picture World*

The Tormented Husband

Released August 30, 1916. Vim Feature Comedies - General Film Company release. One reel. No copyright registered. Release number 21097.

Produced by Louis Burstein. Directed by Harry C. Myers. Unknown if filmed in Jacksonville, Florida or Providence, Rhode Island.

with Harry Myers, Rosemary Theby.

[no synopsis available].

"The domestic peace of the Newlyweds again gets a serious jolt in this number of the Vim Feature comedies, in which Harry C. Myers and Rosemary Theby are now appearing. The picture keeps pace with the previous numbers of the series, both as to plot and the finished acting of the two stars." –*Moving Picture World*

The Chalk Line

Released September 6, 1916. Vim Feature Comedies - General Film Company release. One reel. No copyright registered. Release number 21123.

Produced by Frank Tichenor. Directed by Harry C. Myers. Written by Watkins Eppes Wright. Filmed August 1916 at 44 Franklin Avenue, in downtown and at the Eastern Film Corporation studios in Providence, Rhode Island.

with Harry Myers (*Mr. Love*), Rosemary Theby (*Mrs. Love*), George Reehm (*bookkeeper*), Jennie Nelson (*stenographer*).

Mr. and Mrs. Love (Harry Myers and Rosemary Theby), with their young son, are so happy that hubby is usually late for work. The stenographer in Mr. Love's office who is in love with the bookkeeper places a note and handkerchief in Mr. Love's pocket by mistake. Hubby spills some of baby's milk on his coat and when wifey is cleaning it she discovers the note and demands an explanation from hubby, who knows nothing about it. Wifey decides that she must live in the same house with hubby on account of the baby, but apart. She puts a chalk line on everything in the house, even the maid, and tells hubby that the line is to be considered a six foot wall. A friend of hubby's calls and is much embarrassed when Mrs. Love ignores him when he speaks to her. It is then up to Mr. Love to explain that the chalk line is a six foot wall. The stenographer, in the meantime, is angry because the bookkeeper failed to answer her note and asks for an explanation. She is informed that the note was not in his pocket that it must have been placed in Mr. Love's pocket by mistake. They decide to explain the situation to Mr. Love, and upon calling at the house are confronted by Mrs. Love to whom they explain everything. Mr. Love is holding baby and feeling a damp chill on his

arm he places baby on the floor. Baby gets busy with its little body and rubs out, the chalk line. Wifey returns to the room and is pleased to see the chalk line removed. She awakens hubby, who informs her that he did not remove the line. They miss baby and find him looking at them from under a chair and of course, due to the explanation from the stenographer and bookkeeper Mrs. Love apologizes to hubby, who forgives her. [MPW]

The almost complete absence of the Myers & Theby Vims becomes even more unfortunate when this film and the following film released are viewed. The only examples of their work at Vim, the two comedies show the series to be on par with the Drews and endearing in their own way. Harry Myers and Rosemary Theby play well off of each other, and like the Drews they rely more on situation than slapstick for their humor.

Showing up in this film is an old co-worker of Harry's from the Lubin days, George Reehm. Once an integral part of Walter Stull's and then also Bobby Burns' careers Reehm had left acting in 1915 to go direct for Biograph. When that studio more or less closed up shop in late 1915, Reehm was left unemployed. His joining Vim was announced in the trades on August 5. Another addition announced was Jennie Nelson (along with newly acquired husband William Chamberlain), who had worked with Myers at Lubin and appeared in some of the Myers & Theby Victor comedies. Whether Reehm appears in any other of the Myers & Theby Vims before or after this one remains unknown, he does not appear in the only other extant title *A Strenuous Visit*. While Jennie Nelson certainly traveled down to Jacksonville at some point, it is unclear if she did so when the troupe left Providence following

Myers' feud with Frank Tichenor or later; it is also unknown if Reehm went South at all.

Harry Myers didn't waste George Reehm's presence at Vim, at least not in this film. At the office Harry spills some glue on his desk and uses the inside band of George's straw hat to wipe it off his hands. When George runs an errand to mail a letter he realizes that the hat is stuck to his head. He returns to the office and with Harry's assistance they are able to remove the hat while destroying it at the same time. A great comedy vignette between Myers and Reehm, yet George is subjected to such physical abuse from Harry in an attempt to remove the hat that he must have been questioning his move back before the camera. However, it does show that Myers truly valued the comic abilities of his once and current cohort.

There is some question as to the true author of this comedy. *Moving Picture World* ran a brief article about the issue which read in part: "WHO IS AUTHOR OF "THE CHALK LINE. Understanding that two parties claim to be the authors of his comedy, 'The Chalk Line,' Watkins Eppes Wright wishes to state through the columns of the *Moving Picture World* that he is the sole author and originator of the said comedy."

"That Harry Myers and Rosemary Theby are determined to maintain a high level in their comedy offerings is amply evidenced in this very entertaining number. The plot concerns a domestic fight, owing to the wife's jealousy, which results in the house being divided into two parts indicated by a chalk line. An infant, idolized by both parents, is instrumental in effacing the barrier. Settings for this picture are in notably good taste." -- *Moving Picture World*

"*The Chalk Line*, a Harry Myers-Rosemary Theby Vim comedy, is a feature not to be overshadowed by the most pretentious five-reeler. There are more real laughs in this "refined" comedy than most optimistic can expect, a practical joke, a bottle of glue, and a damp infant formed the nucleus for a decidedly hilarious time." -- *The Oregonian*

A Strenuous Visit

Released September 13, 1916. Vim Feature Comedies - General Film Company release. One reel (840 feet). No copyright registered. Release number 21153. Also known as *The Strenuous Visit; His Strenuous Visit.*

Produced by Frank Tichenor. Directed by Harry C. Myers. Set design by Harry C. Myers. Filmed August 1916 at the Eastern Film Corporation studios in Providence, Rhode Island.

with Harry Myers (*Harry*), Rosemary Theby (*Rose*), Jennie Nelson (*stenographer*).

Harry arrives in town and telephones his college friend, Fred, who has since been married, that while he is in town he would like to meet his wife. Fred notifies his wife, Rose, that he will have a friend home for lunch. Rose goes out to purchase a few things and Harry, who is somewhat a flirt, not knowing that Rose is Fred's wife, flirts with Rose and is snubbed. His persistency, however, angers Rose, who calls a policeman and has him arrested. Harry calls upon Fred to bail him out and, together, they start for Fred's home and, as Rose is busy getting lunch, she fails to hear them enter. Suddenly Fred is called away, and before going tells Harry to make himself at home and while he is looking the place over, Rose is frightened by the sight of the flirt in her home and again calls the same policeman, who arrests Harry for the second time. Fred, who is again called upon to get Harry out, decides to hold him at the office this time and Rose makes up her mind to tell Fred of the experiences. She calls at Fred's office during Fred's absence and is again frightened by the same flirt, and the victim of circumstances is arrested for the third time by the same policeman, Rose accompanies Fred to the station this time and after bailing Harry out for the third time, demands an explanation. Apologies and explanations are in order, after which everyone is

forgiven, and Harry is properly introduced to Rose. Morale — Harry, who thinks he is away from everyone, especially the girls, is quietly fishing, when along comes several beauties and rather than flirt Harry jumps overboard and comes up to find a mermaid facing him. He dives under again, followed by the mermaid and the bubbles are evidence of his end. [MPW]

The police sergeant is an outlandish character with a giant spit curl on an otherwise bald head. He dresses with an open collar, burns incense and has to sniff smelling salts when he hears of Harry's offenses flirting with Rosemary. A decidedly effeminate demeanor, a ribbon bow on his telephone the police sergeant even

sprinkles perfume in Harry's hat. With no mention of this character in the reviews for the film, it would be interesting to know how the public of the day reacted to the overtly gay desk sergeant.

Motion Picture News wrote a story about Harry Myers' unique set designs: "In one of the scenes is shown a police station staged as Harry Myers thinks a police station ought to look, but it is a far cry from the grim abode of the green lamps to Harry's idea. In discussing the setting Mr. Myers says, "I've been in any number of police stations both on my own part and for friends – and on entering them I always had a feeling of 'Lord! I wish I didn't have to go in there!' And after I forced myself in or had someone persuade me to go in, there was still that same creepy feeling that made you feel as though you had committed some crime, and I've talked to a lot of people who had at different times visited the same place and they were of the same opinion." Many of the sets in this, and presumably all of the Myers & Theby films, are rather bizarre. Somewhat a cross between art deco and surreal the sets were used for some scenes with "normal" settings used otherwise making the Myers creation even that more incongruent.

"This is probably one of the most humorous one-reel comedies that Harry Meyers and Rosemary Theby have done. The story is full of laughs, as can be imagined when it is known that Harry is arrested three times for flirting with the wife of his friend Fred, whose home he was invited to visit. Harry is bailed out three times by Fred before introductions are made and explanations offered. Novel settings help the production and the new idea in police stations is funny." -- *Moving Picture World*

"Harry Myers and Rosemary Theby are featured in this amusing little item. Mr. Duprey expects a friend, unfortunately Mrs. Duprey does not know hubby's friend, consequently when "friend" offers to carry Mrs. Duprey's parcel on meeting her in the street, Mrs. Duprey calls a policeman and trouble follows for hubby's pal. Special mention must be given to the artistic settings of these comedies, which imbues the film with a sort of futurist atmosphere." -- *Kinematograph Weekly*

The Honeymoon Car

Released September 20, 1916. Vim Feature Comedies - General Film Company release. One reel (1,000 feet). No copyright registered. Release number 21179.

Produced by Frank Tichenor. Directed by Harry C. Myers. Filmed at the Eastern Film Corporation studios in Providence, Rhode Island.

with Harry Myers (*groom*), Rosemary Theby (*bride*).

A money order arrives in a letter from Uncle. The recipient of the letter is advised to buy a car, get married and make the trip to the Uncle's home in the car. On the way the bridal pair run out of gasoline. The groom walks to the nearest gasoline station and while he is on the way, a tramp holds up the bride and an old maid nurse who was sent along on the trip by the bride's mother. He takes their jewelry and money and makes his getaway. The returning groom is told of the affair and he starts in search of the robber, leaving the bride and maid to refill the tank. Not being able to locate the robber he returns to the car and everything looking to him "all right." They start off. While riding over the bumps, the gasoline tank is lost, the air pressure goes down and the car stalls. Unable to find the cap, he inquires who put the cap on the tank and learns that the old maid had, so the groom replaces the cap with the maid. She takes her place as the "gas cap." He gets up his pressure and they continue. Through the gas station man they learn of the direction of the tramp and while following him, they enlist the aid of a constable. The tramp, who has been making his getaway safe by riding the trunk of another car, is discovered by the driver and treated to the "bum's rush." He soon tires and falls asleep under a tree where he is discovered by the bride as they almost pass him. In order to make the arrest, they have to chase him into a mud puddle. Eventually he is placed in a one man lockup which he easily kicks over and makes his escape. The honeymooners arrive at Uncle's home, but they are so dirty from the fight in the puddle that he refuses to recognize them. They return to the car and sit down on the running board where they try to think of a way to make Uncle realize his relationship to the groom. [MPW]

The *Moving Picture World* felt that "This reel falls far below the high mark set by Harry Meyers and Rosemary Theby in previous Vim Feature Comedies." However, the Myers-Theby comedies were generally well received and it is unfortunate that more don't exist to allow for modern day assessment.

"Rosemary Theby and Harry Myers are effective in this single reel comedy dealing with a pair of newlyweds who are forced to take a chaperon with them on their automobile wedding tour. Several amusing incidents happen on the road in which the chaperon is made to play the goat." -- *Motion Picture News*

Artistic Atmosphere

Released September 27, 1916. Vim Feature Comedies - General Film Company release. One reel (950 feet). No copyright registered. Release number 21209.

Produced by Frank Tichenor. Directed by Harry C. Myers. Filmed at the Eastern Film Corporation studios in Providence, Rhode Island.

with Harry Myers (*Hubby*), Rosemary Theby (*Wifey*).

Wifie reads that every woman must create an artistic atmosphere in her home to avoid becoming old. She thinks she already shows signs of age and takes up painting – the first thing that enters her head. Hubby stands for the litter of artist's paraphernalia all over the house, but objects when wifie decorates his collars with her landscapes, causing him to become the laughing stock of the men in the office. When the wifie gets his best friend to pose as a model for "A Perfect Man," hubby is fired for staying at home, jealously watching lest a love affair develop. Hoping a baby will cure her mania for painting, he adopts one, only to find that babies are not in her line, and he puts it on a rich man's doorstep. A policeman is about to arrest him, but hubby claims he was only going to change its diaper, producing his handkerchief to prove it. He takes it home, gets it to sleep, and goes out to look for work. Wifie tells him to get something artistic. Returning home, he sees the painting outfit flying out the window, finding that the wife has discovered a Caruso in the person of the baby. Hubby is overjoyed to hear that wifie intends to find her "artistic atmosphere" cultivating the baby's voice. [MPW]

Some modern sources list Babe Hardy as appearing in this film but since this was filmed in Providence when Hardy was known to be in Jacksonville those claims are in error. Little is actually known about any of the supporting casts for these Providence-shot Myers & Theby comedies.

"The most effective bit in this single reel offering, featuring Harry Myers and Rosemary Theby, is a baby that can be made to laugh or cry at will. The picture has been well staged with some effective settings and clear distinct photography. The comedy situations are brought about by a young wife who believes that it is necessary to instill an artistic atmosphere in the home, but when this self same atmosphere is responsible for her husband losing his position, he goes to an orphan asylum and adopts a baby, saying that she can devote her artistic energies to the cultivation of the baby's voice." -- *Motion Picture News*.

"A capital little comedy which will appeal to most audiences. It is perfectly clean and wholesome, running its allotted course without exaggerated business, 'slap-stick' or the slightest taint of vulgarity. The story, a slight, one, founded on the not very original theme of a newspaper paragraph leading a young wife to attempt a general reconstruction of her home and the lives of those around her is well told. Mrs. Love gets the craze for "artistic atmosphere" through reading a newspaper paragraph, and begins decorating her household goods. Even her husband's collars do not escape. In desperation he gets a baby from an orphanage, and when Mrs. Love fascinated by the infant's wonderful lung power, declares the cultivation of its voice all the 'artistic atmosphere' she wants, life readjusts itself on rational lines. The acting is excellent, and the staging quite up to the usual standard in these features." -- *Kinematograph Weekly*

A Grain of Suspicion

Released October 4, 1916. Vim Feature Comedies - General Film Company release. One reel. No copyright registered. Release number 21235.

Produced by Frank Tichenor. Directed by Harry C. Myers. Filmed at the Eastern Film Corporation studios in Providence, Rhode Island.

with Harry Myers (*Mr. Love*), Rosemary Theby (*Mrs. Love*).

Mrs. Love sees a bargain in real estate and decides to surprise her hubby by purchasing it and paying for it with her own money. The real estate man calls regularly to collect his payments and upon several of those occasions he is seen by hubby, who, not knowing who he is, gets jealous. He decides not to say anything about it to his wife who decides to say nothing to her husband until the lot is paid for. The continued visits of the real estate man annoys hubby and he decides to put a detective on the case. The detective gets working; he goes to the office of the real estate man and obtains a good look at him; he then decides to spy around the house. He sees the collector call for his regular instalment and notifies hubby that the mouse is in the trap. He enters the house and arrests the real estate man, much to the surprise of his wife. Hubby comes in and when he is acquainted with the facts in the case he pleads for forgiveness. Wifey forgives him. [MPW]

"This number of the Vim Feature Comedies, in which Harry Myers and Rosemary Theby are featured, can only be classed as fair. Although the two players work hard, the story is weak. Many of the subtitles, though, are really humorous. Hubby is jealous over the seeming attention paid his wife by another man. The 'other man' is a real estate agent from whom the wife has bought a lot as a surprise to hubby. He hires a detective and learns the supposed interloper's identity when the former is arrested by the detective." -- *Moving Picture World*

"This is a comedy featuring Harry Meyers and Rosemary Theby and the plot hinges on a husband's jealousy coupled with his stinginess as to 'pin money,' almost breaking up a home. It is only a fair number and does not come up to the standard set by Meyers and Theby in other releases from the same company. The story is very 'forced,' but the acting of the principals and the good photography tend in a way to make up for this fault. There are quite a few laughs and the subtitles are quite funny in themselves. It makes an acceptable release but nothing extra". -- *Motion Picture News*

Their Installment Furniture

Released October 11, 1916. Vim Feature Comedies - General Film Company release. One reel (850 feet). No copyright registered. Release number 21267.

Produced by Frank Tichenor. Directed by Harry C. Myers. Filmed at the Eastern Film Corporation studios in Providence, Rhode Island.

with Harry Myers (*Harry*), Rosemary Theby (*wifey*).

Harry promises wifey a birthday present, but wifey is impatient and instead of waiting for it she goes to hubby's trousers while he is asleep, and helps herself to a roll of bills amounting to $200, which she supposes is her birthday gift. She places it under her pillow and then dreams hubby placed it there. After finding it she thinks her dream has come true and tells hubby he is the dearest man in the world. Hubby goes to the office and is greeted by numerous bills. After making out checks for all of the bills he discovers that his bank account is overdrawn and when he goes to deposit the $200 he finds it missing. In the meantime the money has become a burden to wifey and she goes to town to find someone who will relieve her of it. When hubby questions her about it she thinks he is fooling and tells him he must be hungry. Next day during the progress of the wife's birthday party when everybody seems to be enjoying themselves the collectors with the "N. G." checks come to take away the furniture. It does not take long for them to bust up the party and innocent hubby gets a little "busting up" himself. [MPW]

As illustrated by the adjacent photo, the sets designed by Harry Myers were usually a cross between art deco and cartoon. Often with a futuristic bent they were almost always bizarre.

"A fair number of the Vim Feature Comedies, in which Harry Myers and Rosemary Theby are featured. Novel settings help this reel. Wife helps herself to Hubby's $200 without his knowledge. Next day he makes out checks and overdraws his account. Considerable fun is in evidence when the installment collectors come to take away the furniture during the course of a party because Hubby's checks are 'N.G..' The party is broken up." -- *Moving Picture World*

A Persistant Wooing

Released October 18, 1916. Vim Feature Comedies - General Film Company release. One reel. No copyright registered. Release number 21292.

Produced by Frank Tichenor. Directed by Harry C. Myers. Filmed at the Eastern Film Corporation studios in Providence, Rhode Island.

with Harry Myers (*Harry*), Rosemary Theby (*Rose*).

Rose is a rich young woman who has everything she wants. One day while out in her machine she sees Harry in his machine. His appearance appeals to her and she purposely collides with him. When he goes about his business she follows him and later collides with him again. Harry gets angry and when he reproves Rose she asks him to kiss her hand. As she is so coquettish he does, but when she importunes him to kiss her on the face, Harry refuses, saying he is an engaged man. He then drives home unaware that Rose is following him. When he enters his home Rose "buys" his chauffeur to resign in order that she can disguise herself as a man and take his place. Harry's wedding day arrives and Rose, who is now much in love with Harry, knowing Ruth will marry any man if he has money, decides to prevent the wedding if possible. She drives Harry though mud and water and finally succeeds in putting the car out of commission, therby preventing Harry from being on time for the wedding. Later Harry finds that Ruth has married someone else and decides to take his chauffeur, having learned who his chauffer is. Rose, realizing that she has won, looks at him haughtily. He then says, "I'll give you that kiss now," but she tells him to wait until they have been married. [MPW]

Reviewers frequently mentioned the overall production quality of the Myers & Theby films and that certainly is mostly attributed to Harry Myers' involvement in the films from top to bottom. The directing, writing, acting, even set design all point to Myers, and the great subtitles noted are likely the work of Myers too.

"Harry Myers and Rosemary Theby are featured in this number of the Vim Feature Comedies. The care that the picture has received in its production make it acceptable. Many of the sub-titles are mirthful, as is much of the action. The story hardly gives the two leading characters an opportunity to display their laugh-provoking capabilities. It tells of a young woman's persistent wooing of the man she wants." -- *Moving Picture World*

"Rosemary Theby and Harry Myers are featured in this single-reel comedy, which, though having a trite story, has been exceedingly well produced and directed. The sub-titles deserve especial commendation, some of them being more amusing than much of the action. A young girl falls in love with a young man, who is already engaged to another girl. She does not allow this little thing to stop her, however, and by causing the bridegroom to be late for the ceremony breaks up the wedding. He then decides that he had better marry her after all, and the picture closes to the usual happy ending." -- *Motion Picture News*

Green Eyes

Released October 25, 1916. Vim Feature Comedies - General Film Company release. One reel (880 feet)No copyright registered. Release number 21324. [Some sources list *Home Made Horrors* as released on this date].

Produced by Frank Tichenor. Directed by Harry C. Myers. Filmed at the Eastern Film Corporation studios in Providence, Rhode Island.

with Harry Myers, Rosemary Theby.

Mr. Barrett is jealous of his wife, who is establishing a law practice. A letter is received from a long-lost uncle who proposes a visit in the near future. He is an old bachelor, grown rich from the gold fields. Having endured many hardships, he is looking forward to rest and peace in Mr. Barrett's quiet little home. Just reward shall be theirs for kind treatment. His arrival at an inopportune time is attended with amusing, almost tragic, incidents. Fortunately, however, all ends well with a lesson for Mr. Barrett. [MPW]

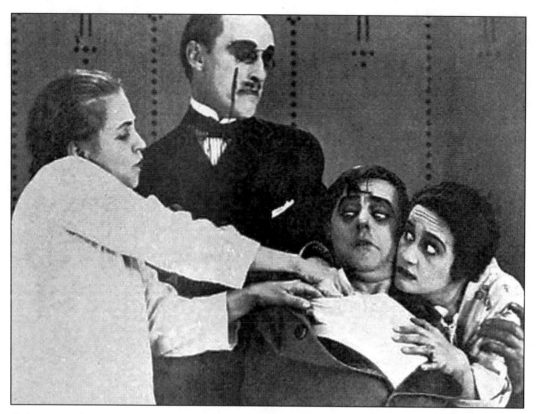

"This number of the Vim Feature Comedies, in which Harry Myers and Rosemary Theby are featured, is better than have been several of their recent releases. There are quite a number of humorous situations, well carried out. The settings, photography, and other details of production add to the film's worth. The jealousy of a young husband furnishes the nucleus of the story. He becomes jealous of a long-lost uncle, who returns, and much fun is made in the film before the happy reconciliation." -- *Moving Picture World*

"This is described as a 'refined comedy,' and it has every right to the title. The stars, Harry Myers and Rosemary Theby, can always be relied upon to provide enjoyment for any class of audience, and we are inclined to think that most people who see it will be sorry when the film ends." -- *Kinematograph Weekly*

Gertie's Garters

Released November 1, 1916. Vim Feature Comedies - General Film Company release. One reel. No copyright registered. Release number 21350.

Produced by Frank Tichenor. Directed by Harry Myers. Filmed at the Eastern Film Corporation studios in Providence, Rhode Island.

with Harry Myers (*Harry*), Rosemary Theby (*Rose*).

Harry is a young business man. Rose, his wife, is jealous to the extreme. Harry, with an eye for beauty in distress, loans a young woman carfare and walks with her to the car to see that she gets the right one. She sees a man coming as they stand waiting for the car and slips a pair of diamond set garter buckles into Harry's pocket. The man accuses the fair one of being Gert the Goat, a shoplifter. She claims Harry as her husband, and says she is a respectable married woman. Harry is too much of a gentleman to call a lady a liar and helps her along by putting his arm protectingly around her. But he does not value his "position" so well when the detective decides to take them both to the station house, where Harry makes a clean breast of it and proves who he is. The sergeant sets him free. Harry hustles home because he will be late for dinner at best. Arrived home, he steals into the flat and finds the dining room dark. Rose seems to be there, so he seizes and kisses her. There is a scream, the lights are turned on and Harry sees Rose at the electric switch while he stands with his arms about the half fainting maid. He squares himself on this, but a moment later when he wipes the perspiration from his dripping brow the garter buckles clatter to the floor. Rose has them in an instant. Harry, trained in lying, is quick to explain that he obtained them for her and that is the reason why he was late for dinner. Then he has to explain why he brought them loose in his pocket and he tells (in a vision) how he was held up, but dashed after the burly ruffian and forced him to give up her property. His wife believes him and he is about to sit down to dinner when the police come in. They took his address when he showed his papers and Gertie confessed that she slipped the buckles into his pocket. The detectives give him his pocketbook and watch, which Gertie managed to get hold of, and they leave him to his fate. [MPW]

The *Motion Picture News* noted in their review of the film that it seemed to have been censored, or more likely heavily edited by the studio prior to release. Perhaps this tinkering with the film after it was finished was one of the sour points between Myers and Tichenor that would eventually lead to Harry Myers and Rosemary Theby leaving Rhode Island. Here is how the review addressed the edited film: "Harry Myers and Rosemary Theby star here in refined comedy. We say refined, advisedly, for evidently the parts of the film that live up to its name have been scissored considerably. Some audiences will be greatly disappointed because the opportunity to work in 'business' of a suggestive nature has been lost."

"This number of the Vim Feature Comedies, in which Harry Myers and Rosemary Theby are featured, is only average. The film is helped somewhat by a few novel sets, and several rather humorous police station scenes. The story is not much, and tells how Harry gets in trouble when a female crook slips a pair of pilfered, jeweled garters in his overcoat pocket. His troubles commence when his wife finds them there." -- *Moving Picture World*

Marked "No Funds"

Released November 8, 1916. Vim Feature Comedies - General Film Company release. One reel (1,050 feet) No copyright registered. Release number 21382.

Produced by Frank Tichenor. Directed by Harry C. Myers. Filmed at the Eastern Film Corporation studios in Providence, Rhode Island.

with Harry Myers (*Harry*), Rosemary Theby (*Rose*).

Harry is a stockbroker, but business is poor and he cannot buy Rose the new automobile coat she wants. He is sitting in the office worrying about last month's rent, when a prosperous stranger is ushered in. The stranger gives an order for ten thousand shares of General Munitions, preferred, and gives his check for ten thousand dollars to cover the margins. Harry is so overjoyed at the order that he does not take the precaution to ask the

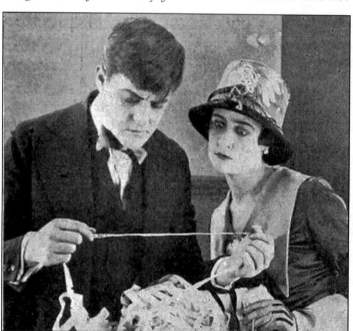

stranger who he is. He 'phones the order to another broker and gets the stock. Then he phones Rose to come down and get the coat. They celebrate the occasion, and next morning Harry goes to the office hoping that more prosperous strangers will come in. He is taken aback when the first visitor is a bank runner with the check marked "No funds." He starts to "flirt" with a nice nickel-plated revolver when he takes a look at the tape. "G. M." is going up by quarters and halves and then some. Harry does not know how to conceal his joy. But in walks the prosperous stranger with a demand for his stock and a check to cover the entire amount. Harry shows him the other check and the stranger explains that he forgot that he no longer had an account there and offers to go over to the bank and get the larger check certified. It looks very much as if Harry would have to be satisfied with a buying commission only, when in walked a couple of huskies who grab the stranger and explain that he is an escaped innatic with a penchant for playing the market. Clearly the stock is Harry's and he takes down a handsome profit. [MPW]

"This number of the Vim Feature Comedies featuring Harry Myers and Rosemary Theby, is an improvement over several of their recent releases. There is a more humorous story, well worked out by Mr. Myers and Miss Theby, and the unusual novel settings." -- *Moving Picture World*

His Wedding Promise

Released November 15, 1916. Vim Feature Comedies - General Film Company release. One reel. No copyright registered. Release number 21408.
Produced by Frank Tichenor. Directed by Harry C. Myers. Filmed at the Eastern Film Corporation studios in Providence, Rhode Island.

with Harry Myers (*Sidney*), Rosemary Theby (*Harriet*).

Harriet married Sidney only on the condition that he promised never to smoke. Sidney remains faithful to his pledge for many months. Harry's struggle to refrain from smoking is watched by his stenographer and clerk. A messenger boy smoking a cigarette delivers a telegram and Sidney orders him from the office before he is tempted to snatch the cigarette from him. Dick, a friend of Sidney's and one-time model for their class, is invited to the house for dinner. He, however, is not the model he once was; he is now a real sporty traveling salesman for a cigarette company. Finally, Sidney solves the difficulty. He is still the perfect husband, but does not mean to allow Harriet to rule him in all things. He has rented a room where he spends an hour each day transacting his business and incidentally smoking to his

heart's content, but his happiness is short-lived, for Jesse Walsh has traced him and tells the wife what he suspects. Here the real trouble begins but Sidney is not deprived of his cigarette. Harriet also is a little inclined to take a "puff" to satisfy her husband. [MPW]

"Quite an amount if subtle humor is found in this number of the Vim Feature Comedies, featuring Harry Myers and Rosemary Theby. At no time will the spectator laugh out loud, but all through the running of the reel he will chuckle, especially if he, like Mr. Love, promised his wife that he would not smoke. That promise made Mr. Love leads almost to a domestic rupture in the Love household, but in the end Friend Husband's cigarette is lit by wifie."
-- *Moving Picture World*

The Good Stenographer

Released November 22, 1916. Vim Feature Comedies - General Film Company release. One reel. No copyright registered. Release number 21440.

Produced by Frank Tichenor. Directed by Harry C. Myers. Probably filmed at the Eastern Film Corporation studios in Providence, Rhode Island.

with Harry Myers (*Mr. Love*), Rosemary Theby (*Mrs. Love*).

Mrs. Love is jealous of Mr. Love's stenographer and insists upon taking her place. Hubby does not like to refuse his wife's request and decides, after she is installed as his stenographer, to get rid of her some way, as the discharged stenographer is a great help to him in business. A friend of Love's schemes to help him. He telephones to Love's office and starts a flirtation with the stenographer (Love's wife). Wifey is indignant and tells Love of the incident upon his return. He informs her that he lost a good customer on account of her impertinence. She goes

to explain to the customer, who tells her that he never phoned. She then realizes she was tricked and decides hubby shall pay the penalty. She quits the job when she is assured of a lot of pretty things. [MPW]

"The story of this number of the Vim Features Comedies does not give Harry Myers and Rosemary Theby opportunities to get across much comedy. It tells of a jealous wife becoming her husband's stenographer, and of how he made her quit the job. The usual novel settings of Mr. Myers help somewhat." -- *Moving Picture World*

Hubby's Chicken

Released November 29, 1916. Vim Feature Comedies - General Film Company release. One reel. No copyright registered. Release number 21466. [Some sources list December 6, 1916 as the release date].

Produced by Louis Burstein. Directed by Harry C. Myers. Assistant director, Jerold T. Hevener [?]. Probably filmed at the Vim studios in Jacksonville, Florida.

with Harry Myers, Rosemary Theby.

[no synopsis available].

Around this time Jerold T. Hevener, who had worked with many of the Vim players while they all were at Lubin, was added to the Vim forces. Hevener's fixation with poultry (he was a prize winning chicken breeder and general animal lover) implies he had began his work as assistant director on the Myers-Theby films by the time of this film's production.

"A fair number of the Vim Feature Comedies, with Harry Myers and Rosemary Theby. Mr. Love, a poultry fancier, gets into a lot of trouble with Friend Wife over a chicken which the wife thinks is the wrong kind of a chicken. However, after she hires a detective and chases Hubby to the station, she finds that Mr. Love has been chasing a white leghorn, and everyone is happy." -- *Moving Picture World*

Charity Begins at Home

Released December 13, 1916. Vim Feature Comedies - General Film Company release. One reel. No copyright registered. Release 21524.

Produced by Louis Burstein. Directed by Harry C. Myers. Assistant director, Jerold T. Hevener [?]. Filmed late November 1916 in at the Vim studios in Jacksonville, Florida.

with Harry Myers (*Mr. Green*), Rosemary Theby (*Mrs. Green*).

Mr. Green, a prosperous architect, is tried by his wife's fads. Her latest one is charity. Over the breakfast table she tells him her plan for various charity affairs. She gives his clothes to beggars and each day the army of solicitors is increased and she sends them to hubby's office. When she learns that hubby turns them away she is dumbfounded. She goes so far as to put a drunken woman to sleep in his bed and it is up to hubby to sleep on the floor. The next day Green gets a brilliant idea. He purchased six dogs and takes them home with him, and when wifey asks the reason she is informed that he believes in animal charity. Trying days follow; he brings home a monkey, several kittens, white mice and an old skate of a horse which he turns loose on the lawn. He next brings home a sick elephant and is confident the elephant will recover if allowed to play on the front lawn with the horse. That night at dinner Green is enthusiastic over plans for a home for stray animals which he thinks would look nice on the front lawn. They then agree to give up their charities and Green makes out a check for the Bide-a-Wee Home and one for the Associated Charities. [MPW]

"A laughable number of the Vim Feature Comedies, with Harry Myers and Rosemary Theby putting over considerable comedy. Rose believes in charity to such an extent that beggars get most of hubby's effects. He cures her by becoming the father of a host of stray animals of all kinds. They soon enter into a compact to keep their home for themselves." -- *Moving Picture World*

They Practiced Economy

Released December 20, 1916. Vim Comedies - General Film Company release. One reel. No copyright registered. Release number 21554.

Produced by Louis Burstein. Directed by Harry C. Myers. Filmed late November-early 1916 at the Vim studios in Jacksonville, Florida.

with Harry Myers, Rosemary Theby.

The Newlyweds, on checking up their month's expenses, are appalled at the size of their bills. They decide to begin at once and economize in everything. He walks to the office to save carfare and loses his hat and tears his clothes. She discharges the maid and in washing the dishes drops an armful of her best china and breaks it. He discharges his office boy and sweeps out the office himself, breaking up furniture and losing his best client by suffocating him in dust. They are invited to the opera that evening and he hurries home to dress. To economize he shaves himself and she presses his trousers. Unaccustomed to shaving, he cuts himself badly and while she runs for a doctor, the flat iron burns through the trousers and ruins the dining-room table. In her haste to get a basin of water for the doctor, she swings the gas jet against the lead water pipe and eventually a hole is melted in the pipe. To save a plumber's bill, he decides to fix the leak himself. She discovers that the dinner is burning up on the stove and pours water on it. The resultant steam burns her hands. He runs for the doctor, and the water pipe, left to itself, floods the house. Unable to go out, they make a scanty supper on crackers and milk, during which he figures up their savings for the day. They find that they have saved $4.20 at a cost of about $900, so he cuts the word "economy" out of the dictionary and tears it up. [MPW]

"Harry Myers and Rosemary Theby indulge in a little more slapstick than usual in this number of the Vim Feature Comedies. The film is more or less humorous. Mr. and Mrs. Love try to save money—Mrs. Love discharges the maid and Mr. Love fires the office boy. Then their troubles begin, and before they are through the house is almost a complete wreck. Mr. Myers is seen in some fairly funny water stuff."
-- *Moving Picture World*

Her Financial Frenzy

Released December 27, 1916. Vim Feature Comedies - General Film Company release. One reel. No copyright registered. Release number 21576. Listed in some sources as *A Financial Frenzy*.

Produced by Louis Burstein. Directed by Harry C. Myers, set designed by Harry C. Myers. Filmed early December 1916 at the Vim studios in Jacksonville, Florida.

with Harry Myers (*I Due Love*), Rosemary Theby (*Mrs. Love*).

I Due Love is gratified by the news that his salary has been raised and goes home to lunch, but instead of finding the usual smiling wife he finds a note saying she has "gone shopping." Packages commence to come in C.O.D. He goes looking for his wife and finds her loaded with bundles; she drags him into a fashionable café and he decides to humor her. Mrs. Love eats the most expensive things and shows hubby more purchases, one of them being a necklace; he is stunned and attempts to bear up by drinking highballs. In the meantime his boss has seen him. His suspicion is aroused by the fact that he is drinking heavily and seems to have bought his wife all sorts of presents. He also learns that Love had not made a deposit at the bank, and has him arrested. After Love has convinced him of his innocence, Mrs. Love explains she has inherited $50,000 from her uncle's estate. [MPW]

Apparently, the interior sets were made to represent a seaside café and were inspired by a photo Harry Myers saw in *Vanity Fair* magazine. The entrance to Myers' own dressing room then became the front of the café.

"A quite entertaining number of the Vim Feature Comedies, with Harry Myers and Rosemary Theby getting over a number of laughs. The financial frenzy comes about when Hubby gets a raise and Friend Wife goes on a shopping tour. The money-spending proclivities of both lead to funny complications, but everything is all right because Mrs. Love has inherited considerable money. A good farce comedy." -- *Moving Picture World*

It's All Wrong

Released January 26, 1917. Vim Comedies - General Film Company release. One reel. No copyright registered. Release number 21670.

Produced by Louis Burstein. Directed by Harry C. Myers. Filmed late 1916 at the Vim studios in Jacksonville, Florida.

with Harry Myers (*Mr. Love*), Rosemary Theby (*Mrs. Love*).

Mrs. Love and her sister, Helen, are told by the minister that every woman should be able to influence at least one man, and when he gives them each a copy of a pledge of total abstinence to get signed they promise to put his advice into practice. Rose loses no time in forcing her rather gay husband to sign and Helen finds it an easy matter to obtain the signature of her sweetheart, Jim. Unfortunately, Mr. Love is met by a number of old friends who insist upon him taking a drink before he goes home, in spite of the pledge, which they ridicule. He falls off the water-wagon and is soon in no condition to dine at home; he, therefore, phones his wife that he is obligated to work late. Jim, who really has to work, also phones that he cannot come. Helen thinks he is not telling the truth and a lonely evening is passed by both women. In the meanwhile Harry ends up the night by dining in a cabaret, and when it is time to leave he can hardly stagger. In a rather helpless condition he is found leaning against a post by Jim, who having finished work, is returning home. Jim consents to help Harry home. Harry insists upon being taken in through the kitchen, where he knocks over a table. The noise awakens Rose and her sister, who immediately think of burglars. Rose dons her husband's clothes and, with a pistol, the women go downstairs to face the burglar. Jim sees Helen with a man's arms around her and denounces her. Rose denounces Jim for having brought her husband home in such a condition. The next morning Harry explains that Jim had not been drinking but had met him and brought him home. Helen decides to ask Jim's forgiveness, and is informed over the phone that within ten minutes he will be a dead man. Helen, Rose and Harry rush to save Jim. When they arrive at his home they find him lying on the floor with a gas pipe in his mouth. They think that he is dead and while Helen is bending over him Jim rises and kisses her. He was only playing dead, and the pipe he had in his mouth was found to be attached to a water faucet. [MPW]

The last Myers & Theby to released by Vim. Myers then spent the first part of 1917 in an aborted attempt at starting up a new company, Encore Pictures, with Marcel Perez. The comedy pair then returned to the vacated Vim Studio and began a brief series of comedies along with Mark Dintenfass that were released by Pathé.

[no reviews available]

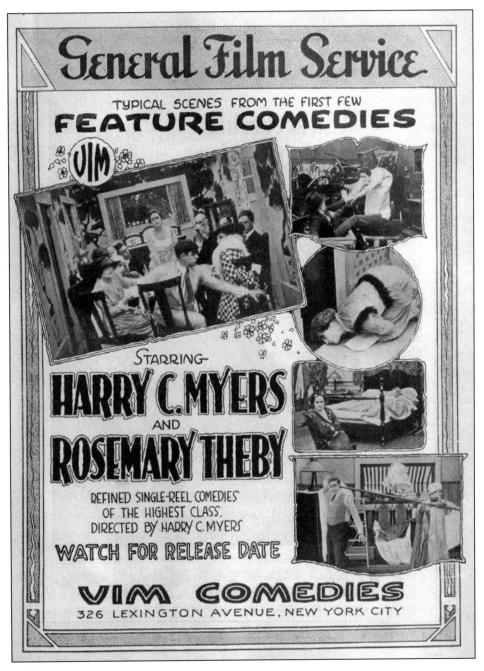

BABE HARDY COMPANY

A Maid To Order

Released October 26, 1916. Vim Comedies - General Film Company release. One reel. No copyright registered. Release number 21328.

Produced by Louis Burstein. Directed by Will Louis. Filmed early October 1916 in Jacksonville, Florida.

with Babe Hardy (*Plump, the lazy husband*), Kate Price (*Kate, Babe's wife*), Raymond McKee (*Raymond, the man of the house*), Florence McLoughlin (*the lady of the house*).

When Raymond's frivolous young wife informs him that household duties were too hard for her, they ask Kate, the cook, where a neat maid can be secured. Kate, being the proud possessor of the luxury of Plump as her husband, instantly sees a chance whereby she can keep the job in her own household and also force Plump to work for his daily bread. Informing the young couple that she knows a jewel of a maid, she hurries home and dresses Plump in some of her clothes. Both Raymond and his wife, impressed with the appearance of the new maid, try to make it as pleasant as possible for her. However, Kate's jealousy comes to the surface when she sees her loving man petted by the young wife and Plump, to his disgust, is forced to submit to the attentions of Raymond. Finally when the young wife discovers her husband flirting with the maid, her anger arises suddenly and she orders Plump out of the house. Raymond intercedes for the maid and matters rest until Kate again catches the wife petting Plump. Then everything is certainly all off and in the confusion Raymond learns that the supposed maid is a man, so between the three-sided attack poor Plump is done up to a frazzle. [MPW + MPW article]

Kate Price joins Vim with this film following a long tenure with Vitagraph and then an ever-so-brief stop at Keystone where she appeared with Roscoe Arbuckle in *The Waiter's Ball*. Price throughout her career appeared in hundreds of films with some of the best to ever appear in front of the camera. In 1916, with just a few brief weeks in between, she made films with perhaps the two best "plus-size" comedians to ever make a silent comedy: Fatty Arbuckle and Babe Hardy.

This film reunites Hardy and director Will Louis with their former Edison cohort Raymond McKee. With a bit of fanfare McKee was signed by Vim, only appearing in two films before quickly disappearing. According to a *Moving Picture World* article from October 21, 1916: Raymond McKee left Vim because he got an offer to be Mabel Taliaferro's leading man in her next two Metro-Rolfe features (the first being *The Sunbeam*). McKee had just finished another Metro-Rolfe feature (*The Wheel of the Law*) when "he went to Jacksonville for the purpose of giving his mother the pleasure of a Florida winter, which she has never yet enjoyed. A stock company engagement made the trip possible from a practical point of view." So basically Vim was a working vacation for McKee.

"Plump becomes a maid in this comedy reel. As such he's the pet of the household, his wife's jealousy starts things. Considerable fast knockabout work is done by the comedians during the running of the reel. The reel has a whirlwind finish when the maid is discovered to be a man. Babe Hardy and Kate Price are a plump pair of funmakers." -- *Moving Picture World*

"Kate Price and Babe Hardy two shining Vim comedy stars will be seen in 'A Maid to Order,' a rollicking comedy in one reel. Kate Price is well known to Natchez fans having been seen in numbers of Vitagraph plays always scoring a hit whenever appearing on the screen. Babe Hardy is a newcomer—he is one of those small fellows weighing three hundred and sixty five pounds and as active as any youngster. Babe is funny, not one of those stagy kind but a real funny screen comedian producing laughter where others fail." -- *The Natchez Democrat* (Natchez, Mississippi)

Twin Flats

Released November 2, 1916. Vim Comedies - General Film Company release. One reel. No copyright registered. Release number 21357.

Produced by Louis Burstein. Directed by Will Louis. Filmed in October 1916 Jacksonville, Florida.

with Babe Hardy (*Babe*), Kate Price (*Kate, Babe's wife*), Raymond McKee (*Raymond*), Florence McLoughlin.

Babe and Raymond, two pals, and tenants in the Riverside Apartments, are both ruled by wives who insist on their remaining home nights. The night of a big poker game at the club, the pals frame up a scheme whereby, appearing to flirt with each other's wives, a fight will follow and in the melee, Babe and Raymond will beat it to the club. The scheme works fine, for after the fake fight is over an ambulance is summoned to carry Raymond off to the hospital. On the way to the hospital, Raymond makes a spectacular escape from the ambulance and reaches the club only to learn that Babe has not yet arrived. Raymond with the assistance of the other club members, masked as burglars, force an entrance into Babe's flat. Kate, Babe's husky spouse, mistaking Raymond and his pals for regular burglars, enters the combat, and routs the entire crowd, reserving Raymond as her last victim. During the confusion, Babe escapes and arrives at the club, where he learns with consternation of the treatment meted out to his club mates. Raymond has fared even worse than the others, and when Kate gets through with him he surely is a fit subject for the hospital, and this time he makes no objection to being carried there, where he is bandaged and put into bed. Babe, in the meantime, has been a heavy winner in the card game and also has partaken of innumerable liquid refreshments. When he arrives at the apartment house he stumbles into Raymond's flat. Mrs. Raymond, waiting well armed for the return of her hubby, brings down with full force on Babe's head the rolling pin meant for Raymond's reception. Stunned and battered, Babe is also carried to the hospital, where he finds himself in the next bed to his pal. [MPW]

Babe Hardy's character's name in Vim publicity materials has been changed from Plump to Babe, but it took the reviewers a few films to pick up on that. This film shows yet another attempt to get away from the wives. For Babe later in his career working as half of Laurel & Hardy it was the lodge meeting or the convention, here it is a big poker game. In those later films, much to Stan and Ollie's credit, they never resorted to attempted adultery in order to get their way. One wonders what Babe or Raymond would have done in *Twin Flats* if either wife had given a favorable response to flirting.

Some newspapers erroneously include Billy Ruge in the cast and one even refers to the film as a Plump & Runt. With Mother McKee fully rested and tired of Florida this was Raymond McKee's second and last Vim comedy. His reunion with his former Edison cohorts (Hardy and director Will Louis) was short-lived as he returned to New York City.

"Portly Babe Hardy and Kate Price, also blessed with avoirdupois, are the chief funmakers in this reel. It is a good knockabout number. The means Plump and his pal take to get out of their flats to the club are funny. Only Raymond gets away, and he brings several of his pals around to Plump's flat. They are routed by Kate, the wife, but hubby gets away and comes home with a bank roll, won at poker." -- *Moving Picture World*

A Warm Reception

Released November 9, 1916. Vim Comedies - General Film Company release. One reel. No copyright registered. Release number 21386.

Produced by Louis Burstein. Directed by Will Louis. Filmed October 1916 in Jacksonville, Florida outside *The Beauty Parlor* at 406 Broad Street, on Riverside Avenue and at the Vim studios.

with Babe Hardy (*Babe*), Kate Price (*Mrs. Price*), Joe Cohen (*Count De Appetyte*), Florence McLoughlin (*Kate's daughter*), Edna Reynolds (*maid*), James Renfro (*a tough*).

Just because Mrs. Price, known to her old associates in Shanty Alley, as Kate, has suddenly acquired heaps of money, she decides that as a suitor for the hand of her daughter, Florence, Babe is as welcome as a glass of poison. Babe is in despair, but learning that Kate is planning a big reception in honor of Count Brokski, to whom she hopes to marry Florence, Babe has his friends kidnap Kate and with the help of Florence and the maid, dresses up In Kate's clothes and receives the guests. What Babe does to the guests and the Count in particular, is a shame, and although the money looks ever-inviting to the Count, nevertheless the wallops handed to him by the supposed mother, takes away all the ardor of the poor Count. Kate, meanwhile, is putting up the battle of her life with the kidnappers, but finally they subdue her and bind her securely. Babe appears on the scene, and after pretending a wonderful fight, succeeds in releasing Kate, and bringing her home.. The grateful mother decides that our hero, even if he is fat and of humble birth, is good enough for her as a son-in-law. [MPW]

From the don't-believe-everything-you-read department: all of the Vim publicity material lists Raymond McKee as Count Brokski; and trade reviews also mention McKee in the role. But it is Joe Cohen as Count De Appetyte, not McKee, who receives all the punishment from Babe while he impersonates the mother, McKee having safely returned to New York City.

Babe Hardy gets three of his buddies to kidnap Kate Price; he should have hired twenty. Kate takes care of the three in quick order, and only when Babe sneaks up from behind and knocks her out does the kidnapping occur. Once dressed as the mother, Babe stands at the top landing of the staircase and poses for all of Florence McLoughlin's friends, only to trip and fall head first down the stairs. When the Count arrives, Babe constantly kicks and pushes the Count about, discouraging any intentions the Count may have had towards Florence. When Babe starts to remove the dress he is wearing, he stops (realizing "someone" is watching) and shyly looks into the camera. Possibly the first sustained example of Hardy's awareness of the camera, one of his most unusual and distinctive traits as a film actor. The film then irises in on Babe's head, and when it pulls back out to a full screen Babe is again dressed in his suit.

A Warm Reception is the only extant example of the films made at Vim by the all-too-briefly organized Babe Hardy Company. It does show that as the lead actor (and soon director) of the unit, Hardy was up to the task. Kate Price is lively and used to great effect (unlike some of the soon-to-come Sparkle comedies), and it seems the teaming of "Plump and Plumper" had some potential had not the internal business dealings of Vim gotten in the way.

"The old comedy idea of a mother who wants her daughter to marry a count is used in this reel. Babe Hardy is seen as the favorite suitor of the daughter, Kate Price is the mother and Raymond McKee, the count. It is the fast knockabout of these three that lend what comedy there is to the film. It is the Count who gets the warm reception being received by Babe masquerading as the mother." -- *Moving Picture World*

Pipe Dreams

Released November 16, 1916. Vim Comedies - General Film Company release. One reel. No copyright registered. Working Title: *Imagination*. Release number 21415.

Produced by Louis Burstein. Directed by Will Louis. Story by Will Louis. Filmed at the Vim Studios in Jacksonville, Florida.

with Kate Price (*Maggie*), Babe Hardy (*Babe*), Joe Cohen (*butler*), Edna Reynolds (*maid*).

Kate, the prize kitchen mechanic of the Goldrox home, has always envied the fair maids she has seen promenading the avenue, and resolves that, no matter what the cost be, she, herself, is some day going to enjoy the life of a society leader. Babe, the driver of one of the city's garbage carts, also has day dreams of the life he would like to lead. In the park one day Kate, adorned in her best, encounters Babe, also attired in his Sunday best. The two entertain each other with stories of the thrills and bores of the lives they pretend to lead, greatly to the delight of the other. When the Goldrox are away for a day, Kate seizes the golden opportunity to indulge in the joys of living the life of the social grand dame of her dreams. With the help of the family servants she invited Babe to the house, where she proceeds to entertain him. Babe, dressed in his overalls, drives up to the back of the house to empty the garbage cans.

He meets Kate coming out of the kitchen with the scraps of the morning meal, and each learns of the deception of the other. [MPW]

"Kate Price and Babe Hardy keep things moving in this comedy reel. Kate is seen as a cook who has social ambitions and Babe is seen as the driver of a garbage cart who would like to step high too. They meet and dressed to their best each tries to make the other believe they are the real goods. A moderately good comedy number." -- *Moving Picture World*

Mother's Child

Released November 23, 1916. Vim Comedies - General Film Company release. One reel. No copyright registered. Release number 21444.

Produced by Louis Burstein. Directed by unknown [possibly Will Louis or Babe Hardy]. Filmed October or November 1916 in Jacksonville, Florida.

with Babe Hardy (*Babe*), Kate Price (*his mother*), Joe Cohen (*Tom*), Florence McLoughlin (*Florence*), Edna Reynolds.

Babe, the pride of Cheestown and his mother's darling, arrives at Tidewater College at the opening of the school term. Babe's idea of a good time is a volume of the Iliad and a bag of peanuts. But after he has laid eyes on Florence, the prize peach of the Co-Eds, he deserts his book long enough to start a mild flirtation with her. This is directly in violation of the rules issued by the upper classmen to govern the conduct of the freshmen. Babe pays no heed to the rules, and thereby incurs the hostility of Tom, the Sophomore leader, who orders Babe to be subjected to the hardest of initiation and hazing stunts. However, after Babe has had a few rough stunts pulled off on him, his mother comes to visit her darling boy and, seeing the way he has been treated, decides to take a hand in the hazing game herself. Disguising herself, she lays in wait for the sophomores, and when they visit Babe's room for the purpose of hazing him, they receive the surprise of their lives. [MPW]

It is hard to develop a strong chronology of when titles were made at Vim, and then when they were released. Best guess would be that this film was made while Vim was still relatively intact, the absence of Ethel Burton indicating that she was still happily making Pokes and Jabbs comedies across the lot. Assuming that is true, this comedy would have been shot in late October, perhaps very early November 1916, and as such directed by Will Louis. However, even if this film wasn't a Babe Hardy directorial effort, it is obvious he was still very involved in the construction of these Vim comedies. *Mother's Child* combines the premises of two earlier Hardy comedies: *Mother's Baby Boy* and *The Simp and the Sophomores*. One British review noted that the school is "evidently a mixed school, which only a very luxurious nation would think of." Back in the day the idea of co-ed school was seen as a luxury or progressive idea, at least by the British.

"The art of conveying humour through the medium of the screen seems to be the monopoly of a very few producers, although many others are adept at providing humour when they are working all they know to hand out the sob stuff. However, the producer of *Mother's Child* has made a bold attempt to break through, and really has succeeded in producing a picture which got several quite hearty laughs from a scanty and generally bored trade audience. Several clever people are more or less wasted on mediocre material. The photography is good and, after all the main thing, *Mother's Child* will probably bring hearty laughter from any good tempered and unsophisticated audience." -- *Kinematograph and Lantern Weekly*

Prize Winners

Released November 30, 1916. Vim Comedies - General Film Company release. One reel. No copyright registered. Release number 21473.

Produced by Louis Burstein. Directed by Will Louis. Filmed early November 1916 at the Vim studios in Jacksonville, Florida.

with Babe Hardy (*Babe*), Kate Price (*Lady Kate*), Billy Ruge (*Billy*).

When Babe and Billy are released from the county jail where they were serving sentences for chicken stealing, they resolve that in the future they will work honestly for a living. However, they are not wonders at keeping their minds on work, for the first job they secure is that of inspectors of the beer at a local brewery. All that they know of inspecting beer is to sample it, and after they have sampled it for a few hours, they couldn't even see the buildings, so, of course, when the boss comes around, they lose their positions. The question of food now beset the Babe and Billy, so to ease their famished stomachs they enter Lady Kate's house where a big masquerade ball is in progress. Finding their way into the cloak rooms they steal everything that they see, but once having secured the silver and other trinkets, they discover that their exit is blocked by the servants, who insist on mistaking them for guests. Forced into the ball room, they are seen by Lady Kate, who immediately gives to them the prize for being the best masqued persons in the room. After basking for a few moments in the sunny smiles of Lady Kate, Babe decides that honesty is the best policy, so he catches the unwilling Billy and forces him to give up all the stolen jewelry. Babe leaves it on the table for Lady Kate, and with his disgruntled pal leaves the house before their deception is discovered. [MPW]

Except for the characters' names and the presence of Kate Price, this is pretty much a latter-day Plump & Runt comedy. Billy Ruge, who was absent from the first few Hardy-Price films, makes a rare appearance in one of the Babe Hardy Company films. This also is the final film Will Louis would direct for Vim.

"Babe Hardy and Kate Price are the funmakers in this comedy reel. Quite a bit of fast amusing action takes place when Babe and his friend horn their way into a masked ball being given at Kate's house. They become a trifle tipsy because of their jobs as beer inspectors and, in stolen plumage, they take the prize at the ball - also the silverware. Babe, however, takes the loot away from his partner and gives it back." -- *Moving Picture World*

The Guilty Ones

Released December 7, 1916. Vim Comedies - General Film Company release. One reel. No copyright registered. Release number 21502 (ETR); 21498 in Motion Picture News on this date but not this specific title.

Produced by Louis Burstein. Directed by Will Louis. Filmed in Jacksonville, Florida. [sometime prior to November 8, 1916]

with Babe Hardy (*Babe*), Kate Price (*Kate*), Billy Ruge (*detective*), Florence McLoughlin (*desk clerk*).

Babe and Kate, two ex-convicts and former underworld pals, have drifted apart since their prison days. Kate has reformed and is now a reporter in a distant city. Babe, overflowing with ideas of how to separate the unsuspected citizens of their hard earned cash, comes to the city. Creating some comment by his free way of dispensing coin, the newspaper sends Kate to interview the illustrious stranger. When Kate recognizes Babe, she almost faints, but Babe, by his suave speech, shows Kate that if she will join him in his scheme they will reap a fortune. The two insert a notice in the paper to the effect that the man who is so anxious to conceal a certain questionable deal had better pay hush money at once to Babe or his arrest will soon follow the exposure. The result of the notice is extraordinary, as it appears that every man in town has pulled off a questionable deal. Just as the two crooks are about to leave the city with their ill-earned gain, their Nemesis appears in the form of an amateur detective, who has overheard their plans. Babe and Kate are arrested. [MPW]

Billy Ruge's last screen appearance with his Vim comedy partner Babe Hardy. It is also Will Louis' last directorial effort to be released by Vim. By the time of the film's release, trade papers were confirming the demise of Plump & Runt, the departure of director Will Louis (who went to Amber Star to direct Billy Ruge) and Babe's promotion into the directorial ranks.

"Babe Hardy and Kate Price get over numerous laughs in this comedy. The portly pair are seen as ex-convicts, but Kate reforms and becomes a reporter. Babe has a scheme whereby he expects to make a lot of money and he induces Kate to work with him. The result of an ad to the effect that if a certain man doesn't pay blackmail there will be dire consequences is funny-- almost every man in town has something to conceal." -- *Moving Picture World*

He Winked And Won

Released December 21, 1916. Vim Comedies - General Film Company release. One reel. No copyright registered. Release number 21556. Erroneously listed as *He Went and Won* a number of times in the trade papers.

Produced by Louis Burstein. Directed by Babe Hardy. Filmed late November 1916 at the Vim studios in Jacksonville, Florida.

with Babe Hardy (*Babe*), Kate Price (*Kate*), Ethel Burton (*Ethel*), Florence McLoughlin (*Florence*).

Kate, president of the Suredeath Street Railway Company, has a daughter Ethel, who is the apple of her eye. Babe, an inventor of a safety device for the controller of the trolley car and possessor of a funny little wink, arrives to demonstrate his invention to Kate. Through the aid of Florence, his confederate, whom he managed to install in Kate's office as a stenographer, Snorky, president of a rival traction company, learns a demonstration will be given on a certain date. Snorky plants a bomb underneath the car so that when the lever strikes a certain mark the bomb will explode. However, Babe has Ethel to accompany him on a trial spin a few hours before the demonstration, and their entrance blocks Snorky's escape.

Finding himself trapped in the death car, Snorky raves and a desperate struggle takes place between him and Babe. Babe overpowers Snorky and hurls him of the roof of the fast-flying car just as the bomb explodes. The explosion throws Babe and Ethel high into the air, but with Babe's usual good luck, he and Ethel land safely in Kate's auto. [MPW]

The first film directed by Babe Hardy to be released; it was not the first film that Babe shot as a director. A *Motion Picture News* reported the changes at Vim this way: "Babe Hardy, the Vim star comedian, is now directing his own company, and is producing some of the best pictures produced at the Vim, Jacksonville studios since their organization. Mr. Hardy is supported by Miss Ethel Burton, Miss Florence McLoughlin, Tom Murray, Louise Carver, Joe Cohen and Bert Tracy. Herman Obrock is the chief cinematographer for the Babe Hardy company, having recently joined the Vim from New York."

This short could have easily been called *Something In* <u>*His*</u> *Eye*, having borrowed its basic premise from the 1915 Novelty film, *Something In Her Eye*, in which Babe Hardy also appeared. This marks Ethel Burton's first appearance with the newly designated Babe Hardy Company, having decided not to move over to Amber Star with the rest of the Pokes & Jabs troupe.

"Kate Price and Babe Hardy are the leading figures in this fun film. There are several little laughs in the reel. Babe is seen as the inventor who has a peculiar wink. The rival tries to plant a bomb in car which is to test Babe's invention, but is himself the victim. Fast action marks this comedy." -- *Moving Picture World*

Fat And Fickle

Released December 28, 1916. Vim Comedies - General Film Company release. One reel. No copyright registered. Release number 21582.

Produced by Louis Burstein. Directed and written by Babe Hardy. Photographed by Herman Obrock. Filmed November 13-18, 1916 at the Vim Studios in Jacksonville, Florida.

with Babe Hardy (*Babe*), Kate Price (*Kate*), Ethel Burton (*Ethel*), Florence McLoughlin (*Florence*).

Babe is happy over his engagement to Florence, but the minute he thinks of breaking the news to her mother, Kate, his dream of joy is ended. For Kate's ex-husband was a pugilist and his friends always considered him "some pug." Yet at home he was Kate's little lambkin, for Kate carried a wallop in each hand that had a bigger kick than a Krupp gun. Babe thought "Safety first" should be his motto; yet, instead of being rough with him when she heard the news, Kate only smothered Babe with hugs. Later, however, Babe meets Ethel, a blonde vampire who drives all thoughts of home and Florence out of Babe's head until the time came to tell Florence that she was no longer a member of the "Engagement club." Kate hears the news and her past training with her ex-hubby stands her to good effect until Babe, declaring truce, proclaims Kate the lady of his choice. Trouble begins between Florence and her mother over the possession of Babe. During the melee Babe escapes and seeks safety at the side of Ethel, only to receive an awful blow when he learns Ethel already owns a husband. Then Babe figured, although her mother may be a little rough, it was cheaper to get married than to work, so Babe beats it back to Florence and Kate, where a happy reunion occurs. [MPW]

This was Babe's first directorial effort, although not the first released. Exact release dates for the remaining Vim Comedies is hard to ascertain. The General Film Company had at this time taken on an official policy of not publishing specific release dates. Publicity and press attention to Vim also was waning by this time.

"An amusing comedy number, with Babe Hardy and Kate Price getting over numerous laughs. They indulge in considerable rough arguments. Both have enough avoirdupois to make this amusing. Babe is the fickle one, and finds out that it doesn't pay to be fickle with the daughter of Kate. Despite a vampire, however, things are brought to a happy close. An acceptable number". -- *Moving Picture World*

The Boycotted Baby

Released January 4, 1917. Vim Comedies - General Film Company release. One reel. No copyright registered. Release number 2162.

Produced by Louis Burstein. Directed by Babe Hardy. Filmed November 1916 at the Vim Studios in Jacksonville, Florida.

with Babe Hardy (*Babe*), Kate Price (*Kate*), Ethel Burton [?].

Among the prohibitions contained in the ordinances of Cordeliaville are "Lovers" and "Babies," and the law is prosecuted in the village by the Women's League, but lovers know no laws and Babe Hardy and Kate Price are no exception. Meanwhile a woman arrives in town with a baby and seeing the notice hides the baby. Babe and Kate find the motherless child and decide to take it home. The Women's League in a body visit Kate's home to protest against further love-making in Cordeliaville. Babe is at the house when they arrive and they find a sheepish expression on his face which perhaps is explained when the new-found baby begins to cry. The scandal is worse than if a murder had been committed in the village of Cordeliaville, and it takes many an explanation and unlooked for circumstance to straighten out the mix-up. [MPW]

Babe, by one reviewer, is described as having a "sheepish expression" on his face when the baby is discovered. One can only imagine the typical shy, fidgety take. He, of course, is embarrassed because we all know what generally causes babies. This short borrows a bit from the Edison comedy *Poor Baby*, which also featured Hardy.

"Babe Hardy and Kate Price are as fat and funny as ever in this comedy reel. The humor is too suggestive at times, the parentage of a baby being laid at the door of two unmarried couples. They live in Cordeliaville where lovemaking is banned and babies taboo. The baby is abandoned by its mother and placed by a tramp at Kate's door. After being transferred around many time, the baby finally reaches its mother's arms by means of the same tramp that first found it." -- *Moving Picture World*

His Movie Mustache

Released January 11, 1917. Vim Comedies - General Film Company release. One reel. No copyright registered. Release number 21626.

Produced by Louis Burstein. Directed by Babe Hardy. Filmed December 1916 at the Vim studios in Jacksonville, Florida.

with Babe Hardy, Kate Price, Ethel Burton [?].

[no synopsis available].

The *Florida Metropolis* makes reference to Babe Hardy shooting a comedy on Hawaiian sets and sporting a mustache. A few contemporary newspapers would advertise the showing of the film in a local theater, and the title is listed on the Vim release schedule published in the trade papers. Nothing else is known about the film.

"A Vim comedy full of fun." -- *Altoona Times* (Altoona, Pennsylvania)

The Love Bugs

Released January 25, 1917. Vim Comedies - General Film Company release. One reel. No copyright registered. Release number 21667.

Produced by Louis Burstein. Directed by Babe Hardy. Photography by Herman Obrock. Filmed in part November 19, 1916 at Cohens Department Store in Jacksonville, Florida.

with Kate Price (*Kate*), Babe Hardy (*Babe*), Ethel Burton (*Ethel*), Joe Cohen (*Cohen*), Florence McLoughlin, Tom Murray, Louise Carver.

Ethel, the daughter of Kate, a boarding house mistress, is loved by Snooky, a social pirate, and one of her mother's boarders. Babe, another roomer at Kate's house, and head salesman at the ribbon counter at Cohen's department store, is also in love with Ethel. On account of Babe's effeminate manners and small salary, Ethel refuses to have anything to do with him. Filled with a craze for diamonds, Ethel secretly covets the beautiful pendant worn by Mrs. Carver, a wealthy roomer living at Kate's domicile. Snooky also covets the pendant, but with an entirely different motive. Watching his chance, Snooky is about to steal the pendant when he is interrupted by Babe, who also has designs on the jewels. Before Babe can escape he is discovered by Mrs. Carver and Babe seeks safety in flight followed by the irate husband of Mrs. Carver. The husband follows Babe, who, after a perilous journey across roof tops, rushes in to the boarding house just as Snooky, with the pendant in his pocket, is trying to escape. He seizes and exposes Snooky, and receives the praise of Ethel and the others. [MPW]

After the filming *The Love Bugs* (and possibly one other Babe Hardy-directed Vim) Kate Price enjoyed a nice Thanksgiving dinner as a guest in the home of Mr. & Mrs. Babe Hardy, and then moved her place of employment to the Amber Star studios. Kate and Babe Hardy would work together again in the 1925 Larry Semon feature *The Perfect Clown*, but for the next few months her primary co-star would be Billy Ruge. Not sure that was an upgrade.

In order to have full run of the store and keep onlookers at a minimum, the Babe Hardy company shot at Cohens Department Store on a Sunday, which while practical did not sit well with much of the local populace that was still used to businesses being closed on that day of the week. Cohens was located at 117 West Duval Street in the St.

James building in downtown Jacksonville. Unlike many filming locations in the downtown area of Jacksonville the St. James building still exists. Restored and slightly remodeled, the building now houses the City Hall.

"A comedy uproar with Kate Price and Babe Hardy." -- *Daily Arkansas Gazette (Little Rock, Arkansas)*

The Other Girl

Released February 1, 1917. Vim Comedies - General Film Company release. One reel. No copyright registered. Release number 21689.

Produced by Louis Burstein. Directed by Babe Hardy. Filmed in Jacksonville, Florida.

with Babe Hardy (*Babe*), Ethel Burton (*Ethel*), Florence McLoughlin (*Florence, a vampire*).

Believing his sweetheart, Ethel, has spurned him, Babe wends his way to a cabaret intent on drowning his cares. He falls victim to the wiles of Florence, a dashing vampire who has discovered that Babe will fall heir to a fortune if he is married within a certain time. She lures him into a mock marriage and then announces her intention of sharing his fortune. Later Babe learns that Ethel has really been the victim of circumstances and she intends to marry him at once. In a quandary, he endeavors to escape from his dilemma, but Florence holds him fast to his supposed marriage vows. The vampire, however, has been followed by Pussey Foot, the detective, who recognizes her and unearths the plot against Babe. Just as Florence and Ethel are about to battle for possession of Babe, Pussey Foot appears and denounces Florence, exposes the mock marriage and reunites the lovers. [MPW]

[no review available]

A Mix Up In Hearts

Released circa February 15, 1917. Vim Comedies - General Film Company release. One reel. No copyright registered. Release number not listed
Produced by Louis Burstein. Directed by Babe Hardy. Filmed late 1916 at the Vim Studios in Jacksonville, Florida.

with Babe Hardy, Ethel Burton, Harry Naughton.

[no synopsis available].

By mid-February 1917, Vim quit publishing specific release dates for their films and little other information on their releases was commonplace, in part due to the fact that by Christmas 1916 there really was no Vim anymore. Modern sources muck up the details, identifying this film as a King Bee comedy. The 1917 release date and the presence of Babe Hardy and Ethel Burton give some clues as to why the mistake is made. Yet the crediting of Arvid Gillstrom as director and the presence of Billy West are totally incorrect.

Babe Hardy and Ethel Burton's last work for the Vim Films Corporation. Around the time of its release, they were both beginning work over at the old Thanhouser studio shooting the first of the King Bee comedies. Directed by Arvid Gillstrom, the King Bee comedies were essentially the Babe Hardy Company from Vim with a new leading man, Billy West. The new company, headed by Louis Burstein and managed by Harry Naughton, gave many of the Vimmies a new lease on their film careers. For Ethel Burton it also gave her a husband. On May 4, 1917 with Babe Hardy and Florence McLoughlin along as witnesses Ethel married Gillstrom in St. Augustine, Florida.

[no reviews available]

FAUX VIM COMEDIES

Terrible Kate

Released January 18, 1917. Vim Comedies - General Film Company release. One reel. No copyright registered. Release number 21644. Studio publicity and other sources refer to the film as *Bad Kate*.

Produced by Frank Tichenor for Amber Star Films Corporation. Directed by Will Louis. Filmed mid-December 1916 at Garrick Studios in Jacksonville, Florida.

with Kate Price (*Kate*), Billy Ruge (*Bill*), Roland Hill (*bartender*), Jobyna Ralston, Jennie Nelson.

In front of a saloon and a private graveyard two cowboys are on the verge of a fight, when Kate looms up in the doorway. The men immediately separate. In No Man's county everyone holds Kate in awe. In one instance, she takes drastic measures to stop a brawl in her saloon, and, as a result, another grave is added to the others in her private graveyard. On another occasion she demonstrates her marksmanship by hitting a reflection in a mirror. One day, however, she meets Bill, a man of iron will, who proves his calibre on his arrival by starting a little gun play after blowing smoke in the faces of a few strangers. As Bill goes to the saloon, he passes the graveyard and the epitaphs on the tombstones set him thinking. At the saloon he introduces himself and treats to drinks. When he refuses to pay, Kate starts a scrap in which Bill is victorious. In another encounter Bill is again the victor. Kate finally becomes submissive, and marries Bill, who is very domineering and is in the act of scolding her when his wife wakes him with the aid of a rolling pin and Bill appeals for mercy. [MPW as TERRIBLE KATE]

The lines between Vim and Amber Star (Jaxon) were very blurry in the last few months of 1916. Released as a Vim Comedy this film was for all intent and purposes a Sparkle comedy. All the players and even the director are the same as the first Sparkles and was filmed at the Garrick Studios where most all of the Jaxon comedies made in Jacksonville were shot. However, this was Will Louis' last directorial effort for Amber Star (many of the Sparkle comedies released in 1917 were directed by Louis but shot before *Terrible Kate*). Louis would begin directing Black Diamond Comedies in early January 1917 splitting time between Jacksonville and the studio's home base in Wilkes-Barre, Pennsylvania.

First known appearance of Jobyna Ralston in the movies, her joining the Ruge-Price Company being announced when production started on *Terrible Kate* The absence of Ethel Burton as well as Florence McLoughlin left the new Amber Star a bit shy in the ingenue department, and Ralston helped fill that void.

"Terrible Kate a roaring Vim comedy also on tonight's bill stars inimitable Kate Price, the funniest woman on the screen." -- *Wilmington Dispatch (North Carolina)*

A Job For Life

Released February 2, 1917. Vim Comedies - General Film Company release. One reel. No copyright registered. Release number 21694.

Produced by Knickerbocker Star Features. Filmed 1916 in Long Beach, California.

with Charles Dudley (*Dud*), Bert Crapoe (*Bert*), Florence Horkheimer (*Little Toddles*), Bruce Smith (*Chief of Police*).

Miss Flo has been reading in the park about two crooks robbing girls. Bert and Dud, who have been reading the ads in the help wanted column, find that there is no position open for their peculiar talent and give it up. Bert goes about his way. He sees Miss Flo and flirts. She is amused and he likes it for encouragement. He sits beside her and plays with her pocketbook. Dud sees Bert take money out of the pocketbook. Determined to get the money Dud steals up behind and tries to grab it. Bert kicks him away. Dud plans to have a notorious gang of crooks abduct the woman and force her to give up the money. Bert has a made a hit with Miss Flo and she suggests they get something to eat. They go to a lunch counter, and, being fond of pie, she begins to "Clean up" everything in sight. In the meantime Dud, having gathered his gang, comes back looking for the girl but she has gone. Dud sees her at the lunch counter and sends one of his men to buy a large number of pies. Dud wins the favor of Miss Flo because he can give her more pie. This starts a pie fight. Dud takes Miss Flo to the park where the crooks grab her and take her to the den. Because she refuses to give up her money, Dud gives her five minutes to agree or be blown to pieces by a bomb. Her father, who is the chief of police, reads about crooks in the park and is worried about his daughter. He goes out looking for her. Bert, who has been looking for his lady love, encounters her father, who mistakes him for a crook. They fight and father knocks Bert down. Bert discovers a footprint of Dud and the girl,, and he and father take up the trail, which leads to the den. They look in the window and see a bomb burning. Father goes after the rest of the police and Bert goes for water. The crooks, looking out the window, see Bert and follow him. Bert runs to the edge of a cliff overlooking the sea, and does not know how to get down. The crooks knock him over, but he bounces back and knocks out the crooks. Throwing the rope which the crooks carried over the cliff, he slides down it, fills his pail with water, and then slides up the rope to the top of the cliff. Bert races back to the den with the water and arrives just as father appears with his force of police. Miss Flo is eventually rescued, and her father in gratitude gives the hand of his daughter to Bert, who thereby contracts "a job for life." [MPW]

The tumultuous times that were the last days of Vim make it hard to fully understand all that was happening. Films shot by what remained of Vim and by the Eastern Film Corporation-backed Amber Star were both being released as Vim Comedies. However, such an arrangement along with the ongoing legal wranglings resulted in gaps in the release schedule. Odd in that while the Vim company was making them and releasing them as fast as they could, Amber Star had many more titles in the can that could have been released at this time, but were held back and released later in 1917 as Sparkle or Jaxon comedies. Nevertheless the lack of releasable product caused Vim (or perhaps the still somewhat attached Melies Manufacturing Company or the General Film Company itself) to buy outside productions for release as Vim comedies. *A Job For Life* was the first of these and since Knickerbocker was also working as a Melies subsidiary, it made some sense that they would be source for surplus product. Most of the Knickerbocker films were directed by E.K. Horkheimer and all were shot in Long Beach, California.

"A Roaring Vim Comedy, with a good laugh in every scene." -- *Republican and Herald (Pottsville, Pennsylvania)*

Nora Declares War

Released February 8, 1917. Vim Comedies - General Film Company release. One reel (850 feet) No copyright registered. Release number 21711.

Directed by unknown. Filmed 1915 at the Eastern Film Corporation studios in Providence, Rhode Island. Likely intended for release as part of the Pelican Comedies brand.

with unknown.

Nora, an Irish cook, is imbued with the idea that she is terribly abused. All the members of the household order her around and the children play pranks which anger her. Her back is turned for a few minutes and the children pepper the soup which she is about to serve to the head of the house, a grouchy old man. It is so strong with pepper that he decides to get after Nora. Just as he is about to chastise Nora, the iceman enters and, thinking that he is crazy, forces a piece of ice into his mouth. Next door Bridget reigns supreme, and Nora cannot understand it. Bridget discloses her methods and Nora decides to try them out. She routs the old man from the kitchen, spanks the children, and everyone in general begins to feel her temper. After getting the members of the household under her control she dresses and informs them that it is her afternoon off. She and Bridget depart to enjoy a few hours of recreation — which is something Nora has not done for some time. [MPW]

The Eastern Film Corporation, the parent company of Amber Star, was an odd entity. Although making films since 1915 they barely released any of them. This comedy is the earliest example of Eastern cleaning out their vaults, which they would do to a greater extent later with the Sparkle Comedies.

"A Vim Comedy which gives you an opportunity to enjoin many good grins as well as some brilliant comedy action." -- *Frederick News-Post (MD.)*

"A very humorous theme, the working cut of which will cause general merriment." -- *The Bioscope*

Happy Nat's Dilemma

Released February 9, 1917. Vim Comedies - General Film Company release. One reel. No copyright registered. Release number 21713.

Directed by unknown. Production credits unknown.

with W.J. Sloane.

Happy Nat, a society drunk, has an engagement with his fianceé, a widow. Through overindulgence he falls asleep and dreams that his fiancée has jilted him because of his drinking, and he therefore decides to become a prohibitionist. He becomes "chartable" and steals a delivery boy's groceries because he sees a blind man and his daughter in want. He also steals clothes for the little girl. When he wakes he remembers his appointment with the widow. His dreams so worry him he decides to quit drinking and then he hustles to meet his intended. [MPW]

W. J. Sloane was the name of a major furniture manufacturer and retailer during the first half of the 20th century. The lead comedian is probably using an alias, this being the only film credit attributed to a W. J. Sloane.

"W.J. Sloane is the chief comedian in this comedy reel. The number has quite a number of laughs, and tells of Happy Nat's dreams. Happy Nat is a bibulous gentleman, but in his dream he becomes a philanthropist. As the reel closes he awakes and goes to keep the appointment he had. A fair reel." -- *Moving Picture World*

The Newlyweds' Mistake

Released February 22, 1917. Vim Comedies - General Film Company release. One reel. No copyright registered. Release number 21750.

Directed by unknown. Production credits unknown.

with George Larkin, Irene Wallace.

Mr. and Mrs. Newlywed decide to spend a day at the beach, but before leaving Mrs. Newlywed insists upon purchasing a little beauty powder. While she is getting the powder her husband decides to get some smokes. Wifey returns first and mistaking a man in a passing auto for Mr. Newlywed gives chase. Hubby in the meantime returns and while waiting anxiously for wifey mistakes a woman for her. He follows his supposed wife in another car. Arriving at the beach both husband and wife search bathing houses, and cafes looking for each other. They search in vain and dejected leave for home feeling that it was a case of mistaken identity. Mrs. Newlywed arrives home first, closely followed by her spouse. Explanations ensue and hubby and wifey decide to spend their future holidays at home. [MPW]

The pedigree of some of the bought films released by Vim is hard to fully discover. George Larkin worked in Jacksonville during 1916 making serials for Kalem, giving some credence that this may have actually been a Vim or Amber Star production. However, Irene Wallace never worked in Jacksonville and was busy working for Victor up in New York City during 1916. The two were known to have made films together in 1915, so there is a good possibility that *The Newlyweds' Mistake* is actually a Selig product.

"A comedy reel with George Larkin and Irene Wallace playing the leads. The newlyweds each mistake someone else for their marital mate. Each gives chase to the wrong party and funny complications follow. An average comedy number." -- *Moving Picture World*

Art and Paint

Released February 23, 1917. Vim Comedies - General Film Company release. One reel. No copyright registered. Release number 21752.

Directed by unknown. Production credits unknown.

with unknown.

Mr. A. Suburb decides to have his dwelling renovated and selects Stooge, a painter with artistic ideas, who has a helper named Boozo, to do the work. Boozo's favorite pastime is reposing in empty dry goods boxes and it is in one of these haunts Stooge finds his trusty assistant. After considerable difficulty Stooge succeeds in arousing Boozo and hooked together with a painter's ladder they depart for the field of endeavor. Upon their arrival they proceed to erect a scaffold and in doing this prove themselves acrobats. Their artistic tastes do not appeal to Mr. Suburb's peculiar fancy and they are dismissed but not dismayed for Dame Fortune smiles sweetly upon them and they become heirs to $5,000. They decide to open a studio and become artists. Their first customer, a six-footer, is not pleased with their conception of him and, aided by his physique, cleans out the studio and deposits the artists in a garbage wagon. Here the dreams of the ambitious painters end. [MPW]

Other than the synopsis and release date little is known about this film, except that it was released as a Vim comedy. One newspaper ad (the majority of which were notoriously incorrect) mentioned this as a Pokes & Jabs comedy while another listed the star as John Dudley. A somewhat educated guess would deem this another bought film, but the vacuum of details make that pure conjecture.

[no reviews available]

Harry's Pig

Released week of February 26, 1917. Vim Comedies - General Film Company release. One reel. No copyright registered. Release number not listed.

Produced by the Harry La Pearl Picture Company. Filmed June 1916 along Fulton Street and other locations in Jamaica, Long Island, New York.

with Harry La Pearl (*Harry*).

Harry La Pearl, a rural favorite, visits the town grocery store to make his weekly purchases, but as he is about to leave he is attracted by a pretty girl, and when endeavoring to make a hurried exit from the store upsets things in general, including the flour barrel, fruit stand, etc. Harry's wife, however, is closely upon his heels and to make his getaway he steals a large pig and rides him through the town closely followed by his wife, the town marshal and numerous others attracted by the amusing sight of Harry riding a pig. Many amusing incidents ensue before Harry's pig finally finds his way back to his pen where Harry is captured by his wife, and he then resolves not to look from the straight and narrow path in the future. [M & MPW]

Most sources give 1884 as the birth year for Harry La Pearl. Either those sources are incorrect or La Pearl led a very hard life. In *Harry's Pig* he appears to be a man in his late 50's, even early 60's and his on screen presence is reminiscent of the older Buster Keaton seen in the beach movies. The film is fairly well made but the timing on all of the gags and pratfalls seems to be a beat or two off, as if they filmed the rehearsal. Or, perhaps because of having primarily worked in the theater, La Pearl and company were playing to the back row of the balcony and not for a screen audience.

The Harry La Pearl Picture Company worked out of the Cedar Manor Hall hotel in Jamaica, New York, the former Firehouse Hotel that La Pearl had bought as an investment and that he and his wife ran. Apparently Mrs. La Pearl provided a little too much room service to one of the guests, and New York papers in August 1916 told stories of La Pearl chasing the man down for writing bad checks but in reality, as one paper noted, actually "the real trouble between La Pearl and [John] Larabee involves the affection of a girl." The story has both happy and sad endings. La Pearl would remarry in 1920, after obviously divorcing the philandering first Mrs. La Pearl, and have a long happy marriage to his wife Loretta. On a sad note Cedar Manor Hall burned on February 26, 1917, ironically just as *Harry's Pig* was being released. La Pearl would continue to call the Jamaica area of Queens, New York home for most of the rest of his life.

"Harry La Pearl has a lot of fun with a porker in this comedy reel. He performs some funny antics as he rides down the main street of the town. His wife and the grocery store man have something to say and do about Harry's exploits, too. There is quite a bit of fast action in this reel and the laughs are not too scarce." -- *Moving Picture World*

Seeing Double

Released week of February 26, 1917. Vim Comedies - General Film Company release. One reel. No copyright registered. Release number not listed.

Produced by Knickerbocker Star Features. Filmed 1916 in Long Beach, California.

with Charles Dudley (*Dud*), Bert Crapoe [?] (Bert).

Dud, a henpecked husband, while doing the weekly ironing burns his hand and decides to seek a more amusing occupation. He leaves by a window and is met by his friend Bert, who has jilted his wife because of her bullets which she serves as biscuits. Bert has been sojourning by a cigar stand and has succeeded in stealing a cigar cutter. The two ex-husbands enter a thirst parlor followed by a cop. The cigar cutter now serves as a weapon of defense and after Bert has succeeded in ejecting the proprietor and the cop, the two ex-husbands take over the thirst parlor and to their delight become highly hilarious, proceeding to invite all who enter to join them on their jamboree. While in hiding the two heroes see double and they decide to visit their wives at Bert's home, where they receive a peppery reception and are forced to retreat to the dog house where, wrapped up in each other's arms, they depart for the land of dreams." [MPN & M]

[no reviews available]

This is Not My Room

Released March 1, 1917. Vim Comedies - General Film Company release. One reel (900 feet). No copyright registered. Release number not listed. May have been released in Latin America as an Essanay comedy.

Probably produced by Kalem. Directed by Harry Millarde [?].

with Ethel Teare.

"The thoughtful husband" decides that wifey is in need of a vacation and therefore sends her away to a quiet summer hotel. Upon her arrival her hand baggage is placed in the wrong room by a "dime-novel crazed" bellboy, who at the same time places another guest's baggage in her room. The similarity of the numbers "66" and "99" is the cause of the error, and when Ethel, a newlywed, arrives to meet her husband she is escorted to her husband's room, but to her astonishment finds a woman's wearing apparel thrown about the room. Ethel decides to make more trouble and therefore removes the lingerie and places it in room 99, where it is discovered by the thoughtful husband," who has also arrived in response to wifey's telegram. In the wee small hours of the morning "the cabaret rounder" returns to the hotel, and when he attempts to retire in Ethel's room a general mixup ensues, which ends in a pink pajama parade and the satisfactory adjustment for everyone. [M]

Ethel Teare started in pictures with Kalem in 1914 working in various units most often in support of John E. Brennan. By mid-1915 Teare had become the chief female comedy support to Ham & Bud in their long running series of comedies. For a time during 1916 Teare was given her own series, but ended her tenure at Kalem back working with Lloyd Hamilton and Bud Duncan. She left Kalem in late 1916, moving first to Keystone and then Fox. This film is likely a leftover from the short-lived Ethel Teare series made for Kalem. For those keeping score the film was released in Spanish-speaking countries as *En Casa Ajena*.

"Hubby decides that wifey needs a vacation and sends her off for a rest. The bellboy, confusing the numbers of the rooms, puts the wifey's handbag in the room of another guest, and when the guest's wife arrives she is surprised to find another woman's handbag in her husband's room. After a mixup things are adjusted satisfactorily." -- *Exhibitors Herald*

A Deal in Furniture

Released March 1917. Vim Comedies - General Film Company release. One reel. No copyright registered. Release number not listed.

Directed by unknown. Production credits unknown.

with unknown.

Stooge, manager and truck driver, of the Fall-a-Part Furniture Company, is successful in selling the complete furnishings for Mr. Groucho's new flat, and arranges to make immediate delivery. Stooge experiences considerable difficulty in loading all the furniture bought. Finally it is placed on the truck and Stooge starts for his destination. Upon arrival at the flat he is met by Mr. Groucho and his wife. The latter insists upon giving instructions and in attempting to follow these instructions Stooge becomes tangled up in the furniture and carpets. Groucho and his wife, assisted by the landlady, attempt to adjust matters by holding on to one end, but they make matters worse, for a tug-o-war ensues and Stooge is knocked out of a window and falls into a garbage can below. In falling he upsets the can and rolls away from the trouble. [MPW]

An example of erroneous newspaper listings shows up *in The Daily Courier* (Connellsville, PA) of March 31, 1917 for *A Deal in Furniture*. The ad for the film mentions George Dudley in the cast, which really means Charles Dudley or perhaps George Larkin? We likely will never know.

"*A Deal in Furniture* will be a rip-roaring comedy with many unusual scenes and situations." -- *The Allentown Leader (Allentown, Pennsylvania)*

Deep Stuff

Released March 1917. Vim Comedies - General Film Company release. One reel (900 feet). No copyright registered. Release number not listed.

Produced by Knickerbocker Star Features. Filmed 1916 in Long Beach, California.

with Charles Dudley (*Dud*), Bert Crapoe (*Bert*).

Dud and Bert are enjoying a stay at a fashionable summer resort. Realizing that in order to continue they will have to raise funds, Dud secures a position as life guard. His wife sees him surrounded by a number of beauties and chases him into the briny, she after him. She forgets she is unable to swim until she is over her head. Dud rescues her and receives a reward of $5,000 for bravery. His pal, Bert, feels that he is entitled to a share of the reward and when it isn't forthcoming he threatens to blow up Dud. Bert places a bomb in Dud's home and Dud enters just in time to plant the bomb behind Bert, who is making his retreat. The bomb explodes and Bert takes a flying trip through the clouds and when he returns his wife receives him with wide open arms. [MPW]

The last of the Knickerbockers released as a Vim. Knickerbocker Star Features were by mid-1916 in essence a brand of the Balboa Amusement Company. Started in 1915, Knickerbocker Star Features were initially produced by Gaumont for release though Mutual. Melies Manufacturing took over the brand and subcontracted with a production company to produce the films for release through the General Film Company (much like they did with Vim). By mid-1916 Melies was unhappy with the product and moved the brand over to the Balboa Amusement Company for production. Balboa kept the brand going long after the demise of both the General Film Company and Melies Manufacturing.

"A seashore comedy of refined mirth and humor, that is side splitting." -- *The Evening Herald (Pottsville, Pennsylvania)*

"Full of laughs and mirthful thrills, this smart comedy proves how big a quantity of good things can be wrapped up in a small parcel." -- *The Bioscope*

Willie Walrus Pays Alimony

Released March 1917. Vim Comedies - General Film Company release. One reel. No copyright registered. Release number not listed.

Directed by unknown. Production credits unknown.

with William Wolbert [?], Ethel Teare.

Willie Walrus, a baker, is ordered by the court to pay alimony, but this Willie refuses to do, as he thinks his wife can earn her own living. Wifey, however, imbued with the militant spirit, decides to force him to pay her and visits the bake shop where Willie juggles the dough. Willie, assisted by his fellow bakers, succeed in getting wifey out of the shop. Knowing she will return again, he decides to poison her by placing rat poison in some candy. His friends see an opportunity to play a practical joke and instead of sending the poisoned candy to Willie's wife, they send her a box of good candy and the poisoned candy is replaced with castor oil nuggets which Willie presents to the cashier. Explanations are now in order, and a reconciliation takes place between Willie and his wife. [MPW]

William Wolbert made at least four other Willy Walrus films for Joker in 1914, and the character appears in a 1914 Sterling entitled *His New Job*. Whether this is another Wolbert film or something different is not known. However, just before she began her long stint in support of Ham & Bud, Ethel Teare made a handful of comedies together with Wolbert in the spring of 1915 for Kalem. So this could be an erstwhile Kalem which may support contemporary newspaper ads that included Bud Duncan in the cast.

"A side splitting Vim comedy of refined humor, full of amusing scenes with a laugh in every foot, a real gloom dispeller." -- *The Evening Herald (Shenandoah, Pennsylvania)*

In Stumpland

Released March 1917. Vim Comedies - General Film Company release. One reel (900 feet). Copyrighted October 11, 1916 (LU9286) by Juvenile Film Corp. Release number not listed.

Produced by Paul H. Cromelin. Directed by James A. FitzPatrick [or possibly Frank Andrews]. Written by Frank Andrews. Produced by Juvenile Film Corporation in New York City circa 1916 for intended release through Sterling.

with Joseph Monahan (*Chip*), Janethel Monahan [*Nell*].

Doctor Stork leaves a little stranger at Chip's house. Chip tells his little friend, Nell, all about the baby sister and Nell wants a little sister, too, so Chip and she ask the doctor where he gets his babies. He tells them in the stumps of trees and they both determine to go baby hunting. On their way they pass the doctor's house and, seeing his baby carriage, take the baby out and run away with the carriage. They hide the doctor's baby under a clump of bushes, where it falls asleep. After looking in a number of stumps and finding nothing, Chip exclaims "there must have been somebody here before us." Nell is disappointed and starts to cry. At last Chip comes to a large stump, and, looking into it calls to Nell, saying, "There's lots of babies here." He pulls out three little rabbits, and they put them into the baby carriage and start homeward. In the meanwhile the doctor and his wife have missed their child. Giving up the search they return home, just in time to see Chip and Nell coming through the fields with their missing baby carriage. They are horrified to see Chip and Nell give the carriage a push over an embankment, and it rolls to the bottom. Thinking their baby is in it they rush to the carriage and drag out the rabbits. The doctor administers a spanking to Chip and all ends happily when the children lead the doctor and his wife to where the baby is hidden. [MPW]

James A. Fitzpatrick directed a number of one-reel comedies for Juvenile Film Corporation that centered around the character of Chip (played by nine year old Joseph Monahan) who often impersonated Charlie Chaplin: *A Chip Off the Old Block, Chip's Backyard Barnstormers* (two reels), *Chip's Elopement, Chip's Rivals* (a print of this title survives at the Museum of Modern Art), *Chip's Movie Co.* and a special two reel production *Chip's Carmen* where young Monahan does his take on Chaplin's *Burlesque on Carmen.* Another production was announced *Chip Van Winkle,* but does not seem to have been released. Additional Juvenile titles included *The World War in Kidland* and *For Sale – A Daddy.* Juvenile's company motto was "Children's Pictures By Children, For Children." The "Chip" series of comedies were released by Juvenile Film Corporation (a subsidiary of the Cosmofotofilm Company) via State Rights beginning in March 1916.

It is possible that this film, *In Stumpland,* was a pilot for the series and picked up by Sterling for distribution (not unlike the first "Pokes and Jabbs" film) but then not released and eventually sold to General Film Company for release under the Vim brand, or possibly made after the above-mentioned films and sold when the Chip series folded.

"A little comedy which, without being wildly exhilarating and remarkable for its humour, will please vast numbers of the picture-going public, more especially the women and children for whom we presume it was produced. It deals with the exploits of two children who having been told various stories about the arrival of infants, accept the doctor's story that he finds them in the stumps of old trees, and, commandeering a pram, go in search of children. The story is well and easily told, the staging is good, and the photography excellent." --*Kinematograph Weekly*

Somewhere in Mexico

Released March 22, 1917. Vim Comedies - General Film Company release. One reel. No copyright registered. Release number not listed.

Produced by the Harry La Pearl Picture Company. Filmed Summer 1916 in Jamaica, Long Island, New York.

with Harry La Pearl.

Harry and Slats, two ambitious farm hands, after causing their employers much grief, decide to depart for a more exciting field of endeavor, and by chance learn that their employer, Hicks, and his brother, John, are preparing to leave for Mexico to locate a lost treasure. Harry and Slats, bent upon getting there first, start out immediately. They arrive at the border line, but as they are not permitted to pass they decide to submarine their way across, their baggage serving as the submarines. They succeed in getting on the other side but learn that Hicks and John have reached the treasure ahead of them. After maneuvering for some time they discover where the treasure is hidden. They array themselves in all kinds of jewels and pose as bull fighters, and soon they are the prides of the town. They enter an arena to fight a bull, but when a burro enters disguised as a Spanish

bull the crowd leaves in disgust. The little town is then attacked by bandits and our heroes sustain their reputation, but when Hicks and John discover that the balance of the treasure is missing they soon find the robbers and a panic ensues. [MPW]

Harry La Pearl was a circus performer almost from birth, as his father headed up the La Pearl Circus. La Pearl worked for his father, eventually moving on to work for both the Ringling Brothers and Barnum & Bailey circuses (before those two merged). Around 1913, he took up residency at New York City's Hippodrome Theatre where he was highly regarded and considered chief of all clowns. David Horsley signed La Pearl (along with fellow Hippodome performer and future Vimmie Spook Hanson) first to his Centaur brand of films and then in mid-1915 to the MinA company.

Also at MinA working is support was comedian George Ovey. When La Pearl departed MinA, Ovey took his place as lead comedian, a role he would keep with Horsley for years, even when Horsley moved over to Mutual and rebranded his films Cub Comedies. The similarity of La Pearl's character and the one that Ovey would take on didn't go unnoticed. Comedian-director Al Ray wrote in an article for *Picture-Play Weekly* that "Ovey's make-up is not his own, in the first place. It belongs to Harry La Pearl. When Harry played leads, and directed for MinA, the same company that Dave [Horsley] owns now, although under the brand of Cub, he wore identically the same make-up that Ovey uses now, and yet they talk about the latter's originality!" So, when watching "Jerry" in the Cub Comedies, remember you are actually watching Harry, or rather the great Harry La Pearl imitator George Ovey.

"Harry La Pearl is cast in a role which suits him in every particular and the picture fairly vibrates with comic absurdities outlined in such convincing fashion that it figures as a perfect riot of fun from beginning to end." -- *Exhibitors Herald*

Nellie's Nifty Necklace

Released March 23, 1917. Vim Comedies - General Film Company release. One reel (845 feet). No copyright registered. Release number not listed. Released in the U.K. as an L-KO comedy on February 4, 1917.

Produced by the L-KO Komedy Company [Henry Lehrman?]. Filmed in Hollywood, California mid-1916.

with Billie Ritchie, Marjorie Ray.

Nellie has many suitors, but she yearns for a necklace. While strolling in the park a policeman becomes enraptured with her charms and gives her the desired necklace, but as Nellie will not satisfy the policeman by kissing him he wants his necklace back. Nellie returns the precious jewelry and Mr. Policeman finds a willing customer in the person of one Billie, a lovesick four-flusher, who is also enraptured with Nellie. Along comes "Long Arm Jim" and soon relieves Billie of his love token. Jim knows woman's weakness and succeeds in selling and reselling the necklace many times – each time extracting it from the purchaser. Billie is the first to discover the loss and is soon joined by the other victims. "Long Arm Jim" is finally captured and the necklace is returned to its original owner – the policeman. Billie, however, succeeds in getting it from the policeman and when he presents it to Nellie he wins her for life. [MPW]

An advertisement in the September 30, 1916 *Moving Picture World* lists this as a forthcoming L-KO title. However the film was not released by L-KO and apparently was sold and released as a Vim Comedy. This was not an uncommon practice, as made apparent by the Vim release schedule around this time. Universal (L-KO's parent company) did this on at least one other occasion when it sold some of Alice Howell's Century product, resulting in her film *Distilled Love* eventually being released by Reelcraft. To further confuse things, *Nellie's Nifty Necklace* was released in the United Kingdom in early 1917 as an L-KO comedy.

"The lure of a necklace and its potent effect in love making is humorously set forth in detail when a fair maiden's fondness for jewelry, as portrayed by dainty Marjorie Ray, leads her ardent suitor through a medley of comic adventures in his desire to satisfy her longings. A policeman is the first to court Nellie's charms by endowing her with the coveted necklace, but failing to obtain a kiss, the minion of the law wants his present back. Billie, the lovesick swain, buys the necklace, and is in turn relieved of it by a member of the light-fingered fraternity. The latter sells and resells his treasure trove, but after a determined hunt by his victims is captured and made to disgorge. How Billie eventually succeeds in winning the girl furnishes a series of laughable incidents, during which the principals keep the action going at top speed." -- *Exhibitors Herald*

"It's as old as the hills, this plot, but it is cleverly done and never drags, the pace is terrific and funny. The park loafer is wonderfully like Billie Ritchie. It is more than useable." -- *Kinematograph Weekly*

Wanted - A Bad Man

Released March 24, 1917. Vim Comedies - General Film Company release. One reel. No copyright registered. Release number not listed.

Probably produced by Kalem. Directed by Harry Millarde [?].

with Bud Duncan, Ethel Teare.

The little town of Hicksville is proud of their new uniformed police force, and when a wire comes that a desperate criminal is at large and that a reward of $500 is offered for his capture, dead or alive, great excitement prevails at the central police station. Bud and Slim, the two new additions to the force, are determined that they will capture the bad man. Their search begins, but Miss Ethel comes between them, and for a time they almost forget that it is their duty to capture, dead or alive, the terrible "Giant George." When the "Giant" comes leisurely walking before them with six-shooters drawn, two brave policemen desert their duty and flee for safety. A riot call is sent in and the town police force finally locate the bad man in his room. When they attempt to arrest him, however, he quietly takes away their revolvers and orders them from his room. Bud and Miss Ethel find a huge mallet, and when the bad man attempts to leave his room it falls from Bud's hands and the bad man falls in his tracks. Bud receives the reward, and peace and quiet once more reign supreme. [MPW]

Filmographies have long listed this title as a Babe Hardy and Ethel Burton film. However, more modern research abilities, such as being able to text search hundreds of newspapers at a time, provide new evidence that this was rather a Kalem throwaway. Pure conjecture would suggest that this was one of the comedies shot during the time Lloyd Hamilton was recovering from a broken leg in 1915. With no "Ham", "Bud" made a number of comedies, some with Rube Miller, to fill out the release schedule and not knowing how long Hamilton would be out may have overstocked their releases.

[no reviews available]

Sally Catches On

Released March 1917. Vim Comedies - General Film Company release. One reel. No copyright registered. Release number not listed.

Directed by unknown. Production credits unknown.

with unknown.

[no synopsis available].

Details don't get much more obscure than with this film: it's listed on the release charts printed in the trade papers, but that is all. While most of the Vim product can at least be traced to the Philadelphia Board of Censors records or have some mention in contemporary newspapers, there are no such appearances by this title.

[no reviews available].

Poor Dad

Released circa late March 1917. Vim Comedies - General Film Company release. One reel. No copyright registered. Release number not listed.

Directed by unknown [Frank Griffin directed *Innocent Dad*]. Production credits unknown.

with John Brennan. [Dot Gould, Gus Erdman appear in *Innocent Dad*].

Arthur and Papa, who are spending a day at the beach become separated; Papa becomes hungry and enters a cafe where he has an argument with a husky waiter which results in a fight and Papa, much frightened, hides under a table. At this moment Arthur enters accompanied by a beautiful girl whom he has become acquainted with through a flirtation on the boardwalk. Arthur and his friend take seats at the table under which Papa is hiding and are served by the husky waiter, Papa thereby getting no chance to escape. In the meantime the girl's sweetheart, who is a villainous looking character, starts in search for her and becomes a raving maniac when he is told she has entered the cafe with Arthur. He draws his gun and dashes into the cafe; Arthur, seeing him coming, quickly disappears. Papa now sees his chance to escape and in making his getaway carries table and all with him. He is seen by the sweetheart, who, thinking he is Arthur, gives chase, taking shots at him. Papa seeks to escape by swimming out in the water and climbing the mast of a sunken ship The lover, foiled, makes use of an old cannon which he finds on the beach and takes shots at Papa, who still clings to the mast. About the third shot the cannon explodes, blowing the sweetheart through the air. After a flight through the clouds he falls on Papa. Both fall off the mast and finish their fight in the water.
[MPW synopsis of Innocent Dad]

John Brennan, who had been Ruth Roland's male lead at Kalem, made his debut at Universal in a Sterling comedy entitled *Innocent Dad* released December 24, 1914. The synopsis for that film refers to his being "poor dad." It is possible that this film (like a number of unreleased Universal titles) was sold to Vim, although this having been previously released would be an unusual exception. Another possibility is that this a Kalem production since others were known to be released under the Vim banner.

"In which John Brennan, one time of the Kalem conpany, makes his debut into the ranks of the Universal. Playing the name part of this comedy, it is poor Dad who gets into a whole lot of trouble when he is the most innocent one of the crowd. There is a grand mix-up in a dining room which is fairly humorous. The picture is a comedy of the average order, nothing startlingly funny, but everything passably humorous." -- *Motion Picture News review of Innocent Da*

When Lena Struck Montana

Released circa late March 1917. Vim Comedies - General Film Company release. One reel. No copyright registered.

Produced by Century Film Company. Directed by Gilbert P. Hamilton. Written by Dot Farley. Photographed by Nick Barrow. Filmed December 10-18, 1915 in Roundup, Montana.

with Dot Farley (*Lena, uncouth servant girl*), George Davenport (*mine superintendent*), Alma Farley (*his mother*), Conrad Wilke, Louis Hathaway, Carl Coverdale, Edith Rhyneta, Iona Davis, Lillian Morris.

Lena is hired by the mother of the mine superintendent and has many mishaps from the moment she gets off the train until she must be unburied from under the coal at the mine. [RS]

Shoot a western comedy in Montana in the dead of winter? Doesn't seem to make a lot of sense, but it was common practice for Producer/Director Gilbert Hamilton and Writer/Star Dot Farley to shoot films in remote places. Farley, who would eventually work at Mack Sennett and later at RKO (playing Edgar Kennedy's mother-in-law) and Hamilton, a former Essanay executive, met while both were working for the American Motion Picture Company. Before heading to Montana the two had shot the similarly titled "Lena Struck New Mexico" in Albuquerque in 1913 where they established the Frontier Motion Picture Company and then the Albuquerque Motion Picture Company. The two had earlier made the Shamrock brand for the St. Louis Motion Picture Company the concept being finding local money dreaming of establishing motion picture production in their town and after a batch of film moving on to the next town. But with the Century Film Company their pattern changed. After filming a handful of films in Roundup they moved production to Los Angeles, ultimately abandoning Montana. The company didn't last too long in Hollywood, ceasing business late in 1916, and with the establishing of the Century Comedies brand around the same time (both shooting at Sunset & Gower) there is often some confusion about the two companies.

When the movie people first came to town there was much fanfare in the *Roundup Record-Tribune* with weekly stories on the film activities. The first announced was supposed to be called *The Outlaw's Christmas* with the second and third titled *Dot's Roundup* (a three reel western) and *Making a Lady of Dot* (a comedy two reeler). Whether any of these were made or released is not known, although since *When Lena Struck Montana* did find a release, albeit via an odd route, the others may have seen the light of day in some fashion. It is known that at some point in the first half of 1916, Hamilton, Farley and company shot the first four reels of another film, *Inherited Passions,* in Montana, finishing the seven reel feature during August 1916 at the Christie Studios in Los Angeles (at that point abandoning Montana, although initially announcing production would happen in both locales). Rumor has it that during the filming, Hamilton also abandoned Farley and the production in order to carry on affair with one of the film's extras. The film was finished with Hamilton and Dot Farley leaving Century at that point. Whether there was anything more than a business relationship between Gilbert Hamilton and Dot Farley is unclear.

When Lena Struck Montana was previewed in Roundup, Montana at the Orpheum Theater on December 30, 1915. A heavy snowfall in the middle of the production gave the second half of the film a much different look than the first segment. Cranking the camera was future Roach director Nick Barrows (credited as Nick Barrow).

Certainly not really a Vim comedy at all, this was the last film released under the Vim brand.

"A whirlwind comedy with a cyclone finish." *The Ottawa Herald (Ottawa, Kansas)*

The Vim Studios. Located at 750 Riverside Drive, Jacksonville, Florida.

JAXON ⊕ FILMS

JAXON FILM CORPORATION

At the beginning of 1917 there was no more Vim, but Amber Star was seeming to hit their stride. However most of their productions, reminiscent of the modus operandi of the parent Eastern Film Corporation, sat in the can but with a few sneaking out as, ironically, Vim Comedies. Jerold T. Hevener took over directing the Billy Ruge and Kate Price films with Will Louis defecting to the United States Motion Picture Co. shooting Black Diamond Comedies over at the old Kalem studio (that company with Louis would return to their home base of Wilke-Barre, Pennsylvania in March). Frank Tichenor went back up north and Jim Carelton, a former Vim cameraman, became the studio manager in Jacksonville.

On January 19, 1917 the local papers reported that Walter Stull was suffering from la grippe (also known as influenza, a sickness that a year later would kill tens of millions). Some time in mid-February, Kate Price left Jacksonville leaving Billy Ruge to carry on making comedies by himself, and the handful of Finn & Haddie comedies with a new partner Walter Stahl. With Kate Price's departure, the use of "Plump & Runt" as a series name disappeared and the umbrella title of Sparkle Comedies took hold. This allowed for Billy Ruge's solo work, a faux Plump & Runt, the Finn and Haddie series, and some old Pelican Comedies to have a brand under which they would be released.

Things began to wind down for Amber Star in Jacksonville in the Spring of 1917. Jerold T. Hevener finished his contract with the studio on April 2nd and sought employment elsewhere. The *Florida Metropolis* reported that Billy Ruge and his company would open the Amber Star studio in Providence on May 1st, noting it was the former Eastern Film Corporation studio (although in reality it remained that).

After completing their first (and only) two reel comedy in late April 1917, the Jaxon Film Corporation closed the studio in Jacksonville and headed north. Boarding the S.S. Apache on May 2, in addition to Bobby Burns and Walter Stull, the trade papers reported that Manager Frank E. Samuels, Jack Dale, Bill Hopkins, Bill Ferguson, Dorothy Cherry, Jennie Nelson, cameraman Leland Coutant, Betty Berlin, Tom Regan, cameraman Howard Green (who had been turning the crank on the Billy Ruge starrers); Margaret Drum, Spook Hanson, Mabel Best, Boots Renfro, Ora Fletcher, Lillian Benjamin, Helen Gilmore, Margaret Gilmore, Dad Bates, and Bobby Ulmer comprised the contingent headed for a new studio home (James Renfro was announced as departing with the troupe; instead he stayed behind and went to work over at the old Vim lot with Harry Myers and Rosemary Theby). Upon arriving in New York City the company would then board a train for their final destination of Providence, Rhode Island.

Although not reported in the main press release regarding the move, Edna Reynolds (accompanying her husband Spook Hanson) and Billy Ruge were also known to have traveled to Providence. Perhaps the plans Amber Star had for Ruge influenced their decision to not include him in the publicity. Upon arrival in

Providence, Ruge was told that his services were no longer required. Ruge had been a local celebrity in Jacksonville and certainly could have found work there had he known his status with Amber Star. With Pokes & Jabbs nearly since the beginning, Ruge had well served the Wizard/Vim/Jaxon brands as a starring comedian and a supporting player; certainly he deserved a better ending than the one Tichenor and associates gave him. The Sparkle Comedies would continue to feature Ruge via the backlog of films he made in Jacksonville, as well as with another batch of Pelican Comedies made in 1915.

When Eastern began to market the new comedies in March 1917 they changed the name of the production company from Amber Star to Jaxon. The name change was somewhat ironic in that soon after the company left Jacksonville for what would be the last time. Had the Pokes & Jabbs unit stayed intact it is likely they would have gone back to Jacksonville to avoid a Rhode Island winter, but fate had another plan.

Roger William Park. Providence, Rhode Island.

After sitting around for a few weeks, Burns, Stull and company finally got to shoot their first comedy in Providence in late April. There had been some concern that the inactivity signaled a waning interest on Eastern's part and some players departed for seemingly more secure work in New York. However, filming did resume and some of the best Pokes and Jabbs comedies were made in Providence.

Using the Eastern studio that sat next to Roger Williams Park, the Rhode Island version of Pokes and Jabbs didn't look all that different than the Florida-produced films, albeit minus a palm tree or two. The romps in Roger Williams Park looked much like those taken in Riverside Park, and in the late 'teens middle class neighborhood streets lined with wood-frame houses looked much alike.

At 3:00 a.m. on August 23, 1917 a fire broke out in the main building of the studio and there was serious damage. A statement from Eastern remarked that by 3:00 p.m. the next day production was resumed, but that likely was Frank Tichenor putting on a smile when the reality was much different. The damage and loss of completed films (apparently footage shot for the government and not Jaxon product) put Eastern on unsure ground. It is unclear if Eastern resumed the filming of the Jaxon Comedies after the fire, or if they did for how long. All indications are that by the end of the year the only production in progress was the serial "A Daughter of Uncle Sam" that featured a production unit totally unrelated to the comedies that had been made. Along with the fire, another factor that may have spelled the end for Pokes & Jabbs was tragedy in Bobby Burns' personal life. His wife,, Violet, passed away in Providence on October 3, 1917 and was buried a few days later in Philadelphia. Certainly for a time Burns just didn't have the heart to be funny, and Stull, back home for the funeral, just decided to stay there and leave movies behind. Whatever the true circumstances that killed Pokes and Jabbs, and despite titles that would be released throughout 1918, the acrobat and the man in plaid ceased to be a comedy team sometime in the Fall of 1917.

JAXON COMEDIES

Are Actors People?

Released June 22, 1917. Jaxon Comedies (series No. 1, No.1) - General Film Company release. One reel. No copyright registered.

Produced by Frank Tichenor. Directed by Bobby Burns and Walter Stull. Filmed circa late May 1917 at the Eastern Film Corporation studios in Providence, Rhode Island.

With Bobby Burns (*Pokes*), Walter Stull (*Jabs*).

[no synopsis available].

The first Pokes and Jabbs made in Rhode Island. With so many Jacksonville produced Pokes & Jabbs comedies in the can, why Jaxon decided to release this comedy first is a mystery. Perhaps it was to show off their home studio, or for no particular reason at all; odd releasing practices were nothing new to parent company Eastern Film Corporation. The July 1, 1917, *New York Tribune* published a story about the Providence studio and mentioned this film, "The first of the new series of 'Pokes and Jabs' films that have been issued by the Jaxon Film Corporation bears the title of *Are Actors People?* The president was showing some Newport swells around the Providence studios when the picture was being taken. Water was squirted, bricks were thrown and all the other things were done that go to make a comedy film. 'Goodness!' exclaimed one of the slumming party, 'Are those people human?' Hence the paraphrase of Mrs. Alice Duer Miller in the title."

"Here a curious question is raised. Are they? Who dare answer? See the picture." -- *General Film Company advertisement.*

"Pokes and Jabs return after a short absence to give us a glimpse of a laughable comedy entitled 'Are Actors People?' Decidedly good." -- *Fairmont West Virginian*

A Ride For Life

Released circa June 1917. Jaxon Comedies (series No. 1, No.2) - General Film Company release. One reel. No copyright registered.

Produced by Frank Tichenor. Directed by Bobby Burns and Walter Stull. Possibly made circa October 1916 at the Vim studios in Jacksonville, Florida.

With Bobby Burns (Pokes), Walter Stull (Jabs), Ethel Burton [?].

Pokes and Jabs work in a grocery store. Jabs is in the delivery system and practices trick riding on his bike. About a year later Pokes, with Ethel, the belle of the town, takes in the sights of a traveling street fair. One show features "Daredevil Jabs," and Ethel recognizes her old suitor as the daredevil trick rider. Pokes is jealous of the acclaim won by the feats of his rival, and undertakes to duplicate anything done by Jabs. His attempt at a "daredevil dive" on the wheel is made unhappy by Jabs who cuts the guy wires of the platform. After a tumble Pokes tries it again, gritting his teeth at the sight of Ethel spooning with Jabs. He mounts the wheel and starts down the steep runway to terra firma. He goes at such a velocity that he plunges far over the tank of water set to receive him, and his bicycle commences to act like an aeroplane. He soars over fields, woods and towns. The last seen of him is far out at sea pedaling zealously into the horizon. [MPW]

The mention of a character named Ethel may indicate that this film was one of the Amber Star comedies made at the Vim studios just prior to the big split between Vim and Amber Star. If the Ethel in the film is Ethel Burton then that would be the case since she did not make any Pokes & Jabbs comedies after Burns & Stull left the studio on Riverside Avenue.

"There's a convulsion in every scene of this one, and the climax shows Pokes pedaling on a bike madly out to sea." -- *General Film Company advertisement.*

Military Madness

Released June 22, 1917. Jaxon Comedies (series No. 1, No.3) - General Film Company release. One reel. No copyright registered.

Produced by Frank Tichenor. Directed by Bobby Burns and Walter Stull. Filmed in Providence, Rhode Island.

With Bobby Burns (*Pokes*), Walter Stull (*Jabs*).

Pokes conducts a clothing store but business is dull, Jabs comes by. Showing Pokes the war news in the day's paper, Jabs suggests he (Pokes) lay in a profitable stock of munitions. Pokes is further inspired by conscripts full of the war spirit coming to him to ask for uniforms. He lays in a supply and business becomes brisk. Suddenly Pokes is called to the front as their commanding officer. In many thrilling skirmishes at the front Pokes is singled out by the enemy. A new invention, a chasing bomb overtakes Pokes, and blows him into the enemy's camp where he fights a hand to hand battle with the champion of the foe. His troops, witnessing the conflict from afar, decide to rescue him. A lasso is thrown to snare the foe, but Pokes is caught instead and dragged over rock and rill—until he awakes and finds Jabs pulling his necktie to rouse him to another war bulletin. Pokes, after his dream, is through with war, and decides that Sherman was right. [MPW]

"Pokes & Jabs do well in this comedy sketch which has plenty of action throughout."
-- *Fairmont West Virginian*

The Rest Cure

Released circa July 1917. Jaxon Comedies (series No. 1, No. 4) - General Film Company release. One reel. No copyright registered.

Produced by Frank Tichenor. Directed by Bobby Burns and Walter Stull.

With Bobby Burns (*Pokes*), Walter Stull (*Jabs*).

Pokes is weary, worn and tired and goes to a doctor. The patients in the doctor's office do not add at all to Pokes' joy. The doctor is busy—not with a patient, but a sweetheart. Pokes interrupts, and for this is given a strenuous examination, and after paying the five dollars fee has to console himself with the advice that he needs a complete rest. The first haven of rest tried by Pokes is home, but as usual when one seeks peace and quiet, the world seems in opposition. Wifey is sewing on the machine. Daughter is entertaining the count in the parlor where he is showing his operatic powers. Pokes tries the roof, but a summer shower drives him in. There the din continues, and Pokes rushes from the house. After much wandering he arrives at the Hideaway Inn, kept by Jabs. Here he is certain of finding rest and quiet. Jabs and the bellboy are asleep. Pokes wakes them and finds there are no vacant rooms. As he is about to depart, Jabs tells him he can have a cot in a quiet hallway for the same price as one of his best rooms, and Pokes accepts and is conducted to the hall. He soon falls asleep, but the hotel turns out to be a sanitarium, and the insomnia patients make Pokes' existence a very Hades. Finally, in desperation, he spies a fire escape under which is a sign, "In case of fire grab ball, jump out window and bounce to safety." Pokes grabs the ball and makes the leap and sinks in the ground up to his neck. With a disgusted look at the contrivance he murmurs that he "Thought the darn thing wouldn't work," and placing it under his head for a pillow, succeeds in sleeping the rest of the night in complete comfort on the cold ground. [MPW]

"The main accomplishment recorded here is a gink getting completely cured of rest." --*General Film Company advertisement.*

The Pearls of Pauline

Released circa July 1917. Jaxon Comedies (series No. 1, No.5) -General Film Company release. One reel. No copyright registered. Working title: *Anything, Any Time, Any Place.*

Produced by Frank Tichenor. Directed by Bobby Burns and Walter Stull. Filmed January 28, 1917 near Garrick Studios in Jacksonville, Florida.

With Bobby Burns (*Pokes*), Walter Stull (*Jabs*), Mack Richards.

Pokes is quite a pool shark, and at the club gives a demonstration of his skill to the amazement of the other members. Jabs, the newly appointed Chief of Police, puts his wife and two daughters into an auto and starts them off on a motoring tour. Before going Mrs. Jabs leaves her valuable pearl necklace with her husband for safe keeping. During the pool game, Billy Berlin, one of the members, rushes in with a copy of the daily paper and shows the members, including Pokes, the defy the new chief has published for the benefit of honest people and the downfall of the crooks. Pokes takes it as a joke, and discounts the ability of Jabs to do what he has promised. Pokes writes Jabs a note stating that he can get anything, any time, any place. Jabs goes at once to the club, where he meets Pokes. Producing the pearl necklace, Jabs wagers Pokes that he will place the necklace in a certain house, and defies Pokes to find it, and bring it to the club. The necklace is placed, and Pokes starts out to get it. After thrilling experience and hair breadth escapes Pokes is cornered in the cellar of the house by the chief and a squad of officers. They search him, but fail to find the necklace. Pokes, with a smile, leads the chief back to the club followed by the others. There Pokes takes off a wig, which no one knew he

wore, produces the necklace, and claims the reward. But to Pokes surprise the "chief" removes a false mustache, and remarks calmly, "I am not Jabs." Pokes, nonplussed, tries to sneak away when Jabs appears from behind a chair, where he has watched the whole affair, and meet Pokes. The laugh is on Pokes, and while he stands there ashamed and thinking that honesty is the best policy. Jabs, with the necklace in his hand, gives him the laugh. A great metamorphosis takes place, which causes Jabs to remark, "Darwin was right." [MPW]

"A Jaxon special comedy featuring those funny acrobatic comedians Pokes & Jabs in a series of hazardous adventures that will sure set you laughing." -- *Lebanon Daily Reporter (Indiana)*

"The author takes the name of a late popular series and makes a crackerjack comedy for Pokes and Jabbs to caper about in. Lots of amusement." -- *Fairmont West Virginian*

Ploughing the Clouds

Released June 22, 1917. Jaxon Comedies (series No. 1, No. 6) -General Film Company release. One reel. No copyright registered.

Produced by Frank Tichenor. Directed by Bobby Burns and Walter Stull.

With Bobby Burns (*Pokes*), Walter Stull (*Jabs*), Jennie Nelson (*Jennie*), Edna Reynolds.

Jabs is an aviation instructor. Pokes loves fluffy haired Jennie Buchdough. Her parents think Pokes is just about right. She does not return his affection. Life holds no further charms and he seeks the river but finds the water too cold. He decides to join the army and die on the battlefield. That will melt her heart. But the physical examination is too strenuous. He finally arrives in front of Jabs aviation field, and Jabs takes him for a flight. While they are in the air Jennie and her parents arrive at the field. When the aeroplane lands Pokes is too wobbly to leave the machine. Jabs hurries to Jennie's side and she gives him a rose and her photograph. He tells her of his new pupil, does not mention Pokes' name, and says, "Watch me loop the loop." He and Pokes ascend. Jabs loops the loop and does other stunts. Pokes says he'd rather get out and walk. Jabs takes Jennie's photo and kisses it. Pokes sees it and learns Jabs is his rival. He grabs Jabs and they fight Jabs is thrown out and lands at Jennie's feet unhurt. Pokes has a terrible time alone. They beg Jabs to save him. Jabs agrees, loads the aero-torpedo cannon and shoots. The machine is blown to atoms, but Pokes floats gracefully down with his umbrella, through the skylight into the laboratory. The rest run out but Jennie remains. Pokes recognizes her and folding her in his arms remarks, "Jabs is a good shot but I win the prize." [MPW]

"A Pokes and Jabs comedy is offered as the fun maker. It is called *Ploughing the Clouds* and presents the favorite actors in a number of funny situations and startling stunts." -- *Fairmont West Virginian*

Counting 'Em Up

Released circa July 1917. Jaxon Comedies (series No. 2, No. 1) - General Film Company release. One reel. No copyright registered.

Produced by Frank Tichenor. Directed by Bobby Burns and Walter Stull.

With Bobby Burns (*Pokes*), Walter Stull (*Jabs*).

Pokes believes himself an artist on the cornet, but the Jabs family across the hall, like the rest of the neighbors, do not share this opinion. They are all annoyed at the noise he makes and finally Jabs tells his wife that he will stop it by getting Pokes out of the house. He finds some difficulty in doing so, however, as Mrs. Pokes keeps a watchful eye on her spouse. He finally succeeds by arresting Pokes, and once out of the house they start out for a good time, which they surely have, getting into all sorts of scrapes as their imagination gets the better of them. They finally arrive home and tell a well connected story, only to be thrown out of the window by their enraged wives. They are not hurt, but the sudden stop at the bottom lands them among the stars, and while Jabs bemoans his fate, Pokes is leisurely "counting 'em up." [MPW]

"One of those funny Jaxon comedies featuring the somewhat different comedians Pokes and Jabs is a whirlwind laugh of acrobatic stunts that will keep you busy counting 'em up." -- *Lebanon Daily Reporter (Indiana)*

The Baggage Man

Released circa August 1917. Jaxon Comedies (series No. 2, No. 2) - General Film Company release. One reel. No copyright registered.

Produced by Frank Tichenor. Directed by Bobby Burns and Walter Stull.

With Bobby Burns (*Pokes*), Walter Stull (*Jabs*).

Pokes and Jabs get work on a railroad, Jabs as chief baggage smasher and Pokes as assistant. Pokes does all the work, while Jabs gets the tips and honors. A messenger from a bank with a million dollars in his grip arrives at the station, followed by Lanky Luke, a crook, and also by a female detective to see that he is not molested. The detective's and messenger's grips get mixed, and when the detective goes to the waiting room to doll up she finds she has the wrong grip. Meanwhile the crook, having knocked out the messenger and taken possession of the grip which he thinks contains the million, is waiting for the train, when the detective accosts him. After a fight, the detective is overpowered and placed on the railroad track. The train is approaching when Jabs, seeing the form on the track, summons Pokes to the rescue. Pokes returns to the station with the fainting female in his arms and is met by Jabs, who relieves him of his burden

and carries her into the station where he receives the hearty congratulations and applause of the crowd. Pokes gets down behind the ticket rail and murmurs: "What's the use of being a hero, anyway?" [MPW]

"Pokes and Jabbs the favorite comedians pull off some very funny stunts in this reel." – *Fairmont West Virginian*

Getting the Coin

Released circa August 1917. Jaxon Comedies (series No. 2, No.3) - General Film Company release. One reel. No copyright registered.

Produced by Frank Tichenor. Directed by Bobby Burns and Walter Stull.

With Bobby Burns (*Pokes*), Walter Stull (*Jabs*).

Pokes and Jabs are forcibly ejected from the Family Vaudeville theater after failing to make good, and find they have between them just eight cents. Jabs discovers a paid-up accident insurance policy in one of his pockets, and in order to collect tries in vain to get injured. Finally Pokes takes a chance. Jabs beats him with a coupling pin, swathes him in bandages, and carries him to the insurance office. He learns that the policy expired two weeks before. Pokes is badly damaged, and has to be taken to a hospital. Prof. Bakem has a theory that by the application of intense heat inanimate bodies may be restored to life. He yearns for a subject to prove it. When the professor remarks that the man who secures him a subject shall claim the hand of his daughter, Percy starts on a hunt. He meets Jabs in front of the hospital, a bargain is struck, and they return to the ward for Pokes, but Pokes refuses to be baked. After a chase, Pokes jumps through a window and lands in the professor's baking pan, and is shoved into the oven. The heat is applied, but the theory is a failure, and the oven explodes. Pokes, after an aerial flight, lands beside Jabs, who is counting the coin Percy has paid him. They divide the money. [MPW]

"The comedy selected today to run with 'Broadway Jones' is 'Getting the Coin' and it is one with a whole lot of fun and action." -- *Altoona Tribune (Altoona, Pennsylvania)*

Tough Luck

Released week of August 11, 1917. Jaxon Comedies (series No. 2, No. 4) - General Film Company release. One reel. No copyright registered.

Produced by Frank Tichenor. Directed by Bobby Burns and Walter Stull.

With Bobby Burns (*Pokes*), Walter Stull (*Jabs*).

Pokes and Jabs are behind with their board and are held up by the boarding house keeper at the point of a pistol. Jabs tells her that they have money hidden in their room and she agrees to wait till they go up and get it. Mrs. Ham goes to market and returns just in time to catch the delinquent about to skip. Jabs escapes, but Pokes is caught by the hair of his head and made to work out the double board bill as cook, waiter and scrub woman. Pokes tries to escape one night, but Mrs. Ham hears the commotion and, mistaking it for burglars, notifies the police. The cop arrives just as Pokes drops out of the window. They grapple and in the scuffle the cop loses his helmet, revealing Jabs. Mrs. Ham from the window recognizes the pair and is furious. Looking about for a weapon of vengeance she seizes the packed trunk and hurls it at them. It hits Pokes in the head. Jabs does his duty and arrests Pokes, who appears in court the following morning a wiser and smaller man. [M & MPW]

"Tough Luck is a Pokes and Jabs comedy with a laugh in every movement." -- *Fairmont West Virginian*

Love Letters

Released circa August 1917. Jaxon Comedies (series No. 2, No.5) - General Film Company release. One reel. No copyright registered.

Produced by Frank Tichenor. Directed by Bobby Burns and Walter Stull.

With Bobby Burns (*Pokes*), Walter Stull (*Jabs*).

[no synopsis available].

Originally *Jolly Tars* was scheduled to be released as part of series number 2 but was withheld and replaced with this title.

[no reviews available]

Play Ball

Released circa September 1917. Jaxon Comedies (series No. 2, No. 6) - General Film Company release. One reel. No copyright registered.

Produced by Frank Tichenor. Directed by Bobby Burns and Walter Stull.

With Bobby Burns (*Pokes*), Walter Stull (*Jabs*), Edna Reynolds.

Pokes and Jabs, clerks in the brokerage office of Adam Fossil, are both smitten with the charms of Edna, the stenographer. Fossil also indulges in an occasional flirtation with her. The baseball season is about to begin and the enthusiasm of Pokes and Jabs is aroused to concert pitch by announcements of the opening game. Old Fossil catches them playing an imaginary game and fires Jabs and sets Pokes to work posting the ledger. Pokes resorts to a little liquid refreshment to brighten his spirits. Edna has a headache and is excused for the afternoon. Pokes writes himself a letter stating his grandma is seriously ill, and is also excused; he meets Edna and they go to the ball game. In the midst of an exciting play Edna discovers the boss is directly behind them, and Pokes sneaks off to another section. Meantime Jabs has entered into a plot with Mill Blutch to rob Fossil's safe. The game is at its height. The last inning score tie and two men out, three men on bases, when the heaviest hitter has an argument with the umpire and is ordered out of the game. Pokes offers to take his place and hits the first ball so hard that it flies into Fossil's window, hitting Jabs on the head just as he has lit the fuse to blow up the safe. Pokes scores a home run and the stands go wild with delight. The safe explodes and the noise arouses Pokes from his slumber. Rushing through the offices, he finds everything going on as usual. Returning to the counting room he throws the bottle of rye out the window, repeating to himself, "never again." [MPW]

[no reviews available]

Speed Demons

Released September 14, 1917. Jaxon Comedies (series No. 3, No.1) - General Film Company release. One reel. No copyright registered.

Produced by Frank Tichenor. Directed by Bobby Burns and Walter Stull. Filmed July 21, 1917 at Narraganett Park in Cranston, Rhode Island.

With Bobby Burns (*Pokes*), Walter Stull (*Jabs*), Ralph DePalma, Barney Oldfield.

Jabs, who is suffering from an attack of speeditis, is hustled off to Dr. Dippy's sanitarium, while Pokes, another auto enthusiast, wanders at large without a car. On the day of the world's championship auto race between Oldfield and DePalma, Jabs escapes and follows the crowds to the race. Pokes goes also and invites himself to ride in Lotta Wealth's speedster, but is ejected. Just then Jabs happens along and with his aid Pokes gains admittance to the

race track, but Jabs is left outside. Seeing the guards on his trail he beats it back to the sanitarium. The race takes place and after many incidents Oldfield wins. Lotta Wealth remarks that she could beat Oldfield's record. Pokes doubts it, so off they went, through fences, over hills, through valleys and over bridges, until they finally run through an open draw. As they are swimming for shore Pokes remarks to Lotta, "I knew when we started you couldn't do it," but her reply is lost in the noise of the waves. [MPW]

Filmed during the Ralph DePalma – Barney Oldfield automobile race which took place July 21, 1917 with several Jaxon cameras capturing the action. A dozen cut-ins of the footage was used in *Speed Demons*. Three races took place at the Narragnsett Speedway the day the Jaxon crew was there to capture the action. Barney Oldfield driving *The Gold Bug* took the 25 mile and 10 mile races while Ralph DePalma in the *Packard 12* won the 15 mile race. Oldfield completed the 10 mile race in 8 minutes and 14 seconds breaking the course record of 9 minutes and two seconds set in 1915 by Eddie Rickenbacher. That equates to the unbelievable-for-its-time speed of 72 mph.

The speedway was located in Narragansett Park in the town of Cranston, Rhode Island which was located just a few miles south of Providence. The site of the speedway was part of the Rhode Island State Fairgrounds, and originally was a dirt oval track where not only the first oval track car race was held in 1896 but where horses raced including the great Dan Patch. When paved in 1915, and possessing 20 degree bank turns the one mile oval become the first super speedway to be built predating even the famous Indianapolis Raceway.

"Another interesting subject on the screen is a Pokes and Jabs Comedy featuring the Jaxon's favorite comedians, Burns and Stull, in a screaming comedy entitled 'Speed Demons.'" -- *Fairmont West Virginian*

The Collectors

Released circa September 1917. Jaxon Comedies (series No. 3, No. 2) - General Film Company release. One reel. No copyright registered.

Produced by Frank Tichenor. Directed by Bobby Burns and Walter Stull.

With Bobby Burns (*Pokes*), Walter Stull (*Jabs*).

Jabs runs a female gymnasium and his motto is "Get all the trust you can and pay no one." His landlord notifies him that if he does not pay the back rent it will be collected by force. Numerous collectors try and fail. Pokes finally gets the job and starts out to collect. Whether it is his winning ways, his dogged persistence or his bullet proof armor that caused his success is unknown, but the landlord is telephoned for and when he arrives at the gymnasium he finds Pokes calmly sitting on Jabs' chest, with Jabs' sweetheart on his lap counting the roll to see if it will cover the amount owed. [M & MPW]

"Pokes and Jabs, the inimitable funmakers, will be seen in their latest comedy scream *The Collectors* and it is a roar from beginning to end." -- *Wilmington Morning Star*

Jolly Tars

Released circa September 1917. Jaxon Comedies (series No. 3, No.3) - General Film Company release. One reel. No copyright registered.

Produced by Frank Tichenor for Amber Star Films Corporation. Directed by Bobby Burns and Walter Stull. Filmed December 5 -9, 1916 at the Duval County Fair in Jacksonville, Florida.

With Bobby Burns (*Pokes*), Walter Stull (*Jabs*), Tom Regan (*grapefruit stand vendor*), Edna Reynolds (*captain's wife*).

Pokes and Jabs ship with Captain Bates as first-class seamen. When the captain wants his bearings they are both asleep but are soon aroused. Up aloft Pokes is amazed at the sights that greet his eye through the telescope. Jabs takes the telescope and wonderful things appear, among them some dancing girls at the county fair. They decide to take French leave, and are soon at the fair. The captain's wife and two daughters are there also, and while the girls accompany their gentlemen friends about the grounds, mother decides to have her palm read. In her haste she leaves the handbag on the bench and Pokes and Jabs discover it, and their joy is supreme when they find in it a roll of bills. They proceed to the fair, and Pokes gives a wonderful exhibition of archery. Mother and the girls witness the arrow shooting and recognize the handbag. Pokes takes to his heels, and just as Jabs is about to be taken off by a policeman the wild animals break loose. Jabs is singled out by one of them and a race for life begins, ending at the of the ship. Jabs is about to give up when he gets the surprise of his life. "Did the bear eat Pokes or did Pokes eat the bear?" [MPW]

The real charm of *Jolly Tars* are the views of the Duval County Fairgrounds that the otherwise nonsensical running about affords. There are pretty girls and a missing handbag but all are excuses for the various vignettes that take place between the chasing around. Towards the end of the film, Pokes accidentally goes into the bear's cage and is apparently eaten. This conveniently allows for the final chase with the entire cast running from the bear to have Bobby Burns missing. Any guesses who is in the bear costume?

The ship Pokes & Jabbs leave for their day at the fair was the S.S. Arapahoe IV of the Clyde Steamship Company that regularly ran between Florida and New York City. The original S.S. Arapahoe was, in 1909, the first ship to send the newly developed S.O.S. distress signal over the wireless. For those keeping score: the ship had lost its power and was drifting off Cape Hatteras, North Carolina but due to the S.O.S. signal was rescued 36 hours later.

[No reviews available]

Wild Injuns

Released circa September 1917. Jaxon Comedies (series No. 3, No.4) - General Film Company release. One reel. No copyright registered.

Produced by Frank Tichenor. Directed by Bobby Burns and Walter Stull.

With Bobby Burns (*Pokes*), Walter Stull (*Jabs*).

Mrs. Gotrox, an enthusiast over the civilization of the Indian, has contributed liberally toward their education, and after the graduation exercises at the agency the commissioner decides to send two chiefs, "Rolling Thunder" and "Tossing Ball," to thank her in person. Mrs. Gotrox plans a novel reception for them. All the decorations are to be Indian, and the guests are to wear Indian costumes. Pokes and Jabs are seated on a freight car enjoying their scant morning repast, when the Indians arrive and ask to be directed to the Gotrox mansion. Pokes and Jabs, mistaking their actions for threats, take to their heels, followed by the two Indians. Finally they find two coupling pins, and when the Indians come up they quickly overpower them. Finding the introductions to Mrs. Gotrox, they decide to become Indians. At least long enough to satisfy the cravings of the inner man. The reception is on full blast when Pokes and Jabs arrive. As a bit of realism, Jabs proceeds to scalp the colored butler. Pokes, not to be outdone, drains the punch bowl and chases the guests and ends up scalping his hostess, exposing her bald head to the company. The two chiefs, hearing the woman scream, rush in. A wild fight follows, and Pokes and Jabs flee, followed by the trusty arrows of the Indians. [MPW]

"Pokes and Jabs masquerade as redmen in this one-reel farce, and do their usual lively stunts." –*Moving Picture World*

Deviled Crabs

Released circa October 1917. Jaxon Comedies (series No. 3, No.5) - General Film Company release. One reel. No copyright registered.

Produced by Frank Tichenor. Directed by Bobby Burns and Walter Stull. Filmed along Wilton Avenue, in Roger Williams Park and at the Eastern Film Corporation studios in Providence, Rhode Island.

With Bobby Burns (*Pokes*), Walter Stull (*Jabs*), Edna Reynolds (*Mrs. Pokes*), Jennie Nelson (*the flirt*).

Pokes, a hod-carrier, has been discharged by Jabs, the contractor, and on his way home he stops at the saloon to drown his sorrows and partakes freely of devilled crabs and beer. When he arrives home the wife seats him before the fire to rest while she prepares supper. Strange sights appear to Pokes. The devil, with Jabs' face, comes out of the fireplace and Pokes signs a bond selling himself to Satan for a rousing good time. His clothes immediately change and money rains on him. Pokes has a great time but the devil is always at his elbow. Finally, he decides to rid himself of Satan or Jabs, whichever it is, and hides under the haystack, but it immediately catches fire and Pokes wakes with a wild cry to find that he has poked his feet into the blazing fire. His wife puts out the flames and says, "Come to supper, we have nice devilled crabs." Pokes' reply is left to the imagination, but there are a lot of broken dishes in the yard the next morning. [MPW]

The drunk Pokes' journey home from the bar is filmed cleverly with the tilting and spinning of the camera giving the audience the full drunk effect. To Burns' credit, his slipping around and apparent losing battle with gravity are perfectly timed with the camera tilts. However, while Burns does fine in the film it is perhaps Walter Stull's best turn as Jabbs. Dressed as the Devil, it is Stull not Burns that is instigating most of the action, and while it is still Burns who does the acrobatics, the sheer joy Stull takes in playing the king of the underworld makes the film.

"Here we have a theme, supposedly humorous, which is based on the dire results of alcohol and dyspepsia caused by unwholesome hankering after devilled crabs. The humour is of the trick order, and mainly consists of the efforts to get safely home of

an indigestion haunted labourer. Pokes gets 'fired' off his job as a hod-carrier. Proceeding homeward, he partakes of liquid nourishment and a free lunch of 'devilled crabs.' Anon the universe spins round him, and everything conspires to get him home in a state which is not at all to the liking of his better-half. He sleeps be the fire, and the devil comes, even as he did to Faust in the long ago, and Pokes signs on for Hades in consideration of receiving

one 'good time.' His week-a-day attire becomes the evening dress of the 'swell,' and under Satanic guidance he sets out for sylvan dells where elfs and beauteous fairies rend his amatory heart. 'Give me one my size,' he pleads, and his plea is answered, but when he stoops to steal a kiss from the chaste red lips, lo! the damsel dissolves and in her place the devil leers at him. Time for payment comes, flames and sulphur fill the air, and Pokes wakes to find his feet on fire and his good wife announcing 'devilled crabs' for supper. Poor fare—the picture, not the 'crabs'—and we seem to be back in the long-ago days of kinematography when watching it. The trick work is as neat and clever as it was fifteen years ago, but the excellent photography might have been used to 'shoot' a more meritorious subject." -- *Kinematograph Weekly*

"Pokes imbibes freely and consumes several devilled crabs. He has a fantastic dream in which Jabs appears as the devil and shows him a good time in exchange for his soul. One of the best numbers in which these comedians have appeared." -- *Moving Picture World*

The Triple Cross

Released circa October 1917. Jaxon Comedies (series No. 3, No.6) - General Film Company release. One reel. No copyright registered.

Produced by Frank Tichenor. Directed by Bobby Burns and Walter Stull.

With Bobby Burns (*Pokes*), Walter Stull (*Jabs*), Jennie Nelson [?].

Percy Hitch, having been ejected from the house by the father of the girl he loves, goes to a den of crooks and solicits their aid. The next day at the breakfast table Mr. Gold receives a blackhand letter, and the whole family become panic-stricken. Two detectives, Pokes and Jabs, are summoned, and they both fall in love with Jennie, the daughter, and it becomes a three-way fight between Pokes, Jabs, and Percy. Pokes wins and the engagement is announced. The wedding day arrives, and when the parson says, "If anyone knows any reason why this couple should not wed, etc.," a tall, stout woman, with nine children, rushes in and throws herself on Pokes' breast, while the children cry, "Pop ! O, Pop !" Unable to explain, Pokes beats it, followed by the children, and when all is quiet the woman lifts her veil, disclosing Jabs, who chuckles to himself, "If I can't win her, you shall not have her either." [MPW]

"Pokes and Jabs are detectives. Both fall in love with the same girl. Pokes' suit is favored and Jabs, in order to prevent the wedding, masquerades as his wife, appearing on the scene with a number of children. An ordinary number, involving considerable slapstick work and a band of ruffians." -- *Moving Picture World*

From Bad to Worse

Released circa October 1917. Jaxon Comedies (series No. 4, No.1) - General Film Company release. One reel. No copyright registered.

Produced by Frank Tichenor. Directed by Bobby Burns and Walter Stull.

With Bobby Burns (*Pokes*), Walter Stull (*Jabs*), Jennie Nelson [?].

Pokes and Jabs, having served their sentence at hard labor, are discharged. Pokes resolves to go straight, while Jabs returns to his crooked associates. Pokes, in order to qualify for a position open to a married man, seeks a wife at a matrimonial agency. There is only one aspirant to double harness available at the time, Jennie, a servant at the prison warden's home, but she is so homely that Pokes loses his nerve and flees. Next he advertises for a wife and Jennie, seeing the ad, answers it, enclosing a photograph of the warden's wife. Pokes starts out for his intended bride. Meanwhile Jabs and his gang have framed up a big job and when Pokes arrives at the warden's house in search of his future wife, he runs into Jabs. Jabs congratulates Pokes on his return to the crooked path and has him hold the bag while he collects the loot. At this moment the warden returns and bursts in upon them, and as a "safety first" precaution, they dive through the window, followed by the warden's bullets. They take refuge in an old barn which proves to be a den of bomb throwers, who are just starting out on an expedition. They are forced to carry the bombs to the house of the intended victim, who proves to be the warden. Refusal being useless, they plant the bomb and are getting away when the warden appears at the window and throws the bomb after them. Pokes and Jabs, in their frantic effort to escape, go straight back to the anarchists' den. The bomb follows and explodes. After an aerial ascension and a long drop Pokes and Jabs regain their senses in the same warden's office who informs them they are just in time to try out the new gallows. [MPW]

"Pokes advertises for a wife. The jail warden's housemaid sends him a photo of the warden's wife as being her own, so Pokes makes love to the wrong party. Jabs is a burglar. They are chased by the warden, land in an anarchists' den, and are finally blown up by a bomb which lands them back in jail where they started. The story involves slapstick, a chase by a bomb and acrobatic work." -- *Moving Picture World*

A Day Off

Released circa October 1917. Jaxon Comedies (series No. 4, No.2) - General Film Company release. One reel. No copyright registered.

Produced by Frank Tichenor. Directed by Bobby Burns and Walter Stull.

With Bobby Burns (*Pokes*), Walter Stull (*Jabs*).

Pokes, man of all work, is obliged by his wife to do the housecleaning. Looking out the window he sees a couple of girls and proceeds to flirt with them. They invite him out, but his wife catches him and promptly brings him back. Jabs, an intruder, climbs up a ladder and into the room where Pokes is at work. Pokes immediately knocks him out and escapes down the ladder, but just misses the girl, so decides to indulge in a revel in the park. This he proceeds to do, getting in wrong, however, and is obliged to beat a hasty retreat up the ladder heading to the bedroom. Meantime Jabs has revived and is chasing Mrs. Pokes over the house when Pokes enters through the window, takes in the situation, knocks Jabs out, tossing him out the window and into the arms of a passing policeman, while Mrs. Pokes beams upon her husband and declare him to be a hero. [MPW]

"When Pokes and Jabbs come, the blues go. This reel is particularly well adapted to these laugh creators, and there is no end to the fun they make." – *Fairmont West Virginian*

How It Happened

Released circa November 1917. Jaxon Comedies (series No. 4, No. 3) - General Film Company release. One reel. No copyright registered.

Produced by Frank Tichenor. Directed by Bobby Burns and Walter Stull.

With Bobby Burns (*Pokes*), Walter Stull (*Jabs*), Jennie Nelson [?].

Pokes is a sport when his wife is not around — when she is, he is meekness itself. A game is going on at the club and Pokes is phoned for, but his wife gets the message and Pokes is sent to bed. Jabs, the policeman, is a sweetheart of Jennie, the maid, and calls for his daily refreshments. Meanwhile Mrs. Pokes has gone out and Pokes wanders into the kitchen. He sees Jabs' coat and hat and hastily donning them escapes to the club. Getting back is more difficult, however, but after exciting experiences with a cops and a burglar, Pokes manages to get home, only to be confronted by Mrs. Pokes. The bold story he tells fails to convince his irate wife, who proceeds to massage him with a wooden lower extremity. Pokes is now studying the game of "Old Maid" and trying to learn to tell the truth and once more make friends with his wife. [MPW]

The *New York Dramatic Mirror's* review that notes this comedy was "made for laughing purposes only" is a bit amusing itself. Why else are comedies really made? Comedies usually are made, not to make a statement about some grand social concept (as lofty film scholars like to assert), but to make people laugh. Jerry Herman, in his musical *Mack & Mabel*, wrote in the lyric about making slapstick movies that "No one pretended what we were doing was art!" Thankfully, it's a sentiment that Burns & Stull also shared.

"Another feature of the robust knock-about type, which depends more on the invulnerable qualities of the players where broken limbs are concerned than anything else. The plot and the story are chaotic — in fact, so mixed up are the events which follow each other with lightning-like rapidity that it is rather difficult to follow the story at all. He wants to go to the club and takes the tunic and helmet of the constable who is courting his maidservant to aid him in his deception. Once at the club, however, he quickly despoils his associates. Meanwhile, a burglar has been at work and cleared his home out. Returning, he is able to best the criminal, but has to explain matters. This he does by giving a vivid description of his abduction by the gang of burglars and the heroic strategy by which he obtained not only his liberty but the return of his property. Burns and Stull put all they know into making the comedy a success, and are supported by several people who spare no pains in assisting the laughter-makers-in-chief." -- *Kinematograph Weekly*.

"While the policeman is making love to the pretty cook, the house is cleaned out by a burglar. Meanwhile, the master of the house, clad in the policeman's uniform, has conducted a profitable gaming house raid, and, returning, it is just in time to capture the thief. When he gives a somewhat imaginative account of these adventures to his wife, she is so skeptical that she knocks him out with her wooden leg which she removes for that purpose. Rapid dexterous knockabout humour is the chief ingredient of this merry little comic, the 'plot' of which consists of a series of vaguely connected incidents presented by a hard-working company of acrobatic pantomimists, the little film should be a useful fill-up." -- *The Bioscope*

"*How It Happened*, the third of the new series of Jaxon Comedies being issued through General Film Company, was made for laughing purposes only. Pokes's adventures in his effort to keep an engagement at the poker club provide continuous amusement. The Jaxon Comedies, with Pokes and Jabs, are meeting with great success, inasmuch as they offer a happy combination to the exhibitor anxious to round out his bill with a one-reel funmaker of high order." -- *New York Dramatic Mirror*

Too Much Alike

Released November 16, 1917. Jaxon Comedies (series No. 4, No. 4) - General Film Company release. One reel. No copyright registered. Working title: *The Man Who Looks Like Me.*

Produced by Frank Tichenor. Directed by Bobby Burns and Walter Stull. Filmed August 1917 at the Eastern Film Corporation studios in Providence, Rhode Island.

With Bobby Burns (*Pokes*), Walter Stull (*Jabs*).

Pokes, an all round good fellow, with a slight inclination to flirt, has a jealous wife, a suspicious brother, Jabs, and an inquisitive neighbor. One day as he emerges from the club a bevy of chickens pass, and Pokes manages to catch one, and is invited to a bathing party the next afternoon. Pokes hurries home to replenish the exchequer. Wifey is hard to win over, but he produces an overdue bill, and she gives him $50 to pay it. However, his hurried departure arouses his wife's suspicions, and with the aid of a telephone she discovers the deception. Just then Mrs. Newsy calls and imparts the news that she saw Pokes at the beach with a bunch of girls. Leaving Jabs and the butler to guard the house the two women start out. Poor Pokes is caught red handed. When he arrives home he makes the bold excuse that it must have been the fellow that looks like him, and apparently gets away with it. However, the following day Mrs. Pokes, Jabs and Mrs. Newsy plan to get even, and the manner in which they do so nearly overcomes Pokes, who sees so many people that look like him that he nearly goes wild. [MPW]

This was the film being shot on August 23, 1917 when a fire broke out at the studio. Although production restarted not long after the fire, the expense to repair the studio undoubtedly influenced Eastern to curtail their film production, at least temporarily, and as such led to the end of Pokes and Jabbs.

"The hero strays away from his lawful spouse and engages in merry gambols with a bevy of fair damsels on the beach. Returning home he is ejected and drowns his sorrows in the flowing bowl. The result is that he sees his double haunting him perpetually and is led into a variety of agonizing adventures in his attempts to escape. The fun in this comedy is all on rough and tumble order, aided by clever trick photography and should prove a likely mirth provoker." -- *Unknown trade paper*

Barnyard Frolics

Released circa November 1917. Jaxon Comedies (series No. 4, No. 5) - General Film Company release. One reel. No copyright registered.

Produced by Frank Tichenor. Directed by Bobby Burns and Walter Stull.

With Bobby Burns (*Pokes*), Walter Stull (*Jabs*), Jennie Nelson (*Jennie*).

The Jabs and Jenks farms adjoin each other and Jennie Jenks and Jabs are sweethearts, much against the wishes of their fathers. However, it takes a lot of watching to keep the lovers apart. Pokes, rudely tossed from his side-door Pullman, arrives on the Jabs farm as old man Jabs, who is stuffing a scarecrow, has gone to the barn for more hay. He takes the scarecrow's place and nearly scares the old man into fits. From then on the place is in an uproar. An article in the paper concerning spooks convinces the villages that devils infest the Jabs and Jenks farms. The police force is summoned and a lively chase follows, but Pokes gets away by converting one of the farm implements into a motor cycle. Jabs and Jennie get married and all live happily ever after. [MPW]

Bobby Burns revisits playing a scarecrow as he did in the 1915 Wizard comedy *In Clover*, and this film is in a large part a remake of the earlier film. However, unlike in the earlier comedy Burns has to deal with Stull in this one. The Chicago Board of Censors commented on the "vulgar actions of girl after being shot in seat" and then she apparently exposed her legs after falling off a bench. Also found objectionable was a pitchfork being planted in a man's backside. Despite its basic lack of originality the *New York Dramatic Mirror* had good things to say about the film, "It is one of the most whimsical laugh-makers yet produced in the series."

"A Pokes and Jabs comedy of rural life in which Pokes disguises as a scarecrow, and later is mistaken for a ghost. He does his usual acrobatic stunts and gets several laughs. There is a good finish, where he rides out of the picture, on a grindstone, by turning it upside down and using it as a bicycle." -- *Moving Picture World*

Breaking In

Released circa November 1917. Jaxon Comedies (series No. 4, No. 6) - General Film Company release. One reel. No copyright registered.

Produced by Frank Tichenor. Directed by Bobby Burns and Walter Stull. Probably filmed in Providence, Rhode Island.

With Bobby Burns (*Pokes*), Walter Stull (*Jabs*), Edna Reynolds [?].

Pokes is a firm believer in the saying, "All things come to him who wait," but his landlady apparently gets tired of waiting for the room rent, and Pokes is obliged to move. Wishing to take life easy he becomes a burglar. But as all first-class burglars have assistants Pokes seeks out Jabs, the champion sledge thrower. Jabs insists that Pokes show his metal before he joins him, so Pokes allows Jabs to break several sledges over his head to prove he is solid. Jabs now consents to become Pokes' assistant. They break into a house which is filled with measles, only to break out quicker. Next they enter the house of athletic Edna, who has long waited to try out a new knockout blow. When Pokes and Jabs come back to life they are protected by Big Mike, the cop, who allows them to play golf for the rest of their lives on the rock pile. [MPW]

"Pokes and Jabs give a great display of slapstick comedy in this single reeler. Pokes having taken a full course in villainy, decides to become a burglar and enlists Jabs as his assistant. They have some highly exciting experiences, first breaking into a house infected with measles, and later falling foul of athletic Edna, who has been waiting for such an opportunity to display her prowess. She vanquishes the couple in short order. They are eventually arrested." -- *Motion Picture News* (reviewed by F.G. Spencer)

Blundering Boobs

Released December 7, 1917. Jaxon Comedies (series No. 5, No. 1) - General Film Company release. One reel. No copyright registered.

Produced by Frank Tichenor. Directed by Bobby Burns and Walter Stull. Probably filmed in Providence, Rhode Island.

With Bobby Burns (*Pokes*), Walter Stull (*Jabs*).

The female member of a vaudeville team, out of a job, accepts a position as teacher in a country school. All of the men fall in love with her; and her partner, disguised as a peddler, sells her fake stage jewelry to them, and they make her a present of the different articles. [MPW]

One review noted that there was "considerable watermelon and vegetable throwing", certainly keeping up the high brow nature of these comedies. Plus, why just settle for tossing about custard pies?

"Burns and Stull are featured in this film, which consists altogether of slapstick work in which a Hebrew peddler, a fair maiden and the members of a rustic fire company engage in a cross-country chase, which ends on the roof of the fire-house, with the blackjacking and a presumable capture of the quarry. There is no plot worth mentioning, the picture being chiefly remarkable for its comic absurdities and the acrobatic feats of the principals." -- *Exhibitors Trade Review*

Disappointed Love

Released December 13, 1917. Jaxon Comedies (series No. 5, No. 2) - General Film Company release. One reel. No copyright registered.

Produced by Frank Tichenor. Directed by Bobby Burns and Walter Stull. Probably filmed in Providence, Rhode Island.

With Bobby Burns (*Pokes*), Walter Stull (*Jabs*).

A pretty rustic maiden engaged in making pies, pauses in her work to greet a bucolic suitor. While the latter consumes some pastry, a rival approaches in the form of a tall stranger. He is chased by the girl's parents, and a merry hunt ensues, during which father falls into a water barrel and is nearly drowned. In spite of the odds against him the stranger wins gloriously, carrying off the damsel. [ETR]

"This number features Burns and Stull in the characters of Pokes and Jabs. Some of the action is funny, but the connecting plot is too slight to get the best effects. The most amusing episode is that in which Jabs tries to kill himself by taking powdered sugar, which he thinks is rat poison." -- *Moving Picture World (reviewed as A Disappointed Love)*.

"The beauteous farm maid's silk-hatted admirer drinks the 'poisoned' milk with which her fleshly rustic love had intended to kill himself. Wild uproars ensues when the mistake is discovered, and the 'dying' swain anticipates his violent end by a series of fierce contortions. All is set right, however, by the chemist's bland admission that it was sugar, not poison, which he sold to the would-be suicide. Deft knockabout business abounds in the unpretentious little 'Pokes and Jabs' comic, which is performed with much energy by a troupe of agile acrobatic comedians in a simple farmyard setting. Quick, bright, and free from vulgarity, 'Disappointed Love' is an entirely usable, if unambitious, playlet." -- *The Bioscope*

"This is a little comedy of the good old-fashioned slap-stick knock-about order. The story is frailer than usual, if anything, the feature might just as well be called 'Fun on a Farm,' as most of the humour is drawn from business with revolving stiles, water butts, infantile pigs, and the other well-known accessories of farm life. Pokes loves the girl, but her parents evidently favour Jabs. Heart-broken, he goes to the chemist for rat poison, but is sugar instead. This he places in milk, and is about to drink fatal draught when the farmer drags him off to his work. The draught is taken instead by his rival, and there is much chasing and acrobatic work before matters are straightened out. The action is quick-moving, and the feature will doubtless be popular with those who like entertainments of the simplest character. Burns and Stull work hard, and the rest of the company do the same in their determination that success shall crown their efforts." -- *Kinematograph Weekly*

"This is brisk knockabout comedy where in Burns and Stull execute some marvelous acrobatics and keep matters moving at a lively rate. There is abundance of clever trick photography in evidence." -- *Exhibitors Trade Review*

He's in Again

Released circa December 1917. Jaxon Comedies (series No. 5, No. 3) - General Film Company release. One reel. No copyright registered.

Produced by Frank Tichenor. Directed by Bobby Burns and Walter Stull. Probably filmed in Providence, Rhode Island.

With Bobby Burns (*Pokes*), Walter Stull (*Jabs*).

[no synopsis available].

"'*He's In Again* is a roaring Pokes and Jabs comedy that will also create enjoyment not to say merriment." -- *The Wilmington Morning Star (Wilmington, North Carolina)*

How It Worked

Released circa December 1917. Jaxon Comedies (series No. 5, No. 4) - General Film Company release. One reel. No copyright registered.

Produced by Frank Tichenor. Directed by Bobby Burns and Walter Stull. Probably filmed in Providence, Rhode Island.

With Bobby Burns (*Pokes*), Walter Stull (*Jabs*).

[no synopsis available].

The last Pokes & Jabbs comedy to be a regular release as part of the series (*Breaking Into Business* which was rebranded a Bobby Burns Comedy and released over two years later was the actual last release). By the time the film was released Bobby Burns had moved on to his next film company, and Walter Stull was just beginning to settle into his post-performing life in Philadelphia.

"A comic number, featuring Burns and Stull as Pokes and Jabs. The plot concerns a henpecked husband, whose wife returns home suddenly to find him having a good time. She breaks up the party in typical burlesque style. Not very new in plot, but quite amusing in spots." -- *Moving Picture World*

Their Model Careers

Released circa December 1917. Jaxon Comedies (series No. 5, No. 5) - General Film Company release. One reel. No copyright registered.

Produced by Frank Tichenor for Amber Star Films Corporation. Written and directed by Walter Stahl. Filmed Spring 1917 at the Garrick Studios in Jacksonville, Florida.

With Walter Stahl (*Finn*) and Billy Ruge (*Haddie*).

[no synopsis available]

By the time these Finn and Haddie comedies were released Jaxon had suspended production of the Pokes & Jabbs comedies and was merely using up its stockpile of films made during their time in Jacksonville. The disappearance of Pokes & Jabbs and then the appearance of Finn & Haddie has caused modern film historians to make the wrong assumption about the sequence in which these films were made, and who appeared in them. Both this film and the next were referred to as "Sparkle Comedies" in some trade papers, and reviewers go back and forth in their references to Walter Stull or Walter Stahl as Billy Ruge's co-star. The similarity of names between the two Walters caused some confusion even in the day as to who actually played Finn to Ruge's Haddie, so modern sources getting it wrong is an honest mistake.

The evidence that it was Walter STAHL not Walter STULL that starred in the Finn & Haddie comedies alongside Billy Ruge.

Most of these comedies were made right around and just after Kate Price's departure from Amber Star in February 1917. Walter Stahl, while directing at Regal in Jacksonville in Spring 1917, was often working at the Garrick Studios where the Sparkle Comedies featuring Ruge were filmed, allowing him the ability to work for both companies. To give added strength to the fact that it was Walter Stahl in these comedies is the fact that during the time frame these films could have been made Walter Stull was recovering from a bout of "la grippe" (a term often used to describe the Spanish influenza), and the posters for the Finn & Haddies mention Stahl by name and depicts the rather tall, slender man (Stull was a medium height and stocky).

"Stull [sic] and Ruge appear in this number as two flirtatious individuals. The latter suddenly inherits his aunt's cloak and suit business, which they conduct in an amusing way. Some of the models make a rather breezy appearance, but there is nothing that will greatly offend." -- *Moving Picture World* [Note incorrect Walter referenced in review]

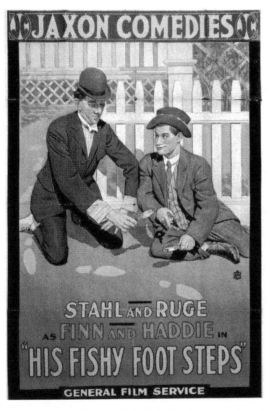

His Fishy Footsteps

Released circa January 1918. Jaxon Comedies (series No. 5, No. 6) - General Film Company release. One reel. No copyright registered. Working title: *His One False Step*.

Produced by Frank Tichenor for Amber Star Films Corporation. Directed by Jerold T. Hevener. Written by Walter Stahl. Filmed January 1917 at the Garrick Studios in Jacksonville, Florida.

With Walter Stahl (*Finn*) and Billy Ruge (*Haddie*), Kate Price [?].

[no synopsis available]

This film belies the notion that Billy Ruge made the faux Plump & Runt comedies with Kate Price and only after her departure from Amber Star did he began making the Finn & Haddie films with Walter Stahl. Evidence would suggest the transition was not so clean. A blurb about this comedy, mentioned as *His One False Step*, appeared in the January 13, 1917 edition of the *Florida Metropolis*, noting that it was written by Walter Stahl, director of Regal productions. The newspaper also noted that Kate Price was in this production, so it seems the Amber Star bosses were tinkering with exactly what to do with their second unit which may have led to Price's dissatisfaction and departure.

"It is a scream. Bring the children." -- *Chickasha Daily Express (Oklahoma)*

Anybody's Money

Released circa January 1918. Jaxon Comedies (series No. 6, No. 1) - General Film Company release. One reel. No copyright registered.

Directed by unknown. Filmed circa 1915-16 at the Eastern Film Corporation studios in Providence, Rhode Island. Originally intended to be part of the Pelican Comedies series.

With unknown.

[no synopsis available]

"A swift stepping comedy of high society life." -- *New York Dramatic Mirror*

Close Shaves

Released 1918. Jaxon Comedies (Series No. 6, unknown number)- General Film Company. One reel. No copyright registered.

Produced by Frank Tichenor for Amber Star Films Corporation. Written and directed by Walter Stahl. Filmed Spring 1917 at the Garrick Studios in Jacksonville, Florida.

With Walter Stahl (*Finn*) and Billy Ruge (*Haddie*).

[no synopsis available]

[no reviews available]

Hash and Horrors

Released circa January 1918. Jaxon Comedies (Series No. 6, unknown number) – General Film Company. One reel. No copyright registered.

Produced by Frank Tichenor for Amber Star Films Corporation. Written and directed by Walter Stahl. Filmed Spring 1917 at the Garrick Studios in Jacksonville, Florida.

With Walter Stahl (*Finn*) and Billy Ruge (*Haddie*).

[no synopsis available]

After his stint with Billy Ruge at Vitagraph ended later in 1918, Walter Stahl (neé Hall) was hired to directed the Spanish comedian Raymond Cacho in a series of comedies for Hispano-American Film Company. The title for the first was announced as *Hash and Horrors* and noted that it was written by Walter Hall. Nothing seems to have come of these films that probably were never made, so perhaps the producers realized the title had already been used.

[no reviews available]

Inspector's Wife, The

Released circa January 1918. Jaxon Comedies (Series No. 6, unknown number)-General Film Company. One reel. No copyright registered.

Directed by unknown. Filmed circa 1915-16 at the Eastern Film Corporation studios in Providence, Rhode Island. Originally intended to be part of the Pelican Comedies series.

With unknown.

[no synopsis available]

"This is a rollicking comedy in which everyone is involved in a series of amusing mixups which move along in rapid-fire order as though fired from a machine gun." -- *Motion Picture World*

In Wrong

Released January 1918. Jaxon Comedies (Series No. 6, unknown number) - General Film Company. One reel. No copyright registered.

Produced by Frank Tichenor for Amber Star Films Corporation. Written and directed by Walter Stahl. Filmed Spring 1917 at the Garrick Studios in Jacksonville, Florida.

With Walter Stahl (*Finn*) and Billy Ruge (*Haddie*).

[no synopsis available]

"Stahl and Ruge surrounded by a score of pretty and dainty pajama clad maidens furnish a riot of fun that is said to be a fast and furious from start to finish." -- *Exhibitors Trade Review*

"*In Wrong*, the second of the new Finn and Haddie Comedies released under the Jaxon brand by General Film Company, presents Walter Stahl and Billy Ruge in a laugh-making stunt of a novel nature." – *New York Dramatic Mirror*

Out and In

Released January 18, 1918. Jaxon Comedies (Series No. 6, unknown number) - General Film Company. One reel. No copyright registered.

Produced by Frank Tichenor for Amber Star Films Corporation. Written and directed by Walter Stahl. Filmed Spring 1917 in at the Garrick Studios in Jacksonville, Florida.

With Walter Stahl (*Finn*) and Billy Ruge (*Haddie*).

[no synopsis available]

Trade paper announced this was the first Finn & Haddie comedy, while perhaps the first to be made it was the penultimate Finn & Haddie released.

[no reviews available]

Her Fatal Shot

Released circa January 1918. Jaxon Comedies (series No. 6, No. 2) - General Film Company release. One reel. No copyright registered.

Produced by Frank Tichenor for Amber Star Films Corporation. Written and directed by Walter Stahl. Filmed Spring 1917 in at the Garrick Studios in Jacksonville, Florida.

With Walter Stahl (*Finn*) and Billy Ruge (*Haddie*).

[no synopsis available]

The last of the Finn & Haddie comedies to be released, and the last work of Stahl before he changed his name to Walter Hall. Within a few months of the film's release Walter Stahl/Hall and Billy Ruge would reunite at the Vitagraph Studios in Brooklyn, New York for a short series of comedies. Although there is no indication that the Finn & Haddie films had any impact upon movie audiences, it is apparent that Walter and Billy enjoyed working together.

[no reviews available]

Marooned

Released circa January 1918. Jaxon Comedies (series No. 6, No. 3) - General Film Company release. One reel. No copyright registered.

Directed by unknown. Filmed circa 1915-16 at the Eastern Film Corporation studios in Providence, Rhode Island. Originally intended to be part of the Pelican Comedies series.

With unknown.

[no synopsis available]

[no reviews available]

Sherman Was Right

Released circa January 1918. Jaxon Comedies (series No. 6, No. 4) - General Film Company release. One reel. No copyright registered.

Directed by Dan Mason. Filmed September 1915 at the Eastern Film Corporation studios in Providence, Rhode Island. Originally intended to be part of the Pelican Comedies series.

With Dan Mason.

[no synopsis available].

A play by this title opened on Broadway at the Fulton Theatre on October 26, 1915 but only ran for seven performances. However, the play's anti-militarism slant gave it life in the suburbs for years afterwards where theatergoers, fearful of America entering the Great War, were receptive to its message. Earlier, a Royal Comedy with this title was released by Mutual in 1914. What little is known about the Jaxon comedy is that it was "an entertaining farce on domestic life" and not a political statement akin to the Broadway play. The phrase itself "Sherman was right" is a response to General William T. Sherman's assertion that "War is Hell", a fact that Sherman with his scorched earth tactics in the Civil War helped to confirm.

"This is an ordinary comedy number, with Dan Mason in the leading role. War, of course, is responsible for the title. Dan is instrumental in forming a home guard. The wives of the members form a league of peace and lock their husbands out, refusing to give them any dinner. Complications are caused by the arrival of a beautiful woman to whom the guard pay considerable attention. However, all is satisfactorily adjusted when the wives learn that the lady is lecturing on national defense." -- *Moving Picture World*

What Will Happen Next?

Released circa January 1918. Jaxon Comedies (series No. 6, No. 5) - General Film Company release. One reel. No copyright registered.

Directed by unknown. Written by Wilfred Clarke, based on his vaudeville play with the same title Filmed circa 1915-16 at the Eastern Film Corporation studios in Providence, Rhode Island. Originally intended to be part of the Pelican Comedies series.

With Wilfred Clarke, Grace Meinken.

He [Wilfred Clarke] impersonates a flirtatious young husband, who goes to a fancy ball and there while imbibing too freely of champagne meets a young woman who he escorts to his own home. There he experiences considerable difficulty in keeping the knowledge of the other woman's presence away from his wife, and the situation is made all the more embarrassing when the husband finds that the unknown woman is the wife of his best friend. [Quad-City Times]

   Wilfred Clarke, apparently a nephew of thespian Edwin Booth, was primarily a vaudevillian with only a brief attempt at motion pictures with his stay in Providence. Debuted in 1906, Clarke played the sketch by this title around the country for a number of years to much success and great reviews. His brother Harry even starred in the sketch for a second company, touring the country around 1909, and Clarke eventually set up "The Wilfred Clarke Players" to put on the sketch in smaller houses without himself in the cast. Many reviews referred to Wilfred Clarke's great comic talent making it somewhat surprising that he was not able to transition into becoming a film comedian.

"Wilfred Clarke and Theo. Carew are playing *What Will Happen Next*, their comedy sketch which is away from the beaten path. It follows a familiar strain of plot construction, to be sure, but in treatment it is full of effective and novel bits of comedy business and talk. Mr. Clarke is a comedian of individuality. His method is quiet and smooth, but he makes his points with certainty and sureness. Another comedian without Clarke's skill would be led to play for his laughs in the sketch by hurry and noise. The piece is of the sort that usually handled in that way. Clarke secures his laughs more legitimately and by the exercise of a higher skill. Miss Carew looks exceedingly well and made an excellent opposite to Clarke. The other two members of the company were adequate to the demands of their parts." -- *Variety* [review of stage version]

Which Was Lucky?

Released circa January 1918. Jaxon Comedies (series No. 6, No. 6) - General Film Company release. One reel. No copyright registered.

Directed by unknown. Filmed circa 1915-16 at the Eastern Film Corporation studios in Providence, Rhode Island. Originally intended to be part of the Pelican Comedies series.

With unknown.

[no synopsis available]

"A one reel subject dealing with the weird adventures of two troublefinders." -- *Moving Picture World*

"Then comes another of those high class Jaxon comedies — the same that are run in New York's great Broadway theatre. Entitled 'Which Was Lucky?' a full reel of high class refined amusement." -- *Wilmington Moring Star*

The Unofficial Maneuver

Released circa March 1918. Jaxon Comedies (series No. 7, No. 1) - General Film Company release. One reel. No copyright registered.

Directed by Dan Mason. Written by Stanton K. Berry. Filmed early May 1915 at the Eastern Film Corporation studios in Providence, Rhode Island. Originally intended to be part of the Pelican Comedies series.

With Dan Mason, Grace Peters.

[no synopsis available]

This was the first film made by the newly opened Eastern Film Corporation in May 1915. The female lead, Grace Peters, was actually a Washington socialite and daughter of Commander George H. Peters, USN (ret.). The scenario writer, S.K. Berry, was a Providence local. Certainly by the time these Pelican comedies were finally released they looked dated.

[No reviews available]

What Occurred on the Beach

Released circa March 1918. Jaxon Comedies (series No. 7, No. 2) - General Film Company release. One reel. No copyright registered.

Directed by unknown. Written by Wilfred Clarke, based on his vaudeville play with the same title Filmed circa 1915-16 at the Eastern Film Corporation studios in Providence, Rhode Island. Originally intended to be part of the Pelican Comedies series.

With Wilfred Clarke, Grace Meinken.

[no synopsis available]

Another of Wilfred Clarke's vaudeville sketches transferred to the movie screen. This sketch, which also was received to rave reviews, was presented around the country circa 1910. Although twenty-five years younger, Grace Meinken became Mrs. Clarke during the vaudeville run of the sketch, perhaps answering what really occurred on the beach. By 1916, the Clarkes owned the Walnut Street Theatre in Philadelphia while continuing to tour in vaudeville. Eventually the two divorced and Meinken married actor Bert Lytell.

"Wilfred Clark and Co. presented *What Occurred on the Beach*. The new sketch contains an abundance of good material and a plot somewhat different from the majority. It can be easily distinguished as Wilfred Clark's work. Grace Meinken is the only one remaining from the old cast. She seems to improve with every performance. *What Occurred on the Beach* easily found favor." -- *Variety [review of stage version]*

An All-Fool's Day Affair

Released circa March 1918. Jaxon Comedies (series No. 7, No. 3) - General Film Company release. One reel. No copyright registered.

Directed and written by Dan Mason, based on his playlet *All Fools Day*. Filmed late Spring 1915 at the Eastern Film Corporation studios in Providence, Rhode Island. Originally intended to be part of the Pelican Comedies series.

With Dan Mason, Tom McEvoy.

[no synopsis available]

Mason's playlet, called an afterpiece since it followed the main attraction, was first produced in 1881.

[no reviews available]

Beating Him to It

Released circa March 1918. Jaxon Comedies (series No. 7, No. 4) - General Film Company release. One reel. No copyright registered.

Directed by unknown. Filmed circa 1915-16 at the Eastern Film Corporation studios in Providence, Rhode Island. Originally intended to be part of the Pelican Comedies series.

With Tom McEvoy (Dick Sturgis), Dean Raymond (Mr. Sturgis), Marguerite Chaffee (Ethel Hollis).

Dick Sturgis asks Ethel Hollis to marry him. Their fathers are old friends, and Dick tells his pal Hollis before his son gets the chance to ask for permission. While happy with the news the two fathers decide to have some fun with the young lovers. Dick is so nervous that he can barely ask Ethel's father for her hand in marriage. Dick is told by his would be father-in-law that he has his blessing but only if Dick can beat him at a business deal. The next morning Ethel overhears her father setting up a deal on the phone and tells Dick so that he can beat him to it. Ethel distracts her father with a drive in the country while Dick takes advantage of the business deal information. That evening old man Hollis thinks he has been double-crossed and laments losing the big deal. He then learns it was Dick that made the deal, and in doing so accomplished the required task to gain his permission for Dick to marry Ethel. [RS]

A severely water damaged print of *Beating Him to It* survives, and enough image remains to follow the plot and assess the filmmaking. Much of it is shot in the country at or near a stately house, the rest of the film are interiors shot at the studio so no real glimpses of Providence are to be seen. Void of any slapstick, the humor is gained through the situations presented and primarily from Tom McEvoy's struggle for courage to ask his future father-in-law for matrimonial permission. Other than being listed by title in advertisements and release charts there is no other trace of this film; that a print surfaced nearly a hundred years later is nothing short of miraculous.

[no reviews available]

Forced Into Matrimony

Released February 1918. Jaxon Comedies (series No. 7, No. 5) - General Film Company release. One reel. No copyright registered.

Directed by Dan Mason. Filmed circa 1915-16 at the Eastern Film Corporation studios in Providence, Rhode Island. Originally intended to be part of the Pelican Comedies series.

With Dan Mason Dean Raymond.

[no synopsis available]

[no reviews available]

Breaking Into Business

Released May 1920. Bobby Burns Comedies for Jaxon Film Corporation. States' rights release. Two reels. No copyright registered.

Produced by Frank Tichenor. Directed by Bobby Burns and Walter Stull. Filmed late April 1917 at the Garrick Studios in Jacksonville, Florida.

With Bobby Burns (*Pokes*), Walter Stull (*Jabs*), Roland Hill (*strong man*), James Renfro (*agency clerk*),

The agent at the O.K. Vaudeville Agency spends too much time "auditioning" one particularly cute actress and gains the ire of the long line of aspiring actresses and actors waiting their turn. One of the would-be actresses goes home and tells her husband, the local strong man, of the agent's insult. Meanwhile the team of Pokes & Jabbs arrive in town and show up at the agency. Foregoing the long line of auditioners, the two show the reluctant agent their talents. Anxious to get back to the pretty actress the agent takes Jabbs into the next room and shoots him out the window and into a trough of water via a trick chair. Discovering Pokes making time with the pretty actress the agent provides him the same fate. By this time the strong man is all worked up and calls the agent promising to beat him for insulting his wife. While drying out their clothes Pokes and Jabbs rescue a young socialite who is atop a runaway horse. Taking her home safely they are given a $500 reward for their efforts. The agent looking to avoid his forthcoming beating puts his agency up for sale. Pokes and Jabbs see the "for sale" sign and determine how to spend their new found fortune. The agent grabs the check and makes a quick exit. The two new agents then quickly go through the long line of auditioners quickly by sending them all out the same window they once experienced. The strong man arrives and looking to beat up an agent goes after both Pokes and Jabbs. They use the trick chair to get rid of the angry husband only to have the former agent, who had learned the $500 check was a phoney, return. He chases the two around the agency to gain his revenge for their bogus business deal. [RS]

Released well after the rest of the Pokes & Jabbs comedies made by Jaxon, this film was actually advertised as part of a Bobby Burns Comedies series that Jaxon was attempting to sell in 1920. Burns does receive sole credit at the beginning of the film but it is the old team of Burns & Stull throughout. The last film that Jaxon would shoot in Jacksonville before abandoning Florida for their home base of Providence, Rhode Island, it is also Pokes & Jabbs' only foray into two-reelers. Just as frantic and nonsensical as their standard product, Burns and Stull handle the double length well with only the slightest increased detail to the plot.

There is some minimal evidence that more unreleased or retooled Poke & Jabbs product came out through Jaxon in 1920. Newspapers reported screenings of two reel Pokes & Jabbs comedies entitled *Way Out West, Black and White, Pokes & Jabbs* and *The High Cost of Cheating*. Other previously released titles such as *Jolly Tars* and *How It Happened* were included in the new series. Whether any of these were shot as two reelers, or more likely combined one reelers is not known. Part of the Bobby Burns Comedies being marketed by Jaxon at the time it is interesting to note that newspapers referred to Burns & Stull as the stars.

[no reviews available]

SPARKLE COMEDIES

A Bargain at $37.50

Released circa 1917. Sparkle Comedies (series No. 4, No. ?) - General Film Company release. One reel. No copyright registered.

Produced by Frank Tichenor for Amber Star Films Corporation. Directed by Jerold T. Hevener. Filmed circa February 7, 1917 in Jacksonville, Florida at the Garrick Studios.

With Billy Ruge, Kate Price, Roland Hill.

Kate and Bill live in a humble cottage, their "family" consisting of a horse, a cow, a parrot, a pig, a goat and kid, a dozen chickens and as many ducks, all living in one room. Their nearest neighbors own a large automobile, and not relishing their snubs Kate and Billy decide to buy an automobile. A bargain is advertised in the paper for $37.50. Not having that amount of money they decide to sacrifice the animals, and proceed to cart the whole lot to town and walk them into a pawnshop. They obtain the $37.50 and buy the auto. Then their troubles begin. The car races over the earth at 109 miles an hour, destroying everything it comes in contact with. They are finally chased to a finish by a dozen sheriffs for exceeding the speed limit, and wind up by diving headlong into a ditch with the whole police force on top of them. [MPW]

Note: Amber Star was originally intending to resurrect the Plump & Runt series with a new Plump.

The production dates on most of the Sparkle comedies are unknown and they were not necessarily released in order. Whether this film was one of the first Sparkles directed by Will Louis or a later one directed by Jerold Hevener is not immediately known. The presence of all the animals, something Hevener liked to use in his comedies, and an ever-so-brief mention in the local newspaper (*Florida Metropolis*) about the production indicate that Hevener was the director.

"Kate Price and Billy Rudge [*sic*] are featured in this number. In order to keep up with their neighbors they sacrifice a varied assortment of live stock which occupies the same living room with them, and buy a second-hand auto, which finally runs away with them, and ends by their being arrested for speeding. Contains a few laughs." -- *Moving Picture World*

Where is My Nightie?

Released circa 1917. Sparkle Comedies (series No. 1, No. 1) - General Film Company release. One reel. No copyright registered.

Directed by unknown. Filmed circa 1915-16 at the Eastern Film Corporation studios in Providence, Rhode Island. Originally intended to be part of the Pelican Comedies series.

With unknown.

[*no synopsis available*]

[no reviews available]

Fresh Air

Released circa 1917. Sparkle Comedies (series No. 1, No. 2) - General Film Company release. One reel. No copyright registered.

Directed by unknown. Scenario by John C. Brownell. Filmed circa early 1916 at the Eastern Film Corporation studios in Providence, Rhode Island. Originally intended to be part of the Pelican Comedies series.

With Tom McEvoy (*Jones*), Paula Stay (*Mrs. Jones*), William Mandeville (*the Bishop*), Warren Cook (*Talbot Tubbs*), Anna Athey (*Mrs. Tubbs*), Herbert Roderick (*Jim Little*), Isabel Daintry (*Maggie Frye*).

Jones, being advised by his doctor to "sleep in the open," and having no sleeping porch utilizes the front veranda, and when night comes Mrs. Jones tucks him in and leaves him. Next morning Mrs. Jones goes out early to feed the chickens and falls into a lengthy conversation with her neighbor. Jones wakes to find a crowd enjoying the unusual spectacle. He rushes to the front door, and finds it locked. The crowd grows. A small boy appears and "sics" his dog on Jones. Jones leaps off the veranda and flees chased by the crowd. Coming to the minister's house he seeks refuge there, finding the door open. The minister and his wife have just left the house. Jones runs upstairs to the minister's bedroom, gets a suit of the ministers clothes and is about to make a getaway when a policeman and his intended bride appear. Jones, afraid to refuse, hunts up a prayer book and does the best he can to perform the ceremony. Jones kisses the bride, the cop hands him a fee, and Jones makes a second attempt to escape when an auto stops in front of the house and a bishop appears. Jones pretends to be a guest, tells him to make himself at home and beats it, only to run into the policeman who, with Mrs. Jones, is looking for the lost husband. The cop is frantic when he learns of the fake ceremony, but finding the bishop is a real minster, he jumps into an automobile, gets Maggie, and they are married by the bishop with Jones and his wife as witnesses. [MPW]

William Mandeville worked for Fred Mace making Flamingo Comedies in 1914, including some time shooting in Jacksonville, Florida. He appears in Eastern's *Cap'n Eri* along with George Bunny. After Eastern he worked with the likes of Flora Finch and Ethel Barrymore. Also amongst the cast in this film is Isabel Daintry who had appeared in Royal Comedies in support of Bobby Burns and Walter Stull, the future Pokes & Jabbs. These Pelican Comedies seem to have been her last film work.

[no reviews available]

The Spy

Released circa July 1917. Sparkle Comedies (series No. 1, No. 3) - General Film Company release. One reel. No copyright registered.

Directed by unknown. Scenario by John C. Brownell. Filmed circa late 1915 – early 1916 at the Eastern Film Corporation studios in Providence, Rhode Island. Originally intended to be part of the Pelican Comedies series.

With Tom McEvoy (*Stephen Wiltstack*), William Mandeville (*Zeb Hunker*), May Abbey (*Patzy Higgins*), Henry Carlton (*Major Lord*).

Stephen Wiltsack, a young designer of ladies' costumes, is sent by his firm to a quiet town to work out a series of fashion designs. A fort is located in the town, and Stephen chooses a spot overlooking the fortifications for his sketching. Zeb Hunger, a wise village constable, jumps to the conclusion that the young fellow is a spy. One night Zeb follows Stephen to his cottage and the young man, surprised at seeing him peeking in the window, points a gun at the constable who, badly frightened, disappears. Stephen laughs while Zeb tells his companions that the city fellow was about to fire when he saw his badge and dropped the gun. One day Stephen sends a message to his firm saying that he is working hard on the fortification grounds. Zeb makes the boy give up the message. His suspicions being confirmed, he rushes madly to the fort and tells the commander that a spy is making sketches. Stephen is arrested. Zeb seizes the drawings and thrusts them in front of the commander's face. The latter drops back bewildered as he finds himself looking at a sketch of a new corset. Stephen explains the situation and the constable is ejected from the house. [MPW]

Like most actors and comedians of the time Tom McEvoy paid his dues in vaudeville. Around 1911 he was appearing in an act entitled *Breaking Into Society* along with his then partner Ford Sterling. According to Sterling, Henry Lehrman saw the act and convinced Sterling to come over to Biograph and with himself, Mabel Normand and Mack Sennett make some movies. Not long after losing his stage partner McEvoy also entered movies in 1912 and worked with many companies including Nestor, IMP, Edison and Kalem. In 1916, McEvoy was announced as the director for a serial based upon the *Bringing Up Father* comic strip but that project never seemed to materialize. McEvoy then went on to direct some of the Johnny Ray comedies.

[no reviews available]

The Trunk Route

Released circa 1917. Sparkle Comedies (series No. 1, No. 4) - General Film Company release. One reel. No copyright registered.

Directed by unknown. Filmed circa 1915-16 at the Eastern Film Corporation studios in Providence, Rhode Island. Originally intended to be part of the Pelican Comedies series.

With unknown.

[no synopsis available]

"A side splitting and hilarious Sparkle comedy. A veritable whirlwind of fun and mirth." -- *The Evening Herald (Shenandoah, Pennsylvania)*

The Water Cure

Released circa August 1917. Sparkle Comedies (series No. 1, No. 5) - General Film Company release. One reel. No copyright registered. May have also been released as *Bertie's Bath*.

Directed by unknown. Filmed circa 1915-16 at the Eastern Film Corporation studios in Providence, Rhode Island. Originally intended to be part of the Pelican Comedies series.

With unknown.

[no synopsis available]

[no reviews available]

A Night of Enchantment

Released circa 1917. Sparkle Comedies (series No. 1, No. 6) - General Film Company release. One reel. No copyright registered.

A younger Dean Raymond

Directed by unknown. Filmed circa late 1915 at the Eastern Film Corporation studios in Providence, Rhode Island. Originally intended to be part of the Pelican Comedies series.

With Marguerite Chaffee (Nora, Mrs. Van Worden's Maid), Dean Raymond (Skuyler Van Worden), Maud Cooling (Mrs. Skuyler Van Worden), Fritz De Lindt (Ferdinand, Chauffeur), Herbert Roderick (Kelley, the policeman).

Pretty Nora, maid of the Van Worden's, beholds the other servants spooning with their sweethearts every night while she, with a heart full of romance, has no beaux. Her dream of a husband is a big handsome fellow, preferably in a uniform. Later she is informed by a fortune-teller that her husband-to-be is near at hand. Not long after, a new chauffeur appears across the street who is soon making love to her. He teaches her to drive the automobile and takes particular interest in Nora's descriptions of her mistress's wonderful jewelry. One bright moonlight night Ferdinand takes Nora to ride, incidentally taking with him a priceless rug from the hall. He speeds up and they go at break-neck speed. Nora begs him to stop, only to discover that her hero is a common thief running away with her mistress' jewels. Nora drops the rug and when the chauffeur goes back for it she drives off, meets a motorcycle cop, tells her story and they return in time to apprehend her former idol just as he is making his getaway. In the policeman Nora finds the man of her heart. [MPW]

Little is known about Marguerite Chaffee who seems to have started working on stage around 1913 but by 1915 all but disappears. Her sole claim to fame seems to be when, in May 1914 while appearing with the LaVerne Company at the Lyric Theatre in Atlanta, she ditched rehearsals to go visit her fiancé Dudley Arthur. She was fined $40, but took the Company to court and obtained a ruling that the fine was illegal. She then quit the company and broke off the engagement.

Dean Raymond made a few other films after his time at Eastern but primarily worked on stage appearing on Broadway frequently in the '20s and '30s. He was married to Maud Cooling who also occasionally worked in film and on stage.

[no review available]

An Attorney's Affair

Released circa August 1917. Sparkle Comedies (series No. 2, No. 1) - General Film Company release. One reel. No copyright registered.

Directed by unknown. Filmed circa 1915-16 at the Eastern Film Corporation studios in Providence, Rhode Island. Originally intended to be part of the Pelican Comedies series.

With unknown.

Lawyer Bard gets a photograph of Grace Knowles, heiress to half a million, with instructions to find her. His wife sees him looking at the picture and, as he leaves without kissing her, becomes suspicious and employs Detective Carter. The detective's wife is Grace Knowles and worked in Smith's cafe before her marriage. The detective follows Bard to the cafe, gets hold of the photograph and finds it is his wife. He overhears Bard telephone to Mrs. Carter and goes home and finds his wife out. He then goes to Bard's house and talks with Mrs. Bard through the window. The lawyer returns and fires a shot at the supposed burglar, but is suspicious. Finally the detective and Mrs. Bard decide to have it out at Bard's office, but, finding he has gone to Smith's cafe, they follow. In the meantime Bard has sent for Mrs. Carter and she while waiting for Bard to return from lunch decides to pay a visit to her old employer, Smith. There she is introduced to Bard, and they have lunch together while he explains her case. In comes Mrs. Bard and the detective. Mrs. Bard accuses her husband of infidelity and he accuses her of intriguing with the burglar. Explanations follow and the party sit down to dinner at the expense of the newly-made heiress. [MPW]

"A screaming Sparkle comedy, with a good laugh in every scene." -- *The Evening Herald (Shenandoah, Pennsylvania)*

Her Peignoir

Released circa August 1917. Sparkle Comedies (series No. 2, No. 2) - General Film Company release. One reel. No copyright registered.

Directed by Charles Pitt. Filmed circa late 1915 at the Eastern Film Corporation studios in Providence, Rhode Island. Originally intended to be part of the Pelican Comedies series.

With Tom Mulgrew (*Ami Simple*), Estelle Wynne (*Janice Simple*), Mrs. Herbert (*Mrs. Gay*), Hamilton Crane (*Mr. Gay*).

Ami Simple and his wife never tire of telling their neighbors, Mr. and Mrs. Gay, of their wonderfully happy and eugenic marriage. One morning Mrs. Simple, struck by a stunning new peignoir in Vogue, decides to have one and goes at once to her dressmaker. Ami returns home to lunch and cannot get in. With the aid of Gay he breaks in through the window and finds a note on the table which reads : "Have gone to have my peignoir cut. Janice." Horrified at the terrible news, Ami calls up the hospital and is told that Mrs. Simple is undergoing ether. Rushing to the hospital he bends over the bed and finds the patient is another Mrs.

Simple. He shows the note to the superintendent, who calls in several doctors for discussion. After trying in vain to discover from their medical books what a peignoir is, they conclude it is some terrible new disease and assure Simple that his wife has probably gone to a specialist. Overcome, Simple enters a saloon and manages to take the edge off his sorrow. Meanwhile Janice returns and Mrs. Gay asks her if the operation was successful. Explanations follow and Janice unwraps a bundle and shows what a peignoir is. Simple wends a crooked path home and when he, too, is told what a peignoir is he flops to the floor. [MPW]

Estelle Wynne, who came from Cincinnati, Ohio, was married to fellow Eastern Film player John C. Wynne, who like director Charles Pitt, and most Eastern players working in Providence around 1915 were primarily stage performers with few if any other screen credits.

[no review available]

Those Terrible Telegrams

Released week of August 11, 1917. Sparkle Comedies (series No. 2, No. 3) - General Film Company release. One reel. No copyright registered.

Directed by unknown. Filmed circa 1915-16 at the Eastern Film Corporation studios in Providence, Rhode Island. Originally intended to be part of the Pelican Comedies series.

With Johnny Ray [?], Emma Ray [?]

Tom Winters and May Summers marry and remove to the city. They are joined later by Jerry Summers who marries Miss June Fall a year later. On the wedding day Jerry joyfully telegraphs his mother that she has a new daughter. On the same day Tom telegraphs his mother announcing the arrival of a new baby. The telegrams arrive together and are misdirected by the local operator. Mrs. Winter receiving Mrs. Summer's telegram and vice versa. The horrified mothers at once set out for the city where, after an amusing scene, everything is satisfactorily explained. [M & MPW]

"'Those Terrible Telegrams' is a roaring comedy featuring the famous Two Rays, vaudeville headliner comedians." -- *Wilmington Morning Star (North Carolina)*

The Stag Party

Released circa August 1917. Sparkle Comedies (series No. 2, No. 4) - General Film Company release. One reel. No copyright registered.

Directed by unknown. Story by Mae A. Hitchcock. Filmed circa 1915-16 at the Eastern Film Corporation studios in Providence, Rhode Island. Originally intended to be part of the Pelican Comedies series.

With Effie Shelley (*Sally*), Tom McEvoy (*Billy Barlow*), Tom Mulgrew (*Bob Temple*), Mildred Bright (*Grace Gilmore*).

Billy Barlow sends Sally a note inviting her to go motoring but drops it, and his sister Betty puts it in his overcoat. Billy finds Sally out, and thinks she does not love him. Meanwhile Bob Temple and Grace Gilmore have planned to elope and ask Billy to help them. On the night of the elopement Sally gives a stag party for her girl friends and Betty provides herself and several others with clothes from her brother's wardrobe. Billy is astonished to find his clothes gone. Finding Betty's invitation to the stag party he sees any chance of getting even with Sally and phones the police a description of the clothes, saying the thieves are at Sally's house. He starts out in his pajamas and overcoat, but is arrested for speeding. He phones Bob to bring him some clothes. Meanwhile the police arrive at Sally's and they are all brought to the station house. Bill has been released, and hearing of the raid he and Bob race to the station house. Explanations follow and Bob, Grace and Bill hasten to the minister's, Grace still wearing make clothes. At the depot Grace and Bill pick up the wrong suitcase and discover on their arrival at the hotel that Grace has a bag full of men's clothes while Bob has the bag containing Billy's pajamas. After mutual explanations Bill and Sally race to the minster's and are married. [MPW]

Mildred Bright made her film debut in 1912 working for Éclair and worked there exclusively until her move to Eastern. After a handful of films she returned to vaudeville and except for a single appearance in 1922 left movies behind her.

"The Stage Party, a rich comedy of a different sort." - Fairmont West Virginian

Bragg's Little Poker Game

Released circa September 1917. Sparkle Comedies (series No. 2, No. 5) - General Film Company release. One reel. No copyright registered.

Directed by Dan Mason. Filmed circa 1915 at the Eastern Film Corporation studios in Providence, Rhode Island. Originally intended to be part of the Pelican Comedies series.

With Dan Mason (Braggs), Dean Raymond.

Late one night Bragg gets a message that a poker game is in progress at a friend's, and manages to leave the house without waking his wife. Soon after a burglar enters the house, followed by a cop. The burglar gets into the twin bed vacated by Bragg and when the cop appears says "Hist! don't wake my wife." The policeman leaves the room determined to wait for the burglar. In the meantime the poker game is raided and all are arrested except Bragg, who escapes and arrives home only to be captured by the waiting cop. He protests that he is Bragg, but his wife, half asleep, says that her husband is in the next bed. and Bragg is led away. Later Mrs. Bragg finds out her mistake and the real burglar is taken by the police. At the station the members of the raided poker party who are all in one cell discover that in the scrimmage a pack of cards has been saved and, with additional partners, the game is continued. [M & MPW]

[no review available]

The little poker game.

Mixed Nuts

Released circa September 1917. Sparkle Comedies (series No. 2, No. 6) - General Film Company release. One reel. No copyright registered.

Directed by unknown. Filmed circa early 1916 at the Eastern Film Corporation studios in Providence, Rhode Island. Originally intended to be part of the Pelican Comedies series.

With Alfred Swenson (*A. Wall Nut*), Marguerite Chaffee (*Hazel Nut*), Lorle Palmer (*Belle Bun*), Edward Lawrence (*Mr. Winslow*), Ione Bright (*His Wife*).

A. Wall Nut and his wife, Hazel, are a happy young people, but the spectre of gray hair threatens to mar their happiness. The young husband is sent to Europe by his firm and cautions his wife not to dye her hair in his absence or he will divorce her. But the sight of fresh gray hairs is too much for her and she goes to the hairdresser to have her locks retouched. Falling asleep, she is frantic to find on awakening that her hair has been dyed a deep and lasting black, and decides to go to California with her sister until the dye wears off. A. Wall Nut is recalled by his firm and wires his wife that he is returning. The Swedish servant receives the message and answers it, cutting down the cable until it reads : "Your wife died. It was terrible. Her sister has taken her to California." Wall Nut receives the message and is overcome. He writes a letter enclosing some money and gives it to a loiterer in the hotel lobby to mail. The latter is a thief and is run down while making off with the letter and money and mistaken for A. Wall Nut. Word is sent to Hazel that her husband has been killed. On the way home Nut tells Mrs. Winslow, a friend, of his wife's death. In the meantime Hazel, waiting at the dock to receive her husband's body, meets Mr. Winslow. Through glasses they see Nut and Mrs. Winslow apparently in close embrace. The boat docks, mutual explanations follow and the reunited Nuts wend their way home. [MPW]

Ione Bright

Alfred Swenson and his wife Lorle Palmer did most of their work on stage having appeared in such productions *as The Vagabond King* and *Quincy Adams Sawyer.* Swenson did make a few films for Lubin in 1912, and they both apparently appear in a few films released by Kriterion in 1915 (both C.K. Film Co. and Alhambra brands). Their primary work at Eastern was with the dramatic company working in Eastern's first big feature production *Strife.* They began their work in Providence on January 8, 1916. Also featured in the cast was Ione Bright who was chiefly a stage actress appearing on Broadway for much of 1916 and 1917 after her brief stay at Eastern. *Mixed Nuts* is her only known screen credit.

"A Sparkle comedy which caused side-splitting laughter throughout." -- *Moving Picture World, from article on Castle Square Theatre in Boston turning into movie house.*

Hearts and Harpoons

Released September 20, 1917. Sparkle Comedies (series No. 3, No. 1) -General Film Company release. One reel. No copyright registered.

Directed by Dan Mason. Filmed circa 1915-16 at the Eastern Film Corporation studios in Providence, Rhode Island.

With Dan Mason, George Bunny.

In a fishing hamlet Captain Peters and Captain Hankins, retired sea captains, are old cronies. Mrs. Scribbler, a widow and writer of sea stories, comes to the town to get atmosphere. On her arrival both old captains fall in love with her and a strong rivalry springs up between them. Captain Hankins proposes a sail down the bay and the widow accepts. Captain Peters bribes Clarence, a hoodlum, to bore a hole in the boat. He then makes a daring rescue of the widow from the sinking yawl, to the discomfiture of his rival. Captain Hankins learns that Captain Peters is responsible for the leaky yawl and determines to get even. Learning that Captain Peters is to take the widow out driving he fixes it with the liveryman to give them a balky horse and later relieves Captain Peters of his prize and turns the tables. That night a duel is proposed, the choice of weapons being harpoons at twenty paces. Just before the signal to begin is given the widow and Jack Martin, who has been trying to induce the lady to marry him, rush in and matters are explained. The two captains make up and Jack leads his widow away. [MPW]

Initially hired by the Eastern Film Corporation to make a series of seagoing films (one, *Cap'n Eri* was actually released in 1915), George Bunny makes an appearance in this, one of the Pelican comedies. Since this film has a seafaring theme itself perhaps it was just easiest to keep Bunny in costume and let Dan Mason use him in the comedy unit Mason was heading. George was the younger brother of the great John Bunny, and there were a number of efforts to develop him into a comedy star after the untimely death of his brother on April 26, 1915. While George found regular work in film he never achieved star status or even an ounce of his brother's fame.

[no review available]

Toodles

Released circa September 1917. Sparkle Comedies (series No. 3, No. 2) - General Film Company release. One reel. No copyright registered.

Directed by Dan Mason. Filmed 1915 at the Eastern Film Corporation studios in Providence, Rhode Island. Originally intended to be part of the Pelican Comedies series.

With Dan Mason.

[no synopsis available].

[no review available]

Bangs Renigs

Released September 1917. Sparkle Comedies (series No. 3, No. 3) - General Film Company release. One reel. No copyright registered.

Directed by Dan Mason. Filmed 1915 in Providence, Rhode Island at the Eastern Film Corporation studios. Originally intended to be part of the Pelican Comedies series.

With Dan Mason (Bangs).

Bangs, a faithful employee in the office of Brewster, a rich merchant, is overjoyed one day to receive a note from the boss inviting him to his country home and stating that he is to be taken into the firm and likewise into the family. Bangs starts off in high spirits and is received with open arms. Next day he is introduced to Brewster's sister, Matilda, and it dawns upon him that he is expected to take Matilda off Brewster's hands. The next morning, in desperation, he tries to escape by the window. Matilda sees him and a wild chase starts through the country. He takes refuge in the river and Matilda follows. Hiding in a clump of bushes he is set upon by an escaped convict and made to exchange clothing. Matilda, mistaking the fleeing convict for Bangs, overtakes him after a long chase. The prison guards come upon them and proceed to drag the convict back to prison, followed by the angry spinster. They come upon poor Bangs and take him along too. At the prison Bangs discovers that the superintendent is a brother lodge member, and he prevails upon him to send him to jail to escape from the clutches of Matilda. Finally, Mr. Brewster's sympathy for Bangs induces him to call his sister off and Bangs remains in jail, a happy prisoner, safe from the pursuing female. [MPW]

"Dan Mason has the leading comedy part in this one-reel farce. It shows how a brother schemes to marry off his old maid sister to a faithful employee, and is fairly amusing."
-- *Moving Picture World*

A Triple Entente

Released circa October 1917. Sparkle Comedies (series No. 3, No. 4) - General Film Company release. One reel. No copyright registered.

Directed by unknown. Filmed circa September 25, 1915 at Oakland Beach, Rhode Island and in Providence, Rhode Island at the Eastern Film Corporation studios. Probably originally intended to be part of the Pelican Comedies series.
With Wilfred Clarke (*Benedict Bann*), Marguerite Chaffee (*one of the "girls"*), Dean Raymond (*police desk sergeant*), Jack Magle (*pilot*).

Benedict Bann arrives at the hotel with his three wives (Amelia, Bedelia and Cordelia). They look to keep him in line, while he looks to sneak out and meet his old friend Tom Single at Flossie Footlight's club. However, not arriving Tom goes to the hotel and learns that his old pal Benedict has three wives. Trying to free up some time for himself Benedict takes each wife on an individual date, only to abandon them as soon as he can. When each wife learns they have been ditched they raise up such a fuss as to get arrested. The desk sergeant releases the wives from jail and instructs his officer to bring in the "Bluebeard." The police and the wives search for Benedict and find him at the club. Benedict jumps out the window and speeds away in a car while the wives beat on the girls that had been entertaining their husband and his friend. The chase ends at the beach where Benedict hops into a bi-plane and flies away. [RS]

The title of the film refers to the alliance struck between Russia, France and the United Kingdom in 1907 that ultimately was one of the factors that led to the Great War. In the film the triple powers are the three Mormon wives that the unhappy husband married for some reason. Amelia is young a relatively pretty, Bedelia is older and beauty challenged, and Cordelia is just old and bossy. One of the few Pelican Comedies that survives in a watchable condition, *A Triple Entente* shows that the films made by the Eastern Film Corporation in 1915 and 1916 were well made and of comparable quality to other films released at that time. However, sitting in the vaults for two or three years didn't do the films any favors and, certainly for 1917 and 1918 audiences, began to look dated.

The October 2, 1915 edition of the *New York Clipper* details the making of *A Triple Entente*: "The Eastern Film Corporation, with studios located just outside of Providence, has engaged Jack Magle, the famous birdman of New England, to appear in several pictures. Before a crowd of several thousand at Oakland Beach, last Sunday Magle made a sensational flight, carrying with him Wilfred Clarke, who is assuming the leading role in the comedy entitled *The Triple Entente*. Several preliminary scenes were taken on the shores of the beach, and then before the eyes of the interested onlookers Mr. Clarke took his place beside Magle, and the airship with the two men ascended high in the air, the picture camera following its many gyrations and dips as it circled the bay. A daring feature during the taking of the scenes for *The Triple Entente* was the flight made by Marguerite Chaffee, leading lady of the Eastern Film Corporation. Miss Chaffee, who holds many records for feats of athletic prowess is an experienced flyer, and the sight of this young girl as she piloted the flying craft through many intricate turns at a dizzy height held the spectators spellbound. *The Triple Entente*, a comedy film showing these scenes, will shortly be released in photoplay houses throughout the country."

"A one-reel sparkling comedy production, full of pep." -- *Decatur Daily Democrat*

Whose Hosiery

Released circa October 1917. Sparkle Comedies (series No. 3, No. 5) - General Film Company release. One reel. No copyright registered.

Directed by unknown. Likely shot circa 1915-16 in Providence, Rhode Island at the Eastern Film Corporation studios. Probably originally intended to be part of the Pelican Comedies series.

With unknown.

Henry Brown, a traveling salesman, with sporty inclinations, buys a pair of gloves in a department store and gets instead a pair of silk hose, while Marie gets the gloves — the exchange being made by the cash girl. Mrs. Brown discovers the stockings in her husband's pocket, and, supposing they are for her, leaves them. Henry pleads a business engagement, and goes off for the night. He meets Marie and gives her stockings. Meanwhile, Mrs. Brown looks for the silk hose, and is surprised to find they have disappeared. Naturally suspicious, she at once decides that her husband is buying stockings for other girls. Her ire is aroused, and she manages to find out where her husband is dining and follows him to the restaurant. Meanwhile, Brown is having the time of his life with Marie and several boon companions. Mrs. Brown just misses them and returns home baffled. The next night she intercepts a note to Henry saying his gloves will be at the Royal Cafe that evening. She trails her husband to the cafe and is horrified to see a young lady wearing the identical silk stockings her husband had carried. Mrs. Brown Herbert pounces on her husband, a wild mix-up follows, Henry manages to explain about the exchange of parcels, and his wife leads him from the café by the ear. [MPW]

"An amusing farce comedy based on the old idea of the customer who gets the wrong package. Brown receives hosiery instead of gloves, gives them to the right girl who is to bring him the gloves the next evening. His wife gets wise, raises a row in the restaurant, but all ends satisfactorily when the girl produces the gloves." -- *Moving Picture World*

Wrong Wrights

Released circa October 1917. Sparkle Comedies (series No. 3, No. 6) - General Film Company release. One reel. No copyright registered.

Directed by unknown. Likely shot circa 1915-16 in Providence, Rhode Island at the Eastern Film Corporation studios. Probably originally intended to be part of the Pelican Comedies series.

With unknown.

Joe Wright and Jim Wright, married salesmen and old-time friends, register at the same hotel in New York unknown to each other. Joe, a newlywed, sends a loving telegram to his wife and the bellboy, whom he has not tipped, adds "follow me" to the message. Meanwhile Jim Wright goes out to see the town. Mrs. Joe, on receipt of the telegram, starts for New York at once and Mrs. Jim, always suspicious of her husband, decides to trail him. The bellboy takes them both to the wrong rooms and Mrs. Jim, hearing a splashing in the bathroom, is about to enter when she sees a woman's picture on the table. Joe, in the bathroom, hears a strange woman's voice and remains in the bathroom under a cold shower. Meanwhile Mrs. Joe, in Jim Wright's room, promptly goes into hysterics at the sight of another woman's picture and awaits her hubby with an umbrella. When Jim returns to his room after a gay night, Mrs. Joe pounces on him and the noise rouses the entire hotel. When the lights are turned on Mrs. Joe discovers her mistake. The clerks realize the error that has been made and hasten to the other Wright's room and get there just as Mrs. Jim is opening the bathroom door. Explanations follow and finally the wrong Wrights find themselves in the right rooms. [MPW]

"A comedy in which two traveling salesmen, each by the name of J. Wright, go to the same hotel. Through the scheming of a bellboy, whom one neglected to tip, their wives appear on the scene, and are shown to the wrong room. Obvious complications ensue. A fair number, with some laughs, but no novelty of plot or situations." -- *Moving Picture World*

Week End Shopping

Released November 1, 1917. Sparkle Comedies (series No. 4, No. 1) - General Film Company release. One reel. No copyright registered.

Produced by Frank Tichenor for Amber Star Films Corporation. Directed by Jerold T. Hevener [?]. Filmed circa late 1916-early 1917 in Jacksonville, Florida at the Hotel Mason and the Garrick Studios.
With Billy Ruge (*Billy*), Kate Price (*Kate*).

Kate and Billy visit a department store, where, Billy, disregarding his wife's presence, pursues a pretty girl whom he sees at the entrance. Kate finds them deeply absorbed in conversation, and after chasing the girl lands Billy on his head. Kate then drags Billy into the dry goods department, where he starts another flirtation, ending in a mix-up in which Kate gets entangled in a bolt of flannel and is dragged around the store. Other departments are visited and the flirtations continue. In the hosiery department Billy becomes enrapt with a beautifully modeled pair of legs in a show case, behind which stands a saleslady in such a position that the legs seem to be hers. Kate enters and another sensation is created. In the shoe department a dashing girl enters, removes her shoes and displays several holes in her stockings. Another flirtation ensues. The husband of the girl, who is of the Bowery type, tired of waiting outside, enters the store and discovers his wife in Billy's arms. He becomes enraged and starts a shooting affray. Billy, in his efforts to escape, catches hold of the parcel basket and goes flying around the store, finally dropping into Kate's lap. Just then the shoe salesman enters with the girl's old shoes, Billy having paid for the new ones, and hands the parcel to Billy, who turns it over to his wife, saying he has bought her a pair of new shoes. She opens the package, finds the girl's old shoes, and, taking Billy across her knees, gives him the spanking of his life. [MPW]

"A slapstick number of no great merit. The comedy has some amusing business but is not one that we could recommend for a refined program. Considerable of the action takes place in a shoe store where the wife of one man flirts with another. A mix up occurs when wife number two comes to search for her husband. Old stuff which the public must be tired of." -- *Moving Picture World*

Pals

Released circa November 1917. Sparkle Comedies (series No. 4, No. 2) - General Film Company release. One reel. No copyright registered.

Produced by Frank Tichenor for Amber Star Films Corporation. Directed by Jerold T. Hevener. Filmed January 14, 1917 in Jacksonville, Florida at the Hotel Seminole and the Garrick Studios.

With Billy Ruge (*Bill*), Kate Price (*Mrs. Runt*), Mack Richards.

Mrs. Runt takes in washing to provide a living for herself and daughter and a lazy husband who devotes himself to the beer can. Finally Kate throws Bill out of the house and he joins a circus, driving a trick ostrich. The circus goes broke and Bill takes the ostrich in payment for his salary. Meantime Kate falls heir to a fortune. She and her daughter arrive at a hotel just as Bill is trying to register for himself and ostrich. They are thrown out and land at Kate's feet, but she doesn't recognize him. Kate's trunk is dropped and, the lid bursting open, Bill smuggles in the ostrich. Bill's room proves to be opposite Kate's, and during her absence Bill goes to release the ostrich and is caught. Kate chases him over roofs, finally down a flag pole which brings Bill upon a hydroplane, Kate close at his heels. Bill catches hold of the rope to the plane and up he goes. Kate secures a motorcycle and a race ensues. Kate goes headlong over an embankment, is thrown into a passing auto and rushed back to the hotel. Just as she is seated in her room Bill comes crashing through the skylight. Kate takes another shot at him and he dives out the window onto the back of the ostrich and rides away, saying, "Back to the circus for mine." [MPW]

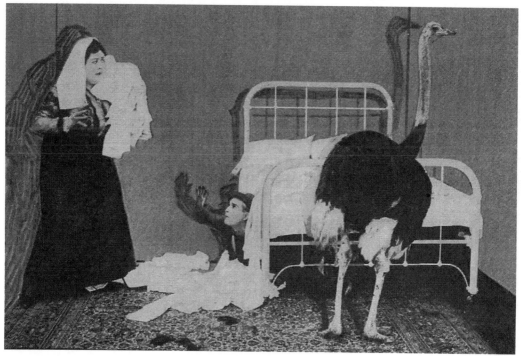

[no review available]

Ambition

Released circa November 1917. Sparkle Comedies (series No. 4, No. 3) - General Film Company release. One reel. No copyright registered.

Produced by Frank Tichenor for Amber Star Films Corporation. Directed by Jerold T. Hevener [?]. Filmed circa January-March 1917 in Jacksonville, Florida at the Hotel Mason and the Garrick Studios.

With Billy Ruge (*Billy*), Jennie Nelson (*Kate*), Kate Price (*Mrs. B. Nice*), Roland Hill (*party guest*), James Renfro (*butler*).

Kate and Bill, living on a farm, dream of the joys of high life. Finally Kate answers an advertisement for a maid to attend a wealthy foreigner and secures the position. Kate soon sees a chance to realize her dream. Miss Adair receives an invitation to a week-end party, and is obliged to send her regrets, giving the letter to Kate to mail. Kate re-writes it, sending an acceptance, and, after her mistress has left town, Kate goes to the party as Miss Adair. Meantime Bill also gets a job with the DeNice family, which is giving the party. He is ordered to take a drink to the baron's room, and spills the liquor on the baron, who promptly hits him. Bill wallops the baron and puts him out of business; then, donning the baron's clothes, he joins the guests and, in the boisterous festivities, gets by. Kate, meanwhile, has made a great hit with a Russian count. Bill insults Kate before the count, who demands satisfaction. Bill has to be dragged out to the field of honor. When the swords clash, Bill gets scared and flees. A long chase follows, and finally Bill is caught in the middle of the big bail room. The count drags Bill over to Kate, demanding an apology, when in comes the real Miss Adair, and with a dramatic gesture says, "She is my maid." At this point the real baron enters and exposes Bill. Both Kate and Bill are thrown out bodily, and the Russian count says, "never again." When they recover their faculties, Bill and Kate admit they have had enough of high life and embrace. [MPW]

The publicity department at the Amber Star Studios must have had a bad day when they released the synopsis for *Ambition*. The character they call Kate is actually played by Jennie Nelson and not Kate Price. Very odd that Kate Price is relegated to being a supporting player and barely appears in the film, and then only to give a reaction or two with no real comedy business. Jennie Nelson does a fine job, but with the studio supposedly developing Price & Ruge as a comedy team, the casting is very odd and the under-utilization of Kate Price almost criminal. The storyline is all over the place, which is bothersome, but then so are the settings, which is enjoyable in that Jacksonville is seen to full advantage. Some business between Billy and the overly tall man that portrays the baron is amusing, with the much shorter Ruge easily slipping between the baron's legs in order to avoid harm. But perhaps a little more ambition is what the scenario writer should have possessed.

"A one-reel comedy featuring Billy Ruge, based on the idea of the country girl who comes to town and gets a job as a maid, while her lover enters the employ of another society swell as a butler. They both attend a reception disguised as guests, are discovered and thrown out. An old idea, presented with considerable slapstick work, but which contains a few laughs." -- *Moving Picture World*

In High Speed

November 22, 1917. Sparkle Comedies (series No. 4, No. 4) - General Film Company release. One reel. No copyright registered.

Produced by Frank Tichenor for Amber Star Films Corporation. Directed by Jerold T. Hevener [?]. Filmed circa January-March 1917 in Jacksonville, Florida at the Hotel Mason and the Garrick Studios.

With Billy Ruge (*Billy*), Kate Price (*Mrs. B Nice*).

Sally and Rube, lovers, go to the city to see the fair. Unaccustomed to city ways, they meet with many accidents and have trouble with the traffic cop, but finally reach the fair grounds. They saunter past a tent on which is a sign reading, "Kiss the Prettiest Girl in Springfield for 50 Cents." Rube breaks away from Sally and goes in. He shows the "prettiest girl in Springfield" a wad of money that he has saved during the past year, and she at once accepts his invitation to see the fair with him. The manager, disgusted at losing his vampire, goes outside, sees Sally and drags her in to take the part. In comes a dandy who becomes stuck on Sally. She refuses to kiss him and proceeds to tell him how she came to be there. Finally Rube's money becomes exhausted and the girl becomes frigid and leaves him. Rube is bewildered, but cured. He sees Sally and her new friend stroll by and appeals to her, but they laugh at him and, crossing the street, enter an automobile and drive off. Rube leaves the fair disconsolately. [MPW]

Each film trade paper had a staff of writers reviewing films and they usually were fairly objective. But sometimes they would publish an "article" that looked like a review but was really nothing more than a studio press release. *Moving Picture World* published the following: "Kate Price and Billy Ruge, fun-makers extraordinary, create the biggest bundle of laughs they have yet turned out in the current release, *In High Speed*, in the new series of Sparkle comedies being distributed by General Film Company. *In High Speed* depicts the heart burnings of a country girl, Sally, her subsequent revenge upon her faithless lover, Rube, and the latter's discomfiture at the hands of a city vampire. This comedy continues to set the pace which makes the new series of Sparkles most desirable program adjuncts." In this case, the legit reviews echoed the studio's propaganda. It is interesting to note that when the Sparkle comedies were reviewed, Kate Price often was not mentioned at all, even though she was known to be in the film, and was a highly regarded comedienne.

"Billy and his rustic sweetheart attend the country fair. He yields to the attractions of a damsel peddling kisses in a booth. A fat sport annexes his girl. After numerous adventures Billy finds his pocket has been picked. He drives disconsolately home in his buggy, while the girl rolls by triumphantly in a big automobile with the favored suitor. The photography is good, the fair settings excellent and Billy Ruge extracts a lot of merriment out of the situations. There is a variety of horseplay in evidence and the film will please admirers of broad comedy." -- *Exhibitors Trade Review*

Monkey Maid Man

Released circa December 1917. Sparkle Comedies (series No. 4, No. 6) - General Film Company release. One reel. No copyright registered. Working title: *Home Made Horrors*. Erroneously listed in some sources as: *Money Maid Man*.

Produced by Frank Tichenor for Amber Star Films Corporation. Written and directed by Jerold T. Hevener. Filmed late January 1917 in Jacksonville, Florida at the Garrick Studios.

With Billy Ruge (*iceman*), Kate Price (*maid*), Roland Hill, Mack Richards.

> *Kate, a maid in the household of Mr. and Mrs. Trude, is in love with Billy, the Iceman. One morning, while serving breakfast. Billy appears, and Kate entirely neglects the family, giving all her attention to the little iceman. Their love-making disgusts Mr. Trude, and he leaves for the office without his breakfast. Later in the day he is induced by a friend to have a drink. Meanwhile Kate and Billy continue to make violent love, and finally Kate escorts him out to the ice wagon. Still unable to separate, they sit on a cake of ice. and the horse starts carrying through the busy streets and finally returns them to their starting point without either of them knowing it. At length Billy succeeds in tearing himself away, promising to return in the afternoon and take Kate to the movies. He enters a saloon with a cake of ice, and clumsily drops it on the foot of a man at the bar who proves to be Mr. Trude, who is not exactly sober. A quarrel ensues, but Billy buys the drinks, and they become friends. An organ grinder enters with an educated gorilla, which creates so much amusement that Mr. Trude and Billy buy the animal, and Mr. Trude decides to take it home. Cautiously approaching the house they see Kate all dressed waiting to be taken to the movies, and Mrs. Trude awaiting her husband's return to dinner. The men stealthily go upstairs to a bedroom. The gorilla's actions cause such a commotion that the women downstairs start to investigate, and entering the bedroom find Billy and Mr. Trude in the arms of the gorilla. Horrified, they rush to a nearby police station, and a squad of policemen are sent out. They rush into the house expecting to find a burglar, and, when they behold the gorilla, make a swift retreat. Finally the owner of the gorilla appears and buys it back. As he leaves the women rush upstairs, and, discovering their dear ones unhurt, all is forgiven.* [MPW]

"Kate is the cook, and Billy is her lover, the ice man. Billy meets the master of the house in a saloon, and they buy a monkey, after partaking quite freely of liquid refreshment. After much excitement they finally dispose of the beast. There are a number of comedy policemen who do ordinary rough and tumble stunts, and Billy has some amusing work with the monkey, which is almost as large as he is." -- *Moving Picture World*

On the Love Line

Released December 22, 1917 [NYDM says Dec 13]. Sparkle Comedies (series No. 5, No. 1) - General Film Company release. One reel. No copyright registered.

Produced by Frank Tichenor for Amber Star Films Corporation. Directed by Jerold T. Hevener. Filmed in Jacksonville, Florida at the Garrick Studios.

With Billy Ruge (*Billy*), Jennie Nelson (*Letty*), Edna Reynolds (*mother*), Roland Hill (*hash house owner*).

Letty, who considers herself the "whole cheese" in the chop house near the car barn in the city, decides to quit and return to the farm, owing to the persistent wooing of Billy, the Beau Brummel of conductors and motormen. Jim, her country sweetheart, goes to town to meet her and arrives in time to see Letty in the midst of a battle royal which results in the wrecking of the chop house. On the way home Billy keeps up his ardent flirtation, much to Jim's annoyance. Billy picks up a card of Count Elec Trick, Special Envoy to H. R. H., King of Shox. He rigs himself up as the count and calls on Letty, who promptly throws Jim over for royalty. The deception is discovered by Letty's father, who intercepts a message from the Count arranging for an elopement. Father decides to forestall the plans, so in the morning he takes Billy's trolley car and dashes to the appointed place, followed by Billy in an auto. Letty thinks Billy is running the trolley and only sees her mistake when it is too late and she is locked in the speeding car. Billy overtakes the trolley, snatches Letty from the window, the auto explodes and they are landed at the abode of the village pastor, who ties the knot as the irate father dashes in and decides to give his blessing. [MPW]

On the Love Line is a pretty well made and funny comedy, unfortunately something rare for Billy Ruge's solo work. Whether some of his other Sparkle Comedies reach this level will likely never be known since, except for *Ambition*, no others are extant. However the real star is Jennie Nelson, who takes on the role of the gum chewing Letty with much vigor. The opening scenes with Letty washing the dishes is very inventive with her tossing dishes onto a conveyor and in a somewhat Rube Goldberg manner the dishes seem to clean themselves using some stop motion camera work. Even when the dishes are cleared from the dining area back to the kitchen the action is handled this way. Stop motion is further used to show the eggs cooking themselves and the plates serving themselves across the lunch counter. Even the signs in the "hash house" show some inventiveness with one of the special of the day being "Eggs on the Half Shell." Billy Ruge for his part is still good old Billy mostly taking pratfalls and mugging but since the rest of the cast is up to the task even he draws a laugh or two. *Exhibitors Trade Review* liked Billy's work in this one: "The comedy is full of brisk rough action and gives the versatile Mr. Ruge numerous opportunities." While *Moving Picture World* thought the film overall was funny, "The action is of a burlesque nature and gets up a fair amount of humor."

To identify where a film was shot is sometimes easy to do, and other times difficult. While it seems obvious that the film was shot in Jacksonville, and shows the Riverside district of the town extensively, the name of the trolley company causes some confusion. Well featured in the film the trolley car bears the company name "San Jose Traction Co." which to most (including this California-born author) would indicate the film was shot in the town of San Jose that sits just south of San Francisco. However, many small villages sprang up around Jacksonville in the early 20th century and one just south of town, and serviced by the trolley system, was the town of San Jose. First assumptions, without double checking, often leads to misinformation even when all other indicators contradict the mistaken thought.

"In the first of his new series of Sparkle Comedies, released by General Film, Billy Ruge appears as a Beau Brummel conductor who puts a lot of speed and dash into his wooing. "On the Love Line " is one of the best comedies Ruge has yet done for the screen, and is a guarantee of other fast stepping laughmakers for comedy lovers." -- *New York Dramatic Mirror*

The Detective

Released circa December 1917. Sparkle Comedies (series No. 5, No. 2) - General Film Company release. One reel. No copyright registered.

Produced by Frank Tichenor for Amber Star Films Corporation. Directed by Jerold T. Hevener. Filmed in Jacksonville, Florida at the Garrick Studios.

With Billy Ruge (*Will Huntem*), Jennie Nelson (*Jennie Million*).

Jennie Million, in town on a shopping trip, is kidnapped along with her chauffeur, coming out of a department store. The chauffeur is kicked out with a note to Jennie's father, a wealthy banker, demanding one hundred thousand dollars for the return of his daughter. The police are notified, and Will Huntem, the world-famous detective, is put on the case. He advises the banker to place a bundle of fake money in the appointed place. He catches one of the gang in the act of taking the money, but in the mix-up his man disappears through a manhole. He follows through the sewers and arrives at a door leading to their den where the girl is tied up.

The gun-men get into a row among themselves and Bill, the detective, dashes in. A fight ensues and he is tied to a keg of gunpowder. They light the fuse and then start in pursuit of the girl who has freed herself. Left to his fate, the detective weeps copiously and discovers a way out by means of his tears. Holding his streaming face over the fuse he sees the fatal spark go out under the flood of salty tears and, tearing his bonds asunder, he grabs a bomb and dashes after the gang. Meantime the girl takes refuge up

the ladder of a water tank, the gang following. Taking in the situation at a glance the relentless detective calls to the fair one to jump into his waiting arms, which she does, while the detective hurls the bomb into the midst of the ruffians. The tank is shattered and the gang fall to earth only to renew the chase with renewed vigor. The father and chauffeur, having witnessed the chase, now dash after the gang and a race ensues, ending in the crooks being precipitated into a raging stream, while the father clasps his daughter in his arms. [MPW]

"Will Huntem, a shrewd and calculating detective, who isn't afraid of anything from bombs to gunpowder, is introduced in the current Sparkle comedy of General Film Company, *The Detective*. Billy Ruge, as Huntem, no sooner emerges from the triumph than he is plunged into another laugh-making adventure. He saves himself from an untimely fate by weeping copiously upon the fuse attached to the barrel of powder upon which he is tied, and returns to the pursuit of the captors of Jennie Million." -- *Motion Picture News & Moving Picture World*

Smashing the Plot

Released circa December 1917. Sparkle Comedies (series No. 5, No. 3) - General Film Company release. One reel. No copyright registered.

Produced by Frank Tichenor for Amber Star Films Corporation. Directed by Jerold T. Hevener. Filmed in Jacksonville, Florida at the Garrick Studios.

With Billy Ruge, Jennie Nelson (*Jennie*).

Jennie, maid of all work in the home of a railroad president, hears the strains of her sweetheart's hand organ outside her window. Tony sends her a note beseeching her to go to a "wop" dance that afternoon, entrusting the note to the monkey, who promptly delivers it to Mr. Barker and his wife who are sitting on the lawn. The note is finally delivered to Jennie and that afternoon they hie themselves to the dance. Here Tony is given a "high sign" by a fierce looking "wop" informing him that his presence is desired at a meeting of the secret society in the basement. He rushes off and Jennie follows and from an adjoining room overhears them draw lots to see who shall blow up the railroad bridge that afternoon as

President Barker passes over it. Tony feels highly honored when he draws the lucky number, but Jennie, hearing that Tony was "framed," springs a trap in the floor and down go several of the "wops." She tries to escape but is captured and made a member of the secret society. She is instructed to blow up Mr. Barker's home, but instead mounts a horse and gallops after Tony who has found a hand car on the track. Then follows an exciting chase, the "wops" having mysteriously appeared on the scene in a carriage. Jennie, seeing they are gaining on her, throws her bomb and blows up the carriage. Mounted police are called out and take up the chase in a patrol, while the "wops" continue on to the bridge in a row boat. Jennie arrives just in time to flag the train and taking the infernal machine from Tony throws it into the boatload of "wops," incidentally pushing Tony off the bridge. She dives over after him and drags him ashore and tells him that blowing up railroad presidents is a "bum job." [MPW]

A monkey has a prominent part in this film and director Jerold Hevener's affection for using animals in his films didn't go without notice by the local press. So much so that Hevener sent word to the *Florida Metropolis* that he was actually more versatile. Writer Tracy Hollingsworth noted in his *Flivvers From Film Folk* column that "Now Jerry Hevener has sent us word that he does direct other things besides animals in his Amber Star pictures, which we knew all the time." It is unknown if the references to directing animals included Billy Ruge.

"In thee current Sparkle comedy, *Smashing the Plot*, Billy Ruge takes the part of an organ-grinder who is persuaded to assist in the destruction of a railroad bridge by a band of anarchists. All sorts of funny complications result, and in the end the plot of the bomb-throwers is smashed." -- *New York Dramatic Mirror*

After the Matinee

Released November 1, 1917. Sparkle Comedies (series No. 5, No. 4) - General Film Company release. One reel. No copyright registered.

Produced by Frank Tichenor for Amber Star Films Corporation. Directed by Jerold T. Hevener. Filmed early March 1917 at the Garrick Studios and the Hotel Burbridge in Jacksonville, Florida.

With Billy Ruge, Edna Reynolds (*Trixie Davenport*), Mack Richards.

Wheeler and Bruce, law partners, go to the Beauty Show where they meet Trixie Davenport, a soubrette. Trixie has been informed by her manager that some big publicity scheme will have to be framed up, as business is bad. The partners escort her to her hotel, exacting a promise that she will drop around to their offices to see them. Trixie and her press agent see possibilities of glaring headlines, and soon the partners receive a telephone message that Trixie is about to pay the expected visit. They suspend work and send the clerks home for the day. Trixie arrives, wine is opened and all cares forgotten. Her press agent, in the meantime, has informed the wives that they are needed at their husbands' offices, and soon the partners are informed by the private telephone operator that their wives are in the outer office. Trixie is hastily togged out in various articles of the men's wearing apparel in the hope that she will pass through unnoticed, but she is careful to disclose her sex to the waiting wives, who are shocked beyond words, and are only prevented from tearing her to pieces by the press agent, who has just entered. The attorneys, hearing the rumpus, take refuge on some rigging which is taking up a safe outside the window. The wives follow, cut the rope, and all land on the sidewalk below, where Trixie and her press agent arrive in time to tell a policeman that it is all just a little publicity scheme which will be explained in tomorrow's newspaper. Having accomplished their purpose they merrily beat it, while the wives take vengeance on their misled husbands. [MPW]

Hotel Burbridge,
Jacksonville, Fla.

The big stunt in the film has Trixie jumping from the third floor of the hotel. Edna Reynolds, with a reported crowd of 500 below, actually does the stunt. The *Florida Metropolis* account of the event mentions that the actress was jumping to "escape from the clutches of that cruel Billy Ruge." So there may not have been any actual acting involved.

It should be noted while Ruge and company were filming outside the Burbridge Hotel, his former partner and temporarily ex-film actor Babe Hardy was inside working as the featured singer with his wife's orchestra.

"A knockabout number of the eccentric type, featuring Billy Ruge. He and his partner in the law business become mixed up with an actress and their wives discover them. The action is of the rough and tumble sort and contains some amusing moments." -- *Moving Picture World*

Double Cross

Released circa January 1918. Sparkle Comedies (series No. 5, No. 5) - General Film Company release. One reel. No copyright registered.

Produced by Frank Tichenor for Amber Star Films Corporation. Directed by Jerold T. Hevener. Filmed in Jacksonville, Florida at the Garrick Studios.

With Billy Ruge.

Bill and Leola, old sweethearts, meet in the park and talk over old times. That evening in their respective homes they are preoccupied and at last the suspicions of Bill's wife and Leola's husband are aroused. They visit Prof. Chiro the next day and the husband is told to beware of a dark young man, while Bill's wife is warned that a blonde is trying to alienate her husband's affections. Each determines to pursue the cause of the trouble and an exciting search follows. Finally, wearied of the chase, they call on Prof. Chiro again for advice, and he tells them to see Jingse, the detective, who occupies the next room to his. They do so, but do not recognize the detective, who is the professor in disguise. Each gives him a portrait to be used in tracing the parties. While visiting the two homes in the discharge of his duties the detective recognizes the originals of the pictures and comprehends the situation. He tells Bill and Leola to be in his fortune telling parlors at a certain hour, and also tells the husband and wife, respectively, to be at his detective's rooms at the same time. He first interviews the husband and wife in his role of detective, collects his money, and then tells them that the professor next door will fix them up. The detective makes a quick change and slides through a door into the house next door, where, as the professor, he again collects. Then bringing the two couples together, an explanation follows. [MPW]

"A rollicking screen comedy with some unusually entertaining situations." -- *Moving Picture World*

The Best of a Bad Bargain

Released circa January 1918. Sparkle Comedies (series No. 5, No. 6) -General Film Company release. One reel. No copyright registered.

Produced by Frank Tichenor for Amber Star Films Corporation. Directed by Jerold T. Hevener. Filmed in Jacksonville, Florida at the Garrick Studios.

With Billy Ruge (*Billy*).

Billie, the chauffeur, has won the heart, but not the hand, of Sussie, the daughter of his employer. Bibbs, a prude, has the parental approbation of his struggle for Sussie's hand. When Sussie shows that she has something to say in the matter, the parents decide it is time to send their daughter to a discipline school. Billie is on the scene at the moment of her departure and receives a note from Sussie telling him she is being packed off to school and begging him not to desert her. While Sussie is introduced into the school, Billie is trying to find an escape for her. He hits upon the plan of getting all the girls out by inviting them to a show. The girls climb out of the windows in their pajamas, dress on the lawn, and leave for the show. When they get to the box office, Billie and Sussie sneak away to get married. In the meantime, Miss Prim discovers their absence and notifies the police, apprising them of the clue left by the program which had been found. Billie and Sussie arrive on the scene just before the police, and Billie manages to fool them while they are seeking the other runaways. Billie then tells Sussie's father that they are married and Dad makes the best of a bad bargain. [MPW]

The last Sparkle Comedy released although there is no way of knowing for sure if this was the last one made. But as such it was Billy Ruge's last work for the Jaxon Film Corporation and his final time before the cameras in Jacksonville, Florida.

"Dad got the worst of it in his encounter with Billie's persistent wooing and Susie's determination to be Mrs. Billie. Dad decides to pack Susie off to a discipline school, but Billie, not to be outdone invited all the pupils to a show, and out of the windows they climbed, pajamas and all – and then Billie and Susie hit the trail for the nearest parson's. It's a riot of laughs from start to finish." -- *Exhibitors Trade Review*

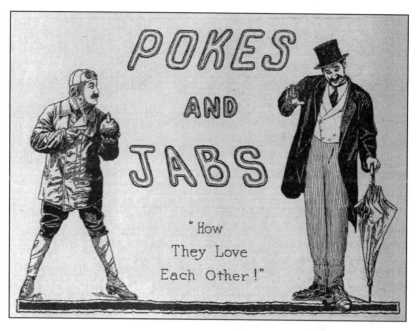

AFTERMATH

By the beginning of 1918 the company that started out as Wizard, morphed into Vim, and transformed into Jaxon was no more. Like oh so many production companies of its time, the entity that made the Pokes & Jabs films (along with some other pretty good comedies) began with a bang and ended with little more than a whimper. Much can always be found about the "new" company hitting the motion picture industry, but rarely is there anyone left to write the press release about the ceasing of production. Vim, with its before and after, lasted just about three years. Over 250 films were produced and/or released by the three iterations, with nearly one hundred of those being Pokes & Jabbs comedies.

There were some attempts by Eastern to keep the Jaxon Film Corporation alive after discontinuing their comedy productions, both as a rental studio and as a producer of new product. In September 1919, Truart had moved into the studio, and then in May 1920 it was announced that Jaxon was making an alliance with producers F.A. Dahme and Luis Seel to produce a series of animated novelties called "Screen Follies" to be released by Capital Films. Around the same time, Eastern created another subsidiary called Photo Products Export Company that began marketing "new" Bobby Burns Comedies as well as a series of films with Billy Ruge (and there is evidence that old Vim comedies were also reissued by Photo Products Export Company). From photographs featured in the trade advertisements for the series it is obvious that, at least with some titles, Eastern was simply rereleasing old Pokes and Jabbs product. In some cases, as with *Breaking Into Business*, they were issuing previously unreleased material that had been sitting in the vaults. It is curious that some of the ads show Bobby Burns sans Walter Stull and dressed in blackface, indicating that they may have been experimenting with the same kind of makeup that would be featured frequently in the Cuckoo Comedies that were yet to come. But Eastern's aspirations to be a leading player in the production and distribution of motion pictures faded. Yet under Frank Tichenor's leadership the Eastern Film Corporation would remain active for decades after the demise of the Jaxon and its other subsidiaries, successfully making educational and industrial films.

With the singular exception of Walter Stull, all of the main players involved with Vim at one time or the other remained in the film industry reaching varying levels of stardom but all achieving steady work in the movie industry. Stull, it appears, had enough. Records indicate that by 1918 he had returned to Philadelphia and took over managing his father-in-law's business. Little is known of his life after his film career. He remained married to his wife Virginia for the rest of his life but no children are indicated in census records. In 1921 the tires on his car were stolen while it was parked in front of his house, and he apparently appeared in a community theater production in 1938, but the photograph and brief mention of his name in the newspaper are the only indication of any involvement in his former life. As a businessman he served on some boards and local committees while living in Philadelphia. Later in life the Stulls moved to a small town just south of Atlantic City, New Jersey. Walter Stull died on November 19, 1946 and was buried in his home town Philadelphia; he was survived by his wife.

Other production companies came into being after the demise of the Vim Films Corporation whose pedigree could be linked directly back to Vim. King Bee, which would make Charlie Chaplin-imitator comedies with Billy West, was pretty much the Babe Hardy unit of Vim with a new director and star. Harry Myers and Rosemary Theby, along with Mark Dintenfass, would take over the Vim lot and briefly continue making Myers & Theby comedies for Pathé. Bobby Burns, again with Dintenfass, would then take over the lot and film his Cuckoo Comedies with many ex-Vimmies, including director Will Louis, as part of the company.

Babe Hardy once remarked that his days with Vim were among the happiest in his life. Certainly the legacy of those three years, be they Wizard, Vim or Jaxon, is great. Some pretty funny comedies were made in what was essentially a testing ground for the futures of some very fine comedians. That fact alone makes the whole endeavor worthy of remembrance.

An ad for the "new" Bobby Burns Comedies. The scene still with Walter Stull and Jennie Nelson gives away the true freshness of these 1920 releases.

Series With Direct Vim Lineage

MYERS & THEBY PATHÉ COMEDIES

By mid-January 1917 Vim was gone. Many of the players had moved over to Amber Star while others picked up work at some of the other studios still in Jacksonville. Babe Hardy, seemingly loyal to Louis Burstein until the end, sang with his wife's band while waiting for Burstein to return with a new film company. Harry Myers didn't wait around. Along with Marcel Perez, he formed Encore Pictures Corporation with the intent of making two-reel Myers & Theby comedies and one-reelers starring Tweedledum. An announcement was made, five acres secured for a studio, and then nothing. For Encore there would not even be a first act.

Then in February, following a lengthy legal dispute with Amber Star, Mark Dintenfass reappeared in Jacksonville and announced he was forming the Myers-Theby Comedy Corporation and would be producing a new series of refined comedies. Harry Myers and Rosemary Theby, having left Jacksonville for New York with the closing of Vim, returned to the Southern city on February 20. The Pathé Exchange was looking to expand the Lonesome Luke comedies to two reels and needed a new supply of one reel comedies. The popular comedies of Myers & Theby provided that product and a variation of comic style. Through never-to-be-fully-understood business dealings, Dintenfass gained control of the old Vim studio and set up shop with many of the old Vim crew making the movies. Myers would direct, Herman Obrock (although he soon bolted for King Bee) and then Eugene French would turn the camera, Jerold T. Hevener (fresh from directing Billy Ruge in Sparkle comedies) was the assistant director and Bert Tracy handled writing the scenarios along with Rex Taylor. Some of the players from other companies that were leaving Jacksonville decided to stay behind and found work at the old Vim lot including Ed Lawrence and Polly Van.

None of the Pathé Myers & Theby comedies survive. They likely were merely a continuation of the well-received comedies they had made at Vim and Victor before that. However not all reviewers were enamored with the new films. The reviewer for *Photo-Play Journal* had much to say about the comedy duo: "A series of comedies in which Harry Myers and Rosemary Theby are starred by Mark M. Dintenfass has been released on the Pathé program, and these latest efforts of this duo make one wonder all the more why they do not separate. They are woefully unsuited to each other from an artistic standpoint. Harry Myers is a top-notch interpreter of serious roles, and he is an experienced director, and we imagine he could show plenty of the essential attributes of a comedian if he were supported by a real comedienne, something Miss Theby is not by any method of reckoning. Candor must be accepted as the means to the end of bettering a condition, and therefore we are constrained to say Mr. Myers needs a new leading lady. Undoubtedly Miss Theby could find a more compatible field in Screenland and there is every indication of her ability running to character work instead of heroics or comics."

Only four of the Pathé comedies were released and both Harry Myers and Rosemary Theby (cohabitating but not yet married) left for the West Coast. Perhaps they took the review in *Photo-Play Journal* to heart, these Pathé comedies were the last time the two would work together on screen on a regular basis. In Hollywood, Theby at first went to work at Universal supporting Lyons & Moran (some of those comedies being directed by Harry Myers); she then would reunite with fellow former Vimite Babe Hardy in a few King Bee comedies, providing the female support for Billy West. Myers would move between supporting and starring roles in features. There was one final attempt to revive their onscreen partnership in March 1921, just after they both appeared in *A Connecticut Yankee in King Artur's Court*, when Dominant Pictures, Inc. announced a series of one reel "New Wed Comedies" to star the pair. The announcement assured readers that those comedies were not reissues, and that twelve had already been filmed; alas, there is no evidence of that having been the case. Around this time, it was also announced that Myers would be writing comedies for Louis Burstein (now spelled Burston) but nothing seems to have come of that either. Harry Myers and Rosemary Theby would eventually marry and both worked regularly, in albeit increasingly smaller roles, until the late 1930s.

The Delicatessen Mystery

Released May 13, 1917. Myers-Theby Comedy Corporation/Pathé Exchange. One reel. No copyright registered.

Produced by Mark Dintenfass. Directed by Harry C. Myers. Photography by Herman Obrock. Filmed March 9-17, 1917 at the Vim Studios in Jacksonville, Florida.

with Harry Myers, Rosemary Theby.

The story of a newlywed couple who, to save expenses, rent their bungalow and become boarders. They soon find out that the landlady has placed an embargo on cooking in the room and the means by which they elude her vigilance provide the comedy. [ETR]

"The plot of this exaggerated 'refined' gem is the troubles of a back-room pair in a city lodging-house, where the landlady rules "no cooking" on the premises. So they go to the delicatessen and smuggle in various "delicacies," first in the landlady's umbrella, and second by the unique idea of winding sausages around the gentleman's belt line. Later they go to the theatre, and take their "leftovers" with them, much to the interference with the olfactory nerves of the audience, who protest emphatically, with a resulting "exposure" in the night court. The fun is not as riotous as it might have been had there been more slapstick, but will please those who like this sort of comedy." -- *Motion Picture News*

"Harry Myers and Rosemary Theby appear for the first time on the Pathé program in 'The Delicatessen Mystery,' a hilarious comedy in one reel. Harry Myers is funnier than he has ever been before and Rosemary Theby prettier than she has ever been before. In addition, there is the most killingly farcical detective ever seen on stage or screen." -- *Moving Picture World*

Jumping Jealousy

Released May 20, 1917. Myers-Theby Comedy Corporation/Pathé Exchange. One reel. No copyright registered.

Produced by Mark Dintenfass. Directed by Harry C. Myers. Photography by Herman Obrock. Filmed circa April 1917 at the Vim Studios in Jacksonville, Florida.

with Harry Myers, Rosemary Theby.

Hubby's lack of interest in his wife causes her to flirt with the iceman and the other trade people. Jealousy at this causes Hubby to start reprisals in bringing into the house a large number of young stenographers. The mix up of the two separate parties form the foundation of the comedy. [ETR]

"This comedy, with Harry Myers and Rosemary Theby, concerns a jealous husband and an equally jealous wife. Each imports a variety of suitors to make the other even more jealous, but eventually matters are patched up in good style. Not much of a plot but containing a number of scenes funny individually." –*Motion Picture News*

"'Jumping Jealousy' can only be classed as an average comedy. It lacks a certain amount of originality, and while it might pull a laugh from some the result is doubtful." -- *Exhibitor's Trade Review*

Rusticating

Released May 27, 1917. Myers-Theby Comedy Corporation/Pathé Exchange. One reel. No copyright registered.

Produced by Mark Dintenfass. Directed by Harry C. Myers. Photography by Herman Obrock. Filmed circa April 1917 at the Vim Studios in Jacksonville, Florida.

with Harry Myers, Rosemary Theby.

The adventures of a young married couple who leave for the country to get a rest, but instead have a more strenuous time than if they had remained at home. [ETR]

"Harry Myers and Rosemary Theby are seen in 'Rusticating,' a one-reel comedy and one of the funniest of the type made famous by this team of farceurs. It tells of the attempt of a city-bred couple to find peace and quiet in the country." -- *Moving Picture World*

"In this Harry Myers and Rosemary Theby take to a farm for rest and fare rather badly. They discover rusticating, with its rainy night, leaky roofs, bees and practical jokes instituted by the farmers, is not at all what it's cracked up to be. This is conventional fare on the whole, but has been treated very well by the actor-director." –*Motion Picture News*

Police Protection

Released June 3, 1917. Myers-Theby Comedy Corporation/Pathé Exchange. One reel. No copyright registered.

Produced by Mark Dintenfass. Directed by Harry C. Myers. Photography by Herman Obrock. Filmed circa April 1917 at the Vim Studios in Jacksonville, Florida.

with Harry Myers, Rosemary Theby.

This is an amusing comedy based on a general mix-up of identities, due to the attempt of a wife left alone to have the house properly guarded. She mistakes a burglar for the detective agency's man, and hubby and a friend and the genuine guardian all get into a mix-up trying to straighten out identities. Wifey, already retired, gets "some scare," but the burglar is finally caught and everything explained. [MPN]

"The wife's sudden visit home, the detective hired to guard the house, the husband's friend on a visit and the real burglar form the run and chase comedy in this production. The plot is simple, relying altogether upon the mistaken identity of the various household and the laugh depends upon the dodging from one room to another in trying to find the real burglar. But still there is enough interest to make this release of value for the varied program." -- *Exhibitor's Trade Review*

CUCKOO COMEDIES

Where Bobby Burns was and what he was doing after the fire at the Eastern Film Corporation studio is a bit of a mystery with only a few clues. The last of the Pokes & Jabbs comedies was released in December 1917, and he did register for the draft on September 17, 1918 in Jacksonville listing Dintenfass as his employer and 750 Riverside Avenue as his place of employment. But professionally nothing is heard of Burns until a single small blurb in the March 28, 1919 issue of *Variety*, which notes that Mark Dintenfass was making series of "Black & White Comedies" at his studio in Jacksonville (the old Vim studios) and that Bobby Burns would star in these comedies that would alternate between those with Burns in blackface and those with him in his standard make-up, hence the "Black and White." The article noted that they had already completed three two-reelers with the first to be called *No Mother to Guide Him*. Nothing more is heard until early August 1919 when the newly branded "Cuckoo Comedies" are officially announced.

Dintenfass, in the interim between making Myers & Theby comedies at the studio and the blackface comedies with Burns, had produced the highly acclaimed feature *My Four Years in Germany*. Will Louis was recruited to direct the new comedies and a cast including Jobyna Ralston (as chief support), Fatty Filbert (soon to be known as Hilliard Karr), Skinny Renfro, May Louis, and Frank Hanson was assembled. Anita Brown would join the troupe a few months later, and Edna Reynolds was mentioned as being in the cast when the latter titles were mentioned.

So the question of when these Cuckoo comedies were actually shot can only be answered with some facts, some guesswork and much confusion. The *Variety* article indicates that at least three Cuckoos were made sometime before late March 1919. It is known that Fatty Filbert, who provided support in those films, started making a series of comedies directed by John Binney for the Florida Film Corporation in 1918 (shot in Jacksonville at the Klutho studios), with the first released in May of that year. These comedies also include Vim alums Bert Tracy and Florence McLoughlin. First called John Binney Comedies but then, when Bert Tracy and Glen Lambert took over directorial duties, relabeled Sunbeam Comedies (not to be confused with the Billy West starring comedies of the same name made by C.B.C. in 1922), the series consisted of at least a dozen two-reelers with the last released in August 1919. It is highly unlikely that Fatty Filbert was making his own comedies and providing support for Bobby Burns at the same time, which means the Cuckoo Comedies were either made sometime in late 1917 or early 1918 before the Florida Film Corporation started production at the Klutho Studios, or perhaps the Binney/Sunbeam films were all in the can by late 1918 allowing time for the Cuckoos to be made before March 1919. Mark Dintenfass was involved in the making of *My Four Years in Germany* for most of the second half of 1917, and by March 1919 was nominated as a candidate for Governor in New Jersey (which may account for the early announcement about the new Bobby Burns comedies followed by little other news) and so not likely, despite trade paper reports, traipsing down to Florida to make movies past March of 1919. While the trades gave the appearance that the Cuckoos were in production well into 1920, the studio on Riverside Avenue had been taken over by the Pioneer Feature Film Company in November 1919. Dintenfass was running National Film Laboratories in Fort Lee, New Jersey by October 1920.

Photo Products Export Company, the successor to Jaxon, ran ads in September 1919, concurrent with the Cuckoo Comedies ads, announcing their own series of Bobby Burns comedies. Some of the ads showed Bobby in blackface, and one of the ads even had a picture of Walter Stull. It is known that these, or at least some of the titles, were leftover Jaxon Comedies ("Breaking Into Business" being an extant example and the only title known to have actually been released). But these ads also show that at some point during his tenure with Jaxon, Burns was experimenting with a blackface character. If these were primarily Bobby Burns solo comedies, when during the Vim/Jaxon years were these made? Perhaps in early 1917 when Walter Stull was recovering from influenza.

It is assumed that Burns went back to Jacksonville immediately after the Pokes and Jabbs comedies ceased production. He was sweet on Will Louis' daughter Mary (eventually marrying her on November 10, 1920), and it was in Florida that Burns had been doing most of his work over the past three years. Just a handful of the Cuckoo comedies were ever made and only one is known to exist. Whether they were made in late 1917, or as the trades suggest during 1919 and early 1920 may never be known for sure.

Adding to the confusion about the first years of Bobby Burns' career after Jaxon are the King Cole Comedies. A series by that name had been announced as early as March 1916 to feature Smilin' Bill Parsons for his National Film Corporation to be released through Pathé. An initial release was announced, *The Artful Dodger*, but it seems Parsons dropped the brand name for his releases. Then in August 1919 the Motion Picture Producing Company of America announced a series of King Cole Comedies to be shot initially on Staten Island then in Brooklyn and starring Sammy Burns. "Camera" magazine mentioned that Sammy Burns had severed his relationship with MPCA in their September 18, 1920 issue. Milburn Moranti starring in a series of King Cole Comedies for release by National Exchanges was announced in April 1921. In August 1921 the trades began listing Bobby Burns as the star of the King Cole Comedies being released by National Exchanges (and there is a single reference that these comedies were also produced by MPCA). Titles announced were *Moonshiners, Strikes to Spar, Bars and Stripes, Jazz Babies, General Nuisance, A Fresh Start* (sometimes listed as *Starting Out in Life*) and *The Shimmy Gym*. The last two titles being the same as Cuckoo releases, indicate that the Bobby Burns version of the King Cole Comedies were nothing more than an effort to repackage the previously released Cuckoo Comedies along with a few made but not issued. No further titles were ever reported and this version of the King Cole Comedies disappeared from the trades by mid-1923.

Bobby Burns had a very long career after suiting up as Jabbs for the last time and wiping off the blackface. Reelcraft announced a number of Sun-Lite comedies starring Burns along with Jobyna Ralston and Billy Quirk (directed by Arthur Hotaling) in June 1921, and there is some indication that, unlike some of the Schiller Productions product, these were produced for release by Reelcraft. Some likely were filmed in Jacksonville. Bobby went on to make Juanita Comedies in Tampa, Florida (later in Orlando) in 1922 - early 1923, and then by December 1923 was hired by Jack White to write Mermaid, Juvenile and Cameo comedies along with former Vimite Al Ray, his first work in Hollywood. For the next 35 years Burns would work regularly as a support comedian, writer and stunt man. He appeared, usually uncredited, in a number of comedies for Hal Roach, including a few with fellow former Vimmie Babe Hardy and his new partner Stan Laurel. Burns also tangled with the Three Stooges, appeared with Harry Langdon and almost countess others. He lived until January 16, 1966 and as such was one of the last surviving Vimmies.

Mark Dintenfass brings visitors to the Cuckoo set.

Starting Out in Life

Released October 19, 1919. Cuckoo Comedies-United Picture Theaters. Two reels. No copyright registered.

Produced by Mark Dintenfass. Directed by Will Louis. Filmed at the Vim Studios in Jacksonville, Florida.

With Bobby Burns (Washington Lincoln Wilson), Will Louis, Jobyna Ralston, May Louis, Fatty Filbert, Skinny Renfrew, Anita Brown.

Hannah, the dusky beauty, will not consider Washington Lincoln Wilson's offer of marriage till that worthy proves himself able to earn his own living. Securing employment a porter at the White Springs Hotel, the coloured coon soon learns that all is not gold that glitters, and that a cheeky lift boy is an adept at sneaking his tips. Also that visitors are a mixture of mean, sober men, generous inebriated persons, old maids, and peaches. Getting mixed up through the numbers of the rooms being changed by the lift boy, our hero, ordered to get the bath ready for an unnamed client, makes a series of mistakes that result in the immersion of the wrong parties, the false imputation of murder for another, and finally his discharge from his position. But the generous gentleman of imbibing habits has tipped him so well that he arrives at Hannah's house with, quite a collection of notes, to discover someone has poisoned her mind against him, and she is about to commit suicide, meeting her just as he is about to end his own troubles in the same way. Mutual love, however, brings about a reconciliation, and helped by his wealth, two dusky hearts beat as one. [The Bioscope, erroneously referred to as *Getting a Start in Life*]

The one extant Cuckoo comedy has the feel and look of its Vim predecessors. Having been shot at 750 Riverside Avenue, with many ex-Vimmies in the supporting cast and with direction (and cameo) by Will Louis it is no wonder. In addition to the racial insensitivity of Burns working in blackface, it is also unfortunate in that most any facial expressions are lost behind the dark make-up.

"The first of the Cuckoo Comedies, 'Starting Out in Life,' has reached the screen. It presents Bobby Burns as its comedian, and he will also be featured in the succeeding comedies. It is too early yet to judge whether blackface work can score upon the screen. Certainly it should be given a thorough trying out. But it strikes us that the Cuckoo people are wise in not depending too much on burnt cork since it is announced that Mr. Burns will alternate as a straight comedian. He is of the old minstrel school in his effort here. And he knows how to score his points in typical low blackface style. But the material given him here is not productive of laughter though at times it sends out a bit of hilarious fun. Bobby Burns appears as a porter in a hotel and he has a busy time of it in discharging his duties. He is discharged himself in the

end though he finds himself a rich man. And that worn out trick of putting on the wrong coat is responsible for his newfound wealth. The comedy is mostly a series of repetitious scenes and the laughter is missing after the second attempt. What is needed in comedies at the present time are original ideas which must be worked out spontaneously. Otherwise bring on the bathing girls. We understand that Cuckoo has a pretty ensemble. But in the comedy's favor is its absence of slapstick. The two reels are clean and wholesome. And such virtues are a credit to the Cuckoo people. Bobby Burns will no doubt hit his stride the next time up when the flaws of his first picture have been fully appreciated by his sponsors." -- *Motion Picture News*, reviewed by Laurence Reid.

"There is some attempt at a coherent story in this comedy, and it depends on the adventures of a darkie who has to make his way in the world to win his girl. He seizes the first chance of work, and with considerable insistency secures a job as the porter in an hotel, in which a good many time-worn tricks are played. Some are too bad, however, and the acting of Bobbie Burns and the fat old toper, who, looking for his bedroom, opens the door of the lift and falls down the shaft repeatedly, has a bright touch. But of the actual material of the comedy one must admit it is commonplace. People expect better stuff than this nowadays."
-- *Kinematograph Weekly*

"Somewhat long drawn out story which. affords Bobby Burns opportunity of displaying his acrobatic agility. Good photography." -- *The Bioscope*

The Shimmy Gym

Released November 30, 1919. Cuckoo Comedies-United Picture Theaters. Two reels. No copyright registered.

Produced by Mark Dintenfass. Directed by Will Louis. Filmed at the Vim Studios in Jacksonville, Florida.

With Bobby Burns, Jobyna Ralston, Edna Reynolds.

[no synopsis available].

One of the Cuckoo comedies that Bobby Burns made sans the blackface makeup.

"Mark M. Dintenfass produced this two-reeler which is being distributed by United Picture Theaters. No reason for producing the affair is evident, there being no story and the incidents which comprise the film certainly are not funny enough in themselves to get more than one or two legitimate laughs. Bobby Burns and Jobyna Ralston are featured. The latter is quite charming, but not funny." -- *Film Daily*

"The greater portion of the action occurs in a gymnasium whither several middle-aged men have gone for the exercise which it is hoped will restore their failing health. A number of young ladies are found in the gymnasium , the usual one-piece gym suits predominating, and complications follow. An airplane and a crematory also figure in the story." -- *Exhibitors Herald*

Sultan of Jazz

Released December 6, 1919. Cuckoo Comedies-United Picture Theaters. Two reels. No copyright registered. Alternative title: *The Sultan of D'jazz.*

Produced by Mark Dintenfass. Directed by Will Louis. Filmed at the Vim Studios in Jacksonville, Florida.

With Bobby Burns (*Sultan*), Jobyna Ralston.

The ship's janitor and his captain are scared at the sight of a whale pursuing the vessel, and Bobby, as a Jonah, is consigned to the vast deep. When he reaches land he discovers himself somewhere in Turkey, and in the midst of a strange crowd. Borne into the presence of the Sultan, who is amusing himself with the ladies of his court, he is threatened with imprisonment. But turning the tables on his warders, Bobby hurries back to the fair creatures' company. Fascinating the king with a demonstration of a native game of his own native country, in which dice play a prominent part, Bobby begins to enjoy the fun, regardless of the fate of those he has penned up in a hot-air prison. But retribution in the shape of Bolshaviskers plotting against the Sultan, is on his track, and by means of pretending to heap honours on his

woolly head, the royal host hopes to escape furious measures of the revolutionists. In addition there is a roaring lion, and some furious females, and other excitements of an alarming kind in store for the waif of the sea. How Bobby copes with them all is shown in lively fashion, till he decides to fly while the flying is good, back to the captain, who receives him with the enthusiasm one might expect would be accorded to a friend with a bottle of rum, to be had for the asking. Full of funny incidents of a highly extravagant nature, Bobby Burns and a bevy of pretty girls work hard to make the fun fast and furious. The photography is good throughout. [The Bioscope]

Bobby plays a Sultan in blackface, and apparently Jobyna Ralston wears some "exceptionally startling" costumes. While it appears the film is not extant, the fate of one print is known. In November 1920 the film ran at the Newcomb Theatre on Canal Street in New Orleans. It caught on fire, but thanks to an automatic sprinkler system in the theater no one was injured. The theater reopened the next day, the Cuckoo comedy being the only casualty of the incident.

"A sketch of the astonishing adventures of the nigger ship-purser, who is thrown overboard for his lack of skill in mixing the skipper's drinks, and finds himself involved in a series of exciting incidents in the Sultan's palace. Bobbie Burns himself is funny, but in the comedy itself there are few incidents which exhibit a very high standard of humour. There is a lot of chasing in and out of the Djazz palace, much trapdoor work, and a group of harem beauties. There are several laughs, but on the whole the comedy is of an out-of-date type." -- *Kinematograph Weekly*

"The story permits of much comedy and keeps the Cuckoo girls much in evidence because its scenes are laid in the harem of a Sultan." -- *Motion Picture News*

All Out of Luck

Released circa November 1919. Cuckoo Comedies-United Picture Theaters. Two reels. No copyright registered. Alternate title: Out of Luck.

Produced by Mark Dintenfass. Directed by Will Louis. Filmed at the Vim Studios in Jacksonville, Florida.

With Bobby Burns, Jobyna Ralston.

[no synopsis available].

[no review available]

Jobyna Ralston and Bobby Burns in an unidentified Cuckoo, possibly "All Out of Luck".
Lack of a published synopsis or extant film print deny the ability to confirm.

Ball Bearing But Hard Running

Released February 29, 1920. Cuckoo Comedies-United Picture Theaters. Two reels. No copyright registered. Released in the U.K. as *No Mother To Guide Him*.

Produced by Mark Dintenfass. Directed by Will Louis. Filmed at the Vim Studios in Jacksonville, Florida.

With Bobby Burns, Jobyna Ralston.

Bobby, the dude, buys a cheap diamond ring from a suspicious-looking stranger, bestows it on his girl, and finds himself charged with theft. A stern judge, a discerning jury, and a rapid change into convict's garments, are the next events of his blameless life. Later on subterfuges to escape work, and an escape in company with a fellow-sufferer, and the equal division of one nice, roomy suit between them. For a while Bobby dons the coat, his pal inserts himself into the trousers, and carries him on his shoulders. And now strange events happen at the Hotel Camouflage, and curiosity beholds frightful sights through keyholes. And the poor man whose clothes were stolen while he bathed, gets assistance to track them down. But Bobby's luck is on the mend, for just in the nick of time he reaches the girl's house, and by a lucky chance, sheds prison stripes, and gets his compassionate mother-in-law-to-be and his girl to cover up his retreat. [B]

Another of the releases that features Bobby Burns sans the blackface make-up.

"The revels of the convicts, and the wild efforts of the law to inspire order, make for laughter in this hilarious Cuckoo Comedy." -- *The Bioscope*

KING BEE COMEDIES

Early in 1917 while many of his former colleagues were churning out comedies at the Garrick studios for Amber Star, and other of his ex-Vim cohorts were forming their own production companies, Babe Hardy waited for the return of Louis Burstein and a resumption of Vim production. During the interim Hardy entrenched himself as the featured singer and entertainment coordinator for the Burbridge Hotel where his wife Madelyn had been leading the orchestra for some time. Ethel Burton, Florence McLoughlin, Joe Cohen and the rest of the Babe Hardy Company also seemed to be on hold for what became not a resumption of Vim but a new endeavor.

It was announced on February 17, 1917 that comedian Billy West had signed a contract with the Caws Comedy Corporation, a new company organized by Samuel Cummins, Charles Abrams, Arthur Werner and Nat Spitzer (the first letter of their last names, C-A-W-S, creating the firm's name). However, within just a few days the contract was voided in order to allow yet another new company, Tip Top Comedies, to employ the Chaplin imitator. Most of the principals at Tip Top were the same ones that had formed Caws, but Cummins was jettisoned in favor of Louis Burstein who became the president of the new company. A month later on March 18, 1917 the new company, soon to be rechristened as the King Bee Films Corporation, began production in Jacksonville. With the old Vim studio over on Riverside Drive occupied by Myers & Theby, the recently vacated Thanhouser studio was rented. Coming along with Billy West from New York was his wife Ethlyn Gibson and director Arvid Gillstrom. Already in town and ready to go to work were Babe Hardy, Ethel Burton, Florence McLoughlin, Harry Naughton, Bud Ross, Polly Van, and Joe Cohen.

King Bee would only stay in Jacksonville for as long as it took to make five two-reelers and after temporarily relocating to Flushing, New York for a single comedy, made five films at another old Vim stomping ground, the former Horsley studio in Bayonne, New Jersey.

Then with the decline in Florida, particularly Jacksonville, as a production center, King Bee did what most film companies were doing. Instead of chasing the good weather between New York and Florida, they up and moved to California. Doing so they lost some of the old Vimmies such as Florence McLoughlin and Joe Cohen, both of whom returned to Jacksonville. Also gone temporarily was Mrs. Gillstrom, Ethel Burton, but after the first few films made in Hollywood she ended her extended vacation and went back before the King Bee cameras.

Out in Hollywood, little-by-little King Bee shed more of its Vim heritage. Harry Naughton, who had married Louis Burstein's niece Mildred, left the company since as a responsible married man he needed a real job and went to work for a shipping company and moved to the Bay Area. Even though Rosemary Theby came to work at King Bee briefly, by the time the company morphed into the Bull's Eye Film Corporation all vestiges of Vim were gone; including, after a single film released by Bull's Eye (but probably produced while still King Bee), Babe Hardy.

With the reorganization of King Bee into Bull's Eye, Hardy tired of being in the midst of another Burstein turmoil and found work at L-KO where he again assumed star status, although he also occasionally provided support for the likes of Harry Gribbon. After his brief stay at L-KO, Babe moved on to Vitagraph, first in support of Jimmy Aubrey and then Larry Semon. By 1926 he found himself at the Hal Roach Studios where he teamed with Stan Laurel, and the rest is history and well known.

Only the King Bee comedies produced in Jacksonville are listed here. For a complete study of the King Bee titles please refer to the book, **Laurel or Hardy: The Solo Films of Stan Laurel and Oliver "Babe" Hardy.**

Back Stage

Released May 15, 1917. King Bee Films Corporation/states' rights release. Two reels. No copyright registered. Working Title: *The New Stage Manager*.

Produced by Louis Burstein. Directed by Arvid E. Gillstrom. Photographed by Herman Obrock. Edited by Ben H. Cohen. Filmed at Thanhouser studios in Jacksonville, Florida.

with Billy West (*Props*), Ethel Burton (*Ethel*), Babe Hardy (*Babe*), Leo White, Florence McLoughlin, Polly Van, Joe Cohen, Budd Ross, Ethlyn Gibson.

Props, the stage man, and his assistant at the Orpheum Theater, Plunkville, divide their time equally between drinking and attention to duty. The Wiggle sisters, an Hawaiian act, arrive and demand the star's room, and there is a rumpus when Props declines to accede to their request. But Props relents when Babe, the strong man, and his wife, Ethel Burton, arrive, for Props has an eye for beauty. Props is forever getting in the way of the performers and causing unmeasured confusion. His bibulous assistant has an unfortunate propensity for dropping the curtain at wrong moments. However, the audience in front likes the show, and the philosophy of Props appears to be "I should worry." The strong man and his wife present their act, assisted on the stage by Props, who is always in the way. The curtain descends, leaving the strong man alone on the stage. The audience thinks this is part of the show and applauds accordingly. But to the succeeding act, "Rags and Riches," a serious drama, they tender a hostile reception and leave the house. Meanwhile the strong man, returning to his dressing room, finds Props making love to his wife and there is a fierce altercation. But Props escapes punishment and appears to be immune from the attacks. [MPW]

Billy West's wife Ethlyn Gibson moved from her usual lead role aside her husband to a supporting role to the deference of Ethel Burton as the leading lady. The casting as such may have been due to Burton's long tenure in Jacksonville and her fine work with Vim. Or perhaps her superior talent and beauty played a part. Her looks and engaging personality certainly did not go unnoticed by the film's director. Shortly after the production of *Back Stage* concluded Ethel Burton become Mrs. Arvid Gillstrom. On May 4, 1917 the two motored to Saint Augustine with Babe Hardy and Florence McLoughlin coming along to serve as witnesses and were married.

Arvid Gillstrom had worked at Keystone but the King Bee publicity department stretched the truth a bit when they said that Gillstrom had directed the real Chaplin. Someone who had actually worked extensively with Chaplin, Leo White, was a welcome addition to the company. Babe Hardy stepped over from lead comedian to chief support smoothly, and certainly all the other Vimmies were happy to be back at work.

"Under the direction of Arvid E. Gillstrom and supervision of Louis Burstein, a funny comedy has been produced in 'Back Stage.' Of course the story is an impossible one, but it still has merit. The trials and tribs of the artists and other men necessary to run a theater are well enacted by Billy West, and a good cast." -- *Exhibitors Herald*

The Hero

Released June 1, 1917. King Bee Films Corporation/states' rights release. Two reels. No copyright registered.

Produced by Louis Burstein. Directed by Arvid E. Gillstrom. Photographed by Herman Obrock. Edited by Ben H. Cohen. Filmed at Thanhouser studios in Jacksonville, Florida.

with Billy West (*The Hero*), Babe Hardy (*his rival*), Ethel Burton (*a society girl*), Leo White (*the count*), Budd Ross (*the butler*), Polly Van (*the mother*), Florence McLoughlin (*shy maiden*), Frank Lasnler (*thug*), Ben Ross (*proprietor*), Joe Cohen (*the dude*), Frank Bates (*bartender*).

Billy, the waiter in Mack's Cafe, has high ambitions. While he chases the tall glasses of foaming brew for his customers, his mind is filled with visions of fair dames clamoring for a nod or smile from him. As a waiter in a cheap cafe he is decidedly a frost, his only asset being an ability to handle rough patrons. During his leisure hours he wanders through the park flirting with the girls. His flirtations with the sweetheart of the Count get him in bad, and he is invited by the Count to indulge in a duel to the death. Billy espies Ethel struggling with two ruffians who have beaten up Babe. Billy routs the thugs and escorts Ethel home. Ethel's ma is one of those grand dames whose first question to all strangers is, "Where is your family tree planted?" When she gives Billy the once over, Billy feels like an angleworm on a hook, but he comes back strong and flashes the Count's card before mother's eyes. The card wins Billy an invitation to Ethel's reception, much to the chagrin of Babe who is jealous of him. At the reception Billy gives a fine imitation of how to behave in society. Just when he is having the time of his life, Billy remembers that it is time to be back on the job, so without even pausing to say goodbye, he is on his way to the cafe. The wine he consumed during the reception gets in its work, and Billy is in wrong more than ever. Babe has learned that Billy is an impostor, and he has discovered the cafe where he works. With the desire to show up his rival, Babe invited Ethel and other guests to go on a slumming trip and escorts them to the cafe. The first Billy knows of Ethel's presence is when he attempts to take her order, and then tries to pass himself off as a guest. This strategy is frustrated by Babe, who openly denounces Billy and in the mix-up that follows Billy not only gets the gate from Ethel, but a trimming from Babe as well. [MPW]

After having touched on Chaplin's *The Property Man* with the first King Bee release, this time around it is a reworking of Chaplin's *Caught in a Cabaret*, with a bit of *In the Park* rounding out the film.

"The Hero, directed by Arvid Gillstrom, under the supervision of Louis Burstein, is virtually two reels of laughs. Several new and old situations are brought in. This together with a story which really has a plot make it merry throughout. Billy West as the hero with his huge feet and loose pants affords much enjoyment. A good deal of slapstick is used but never fails to amuse. Ethel Burton is good playing opposite Mr. West. Others in the cast are Babe Hardy, Leo White, Budd Ross, Florence McLoughlin and Joe Cohen." -- *Exhibitors Herald*

Dough-Nuts

Released June 15, 1917. King Bee Films Corporation/states' rights release. Two reels. No copyright registered. Also known as The Bakery.

Produced by Louis Burstein. Directed by Arvid E. Gillstrom. Photographed by Herman Obrock. Edited by Ben H. Cohen. Filmed at Thanhouser studios in Jacksonville, Florida.

with Billy West (*Billy, the new baker*), Ethel Burton (*Ethel, the cashier*), Babe Hardy (*Babe, the chef*), Leo White (*Camembert, the proprietor*), Budd Ross (*Boob, the assistant*), Florence McLoughlin (*waitress*), Joe Cohen (*Pierre*), Frank Bates (*his pal*).

It was not Ethel's fault that she caused hostilities between all the men at Camebert's Bakery and Lunch Room. She simply had to flirt with men and every man she smiled at swore to have her as his own or die. When, however, Pierre, the excitable Italian baker tried to force Ethel to keep away from Babe, the sweet young cashier refused, and told Pierre many things not exactly complimentary. So when Billy happened to enter tin-bakery in search of a "hand out" he interrupted Pierre in the gentle game of choking Ethel. Billy hands Pierre a few swift jolts that result in the undoing of Pierre, much to the delight of Ethel and Camebert, the proprietor. After a few smiles from Ethel, Billy hires himself as a baker, thereby immediately incurring the hostility of Babe. Billy attempts feats of bakery unheard of, and succeeds in making the most wonderful designs in pies and crullers. Everything goes fine until Billy pushes the boob into the bake ovens, causing the boob's trousers to catch fire. Then in the attempt to quench the flames, Billy manages to drench the proprietor with a bucket of water. These little things help to put Billy in wrong with everybody but Ethel, who still smiles at him. The real trouble occurs when Babe discovers that Ethel has not only flirted with Billy but has actually kissed him. Babe allies himself on the side of Camebert and the Boob, and all three declare war on the hapless Billy. Billy succeeds in passing through the blockade and reaches the bakery intent only on "safety first." In the bakery, however, he finds escape cut off by Pierre and a pal who have returned to blow up the establishment. With the two forces closing down on him, Billy is powerless and only by use of judicious sprinting and good headwork did Billy finally manage to escape. [MPW]

While the gags and even plot (mimicking *Dough and Dynamite*) harken back to the Keystone-era Chaplin, this is the first King Bee where Babe Hardy puts on a full Eric Campbell persona giving the audience quite the cross section of Chaplin reenactments between Keystone and Mutual. The film is paced like a Keystone comedy with flour thrown about and even a pie or two, yet Hardy blusters and stomps in a manner of which Mr. Campbell would certainly be proud.

"The plot and its resultant action are cast in and around a bakery, and the farcical complications that ensue on account of the jealousies caused by pretty Ethel Burton between the diminutive Billy West and the ponderous Babe Hardy are said to be funny in the extreme." – *New York Dramatic Mirror*

Cupid's Rival

Released July 1, 1917 King Bee Films Corporation/states' rights release. Two reels. No copyright registered. Working Title: *The Artist*.

Produced by Louis Burstein. Directed by Arvid E. Gillstrom. Photographed by Herman Obrock. Edited by Ben H. Cohen. Filmed at Thanhouser studios in Jacksonville, Florida.

with Billy West (*Billy, the janitor*), Mary Taylor (*his wife*), Babe Hardy (*Daub, a poor artist*), Ethel Burton (*Ethel, his sweetheart*), Leo White (*Hyflyer, a rich artist*), Budd Ross (*Mike, the bellboy*), Joe Cohen (*Dough, the landlord*), Ethlyn Gibson (*a model*), Florence McLoughlin (*dancer*).

Billy, the janitor of the De Luxe Studio apartments, is ordered by Hyflyer, the fashionable artist, to serve breakfast immediately. Billy's wife prepares the meal and Bill departs upstairs with a tray of chicken. In the same apartments resides Daub, a young, impoverished artist. The only way that Daub can avoid eviction is by accepting a commission from Dough, the landlord, to paint the latter's picture. Inspired by the love of his sweetheart, Ethel, Daub starts nobly on his work. However, his ambitions are shattered when he sees Ethel entering the studio of Hyflyer, his despised professional rival. Infuriated at the sight, Daub bursts into Hyflyer's studio. Here the scene he beholds destroys all of his remaining reason, for he finds Ethel tenderly stroking Hyflyer's head. Little does Daub realize that Hyflyer has been felled by Billy, who has mistaken the artist for Mike, the elevator chauffeur. Daub seizes a large life-like painting of Ethel that is standing on a nearby easel and smashes it over the head of the unlucky Hyflyer. Tearfully Ethel explains that she had posed for the painting only because the proceeds of its sale would be utilized to defray the expenses of their coming wedding. Hyflyer bemoans the loss of his prized canvas as the date of the exhibition is only a day off. In Daub's studio, another tragedy has in the meantime occurred. Mike has seen a mouse enter under the door to Daub's studio and has followed it, armed with a club. Finding the mouse creeping along the top of the finished portrait of Dough, Mike aims a killing blow at the mouse, only to miss, and the club rips through the canvas. Horrified, Mike gazes at the result of his ill-aimed blow, when Ethel realizes what will happen when Dough is told of the mishap to the picture. Mike conceives the idea of dressing himself up to resemble the painting and impersonating the landlord's canvas. The idea is so successful that on the day of the exhibit none of the guests realize that the paintings which are supposed to represent Ethel and Dough are reality flesh and blood substitutes. None except Billy, who has discovered the ruse only through an accident. As soon as Billy learns that his hated enemy, Mike, is sitting in the easel, Billy arms himself with a heavy mallet and proceeds to reek vengeance on Mike. Consternation reigns among the guests, who promptly proceed to take summary action upon Billy. [MPW]

Ethlyn Gibson appears as a model wrapped in gauze holding a pot. Billy while vacuuming the hallway accidental catches the end of the gauze and sucks up the material, spinning Ethel around in the process. The more she spins the less clothed she becomes, with an opportune edit to the next scene just in time. But the absence of nudity was more likely at the hand of a censor than the filmmakers. King Bee was known to not let modesty ruin a good laugh.

In order to investigate his erroneous belief that Ethel is stepping out on him, Babe dresses as a woman in order to catch the two in the act. A rat crawling up his skirt causes Babe to run around the studio eventually revealing himself when his wig falls off. He and Ethel make up but the running around has caused the portrait to be destroyed, so Ethel poses as the portrait for the gallery showing. When Budd Ross interacts with Babe in the film it gives us another glimpse of how Babe works well with a smaller comedian, although in this film more reminiscent of Plump & Runt than Laurel & Hardy.

"Ethel Burton, as the poor artist's sweetheart, adds much to the fun making of the picture. Ethlyn Gibson, as the model plays her part well. Billy West doesn't leave the spectator in doubt as to the fact that he is still a talented comedian. The cast also includes Leo White, Babe Hardy, Budd Ross and Florence McLoughlin." -- *Motography*

The Villain

Released July 15, 1917. King Bee Films Corporation/states' rights release. Two reels. No copyright registered.

Produced by Louis Burstein. Directed by Arvid E. Gillstrom. Photographed by Herman Obrock. Edited by Ben H. Cohen. Filmed at Thanhouser studios, along the Ortega River and in Stinson Park (4045 San Juan Avenue) in Jacksonville, Florida.

with Billy West (*Billy*), Babe Hardy (*Babe*), Florence McLoughlin (*Florence*), Budd Ross (*Budd*), Ethlyn Gibson, Leo White, Joe Cohen.

Billy, a confidence man arrives in Squashville, a lumber town. He sees Babe, the daughter of the village doctor, disporting herself on the banks of the river. Learning that her father is the richest man in the village, Billy begins to beguile the shy, simple miss with tales of life in the big city. The innocent miss falls into his snare and gives her tender heart to the black rascal. Billy, scenting spoils that far exceeds his expectations, summons Florence, his confederate, and two crooks to come to his assistance. Budd, the village boob and life-long suitor for Babe's love, is the one stumbling block in Billy's path -to the successful culmination of his plans. The doctor, returning home after a professional visit, discovers Billy about to make off with all the money in the office safe. Learning from Babe that the villain has beguiled her into opening the safe, the doctor orders Billy out of the house and administers a well-deserved spanking to his too trusting daughter. Upon the arrival of Florence and the crooks, Billy orders his woman confederate to win the love of Budd and to keep him out of the way of the villain. Florence enraptures the country boy and succeeds in keeping him at a safe distance, leaving the villain, Billy, to work in safety. Taking the place of a man who has been shot in a gambling fight, Billy succeeds in gaining an entrance into the doctor's home and persuading Babe to elope with him. The doctor, discovering the plot, rushes to the church just in time to stop the marriage and drags Babe back to the house. Infuriated at the continued failure of his evil plans, Billy resorts to violence and has his two henchmen waylay the doctor, and carry him to the sawmill. Here Budd discovers conspirators placing the doctor upon a log, and threatening to saw him into halves unless he consents to the marriage of Billy and Babe. Horrified at the sight, Budd rushes off to notify Babe and to secure aid of the local police force. Babe arrives on the scene just in time to save her father from the cruel saw and the police arriving shortly after arrest Billy and incarcerate him in the local jail. Florence and the two crooks, who managed to avoid arrest, proceed to steal the jail. Placing the jail on a commandeered wagon, the crooks drive off with the police force in pursuit. Inside the jail Billy is urging his pals to greater efforts when a wheel of the wagon breaks off, and the jail and its sole tenant is hurled into the water. Florence's devotion to her lord comes to the surface and, diving into the water, she reaches the jail, and the two drift far out of the confines of the little village, while Babe, realizing the worth of the love of her rustic sweetheart, Budd, finds contentment and peace in his arms. [MPW]

After *The Villain* was in the can King Bee vacated the Thanhouser studio and headed north. This would be the last time Ethel Burton or Babe Hardy would film in Jacksonville. Both had fond memories of the town and particularly of their time with Vim. Florence McLoughlin would go with the rest up to New York but when King Bee headed west she returned to Jacksonville and worked on the Sunbeam and Cuckoo comedies. McLoughlin married in 1918 and moved to Ohio.

"Billy West in 'The Villain,' the sixth [sic] comedy bearing the King Bee trademark. He is assigned the highly contracted role of which he makes the most. He plays the part of a gay villain who, descending upon a peaceful village, makes love to the belle of that Arcadian spot. From the simple situation springs innumerable happenings of both a dramatic and a ludicrous nature. Billy and his confederates actually commandeer a jail which is swept away by a flood. In another part of the picture, a new murder is committed in a sawmill. These horrors only serve to accentuate the droll comedy incidents which pervade in the offering in which besides Billy West, Babe Hardy, Leo White, Budd Ross and others are prominent." -- *Moving Picture World*

The King Bee Company: Top row: Harry Naughton, Arvid Gillstrom, Herman Obrock. Middle Row: Ethlyn Gibson, Budd Ross, Polly Van, Billy West, Ethel Burton, Joe Cohen, Florence McLoughlin. Bottom row: Leo White, Babe Hardy.

BILLY RUGE'S LATER FILMS

Not much is known about Billy's activities between his unceremonial firing by the Eastern Film executives in May 1917 and his arrival at the Vitagraph studios in mid-1918. What was known about Vitagraph's activity around that time was that most of their comedy production (Larry Semon, Jimmy Aubrey) had moved or was in the process of moving to the West Coast from their Brooklyn studio, and there was a void to be filled. Vitagaph's choice to flesh out their production schedule was an odd one. Walter R. Hall was hired to direct and star in a series of comedies, yet Hall apparently had no previous film experience... or did he? After leaving Jaxon, and perhaps in response to America's entry into World War I, Walter Stahl turned in his somewhat Germanic last name and renamed himself Walter Hall. Basically Finn and Haddie (minus those character monikers) moved their act to Vitagraph.

Beginning with *Dukes and Dollars*, which was released on August 19, 1918, Ruge would appear with Hall in five comedies that Hall both wrote and directed (Frank P. Donovan would take over directing on a on a sixth and final entry, *Boobs and Bumps* that featured Don Barclay instead of Ruge). In usual Vitagraph fashion these films all have alliterative titles: *Dukes and Dollars, Wild Women and Wild Waves, Stripes and Stars, Hula Hulas and Hocus Pocus, and Daring and Dynamite*. With the exception of a fragment of *Stripes and Stars* these films are lost, but what does survive shows that Billy Ruge was the stronger comedic talent in the makeshift partnership, a fact that may soften the lament that the other films are not extant.

After *Boobs and Bumps*, the short series ended and Walter Hall was gone, but Donovan along with Ruge went into production of another film at Vitagraph. Although the film, *Bullin' the Bullsheviki*, started out at the Big V's Brooklyn studio, production moved over to the Paragon studios in Fort Lee, New Jersey and morphed into an independent production made by the one-off Eff and Eff Productions. Now being shot at feature length, the film starred Marguerite Clayton; other notables in the cast were Patsy De Forest (former Lubin star), Pearl Shepard (who had just also appeared in a few of the Hall-Ruge Vitagraph comedies), and Lou Marks. The latter two had appeared the previous year (along with ex-Vimmie Florence McLoughlin) in a series of Three C Comedies that Donovan had directed; Shepard was also a Wizard alum. This would be Billy Ruge's second and final appearance in a feature film (the first being his film debut in 1914's *Fantasma*).

In April 1919, Ziegfeld star comedian Johnny Dooley began filming a series of comedies at the old Biograph studio. Under the umbrella of his own Johnny Dooley

Film Comedies, Inc. the planned twelve two reelers were to be directed by Jack Shultz with Harry Keepers, who had been Myers & Theby's regular cameraman in Jacksonville, on camera. The series was to be written by Bide Dudley based on his "The Office Force" humorous newspaper stories. In support would be Martha Mansfield, Tom Blake, Tom Cameron, Edna Murphy, Tiny Douglas, Lillian Hall, Sophie Tucker, Edna Murphy and Billy Ruge. The cast would be augmented by "The Famous Dooley Beauty Brigade", a group of twenty young would-be actresses. It is known that Billy Ruge appeared in the third comedy filmed, but it is unclear if he appeared in any others.

Following the Dooley comedies, Ruge next found work with Emil Harder. A stage actor who had done some film work for Mirror Studios, Harder formed Sunshine Films, Inc. in early 1918 with the intention of producing 52 comedies a year to star former Biograph comic Gus Pixley (Sunshine Films, Inc. should not be confused with the Chicago company with a similar name or the more well-known Fox Sunshine Comedies). These comedies featured Pixley supported by Tom Ward, although there is some evidence that Ward also directed these comedies or at least the ones not directed by Harder himself. Taking on the brand name of "Moon Comedies," these first Pixley starrers were released in January 1918. Moon Comedies, some with Pixley, others with different comedians (including Gus "Shorty" Alexander formerly Jeff of the Mutt & Jeff comedies, *Lola Venus* and *Funnyface Ascott*) continued to be made well into 1920 when Sunshine Films, Inc. also started a series of comedies starring the Harder Kiddies (Emil, 7 and Alec, 3) and the Funful Comedies brand featuring Billy Ruge.

Concurrent with the release of the Funful Comedies, Billy Ruge reappeared in a number of comedies released by Photo Products Export Co., a subsidiary of Eastern Film Company. Announced as "new" comedies, it is more likely that these were reissues of Sparkle Comedies, although some may have been unreleased comedies made by Ruge in Florida during the first half of 1917. Adding to the confusion was the fact that Harry S. Stone, who was the principal behind the Film Sales Company who represented the Funful Comedies, had just left Photo Products Exports to take on that role. Little is known about the Photo Products Export offerings other than general announcements made in trade advertisements with no actual titles being mentioned. Also in 1920 the Joy Film Co. announced a series of Billy Ruge comedies but beyond a mention in the trade papers nothing seems to have come of them.

A few of Ruge's Funful comedies survive. *Brandy's Cocktail*, which features Harder and Ruge out of character discussing the film's plot in a brief prelude to the comedy, is very stagey with little action and incredibly poor direction. Ruge does an acrobatic fall or two but is unable to pull the poorly made Funful film up from gross mediocrity. Little known actress Erin Shannon was announced as being Ruge's chief support in these comedies leading his "bevy of beauties," and the film does feature a number of attractive females although it's hard to detect which is Shannon. Another Fulful film, *Rattlin' the Bones*, is so devoid of comedy or any production values that it is unwatchable. A somewhat interesting footnote to Billy Ruge's work with Emil Harder is the film *Uncle's Nephew* which was released in the New York City area on April 4, 1921. The *New York Daily News* ran a "Man With the Funniest Face" contest with the chance to star in a Sunshine Films comedy as the prize. Albert Hawker, bellboy at the Continental Hotel, was the winner. Emil Harder also shot over forty participants and put together a film that ran at B.F. Moss' Broadway Theatre the week of April 4, 1921 to select a funniest face comedienne. A winner would be selected based upon audience applause, with first prize the opportunity to make a film for Harder. *Variety* was not so polite when critiquing Albert Hawker writing, "As a comic Albert will never win any contests." Billy Ruge, who appears in the film, again apparently was the stronger comedian by default. All in all, it is no wonder that the Fulful Comedies proved to be Ruge's final film work. Billy Ruge was limited in his abilities as a screen comedian (although he did have his moments alongside Babe Hardy or Kate Price), but these comedies were so poorly made that they would have proven to be the death knell to even the most capable of comedians.

By the end of 1920, Emil Harder was moving his focus toward feature production with films such as *The Nth Commandment* starring Fernando R. Elizondo and Halina Bruzovna, and would continue to make features (many shooting in his native Switzerland) into the late 1920s. Funful Films, like the Moon Comedies, faded away by mid-1921. Billy Ruge decided to go back into vaudeville and resurrected his old Froebe & Ruge act, but with no Froebe in tow Ruge recruited Joe Rose and rechristened the act Ruge & Rose. Published reviews show Ruge & Rose working steadily but mostly to extremely negative reviews. Perhaps the toll of being a highly acrobatic comedian was being to show on Ruge who was well over 50 by this time. Trade papers track the act into 1924 but then Ruge & Rose seem to disappear.

COMPLETE BILLY RUGE FILMOGRAPHY
(except for films made during his Wizard-Vim-Jaxon tenure)

Prior to Wizard-Vim-Jaxon:

Thomas A. Edison, Inc:
Fantasma (Edison, December 19, 1914). Five reels.
Martha's Romeo (Edison, April 20, 1915). One reel.
The Idle Rich (Edison, April 27, 1915). One reel.
The Real Dr. McKay (Edison, May 3, 1915). One reel.
Nearly A Scandal (Edison, May 12, 1915). One reel.
Chinks and Chickens (Edison, May 19, 1915). One reel.
All Cooked Up (Edison, May 25, 1915). One reel.
Cartoons in the Barber Shop (Edison, June 2, 1915). One reel.
McQuade of the Traffic Squad (Edison, June 12, 1915). One reel.
The Breaks of the Game (Edison, June 26, 1915). One reel.
Cartoons in the Laundry (Edison, July 14, 1915). One reel.
The Hand of the Law (Edison, December 17, 1915). Three reels.

Billed as William Ruge in most of these early appearances.

Post Wizard-Vim-Jaxon:

Walter Hall series:
Dukes and Dollars (Vitagraph, August 19,1918). Two reels. 797 feet.
Wild Women and Wild Waves (Vitagraph, September 16, 1918). Two reels. 850 feet.
Stripes and Stars (Vitagraph, September 23, 1918). Two reels. 798 feet.
Hula Hulas and Hocus Pocus (Vitagraph, September 30, 1918). Two reels. 854 feet.
Daring and Dynamite (Vitagraph, December 9, 1918). Two reels.

Bullin' the Bullsheviki (Eff & Eff, 1919). Five reels.

Johnny Dooley Comedies (released 1920):
A Social Sleuth
Bobby the Office Boy
Hearts and Arts
Pep
Private Preserves
Some Mind Reader
On the Inside

Funful Films:

(Sunshine Comedy Co. through Film Sales Company) released circa September 1920 through early 1922. Directed By Emil Harder and co-starring Erin Shannon. One reel (except as noted):

Billy's Brides
Bone Dry Blues
Brandy's Cocktail
Do-Re-Me-Boom
Harem Scarem
He Got It
His Bed Sheet
His Watch Hound
Hot Dog
It's A Live One
Lolly Pop's Daughter
Money Talks
Nutt In (erroneously aka *Nest In* or *Not In*)
Powder Puff Pirates
Rattling the Bones
School for Skirts
The Painter
The Three Jokers
Two Knights
Uncle's Nephew (Two reels)
Will It Come to This?
Winning a Widow

Billy and the Ladies in "Harem Scarem"

The Funful Comedies were all but ignored in the American trade journals and newspapers, rightfully so. But the British trade magazines did comment on the films albeit not also in a favorable way:

"FUNFUL COMEDIES. Featuring Billy Ruge. Very elementary humour of a strong American flavor is dispensed in these unambitious comedies, which are played by a small company of knock-about artists and pretty girls. The productions lack technical finish, but they are, perhaps, adequate to the class of entertainment they present. As fill-ups at "popular" houses where the broadest type of fun is in demand, these films should prove a useable series. They could be improved by some editing. "HE GOT IT." A more or less haphazard series of scenes between girl brigands, moonlighters and a comic bear. The jokes are directed largely against prohibition, and do not appear to have much point for English audiences. "BONE DRY BLUES." Two comedy tramps search for beer in the dry United States of America and, after finding it, dream that they rescue two pretty girls. "IT'S A LIVE ONE." An impoverished sculptor (who also apparently conducts a girls' gymnasium) makes love to the millionaire's ugly daughter, and wins her father's consent to their marriage by palming off upon him a pretty girl as a statue. "WINNING A WIDOW." A tramp poses as a count whose clothes he has stolen, and makes love to pretty girls, hut is compelled finally to marry Ida Bona, the ugly widow, in order to avoid gaol." - *The Bioscope*

"It cannot be said that these comedies rise above the commonplace in any detail. The story is generally feeble, and although there is a certain amount of slapstick fooling, the general tone of humour is very broad and not particularly clever. Perhaps one of the reasons why they appear so weak is that none of the situations mimic or make fun of real life, and instead of relying on ingenious impersonal stunts every opportunity is taken to display bathing belles or ladies in gymnasium costumes in which the chief point consists in their being so attired. The photography and lighting are good, but the class of production is very third-rate, and only likely to attract uncritical audiences except in one or two instances. The same types and actors appear in each. "He Got It." — Billy using his gun in strange fashion finds a rocky country full of ladies also with guns, and endures some chases from them and from a sheriff, who has dressed up as a bear. A lady sheriff in spectacles watches him make love to one of the belles with envious eyes, and is pleased when the bear takes the latter's place and causes confusion. The story is the feeblest of the series, and Billy's maneuvers with his gun not very inspiring. The bear incident may appeal for its sheer absurdity, otherwise there is little to recommend. "Done Dry Blues" — Billy, a workman suffering from prohibition, sniffs at an intriguing smell, and accompanied by a friend locates the beer barrels in a cellar and imbibes without delay. Two young ladies become attached to them, and join them in a ride in a car, when these pleasant episodes are found to be part of Billy's dream, which was only good while it lasted. There is some very mild fun to be extracted from Billy's discovery, which perhaps would carry more point in the country where the film was made. For the rest the antics are net very amusing. "It's Live One." — The live one is a so-called statue with which sculptor Billy wishes to propitiate his would-be father-in-law having met the young lady in a school gymnasium. The obliging poseuse not only succeeds in looking like the real thing, but becomes a second wife to father-in-law. The young lady is made the same type as in all the other comedies — a long-faced spectacled, toothless individual, and can hardly be amusing, as she is so often repeated. At first sight she may seem humorous, however. "Winning a Widow." — A duke is expected at a hotel, and instead of falling in love with the right widow is forced into a bathroom situation with a toothless, spectacled housemaid, and on being told he must either marry her or go to gaol, says he will do the former as the prison is the worst in the country. Billy as the Duke is fairly funny, but there is nothing much to be said for the general trend of the humour. "Nest Inn." — Garrisoned by portresses in tights and overlooked by porter Billy, the building becomes infested with mice, which cause trouble among the sleepers, who include a rich woman and her daughter. Billy comes to the rescue, and is rewarded with the hand of the latter. The young ladies are not very entertaining, but the mice may raise some laughter." -- *Kinematograph Weekly*

Riverside Drive, Main Street and Riverside Park in Jacksonville, Florida.
The places where once movies were made.

CAST OF CHARACTERS

AIKEN, SPOTTISWOODE *(April 16, 1868-February 26, 1933)*. Born in Scotland as Francis Spottiswoode Aiken. A trained Shakespearean actor, Aiken worked on the stage in America until making his film debut with Lubin in 1910. After Lubin he worked often with D.W. Griffith (including *Birth of a Nation*). Like most he moved to Hollywood but his roles diminished after a messy divorce in 1922 from his wife Marion, who claimed that he forced her to live with a wealthy man in order to extort money from the man for adultery. He died in Los Angeles.

AIKEN, THOMAS *(c.1887-November 5, 1926)*. Little is known about Aiken who appeared in a number of Lubin comedies around 1912 and then did some work for Essanay in 1915. Not even the Philadelphia City Directory lists him, unless he had a side business as a "remover of dead animals." Aiken was active in vaudeville both before and after his time in the movies. Born in Chicago, he passed away in Wheeling, West Virginia.

ANDREWS, MELBA *(1897-March 2, 1972)*. A local Jacksonville girl that is known to have appeared in three Vim comedies, her only known film work.

BAKER, WALTER *(January 10, 1892-April 3, 1934)*. Born Walter Charles William Baker in Hamburg, Germany and came to America in 1912 by way of Brazil. Worked at Vim as a crew member and was part of the company that went to work in Providence, Rhode Island for Jaxon. A mechanic and chauffeur by trade, Baker eventually returned to Jacksonville where he died leaving his widow Mary.

BATES, FRANK Joseph *(June 27, 1887–August 2, 1933)*. Another in the long line of Philadelphia-born comedians, also passed away in that city. He may or may not be the same Frank Bates that was an actor for Biograph circa 1915. This Frank Bates was known as Dad Bates while at Vim. Later worked for King Bee but that association ended when he was inducted into the Army and served overseas during World War I. He did return to Jacksonville after the war and worked for the Pioneer Film Company on the "Facts and Follies" series.

BEST, MABEL *(18??-19??)*. First known film work was with Gaumont in Jacksonville in early 1916. Then went to work for Vim and eventually Jaxon. She was amongst the company that went to Providence, Rhode Island in 1917. Known as a singing comedienne, "the pleasing miss at the piano", she also appeared in vaudeville, working in the "Red Pepper Revue" in the mid-twenties.

BLETCHER, BILLY *(September 20, 1895-January 5, 1979)*. Born in Lancaster, Pennsylvania. Started his film career with Vitagraph around 1914 before moving to Wizard in 1915. Went with the newly christened Vim Comedies to Jacksonville where he stayed until late Summer 1916, leaving before the studio's demise. Ended up in Hollywood working first for Christie and then numerous other studios, occasionally starting in his own comedies. Worked extensively in Hollywood for the next five decades in both film and on radio. Married Arline Roberts on December 7, 1915.

BOEHM, ERNEST Arthur *(January 22, 1889-19??)*. Born in Berlin, Germany. Worked as director and interpreter for Marcel Perez, both in Europe and when Perez moved to America. Apparently had some association with Universal circa 1915 and served in the German army for two years but little otherwise is known about Boehm. He is not mentioned in the trades past his brief time at Vim, except he is known to have worked for Erbograph Co. in New York City in 1917, his association with Perez apparently having ended.

BOWERS, BILLY (c. 1862-19??). Born in Pennsylvania. Worked as a blackface comedian in vaudeville before entering movies with Lubin, for a long time with Dumont's Minstrels. Also worked at Wizard and his last known credits were working at Thanhouser and Conquest Pictures. He was married (Mary) and had a daughter (Edith).

BRENNAN, JOHN *(July 17, 1865-December 27, 1940)*. After working in vaudeville found work at the Kalem studios in Los Angeles where he became a popular comedian, often working with Ruth Roland. Brennan moved to New York around 1916 and after appearing in a few films all but disappeared. There were a few mentions in the trades about comebacks that never happened. Died in Los Angeles.

BRIGHT, IONE E. *(May 11, 1887-August 17, 1976)*. Born and passed away in California. Primarily a stage actress, Bright worked briefly for the Eastern Film Corp. in 1915 and reportedly worked for Mirrors Films in 1916. She appeared on Broadway as early as 1910 and as late as 1937. Interesting to note that in the early 1940s Bright shared an apartment in Manhattan with actor Wilfred Clarke, also an Eastern Film Corp. alum with whom she frequently appeared on stage throughout her career.

BRIGHT, MILDRED *(May 30, 1892-September 27, 1967)*. Born in New York, died in California. Made her Broadway debut in the 1909 play *Havana*, then worked from late 1912 through 1914 for Éclair American where she met her husband actor Robert Frazer, a frequent co-star. After making a few films for Eastern Film Corp. she returned to the stage making only the occasional movie with her husband before retiring from acting in the early 1920s having moved with her husband to Hollywood.

BROOKE, MYRA (c.1865-February 9, 1944). Born in England. Stage actress that started working in movies in 1915 for Reliance, followed by work with Wizard, Gaumont, Metro and Thanhouser among others. Her long stage career included stints on the Frohman and Shubert circuits. Brooke, often billed as Brooks, appeared regularly in blackface. She retired in the mid-1920s and did housework for an income.

BROWN, MAXINE Velma *(April 11, 1897-December 27, 1956)*. Born in Denver, Colorado, died in Oakland California. From the age of 5 worked primarily as a stage actress. Brown appeared on film for Komic in 1914 and then for Edison in 1915 and 1916 where she worked with Babe Hardy in a few films. After leaving the movies, Brown worked extensively on Broadway before being one of the first name actors to transition over to the new medium of radio in 1924.

BUNNY, GEORGE Edwin *(July 13, 1868–April 16, 1952)*. Born in New York City, died in Hollywood. George was signed by Eastern Film Corp. soon after the death of his famous brother John Bunny in 1915. There is no record of George being involved in show business prior to his brother's demise and the exploitative aspects of his likeness to his brother were not missed by the trades. Other than at Eastern, George's only other films with him as the lead was, in a series of short comedies made for National Film Corp. in 1921. Otherwise he was mostly a bit player.

BUNTING, EMMA *(June 5, 1886-1957?)*. Born in Sarahsville, Ohio. A major vaudeville performer beginning around 1903 quickly forming her own stock company and working in vaudeville for the next three decades. She settled in New York City in the 1930s and her last credit is on Broadway in *You Can't Take It With You* in 1945.

BURNS, HARRY *(July 20, 1882-January 9, 1939)*. Born Jacob Elman in Russia, Burns worked first in vaudeville then in the movies. Worked as both an actor and director eventually moving into working in moving picture trade publishing. Was married to Dorothy Vernon and was comedian Bobby Vernon's stepfather. Died in Los Angeles, having suffered a heart attack while driving.

BURNS, VIOLET *(1889-October 3, 1917)*. First wife of Bobby Burns (they were married in 1908). She appeared in Lubin and Vim comedies, and wrote a few. It was her death in Providence, Rhode Island that likely was the last straw for the Pokes & Jabbs series. She was buried in Philadelphia.

BURSTEIN, LOUIS *(March 4, 1877-March 25, 1923)*. Born in Russia, and died in Pomona, California when his car hit a train. Burstein was one of the attorneys that represented the Motion Picture Patents Company and just before the demise of the "Trust" went into motion picture production himself. He was the founder of Wizard, Vim and King Bee comedies. When King Bee dissolved, he changed the spelling of his last name to Burston and went into feature production.

BURSTEIN, MILDRED *(February 24, 1891-February 20, 1983)*. Born in Kovno, Russia and came over to American and lived with her uncle Louis. Worked in the Vim front office, and often ran the studio in her uncle's absence. Married Vim & King Bee studio manager Harry Naughton in December 1917. Harry then took a real job with a shipping line out of San Francisco, and the two traveled the world before settling down in the Bay Area.

BURTON, ETHEL *(October 23, 1897-May 15, 1985)*. Born in New York City. Talented and beautiful Ethel was Pokes & Jabbs main female support during the days of Wizard and Vim. Stayed with the Burstein/Hardy faction after the split up of Vim and worked as Billy West's female lead in the first King Bee comedies. She married King Bee director Arvid Gillstrom on May 4, 1917 in St. Augustine, Florida with Babe Hardy and Florence McLoughlin as witnesses. She only occasionally appeared in films once they moved to Hollywood. Her last recorded appearance was in the "So This America?" series that Gillstrom directed for Paramount. They had a tumultuous marriage due primarily to Gillstrom's drinking. The two separated as early as 1925 and after a number of aborted reconciliations divorced in 1931. There are unverified accounts that she was an extra in *Swiss Miss* (1938). She died in Orange, California having married Clarence Anderson and then a Mr. Palmer.

CALHOUN, JULIA (*February 6,1872-April 28, 1923*). Born and died in Philadelphia. Born Julia Earnest she used the last name of her second husband Kirt Calhoun as her stage name working in his touring Calhoun Opera Company until their divorce in 1898. While continuing stage she became Mrs. Lawrence Schwartz briefly until his sudden death in 1902. Made her screen debut in 1912 for Lubin and worked regularly with the Gay Time unit until it was disbanded in 1915. Calhoun only worked sparingly after that.

CARLTON, JAMES L. (*July 2,1877-19??*). Began his work in the motion picture business in 1903 and joined Gaumont Paris in 1905. By 1910 had formed Carlton Laboratories which was a lab, equipment manufacturer, rental studio and production company (initially in Coney Island, but finally in Yonkers). The company was affiliated with the Motion Picture Distribution and Sales Company, where Carlton was a director (Louis Burstein being another). Left his namesake company and went to work for Universal briefly in 1912 before returning to Carlton Laboratories in 1913. That entity was consumed by Reliance in 1914 and Carlton again left the firm. Carlton worked at various motion picture companies, including Vim, before reestablishing Carlton Laboratories in 1929. Born in Michigan.

CARVER, LOUISE (*June 9, 1869-January 18, 1956*). Born Louise Stieger in Davenport, Iowa. Worked in vaudeville since he was a teenager appearing at one point as part of a "sister act" called Carver & Pollard. She often worked with Tom Murray whom she married in 1910. She and Murray dabbled in film during 1916 working for both Eagle and Vim. After another long stint in vaudeville, she settled down in Hollywood beginning a long film career working at the Mack Sennett studios and as a character actress.

CHAFFEE, MARGUERITE (*May 29, 1887-May 1966*). Born in Ohio, but considered Georgia home. Unlike many of her counterparts Marguerite was not born on stage but rather got the acting bug in college. She graduated from Ohio Wesleyan College and did postgraduate work at Emerson College. She did tour the country as a dramatic reader during her time in school, and became a full time entertainer after finishing her studies. Her stage credits are brief and her film credits almost non-existent. Other than her work for the Eastern Film Corp. Chaffee is known to have done some film work for Mutual. She left acting at the end of the 'teens, became an interior decorator and married in 1925.

CHAMBERLAIN, WILLIAM (*November 28, 1887-May 30, 1954*). Chamberlain, who was married to Jennie Nelson, worked at Lubin circa 1912. Along with his wife he went to New York City and found work at various film companies as an actor and director. Chamberlain went to work with Vim in 1916. When Jaxon ceased operations he along with his wife and her two children moved to San Francisco where he became the assistant manager of the Fremont Hotel. Born in Philadelphia he died in Los Angeles.

CLARKE, WILFRED *(June 11, 1867-April 27, 1945)*. Born in Philadelphia, Clarke spent most of his childhood in England where his father appeared on the London stage. Part of the infamous Booth family of actors (his mother was John Wilkes Booth's sister), Clarke returned to America upon his father's death and for the next four decades worked steadily on stage. Twice married, one of those marriages was to actress Grace Meinken in 1910. Clarke lived with actress Ione Bright when he passed away in 1945 in New York.

COHEN, JOSEPH *(18?? – 19??)*. Claims that Cohen was once part of the Fred Karno company cannot be substantiated. Cohen did work on the stage in England from about 1907 to 1914 as part of a "Hebrew comedy" duo known as Lowenworth & Cohen. In the twenties Cohen returned to England, worked on stage again with Sam Lowenworth, then with Murray Leslie and finally Len Jackson. He went back to Jacksonville later in life, and in the early 1970s refused to talk with film historians without being paid first.

COOLING, MAUD *(May 5, 1872-June 11, 1966)*. Born Maud Josephine Hawkins in Fergus, Ontario, Canada. Maud began acting around fifteen coming from a family of performers. She spent some time in France on the Parisian stage, but returned in America in time to marry actor William Taggart (Dean Raymond) in 1891. The two left the stage briefly around the turn of the century and ran a hotel in Niagara Falls. Returning to the theater, Maud, both with and without her husband, remained on the stage into the Thirties, including a stint on Broadway. Her brief film career in addition to working for Eastern Film Corp. included work with Goldwyn and Pathé. A widow for almost two decades, Maud died back home in Canada.

CRAPOE, BERT *(18??-19??)*. Virtually nothing is known about Crapoe except his last name may not actually have an "e" at the end. Apparently he was spotted selling hot dogs at The Pike (a popular but now long-gone amusement area in Long Beach, California) and doing a pretty good Chaplin imitation. His only film work appears to be at the Balboa studios (also in Long Beach) in support of Charles Dudley, a few of those Knickerbocker comedies being released under the Vim brand.

DAINTRY, ISABEL *(c.1884-19??)*. Born in Denver, Colorado, Isabel moved to England when her widowed mother married a British man. Educated in fine boarding schools, Isabel began performing at an early age and on occasion before royalty. She returned to America in 1908 along her with step-sister who became known professionally as Mary Murillo (a prolific scenario writer for films). Working on stage, Isabel found some work on films with Thanhouser around 1910, and then again in 1913 with Reliance and its comedy brand Komic. Her last film work was for the Eastern Film Corp.

DINTENFASS, MARK *(April 17, 1870-November 23, 1933)*. Born in Tuchow, Austria (now Poland). Dintenfass was the founder of the Champion Film Company and one of the organizers of the Universal consolidation of studios. He became associated with Vim midway through its existence and never meshed well with Louis Burstein or later Frank Tinchnor. After the demise of Vim, he leased the studio previously used by Vim and produced a short series of comedies featuring Harry Myers and Rosemary Theby. He then went back to New York, produced the feature *My Four Years in Germany* (1918) and ran (unsuccessfully) for Governor of New Jersey. After that he returned to Jacksonville and produced the Cuckoo Comedies starring Bobby Burns. Dintenfass left the production side of the movie business and operated National Film Laboratories in New Jersey until his death.

DUCEY, LOUISE *(1879–1955)*. Louise, maiden name unknown, married John Ducey, a successful plumber, in 1901 and worked in the hosiery business. She transitioned into acting around 1906 and in 1910 separated from her husband (although they would maintain a relationship until his death in 1921). Her film career started at Reliance in 1913 and she transitioned over to the Komic/Royal unit; she was also briefly at Biograph and appeared in the Clara Kimball Young feature "Camille." Her last known work on stage was in *The Wildcat* in 1921. She remarried in 1927 and helped her husband run a hotel in Malborough, New York.

DUDLEY, CHARLES *(October 1, 1883-March 9, 1952)*. Born Charles Dudley Heaslip in Fort Grant, Arizona. Long term lead comedian with the Balboa Amusement Producing Company beginning in 1914. After Balboa he worked for the likes of Century and Vitagraph in increasingly lesser roles. Dudley made his last film as an actor in 1924, moving behind the camera as a makeup artist. He died in Los Angeles.

EDWARDS, JOHN *(June 1877 – 19??)*. Born in Indiana, Edwards reportedly worked on stage in Australia around the turn of the century. Back in the U.S. around 1906 he was part of the "Honolulu Minstrels" where his go-to role was as Uncle Rufus. By 1910 he was married to Mattie Edwards and working as an actor in New York City. His only known film work was at Lubin between 1913 and 1916.

EDWARDS, MATTIE *(c.1880–19??)*. Born Martha Hughes In New York City, married John Edwards in 1902 in Washington, D.C. After appearing in Lubin comedies she did additional film work for Ebony Comedies and then Oscar Micheaux. Little else is known about Edwards, but much misinformation abounds.

FARLEY, DOT *(February 6, 1881-May 2, 1971)*. Dorothea was born in Chicago and made her first film there in 1910 for Essanay. For most of that decade she appeared in comedies produced throughout the country by various film companies that she and director Gilbert Hamilton created. Once settled for good in Hollywood, Dot had a long tenure at the Mack Sennett Studios, and then as Edgar Kennedy's mother-in-law in the long running "Average Man" series at RKO. She never married and died in South Pasadena, California.

FLEMING, MAMIE *(April 25, 1886-December 31, 1953)*. Born Mary E. Fleming she began her stage career so early she was often referred to as "little" Mamie Fleming early on. Later press accounts centered on her being a very attractive and talented comedienne-singer. She formed her own company around 1902, disbanding it in 1908 and working solo for a few years. In 1910 she joined the Anna Held Company briefly before working for two years for Jesse L. Lasky. In 1912 she went back to solo work but in July 1913 she married L. Montgomery Weidner retiring from the stage and starting a family. Described as a "local favorite" in Philadelphia newspapers she was born there and passed away in Phoenixville, PA.

FORD, RAY *(August 14, 1885-January 10, 1925).* Born in Manchester, England. Born Angela Maycock, Ray (sometimes spelled Rae) appeared in vaudeville and was a Ziegfeld girl appearing in the famous Follies. Ray only had a few screen credits., later becoming Mrs. Robert Hunt. She died suddenly in Sheepshead Bay, New York.

FOREPAUGH, JOHN A. *(August 9, 1852-June 8, 1895).* Forepaugh was the nephew of Adam Forepaugh a circus entrepreneur who often dealt with P.T. Barnum. The younger Forepaugh worked for his uncle's circus business in various capacities. In 1884 when his uncle purchased the Bijou Theatre in Philadelphia the nephew took over the management of the renamed Forepaugh Theatre. His wife Luella assumed management of the theater upon his death. He was born and died in Philadelphia.

FOREPAUGH, LUELLA *(November 10, 1857-January 28, 1959).* Born Luella Brown, she married (using the last name Hutchinson) John Forepaugh in 1883 just before he became manager of the Forepaugh Theatre. She had, since her teen years, been a rider in the circus. When her husband died she became the manager of the theatre. She remarried to George Fish who himself worked in theater management. Forepaugh was born in Yolo, California and passed away in San Mateo, California at the age of 101.

GAHRIS, ROY *(Jul 13, 1885-1943).* Leroy briefly appeared in and directed movies during the mid-teens. Served as a Captain in the U.S. Army during World War I, then moved from New York to Connecticut and operated his own business. He died in Dade County, Florida.

GILMORE, HELEN *(January 4, 1862-November 16, 1936).* Helen had a long career in vaudeville before landing on Broadway where she regularly appeared in 1912 and 1913. Helen made her first film for Kalem in 1913 and worked mainly in short comedies for the next 15 years. She regularly worked at Vim, in Mutual's Cub comedies, and later in her career mainly at the Hal Roach Studios. Born in Washington, D.C. and passed away in Los Angeles.

GLYNN, ELSIE *(May 20, 1897-March 5, 1981).* Elsie worked in vaudeville and on Broadway briefly before joining Thanhouser around 1919. By 1911 she was working at Lubin but left in 1912 to return to stage work. After some time on Broadway and a single film appearance for Mutual, Glynn married Leo Weil, a lawyer from Chicago. She continued acting until the birth of a daughter and son. Records indicated she was widowed some time before 1940, and although a long-time resident of Chicago, died in Norfolk, Virginia.

GODFREY, RAE [Zelma Ray] *(c.1897- 19??).* From Coquille, Oregon, Rae (often spelled 'Ray' in the trade press) arrived at the Vim Studios in April 1916 after some time performing in acrobatic and swimming acts. She worked mainly with Plump

& Runt. Along with Robin Williamson and Anna Mingus, Rae left Jacksonville for Hollywood in October 1916. For the next two years she found steady work at L-KO and then Triangle, but by 1919 her screen credits disappear. She had married, given birth and divorced all within a few months of late 1919- early 1920. The child was her second; the first was fathered by a Jacksonville doctor (she was pregnant when she left JAX). The 1920 census was the last known mention of Rae, showing she lived in Los Angeles but with neither child.

GRANT, (HENRY) CLAY *(November 27, 1885-November 30, 1953)*. Worked as a professional cartoonist, in vaudeville and then made films for Crystal, Imperial (where he appeared with Weber & Fields as well as Bert Tracy), and Mittenthal in support of Heinie & Louie. Following work at Wizard and Vim he went to work for Peerless where he was injured on the job and ended up suing the production company. The incident ended Grant's acting career and he went into production work. Beginning in 1919 he spent the rest of his life working for Fordel Films, Inc.

GREEN, HOWARD [William Howard Green] *(August 21, 1895-Februray 28, 1956)*. Born in Rhode Island, Greene first found work with the Eastern Film Corporation and then worked for Eastern's subsidiary Vim. By the mid-1920s he was working for the major studios in Hollywood, and became well known as one of the better color cinematographers. Often nominated for Academy Awards for his work, Greene was steadily employed until his death.

HANSON, FRANK "SPOOK" [Otto Henry Hanson] *(June 14, 1873-June 16, 1924)*. Well known New York Hippodrome clown working often with fellow clown Harry La Pearl. Frank signed with David Horsley (Centaur then MinA brands) in 1914 to support La Pearl in his new comedies. Moved to Vim when Horsley left for the West Coast. Married in 1915 to Edna Reynolds the two also worked at Jaxon and in the Cuckoo Comedies. Born in Brooklyn, he died with his wife at his side in New York City.

HARDY, BABE *(January 18, 1892–August 7, 1957)*. Born Norvell Hardy in Harlem, Georgia, Hardy adopted the first name of Oliver in tribute to his father. Babe, as he was known both personally and for much of his career professionally, made his first movie for Lubin in 1914 working in Jacksonville, Florida. Leaving Lubin, he worked in the New York City area until he returned to Jacksonville upon having joined Vim (and before that Wizard). The co-star of the Plump & Runt series, Babe would eventually direct his own company during the last days of Vim. He next worked for King Bee which, after a few films in Jacksonville, took him back to New York City and then Hollywood. Once there, he starred in his own series for L-KO and then as a main support for Jimmy Aubrey and eventually Larry Semon. By 1925 he was working at the Hal Roach Studios and being directed in a number of comedies by future partner Stan Laurel. After a thirty-year career as one-half of the screen's most beloved comedy team (plus a handful of solo appearances), Hardy passed away in North Hollywood.

HEVENER, JEROLD T. *(April 30, 1873-April 17, 1947).* Started with Lubin around 1912 and worked as both an actor and a director. Then worked with Scarlet, Mittenthal Brothers and Colonial before heading up Wizard's second unit. After some freelancing around New York, he ended his film career directing Sparkle comedies and assisting Harry Myers with the Myers-Theby Pathé comedies made in Jacksonville. He spent the rest of his life running a paper hanging business, and died in New Brunswick, New Jersey.

HIERS, WALTER *(July 18,1894-February 27, 1933).* His first film work was under the direction of D.W. Griffith at Biograph. Hiers next worked briefly for Edison and then Lubin. Bouncing around New York film companies, Heirs appeared in films by Frohman, Equitable, Wizard and Vim. After spending most of 1916 at Thanhouser he moved on to primarily feature work where he obtained stardom. By the advent of sound he worked less and less, passing away in Los Angeles at the age of 39.

HILL, ROLAND *(February 3,1884-May 27, 1951).* A traveling salesman from Danville, Virginia that settled in Greensboro, North Carolina, in August 1916 Hill convinced local businessmen to set up Gate City Pictures Company to feature him as the star performer and to build a studio in town (apparently never built with filming actually done in Jacksonville). At least one of the reported films was made (*Roland's Lucky Day*), directed by Albert W. Hale and also featuring Beverly Deveron. Smilin' Roland ended up working briefly in Jacksonville for Amber Star (some of his films came out via Vim, others were Sparkle comedies). After Amber Star went north, Hill returned to Greensboro and along with Walter Stahl set up Hi-Ro Comedies, and at least one comedy (*Oswald's Weekend*) and a few local interest films were made. By 1918 Hill gave up acting and became a successful theater owner, with venues throughout both Carolinas. He died in Lynchburg, Virginia.

HOLTON, BETTY *(18??-19??).* Holton's first known work was the Ivan Film Co. in 1914 and her last was to be *My Country First* with Tom Terriss in 1916 but apparently was replaced by Helene Ziegfeld. Trade papers reported that she had worked for Famous Players and Metro but her Wizard work is the only other specifically mentioned. Little else is known except that she was a local New York City girl.

HOPKINS, JACK *(March 17, 1876 -19??).* Older brother of comedienne Mae Hotely, he was born in Buffalo, New York. Hopkins got his first film work in support of his sister at Lubin. He then worked steadily for the remainder of the silent era appearing in both comedies and dramas (often billed as John Hopkins). One of his last roles was in support of "comedian" Al Joy in *The Helpless Helper*.

HOPKINS, WILLIAM R. *(c.1872-19??).* Hopkins, apparently no relation to Jack Hopkins or Mae Hotely, started working for Lubin in 1912. When Lubin closed down its Jacksonville studio, he stayed behind and worked for Gaumont until they too left Florida. Married to the former Mae Sheppard, Hopkins became a grocer and lived in Jacksonville thereafter.

HOTALING, ARTHUR *(February 3, 1873-July 13, 1938)*. Born in Albany, New York, he worked in vaudeville as partner to Fred Mace in an act known as "Mace & Douglas" (Hotaling's middle name being Douglas). By 1896, Hotaling was working at one of the nation's first movie theaters, located in Atlantic City; the embryonic film showplace was ran by the Kiefaber Bros. Soon afterwards he found work with the Lubin Manufacturing Company in Philadelphia and quickly became Sigmund Lubin's boy wonder. Starting out as a projectionist, Hotaling worked his way up to becoming the company's primary comedy film director. Around 1904 he married May Hopkins (often spelled Mae), and in 1910 recruited her to be the star of the new comedy film unit, known as Gay Time comedies, that Hotaling was forming for Lubin. For the next five years the two were responsible for most of Lubin's comedy product. Hotaling left Lubin in 1916 and headed west working for Essanay and Universal over the next few years. Work dried up by the end of 1918 and Hotaling only worked sporadically after that. While enroute with his wife and daughter from his home in Palm Springs toward San Pedro and a sailing to Honolulu, Hotaling suffered a fatal heart attack.

HOTALING, GARRY *(July 16, 1884-February 4, 1950)*. Younger brother to Arthur, Garry was also born in Albany, New York. He came to work for Lubin in 1912 and by the next year was a chief camera operator working primarily on the Gay Time comedies directed by his brother. In 1916 he moved over to Vim where he was the primary cameraman on the Plump & Runt series. When most film production left Jacksonville, Hotaling stayed behind and worked as a ship fitter. He migrated back to upstate New York in 1922, married a local girl and went to work for the YCMA in Utica, a job he held for the rest of his life.

HOTELY, MAE *(c.1879-19??)*. Born May Vera Hopkins in Buffalo, New York. The spelling of her first name varies between Mae and May, but in 1902 married film director Arthur D. Hotaling giving her his last name. Her stage name then being a play on her married last name. It is unknown if Hotely did much stage work prior to entering movies with Lubin around 1910; she may have just been a convenient choice since her husband had been with Lubin for a decade. But she became the lead player of the "Gay Times" comedy unit for the next five years. When her husband left Lubin she retired from the screen, making only one or two appearances in the movies after that. She lived with her daughter in Palm Springs, California the last known reference being the 1940 census.

KEEPERS, HARRY *(April 6, 1883–September 17, 1963)*. Keepers got his start as a cameraman in the movie business working for Vitagraph and circumnavigating the globe for them in 1912-13, something he would do again in 1919-20 for Educational. He worked fairly steady during the teens and early 1920s but never at one studio for too long. After 1923 worked exclusively shooting industrial footage for various companies. Ended up later in life working as a film projectionist in and around Los Angeles. Keepers was born in Newark, New Jersey and passed away in San Diego, California.

KENDIG, WALTER *(September 1888-October 13, 1915)*. Another native Philadelphian, Kendig appears in Lubin comedies as early as 1909. A supporting player with the Gay Times troupe he left Lubin around the time of the Stull-Reehm-Burns exodus and went to work with the trio at Komic. In 1915 he became "Louie" to James Aubrey's "Heinie" in the Mittenthal Comedies series "Heinie & Louie." Kendig along with a co-worker were traveling the streets of Yonkers on his motorcycle when they hit a trolley car. Kendig suffered multiple injuries and died from a fractured skull. Even at such a young age Kendig was already a widower, his wife and son having previously passed away. With little fanfare or notice, Mittenthal hired a new "Louie" never really letting the public in on the switch.

LA PEARL, HARRY *(October 10, 1884-January 13, 1946)*. Born William Harry La Pearl in Danville, Illinois into a family of circus performers. He made his debut doing a trapeze act in his father's show ("J.H. La Pearl's Allied Show") at the age of 5. Leaving the family business as an adult he went to work as a clown for Barnum & Bailey and then at the New York Hippodrome. He made his first films for IMP and Vitagraph but by 1915 was starring in a series for MinA when David Horsley moved his operation to Hollywood. Remaining in New York, La Pearl ended up setting up his own production company in Yonkers to no success. La Pearl appeared in a few features, his last screen appearance being in *Polly of the Circus* (1919) for Goldwyn. Later in life he gave us the clown act and with his second wife Loretta ran a boxing dogs act. He died in Los Angeles and Loretta carried on with the dog act.

LARKIN, GEORGE *(November 11, 1885–March 27, 1946)*. Known as a daredevil performer, Larkin got his start with Pathé and then Éclair in 1912. He dabbled at Lubin and then back at Pathé, but by the end of the year found a home at Kalem primarily in support of Ruth Roland. That work brought him to the West Coast where he then worked for Universal and Selig. Back at Kalem in 1916 he started the very successful *Grant, Police Reporter* serial which ran for 29 episodes. After divorcing his first Wofe Dolly he married his co-star Ollie Kirby. He continued to work for the remainder of the silent era although most of his lead roles were with lesser companies. Larkin and Kirby moved to New York City where Larkin worked as a magazine illustrator. He died in New York City, his birthplace.

LAWRENCE, ED *(c. 1867-July 18, 1934)*. Lawrence was the son of 19th century actress May Nino and made his stage debut at age 3 in Mobile, Alabama (his home state). Primarily a stage actor, he worked for the Peruchi Players for almost his entire career, the only gap being the nine years he worked in support of Mabel Paige, during which time both he and Paige dabbled in the movies. Both companies he worked for toured primarily in Florida and the southeast United States, making him somewhat of a local celebrity. He passed away in Jacksonville, Florida.

LITTLE JERRY *(July 20, 1892- October 15, 1976)*. Born Jerry Albro, he used the name Jerry Austin in his later film career, stood three feet seven inches tall but owned a deep baritone voice. He worked extensively in vaudeville and at one point on Broadway in support of John and Ethel Barrymore in "Claire de Lune" which ran in 1921. Reportedly worked at Universal, Keystone and Fox in the mid-teens as well as at Wizard. Austin did have a resurgence of a film career in the late 1940s appearing in "Saratoga Trunk" and a few other features. He was arrested in 1940 for rape in a pornographic photo sting in New York City. Known as "The Mite of Mirth" and "The Smallest Man With the Biggest Voice" Austin was born in Odessa, Russia (now Ukraine) and died in Los Angeles.

LOUIS, WILL *(June 24, 1873–December 6, 1959)*. Born William Reteneller, a name he kept in his private life, Louis first worked on the stage. In 1903 he was in the cast and a stage manager for the Forepaugh troupe working out of Philadelphia. He first went into film work at Lubin in the Gay Times unit, his earliest known work in 1909. He stayed with Lubin until 1915 when the Gay Time unit was disbanded. While at Lubin he increasingly spent more time behind the camera than in front, at one point being the primary director of the studio's "colored" comedies. He moved over to Edison in 1915 where he worked exclusively as a director, then was brought in to Vim in 1916 to direct the Plump & Runt series. After leaving Vim, Louis briefly worked for Jaxon, and then directed Leatrice Joy at United States Moving Picture Corporation in Wilkes-Barre, Pennsylvania, as well as back in Jacksonville. Remaining in Jacksonville, he then found work directing Cuckoo Comedies and finally for the Florida Film Corporation. Louis stayed in Jacksonville after the film industry left and opened up a costume shop just about five blocks down the street from the old Lubin/Vim studio on Riverside Drive. His daughter Mary married Bobby Burns after the death of Burns' first wife. Louis started life in Woodfield, Maryland and passed away in Los Angeles. [Counting his time at Lubin, Edison and Vim, Louis ended up directing Babe Hardy in more films than any other director.]

MANDEVILLE, WILLIAM *(c.1863–April 19, 1917)*. Primarily a New York City based stage actor, Mandeville was on Broadway well before the turn of the century. He appeared prominently in the 1893 Broadway hit "That Sister of His." He only occasionally ventured into the movies, first with Majestic and then under Fred Mace's direction at Flamingo. He worked at Eastern in 1915, and did his last work for the Creative Film Corp. in 1917. Born in Louisville, Kentucky, Mandeville died in New York City.

MANN, FRANCES *(June 11-1893-October 15, 1970)*. Also known in film as Frankie Mann, she was born in Millhall, Pennsylvania. She worked at Lubin and then other East Coast studios until she married in 1923 (making only three more appearances on screen after marriage). Her sister Alice Mann was also an actress. Mann died in Hollywood, Florida.

MARKS, GEORGE *(c.1852-1932)*. Marks was on the stage around the turn of the century. In 1910 he was listed as an actor in motion pictures and in Philadelphia, which would mean he did some work for Lubin. Went to Jacksonville to work at Vim and then later the Florida Film Corp. Born in New York City, died in Jacksonville, Florida. Not the George Marks that was part of the famous Canadian vaudeville company "The Marks Bros. Company." He's also not the film editor that worked in Hollywood during the early 1930s.

MASON, DAN *(February 9, 1853–July 6, 1929).* Mason appeared on stage for well over 40 years before making his first movie. First appearing in vaudeville in the early 1870s, he worked for a long time with the Theatre Comique troupe and by the turn of the century was well known as an old timer. Mason started out with Edison in 1913 but bounced around various film companies between stage engagements for the rest of the decade, including a spell making Pelican Comedies (eventually released as Sparkle Comedies) at Eastern in Providence, Rhode Island. He then gained his greatest film fame as the Skipper in the Toonerville Trolley comedies and as Pop Tuttle in a derivative comedy series named for his character. His last few years were spent playing supporting roles in features. Born in Syracuse, New York, Mason passed away in Bearsville, New York.

McEVOY, TOM *(December 13, 1885-February 18, 1944).* Born Thomas J. MacEvoy in Philadelphia. Worked in vaudeville along with Ford Sterling. When Sterling was hired by Mack Sennett (initially at Biograph), McEvoy also left the stage and found work at various New York City-based film companies. He had steady work but not necessarily plentiful, at least in terms of credited appearances. In 1915, he had a stint with Eastern in Providence, Rhode Island and then in 1917 directed a series of Johnny and Emma Ray comedies. McEvoy then seems to have left the filmmaking side of the industry, later in life he worked for Columbia Pictures in one of their regional film exchanges. Died in Manitowoc, Wisconsin.

McKEE, RAYMOND *(December 7, 1892–October 3, 1984).* Born Eldon Raymond McKee in Keokuk, Iowa, and reportedly started working on stage at the age of 3. He made his first films for Lubin in 1912 and worked steadily in the "Gay Time" unit until it was disbanded in 1915. Together with Will Louis and Babe Hardy, McKee found work at Edison where he stayed until briefly leaving to work at Vim in 1916. McKee returned to Edison, this time mostly working in features, until he was recruited into the U.S. Army. McKee was in the Army from March 1918 until May 1919 and served with honor in France. He made his way to Hollywood and worked in both shorts and features, his main claim to fame being the star of "The Smith Family" series of comedy shorts made for Mack Sennett. After the series ended in 1929, McKee worked a few more years for various studios but then left film acting. After composing music and writing radio scripts he eventually retired to Hawaii. He married fellow film star Marguerite Courtot in 1923, and the two remained married until his death in Long Beach, California.

McLOUGHLIN, FLORENCE *(May 23, 1898-December 15, 1972).* McLoughlin was born in Richmond, Virginia and moved with her family to Jacksonville, Florida, where her father worked as a ship builder sometime in the first decade of the 20th century. One of many local young women who went to work for the movies in JAX, McLoughlin stood out due in part to being particularly energetic. She was a mainstay in the Plump & Runt unit and then continued with her good friend Babe Hardy at Vim and later with King Bee. When King Bee went to New York City, so did McLoughlin, but when the company moved to California she stayed behind. McLoughlin continued to work briefly in New York (she appears in a few Three C comedies, but then returned to Florida. Her last film work was at the Florida Film

Company in support of Fatty Filbert. McLoughlin fell in love with a returning WWI veteran named Lewis Gilger; the two married, moved to Ohio, and raised two children. She died in Rocky River, Ohio.

McLEOD, ELSIE *(December 5, 1892-19??)*. Her last name often misspelled MacLeod and less often as McCloud. Born in Jersey City, New Jersey, Elsie made her first film appearances in 1912 for Edison and worked there steadily for the next two years. Moved on to work for Powers, Kalem and Imp. She was Marcel Perez's leading lady in his first American film *A Day at Midland Beach* made in 1915. Brought into support Perez at Vim she did the same for Plump & Runt when Perez defected to Eagle. When she left Vim, it was first reported she'd be going to the United States Motion Picture Corp. to act and direct in her own comedies. However, she returned to New York and found work in feature films until retiring from the screen after marrying Edwin Westgate. Other than divorcing Westgate in 1933, little is known of McLeod's post-film life.

METCALFE, EARL *(March 11, 1889–January 26, 1928)*. Metcalf was working on the stage when in 1912 an offer from Lubin to appear in movies caused him to buy out his stage contract and travel to Philadelphia. He worked for Lubin for a few years and then moved into feature work for various companies, usually no higher billing than second male lead. His last work was in a serial centered around aviation (*Eagle of the Sky*). During a flying lesson, Metcalfe either jumped or fell from the aeroplane to his death. Born in Newport, Kentucky, the fatal incident was in Burbank, California.

MILLER, BEATRICE *(c.1897- 19??)*. An English actress she made her Broadway debut in 1915 in *Mrs. Boltay's Daughters* after having worked a few years on the London stage. She worked regularly on Broadway as well as in touring companies. Her last stage credit was in *Carousel* in 1947.

MINGUS, ANNA LEE *(November 15, 1894–June 10, 1979)*. Married to Robin Williamson (July 13, 1914) after two very brief previous marriages. Appeared in small parts while at Vim but otherwise did not work in the movie business. After Williamson's death, she eventually moved from Los Angeles back to her home state of Texas and married Carleton Bull.

MULGREW, TOM *(September 25, 1889–December 1954)*. Mulgrew was born, raised and died in Providence, Rhode Island. After his brief tenure with the Eastern Film Corporation, Mulgrew worked with local stock companies and was known as a "song and dance" man. He eventually opened up his own talent agency and was a popular Master of Ceremonies at local events.

MURRAY, TOM *(September 8, 1873–August 27, 1935)*. Born Thomas Henderson Murray in Stonefoot, Illinois, Murray was not the Tom Murray that led a blackface minstrel troupe (although he did often work in blackface) nor was he the well-known vaudeville theater manager of the same name. Rather Murray was a comedian that worked in the team of Gillihan & Murray, at least until 1910 when he married Louise

Carver and they formed their own act. In 1916 Murray (and Carver) went to work for the Eagle Film Co. as chief support for Marcel "Tweedledum" Perez. They then joined the Babe Hardy company at Vim. They worked regularly Hollywood in the early and mid-1920s, but their work fell off by 1926. A series called "Rolling Stones" to star Murray and Jimmie Adams shot in color was announced in 1930 but nothing came of it. Murray did find regular work on his own "Ranch Boys" radio show that included Jimmie Adams broadcast from KTM-780 AM in 1930 (the group sans Murray but with Jimmie Adams appeared in a number of Charley Chase shorts around 1931). Started his *Beverly Hill Billies* show on both KFI and KECA then KFWB a few years later. He was father of Evangeline and Kathleen (from his first marriage) who were famous on stage as the "Murray Sisters." Murray passed away in Los Angeles.

NAUGHTON, HARRY *(March 6, 1885-October 13, 1962)*. College educated Henry Joseph Naughton followed in his relatives' footsteps and went to work in banking. By 1915 he was living in New York (sharing an apartment with Raymond McKee and Bert Tracy) and met Millie Burstein falling madly in love. He gave up banking and took a job as studio manager for Millie's uncle Louis who had formed Vim working in Bayonne, New Jersey. Naughton was known to occasionally appear on camera as a heavy or person in authority. Naughton and Miss Burstein dated throughout Vim's tenure in Jacksonville and Naughton remained in Louis Burstein's employ taking on similar duties at King Bee which led him to Hollywood. The couple finally wed in January 1918 and Naughton, feeling the responsibilities of a married man, quit the movie business and obtained a job in the shipping industry, moving to the San Francisco Bay area. Working initially for the Pacific Mail Steamship Company, the work afforded the couple the ability to travel and live abroad (they lived briefly in Hawaii). Their son Daniel served with distinction during WWII. Later in life, Naughton worked in the oil industry. He passed away in Hartford, Connecticut.

NE MOYER, FRANCES *(September 29, 1896-December 1981)*. Ne Moyer started in movies in 1910 and was with the Gay Time unit the entirety of its existence, her older sister Marguerite joining her early on. After that company was disbanded, Frances stayed in Jacksonville and went to work for Kalem. Her final screen credit was the leading role in 1919's *The Law of Nature*, released by Arrow. Despite glowing reviews, Ne Moyer then retired from the movies and married Donald McCruden, a publishing executive. She died in North Salem, New York.

NE MOYER, MARGUERITE *(c.1892-September 23, 1951)*. Like her younger sister, Marguerite Ne Moyer was born near Buffalo, New York. How either got to Philadelphia to eventually work as actresses is a mystery. When Lubin broke up the Gay Time unit, Marguerite left the movie business, went back home and married an auto dealer-turned-postmaster-turned-bank executive named Henry Crandall. She died in Buffalo.

NELSON, JENNIE (c.1883 – 19??). Born in Copenhagen, Denmark, Jennie Vanhart was a mother of two when she entered the movies in 1910. Reverting to her presumed maiden name Nelson, the Philadelphia housewife made her movie debut with Lubin and worked mostly in their dramatic unit for the next three years. She divorced her husband in 1913 and one week later married her fellow Lubinite William Chamberlain. The two soon moved to New York City and found work with Gaumont and Victor among other film companies. In 1916 they signed on with Vim and worked initially with the Myers-Theby unit in Providence, Rhode Island. They continued with Vim and then Jaxon in both Jacksonville and Rhode Island. Following the demise of Jaxon Comedies, Jennie and her husband moved to San Francisco.

OBROCK, HERMAN *(February 14, 1887-June 26, 1939)*. Henry, Jr. was born in New York but no one, even Obrock himself, is sure where. He got his start as a cameraman for Pathé (the first to work for the firm in America), then Gaumont and usually shot actuality or newsreel footage. Made his first trip to Jacksonville in 1913 turning the crank for Gene Gauntier. By 1917 Obrock was in Jacksonville again working for the Myers-Theby company and then King Bee. Working with Reelcraft he found his way back to the New York area in the early 1920s, dabbled in producing his own films, worked briefly for Jack Roach shooting the faux Our Gang short *Their Day Out* using local Pittsburgh children in 1928, shot newsreel footage for Universal and by the early 1930s settled in working for Photocolor where he developed some advance color film processes. Erroneously mentioned by the name O'Brock in the trades his family was of Dutch-German heritage. A very tall large man Obrock is easily recognized in behind-the-scenes stills. He died in Brooklyn, New York.

OUTEN, JOSEPH *(September 13, 1885 – 19??)*. Little is known about Outen who was one of the few professional African-American actors brought into Lubin's "colored" unit. He had worked at Lubin since around 1910 and before that appeared on stage as part of Bundy's Georgia Minstrels in a duo act called Gibson & Outen. Reportedly part of the act was Outen's spot-on impersonation of Bert Williams.

PAIGE, MABEL *(December 19, 1880-February 8,1954)*. Born in New York City to Frank and Doris Roberts (Paige was her mother's maiden name) who were vaudeville performers. For nearly thirty years, she headed her own stock company touring mainly the South, with the Mabel Paige Theater in Jacksonville as home base. Along with her husband/manager Charles W. Ritchie, she dabbled in movies in the mid 'teens. Giving up her own company, Paige went to work with the Peruchi Players, working sporadically while raising her children. After the death of her husband she went to work on the stage in New York. The success of the Broadway play "Out of the Frying Pan" brought her to Hollywood when Paramount intended to film the play in 1942. She then became a much-employed character actress in movies and on television. She died in Van Nuys, California during a rehearsal.

PALMER, LORLE *(c.1979 – July 21, 1952)*. Born as Lorle Irine Burns in Pittsburgh, Pennsylvania, her first name often misspelled Lorlie. Palmer worked on the stage with the Shubert Stock Company among others. She was first married to William Bradley and then in 1906 to Alfred Swenson. She and Swenson were 'name above the title' stars for many touring plays throughout the 'teens. They only briefly flirted with movies with Eastern and then Kriterion in 1915. Palmer continued on the stage until her husband settled down in New York around 1924 to concentrate on radio work, she apparently then retired from acting. She died in New York City.

PEREZ, MARCEL *(c.1885–February 8, 1929)*. Perez was known by a number of different first names including Marcel, Fernandez and Fernandea (although it seems that last may have been more a typographical error). He gained fame by his on-screen character name Tweedledum, later shortened to Tweedy, and in Europe as Robinet. Perez came to America in 1915 at the height of World War I since that conflict greatly impinged upon film production in Europe. Inexplicably he was called Bungles during his brief time at Vim in 1916, but swiftly left Vim for Eagle. Back as Tweedledum, Perez wrote, directed and starred in numerous highly underrated comedies over the next half-dozen years. The loss of a leg curtailed his work in front of the camera. He passed away in Los Angeles.

PETERS, GRACE *(December 21, 1884-April 9, 1948)*. Born in Washington, D.C. where her father served in the higher echelon of the U.S. Navy. A star of the Washington social circle Peters was twice married, her second husband John O. Johnson a government official himself. She began doing stage work in 1914 and was associated for a time with George M. Cohan. Her short visit to Providence, Rhode Island resulted in her only film work. Peters remained on the stage until her second marriage, and then continued her life as a Washington socialite. She died in Charlottesville, Virginia.

PRICE, KATE *(February 13, 1872-January 4, 1943)*. Born Katherine Elizabeth Duffy in Blackpool, County Cork, Ireland, Price was the preeminent corpulent comedienne of the silent era. She started at Kalem but spent most of her pre-Vim career at Vitagraph, and after Vim worked steadily for the next twenty years. Few, if any others, worked in support of Sidney Drew, Larry Semon, Fatty Arbuckle, Buster Keaton and Babe Hardy in their career; Price did. She was married to stage actor Joseph Price Ludwig, created her stage name using his middle name, and worked alongside him in vaudeville. She spent the last decades of her life as a widow. Price died at the Motion Picture Country Home in Woodland Hills, California.

RALSTON, JOBYNA *(November 21, 1899-January 22, 1967)*. Born in South Pittsburg, Tennessee, her last name was originally spelled Raulston. Her first film was in late 1916 with Amber Star. She continued to work with Bobby Burns for the next few years in Cuckoo Comedies and then a few Reelcraft releases. After appearing as the Marx Bros. first leading lady in *Humor Risk* she moved to Hollywood and worked at the Hal Roach Studios. She took over for Mildred Davis as Harold Lloyd's on screen leading lady, and then moved into feature film work. Married three times, her last was to actor Richard Arlen. She died in Woodland Hills, California.

RAY, AL *(August 28, 1897 – February 8, 1944)*. Often credited as Albert Ray he started out in movies while still in his teens, including directing his first film just before he turned 18. During the mid-teens he acted in and directed films, including helming Ben Turpin shorts for Vogue, followed with a brief tenure at Vim. He gave up acting in movies around 1921 and concentrated on writing and directing. He directed at Fox, Educational (where he directed Cliff Bowes) and Paramount, eventually ended up working for poverty row studios. Actor Charles Ray was his cousin. Born in new Rochelle, New York, he died in Los Angeles.

RAY, MARJORIE *(July 9, 1890-July 22, 1924)*. Born in Kansas City, Missouri, Ray moved to New York at a young age to become an actress. She joined Dan Russell's "Matinee Girls" and eventually married the actor. The two moved to Hollywood and film work at L-KO. When the movies didn't pan out Ray went back to work on stage with Russell, and then solo after their divorce in 1920. She died in San Diego, California from complications from drug addiction.

RAYMOND, DEAN *(December 13,1864-December 16, 1948)*. Born William Taggart in Ontario, Canada. Married Maud Cooling, also a stage performer, in 1891. The two left the stage briefly around the turn of the century and ran a hotel in Niagara Falls. Returning to the stage both with and without his wife, Raymond remained on the stage into the Thirties regularly working on Broadway through the 20s and 30s. He worked at Eastern Film Corp. in 1915 and various New York film studios for a few years before settling into stage work. Raymond made a few Vitaphone shorts in 1935. He passed away back home in Ontario, Canada.

REEHM, GEORGE *(July 18, 1881 – June 27, 1936)*. Reehm began his film career in his hometown of Philadelphia going to work for Lubin in 1909. When Walter Stull arrived at Lubin the two became known as the Lubin Twins. Reehm worked as both comedian and assistant director. He left Lubin along with Stull and Bobby Burns to work for Komic in 1914, where as a trio they wrote, starred in and directed their own comedies. In 1915 Reehm left the other two to take up as a director over at Biograph, then in 1916 showed up at Vim working in the Myers & Theby unit when they filmed in Rhode Island. Reehm left the movie business briefly and managed a mill during the Great War. Back in the movies he moved around directing for Pan-American Motion Picture Company among other itinerant film companies. By 1922 he found himself in Hollywood working initially in the Hal Roach Studios' scenario department. Reehm continued to work in movies primarily as an assistant director until in 1927 when he moved to Hawaii and worked as a publishing salesman. He died in Honolulu.

RENFRO, JAMES *(September 30, 1892-March 2, 1962)*. Born in Dennison, Texas. Pretty much just a bit player for Vim and then later the Myers-Theby Pathé comedies and the Florida Film Company. Like most others, he left Florida in the late 'teens for California but spent a good deal of time touring the world with the W.H. Rice show. Married a few times, ended up along with his third wife Madie working as dog trainers in Hollywood. "Buster", "Oscar" and then "Daisy" from Columbia's "Blondie" series were their dogs. Known in Hollywood as Rennie Renfro, he died in Shasta, California.

REYNOLDS, EDNA *(February 10, 1888-January 2, 1960)*. Born Edna Mable Koch in New York City, and early on married a man named Johnson who passed away in 1913. Needing employment, Edna went to work in the movies. She married fellow actor Frank "Spook" Hanson in 1915 and became his widow in 1924. Quitting the movies she married for a last time to Arthur J. Kelsey and the two ran Kelsey's Pine Rest Cabins in Howell Township, New Jersey, where Edna was known to have run a bookmaking operation. Widowed once again in 1948, Edna remained in Howell Township until her death twelve years later.

RIDGEWAY, JACK *(c.1865-January 28, 1929)*. Born John D. Ridgeway in Pennsylvania, he passed away in Los Angeles. Made his first film for Lubin in 1911 and like many others had to find work elsewhere in 1915. After some work in New York, he went to California and bounced around from Universal to Fox to Vitagraph. His last known screen credit is from 1921.

RITCHIE, BILLIE *(September 14, 1877–July 6, 1921)*. Ritchie played the drunk in Fred Karno's "Mumming Birds" prior to Charlie Chaplin and in America as early as 1905. But his permanent immigration to the U.S. didn't happen until after Chaplin found fame at Keystone. While legitimately an influence and pre-cursor to Chaplin he is most often viewed as just another imitator. Ritchie started his brief movie career at L-KO, then went to Fox and made his final films with his first director at Henry Lehrman Comedies. Born in Glasgow, Scotland, he died in Los Angeles, California, from injuries incurred while filming.

RITCHIE, CHARLES *(May 21, 1893-July 14, 1979)*. Little is known about Ritchie, who began his film work at Wizard. Although listed as part of the cast, he was more likely one of the cameramen. He worked in that capacity for Herbert Brenon from late 1915 until his enlistment in the Army in 1918. After the war he made his way to California, married and went to work for the County of Los Angeles. Born In New York City, he passed away in Los Angeles. Not the same Charles Ritchie that was married to Mabel Paige.

ROSS, BUDD *(November 8, 1873-March 19, 1933)*. Ross worked on stage from a very young age but first came to great notice around 1909 as part of the Princess Stock Company (based in San Francisco) that also featured the likes of Fred Mace. He next worked as a replacement cast member of the long running road show version of *Babes in Toyland*. He worked in an act with Gus Pixley for a time and the two made it to New York City and entered movies. Ross worked for a few years with various film companies such as Biograph, IMP and Gem but in 1915 was made writer and prime support for Gaumont's Casino Star comedies. In those a different "famous" star took the lead and Ross along a standing stock company filled in all the other parts (as in W.C. Fields' *Pool Sharks* for example). Eventually Ross became the star of the series. In 1917 he became part of the supporting cast of the King Bee comedies, then worked at Vitagraph both as a comedian and writer. Ross worked fairly regular for the rest of the silent era but like many others his work tailed off at the beginning of the 1930s. Ross was born Springfield, Illinois (some sources give the date as 1868) and died in Los Angeles.

RUGE, BILLY *(August 16, 1863-October 19, 1955)*. Born in Plattsburgh, New York. Ruge started out as a contortionist-acrobatic comedian in a stage act with Harry Loa called Loa & Ruge, first working in the John B. Doris Inter-Ocean Circus & Menagerie around 1886. By 1888 Loa was replaced by William Frobel, with the act continuing as Frobel & Ruge. However, Frobel retired from the act in 1899 due to injuries and Charles Ruge (Billy's brother) assumed not only Frobel's place in the act but his stage name. The act, with intermittent solo turns by Ruge, remained on stage until Ruge's entry into movies in 1914. The act had gained international acclaim and due to his superior stage work, Ruge was cast in Edison's *Fantasm* and remained at Edison (usually billed as William Ruge) until his departure for Wizard in mid-1915. Ruge continued with Vim and then Jaxon appearing in his own series, teaming at Vim with Babe Hardy and at Jaxon with Kate Price. After his involuntary departure from Jaxon he went to work at Vitagraph. His final films were made as Funful Comedies in 1920-21. He tried to revive his stage act as Ruge & Rose but limited bookings and bad reviews ended Ruge's entertainment career. He died in New York City.

SCHRODE, JOE *(18??-19??)*. Schrode as a clown and acrobat was part of the Philadelphia Central YMCA team that competed nationally in gymnastics. His first big break in vaudeville was meeting Fred Stone (of Montgomery & Stone) who was preparing to mount *The Wizard of Oz* for the stage. Schrode developed an alternative character to Toto the dog called Imogene the Cow and worked on the highly successful play for years. Much like Bobby Burns' stage work, Schrode's forte became playing animals, essaying the role of Tige in Buster Brown plays as well as horses, lions and dinosaurs. He did briefly attempt film with Komic, Wizard and Vim most assuredly due to his knowing Burns (another *Oz* alumni). Later in his stage career he again went to work for Fred Stone.

SHELLEY, EFFIE *(18??–19??)*. Other than her brief time at the Eastern Film company, and that her last name was often spelled Shelly, little is known about this actress. She did have a lead part in George M. Cohan's *The Royal Vagabond* on Broadway and appeared to work in the chorus in another play after that.

SHEPARD, PEARL *(January 17, 1902-September 3, 1993)*. Born Pearl Ginsberg in New York City, she was the daughter of a New York City furrier. As a child Shepard won the prize of a movie career at a charity ball in 1912, and apparently worked for Thanhouser as her reward. Her first recorded work was for Wizard. Although never directly working for Vim a few of her Wizard appearances were released as Vim Comedies. Shepard then regularly worked for director Frank P. Donovan appearing with Lou Marks and Oom Paul in Three C Comedies. When that company failed to pay the team they all moved over to Diamond Comedies. Shepard, who also worked on Broadway, continued to work into the early '20s when in 1923 it was reported she married Egyptian Prince Mohammed Ali Ibrahim and moved to Paris. She returned to America in 1935 never having been married due to the Prince's father not approving of his son, a Muslim, marrying a Jewish woman. Shepard died in San Diego, California.

SLADE, BILLY. *(August 26, 1884-May 8, 1950)*. Born William Snaden in Manchester, England, he served in the British Army and then in 1911 migrated to the U.S. In 1915, he married Florence Yerex and moved from Michigan to Jacksonville to work for Eagle. Made a few films for Vim at that time but was primarily chief support for Marcel "Tweedledum" Perez for about two years. Then went to work with Victor Moore in Klever Comedies. Slade also made movies for various studios in New York City and worked as a property manager at Fox before leaving the film industry in the early 1920s. Slade got involved in real estate and then moved back to Michigan and ran a boarding house. He died of a heart attack in Ann Arbor, Michigan.

SPRAGUE, NORAH *(April 25, 1892-November 22, 1942).* Norah (first name often spelled Nora) began acting in local productions in her hometown of Lima, Ohio. After graduating from Western College at Oxford she moved to New York City in 1914 to live with an aunt and give show business a try. She was cast in *The Misleading Lady* midway through its Broadway run. She reportedly found film work at Equity during the Summer of 1915, and then with Wizard. Norah had very few screen credits, mostly notably in the 1918 Mabel Normand feature *Dodging A Million*. She did work regularly on stage for a time appearing on Broadway in the 1918 Jerome Kern play *Rock-A-Bye Baby* and was also with the Ziegfeld Follies. Her last screen credit was with Johnny Hines in 1922's *Torchy and Orange Blossoms*. She called off her wedding to Addison Gatling (nephew of the rapid fire gun inventor) in 1920 and remained single all her life. After retiring from the stage, she became a life insurance salesperson.

STAHL, WALTER. *(May 26, 1887-March 30, 1950).* Born Walter Richard Stahl in New York City, he changed his last name to Hall during World War I to get away from the Germanic surname. A cartoonist for Success Magazine and daily newspapers, Stahl began writing and directing films for Regal. This led him to Jacksonville where he did the same for the Finn & Haddie series made by Jaxon. With the name change, he moved back to New York City and made a short series of films for Vitagraph alongside his Jaxon co-star Billy Ruge. Done with acting by 1919, Stahl went behind the camera full time as a writer, director and editor. He spent much of the twenties in Germany working for UFA (an ironic move for someone who had so decidedly distanced himself from his German heritage). He returned to America to work as a salesman, and by 1940 had become a theater manager. Married To Pauline Gollnik in 1917, Stahl died in Caldwell, New Jersey.

STULL, DANIEL *(September 1864-March 6, 1936).* Born, raised and died in Philadelphia Daniel Stull was 14 years older than his actor brother. Although not involved in the film business most of his life (he was at one time a steamfitter), Stull worked briefly in the props department at Vim; most certainly a bit of nepotism helping him secure the job.

SWENSON, ALFRED. *(October 15, 1879-March 28, 1941).* Started on stage as a teenager for his local dramatic company in his native Salt Lake City. A decade or more of stage work led to a brief stint with Lubin making movies in 1912. In 1915 he made a more concerted effort at movie acting and worked for various companies including the Eastern Film Corporation. Swenson then returned to the stage until radio acting provided him with his profession for the remainder of his life (notably on *School of the Air*). Married to Lorle Palmer in 1906, Swenson passed away in Richmond, New York.

TEARE, ETHEL *(January 11, 1894-March 4, 1959).* Although credited as appearing in vaudeville there is no trace of Teare until 1914 when she began a four year run as Ham & Bud's female support at Kalem. Born in Phoenix, Arizona, Teare lived with her family while in Los Angeles. She worked with others at Kalem and occasionally took the lead. After Lloyd Hamilton and Bud Duncan parted ways so did Teare depart Kalem. For the remainder of her career she worked for Mack Sennett and in Fox Sunshine comedies. In 1924 she married banker Frank F. Risso and moved to the Bay Area in Northern California. The two had three children (including a set of boy-girl twins). Teare passed away in San Mateo, California.

THEBY, ROSEMARY *(April 8, 1892-November 10, 1973).* Born in St. Louis, Missouri, Theby found her way to New York and made her first movies for Vitagraph, appearing in both comedy and drama. After a stint with Reliance she was brought over to Lubin with the specific intent of starring beside Harry Myers in 1914. The two left Lubin and headed for Victor in 1915 with their professional (and presumably personal) relationship firmly cemented. Mid-1916 they started their series of domestic comedies for Vim. A series of similar comedies for Pathé followed the Vim series. With Myers she moved to Hollywood and found work in features as well as comedy shorts. Romantically involved with Myers early on (even though he was married with children) the two finally wed in 1926. They rarely worked together in Hollywood and both saw their roles become increasingly smaller and more infrequent. After Myers death in 1938, Theby eventually slipped away from the movie business. She passed away in Los Angeles.

TICHENOR, FRANK *(May 5, 1880-May 6. 1950).* Tichenor started out as a photographer, becoming president of General Film Company during its peak of activity. He then became President of Eastern Film Corporation, overseeing the acquisition of the Vim Films Corporation in 1916. By the early 1920s, he had converted Eastern to producing educational films and stayed with the company for most of the decade, then became a magazine publisher including the aviation-centric *Aero Digest*. Tichenor and his mistress (later wife) drove Charles Lindbergh to Curtiss Field on the morning of his famous transatlantic flight. Tichenor died in Connecticut.

TRACY, BERT *(June 16, 1889 – 19??).* Born Francis Herbert Louis Tracey in Manchester, England, he was part of the Fred Karno troupe that came to America in 1912. Tracy found film work with Kalem and then Lubin. He eventually made it to Florida working with Vim as comedian, scenario writer and assistant Director. After the demise of Vim he worked briefly with Myers & Theby in their Pathé comedies, then directed some of the Sunbeam Comedies made in Jacksonville and also directed Bioscope films in Tampa. He briefly worked in Hollywood in the early twenties but by 1927 had returned to England. His work there is not well documented but he is known to have directed George Formby in his first film *Boots! Boots!* (1934). Later in life he was employed as a dresser for Laurel & Hardy during their British tours. His named is often spelled Tracey with his first full first name Herbert occasionally used.

ULM, BRUNO *(May 27, 1866-December 25, 1937).* Born in Germany, Ulm worked as a scenic artist for Vim and later did the same for film studios in Hollywood. He died in Los Angeles from a car accident on Christmas Day. Ulm was survived by his wife Berdiana and three children.

WALKER, BEN *(December 14, 1874-June 13, 1963).* Often confused with Benjamin Walker of Mackle & Walker, also a stage actor, who died in 1924. This Ben Walker was born In New York and after some stage work made his film debut in *Bottled Love* for Herald Films (the film also featured Budd Ross). He then went to work for Lubin followed by occasional feature film work between stage engagements. Married to Catherine, little is known of his life after his last screen credit in 1927.

WALLACE, IRENE *(August 13, 1898-June 10, 1977).* One of her first jobs on stage was as one of "May Ward's Dresden Dolls." Her first film work was in 1913 for Universal, moving to Selig in 1915 (first in Chicago then Los Angeles). She was back on the East Coast by 1916 where she briefly worked with Roscoe Arbuckle. Wallace left the movies to work on Broadway and then vaudeville, but returned to film work for Selig in 1920. After a few films she left the screen for good.

WATSON, SLIDING BILLY *(1876-1939).* Born William Shapiro and self-claimed inventor of the banana peel slip gag. Watson worked in vaudeville his entire career and gave Fanny Brice her first break in show biz casting her in his *The Girls of Happyland* revue. Also helped a young W.C. Fields early in the juggler's career. Though they were estranged at the time, Watson's wife Helen was murdered in 1926 in an argument with a patron of her club over her pet dogs. Watson worked on stage regularly until his death.

WESTON, HOD *(18??-19??).* Billed as an Irish comedian, "Happy Hod" Weston worked in vaudeville from as early as 1903 appearing for a time with the Flaming Arrow Company and then the Billy "Swede" Hall Company. He settled around New York City, but other than his brief work in Wizard Comedies not much else is known about Weston.

WILLIAMSON, ROBIN EUGENE. *(June 30, 1889- February 21, 1935).* Made his first movies for Lubin, but in the Romaine Fielding unit and not the comedy unit. After work at Vim, he traveled to California with his wife Anna Mingus and found work directing Ben Turpin at Vogue. Having given up performing, Robin directed some films sporadically after that, with his claim to fame being the director of Stan Laurel's first film (*Nuts in May*, 1917). Briefly worked at Hal Roach in 1923 directing Stan again in one film (*Scorching Sands*). Born in Denver, Colorado, Williamson died in Los Angeles.

WOLBERT, WILLIAM. *(November 18, 1883–December 12, 1918).* Born William Augustus Mintzer in Petersburg, Virginia. Worked on stage with his first appearances happening circa 1908. By 1910, he was based in Los Angeles and his first known film work was for Balboa as an actor and occasional director in 1913. Wolbert then moved over to full time directing by 1916, working on feature films for various studios. He was married to Maggie Desmond (*aka* Marcella Hazel O'Brien), although they apparently had a child together while she was still married to another. After his death, in Glendale, California, Maggie married film director Alf Goulding.

WROTHE, EDWIN LEE. (November 19, 1871 – August 6, 1922). Born in Omaha, Nebraska. Professionally billed as Ed. Lee Wrothe. Part of a vaudeville trio that also included Harry Watson, Jr. (of later Musty Suffer fame) and George Bickel. The trio appeared on Broadway a number of times circa 1904. Wrothe broke up the trio in 1906 and went solo. His act usually featured the character of Janitor Higgins. During the 'teens and early twenties he toured in tandem with Slidin' Billy Watson. Wrothe died in Bayside, Long Island from complications related to an arm injury suffered while performing on stage in a sketch entitled "In Now." Was married to Jennie Hand Mills.

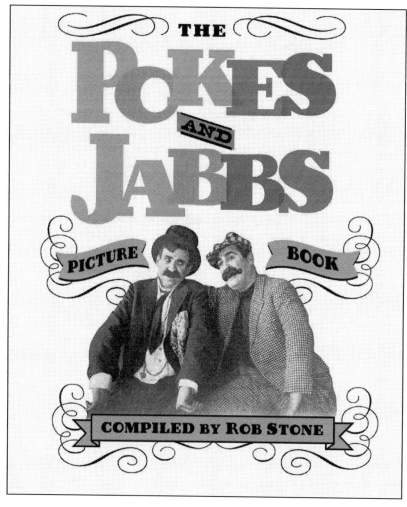

More about
the before, during and after of the Vim Films Corporation
can be found in the companion book:
THE POKES AND JABBS PICTURE BOOK
also available from Split Reel LLC.

INDEX

H

N

W

SPLIT REEL LLC

P.O. Box 946 · Culpeper, VA 22701
info@split-reel.com · www.split-reel.com
(540) 521-9826

Split Reel LLC publishes books and other media related to the performing arts. We specialize in silent film with a focus on providing detailed, deeply researched works that highlight lesser-known aspects of the entertainment industry.

Made in the USA
Middletown, DE
26 July 2022

69984026R00267